Live Music in America

Live Music in America

A History from Jenny Lind to Beyoncé

STEVE WAKSMAN

OXFORD
UNIVERSITY PRESS

Oxford University Press is a department of the University of Oxford. It furthers
the University's objective of excellence in research, scholarship, and education
by publishing worldwide. Oxford is a registered trade mark of Oxford University
Press in the UK and certain other countries.

Published in the United States of America by Oxford University Press
198 Madison Avenue, New York, NY 10016, United States of America.

© Oxford University Press 2022

All rights reserved. No part of this publication may be reproduced, stored in
a retrieval system, or transmitted, in any form or by any means, without the
prior permission in writing of Oxford University Press, or as expressly permitted
by law, by license, or under terms agreed with the appropriate reproduction
rights organization. Inquiries concerning reproduction outside the scope of the
above should be sent to the Rights Department, Oxford University Press, at the
address above.

You must not circulate this work in any other form
and you must impose this same condition on any acquirer.

CIP data is on file at the Library of Congress

ISBN 978-0-19-757054-8 (pbk.)
ISBN 978-0-19-757053-1 (hbk.)

DOI: 10.1093/oso/9780197570531.001.0001

Paperback Printed by Integrated Books International, United States of America
Hardback printed by Bridgeport National Bindery, Inc., United States of America

Dedicated to my parents, Marvin Waksman (May 8, 1929–May 13, 2013) and Jeanne Waksman (April 12, 1930–December 19, 2018).

Contents

Preface and Acknowledgments   ix

Introduction: Toward a History of Liveness   1

1. Selling the Nightingale: Jenny Lind, P.T. Barnum, and the Management of the American Crowd   30

2. Staging the Spiritual: The Fisk Jubilee Singers and the Postbellum Public Sphere   78

3. Economies of Performance: Tony Pastor, Ernest Hogan, and the Emergence of Vaudeville   120

4. Remaking Liveness: The Social Geography of Early Jazz   171

5. Culture High and Low: Reinventing Concert Music   224

6. The Perfect Package: Rock 'n' Roll Concerts in the 1950s   292

7. Crowds, Chaos, and Community: Music Festivals from Newport to New Orleans   345

8. The Politics of Scale: Arenas, Stadiums, and the Industrialization of Liveness   418

9. Staging Hip-Hop: Race, Rap, and the Remapping of Musical Performance   478

10. Conclusion: A Homecoming   540

Notes   571
Index   647

Preface and Acknowledgments

Professional Elvis Presley tribute artist Dwight Icenhower performed at the historical Stuart's Opera House in the southeastern Ohio town of Nelsonville on March 7, 2020. Then the COVID-19 pandemic shut everything down, and Icenhower's performance career was put on hold, as were the plans of his most dedicated fans. When Icenhower made his first return engagement to Stuart's in over a year in March 2021, one of those fans—Sue Paszke—could barely contain her excitement. Profiled in *The Atlantic*, Paszke would have Icenhower autograph her favorite scarf each time she saw him perform. In March 2020, she received her ninety-ninth autograph. Struggling through the pandemic with pneumonia and a series of other health problems, she was unsure she would get her hundredth, but on March 13, 2021, Paszke reached her milestone. A friend of Paszke's and fellow Icenhower devotee, Betsy Naseman, explained why the concert was so important to them coming out of the depths of the pandemic: "I needed one of Dwight's shows in ways I can't really describe . . . We all need that human connection. I didn't have it. None of us did. And that's not normal. That's why today felt so good. It felt like normal again."[1]

In the midst of the shutdown that accompanied the spread of COVID-19 (and has not entirely been lifted as of this writing), live music came for many to stand for what we have lost, individually and collectively. Its very "liveness" assumed new salience as death tolls mounted from the virus, offering aural, visual, and tactile memories of a time when we could be around other people, other bodies, without an overarching fear of contagion. Those same qualities have made live music into one of the most resonant symbols of a return to normalcy as life in the US and around the world has begun to open up again, however haltingly. As reported by *Atlantic* writer Tim Alberta, it is an index of survival that operates on multiple levels: for the participants, performers, and audience members alike; for performance venues and institutions such as Stuart's Opera House, which have managed to re-open after more than a year of near-complete inactivity; and for towns and communities like Nelsonville, where economic hardship was already rampant before the pandemic and has only worsened, but where the persistence of a long-standing music institution—and even more so, of the activities that are housed there—holds out some hope that recovery may still be possible.

When I began researching this book in the fall of 2008, I never envisioned a scenario like the one we have been living through in which live music all but disappeared for months on end. I have opted not to engage at length with the impact of the COVID-19 pandemic, apart from a few pages appended to the book's conclusion that serve as a kind of coda. The bulk of this book was written before the restrictions imposed by COVID-19 took hold. After twelve years of work on this project, I was not able to rethink the framework of the book in a way that made space for the pandemic and its impact. Also, writing a book with such a broad historical sweep, I do not feel like we have enough perspective on the longer-term implications of the current pandemic to be able to offer any satisfying insights. Still, I cannot ignore the reality that surrounds us and the certainty that this book will be read differently now than it would have been if it were released in January 2020. For me, this history feels more urgent now that we have seen just how fragile live music can be.

My work on the history of live music has been fortified by the collections of several libraries and archives around the US. I first want to thank the staff at the Josten Performing Arts Library and the Neilson Library of Smith College, especially Marlene Wong, Janet Spongberg, and Chris Ryan, for helping me locate key items and tracking down my often-complicated interlibrary loan requests. The research on this book truly began with a trip to the American Antiquarian Society in the fall 2008, where I immersed myself in historical sheet music and news reports of Jenny Lind's US tour. Three years later, in fall 2011, I had the good fortune of being the very first scholar to conduct research at the Rock and Roll Hall of Fame Library and Archives. Over two trips to the Rock Hall archives the staff were incredibly helpful and accommodating, and some of my most exciting research finds came from their collections. Special thanks to Jennie Thomas, Andy Leach, and Anastasia Karel. At the Hogan Jazz Archive at Tulane University, Bruce Boyd Raeburn and Lynn Abbott provided crucial help with navigating their vast collection; and at the Institute for Jazz Studies on the Newark campus of Rutgers University, Tad Hershorn generously made his research files on Norman Granz available to me. Multiple trips to the New York Public Library for the Performing Arts at Lincoln Center were instrumental to my research on vaudeville and hip-hop, while the Schomburg Center for Research in Black Culture contributed substantially to my thinking about the connections between vaudeville and early jazz. The Ralph Rinzler collection at the Smithsonian's Center for Folklife and Cultural Heritage proved to be a treasure trove of information about the Newport Folk Festival, and my time there was made more productive with the help of Greg Adams and Jeff Place. Also vital were the American Folklife Center at the Library of Congress; the Special Collections division at Georgia State University, home of the papers of concert promoter Alex Cooley; and the archive of the New Orleans Jazz and Heritage Foundation, where Rachel Lyons and Dolores Hooper provided much valued assistance.

Additional help procuring illustrations came from Brianne Barrett at the American Antiquarian Society, Robert Spinelli at the John Hope and Aurelia E. Franklin Library of Fisk University, Melissa Weber at the Hogan Archive, Agnieszka Czeblakow at Tulane University Special Collections, Tom Lisanti and Andrea Felder at the New York Public Library, Ben Ortiz at the Cornell University Hip-Hop Collection, Jennie Thomas and Justin Seidler at the Rock and Roll Hall of Fame Library and Archives, Laura Zepka at Williams College Special Collections, Alexa Antopol at Fisher Dachs Associates, and Kathleen Sabogal at the Carnegie Hall Archives. Special thanks go to John Kane, who helped me reach David Marks, photographer of the wonderful image of Bill Hanley at Woodstock that appears in Chapter 7.

Throughout the more than a decade that I worked on this book, my academic world has continued to revolve around the International Association for the Study of Popular Music, or IASPM. Between the annual US chapter conferences and the biannual international conferences, I have presented portions of nearly every chapter of this book at one or another IASPM event. More than that, the organization has provided me with a steady base of support and community that extends well beyond my home institution, and I was glad to pay some of that back by serving a term as US chapter president from 2017 to 2019. Thanks especially to Tim Anderson, Alexandra Appoloni, Andy Bennett, Monique Bourdage, David Brackett, Matt Brennan, Lori Burns, Mark Butler, Theo Cateforis, Norma Coates, Martin Cloonan, Amy Coddington, Laina Dawes, John Dougan, Kevin Fellezs, Paul Fischer, Robert Fink, Simon Frith, Robbie Fry, Reebee Garofalo, Daniel Goldmark, Karl Hagstrom Miller, Jason Hanley, Anthony Kwame Harrison, Stan Hawkins, Sarah Hill, Robin James, Beverly Keel, Keir Keightley, Elizabeth Lindau, Kimberly Mack, Andrew Mall, Fred Maus, Charles McGovern, Katherine Meizel, Esther Morgan-Ellis, Diane Pecknold, Alex Reed, Barry Shank, David Shumway, Mandy Smith, Gus Stadler, Matt Stahl, Victor Szabo, John Troutman, Elijah Wald, Gayle Wald, Oliver Wang, Eric Weisbard,

Christi Jay Wells, and Brian Wright. Also, a shout out to my extended popular music and media history friends, scattered around many organizations and institutions: David Ake, Esther Clinton, Mike Daley, Jan-Peter Herbst, Brian Hickam, Jessica Holmes, Mark Katz, Roger Landes, Lauren Onkey, Ann Powers, Carrie Rentschler, Christopher Smith, Jonathan Sterne, Sherrie Tucker, and Jeremy Wallach.

Closer to home, Smith College has been the place where I hang my professional hat for more than two decades. Smith has provided support for *Live Music in America* in myriad ways. Sabbaticals in fall 2008, fall 2011, spring 2015, and academic year 2019–2020 gave me the time I needed to conduct research and writing over the life of the project. I dare say I could not have brought a project of this scope and scale to fruition without these regular breaks in my teaching schedule. Two Smith student research assistants, Emily Seaman and Sara Aboulafia, helped me gather resources while I was first getting this project off the ground, for which I remain grateful. President Kathleen McCartney's selection of me to be the Sylvia Dlugasch Bauman Professor of American Studies, an appointment I held for five years, provided valuable research funds and a forum to present my work to an audience of my colleagues. As the book neared completion, Smith contributed a generous subvention toward the costs of publication, while the receipt of a Jerene Appleby Harnish '16 Fellowship afforded me critical funding to cover the costs of photo permissions and licensing fees. Atop it all are the many great colleagues I have (or have had, in some cases) in the Music Department and American Studies Program at Smith, as well as across the College, with whom I have shared conversations, drinks, meals, and general conviviality: Nalini Bhushan, Peter Bloom, Brigitte Buettner, Floyd Cheung, Jaz Dand, Judith Gordon, Michael Gorra, Anna Goudreau, Ambreen Hai, Laura Kalba, Alexandra Keller, Jen Malkowski, Rick Millington, Andrea Moore, Christen Mucher, Tom Roberts, Kevin Rozario, Margaret Sarkissian, Linda Shaughnessy, Ruth Solie, Kate Soper, Marc Steinberg, Andrea Stone, Michael Thurston, and Frazer Ward.

I wrote a very early raw draft of chapter one of *Live Music in America* for a writing workshop organized by Louis Meintjes at Duke University. I thank Louise and the other participants in that very small workshop—Michael Kramer and Jessica Wood—for creating such a welcoming space in which to break ground on this endeavor. Many others provided the opportunity to present portions of this book while it was at various stages of work-in-progress. Thanks to all of the following: at University of Liverpool, Anahid Kassabian, Robert Kronenburg, Marion Leonard, and Rob Strachan; Simon Frith, Martin Cloonan, Matt Brennan, and Emma Webster for putting together "The Business of Live Music" conference at University of Edinburgh, where live music studies first announced itself as something approaching an academic field; at Syracuse University, Theo Cateforis for the opportunity to speak to the Mobilizing Music seminar; at McGill University, David Brackett, Georgina Born, and Mimi Haddon for hosting an enlivening symposium on Music and Genre; at Northeastern University, David Herlihy, Andrew Mall, and Rebekah Moore; at New York University, Samuel Chan, Maureen Mahon, Kelso Malloy, and David Samuels; Brian Wright and Chris Reali, for the invitation to speak to the Popular Music Study Group of the American Musicological Society; Simon Zagorski-Thomas, for the United Kingdom and Ireland branch of IASPM; and at University of Huddersfield, Jan Herbst and Rosemary Lucy Hill.

To Maria Damon and Carol Mason, two friends from my days at the University of Minnesota, I eat a bowl of whipped cream and sip a dry gin martini in tribute to our years of friendship.

To the musical and creative arts community in Northampton and its environs, thank you for bringing me out of my shell and inspiring me to want to play music in public and for providing much stimulation to the eyes, ears, and other senses. I reserve my deepest appreciation for my band mates in the Electric Eyes (maybe now defunct, maybe not), Adam Douthwright, Fred Fernandes, and Matt Medeiros, as well as close musical companions Joe Pater and Frank Sinistra. For making the Pioneer Valley such a vibrant place to be, power chords of praise to Monte Belmonte, Peter Blanchette, Madeline Weaver Blanchette, Ann Hackler, Dave Hayes, June Millington, Jim Olsen, Priscilla Page, Tanya Pearson, Jim and Nicole Shea (FOE Gallery RIP), Glenn Siegel, and Jeremy Smith.

At Oxford University Press, Suzanne Ryan Melamed offered the first stirrings of encouragement for this project during a long conversation at the Society for Ethnomusicology conference. When she stepped away, Norm Hirschy graciously welcomed me on board and his enthusiasm for this book has been essential. All thanks, as well, to the incisive anonymous reviewers who championed the book's publication.

Final thanks go to the American Musicological Society for providing a publication subvention through its General Fund, supported in part by the National Endowment for the Humanities and the Andrew W. Mellon Foundation.

This book is dedicated to the memory of my parents, Jeanne and Marvin Waksman, both of whom passed away during the years when I worked on it. I have no more words. You are always in my heart.

Introduction

Toward a History of Liveness

Starting in the summer of 1988, Bob Dylan embarked on what has since been dubbed the "Never Ending Tour," which continued unbroken until the onset of the COVID-19 pandemic in 2020. Over a century earlier, the American piano virtuoso Louis Moreau Gottschalk undertook a similarly exhaustive concert tour schedule throughout much of the decade of the 1860s. From 1862 until his death in Brazil in 1869 at age forty, Gottschalk toured almost incessantly and across a geographic scope that encompassed much of the US and many areas of Latin America, where he spent the last four years of his life. His efforts were enabled by a confluence of key developments: the growth of new travel networks, most notably the railroad; the construction of public performance halls across an expanding range of American towns and cities; and the rise of a commercial concert economy that allowed professional artists of sufficient drive to concertize with nearly uninterrupted regularity.

During much of this time, Gottschalk kept a detailed diary full of insights about the peculiar life of the touring concert musician. There one gets a sense of the sheer pace of the pianist's activity, as in this entry from 1864: "Last month, June, I gave thirty-three concerts in twenty-six days. In fourteen months (during which I have remained idle only fifty days) I have given more than four hundred concerts and traveled more than forty thousand miles by railroad."[1] Such endeavors were bound to take their toll, and in one of the diary's most vivid entries, Gottschalk expands at length on the grind of being on the road, day after day, for weeks at a time:

> As in the past, I continue to be whirled in space . . . *Pianistomonambulist!* Everything is foreseen, everything is marked out, everything is regulated in my peregrination. Thanks to the experience of my agent, I know in advance, within a few dollars, the amount of the receipts in a town of a given number of inhabitants. I know, with my eyes shut, every one of the inextricable cross-threads that form the network of the railroads with which

New England is covered . . . In my black suit at 8 o'clock I salute my audience, and give them *Il Trovatore* . . . At ten o'clock I carry off my patriotic audience to the belligerent accents of *The Union* fantasia, and at half-past ten I throw myself, exhausted and depoetized, into the prosaic arms of the blessed Morpheus . . . Then morning, breakfast in a hurry, and alas! five, six, seven, eight, or ten hours of railroad, and always the same thing—the crowd, and to be isolated![2]

Gottschalk's cutting account unfurls the frustrations of the working musician of the 1860s, which were much like the frustrations of the working musician of the 1980s, or the 2010s. Tedium, repetition, routine—what the audience might take to be the thrill of a singular performance, the performer may see as one in a string of endless, and endlessly similar experiences. Yet the sheer regularity that Gottschalk describes should also provoke our wonder. There was already such a system in place that, by the 1860s, an artist could range widely across time and space while knowing where he would be working from one day to the next, how many people he would be playing to, how much revenue he had generated, and the shape of the program he would offer. These elements, as much as the short burst of time when the performance happened, are fundamental to the phenomenon of live music as we know it.

Jump ahead to the 1970s, when arena rock had solidified as the dominant mode of live music production. Railroads had been replaced by a combination of air travel, tour buses and—for the biggest tours on the road—tractor trailers that were necessary to move the elaborate staging materials from one performance location to the next. Largely unchanged, though, was the routine of the concert tour. Documents from Led Zeppelin's 1977 US tour capture the pace in far less personalized terms than Gottschalk's tour diary. Led Zeppelin, of course, is among the most notorious bands in rock history for their on-the-road escapades concerning the pursuit of groupies, destruction of hotel rooms, and other associated acts that epitomized the Dionysian impulses believed to infuse the music and surrounding culture. As out of control as they often appeared, they and other bands like them still had to observe the rigid time discipline required of a band on the road. The master tour itinerary captures this discipline in a series of highly organized grids that offer essential information for each stop on the tour: city, state, day of the week, date of the month, information about the venue, hotel, and the promoter for the show, the time at which the rigging (set-up) for the show was scheduled to start, estimated time of arrival at the destination, proposed travel route, and estimated time of departure.[3] Unlike Gottschalk, who had a single agent to guide him on his way, Led Zeppelin in 1977 had a whole entourage whose job was to make sure that whatever antics the members of the band got into on any given night, things were ready to move to the next stop so that the tour remained on track.

Appended to the master itinerary was a separate travel schedule assembled by Travel Service of America, who had the responsibility to ensure timely travel for the entirety of Zeppelin's touring entourage. Mitzie Calder, an agent for the company, put together a cover letter in which she appoints herself the "Den Mother" for the tour and offers instruction in a caring but firm voice: "Your 'Den Mother' will be with you all the way. Do not hesitate to contact me with any problems in travel or lodging you might have." In the accompanying document, basic details about hotels and air travel schedules are supplemented by recommendations for restaurants at each stop, and very specific guidelines for moving on to the next destination: "Proceed directly through Security and go to the Flagship Suite between gates 6 & 7. Be there no later than 11:45. Salty Dogs and Bloody Marys will be served." At times the tension between the orderliness of the travel plans and the realities of a rock band on tour come to the surface, most notably in a brief note beside the tour's reservation at the Omni Hotel in Atlanta: "Please put best foot forward. This hotel did not want to take us. Dress as neat as possible." Overall, though, the tone is markedly upbeat and meant to keep the band and even more so, its road crew moving efficiently through to end of the first leg of the tour on May 1, when the Dallas-based Showco crew would be able to return home for a brief rest, signaled on the itinerary with the following: "Hotels: Home. Meals: Home cooking . . . Sightseeing: Loved ones. Transfers: Any old way . . . See you on May 17."[4]

* * *

The details, large and small, that connect the experience of Louis Moreau Gottschalk touring across the US and Latin America in the 1860s and Led Zeppelin touring across the US in the 1970s are essential to the fabric of this book. How artists get from place to place is inseparable from the economy of live performance in which they work. Live music matters because of the depth and intensity of experience that it projects to its audiences; because of the ways in which it instantiates deeply held values shared by a wide swathe of the listening public—or deeply held values that become the basis for conflict between one constituency and another; because it has served as one of the primary means according to which people have come together in collective enjoyment. It also matters because it has served as one of the driving engines in the business of music and the industrialization of music production, existing in a dynamic relationship with the selling of sheet music and then sound recordings. In writing a history of live music in the US covering one-hundred and fifty years, I have placed all of these factors in the foreground at different times, viewing performers, audiences, media commentators, and a variety of live music producers (promoters, agents, sound and stage technicians) as central players who have shaped what live music means and how it has evolved. In doing so, I have tried to think as broadly as possible about what I would call the enabling conditions of live music. A core question that occupies the heart of this book is the deceptively simply formulation: What allows live music to happen? Asking this question, I seek to connect what occurs behind the scenes to what takes place on the stage and to highlight the ways in which live music is something that is very deliberately produced and does not just spontaneously materialize.

Thinking about live music in this way entails thinking about "liveness," those qualities that define musical performance as a discrete phenomenon and confer upon it a special character. There are many qualities of live music, or live performance more generally, that may seem essential and transhistorical. Live music is ephemeral. A performance happens and then it is over. If it is reproduced, the reproduction is not a part of the performance but something else, an attempt to capture and preserve the fleeting sensations of the moment. It is moreover situated not only in time but in place. Live music occurs in particular types of spaces. Sometimes these spaces are designed specifically to house such performances; at other times, they are appropriated and repurposed to that end, as is the case with just about any bar or restaurant where live music is presented.[5] In either case, the place where live music occurs has a fundamental impact on the performance itself and upon the audience's experience of that performance. Live music depends upon the co-presence of, at a minimum, one or more performers and one or more members of an audience. For reasons I will explain subsequently, I consider live music to be a public phenomenon. It is not something that happens alone. Following from this, live music is connected to the experience of collectivity. It inherently involves groups of people, and the size and character of those gathered is often as much a defining aspect of the live event as the musical performance itself.

While these characteristics may seem to apply to live music writ large, in writing a history of the subject I have stressed the ways in which the defining elements of live music and perceptions of liveness have changed over time. There are continuities to be found in this history to be sure, as the opening juxtaposition of Gottschalk and Led Zeppelin should make clear; but live music has been far from static even at the level of its core qualities. In considering the historical character of live music, I take an important cue from performance theorist Philip Auslander's influential work, *Liveness*, in which he analyzes the interrelationship between live and "mediatized" forms of cultural expression. Rejecting any absolute distinction between live performance and modes of mechanical and electronic representation such as sound recordings, film, and television, Auslander posits: "To understand the relationship between live and mediatized forms, it is necessary to investigate their relationship as historical and contingent, not as ontologically given or technologically determined."[6] The historical particularity of live performance, and the contingency of those qualities that convey a sense of "liveness," is a running theme throughout this book, from Jenny Lind's first appearance before a New York audience in 1850 to Beyoncé's performances at the Coachella festival in 2018.

Choosing to begin this history in the mid-nineteenth century, I take issue with another of Auslander's principal claims. Expounding upon his understanding of the interrelationship between live performance and media technologies, Auslander asserts:

> I propose that, historically, the live is actually an effect of mediatization, not the other way around. It was the development of recording technologies that made it possible to perceive existing representations as "live." Prior to the advent of those technologies (e.g., sound recording and motion pictures), there was no such thing as "live" performance, for that category had meaning only in relation to an opposing possibility."[7]

This assertion has become something of a commonplace in studies of live performance, musical and otherwise. It has a compelling logic and there is no small degree of truth to it. Yet it suffers for being inexact and also for drawing too strict of a line between the time before and after the advent of mechanical reproduction. Even if we prioritize the rise of sound recordings and film as the events above all that cause "liveness" as a discrete phenomenon to emerge, it has never been clearly shown—by Auslander or anyone else—when exactly this happens, and how. Before these technologies had become routine, meanwhile, other kinds of "mediatization" were in place—sheet music for one; journalistic accounts of live performance, for another; music venues, for another still. If we are going to understand the relationship between the "liveness" of live music and what Auslander calls mediatization, then, we need to refine our understanding of how media works in relation to live music beyond a simple emphasis upon recording technologies.

* * *

By the middle years of the nineteenth century, the perception began to emerge that there was something singular about the experience of live music, that its very liveness exerted a particular sort of attraction and offered a distinct sort of pleasure. To give one especially vivid example, I turn to a passage that is often cited in histories of nineteenth-century popular culture. It comes from journalist George Foster's sensationalist 1850 account of urban nightlife, *New York by Gaslight*. The setting is a dance house owned by Pete Williams, a place that had gained notoriety some years earlier when Charles Dickens wrote about it in the account of his travels across the US and had since been nicknamed Dickens's Place. Foster's language brings his reader into the setting as though he is leading a guided tour. After paying a shilling for admittance, Foster settles himself and his reader in to enjoy the "orchestra," which consists of fiddle, trumpet, and bass drum. "With these instruments," notes Foster, "you may imagine that the music of Dickens's Place is of no ordinary kind. You cannot, however, begin to imagine *what* it is." The writer continues:

> You cannot *see* the red-hot knitting needles spirted out by the red-faced trumpeter, who looks precisely as if he were blowing glass, which needles aforesaid penetrating the tympanum, pierce through and through your brain without remorse. Nor can you perceive the frightful mechanical contortions of the bass-drummer as he sweats and deals his blows on every side, in all violation of the laws of rhythm, like a man beating a baulky mule and showering his blows upon the unfortunate animal, now on this side, now on that. If you could, it would be unnecessary for us to write.[8]

That this passage was published in 1850 should give pause to anyone seeking to claim that live music only acquired a peculiar aura of its own after sound recordings had become pervasive.

Cultural historians have used Foster's account to uncover the existence of a distinct working-class culture existing in the midst of mid-nineteenth-century Manhattan. In Eric Lott's valuable study of blackface minstrelsy, *Love and Theft*, it arises to document the thin line between popular entertainment and political confrontation, an impulse that comes to the surface when Foster describes how the dancers at Dickens's Place, "wild with excitement, like Ned Buntline at Astor Place, leap frantically about like howling dervishes."[9] The Astor Place Opera House was the location of an 1849 conflict between elite and working-class New Yorkers that stands as one of the signal moments in the historical relationship between "high" and "low" cultural formations, and will be discussed at greater length in Chapter 1. For now, what stands out in Foster's description of the musical action at Dickens's Place is the self-consciousness with which he addresses the gap between the event as it happened and his written portrayal. The "live" is here construed as ephemeral, fleeting, inaccessible to those who weren't there except through the eyes, the ears, and the words of one who was present.

Another musical event of 1850 further attests to the power attributed to the live act, but on a much grander scale: the US concert debut of Jenny Lind, the subject of the first chapter of this book. By the time she appeared on the stage at New York's Castle Garden on the evening of Wednesday, September 11 of that year, Lind had been subject of the largest publicity campaign waged on behalf of a single performer up to that time, orchestrated by the manager of her concert tour, P.T. Barnum. The result of the widespread circulation of Lind's image, music, and descriptive accounts of her character was a heightened sense of anticipation regarding her first in-the-flesh concert appearance. Prominent critic John S. Dwight, writing in the New York *Daily Tribune*, could barely contain his excitement in recounting Lind's appearance before the Castle Garden crowd:

> Now came a moment of breathless expectation. A moment more, and Jenny Lind, clad in a white dress which well became the frank sincerity of her face, came forward through the orchestra. It is impossible to describe the spontaneous burst of welcome which greeted her. The vast assembly [reported attendance was nearly six thousand] rose as one man, and for some minutes nothing could be seen but the waving of hands and handkerchiefs, nothing heard but a storm of tumultuous cheers.[10]

Such a momentous response to the sheer appearance of Lind was the product of a burgeoning commercial culture in which live musical events were already part of a larger media system. Lind herself was the prototypical star who became intimately familiar even as she remained distant from the swelling crowds that gathered to hear her fabled voice or simply to satisfy their curiosity concerning what all the fuss was about. As such, she personified those qualities of celebrity described so evocatively by media scholar P. David Marshall: "The celebrity . . . is not distant but attainable—touchable by the multitude. The greatness of the celebrity is something that can be shared and, in essence, celebrated loudly and with a touch of vulgar pride. It is the ideal representation of the triumph of the masses."[11] While sound recording might have amplified the power of such stars, in many ways it only enhanced a long-established phenomenon. Indeed, the longing to be in the presence of such a musical celebrity may have been stronger in the era before sound recording, for the simple reason that only in concert could one actually hear Lind sing.

We might wonder if the aura attached to the live appearance of a star performer has lost some of the force it had in Lind's day. Where does liveness reside in a culture where communication has become instantaneous, where being in the moment is so often filtered through screens and social media platforms that convert lived experience into stored memory in the click of a button? And yet, consider the outpouring of excitement and commentary that attended to Beyoncé's appearance at the Coachella Valley Music and Arts Festival in 2018, which was quickly dubbed "Beychella" in tribute to the artist. I will return to this performance in the conclusion of this book, but for now want to highlight the complex sense of immediacy that accompanied the opening of Beyoncé's Coachella set.

In a dialogue on the entertainment website *Vulture* titled, "What It Was Like to Be in the Audience for Beyoncé's Historic Coachella Show," critic Dee Lockett offered her impressions:

> The moment I saw her drum major signal the start of the show, I was reminded of Beyoncé's last Super Bowl halftime show [in 2016] . . . which began similarly. What I was not prepared for was the parting of the drumline to reveal Bey, dressed in Balmain as a Nubian queen. The cape! The headdress! It was all too much. And then the scaffolding tilted back and elevated to uncage the rest of her 200-person marching band sitting atop bleachers. We were at a pep rally! I think it took others a half-second to realize the setup, which might account for our looks of bewilderment. But make no mistake, when Bey descended the stairs in her BΔK sweatshirt and "Crazy in Love" dropped, the whole field was bumping.[12]

Lockett and fellow reporter Kyle Buchanan proceed to reflect on the way that concertgoers were torn between the desire to document the performance happening before them, holding out their cell phones to get the right shot, and their desire to be attentive to the performance itself undistracted by the small screen in their hands. This juxtaposition has become utterly commonplace and represents a new stage of precisely the sort of mediatization that Auslander discusses throughout *Liveness*, wherein the performance as such and the act of recording or otherwise mediating the performance become all but inseparable. Still the sheer thrill of being present ultimately remained intact, as did the pleasure that derived from sharing that experience of presence with so many thousands (in this case tens of thousands) of others. As Buchanan explained: "For those of us in the crowd, it was impossible to miss the dozens of band members backing Bey on those risers, and their joy powered ours. I saw it reflected on all of our exhilarated faces, a communal experience that I'll never forget."[13]

Elsewhere I have discussed such moments as these, when a musical crowd takes pleasure in its very sense of itself as a crowd, as an instance of "discharge," using the phrase derived from novelist and social philosopher Elias Canetti. In Canetti's terms, the discharge refers to a time when "distinctions are thrown off and all feel *equal* . . . It is for the sake of this blessed moment, when no-one is greater or better than another, that people become a crowd."[14] This experience is essential to the role that live music has played in public life. Indeed, it is one of the most potent ways in which individuals have found pleasure while being not just in public, but being part of a public, collective body.

* * *

Prior to the broad dissemination of mechanical reproduction, many musical performances did not happen before an audience. Of course, this remains true today, but in the absence of sound recordings and radio, let alone streaming music services, it had a different salience. The basic fact that music generally had to be *played* to be heard or enjoyed gives Auslander's insistence upon the belated recognition of "live music" a measure of credibility. Encounters with musical performance were not in themselves exceptional throughout much of the nineteenth century, perhaps especially among the middle classes for whom a sort of domestic music making based around the piano became increasingly common. When John Philip Sousa warned of the dangers of "canned music" in a now-famous 1906 essay, "The Menace of Mechanical Music," he wrote in defense of a musical culture in which the possession of a certain modicum of musical skill had become the norm.[15] "Live music" as such did not have a clear other in this context, a term against which its difference could be posited.

Instead, I would suggest that the operative difference in the era before mechanical reproduction was that between "public" and "private" music making. We can observe the importance of this dichotomy in the multifaceted position of the piano in nineteenth-century musical life. In both Europe and the US, the piano became central to an emergent form of middle-class domesticity.[16] It served as a tool to promote values of cultivation, discipline, and civility; and these values were transmitted through a growing system of formal music instruction that concentrated upon the training of young women. The goal of such instruction was precisely not to foster a fully realized virtuosity, the effects of which were perceived to be disruptive of the proper bourgeois home. Rather, the private sphere hosted a more temperate style of musicianship, in keeping with its association with feminine reserve and virtue.

Public piano performance in the middle and later years of the nineteenth century was a far more demonstrative endeavor and was almost as thoroughly masculinized as private piano performance was thoroughly feminized. Virtuoso pianists became culture heroes of a sort, and in the US assumed a growing prominence throughout the decade of the 1840s. They were heroes of a decidedly ambivalent kind, however, provoking anxiety and adulation in roughly equal measure as critics like the aforementioned John S. Dwight worried about the degree to which their flamboyant pyrotechnics detracted from the more purely musical qualities of their work.[17] In Europe Franz Liszt became a model for this modern form of piano performance, exciting interest throughout the 1830s and for decades following. Liszt never visited the US, but starting with the 1845 tour of the Austrian pianist Leopold de Meyer, concerts by touring pianists—others including the French virtuoso Henri Herz and, in 1853, the American debut of Gottschalk after years of European study—became occasions for debate about the proper role of music in the public sphere.[18] A number of issues followed these artists as they made their way across the American landscape: Is music's role to entertain or to elevate? Should the performer be in service to the composed work, or should the work be the vehicle for inspired performance? Can musical greatness coexist with virtuosic spectacle? Is there a single musical public or multiple publics, and if the latter, should the taste of any one segment of the public predominate?

Musical performance played an integral role in the formation of a modern public sphere, a process which had begun at least a century before the regular incursion of touring piano virtuosos upon North American soil. Social theorist Jurgen Habermas accords a significant but often unrecognized place to music and the arts in his foundational account of the public sphere. Talk about the arts was prevalent in the salons and coffee houses of France, England, and Germany, where he locates an emerging public of critically thinking citizens in the eighteenth century. What gave that talk an especially transformative character was its relative accessibility, which Habermas credits to the growing influence of commerce upon artistic production and consumption such that prior systems of exclusive, elite patronage began to break down. He explains in a key passage: "the same process that converted culture into a commodity (and in this fashion constituted it as a culture that could become an object of discussion in the first place) established the public as in principle inclusive."[19] For Habermas musical concerts reflected this transformation in a pronounced fashion. When concerts that were sponsored by religious institutions or noble courts gave way to concerts that were more squarely commercial in character, they became open to a broader—if still highly circumscribed—public. Just as significant, the role of music changed in these proceedings. It became valued more as a thing in itself and not as an adjunct to religious ceremony or courtly socializing. As a result, "For the first time an audience gathered to listen to music as such—a public of music lovers to which anyone who was propertied and educated was admitted. Released from its function in the service of social representation, art became an object of free choice and of changing preference."[20]

In the US, as in England, much of the formal and documented concert activity in the colonial and early national period occurred under the auspices of musical societies that presented performances for a restricted segment of the public, typically white men of means and property who paid to subscribe to a given concert series that was essentially staged for their benefit. The St. Cecilia Society in Charleston, South Carolina, established in 1766, is generally credited to have been the first such society in the colonies to have had any lasting impact, remaining active until 1820.[21] Society historian Nicholas Butler has shown that admission to St. Cecilia subscription concerts was not limited to members, but that the ticket policy struck a fine line between "exclusivity and hospitality." He outlines four types of tickets that the Society offered for its performances: "season tickets for members, tickets for ladies, single tickets for gentlemen strangers, and season tickets for strangers," stranger being the term for a non-member of the society.[22] The separate category of tickets for ladies suggests something of the imperative to regulate women's concertgoing along different lines from that of men during the time. Butler further notes that "gentlemen strangers" could receive a single ticket for an entire concert season but women could only procure tickets for one performance at a time, ensuring that male concertgoers enjoyed special privilege of access. For all attendees, meanwhile, tickets had to be obtained in advance and were unavailable on the night of a performance, a further mechanism to preserve the desired level of social exclusivity. Perhaps it is needless to say that the city's majority black population was not welcome at these concerts.

By the time we reach Jenny Lind's American debut in 1850, this restrictive sense of the musical public had given way to something far more expansive, if not as all-inclusive as some observers wanted to believe. More than any event that preceded it, Lind's US concert tour instantiated a tendency that remained a defining aspect of the nation's musical life: a running concern with musical crowds as an index of public character. The crowds that gathered at Patrick Gilmore's two Peace Jubilees in 1869 and 1872, that filled Carnegie Hall for a jazz concert by Benny Goodman in 1938 and stood at the steps of the Lincoln Memorial to hear Marian Anderson sing in 1939, that attended the Newport Jazz and Folk Festivals and rock festivals such as Woodstock, and that made arena concerts into the dominant mode of live music production of the late twentieth century—these disparate events indicate the degree to which the impulse to gather the largest crowd possible has been a recurrent theme in the history of American live music. More often than not, the pursuit of the crowd has a decidedly commercial orientation, following upon Habermas' claims about the conversion of culture into a commodity. Capitalism alone does not explain the production of musical crowds, however, which depend on a variety of other factors: urbanism, the concentration of population in such a way that large public gatherings are possible; nationalism, often invoked to invest the collectivity of the crowd with larger significance (as we will see, Jenny Lind concluded her debut concert with a special composition, "Greeting to America"); and the differentiation of society along lines of class, ethnicity, age, and gender, among other factors, which intensifies the crowd's importance as an act of "bringing together" (and also of keeping apart). Musical crowds are a distillation of the "imagined community" that Benedict Anderson has identified at the core of modern nationalism.[23] They embody in material form music's capacity to generate a social field that is at once embedded in larger systems of meaning and power and marked by relative autonomy.

This is not only a book about large-scale events. Most live music happens on a smaller scale and size is not the only, or best, measure of social impact. Consider the contrast between the scene described by George Foster at Dickens's Place and the scene that accompanied Jenny Lind's debut at Castle Garden. Much more than order of magnitude distinguishes these two happenings. Although Lind's concerts were celebrated for representing the full range of American social life, they also particularly embodied an emerging form of middle-class respectability. The music and dancing at Dickens's Place existed on a much "lower" end of the social ladder, a sphere where black and white participants mixed more freely, where music coexisted with the imbibing of alcohol and with sexual commerce, and where a sort of "public intimacy" was enacted that grew in visibility over time and was one of the factors that contributed to the emergence of jazz in the early decades of the twentieth century.

The tension between these different registers of cultural life—the respectable and refined and its lowdown, less inhibited counterpart—is one of the defining facets of live music history in the pages that follow. Contests over taste that followed from this division were in many ways the byproduct of the foregoing changes described by Habermas. As culture became increasingly subject to market forces, taste became personalized and individualized while also assuming greater importance as a marker of social status and class position. Cultural historian Lawrence Levine documented the increasingly rigid boundary that distinguished "highbrow" and "lowbrow" forms of art and culture over the course of the nineteenth century. For Levine, the process through which high culture—classical music, opera, Shakespearean drama, fine art painting and sculpture—was defined as an almost sacred realm apart from ordinary life was driven by social and economic elites who wished to guard their privilege in the face of overwhelming social change.[24] Importantly, Levine shows that these attitudes did not just exist in the abstract but had decided material consequences: the creation of high art institutions such as the modern concert hall, and the accompanying assumptions about how members of the audience were expected to conduct themselves in such a space—in silence and with full concentration directed toward the music or other works on offer—arose out of the growing faith that "true" art entailed a disposition of serious contemplation.

Yet popular culture not only held its ground but expanded its influence in the face of high culture values. Vaudeville created a forum where popular entertainment could be accommodated to certain notions of middle-class respectability. Jazz began its move into the concert halls of high culture early in its history, eventually upending the strict divide between high and low in musical terms. By the rock era of the 1960s and 1970s, the pattern of cultural hierarchy had transformed dramatically, as described by philosopher Bernard Gendron: "In the cultural competition between popular music and high art, popular music has won, not by rising 'higher' than high-cultural music . . . but by making the latter less culturally relevant where it matters."[25] Throughout these various shifts, live music has remained a primary medium through which questions of artistic and cultural value are contested and put into practice; and these points of contest are inextricable from music's place in American public life.

* * *

Returning to the phrase "live music" itself, Philip Auslander is right to suggest that it is a distinctly modern invention. A brief genealogy of the term reveals much about the connection of "liveness" to broader changes in media, culture, and technology. Among the earliest instances in which the discrete phrase "live music" can be found in print is an 1853 newspaper advertisement for a collection of sacred music titled *The Dulcimer*, compiled by music editor I.B. Woodbury and first published in 1851. The text of the ad proclaims in bold print that *The Dulcimer* is a "Live Music Book," and makes a comparison to the recently published sensation, Harriet Beecher Stowe's *Uncle Tom's Cabin*. Like that famed and inflammatory publication, *The Dulcimer* "talks and sings like a live book. Attention is awakened, the thoughts are arrested, the sympathies touched, curiosity aroused."[26] The use of "live" here refers to the power of Woodbury's collection to translate the content on the printed page into material that the reader would be compelled to enact, to convert into music (dare we say, live music) as Stowe's book stirred readers into sympathy with the cause of anti-slavery.

Other early references to live music scattered throughout newspapers of the 1860s and 1870s are similarly idiosyncratic. A shift is observable as the twentieth century approaches. An 1890 edition of the *Worcester Daily Spy* titled its performance review column, "Live Music and Drama," although only two columns appeared under that heading.[27] A smattering of further references to "live music" appears throughout the 1890s: a brass band draws a crowd with its "live music" in Dallas prior to a speech by Texas gubernatorial candidate Gustav Cook; also in Dallas, in 1892, "live music" is an advertised attraction at a meeting of the Y.M.C.A. that also features a sermon on "The Word—How Have You Received It?"; and in 1898, a Republican political rally in Rockford, Illinois, offered "live music" provided by two singing quartets.[28] By this time recorded music was beginning to have more impact, with the phonograph and the gramophone competing for the attention of a still-nascent record-buying public. No explicit reference is made in any of these articles to the presence of sound recordings, however. If anything connects these stray items, it is that all of these events are not expressly musical performances. It would appear that in its early formulation, live music was used to designate music that appeared in settings where it was not a primary feature but added value to a social gathering that was otherwise organized around religion or politics, two principal areas of nineteenth-century public life.

Moving into the twentieth century proper, two sheet music advertisements appearing in the weekly theatrical newspaper the *New York Clipper* offer a telling use of the word "live" in association with music, one that appeared in 1906 and one that appeared in 1919. In the first, seen in Figure 0.1, the F.B. Haviland Publishing Co. advertises nine new songs under the heading, "Real Live Songs for Real Live Singers (You're One) by Real Live Authors."[29] This seems to be a distinctly modern usage of the word "live" in connection with music—although it is important to note that the operative phrase here is not "live music" but "live songs," and secondarily "live singers." The second ad, issued thirteen years later by the McKinley Music Co., uses almost exactly the same phrase for the same purpose of selling new songs in their published, sheet music form: "Live Songs Live Singers Are Singing."[30]

These two examples clearly mirror each other, and their situation in ads for sheet music is of primary significance. I believe the motivation for these proclamations is in fact the growing impact of sound recordings upon the commercial music economy. Recordings are the implicit referent that makes these claims of "liveness" meaningful. However, given that background, it is notable that what is being characterized as "live" is not the performance of songs per se, but songs in their published form, as sheet music. How are these songs "live"? They are live because they are written to be sung by performers on a stage. The logic of promoting and establishing "liveness" as something

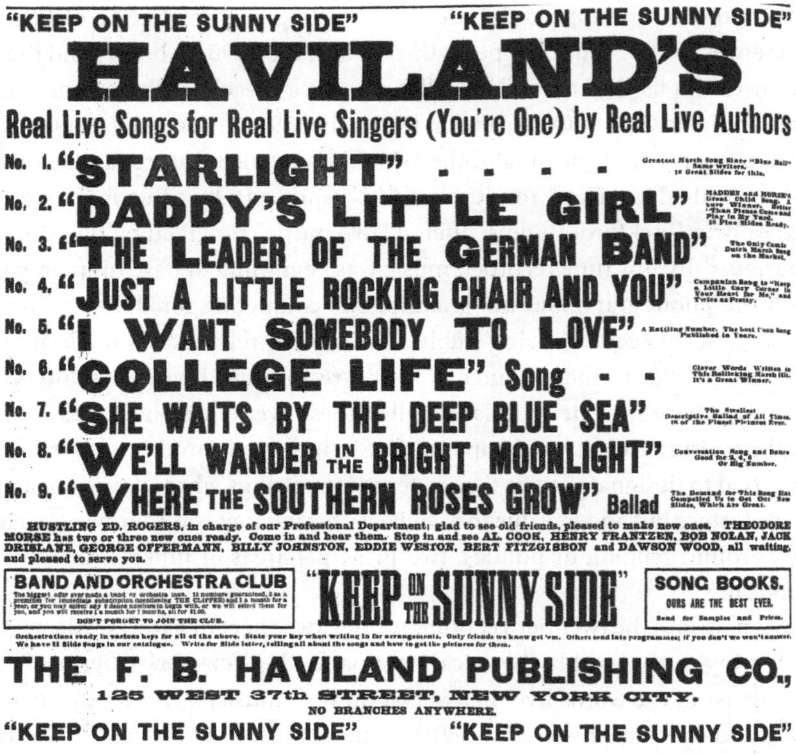

Figure 0.1 "Real Live Songs for Real Live Singers (You're One)." This 1906 ad for the F.B. Haviland Publishing Co. marks an early published instance in which music was described as "live" with a modern inflection. From the *New York Clipper* (February 2, 1906).

discrete here is thus indirect: published songs are "live" because they are designed for theatrical performance, whereas recorded songs, it is suggested, lack this liveness since they only exist in mechanical form. Or to put it differently, the rhetoric of "liveness" here is used not to authenticate live music as such, in opposition to recorded music. Instead, it is used to valorize an alternative, already-existing mode of musical reproduction.

Next we come to a 1916 article in *Moving Picture World*, a trade journal for the still-young film industry. The rise of film exhibition as a form of popular amusement had consequences for musical performance that were, in a sense, as momentous as the spread of sound recording. In 1916, *Moving*

Picture World writer W. Stephen Bush reported on the recent success of the Knickerbocker, a New York movie house managed by S.L. Rothapfel, an influential theatrical impresario who would later found the noted Roxy Theater in New York. Among the improvements that Rothapfel was said to have made in the theater since taking it over was a revitalized musical program that was a part of each show. Under the heading, "Music Means Life," Rothapfel articulated his philosophy concerning music's place in the movie house: "The orchestra is there to charm the audience, of course, but the first thing necessary is to wake them up. Let them know there is music in the house; the drooling dirges may be all right for a first-class Chinese theater, but a place that caters to live Americans wants plenty of live music."[31]

The importance attached to this aspect of Rothapfel's programming policy offers evidence of a key facet of early film history: that the "silent" film era was anything but silent.[32] Music provided by a single musician in smaller theaters, and by orchestras in larger theaters seeking broader patronage, was an integral part of the show. Liveness, and live music specifically, here becomes valued not for its difference from recorded music, but as an alternative to music that is more somber, melancholy or restrained. This "live" quality, according to Rothapfel, is needed to keep the audience alert while watching a silent film, where the music was to awaken spectators to avenues of emotion and experience that the images themselves could not always express. That Rothapfel connects liveness to the uniquely "American" character of the audience adds an unexpected layer of racial connotation, but also reflects the tension existing at the time between entertainment houses that were geared toward local, ethnic enclaves and those seeking to appeal to a wider mass viewership of the sort that Rothapfel pursued.

A 1921 advertisement for Conn wind instruments brings another, rather different sort of connotation to "live music." Here the purpose behind the phrase is to sell musical instruments, and specifically saxophones. Encouraging readers to devote themselves to the "profit and pleasure" that music can bring, the ad copy continues: "Wherever folks gather nowadays music is in demand . . . Here's an opportunity for **you**. Doesn't *live music* thrill you; doesn't the rhythmic surge of a popular selection make **you** want to play?"[33] Enhancing this effort to evoke the "thrill" of live music is a triptych of pictures, portraying Paul Whiteman, who in 1921 was on his way toward becoming the most widely recognized jazz bandleader in the US; Ted

Lewis, known for his comedic antics as well as his saxophone playing, whose popularity as an American bandleader at the time rivaled Whiteman's; and Matthew Amaturo, a multi-instrumentalist with the Chicago-based Benson Orchestra, one of the most popular dance orchestras of the era. Tellingly, all three of the musicians are white, for white artists became the most visible public face of jazz starting with the success of the Original Dixieland Jazz Band in 1916–19 and remained so throughout the 1920s. Meanwhile, the ad invokes "live music" to spur the reader toward visions of professional success, suggesting that the new popularity of jazz has created opportunities for musicians to profit from playing their instruments.

Early discourses surrounding live music cannot be reduced to a single point of emphasis, as these examples attest. Recording technologies figure in most of these instances but their influence is far from determining. We see above all how much emergent recognition of live music depended upon the particularities of context: live music meant one thing in the effort to promote sheet music as a more worthy commodity than sound recordings, and something quite different when employed as a stimulant to the passions of film spectators. The ad for Conn instruments, in turn, offers clear indication that, in the early 1920s, live performance remained the linchpin of a professional musician's career despite what was by then a marked increase in the circulation of commercial sound recordings. Live music is not being invoked here as a safeguard against the impact of recordings, but as the surest and most established path to professional success.

This inflection changed over the ensuing decade as the market for recorded music continued to expand and, more importantly, sound recordings began to appear in settings once dominated by "live," performing musicians. Movie houses once again were integral crucibles of change. The incorporation of recorded soundtracks into film exhibition, which became routinized in 1926 and 1927 with the Warner Brothers Vitaphone system, led to the rapid and systematic dismissal of thousands of union musicians around the US from regular employment in movie theaters. Compounding the situation was the mounting popularity of sound films, which caused a steep decline in vaudeville theater patronage as well, such that professional musicians were losing ground on two fronts at once. By the end of the 1920s, as historian James Kraft has shown, the American Federation of Musicians under the leadership of Joseph Weber mounted a concerted campaign to promote the presentation of live music in theaters and oppose its replacement by sound recordings or what was termed "canned music" in the organization's rhetoric.³⁴ The opposition between "live" and "recorded" music first assumed real coherence and a measure of consistency in public discourse through the AFM campaign.

Surveying a series of ads placed by the AFM in the classical music news publication, *Musical America*, during the years 1929–1931, several features come to light. Most obvious is the use of a rather demonic looking robot as a surrogate to characterize the threat posed by "canned music." In the earliest 1929 ad, shown in Figure 0.2, the robot offends all notions of good music and good taste—pictorially savaging a harp, and verbally accused of imposing his will upon the unsuspecting masses, as the ad asserts:

> There has been no public demand for Canned Music. The Robot has simply claimed the stage without invitation. Having no ears he is undismayed by the lack of applause ... At best Mechanical Music in theaters is a substitute for the Real Thing, just offered as something that "will do" ... Actually, exploitation of Canned Music represents an attempt to prove that Music can be dispensed with in the theater, for Canned Music lacks power to produce emotional reaction and therefore is not music at all in any true sense.³⁵

Significantly, in this first ad, the phrase "live music" or its approximation is nowhere to be found. "Canned music" is juxtaposed with "real music," setting forth a clear dichotomy in which the human is contrasted to the mechanical, and authenticity is affirmed in the face of artifice.

Two months later, in January 1930, the terms of the AFM's campaign take a turn. The musical union makes an appeal to mothers, claiming that the various forces of modern life pose obstacles to a mother's hopes for her children and family: "Humanizing culture is spurned ... Adolescents mock marriage. Crime is luring youth to ruin."³⁶ Amidst this litany of supposedly degrading forces, "the Machine" looms as a "soulless master," standing for all the forces that rob humans of control over the circumstances of their own lives. Against this background, according to the AFM, canned music, or "machine-made sound," is now opposed to "living music." The choice of words is telling. Living music here is infused with deep moral significance. It suggests the degree to which music—"real" music, performed by human musicians in a theatrical setting—might be understood to stand with civilization against barbarism, to protect innocence in the face of demoralization, and ultimately to be essential to the maintenance of humanity writ large. The invocation of highbrow cultural values here suggests how exclusionary this formative

Figure 0.2 In an ad campaign started in 1929, the American Federation of Musicians used an ominous-looking robot to embody the threat that "canned" or mechanical music posed to "real," live music. From *Musical America* (November 25, 1929). Courtesy of the American Federation of Musicians.

discourse on live music was, and how much the AFM aligned its vision with conservative cultural norms.

Further implications of the AFM's campaign come to the surface in two subsequent ads from 1931. Racially discriminatory imagery joins the effort to stigmatize "canned music"—the robots in both these ads are notably darker in appearance than the white figures they are shown to be threatening. Depicted in Figure 0.3, the first, from the October 25 issue of *Musical America*, portrays the robot—who has the label "canned music in theaters" appended to his side—as an unwanted suitor sitting on the couch next to a white woman with an Ancient Greek kithara beside her, meant to signify the purity of the "living music" tradition. In the background, an older white man who is cast as a father figure and holds a newspaper that identifies him as the "music loving public" appears shouting, "When Is That Young Man Going Home!"[37] The second ad, published a month later, depicts the robot as a dark-complexioned nurse trying to administer an unwanted medicine to a young white girl who cowers in fear against a wall. In a caption, the robot says, "Take it, dear, it's genuine music;" and the "wise child"—who is labeled a "theatergoer" in the illustration—rejoinders, "It's only more of that old canned sound, and I'm tired of it."[38] These attacks seem to implicitly target jazz, blues, and other musical styles that are less "legitimate" within the hierarchical sense of culture that the AFM upheld in its campaign. More than that, the recourse to such stark racially coded imagery makes it clear that the AFM aligned "living music" with ideas about culture and civilization that were inextricable from whiteness, and the organization used the fear of racial impurity to generate support for its cause.

In this formative moment of live music discourse, two prominent impulses come to the fore. The promotion of the unique value of "living" music was a critical strategy in the effort to preserve musical employment in settings where union musicians were losing jobs. It was also, though, a failed strategy. Much could be said—and has been said—about how that failure was inevitable given the tide of technological and cultural change, but the second primary impulse at work in these ads contributed to that failure as well: the effort to align live music with highbrow cultural values. Here the AFM evinced a strategy it would rely on for decades moving forward. Sociologist Michael Roberts has shown in a recent book that throughout the 1960s, the American musicians' union at national and local levels resisted forms of popular music that were predominantly associated with African Americans, young people, and working-class audiences.[39] We see the roots of these attitudes in the

Figure 0.3 Another installment in the American Federation of Musicians ad campaign. In its ongoing defense of "living music," the AFM here portrays the robot with a darkened complexion, suggesting a link between "canned music" and musical blackness that is shown to pose a threat to the sanctity of music and, by implication, white womanhood. From *Musical America* (October 25, 1931). Courtesy of the American Federation of Musicians.

AFM's efforts to denounce "canned music" in its campaign from 1929 to 1931. The mobilization of high art rhetoric by those defending the labor of musical performance may be one of the great ironies of musical history, and it bespeaks how much more was at stake than a simple opposition between "live" and "recorded" music would suggest.

* * *

As the foregoing makes clear, the history of live music that follows is much more than an overview of great performances. To the extent that the history of live music has already been written, the "great performance" model has often been used in both academic and popular accounts. Some books cover a range of concerts or events considered influential or exceptional, seeking to create a sort of canon of great concerts that may parallel the many lists of great albums, songs, or artists that always proliferate.[40] Others focus more on a single event, using it as a lens for discussing a given artist's career, the state of a particular genre (jazz, folk, rock), and the ways in which a concert can serve as a flash point for larger social and cultural concerns.[41] Certain live music events have generated a whole literature unto themselves, none more so than the Woodstock Festival of 1969, which has inspired memoirs, oral histories, and academic reflections, along with more straightforward historical accounts.[42] Many of these works are illuminating but few delve very deeply into broader questions about how live music matters and none consider the place that it has occupied in American culture and in the evolving shape of the music business over time and across genres in the way that this books strives to do.

My choice to write a book covering the history of live music with such a wide-angle lens arises from my personal history and my trajectory as a writer and scholar. I make no claims to be a record-setting concert attendee, but according to my rough count I have seen nearly eight-hundred music shows in my life as of this writing. In my last book on heavy metal and punk, I recounted that I attended several concerts a year during my high school years growing up in Simi Valley, California, starting in 1983. Mostly these were hard rock and metal shows by the likes of Van Halen, Iron Maiden, and Judas Priest, at the two primary arena venues in the Los Angeles area, the L.A. Forum and the Long Beach Arena. When I went away to college in Berkeley, my live music habits changed dramatically. Small venue shows became the norm and I saw a much wider range of music than had been available to me in my former suburban life. Rock remained at the core of my live music going but it was much more likely to be punk and indie—X, Sonic Youth, Jane's Addiction, the Butthole Surfers, Firehose, and the Swans are just some of the great shows I recall from that time, along with local favorites Primus who were just starting to attract a larger following. Added to this, I attended two installments of the San Francisco Blues Festival in 1986 and 1987, having my mind blown that first year by Buddy Guy and Junior Wells; saw jazz at venues as varied as Berkeley's Greek Theater (where I saw Miles Davis) and the great Oakland jazz club Yoshi's (where I saw guitarists John McLaughlin and Bill Frisell, on separate nights); and a healthy portion of avant-garde and experimental music that was often curated by local guitarist Henry Kaiser and housed in the Berkeley student union. Arena and stadium shows were an occasional thing during these years—David Lee Roth at the Cow Palace, Motörhead at the Kaiser Auditorium, U2 and the Rolling Stones (separately) at the Oakland Coliseum, and a handful of others.

This eclecticism has characterized my live music habits ever since. I am that breed of cultural omnivore that has arisen in recent decades as a new kind of sophisticate, displacing the older highbrow model.[43] In my current life in Western Massachusetts, I regularly patronize concerts of indie rock, singer-songwriters, metal (when I can find it), jazz, classical music, folk and bluegrass, hip hop, and various world music traditions. During 2019 alone, I saw J. Mascis, the Hot 8 Brass Band, the Indigo Girls, Blue Öyster Cult, Rhiannon Giddens, Mitski, Billy Cobham, Mike Watt, and South African underground band BCUC, among others. When I travel, I often make a point of seeking out live music at least once during my journeys. On a recent visit to Australia, I saw the brilliant Japanese noise artist Merzbow do a show at a Melbourne art space. Periodic trips to New York and New Orleans give me access to artists that are less likely to make it to the small college town where I live. And, pre-pandemic, I played a smattering of local gigs as the lead guitarist with the psychedelic indie rock band, the Electric Eyes. My lifetime of gig attendance—and occasional performance—infuses this book. It informs my curiosity about live music and stirs my conviction that live music is a defining element of American culture that has never really gotten its due.

Digging into the intersecting histories of heavy metal and punk for my book, *This Ain't the Summer of Love*, I wrote about arena rock as one of the main factors that contributed to the emergence of metal and made it appear a socially significant phenomenon. Metal in the early 1970s became the music preferred by a segment of the rock audience that showed a strong disposition to want to gather in large crowds. Having grown up attending arena shows, I was fascinated with how these enormous spectacles had become so conventional; and upon finishing that book, I was left with a lot of lingering questions about how much arena rock was a historically unique occurrence. Sorting through my accumulated memories of studying US history and culture, I recalled having read P.T. Barnum's autobiography as a graduate student, in which he discusses among other topics his promotion of the Swedish concert singer Jenny Lind. It so happens that Lind has a peculiar relationship with Northampton, Massachusetts, where I currently live. She performed in Northampton in 1851 and 1852, during the latter phase of her US tour; but more than that, she spent her honeymoon in Northampton after marrying her accompanist, the pianist Otto Goldschmidt, and reputedly gave the town its cherished nickname, "Paradise City." Spurred by this combination of local history and general curiosity, I went back to Barnum's account of his work with Lind and then began researching her tour in earnest. You could say, then, that this book has its genesis in my efforts to think through the historical parallels between Jenny Lind and Grand Funk Railroad.

At the time that I began to work on this book, record industry revenues had been in steady decline for the better part of a decade due to increased availability of streaming music on the internet. During the same time period, live music revenues were growing almost as dramatically as recorded music sales were declining. According to data compiled by music industry scholar Peter Tschmuck, US sales of recorded music reached a high point in 1999, with over $14 billion in combined sales of compact discs, vinyl albums, cassettes, and music-related videocassettes. By 2009, that total was cut by more than half, to just over $6 billion in sales, of which nearly a third was generated by digital music files.[44] Overall gross revenues generated by live music ticket sales in the US, by comparison, were $1.5 billion in 1999, at the time an industry record according to the leading concert industry publication, *Pollstar*.[45] That figure rose steadily for every year of the ensuing decade, so that by 2009, concert industry revenues reached $4.6 billion.[46] In other words, in 1999, recorded music revenues topped live music revenues by a factor of nearly ten to one. A decade later, the ratio was more like three to two. Moreover, these tabulations do not take into account all the other revenue generated by live music that is not included in ticket sales information, from service charges on tickets to parking to food and alcohol and the ever-important band merchandise.[47] It is fair to say, then, that one of the major transformations of the twenty-first-century media economy is that the live music industry has achieved a degree of relative parity with the industry for sound recordings that it has arguably not enjoyed since the 1940s, if not before.

For years prior to this point, popular music scholars and critics had treated the record industry as though it was the music industry writ large. There was comparatively little work on live music as an industry or as a cultural phenomenon more generally when I first had the idea for this book. That position is no longer tenable, and thankfully, the situation has started to change. Studies of live music have begun to proliferate, with music festivals and the concomitant process of "festivalization" having become a particular focus of concern.[48] Most notable has been the ongoing work of the scholarly team comprised of Simon Frith, Matt Brennan, Martin Cloonan, and Emma Webster to document the evolution of live music in the U.K. from 1950 to the present. Their three-volume work sets a new standard for live music scholarship that thinks through questions of economy, performance, policy, musical labor, and social impact.[49] I see my book as a sort of companion volume to theirs. Together they will hopefully inspire more "big picture" thinking about live music and its current and historical value.

One passage in the first volume of Frith and colleagues' history especially resonates with my own efforts. Here, they seek to explain how a focus on live performance rather than recordings changes the terms according to which we understand the shape of popular music history from the vantage point of the working musician. In particular, they are concerned with the period in the 1950s when rock 'n' roll first began to influence British society. To emphasize live performance means the following, they argue:

> First, it makes clear that changes in musical taste and performing practice are more gradual and complex than is suggested by comparing lists of best-selling records ... Second, it reminds us that musicians' lives do not begin and end with their recordings. For most artists, careers begin long before they reach a recording studio and continue long after their records cease to appear in the charts ... Third, professional musicians are ... remarkably adaptable, and a historian can only be impressed by their unquenchable ability to take on new styles and sounds to meet market demand.[50]

The upshot of this perspective is that rock 'n' roll no longer appears as the "revolutionary" occurrence it is so often portrayed to be. Instead, it appears as the outgrowth of a complex web of interlocking developments that gradually took hold as a dominant force, while other tendencies remained intact. What matters for my purposes, more than the specific case about rock 'n' roll, is the suggestion that by putting live music in the foreground we see music history differently. That is, at root, the premise of this book as well.

* * *

The chapters of this book unfurl a narrative with many layers and multiple threads. Certain chapters revolve around specific performers (Jenny Lind, the Fisk Jubilee Singers, Ernest Hogan and Tony Pastor). Others cohere more around particular genres (jazz, rock 'n' roll, hip-hop) or types of venues (concert halls, festivals, arenas and stadiums). In all cases, I have selected historical figures and events that have some significant bearing upon the larger shape and trajectory of live music, its cultural impact, and its economic underpinnings. Starting the book with chapters on Lind and the Fisk Singers, I deliberately put women and black artists in the foreground. The importance of live music as a medium through which relations of power and inequality have been negotiated is a running concern in this book, which I see as an important counter to those who herald live music as an uncomplicated means for forging "togetherness." How live music establishes the terms according to which some sense of togetherness, or collective belonging, might be felt is itself one of the central questions that pervades the various chapters that follow.

One bias that I will admit to at the start is that I have privileged larger-scale live performances over smaller ones. Both types figure prominently in the pages ahead, and some chapters—on vaudeville, and especially Chapter 4 on early jazz venues—concentrate more on smaller-scale events. However, as alluded to earlier, my curiosity about live music was piqued by thinking about the arena concerts of my youth and the search for historical precedents. To put it bluntly, I find events that draw large crowds unusually compelling for the way that they embody the capacity of live music to assume broadly representative significance regarding the "public" at large or specific segments of the public who become uniquely visible by gathering in one place, drawn together by common interest in a given artist, genre, or set of values. Such large-scale events have also been primary drivers of economic growth and transformation throughout the history of live music, providing a line of continuity between the nascent mass marketing efforts of P.T. Barnum in the

1850s, the agents and promoters who built the arena and stadium concert economy in the 1970s and 1980s, and the multinational corporations that have promoted the renascence of American music festivals in the twenty-first century. Much excellent work has been done already on varieties of smaller-scale live music—jazz clubs and lofts, punk and indie music clubs, folk music coffeehouses, underground hip-hop venues, performances spaces dedicated to contemporary art music. We still await a study that stitches these multifarious strands of activity together.

Another core organizing principle that weaves its way through this book might be called creative juxtaposition. I find that the most compelling insights often come from setting two seemingly disparate subjects in relation to each other to see how they might reveal something new. Sometimes the juxtaposition operates between chapters, as with the opening pair of chapters on Jenny Lind and the Fisk Jubilee Singers, where obvious differences in the race and class of the performers exist alongside crucial parallels in the appeal made to middle-class tastes and sensibilities and the effort to present live musical performance as an almost sanctified kind of endeavor. The final two chapters of the book enact a comparable juxtaposition, in this case between the genres of rock and rap, to bring into stark relief some of the ways in which racial inequities continued to shape the field of live music performance and production into the end of the twentieth century and the beginning of the twenty-first.

Several individual chapters employ this principle of juxtaposition internally, starting with Chapter 3 on variety and vaudeville performance, which combines the stories of the black performer and songwriter Ernest Hogan and the white performer and impresario Tony Pastor. Here, as above, putting these figures in dialogue is a means to observe how race mattered to the evolving field of live music, as black and white artists had different opportunities open to them and distinct obstacles to overcome when they appeared before the public. In other chapters, I explore what I take to be unexpected and essential interconnections between distinct music genres. Chapter 5, on the changing culture of the concert hall in the first half of the twentieth century, foregrounds the intersecting paths of jazz and classical music during a crucial period of transformation in the history of both styles. Writing about music festivals in Chapter 7, I purposefully do not limit myself to festivals associated with a single genre, but cross permissively between jazz, folk, and rock festivals to put forth a more holistic portrait of the festival as a dynamic live music form. Pursuing this approach is necessary to write what I consider to be a proper history of live music, because live music does not belong to any one genre and does not work in just one way. Researching this book, I became excited at several points as I began to see connections that I had not seen before, and I hope I am able to pass that excitement along to my readers. Let the show begin.

1
Selling the Nightingale
Jenny Lind, P.T. Barnum, and the Management of the American Crowd

Jenny Lind bade farewell to the American public from the concert stage on a Monday night, May 24, 1852. It had been nearly two years since she made her debut at New York's Castle Garden on September 11, 1850. During the intervening time she had toured widely across the US and as far south as Havana, Cuba, was intensively lionized by the press and large segments of the American public but also had become, increasingly, a target of criticism, especially after having dissolved her partnership with the illustrious and infamous showman P.T. Barnum the previous year. Now, she appeared as Madame Otto Goldschmidt, having married her Jewish accompanist and musical director and taken his name during the course of her American travels. For the most moralistic segment of the public, some of the glow of innocence and charity that had surrounded the singer had rescinded since the first rush of acclaim that accompanied her US debut. Nonetheless, here she was, back on the same Castle Garden stage performing a program that was designed to evoke the sensation of that earlier landmark event.

Amongst those in the audience was John Sullivan Dwight, who was gaining a reputation as the most noted music critic in the US. At the time of Lind's debut, Dwight—although he was based in Boston—was hired by the New York *Daily Tribune* to cover her initial run of concerts. When Lind performed her farewell concert in 1852, Dwight had just begun his own namesake publication, *Dwight's Journal of Music*, which carried his review of the performance in its eighth issue. His observations conveyed none of the ambivalence that had surrounded Lind in the latter part of her American sojourn. Instead, as he had done upon first hearing her in 1850, he waxed rhapsodic not only about Lind, but about those gathered to listen:

Castle Garden, last night, presented a spectacle, the like of which we hardly hope again to witness in our mortal life. Think of *seven thousand* faces, lit with sad enthusiasm, looking from every part of every circle of the vast area and gallery, so brilliantly illuminated, turned all to one focus, to greet and to enjoy, for the last time, face to face and audibly, the presence and the almost more than mortal music, of a woman who, in eighteen months, by the mere divine right of goodness and of a matchless voice conscientiously trained to perfect obedience to the highest inspirations of Art, has established a sort of moral and ideal empire in the hearts of this whole people, rude and cultivated.[1]

Dwight's conviction about the transformative effect that a singer such as Lind could have upon the American public was in line with his general faith in the transcendent power of music when it was brought to an especially high point of cultivation. Most striking is his focus on the crowd as the best index of this transformation and the power that Lind exerted over the collective imagination. Jenny Lind mattered, for Dwight and her other most ardent champions, because of the way that she was perceived to combine artistic brilliance and moral elevation; and these qualities could be observed in the way that she constituted by her very popularity a mass audience that could be taken as a sign of civic decorum, during a time in US history when crowds were more often construed as evidence of social disorder.[2]

At the time that she first arrived in the US, Lind was far from the first foreign musical celebrity to tour the country. Indeed, the history of American music performance during the first half of the nineteenth century can be rendered as a series of visits by foreign artists who had varying degrees of impact on public tastes and desires: from the Garcia family troupe who came in 1825 and established Italian opera as the estimable but elusive height of musical pleasure for a select audience, to the visits of competing English opera singers such as Jane Shirreff, John Wilson, and Arthur and Anne Seguin in the 1830s and early 1840s, to the mid-1840s appearance of instrumental virtuosi on piano (Leopold de Meyer and Henri Herz) and violin (Ole Bull).[3] The commencement of Lind's tour in 1850 was in many ways a culmination of this strain of European influence on the American musical landscape, through which touring European musicians recast the relationship between popular and cultivated strains of musical performance in the US.

And yet, construing Lind in this manner does not do justice to the sheer scale of exposure and success that accompanied her American sojourn. Earlier touring artists had achieved considerable notoriety, including operatic vocalist Maria Garcia (later known by her married name, Malibran), who appeared with the Garcia troupe in 1825 and remained among the most acclaimed sopranos of the nineteenth century long after her untimely death at the age of twenty-eight in 1836. But no previous touring artist engendered such widespread desires, such longing to hear her treasured voice and see her expressive countenance; nor did any previous artist give rise to such an explosion of efforts to represent her, both verbal and visual. Above all, no earlier touring artists, and few who came in the following decades, were met with such crowds at every turn. With Jenny Lind, music entered the American public sphere in a new way. It became part of something akin to what would, in the twentieth century, become termed "mass culture."

One could well argue that such a provisional form of mass culture had already begun to arise in the 1840s, a decade that saw the explosion of American print culture and, in the realm of entertainment, the dramatic growth of blackface minstrelsy. The crowds drawn to minstrelsy were of major importance to the growth of US popular culture and were in many ways the precondition for the success of Jenny Lind. But the crowds that flocked to see Lind were notably different for reasons that went beyond size (Lind's initial American concerts at New York's Castle Garden were reported to have drawn between six and eight thousand people each). Eric Lott, W.T. Lhamon, Dale Cockrell and others have argued that blackface minstrelsy—especially in its earliest phases in the 1830s and 1840s—largely appealed to an audience of urban white working-class men.[4] Lott has made a compelling case for the ways in which minstrelsy refracted issues of class and gender through the more overt mechanisms of racial performance and representation during a time of immense social transformations. As he asserts, "minstrelsy helped constitute a break . . . between elite, genteel, and low cultures which would be fundamental" by the twentieth century.[5] Lind's audiences were shaped by these same divisions but were less well defined in their social characteristics. The sheer magnitude of the public interest in Lind ensured that no one social group would rule the crowds that attended her performances, and newspaper accounts routinely commented on the heterogeneity of her audiences in most regards other than race: women as well as men were in attendance, old as well as young, and a broad range of classes from working-class roughs to the most respectable gentlemen. This heterogeneity made Lind into a figure with mass appeal of a decidedly modern character: rather than clearly appeal to one social group to the exclusion or the consternation of others, she conveyed a complex range of appeals that cut across social distinctions and lent itself to multiple readings.

Lind's broad appeal was not simply a unifying or homogenizing force. Bringing a broad cross section of people together, her concerts also operated as sites of conflict, sometimes overtly, sometimes in more subtle ways. In this regard, Lind's concert tour did extend the dynamics of blackface minstrelsy and other entertainments of the 1840s, something about which we should hardly be surprised. Only a year previous to her arrival in September 1850, after all, the Astor Place Riot had shown to what degree the staging of culture had become contested terrain in mid-nineteenth-century New York.[6] Although the source of the unrest concerned not music but theatrical performance—with working-class advocates of rugged American actor Edwin Forrest protesting the more refined Shakespearian approach of British actor William Macready—it was no idle detail that the site of the riot was the Astor Place Opera House, which in its short two year existence had become the center of the New York elite's efforts to create a space of cultural privilege in which they could exhibit their prestige.

Lind herself was much more in line with the values represented by Macready than Forrest, but she and her tour manager, P.T. Barnum, made a strategic choice in circumventing Astor Place when selecting a location for her New York concerts. Nonetheless, by seeking to extend her public to a relatively broad cross section of mid-nineteenth-century urban America, Lind and Barnum stepped into a potential minefield and did not emerge completely unscathed. In her earliest New York concerts and her appearances in other cities such as Boston, the main conflicts arose over access to tickets and access to seats. Tickets for the concerts were priced at a very high $3, with cheaper $2 and sometimes $1 admission available for less choice seating locations or for promenade tickets that allowed the spectator to stand at the edge of the hall. But Barnum pushed the prices considerably higher by selling the prime tickets at auction, realizing average costs of above $6 per ticket and turning the privilege of purchasing the first ticket to any segment of Lind's tour into an occasion to bid for status and recognition. Resentment was bound to result from such practices, especially when at Lind's first Castle Garden concerts spectators who had bought their tickets at auction at inflated prices had their seats stolen from them by promenade ticket holders who used their $1 admission to grab the best seat they could find. For Barnum, the effort to balance maximum profit with crowd control and the perception of fair practice remained an ongoing struggle until he and Lind dissolved their contract in June 1851. Meanwhile, broader tensions at times flared around Lind's appearances to the point where, in cities such as

Pittsburgh and Hartford, they resulted in smaller scale echoes of the struggle over the public sphere instantiated by the riots at Astor Place.

Where's Barnum?

Addressing what he calls "the Jenny Lind Enterprise" in his widely read autobiography, P.T. Barnum presents his promotion of the singer as one of the defining moments in his long career as a master of American amusement. Recounted Barnum:

> And now I come to speak of an undertaking which my worst enemy will admit was bold in its conception, complete in its development, and astounding in its success... That I am proud of it now I freely confess. It placed me before the world in a new light; it gained me many warm friends in new circles; it was in itself a fortune to me—I risked much but I made more.[7]

Barnum here composes the groundwork for a narrative that is, in a sense, foundational to the business of American entertainment, and live music especially. At the center of the story are two terms, risk and reward. By Barnum's account, it was his decision to take the risk of bringing Jenny Lind to the US that set a whole chain of events in motion that culminated in one of the transformative episodes in American cultural history. He took that risk knowing full well that it would be difficult, because however much he may have possessed unique abilities to cater to public demand, he also recognized that the public's desires were not so predictable: "'The public' is a very strange animal, and although a good knowledge of human nature will generally lead a caterer of amusements to hit the people, they are fickle, and ofttimes perverse."[8] Yet the risk was worth taking, and more than that, it justified for Barnum the scale of his reward, the massive earnings that came his way when his hunch about Jenny Lind's appeal proved right. Only those who risk are the rightful earners of profit: in this assumption, the business of concert promotion provided a template for the moral economy of capitalism writ large.

As for Lind, her American celebrity preceded her appearance in the US by some years. Born in 1820 in Stockholm, Sweden, she had begun her performing career at a young age, but her notoriety in Europe truly excelled over the course of the 1840s. An early turning point came in December 1844 when Lind debuted in Berlin, assuming the lead role in *Norma*, Vincenzo Bellini's 1831 opera whose title role had already become a proving ground for some of the era's most celebrated sopranos.[9] Nearly three years later, in May 1847, Lind first performed in London in Giacomo Meyerbeer's *Roberto il Diavolo*, and her star rose to further grand proportions, while reports of her activities became increasingly common in the burgeoning American press. During this initial run of performances in London, the image of Lind began to take hold that would be so integral to her American success. Music historian George Biddlecombe highlights the portrayal of Lind by London critic Rumsey Forster, who claimed that the singer's presence onstage conveyed to her audience "the saint-like purity of her mind and heart." According to Biddlecombe, this was "the first assertion of Lind's sanctification, which would last well into the twentieth century."[10]

Barnum aggressively pursued the opportunity to bring Lind to the US on the strength of the reputation she had earned in Europe, and on the value that he attached to her association with feminine virtue. As he admitted in his autobiography,

> although I relied prominently upon Jenny Lind's reputation as a great musical *artiste*, I also took largely into my estimate of her success with all classes of the American public, her character for extraordinary benevolence and generosity. Without this peculiarity in her disposition, I never would have dared make the engagement which I did.[11]

While these qualities had already implanted themselves in the public mind to a good degree, Barnum's own mastery of the techniques of publicity amplified Lind's existing recognition into something even larger, at times seeming nearly inescapable. Musicologist Mark Samples has suggested that Barnum's promotional efforts on Lind's behalf constitute one of the earliest concerted efforts to create a "brand" around a musical star in the US, which was defined around the interlocking qualities of celebrity, artistry, and charity.[12] That Barnum's own celebrity was itself already established facilitated the process of making Lind into one of the most widely recognized figures in nineteenth-century America. Yet Barnum's sponsorship, and his preceding success in the sphere of unabashedly popular culture with his American Museum, also made Lind's tour into something far more complicated than it might have been. With Barnum behind her, Lind stood at the boundary between the common and the refined, the low and the elevated, in a markedly pronounced manner.

The interrelationship between these different spheres of musical and artistic expression was in flux throughout the nineteenth century. Indeed, the very notion that there were distinctions to be made between the "high" and the "low" was itself novel. William Weber, surveying changes in concert programming over the course of the century in Europe and the US, observes pointedly, "The concept of classical music should be seen as pioneering rather than conservative during the first half of the nineteenth century. Endowing older works with canonic authority ... made a fundamental break with musical tradition."[13] This impulse toward classicization of music and other cultural forms was increasingly aligned with the values that cultural historian Lawrence Levine has described as "sacralization," which in the US began to come more to the foreground by mid-century. Associating the principles of sacralization with the music criticism of John S. Dwight—the very same Dwight who so vociferously praised Jenny Lind upon her debut and farewell concerts alike—Levine defines it as the search for "an art that makes no compromises with the temporal world; an art that remains spiritually pure and never becomes secondary to the performer or to the audience; an art that is uncompromising in its devotion to cultural perfection."[14] This emergent ideal of sacralized art also fostered more socially exclusivity than what came before, wherein a kind of eclecticism had been predominant, serious and light forms of expression were often presented side-by-side, and audiences too had been comparatively more heterogeneous than they would be as the century proceeded.

Jenny Lind's appearance in the US came at a time when calls for musical elevation were becoming more pronounced, but when the sacralization of classical music was very much a work in progress. If anything, Lind herself was sacralized more than the music that she sang. As portrayed by Barnum's publicity machinery, Lind became the living embodiment of one of the most potent icons of the era: the sentimental heroine. She was defined by her talent and musical excellence, but also and often more importantly, by her virtue and her charity. A key element in Lind's image of moral fortitude was her decision upon coming to the US to appear only as a concert singer, and not to perform in more squarely theatrical operatic productions in which she would be acting and assuming a role for an entire performance. In the moral climate of mid-nineteenth-century American culture, a wide segment of the public viewed the world of theater with suspicion and believed theatrical entertainers to be of dubious character. Although she made her European reputation performing opera, Lind had been questioning this aspect of her career for several years prior to arriving in the U.S; and made her exclusive appearance in concerts, not operatic performances, a condition of her contract with Barnum.[15] Appearing only as a concert performer allowed Lind to avoid some of the stigma attached to the theatrical arts. It also meant that she presented herself to the American public *as* herself, which facilitated the elision of any difference between her artistic persona and her "true" self in the public mind. Such maneuvering was one of the ways in which Lind, as a female performer, could be subjected to the intense amount of public adulation and scrutiny that would surround her at a time when women—and especially "respectable" women of the middle classes or the elite—were more commonly and comfortably associated with the private domestic sphere. Yet Lind's public standing also demonstrates a point made by historians of mid-nineteenth-century America: that sentimental values were not only oriented toward the private sphere, and that women often used sentimentality to gain access to public life in ways that might otherwise have been forbidden.[16]

Barnum himself partook in the culture of sentiment, not only in the rhetoric he used to promote Lind but in his self-promotional efforts as well. As such he demonstrates another often overlooked aspect of nineteenth-century cultural history, that while sentimentality—the culture of intense feeling and sympathy—was most often associated with women's experience, it could also be used by men as a way of negotiating their own relationship between the public and private spheres. Barnum's prominence as a temperance advocate is especially notable in this regard, for as literary scholar Glenn Hendler has asserted, the temperance movement gave rise to some distinctly masculine forms of sentiment, with reformed alcoholics often confessing their past sins through a veil of tears and heavy emotion.[17] That Barnum gave temperance lectures at many stops along the way of his tour with Lind only reinforces the importance of this connection, and suggests that he was well attuned to the power of sentimental rhetoric by the time he arranged for Lind to visit the US. He was furthermore aware of the instrumental role that the promotion of Lind's virtue could have to his own reputation. As Bluford Adams observed in his study of the showman, Barnum regularly reminded the public of his role in Lind's American tour during the last decades of his life, because "Lind stood for everything that, in the minds of many Americans, Barnum was not: privacy, artlessness, sensibility, charity, innocence, and piety."[18]

Selling Jenny Lind

Barnum was not the only one charged with the task of selling Lind. Lind's US appearance became the occasion for all manner of efforts to use her image or her reputation for commercial purposes. W. Porter Ware and Thaddeus Lockard, authors of the most detailed study of Lind's tour, note that from the moment of her arrival in the US, Lind's name was used to sell "gloves, bonnets, riding hats, shawls, mantillas, robes, chairs, sofas, pianos" and a host of other items.[19] One of the consumer items most closely linked to Lind's talents was sheet music, production of which had entered a period of growth in conjunction with the rise of domestic music making among middle class Americans. Sheet music served a number of potential functions for patrons of Jenny Lind's music: it could be a way for a listener to familiarize herself with some portion of Lind's music prior to hearing her perform, could be a substitute for hearing her in concert for those who could not afford the cost of a ticket, could be a souvenir of Lind's performance after the fact, or could be a way of possessing some part of Lind's talent, all the more so if one sought to recreate the music on the page for oneself. Sheet music was also notable for its visual appeal. Many of the songs printed in association with Lind featured illustrations of the singer, some quite lavish in detail, as can be seen in Figure 1.1, thus affording the buyer pleasure even if she did not possess the requisite ability to play the song in question.

A series of advertisements published in the days leading up to Lind's arrival in New York offers some sense of the strong competition that arose in efforts to turn her name into a marketable commodity, and sheds light on the peculiar cultural position that Lind occupied at the time. The ads appeared in several locations including the *Morning Courier and New York Enquirer*, one of the leading daily newspapers of the era. In the August 29 edition of the *Courier*, the three ads were placed in succession, one following the next in a single column.[20] At the top was an ad by the music publisher Samuel Jollie, who promoted his acquisition of the exclusive rights to publish all the music to be sung by Lind on her forthcoming American concert tour. Jollie warned readers that other music publishers who might issue Lind's music did not have such an arrangement and therefore would be promoting the music that Lind had sung in Europe, not the music she would sing in America.

Directly beneath Jollie's ad was a second, by William Hall & Son. In effect, Hall & Son affirm the claims of Jollie but turn those claims around. Hall had acquired the exclusive rights to republish *European* editions of Lind's

Figure 1.1 This sheet music cover from 1850 surrounds the figure of Jenny Lind with flowers, birds, and angels, as well as various spectators standing in for her audience, representing the ways in which she was turned into an icon of idealized femininity. Courtesy of the American Antiquarian Society.

music in the US. This was not to be regretted but to be seen as a mark of their own edition's superiority, so they claimed: "It is an easy matter to alter a composer's music, and *Americanize* it in some way, in order to obtain a copyright and then endeavor to palm it on the public as a genuine article—but we may be assured that Miss Lind will not sacrifice her fame by adopting new fancies and styles of singing to please or fill the coffers of an American music seller. We would as soon expect to see her turn Negro Minstrel and sing Emma Snow."

Then came the third and final ad placed by another competing publisher, William Vanderbeek. Vanderbeek ridicules both of his competitors and their claims to represent the true music of Lind. He has no exclusive agreement of any kind, but still promises to publish a wide selection of Lind's music in a set of pleasing and accurate editions. Establishing the value of his Lind library, Vanderbeek directly responds to the language of Hall's ad to further promote his own offerings: "The subscriber does not expect to see *Jenny Lind* turn Negro minstrel and sing *Emma Snow* or *Kate Lorraine*; but since he once touches upon this subject, he takes this opportunity to inform his patrons, the public in general, and *Jenny Lind* in particular, that the large catalogue of his publications contains, besides all the good, new, and fashionable music, a most excellent selection of Ethiopian airs, which he takes pleasure in offering to the public."

These three advertisements say much about the process of turning Jenny Lind into a commodity and reveal something of the context surrounding her concert tour and the values that were projected onto her at the moment that the tour was set to begin. As the ads make clear, Lind was seen to inhabit a distinct sphere from the realm of purely popular musical entertainment, connoted by the repeated references to "negro" minstrelsy. These references themselves are telling, however, not just for the way they draw a distinction between Lind and minstrel performers but because they suggest that, however removed Lind may appear from lowly minstrel tunes, the popularity of minstrelsy is part of the background against which any judgments of her will be made. In effect, drawing attention to Lind's proximity to blackface minstrelsy while disavowing any possible connection she might have was a way to enhance her aura of Northern European whiteness, an aspect of her persona that was integral to the image of moral and sexual purity she was perceived to project.[21]

While Lind might never stoop to sing a minstrel song, her music when published was part of the same sphere of musical commerce, something that William Vanderbeek alone was bold enough to admit. This was true not only of Lind but of operatic music in general, which occupied a space somewhere in between the emerging discourses of "classical" and "popular."

Musicologist Charles Hamm asserts that sheet music versions of favorite selections from operatic works were prevalent in middle-class homes from the 1830s forward:

> All evidence insists that [operatic music] was indeed performed in the American parlor and that these operatic songs became part of the popular song repertory. They were printed and sold in the same form, by the same publishers, in quantities equal to and even greater than earlier successful songs. In numerous anthologies published later in the century... Bellini is found side by side with Thomas Moore, Henry Bishop, Henry Russell, the Hutchinsons, and Stephen Foster. There was not as yet a stylistic distinction between popular and classical music; popular music was simply whatever sold the most copies and was known to the most people.[22]

Hamm reinforces his point by further noting that Jenny Lind's own concert repertory included such parlor favorites as "Home, Sweet Home" and "The Last Rose of Summer" alongside operatic arias by Bellini, Meyerbeer and other noted European composers. The relative fluidity of Lind's song selection made her, in the words of Levine, into a figure that "symbolized the best of European culture without an aura of exclusiveness."[23]

Also revealing in these sheet music ads is a struggle to represent the "true" Lind. Was Lind best portrayed through her past success in Europe or through her anticipated success in the US? Was one version of this repertory clearly more authentic to her artistry than another? These were the terms according to which Jollie and Hall competed to be the rightful publisher of Lind's music in New York. From Jollie's ad, one can gather that however much Lind's European success made her appearance in the US of note, Americans would do best to make her music their own. From Hall, in turn, a more critical message arises, not just of Jollie's marketing claims but of the broader prospects of Lind in the US: that "Americanizing" Lind would be akin to taking away that which is most valuable in her music and her character. Vanderbeek's repudiation of both claims, meanwhile, suggests that the effort to establish the authenticity of a performer and her work was an instrumental way of creating a market but was not the only available approach. Lind might elevate and inspire, but in Vanderbeek's more forward address to potential consumers, she might also simply give pleasure.

Crowds and the Public Sphere

Addressing the social significance of rock music festivals from a twenty-first-century vantage point, pop music critic and scholar Gina Arnold has asserted:

> Rock festivals are where the masses now choose to participate in public life. Beginning with Newport and Woodstock and the Isle of Wight... certain festivals have imprinted themselves on the media as being events of great cultural relevance and importance. Hence, in the crowd's mind, these spaces are where participants may believe they are *participating in history itself*.[24]

Music festivals are a topic for a later chapter, but the tendencies that Arnold observes starting in the late twentieth century have their roots over a century earlier. The American tour of Jenny Lind is a significant milestone in the conversion of musical crowds into an instantiation of the spirit of public life. While this was partly a matter of scale, it was more pointedly a matter of context, as events of the recent past made the crowds that attended Lind's concerts into a phenomenon that was believed to be of great historical consequence to the cultural history of the American nation. Specifically, the Astor Place Riot that took place on May 10, 1849, laid the groundwork for a new sort of politicization of the crowds that attended artistic and cultural events.

The riot at the Astor Place Opera House was not an entirely singular event. Theater riots had been mounting in the US, and in New York City particularly, since the 1820s. At least six major riots had happened in New York theaters between 1825 and 1849.[25] Riots were prompted by a range of factors, but the stimulus was often the offense taken by a sector of the audience at the pretenses of visiting British artists, as with the Astor Place Riot, which was directed most explicitly against the British actor William Macready. Behind these apparent patriotic impulses lay two deeper strains of conflict that intensified throughout the period. First, the massive growth of industrial capitalism in the US during these years generated new sensibilities concerning the relationship between class and culture. Audiences had long considered themselves to have the right to "act out" during theatrical performances—to interrupt a performance, whether to demonstrate approbation or to denounce or ridicule what was being offered on stage.[26]

This right became increasingly called into question, though, as an emerging middle class asserted new norms of decorum in public life, which had the effect of seeking to contain working-class forms of expression. Exacerbating the tension was the second major shift that occurred: the business of American entertainment was growing along with the expansion of industrialism, which led to a proliferation of theaters in New York. Whereas previously, diverse sectors of the audience would be likely to gather in a single theater, more and more the audience became divided along class lines and more materially according to theatrical location and neighborhood. This increased separation of different classes of audiences from each other magnified the perception that the world of theatrical and musical entertainment was growing more exclusive than before, and at times provoked audiences to take action as a means of asserting their basic right of belonging to the sphere of public entertainment.

Italian opera—that is, opera performed in the Italian language, using the ornate style of singing known as *bel canto*—was one of the primary areas in which the effort among cultural elites to create spaces of their own took hold most powerfully. The Astor Place Opera House was one of several initiatives to establish a dedicated opera house that would serve the interests of more wealthy theatergoers. Comparatively more successful than these earlier ventures, at least in the short term, the relative exclusivity of the Astor Place Opera House was inscribed in its very location at Eighth and Lafayette Streets, now part of the bohemian chic East Village but at the time adjacent to an upper-class neighborhood well to the north of more popular entertainment districts. Inside the theater, a sort of hierarchy was built into the physical layout in a manner best described by opera historian Katherine Preston: "Those individuals who could afford the 50 cent admission to only the old upper gallery, now renamed the 'amphitheater,' found that section of the house to be 'the most uncomfortable and ill-contrived place imaginable.' Even worse, the view of the stage from the gallery was almost completely blocked by a huge, ornate chandelier."[27] On the other hand, the area on the floor nearest to the stage—historically called the "pit" and priced low to admit a broad cross section of theatergoers—was now renamed the "parquette" and fitted with armchairs to justify a higher admission price. Most luxurious were the two rows of elevated boxes that were available by seasonal subscription to the most committed patrons of the house, which were furnished with sofas and lounges upholstered in purple velvet.[28] This arrangement was in the service of a theater that was designed as much to allow the fashionable inhabitants of the boxes to be on display as it was to present the finest operatic and theatrical entertainment.

That the British actor William Macready was appearing at Astor Place in the role of *Macbeth* was partly a matter of happenstance, a reflection that in the nineteenth century even the most exclusive opera houses did not just present opera.[29] Yet Macready's appearance there also indicated that he was a favored actor among a more elite segment of the New York theater audience than most of his contemporaries, including his rival, the American Edwin Forrest. The two actors specialized in Shakespearean roles but approached the task quite differently, with Forrest often displaying a brusque masculinity and Macready embodying a more refined, classically trained style. Conflict between them stemmed from a sequence of events that had gathered force during the 1840s, most notably Forrest's disappointment when he toured England mid-decade and had trouble drawing audiences, a circumstance he blamed on Macready who was influential in British theatrical circles. When Macready visited the US in 1849, Forrest challenged him directly by performing the same roles at another New York theater, the Broadway. Supporters of the American actor, meanwhile, took it upon themselves to confront Macready and halt his ability to perform.

On Monday, May 7, Macready's opponents jeered and threw objects at the actor during his performance, leading him and the whole company to abandon the stage early, leaving the play unfinished. Macready planned at that point to forego further scheduled appearances and return to England; but a segment of New York's cultural elite that included authors Washington Irving and Herman Melville issued a public card imploring the British artist to continue, while promising that "the good sense and respect for order prevailing in this community, will sustain you on the subsequent nights of your performances."[30] Riot historian Peter Buckley suggests that the card changed the stakes of what was transpiring, converting a more familiar "theater riot" into a "riot *about* the theater—a contest for control over this 'public' place and the forms of behavior appropriate to it."[31] Macready's next appearance at Astor Place on Thursday, May 10, consequently drew a much larger and fiercer force of opposition. Inside the opera house, a fairly small number of protesters hissed, hurled insults, and threw objects at the stage, their actions drawing decisive response from police stationed in the theater who pulled them from the audience and sequestered them, allowing that night's performance of *Macbeth* to run to its conclusion. Outside, however, a crowd of ten thousand or more was gathered on the streets surrounding the opera house, throwing stones at the windows and shouting their resistance to Macready in a manner that was clearly audible to those gathered within. At the order of New York City mayor Caleb Woodhull, military detachments were called to exert control over the crowd gathered in the streets. Pelted with stones and subject to intense verbal abuse, the soldiers were given the charge to use their weapons to force the crowd into submission. Several volleys of shots were fired, and by the time the night's events had played out, more than twenty New Yorkers had been killed and several dozens more wounded.[32]

During the days and weeks that followed, commentators expressed despair about the loss of life while questioning how and why the situation had escalated to the point that it had. Two primary perspectives, very much at odds, rose to the surface. Many of the city's daily newspapers expressed ultimate support for the use of violence, however regrettable, claiming that the preservation of social order in the face of such "rowdyism" as was on display required sacrifices to be made. Typical of this view was the proclamation by the *New York Commercial Advertiser*: "Frightful and lamentable as is the loss of life on such occasions, there is no middle course between vigorous repressive action and the abandonment of the city to mob rule. Authority must be sustained—its power must be enforced."[33] Against this view, which placed blame for the riot squarely on the shoulders of those opposed to Macready, arose another that examined the sources of the conflict with a more critical eye. An article in the *New York Atlas* took to task those who issued the public card encouraging Macready to perform despite the resistance against him: "When the card in question was issued, the original controversy... sunk into oblivion. And the contest, at once, assumed the aspect of a war between *castes*, and classes, and parties. It at once arrayed the Rich against the Poor."[34] Elaborating on this view was a piece in *Home Journal* magazine that attributed the riotous impulses exhibited by Macready's opponents to the exclusivity that the Astor Place Opera House was built to exemplify, and especially highlighted the "aristocratizing of the Pit" that made less moneyed theatergoers feel unwelcome.[35] Infusing all sides of the debate were fundamental questions concerning the "rights" of theater audiences: should the rights of those who favored Macready and wished to see him perform outweigh the rights of those who opposed him and wanted to prevent him from taking the stage?

In the recent past the answer to this question would have been far from straightforward. However, as media historian Richard Butsch has argued, the Astor Place Riot was a turning point in casting mass public action as an illegitimate facet of American public life. Butsch examines the interrelationship between the key terms, "crowds" and "publics," which fluctuated over the course of the nineteenth century. Prior to Astor Place, newspapers and other organs of public discourse had generally recognized the rights of audiences to interrupt theatrical performances and to otherwise assert their interests on a collective scale. Crowds, then, were not perceived as inherent disorderly; or rather, the disorder they practiced was understood to be acceptable under the right circumstances. The riot strengthened a tendency to construe the crowd as a "mob," an irrational force that posed a more sustained threat to the existing social hierarchy. Following Astor Place, the tenor of published commentary regarding public gatherings assumed a more consistently disparaging character and became more forcefully defined along lines of class.[36] A gathering of working-class people was perceived as a threat to public order and calls for decorum became more insistent on behalf of the interests of respectable middle-class citizens. In effect, crowds were increasingly defined as something in opposition to legitimate public bodies, and crowd control became conceived more as a requisite aspect of organizing public sociability.

Much as Jenny Lind's appearance in the US came at a time when the boundaries between the popular and the elevated were beginning to be redrawn, she also came at a time when the meaning of the crowd, and the meaning of public social life more generally, was in a phase of transition. That she drew such large crowds upon her arrival and then to her first several concerts in New York and elsewhere, was a source of widespread fascination and concern. New York newspapers and magazines were littered in the days following her arrival with detailed descriptions of the crowds that greeted Lind and went to her concerts; and embedded within these descriptions were some powerful social judgments about what these crowds signified about the state of music and public life in America. Ultimately, no single view clearly prevailed, but what comes through most profoundly in these accounts is the extent to which chroniclers of Lind's visit to the US saw themselves engaged in a broad effort to define the terms of the musical public sphere, to raise issues about who should be allowed in this sphere and who should not, about the extent to which this sphere should be governed by commercial considerations or by higher ideals. The sheer magnitude of the enthusiasm surrounding Lind made these questions seem pressing, and the dialogue that ensued would continue to resonate in the years and decades that followed.

The Arrival

Jenny Lind arrived in New York harbor on the afternoon of Sunday, September 1, 1850, as a passenger aboard the Atlantic, a large steamship that had left from Liverpool eleven days prior on August 21.[37] The American public had been kept apprised of Barnum's plan to bring her to the US and of the progress toward her arrival for several months already, with a steady stream of print publicity building anticipation for the event. Reports of Barnum's contract with Lind circulated widely, and the details of the contract—which guaranteed the singer a minimum $150,000 payment for the performance of up to one hundred and fifty concerts, plus a percentage of the gate receipts—did much to stir the public imagination. Barnum also used such tools as a songwriting contest to build interest in Lind, through which individuals were invited to submit a set of lyrics for the singer to recite by way of greeting her American public, and which would be set to music by her concert conductor, Jules Benedict. Although the contest generated both criticism and satire, it also drew several hundred submissions and heightened the sense that Lind's appearance would be an event of some significance.

However effectively Barnum had built a sense of expectation around Lind in the weeks and months leading up to her arrival, the scene that met Lind as the Atlantic approached New York that Sunday—depicted in Figure 1.2—could not have been fully anticipated. The occasion was akin to other mass public ceremonies that became common in antebellum New York and other American cities. Less than two months earlier, for instance, a procession of an estimated forty thousand people marched through the streets of New York to commemorate the passing of President Zachary Taylor.[38] That a comparably sized crowd came to meet Lind testifies to the degree to which her arrival had the air of a citywide, if not a fully national, holiday. Some sense of the sheer size of the crowd can be gathered from the report of the *Morning Courier*:

> Long before the gallant steamer hove in sight, the vicinity of West st., for the length of a dozen blocks, was densely thronged with more than 30,000 persons, who were anxiously awaiting her arrival . . . The steamer at last appeared. The multitude swayed with excitement, as the *Atlantic* neared the wharf, and the most enthusiastic cheering broke forth, which must have given the beautiful Swede some idea of the cordiality of an American welcome.[39]

Figure 1.2 An artist's rendering of Jenny Lind's arrival in the US on September 1, 1850, in which the singer is dwarfed by the surrounding crowd of people gathered to welcome her at New York harbor. Reproduced from P.T. Barnum, *Struggles and Triumphs, or, Forty Years' Recollections* (Buffalo, NY: Warren, Johnson & Co., 1872).

The writer for the *Daily Tribune* paid more attention to the character of the assembled mass, as well as the ways in which members of the crowd took advantage of every available space to get a glimpse of the hallowed singer:

> As we neared Canal st. pier, the interest was increased by the spectacle of some thirty or forty thousand persons congregated on all the adjacent piers and shipping, as well as all the roofs and windows fronting the water. The spars and rigging of vessels—the bulkheads along the wharves, and every other spot commanding a sight, were crowded, while every fender at the Hoboken st. Ferry House was topped with a piece of living statuary ... From all quarters, crowds of persons could be seen hurrying down toward the Atlantic's dock. The multitude increased so rapidly that we began to fear there would be difficulty in making a way through it. The distinguished visitors all expressed their astonishment at seeing so many well-dressed people in the crowd. Mdlle. Lind, especially, was very much struck with the

air of respectability which marked the thousands assembled. Turning to Mr. Barnum, she asked, "Have you no poor people in your country? Every one here appears to be well-dressed."[40]

With the Astor Place riot still fresh in the public memory, such testimony regarding the well-dressed, respectable character of those gathered effectively neutralized the assembly, making it seem as though it posed no severe threat of disorder. In a sense, the crowd became an emblem of the city of New York itself, its individual bodies populating both the city's built structures and the streets designed to allow their passage.

Yet this apparently benign crowd was not so easily contained either in practice or in representation. The above passages contain an ambivalent mix of sentiments that conveyed the charged atmosphere surrounding any crowd of this size: anxiety mixed with enthusiasm, fear mixed with astonishment. When Lind finally appeared and made her exit from the Atlantic onto the shore and into an awaiting carriage, the crowd's enthusiasm reached a level where decorum was in danger of being breached. The carriage was surrounded and immobilized, and the collective desire to pay tribute to Lind became almost akin to holding her hostage:

> At this moment, was heard a wild hurrah at the gate, such as proceeds from besiegers when they enter the breach they have made in the wall or gate of a city. The people who had been kept off with hard fighting by the police, at length made one tremendous rush . . . and this heightened the excitement to a pitch of wild tumult . . . There appeared to be no hope of getting through the crowd. The driver had only to battle for it; he whipped the horses, which he found to be useless, and then he whipped the crowd, when immediately the Nightingale put her head out of the window, and said, with much excitement, "You must stop; I will not allow you to strike the people; they are all my friends, and have come to see me." This sentiment was received with a deafening cheer, and the crowd made way themselves, influenced by the soft, persuasive accents of the Swedish Philomel.[41]

The people, in this scenario, are on the border between human and animal. Unmovable and uncontained, they are whipped like the horses that draw Lind's carriage (and perhaps in a more displaced sense, like the slaves whose bondage was a growing source of national tension).[42] By the writer's account, only Jenny Lind herself has the power to fully humanize the proceedings and restore order. In this story and others, Jenny Lind was widely cast as a figure that could tame the wilder passions of humanity not through force but through the influence of compassion and sympathy. Indeed, it was these qualities that made her a woman who could inhabit the public sphere without fear of losing her virtue.[43]

* * *

Once Lind was ensconced in her New York residence at the Irving House, the buildup toward her first concert began. The night of her arrival, standing upon the Irving House balcony, she was serenaded by the New York Musical Fund Society before a crowd almost as large as that which had greeted her earlier in the day. In the days that followed, almost every move she made was documented in the city's daily papers and more widely.[44] Perhaps the most pressing order of business was the selection of a site for her debut. A new concert hall had begun construction in the weeks leading up to her arrival but remained incomplete. She and Barnum thus toured the city's principal concert venues, and eventually settled upon the capacious Castle Garden. Located at the Southern tip of Manhattan, on the waterfront promenade area called the Battery and near the harbor where Lind first touched ground in the US, Castle Garden was a semi-enclosed structure that had a seating capacity estimated at around six thousand, with room for many more standing patrons. Attending an Italian opera company performance in summer 1851, lawyer and avid music patron George Templeton Strong described the overall charms of Castle Garden in a diary entry: "Perhaps there is hardly so attractive a summer theatre in the world as Castle Garden . . . Cool sea-breeze on the balcony, where one can sit and smoke and listen and look out on the bay studded with the lights of anchored vessels."[45] Appearing in early September, Lind's concerts would benefit from the venue's proximity to the water and open character.

Having chosen the site for Lind's concerts, Barnum began the task of advertising the event and arranging the sale of tickets. The first concert was set to occur Wednesday, September 11, and ads for the event first appeared on Thursday, September 5. Providing the full musical program to be performed by Lind and her supporting musicians—including conductor and pianist Jules Benedict, Italian baritone Giovanni Belletti, and an orchestra of sixty musicians—the first ads also noted that tickets were priced at $3 but that "Choice of places will be sold by auction at Castle Garden, at half-past 10 o'clock, on Saturday morning, 7th Sept., inst."[46] The decision to sell choice tickets via auction did not originate with Barnum. His biographer Neil Harris recounts that when touring the South in the early 1840s, the impresario observed the manager of Viennese dance sensation Fanny Ellsler using the same tactic, and took away the lesson that "culture could pay."[47] Sale by auction allowed Barnum to generate higher revenues through bidding than fixed admission prices would allow, but the *New York Tribune* offered another motive more sympathetic to Barnum: concern that ticket dealers would purchase large blocks of tickets at lower prices and sell them to the public at highly inflated prices. The auction system gave Barnum and his agents greater control over the process through which tickets would be sold and, ostensibly at least, gave all who attended the auction equal opportunity to obtain the tickets of their choice.[48] Meanwhile, supporting the notion that ticket agents were ready to seize the opportunity to capitalize on the desire to see Lind, the advertising columns of the *New York Herald* contained a growing number of notices offering seats to Lind's first concert at prices from ten to twenty dollars or more in the days leading up to her debut.

Staging an auction to sell tickets for Lind's concerts had another beneficial side effect: the auction became a significant attraction in its own right and stirred yet more publicity for the singer's imminent American debut. Newspapers estimated attendance at the Saturday morning affair at between three and four thousand, despite the potentially inhibiting factors of rainy weather and the decision made by the organizers of the auction to charge admission—a decision that was apparently made without consulting Barnum, and that caused some dissension in the press. That many of those in attendance came as spectators rather than bidders was clear from the fact that only about fourteen hundred tickets were sold that first morning. If there was excitement to be had, it came mainly from the bidding for the first ticket, which was described in a breathless manner by the *Tribune*:

> The first bid was $20. From this starting-point the calls grew louder and more energetic. "Twenty-five"—"Thirty"—"Thirty-Five"—"Forty"—"Sixty"—"Seventy-five"—"Eighty." ("Give me the $100," cried Mr. Leeds [the auctioneer]) "Ninety"—"ONE HUNDRED" (Auctioneer—"I've got it!")—"One Hundred and Five," ("A very low price!" Mr. Leeds) "One Hundred and Ten"—"Twenty-five"—"Thirty"—"Forty"—"One Hundred and Fifty"—"One Hundred and Seventy-five"—"Two Hundred" (Loud cheers)—"TWO HUNDRED AND TWENTY-FIVE" ($225). Here there

was at last a stop, and curious glances were shot around to discover the fortunate candidate. "Genin, Hatter!" was announced.[49]

No subsequent bids matched the extravagance of this one, but overall receipts for the auction were reported to have topped $9,000, and the average price per ticket paid at the auction exceeded six dollars, more than double the advertised ticket price. A second auction, held Monday, September 9, sold an additional three thousand seats, so that total auction sales for Lind's debut were a shade below 4,500, at a total cost of almost $25,000—an average ticket price of $5.53, according to the *Tribune*.[50]

Reporting these dollar amounts, and even more so spurring members of the public to compete for the opportunity to purchase tickets to see Lind, did much to feed the enthusiasm surrounding the singer. Popular music scholar Daniel Cavicchi has said of Lind's American tour:

> A Jenny Lind concert, as managed by Barnum, did not simply offer a performance of *music*; through its multiple events and diverse appeal, if offered a more complex and layered performance of *America's commercial music culture* ... Barnum was inviting Americans to examine—and enjoy—their own participation in Lind's tour ... He made participation in commercial exchange an exciting opportunity to be "in" on something.[51]

The ticket auction was the most audacious and conspicuous aspect of Barnum's promotional techniques along these lines. Auctions were not held for all further Lind concerts in New York, but the ritual initiated by Barnum preceding Lind's debut would be repeated in most cities that she visited, and at each stop served the dual function of raising considerable revenue and generating publicity. Over time, the prices paid for Lind's tickets would stabilize, but in the first weeks of her tour, bidders showed remarkable willingness to vie for the honor of exceeding all earlier bids. When Lind left New York for a brief series of concerts in Boston, bidding for the first ticket eclipsed the inflated price paid by Genin the hatter by almost threefold. That the winning bidder, Ossian Dodge—who paid $625 for the first ticket sold to Lind's Boston debut—was himself a public performer suggests the extent to which the publicity surrounding Lind had an almost viral sort of impact: as Lind herself was publicized, so was she readily used to help publicize others. Moreover, Dodge's excessive bid gave rise to one telling instance of cross-media promotion: a lithograph of Dodge greeting Lind and Barnum while making payment for his $625 ticket circulated widely and was used as a sheet music cover for the publication of one of Dodge's own songs, "Ossian's Serenade."[52]

Jenny Lind Performs

On Tuesday, September 10, the day before Jenny Lind's first concert, P.T. Barnum issued the following public announcement:

> Every seat for Wednesday night has been dispensed of. The purchasers can procure their tickets during this day at the office of Castle Garden. Those holding yellow tickets will the better secure their seats by going on Wednesday night at about 5 o'clock. Those holding red and blue tickets should arrive about 6 o'clock. All places forfeited unless possession is taken before 8 o'clock. A few promenade tickets may be obtained at the American Museum. Price $3. No money will be taken at the doors on the night of the concert. The gentlemen engaged as ushers will please be punctually at the garden at 3 P.M. on Wednesday, in order to learn their duties.[53]

As Barnum alludes to above, tickets were color coded to better help attendees find their seats. Yellow tickets were in the center of the venue, red and blue on either side. (See Figure 1.3) The seats themselves were color coded to correspond to the color of the ticket, and yellow, red, and blue colored lights were positioned in the hall to clearly demarcate the sections. Clearly crowd behavior and crowd control were high on Barnum's list of priorities as the concert approached. We see here how the selling and distributing of tickets was not a strictly financial consideration but also an issue of public order and safety. Such pronouncements would be issued throughout Lind's initial run of concerts in New York, and they indicate the manner in which an event of this scale required the organizers to engage in a kind of public pedagogy, seeking to train the public in how to gather so that they would not create undue disturbance.

By most accounts, Barnum's efforts in this regard worked surprisingly well on the evening of Lind's debut. Although an enormous crowd of people surrounded the outside of the hall, observers were generally struck by the relative ease with which ticket holders were able to enter Castle Garden and procure their seats, ease that was facilitated by the large police presence. The

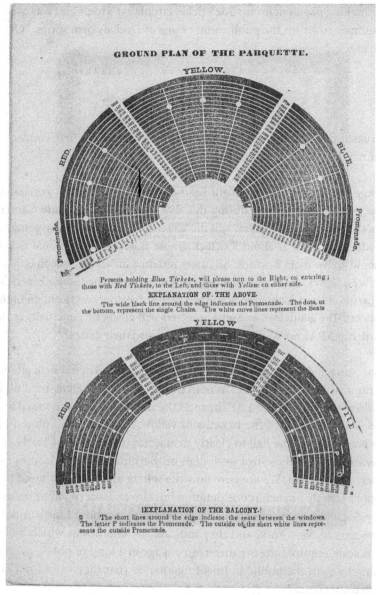

Figure 1.3 This floor plan appeared in the program for Jenny Lind's earliest concerts and explained to concertgoers the division of Castle Garden into distinct ticketed sections coded with the colors red, yellow, and blue, along with a space for promenade ticket holders. Courtesy of the American Antiquarian Society.

biggest challenge to the order of the event came from the water. Newspapers reported that a number of individuals sought to circumvent the carefully guarded entrance to Castle Garden by riding small boats along the water proximate to the rear of the hall. Some of these spectators seemed satisfied with having a more favored position from which to hear the concert; others went so far as to try to crash the event but were successfully repelled by the efforts of the police.

The maintenance of order was more striking for most commentators due to the size and character of the audience that gathered to see Lind perform, shown in Figure 1.4. Although estimates varied, the major news accounts claimed anywhere from five thousand to eight thousand in attendance at that first concert. Among the more notable features of the audience was its overwhelmingly masculine composition. Lind was widely championed for her feminine virtues, but the general opinion was that most "respectable" women were too much concerned with the potential for unruliness to have felt safe attending a public event of such magnitude. Descriptions of the audience for Lind's subsequent New York concerts made a point of observing that the proportion of women to men rose considerably as Barnum demonstrated his propensity for effective crowd control. But this first concert appears to have drawn an audience containing far more men than women.

Of arguably greater consequence was the mix of social classes that attended the event. Although the published accounts are impressionistic, there is nonetheless enough consistency among commentators to safely generalize about the social character of Lind's audience. According to the *Message Bird*, a biweekly New York music magazine that typically featured a semblance of early highbrow cultural commentary:

> In spite of the high bidding for tickets for the first two nights, the assembly was not a display of fashionable aristocracy. You looked round in vain for signs of that. If it were there at all, its usual glaring prominence was softened down ... into the general level of genial and refined humanity. By the third night large representations from the two extremes, the Bowery boys and the "upper ten," were palpably present. Who but Jenny Lind could have assembled *such* an audience?[54]

The *Herald*, whose editorial voice was shaped by the populism of publisher James Gordon Bennett, was if anything even more sanguine in its assessment of the social significance of the gathering. "Never did a mortal in this city,

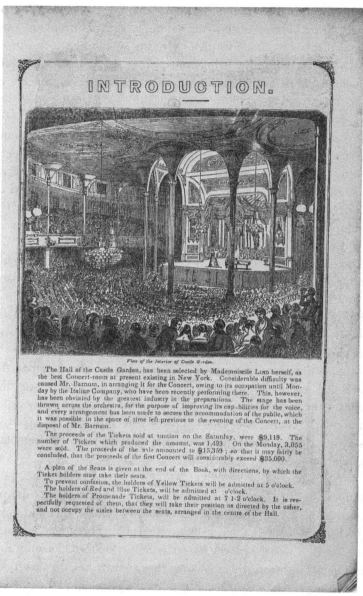

Figure 1.4 Jenny Lind at Castle Garden, in an illustration that appeared in her concert programs in the days and weeks immediately following her New York debut. Courtesy of the American Antiquarian Society.

or perhaps in any other, receive such homage as the sovereign of song received from the sovereign people, on this memorable occasion," exclaimed the writer for the *Herald*. The article continued:

> We say from the sovereign people; for it was not the aristocracy who were there: it was the middle-classes—the mechanics and the storekeepers, with their wives and daughters and sisters, presenting an array of dazzling beauty, in which the upper ten were as lost as a drop of water in the ocean. In the old country, none but royalty and the aristocracy could afford to pay such prices, even for one night, to hear the Nightingale sing. Here, the majesty of the people were present, and presented such a spectacle as we have never seen before. From the ceiling to the stage it was one dense mass of human beings, and the passages all around were filled with those who were fortunate enough to obtain promenade tickets. Yet there was no confusion . . . there was a seat for everybody, and everybody had a seat corresponding with the number of his ticket.[55]

These two passages, from two very different publications, offer the dominant public interpretation of the significance of Jenny Lind's concerts, and her debut in particular. Lind, and arguably Lind alone (in cooperation with Barnum, of course), transcended the social divisions that had all too recently driven a wedge into New York's cultural landscape. Without having sung a note in public yet, her sheer ability to draw a crowd attested to the existence of a cultural middle ground where opposed social groups could join together and to the potential for cultural democracy that still resided in the US despite the apparent growth of disparity and conflict.

With the crowd having been assigned such importance, what actually happened when Jenny Lind stood before it to sing? According to the scheme of that night's concert program, the Castle Garden audience had to wait through two introductory works before Lind made her entrance. Opening the concert, conductor Jules Benedict led the orchestra through the overture to German composer Carl Maria von Weber's opera, *Oberon*; following which was a song from Italian composer Gioachino Rossini's opera, *Maometto Secondo*, that featured the baritone Giovanni Belletti, Lind's performing companion throughout the duration of her tour. Only then did Lind emerge. Her appearance had an air of drama best captured by Richard Grant White, writing in the *Morning Courier and New York Enquirer*:

There was then an impatiently borne interval, the doors at the back of the stage opened and a young woman a little above the middle height, not very robust in figure, with deep, earnest, blue eyes, a mobile mouth expressing both sweetness and determination, came rather awkwardly down between the music stands of the orchestra. The audience immediately burst into applause; she curtsied very deeply with a sort of heart-felt expression, and the audience sprang to their feet, and shouted, screamed, and waved their handkerchiefs, till the young woman seemed oppressed with the homage, and, in fact, stunned with the din. When the people were tired of this manifestation they stopped. The deathlike stillness which pervaded that vast assemblage in the moment after the symphony ceased, and before she parted her lips, was the profoundest, most imposing homage which could have been paid to the genius of Jenny Lind.[56]

If the audience paid tribute to Lind with its silence, creating an aural void to be filled by her voice, the explosion of applause that met Lind upon her appearance seems to have left her somewhat bewildered. Her first scheduled selection, the aria "Casta Diva" from Vincenzo Bellini's massively popular opera, *Norma*, had been a showcase for flights of vocal virtuosity since it first premiered in the US almost a decade earlier; and was moreover taken from the same opera in which she had made her debut before the German public in 1844. Singing it in rehearsals leading up to her concert, Lind had left a powerful impression on those auditors in attendance, including many journalists. But in concert, the piece started awkwardly and to a significant extent fell flat. While she regained some of her poise and vocal strength at the end of the song, the general impression was that Lind's first public vocal performance in the US did not quite meet the incredibly high expectations that surrounded her.

The story of Lind's debut was not a story of disappointment, however. If anything, it was a story of variety. The singer would appear on stage four more times during the evening, and each selection presented her in a distinct musical setting. Her next vocal effort, following a piece for two pianos featuring Benedict and noted virtuoso Richard Hoffman, was a vocal duet on another song by Rossini, which paired her with her baritone counterpart, Belletti. For many critics this was the vocal highlight of the concert, and it demonstrated in a way "Casta Diva" did not that Lind had the power and passion suitable to the performance of Italian opera—a point, however, on which there was far from unanimous agreement, as we will see. Next, after an intermission and another instrumental overture, this time devoted to one of Benedict's own compositions, Lind sang as part of a trio for voice and two flutes, in a composition written expressly for her by the eminent German composer Giacomo Meyerbeer, extracted from his opera, *The Camp of Silesia*. One further solo turn by Belletti led to the climax of the concert, which showcased Lind in one of the songs for which she would become best known during the extent of her concert tour: "The Herdsman's Song," otherwise called the "Echo Song," one of several "Swedish melodies" that Lind would sing (in Swedish) over her several months of touring. The song was notable for Lind's impersonation of a mountain herdsman calling to his sheep and having his voice echo back to him from the mountains. Lind displayed great vocal skill and no small degree of crowd-pleasing trickery in the effect through which she rendered the sound of the echoing voice. According to Herrman Saroni, editor of *Saroni's Musical Times*, the oddity of the composition at first left the audience stunned; but by the end of the first verse, they let loose a "long restrained enthusiasm" that grew into "deafening cheers, hurrahs and *bravos*" as she began verse two. By song's end the response was stronger still, such that "Lind had to repeat it, and if she had acceded to the desires of the audience, she would probably be singing it this very moment at Castle Garden, so enthusiastic and unsatiable [sic] were they in their approbation and clamors for a second encore."[57]

Closing the concert was the "Greeting to America," the winning song from the contest Barnum had sponsored in the weeks leading up to Lind's arrival. With lyrics by American poet and writer Bayard Taylor, and music by Lind's conductor, Jules Benedict, the "Greeting" was something of an anticlimax to the concert in the wake of the crowd-stirring "Echo Song." However, it carried great symbolic importance for the way it expanded the dimensions of the imagined community for whom Lind sang, portraying her as singing for an audience that is not just citywide but national in scope:

> I greet with a full heart the land of the west,
> Whose banner of stars o'er a world is unroll'd;
> Whose empire o'er shadows Atlantic's wide breast,
> And opes to the sunset its gateway of gold.
> The land of the mountain, the land of the lake
> And rivers that roll in magnificent tide—
> Where the souls of the mighty from slumber awake,
> And hallow the soil for whose freedom they died.

Giving voice to this lyrical portrait of America's manifest destiny, Lind offered herself as testament to the progress of the American people, whose geographic expansion was justified in cultural as well as imperial terms.

It was left to Barnum, though, to have the evening's last word. Responding to boisterous calls from the crowd asking, "Where's Barnum?" the impresario appeared on the stage, assuming an air of humility in the face of Lind's artistry. He would refrain from singing the praise of her musical talents, he said, which had already been demonstrated for all to hear; but he wanted to draw attention to another of Lind's great qualities, her charity. Boldly announcing the terms of his contract with Lind, which entitled her to half the net profits of every concert, he claimed that she had insisted that the whole of her share of the first night's receipts—which he said was "in the neighborhood of $10,000"—would be donated to various charitable causes.[58] Barnum then enumerated each of the causes and the sums they would receive, twelve in all, ranging from the Fire Department Fund and Musical Fund Society at the top, to ten further associations including a number of asylums housed in the city (Colored and Orphan Asylum, Lying in Asylum for Destitute Females, Old Ladies' Asylum, etc.).[59] Barnum's maneuver reinforced much of the advance publicity he had circulated concerning the singer, and transmitted a message also at work in many reviews: that Lind's voice, however powerful and pleasing in its own right, could not be fully appreciated apart from her character. As Herrman Saroni wrote in concluding his review: "Not the great artist alone do we worship, but the *true woman*, fresh with all the graces and beauties of unsullied nature, radiant and powerful as an angel, with God's best gift, a pure and loving heart . . . Her mission is not alone to delight and enchant, but to bless and elevate."[60]

* * *

Over the course of the next two weeks, Lind would perform five more concerts at Castle Garden before leaving for Boston, where she would perform next. These concerts, and the surrounding discourse, solidified perceptions of Lind that provided the foundation for her reception as the orbit of her touring activity expanded. Accounts of her near-angelic devotion to charity and religious faith persisted throughout this phase, echoing the publicity image that Barnum had spent so many months constructing prior to her arrival. As the performances accumulated, though, critics became more ready to comment upon the distinctive qualities of Lind's vocal capabilities and the content of her programs. They also continued to express surprise and wonder at the size and character of her audiences. Lind's status as a figure who could unite a heterogeneous public remained strong in this evolving set of impressions. However, her very popularity raised concerns among some critics who wished for more separation between "high" and "low" elements of culture than she was willing to provide; while others debated the cultural underpinnings of her singing approach, questioning whether her style was the most refined.

On this last point, the defining issue was how Lind's "Northern" cultural disposition bore upon her vocal and expressive talents. In the operatic vocal field into which Lind entered in the US, the pinnacle of art was considered—at least by an influential sector of the listening public—to have been reached by Italian singers, who were thought to be best suited to render the esteemed works of operatic composers such as Rossini, Bellini, and Donizetti. A Swede whose main performing experience outside her native land had come in Germany and England, Lind was judged to be remote from this Italian operatic school, in contrast to her most celebrated predecessor, the famed Malibran, whose parents were from Spain and whose father Manuel had spent years performing in Naples before relocating to London.[61] Since the Garcia family's time in the US, Italian opera had been pivotal for a key group of elite New Yorkers who had sought to demarcate a space of exclusivity for themselves through artistic patronage—one result of which, arguably, was the Astor Place riot. To defend the Italian school as the height of musical, and especially vocal, expression was therefore to uphold a value system aligned with social privilege. Lind's success, in turn, suggested that the terms of that privilege were shifting as a new set of standards came into play.

In her analysis of race and auditory culture, Jennifer Stoever asserts that what she calls the "sonic color line" has "enabled the dominant white culture to classify particular sounds as identifiably and essentially 'black,' fixing race in a sensory domain already branded as emotionally potent and unpredictable."[62] Pitting "Southern" and Italian against "Northern" and Scandinavian—and by extension, Anglo-Saxon—followed a parallel logic. This critical debate was not about white against black, at least not explicitly, but was in effect about the whiteness of whiteness, defined in relation to those qualities that were imagined as embodying the height of civilized expression. At stake as well was a fundamental question regarding the proper role of musical art. Should a singer such as Lind stir the passions with maximum impact, leaving listeners in a heightened emotional state; or should she appeal to other faculties, offering what some perceived as a "higher," more contemplative kind of cultural experience?

Making the most elaborate case for Jenny Lind's artistic limitations was Richard Grant White, the music critic for the *Morning Courier and New York Enquirer*. Like those of most daily newspaper critics of the time, White's reviews of Lind's first two concerts joined in the general excitement that her performances had generated and carried little suggestion of criticism. Responding to her third Castle Garden appearance, however, White shifted gears. He had great appreciation for Lind's talents as a singer, but from her first concert forward he felt that something was lacking. Explaining that he wanted more occasion to hear her before revealing his thoughts, White now came forward: "we must bear witness to the correctness of our first impressions, and, strange as it may appear, declare that we find this famous *prima donna*, whose every note is delicious sweetness, this warm-hearted impulsive woman whose every act is sympathy and kindness, a cold and unimpassioned artist."[63] The critic built his case with meticulous detail and somewhat tortured logic. He distinguished between the technical features of Lind's vocal approach and the expressive aspects. She displayed as much technical polish as anyone could want to hear, each of her most demanding selections demonstrating "the same beautiful phrasing, the same purity of intonation, the same finished exactness of execution, and the same marvelous ease which made exactness seem a grace."[64] Yet the very purity of her technique, claimed White, left little room for true emotion to reveal itself. White then went a step further, ascribing the "coldness" of Lind's singing to her geographic origins and her ethnic character. Claimed the writer:

> Jenny Lind is thoroughly and essentially Scandinavian in nature, and such a nature can never, as we believe, acquire that power in vocal expression which is natural to those of Southern clime and blood. With the Northern nations vocal music seems naturally to confine itself to the proper execution of forms of melody and harmony; in the South it is a passionate utterance.[65]

Affect here becomes linked to nation, race, and ethnicity. Jenny Lind's Northern character allowed her to personify beauty of form and virtue in spirit; but it barred her, by White's logic, from exercising the passions to a degree that would leave the listener fully satisfied.

The counterargument came from various quarters. A critic for the *Evening Post* made the case forcefully: "People talk and write about Jenny Lind as if she had assumed the character of an Italian prima donna; whereas she pretends to be nothing more nor less than a northern singer, to our apprehension a more interesting, because more rare species of artist."[66] Expanding on this train of thought was the *New York Herald*, which consistently made the case for the unique value of Lind's "Northern" disposition during her first run of concerts. Responding to Lind's second New York performance, the *Herald* critic stressed that her "soft trills" and "high notes" surpassed those of her contemporaries: "Here it is, that the voice of Northern Europe contests for the palm with the delicious feeling and soul-like energy which characterize the tones and utterance of the sunnier South. The voice that could produce the 'Herdsman's Song,' never could be fed on anything warmer than cold air."[67] A follow-up article in the *Herald* cast Lind as a "Northern Light" whose rise to prominence marked nothing short of a turning point in the progress of art and culture. In music, the writer joined Lind's ascent with the recent success of the Norwegian violinist Ole Bull, proclaiming about the Swedish singer: "All feel her power, all go mad who see her . . . It is new—it belongs to the new northern civilization just as much as the magnetic telegraph does . . . It is electric—it belongs to the new age—it has no affinity for what has gone before."[68]

Weighing most strongly on the matter was John S. Dwight, whose reviews of Lind for the *Tribune* increasingly engaged in a kind of rivalry with those of White for the *Morning Courier*. Like White, Dwight couched his understanding of Lind's expressive power in a broader philosophy of how music should work upon its listeners. She projected a degree of self-possession that, in Dwight's judgment, made her uniquely compelling. Reviewing Lind's second concert, the critic observed: "She sings herself. She does not, like many skillful vocalists, merely recite her musical studies . . . her singing . . . is her own proper and spontaneous activity—integral and whole." This wholeness gave Lind's art a depth that went beyond what Dwight took to be superficial emotion: "True Music, true art can work deeper effect than tears."[69]

Following Lind's third concert, Dwight turned his attention to the question of cultural provenance. Having been especially moved by her rendition of the aria "*Non Parventar*" from Mozart's opera, *The Magic Flute*, the critic expounded:

> It is narrow criticism which imprisons such a singer within the partial scope, albeit classical, of the Italian School . . . True, you would not say of her, in the conventional Italian sense of the word, what is often said in first

acknowledgment of a good singer: "She has *style*" . . . If we are to limit style to that sense, Mdlle. Lind has more than style: she has genius—Northern genius, to be sure.[70]

With the peculiarly "Northern" character of Lind's talent established, Dwight proceeded to offer a critique of the Italian operatic style. Where White associated Italian singers with unfettered passion, Dwight saw these same singers purveying "a very cheap kind of superficial, skin-deep excitability that usurps the name of Passion." And while Dwight was willing to admit that Italian composers and singers alike had a true gift for melody, he nonetheless stressed that "it is not in the genius of the Italian School to produce or hardly to appreciate such a new revelation of song as this human nightingale or canary of Sweden."[71] For Dwight, the singularity of Lind lay in the way that she translated the artistic impulses of Northern European orchestral music into the realm of vocal art. Hers was the art of refined, thoughtful expression, not devoid of emotion but striving toward a style whose effects were not immediately felt, but would leave a more enduring mark upon the listener.[72]

As much as Dwight praised Lind's artistic gifts, he was not uniformly pleased with the substance of her concerts. The one point above all that left him wanting more had to do with the selection of music that she presented. In this he was joined by a handful of other commentators including music publisher Herrman Saroni. Here we see the nascent values of "highbrow" cultural criticism moving to the foreground. Even from the first concert, Dwight complained, "we have yet to hear [Lind] in the kind of music which seems to us most to need and to deserve such a singer—in the Agatha of *Der Freyschutz* [sic.] [an opera by the German composer Carl Maria von Weber], and in Mozart and the deep music of the great modern German operas."[73] She included some such works as her Castle Garden run continued, but Dwight continued to insist that the heights reached by Lind as a vocalist were not matched by the material she sang. As delighted as he was by her inclusion of an aria from Mozart's *The Magic Flute* in her third and fourth concerts, Dwight still wanted more: "We ask to have more of the classic masterpieces, not merely from the one fashionable school of modern Italian opera, with a sprinkling of ballads; but also from the masters with whose music her soul and her Northern genius are most kindred—from such as Mozart, Beethoven, Mendelssohn, or Franz Schubert."[74] The sort of programmatic purity Dwight desired was hardly conventional practice at the time, and evinces music historian William Weber's claim, cited earlier, that the idea of classical music was not conservative but transformative through the first half of the nineteenth century. Dwight was outlining an ideal notion of a classical canon rooted in Germanic musical works that gained significant authority in the second half of the nineteenth century but was not yet fully in place. This issue was another subtext of the battle between "Northern" and "Southern" cultural influence being waged through the reviews of Lind's early performances.

Saroni, who shared Dwight's preference for Germanic works, blamed the imbalance of Lind's programs on her desire to please the multitudes of listeners that came to hear her. By his estimation, too much of her time was spent "with those pieces, in which she enters into competition with the ventriloquist, the equilibrist, with the magician, and with the circus-riders"—this referring primarily to the overwhelmingly popular "Herdsman's Song" with its seemingly supernatural echo, but also to analogous pieces rendered by Lind such as the "Bird Song," another selection that called upon her great mimetic powers. Insistently concluding her concerts with these works that were marked crowd pleasers, Saroni charged that her status as the "Queen of Song" was being supplanted by the less dignified title, "The Slave of the public."[75] Dwight agreed up to a point, complaining in his review of Lind's fifth concert that her programs were assembled with "a too timid and exclusive eye to gratifying public taste." However, he continued also to celebrate the sheer magnitude of her success, as measured by the size of her audiences, much as he had done since her Castle Garden debut. If Lind wished too much to please the crowd, it was because she was "evidently most herself and most inspired when she sings most for *all*."[76] The ambivalence underlying these views typified the peculiar position that Jenny Lind occupied in the culture of the era: hailed as a figure whose popularity held out the promise of elevating public taste and criticized for the very gestures that made her so popular.

Thrown Stones and Shattered Glass

By the time Lind finished her initial run of concerts at Castle Garden, press reports estimated that her audiences had grown to some eight thousand or more. Writers who had been surprised at the size of the crowd for Lind's first performance were continually struck that her audiences kept growing with each concert. Many explanations were posited: that word of mouth and media reports confirmed that Lind was indeed a singer worth hearing, whereas at her first performance audiences were going on faith; that the run of concerts proved Barnum's talent for managing an event of such large proportions, instilling more confidence in the safety of the proceedings. When Barnum announced that Lind would leave for Boston after her sixth concert, it also created a feeling of scarcity that undoubtedly led more people to rush to see her. Although she would return a month later, in late October, for another, longer run of concerts in New York, those would be held in a different and smaller venue—Tripler Hall, a newly built concert hall that had been intended to house Lind's debut but had not been completed in time. Lind would continue to test the capacity of halls in other parts of the country, but never again would she appear in the US before crowds as large as she did during her first run at Castle Garden.

Barnum, meanwhile, continually adjusted his approach to promoting and producing the concerts as they proceeded. After the second concert, he publicly announced that no more tickets would be sold at auction for Lind's remaining New York appearances and that prices would be fixed at a range from two to six dollars for reserved seats, with promenade tickets selling for a dollar.[77] The promenade tickets, which allowed patrons to enter the hall and stand in any suitable available space, became a running cause for concern. Promenade ticket holders routinely grabbed any empty seat, at times leaving those who held the tickets for the same seats standing or having to get in a near-altercation to claim what they had purchased. Ushers were there to mediate the situation but the sheer number of promenade ticket holders—several hundred per concert—made the situation difficult to manage. With each concert Barnum created new controls to try to contain the tension caused by the promenade tickets. First, the rule became that all seats were considered to be held for ticket holders until after the conclusion of the opening overture performed by Jules Benedict and orchestra, at which point promenade ticket holders could take any seats that remained open.[78] When that regulation failed to prevent the rush for seats, Barnum experimented with admitting the promenade contingent only a half-hour before the appointed start time of eight o'clock in the evening; and then with only selling the promenade tickets immediately before the concerts and allowing purchasers into Castle Garden just before the concert started. Yet this created even more of a rush for position at the fifth concert and disrupted the early moments of the performance quite considerably.[79] At Lind's sixth Castle Garden concert—her last before departing for Boston—the problem of the promenade tickets was provisionally solved only by the simple fact that it was so crowded that there were no more seats to be had by the time the non-seated ticket holders entered the hall.[80]

Barnum's continued reliance on promenade tickets was a major factor in the first significant disturbance to occur at one of Lind's concerts. The episode happened at the last of Lind's run of concerts in Boston, which stretched from late September into the middle of October 1850 (with a brief detour for a single concert in Providence, Rhode Island, on October 7). Throughout most of her Boston appearances, Lind and company sang at the Tremont Temple, a theater that also served as a religious meeting place and was the largest available performance venue in the city proper, with a capacity of just under three thousand. From her first Boston concert on the evening of Friday, September 27, until her last at Tremont Temple on Thursday, October 10, Lind performed without incident, drawing a level of acclaim that approached the reception she received in New York. Wishing to accommodate larger audiences than the Tremont Temple would allow and to reach concertgoers coming from other points in New England outside Boston, Barnum then scheduled two concerts for the Fitchburg Station Hall, advertised in Figure 1.5, a much larger venue holding closer to five thousand that was housed in a railroad depot in Fitchburg, several miles northwest of Boston. While tickets for Lind's concerts at Tremont Temple were priced at three dollars, with much higher prices being paid at auctions for the first two performances, at the Fitchburg concerts the tickets were sold for a more affordable range of $3, $2, and $1, the latter being the price for promenade tickets.[81]

Worries about the suitability of the Fitchburg Station Hall as a concert venue arose as soon as it was proposed. Some feared that the hall was not built on a strong enough foundation to support the thousands of concertgoers that would attend. Others thought that it lacked proper acoustics or comfort to allow an audience to fully enjoy Lind's concerts. Following the first of Lind's two concerts there, the *Boston Evening Transcript* observed,

> Much cannot be said of the hall as a place for music, but notwithstanding, Miss Lind and Belletti both accommodated themselves in the most admirable manner to the difficult task of overcoming the architectural inappropriateness of the building ... Nearly every window of the hall was necessarily open, in the absence of different means of ventilation, thus admitting sounds from the street; yet apparently every note was so clearly vocalized that it was distinctly heard in the most remote corner.[82]

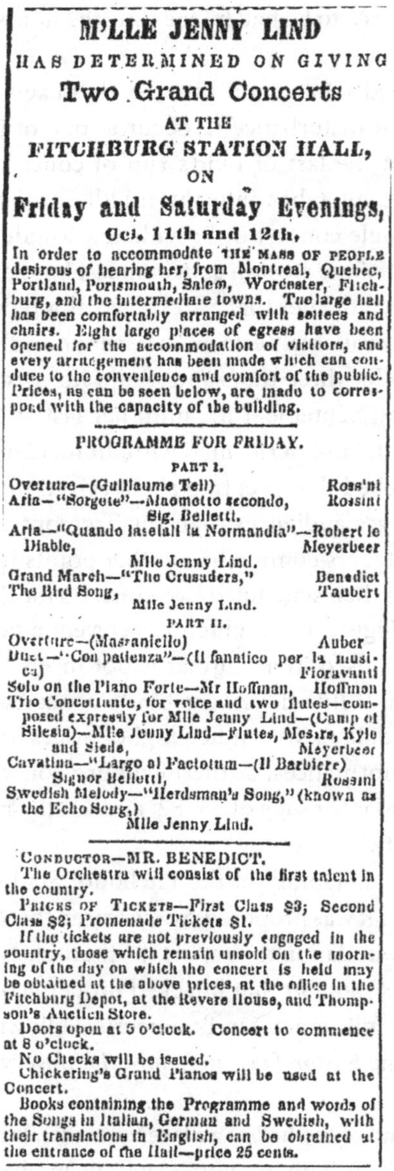

M'LLE JENNY LIND
HAS DETERMINED ON GIVING
Two Grand Concerts
AT THE
FITCHBURG STATION HALL,
ON
Friday and Saturday Evenings,
Oct. 11th and 12th,

In order to accommodate THE MASS OF PEOPLE desirous of hearing her, from Montreal, Quebec, Portland, Portsmouth, Salem, Worcester, Fitchburg, and the intermediate towns. The large hall has been comfortably arranged with settees and chairs. Eight large places of egress have been opened for the accommodation of visitors, and every arrangement has been made which can conduce to the convenience and comfort of the public. Prices, as can be seen below, are made to correspond with the capacity of the building.

PROGRAMME FOR FRIDAY.
PART I.

Overture—(Guillaume Tell)   Rossini
Aria—"Sorgete"—Maometto secondo,   Rossini
    Sig. Belletti.
Aria—"Quando lasciai la Normandia"—Robert le Diable,   Meyerbeer
    Mlle Jenny Lind.
Grand March—"The Crusaders,"   Benedict
The Bird Song,   Taubert
    Mlle Jenny Lind.

PART II.

Overture—(Masaniello)   Auber
Duet—"Con patienza"—(Il fanatico per la musica)   Fioravanti
Solo on the Piano Forte—Mr Hoffman,   Hoffman
Trio Concertante, for voice and two flutes—composed expressly for Mlle Jenny Lind—(Camp of Silesia)—Mlle Jenny Lind—Flutes, Messrs, Kyle and Siede,   Meyerbeer
Cavatina—"Largo al Factotum—(Il Barbiere)
    Signor Belletti,   Rossini
Swedish Melody—"Herdsman's Song," (known as the Echo Song,)
    Mlle Jenny Lind.

CONDUCTOR—MR. BENEDICT.
The Orchestra will consist of the first talent in the country.
PRICES OF TICKETS—First Class $3; Second Class $2; Promenade Tickets $1.
If the tickets are not previously engaged in the country, those which remain unsold on the morning of the day on which the concert is held may be obtained at the above prices, at the office in the Fitchburg Depot, at the Revere House, and Thompson's Auction Store.
Doors open at 5 o'clock. Concert to commence at 8 o'clock.
No Checks will be issued.
Chickering's Grand Pianos will be used at the Concert.
Books containing the Programme and words of the Songs in Italian, German and Swedish, with their translations in English, can be obtained at the entrance of the Hall—price 25 cents.

Figure 1.5 Advertisement for Jenny Lind's two concerts at Fitchburg Station Hall outside of Boston. The ad stresses all the efforts taken to ensure the audience's comfort, but the venue was generally judged unsuitable and gave rise to the first significant disturbance to arise during Lind's American concert tour. From the *Boston Daily Bee* (October 11, 1850).

Lind's ability to fill even the largest and most crowded venue with the sound of her voice without losing her musicality had drawn comment throughout her Castle Garden run. That capability served her well at the Fitchburg Station Hall and was indeed necessary to hold the audience's attention in the unventilated, noisy, and overcrowded space.

At the second of Lind's concerts at the hall, and her last scheduled for this visit to Boston, trouble arose from a confluence of the bad qualities of the venue, the poor management of admitting ticketholders, and mounting public suspicion over Barnum's handling of the production details. Boston newspapers expressed far more dissatisfaction with Barnum than their New York counterparts. Even as they trumpeted Jenny Lind's virtues, they commonly charged Barnum with employing his tactics of "humbug" to get every cent he could from the singer's performances. Feeding the distrust was the pressure exerted by speculators who bought large blocks of tickets and resold them. Some observers posited that Barnum himself might be working in partnership with the speculators to raise prices and boost demand, an accusation that he repeatedly denied. Either way, this situation aggravated what was already a growing disparity between those willing and able to pay for the highest priced tickets located in the best portions of the house and those who could only afford the low-priced promenade tickets. While not quite on the order of the class conflict that underpinned the events of the Astor Place Riot, the manner of selling tickets and then admitting concertgoers to Lind's performances nonetheless highlighted these differences between segments of the audience under the banner of inclusivity, building the basis for resentment on all sides.

Conflict began to stir outside the entrance to the Fitchburg Station Hall in the hours leading up to Lind's concert on Saturday, October 12. Promenade ticket holders gathered *en masse* as they were wont to do, likely joined by others who held no tickets but wanted to join for the sake of being part of the excitement. Kept waiting on the street as the hour of the concert's start approached, the crowd interfered with the ability of other ticket holders to enter the venue. As a writer for the *Boston Courier* put it: "The street in front of the hall was blocked up with all sorts of persons, who continued to press forward, and who determined, if they could not enter the hall themselves that no other should."[83] The real trouble, however, came once people had made their way into the hall. Because of the crush outside, the "promenaders"—as they were called—got in earlier than they were supposed to and began claiming empty seats. Their actions caused sections of the audience to close in upon itself at various points at the back of the hall near the entrance, which was made worse by the lack of ventilation. What ensued was most vividly described by a reporter for the *Daily Atlas*:

> The hall was not capable of containing the immense crowd which rushed like a deluge onward, shouting, shrieking, and crushing. The windows at the entrance of the hall were all broken, wherever a foothold could be obtained upon the sashes; the wall itself was broken through to obtain a standing place upon the mop board . . . and this took place amid the excited roars of some hundreds of angry men, who had paid for a comfortable standing place, but found themselves almost suffocated by a crush of human beings greater than was ever before packed inside of a public building in Boston.[84]

According to two Boston papers, the *Herald* and the *Daily Bee*, at this point a riot was narrowly averted.[85] Following the opening overture for the concert, which was all but inaudible from the tumult, musical director George Loder came to the front of the stage and offered that anyone who was dissatisfied could leave and apply for a refund from Barnum. When Lind sang her first selection of the evening, Handel's *I Know That My Redeemer Liveth*, things quieted further. Indeed, by some accounts, the whole episode paid additional testimony to the singer's unique ability to bring calm amidst chaos. Yet the overall impression left by the concert was one of unrest, with Barnum being given primary blame for the way things had gotten out of hand.

Three first-person accounts help us to understand how the events of the concert appeared to its participants. One of the ushers hired by Barnum wrote a scathing letter to the *Boston Herald* in which he described how the showman haggled with early arrivals at the Fitchburg Station Hall who were met with a whole area of unoccupied seats. Barnum told them the seats were all taken but then contradicted himself by saying they could acquire access to the seats by paying an extra dollar. It was left to the ushers to further guard the seats from intruders, a task made more difficult by the bad faith that Barnum had engendered.[86] A concertgoer who held a promenade ticket wrote of his experience to the *Gloucester Telegraph*, recounting how after purchasing his ticket outside the hall, he and a friend "placed ourselves at the end of the rope, which was secured by police to prevent the crowd from filling up the passage-way, which was kept open to allow the three-dollar ticket holders, who were the aristocracy of the concert, to enter."[87]

Here we see how the different strata of tickets imposed a sort of class divide that was made palpable by the process through which concertgoers entered the venue.

The antagonism that stemmed from the circumstances of the concert came through clearly in a diary entry by upper-class Boston resident Caroline Healy Dall:

> No one could conceive a more horrible crowd ... When I heard the cry for water, air, open the windows &c.—who come from desperate dying men—in choked voices—I felt what must come. I made several calm attempts to get out, but there was no possible means of egress, and a disappointed crowd were storming without—The noise and tumult was now so great—windows breaking and panels giving way—that we heard not one syllable of the opening, Der Freschutz [sic] ... I have seen crowds before, but I never imagined what a suffocating crowd would be.[88]

Dall's anxious recollection, combined with the others, shows just how precarious was the balance that Barnum sought to strike in his promotion of Lind's concerts between the maximization of profit and the provision of sufficient security and comfort to ensure order. When all worked as it was designed to do, the result could appear as the embodiment of social harmony. If things went awry, though, the unsure scaffolding was laid bare, and the heterogeneity of the crowd became a cause for resentment and a source of fear.

* * *

Problems akin to those encountered in Boston continued to arise intermittently throughout Lind's subsequent touring endeavors and became more frequent during a stretch in the spring and summer of 1851. A stray reference to Lind in a Portsmouth, New Hampshire, newspaper story captured the undercurrent of resentment that her concerts generated over time. On the surface the article had nothing to do with Lind but was about the trend of manufacturing cheap brass clocks. In emphasizing the low cost of these items, the anonymous writer noted that many clocks could now be purchased for "a song," and a song of much lesser price than those offered by Jenny Lind when she sang onstage. Expanding on the digression, the article then asked: "why cannot Jenny, in the height of her generosity give a concert for *the poor*? —not the proceeds of the concert, but the concert itself! Why can she not go over the country and sing at one dollar a ticket? In this way she might pile up a million in a short time."[89] Lind's charity may have been widely celebrated but here we see a gap in the logic whereby she was promoted to the public. Represented so often as a singer for "the people" at large, her concerts remained inaccessible to many who hoped to see her; and that basic fact colored the reception she met at many stops along the way.

Following a southward turn in her touring itinerary that took Lind from New Orleans to Louisville, Kentucky, Lind visited Cincinnati in April 1851. Excitement was high, and at the auction for tickets—a sales strategy that Barnum retained when visiting new locations—the first ticket commanded a price of $575, the highest paid since the initial weeks of her tour the previous fall. Her concert in Cincinnati was subject to considerable disruption, however, when a large gathering of men and boys clamored for the shutters of the Sycamore Street Theater to be opened so they could have more opportunity to hear her from the street. Lind continued to perform without undue interruption, but police were called and fired shots over the crowd to scare them into dispersing.[90] When Lind performed in Pittsburgh just a few days later, a similar scene took place, but in this case the crowd outside took the additional step of throwing stones at the windows of the performance hall, some of which were directed at Lind's own private room, which upset the singer greatly.[91] Both incidents demonstrate that apart from the divisions between seated concertgoers and promenade ticket holders, Lind's audience was further segregated along class lines by the presence of what Bluford Adams described as "huge crowds drawn mainly from the lower classes [that] filled the streets outside, hoping to catch the singer's voice through an open window."[92] This latter division was if anything more combustible than that between attendees inside the hall, since the street crowds were more expressly excluded from the proceedings and had less investment in maintaining order.

Maybe the most confrontational occurrence of Lind's entire tour came in July, when Lind performed at Hartford, Connecticut. Notably, this concert came after she had terminated her arrangement with Barnum. The initial contract between the singer and the showman required her to perform one hundred and fifty concerts during her time in the US, but the pair renegotiated the terms shortly after Lind's debut, at which point an escape clause of sorts was added that gave Lind the right to end the agreement after sixty concerts and again, after one hundred.[93] Lind chose to exercise her right shortly after the concert in Pittsburgh, as her hundredth concert was approaching. There is no clear suggestion that the recent near riots were the main stimulus for her decision. Barnum claims in his autobiography that members of Lind's entourage had been encouraging her in this direction for some time, but as tour historians Porter Ware and Thaddeus Lockard point out, there were many reasons why the singer might have wanted this move. She was tired from the constant touring over nine months under Barnum's management, and his hard-sell tactics had not always sat well with her own wish to appease the public.[94] Once the decision was made, they carried it out quickly. Lind and Barnum parted ways after her ninety-third American concert in Philadelphia, and Lind agreed to pay Barnum a sum of $7,000 for the concerts she had not performed for him fewer than one hundred. From that point forward, Lind handled her American concerts on her own with the assistance of trusted advisers, including Max Hjortsberg, her personal secretary and cousin; Charles Seyton, whom she had hired during the tour to keep account of ticket sales and manage her earnings; and Otto Goldschmidt, the pianist who would eventually take over as her musical director and, in February 1852, would marry Lind.

For as long as Lind performed under Barnum's auspices, he functioned as a lightning rod for most of the bad sentiment that might have stemmed from the manner in which her concerts were promoted. Now she had less of a shield. Her first several concerts after their break, in Philadelphia and Boston, were already planned and went relatively smoothly. Lind next turned her attention westward for a series of concerts in the Connecticut River Valley. First came Springfield, Massachusetts, then the smaller city of Northampton to the north, and then down to Hartford, all in the days surrounding the Fourth of July 1851. The events surrounding this short stretch of performances encompass the highs and lows of Lind's tour of the US.

Springfield would be Lind's home base throughout this portion of her tour, from which she pivoted to her concerts north and south. Ticket sales for the Springfield performance, held on Tuesday, July 1, were accompanied by a measure of unruliness. A very large crowd gathered within and outside Marsh's Music Store where tickets were available, and ninety-degree temperatures created a situation where, according to the *Springfield Republican*, "the sweating [was] profuse, and the swearing (we are sorry to say) somewhat like that of the Army in Flanders."[95] Such uncomfortable confines led tempers to flare and altercations broke out, with windows to the store being smashed, but police quickly responded and restored a kind of calm. The concert itself was deemed a success, filling the city's Old First Church. Lind sang several of the pieces for which she had become best known, including the aria "Casta Diva" and set pieces the "Bird Song" and the "Echo Song," as the "Herdsman's Song" was now called. Drawing especial favor from the audience was her addition of the Scotch song, "Comin' Through the Rye," which was not planned according to the printed program but had been requested by members of the public in the days leading up to the concert. As was common by this point in her touring efforts, a large crowd also assembled outside the church during the performance but remained in good spirits and could be heard inside the venue cheering Lind after many of her selections.[96]

Two days later, Lind performed at Northampton's First Church. Prior to the concert there was concern about whether the city housed enough people to generate a sufficient audience for Lind—its population of 5,278 was less than half of that residing in Springfield, which had 11,766 according to the 1850 US Census.[97] It was a point of civic pride, then, that the Northampton performance drew nearly one hundred more concertgoers than the Springfield concert. A writer for the *Springfield Republican* proclaimed that the two concerts together represented an important achievement for Lind as well. Her ability to draw sixteen or seventeen hundred people at prices running from two to four dollars per ticket was exceptional in an area where "the best of musical performances . . . rarely draw over 300 or 400 people at 25 cents a ticket." Added the *Republican*, "She is now venturing out of the pale of fashion and commercial wealth, and receiving the pure and unpolluted incense of country hearts."[98] A woman attending the Northampton concert offered her perspective in the pages of the city's *Hampshire Gazette*, noting that in presence of Lind, "all, tonight, ceased to be strangers! What a little Republic we were, here in the heart of New England, worshiping in that time-honored church!"[99]

That sense of idealized musical community quickly dissipated when Lind reached Hartford. Once again, as in Boston and other settings where crowds grew restless, a primary source of conflict was the work of ticket speculators in running up the price of admission. According to one account, the local concert manager worked with nefarious motives. Sale of tickets were to commence at ten o'clock in the morning the day before the concert, but the doors were not open until noon, at which point a map of the venue showed that many of the best seats had already been procured.[100] Whether or not the manager did in fact collude with speculators was never proven, but the perception spread and ticket prices rose well above those advertised. It did not help matters that the Fourth Congregational Church that held the concert only admitted eleven or twelve hundred people, a far smaller capacity than either the Springfield or Northampton concerts in a city with a larger population. As a result, the crowd that gathered outside the church during the concert was considerably larger than the audience inside. Indeed, the demand to catch sight or sound of Lind was so great that people were willing to pay as much as a dollar for a rooftop seat outside the venue.[101]

On the evening of Saturday, July 5, Lind's concert began at seven o'clock in the evening. Lind and company got through about half of their scheduled program before commotion from the crowd outside began to interrupt the performance. As had been the case in Cincinnati, the windows to the church had been kept shut, most likely to minimize disturbance from those outside but taken by the crowd to be a means of preventing them from enjoying the performance. A round of constant shouting commenced, and some threw stones at the windows to break them open. On stage, Lind became visibly flustered. At one point, the suggestion came that if she would show herself at the window to greet the outside crowd, it would help to settle things, but neither Lind nor the audience inside the church received this well. Lind responded to the situation by rushing through her remaining selections, omitting other features of the program to reach an early conclusion, as was recounted by the *Connecticut Courant*: "After the Bird Song, which was but partially heard from the shouts of the mob, she very judiciously hurried through the rest of the programme, and was evidently so frightened as to be unable to do justice to the two closing pieces—'Home, Sweet Home,' and the 'Echo Song.' This was the reception of Jenny Lind in Hartford!"[102]

One unresolved question emerges from the events at Hartford and other instances in which Lind's concerts gave rise to public disorder: did these crowds cause commotion out of a desire to hear Lind, to participate in the mass adulation that her celebrity had generated; or out of a desire to silence the singer? There is little evidence to suggest that Lind ever stimulated the sort of antipathy stirred by the likes of William Macready. Even those newspaper accounts most critical of the crowd behavior in Boston, Cincinnati, Pittsburgh and Hartford were premised on the assumption that no harm was ever intended toward Lind herself. In fact, reports often went out of their way to suggest that the crowds were in complete sympathy with Lind, even in Hartford. One reporter captured the complex motives of the crowd: "There did not appear to be any disposition to commit violence, but a malicious determination to prevent Miss Lind's voice from being heard, and to break up the concert."[103] While some of the crowd was undoubtedly there for the chance to hear and maybe see Lind, however imperfect the circumstances, another portion appears to have been motivated by resentment that had several possible causes: a feeling of exclusion, a sense of unfairness, and also perhaps the perception that the norms of middle-class civility that surrounded Lind were remaking the public sphere into a place where they felt less welcome.

Speculations

A satirical article in the *New York Daily Tribune* purported to convey the impressions of a Wall Street bank note reporter regarding Jenny Lind. The job of such a reporter was to discern the legitimacy and solvency of the bills used for purposes of exchange. Working as a sort of "counterfeit detector," the reporter was therefore said to be in a good position to judge whether the notes sung by Lind were "genuine." Unsurprisingly, Lind was found to have the requisite degree of authenticity by the representative of Wall Street finance, but the terms according to which the article praised Lind are telling. In the logic of mid-nineteenth-century finance, Jenny Lind's success was the result of the fact that "she is the producer or creator of her own commodity—a commodity of which there are not, and never has been any 'samples,' excepting her own in the market."[104]

This construction of Lind as a singular commodity cuts to the heart of what made her US tour of the early 1850s such a signal moment in the history of American musical life. It also raises another question that remains difficult to resolve, concerning how much Lind herself was the author of her own commodification. Lind's agency in her concert career was notable. Her insistence on singing only in concerts, not in staged operas, established a background around her persona and her artistry that was integral to her public reception. She seems to have exerted a determining choice over what material she sang, and the insistence upon her charity was a reflection of her values as much as it was a projection that converted her virtue into an item to be consumed. Her signal innovation may have been to transfer what historian Karen Halttunen has called "genteel performance" to the concert stage. For Halttunen, genteel performance was typically enacted at home, in the middle-class parlor where women entertained guests and participated in rituals of social distinction and politeness designed to reconcile the cultural imperative to display sincere emotion, on the one hand, and emotional restraint on the other.[105]

Lind similarly alternated between these poles of restraint and sincerity, evident in the interplay between her refined vocal technique, which signaled to her audiences that she was in control of her artistry; and her accent on virtue and faith, which conveyed a strong aura of sincerity. Lind's ability to work between these registers elevated her performances to the point that aesthetics and public morality became inseparable.

What Barnum brought was the requisite willingness to take the risks necessary to promote Lind's appeal beyond the middle-class audiences already disposed to identify with the values that she personified. Lind's success was likely guaranteed with or without Barnum; but he gave her a kind of stardom that extended far beyond the segment of the public that attended her concerts. Newspaper reports and disgruntled crowds decried the work of speculators who drove up the price of tickets to Lind's concerts, but Barnum was the ultimate speculator. Every move he made in his promotion of the singer was a calculated risk designed to maximize exposure and profit. Above all, he chanced that he could draw crowds of unusual size and heterogeneity and maintain sufficient control that the public would remain willing to trust him with their safety and so pay for the benefit of hearing Lind sing. Secondarily, he gambled that he could charge far higher prices for admission than had been customary and not alienate the public that he had so arduously cultivated with Lind's collaboration—an effort that threatened to put his appeal to the public at large in jeopardy. That the veneer of order was upset multiple times during Lind's tour indicates just how much uncertainty surrounded the enterprise, and how provisional the efforts of the singer and the showman were. More than a century before the term "arena rock" assumed currency, Barnum invented a nineteenth-century version of the same phenomenon, creating a model whereby concerts of significant scale could be reproduced for a national market, supported by the adulation of a charismatic celebrity whose appeal cut across lines of gender, class, and competing ideals of cultural value.

2

Staging the Spiritual

The Fisk Jubilee Singers and the Postbellum Public Sphere

The road traveled by the Jubilee Singers from Fisk University was at first a rocky one. Many a writer has told of how they met with a mix of indifference and hostility in their first two months of concertizing, following the decision of headstrong chorus director George White to lead the group on tour in the fall of 1871 to raise money for the financially troubled school. Only when they arrived at New York in late December of that year did the troupe of singers begin to find any significant success with the public. Much of their new recognition came from the patronage of Henry Ward Beecher, among the most widely known and admired ministers in the US, who hosted the Singers at his Plymouth Church in Brooklyn and made his endorsement for them in no uncertain terms. Gustavus Pike, then an officer with the American Missionary Association and soon to become the business manager for the Fisk Singers, first encountered the singers on this occasion, and well remembered the impression made by the opening hymn they sang that evening, "O, How I Love Jesus!" in which the chorus's male singers "mingled their voices in a melody so beautiful and touching I scarcely knew whether I was 'in the body or out of the body.'"[1]

Patronage alone was not responsible for the mounting success of the singers. In his published account of their first American concert tour, Pike posited a more general explanation for the troupe's favorable reception, drawing an analogy to the now forgotten Evangelical comedian John Gough, who provided entertainment for those whose religious scruples typically kept them away from the theater. Gough's success, said Pike, "suggests to me that there may be such a thing as supplying a wholesome demand for entertainment to a class of persons who have too much principle or taste to accept the popular entertainments that come within reach." Regarding the Jubilee Singers, he continued:

> Good people understood full well that the singing of the Fisk students was sufficiently enjoyable before they reached New York; but did the large class of Christians, who would scarcely patronize negro concerts, deem it respectable to attend those of the Jubilee Singers? Was there not so much odium attached to negro concerts, as represented in burnt cork minstrels, that people of taste and character did not think it becoming to rush in crowds to a paid concert given by negroes?[2]

The appearance of the Singers at Beecher's church, then, was according to Pike the first step in the process—deliberately cultivated by the managers of their affairs—of making it *popular* to attend their concerts. The aura of moral rightness that surrounded the Singers was integral to their reception, even more so given the hurdles they had to overcome as a black performing troupe at a time when blackface minstrelsy continued to dominate public portrayals of African Americans on stage and in song.

The legacy of the Fisk Jubilee Singers has been much debated, and in recent years their endeavors have become better documented due to the efforts of historians and musicologists committed to reconstructing and interpreting the troupe's career.[3] For many, their significance lies principally in the way they made the black spiritual into a publicly recognized genre of song, which then leads to important questions regarding whether the spiritual as performed by the Jubilee Singers was more or less faithful to the "folk" version of the spiritual that had emerged among African American slaves in the decades leading up to the Civil War.[4] Yet the Fisk Singers have another sort of significance, to my mind of broader consequence, as the first African American singing group to become widely recognized outside the context of blackface minstrelsy. With the emergence of the Jubilee Singers, and their extensive concert tours throughout the US and Europe during the decade of the 1870s, black music became dramatically repositioned as an element of American public life. This is not to say that the Fisk Singers escaped the legacy of minstrelsy in one fell swoop. Blackface performance remained very much a part of the cultural environment in which the Jubilee Singers dwelled, and at times its logic bore upon the troupe quite forcefully, especially as a wealth of competing ensembles arose to capitalize upon the group's success. Nonetheless, the Fisk Jubilee Singers in their performances and their wider touring endeavors demonstrated and typified a new mobility among African Americans that was both literal and figurative. Their mobility coexisted with an impulse toward remembrance, retaining a key element of slave culture and re-presenting it to the public, which made their achievement all the more complex in its effects upon the cultural perception of African Americans during a pivotal period in American race relations.

Important as were the Jubilee Singers as a representative and exceptional troupe of African American performing artists, they also exemplify the status accorded to music in the years after the Civil War as a potential source of reconciliation and a voice of conscience against the continued specter of violence and racial reaction. When they appeared on the program of the massive 1872 World Peace Jubilee organized by bandmaster Patrick Gilmore, they furthered their own pursuit of recognition and aligned themselves with one of the most prominent musical events of the era, intended to demonstrate music's ability to communicate across national and cultural boundaries. Although the success of Gilmore's affair was questionable in many regards, its design—and the place of the Jubilee Singers within it—warrants attention for the way it sought to mobilize music as a key cultural resource at a time of great social and political conflict. It also foreshadowed the Singers' subsequent move onto the world stage through their extensive tours of England and, later, parts of continental Europe, where they found some of their greatest success and made some of their most outspoken political gestures, such as their participation in the "slave circular" debate that broke out in England at the end of 1875 and carried into the first months of the ensuing year.

Gaining Recognition

When the Fisk Singers first came to wider public attention at the end of 1871, there was little precedent for what they presented. African Americans had provided musical entertainment throughout much of the slave era, but on those occasions when they appeared in more formal concert settings, they presented what then passed for concert music, the mix of familiar popular melodies, program music, and operatic or classical airs akin to that featured in the programs of Jenny Lind.[5] Blackface minstrelsy was popularly recognized as the principal venue for the performance of music that was more squarely associated with African Americans from the 1840s forward but, leaving aside the endless conundrum concerning the degree to which minstrel music bore any direct correlation to music played by black Americans, black performers were few and far between in minstrelsy until after the

Civil War.[6] The white performer in blackface was the primary public representative of black music and culture until well into the nineteenth century, a circumstance that would have enduring repercussions upon popular representations of African Americans. Moreover, when African Americans began to enter the field of professional performance in increasing numbers after 1865, they typically did so while conforming to the constraints of the minstrel stage, acting out stereotyped images and sounds of blackness that had already become conventional through decades of prior circulation. The singing of black spirituals pursued by the Fisk Jubilee Singers marked the most decisive break yet with this established set of performance conventions and created an important new repertoire of practices through which black music and, perhaps more importantly, black musicians could achieve public recognition.

For all they did to recast the mold of public black musicianship, the Jubilee Singers did not enjoy complete autonomy. Its members toured as representatives of Fisk University, one of several black institutions created by Northern reformers after the Civil War to assist the advancement of the freed black population. Located in Nashville, Tennessee, Fisk was opened in January 1866 under the auspices of the American Missionary Association (AMA), a Protestant abolitionist organization with a strong Evangelical cast. The Jubilee Singers emerged out of a choral group organized by George White, who was the school's treasurer and was married to the sister of one of its founding figures, AMA officer Erastus Cravath. As early as May 1867, White staged two nights of public performances at Masonic Hall in Nashville to raise funds for Fisk that featured some of the school's best singers, including seven who would subsequently become members of the Jubilee Singers: Georgia Gordon, Jennie Jackson, Josephine Moore, Maggie Porter, America Robinson, Thomas Rutling, and Eliza Walker.[7] In the years that followed, White's ambitions grew in conjunction with his perception as Fisk treasurer of the school's constant financial pressures. However, the AMA leadership, which had a significant hand in Fisk's governance, was deeply wary of relying upon a troupe of black singers to represent its needs to the public.[8] When White decided after much negotiation to begin to travel with the singers outside of Nashville in 1871, he continued to face resistance from the organization. Even after the Fisk singers became a proven success, the power struggles between White and other leaders at Fisk and within the AMA shadowed the troupe's career and bore upon White's interactions with the singers themselves.[9]

White's influence upon the work of the Fisk singers cannot be overstated. It was he, for instance, who came up with the name "Jubilee Singers" at the end of 1871 to better distinguish them from the more prevalent touring minstrel companies with whom the ensemble was commonly compared. He also chose the singers who would accompany him and represent the school on tour, a process that involved considerable negotiation with trepidatious parents who, though trustful of White's motives, feared the geographic separation and the interruption of their children's education that such an endeavor would entail.[10] The young singers, for their part, volunteered their services with considerable enthusiasm. There were ten members of the original touring ensemble, four men and six women, who were organized to allow for vocal arrangements that followed the standard SATB (soprano–alto–tenor–bass) style common among formally trained choral groups. Jennie Jackson and Maggie Porter were the company's sopranos; another soprano vocalist, Phebe Anderson, remained only a few weeks before leaving due to her father's ill health. The alto roles were taken by Eliza Walker and Minnie Tate, the latter being the youngest member at only fourteen years old at the commence of the tour. Benjamin Holmes and Thomas Rutling provided the tenor parts and singing the bass parts were Isaac Dickerson and Greene Evans. Rounding out the troupe was Ella Sheppard, whose role was multifold, serving as primary musical accompanist, soprano voice, and White's musical assistant. Figure 2.1 captures this version of the ensemble, sans Anderson. Most of the members of this first touring company of Fisk Singers had been born into slavery—Jennie Jackson and Minnie Tate being the two exceptions—a detail of their personal histories that was used by White and others promoting the ensemble to generate sympathy and create a sense of social advancement around the Singers that could be credited to Fisk and to the Christian philanthropy of the AMA.

Once on tour, White prompted a substantial innovation by featuring an increasing proportion of spirituals in the troupe's concert programs. Sandra Graham has pointed out in her meticulous research on the Singers that their earliest concert programs throughout the months of October through December 1871 were rather eclectic and contained a considerable amount of more secular material, including some comic songs that had hints of minstrelsy.[11] The range of material presented was likely devised by White to appeal to the broadest range of potential listeners, but it also reflected the preferences and inclinations of the group's African American members, who wanted to spotlight their trained voices on more "cultivated" music and

Figure 2.1 The Fisk Jubilee Singers as they appeared in 1871. From left to right: Minnie Tate, Greene Evans, Isaac Dickerson, Jennie Jackson, Maggie Porter, Ella Sheppard, Thomas Rutling, Benjamin Holmes, and Eliza Walker. Courtesy of Fisk University, John Hope and Aurelia E. Franklin Library, Special Collections.

on songs that would be recognized as like those rendered by other professional performers. Ella Sheppard recalled some forty years later that, only after much encouragement by White and Fisk principal Adam Spence, she and the other singers consented to perform the spirituals. As Sheppard remembered: "The slave songs were never used by us then in public. They were associated with slavery and the dark past, and represented things to be forgotten . . . We finally grew willing to sing them privately, usually in Professor Spence's sitting-room, and sitting upon the floor . . . we practiced softly, learning from each other the songs of our fathers . . . It was only after many months that gradually our hearts were opened to the influence of these friends and we began to appreciate the wonderful beauty and power of our songs; but we continued to sing in public the usual choruses, duets, solos, etc. learned at school."[12]

Despite the reticence of Sheppard and the other singers, the religious content of their performances drew favorable early notice as they began to tour. A detailed and laudatory review in the *Cincinnati Gazette* followed the Fisk Singers' appearance at two of that city's churches on October 8, 1871.

"Remarkable Praise Meetings," read the headline, and the accompanying story gave background regarding the Singers' association with Fisk and the AMA before offering readers a description of the previous night's concert at Seventh Street Congregational Church. The report characterized the music as "strictly devotional" and added: "The pieces rendered were mostly the quaint hymns which the colored pupils of the South were accustomed to sing when in slavery."[13] The absence of secular material can be explained by the fact that this was a church appearance where no admission fee was charged, the sort of performance for which the Fisk Singers emphasized the sacred aspects of their repertory. According to the anonymous reporter, the "masterpiece" of the evening was "Go Down, Moses," a song that was notably the first black spiritual to have had its music and lyrics published in full a decade earlier, in 1861.[14] Whether the song's familiarity accounted for its impact is unclear from the *Gazette*'s account, but the reviewer credits the Fisk Singers with potently conveying its mix of pathos and empowerment, noting that its beginning was "sad, earnest, and pathetic, as its theme demanded. Then came the destruction of the Egyptian host in the Red Sea, and the deliverance of the fugitive Israelites. Here the music swelled into rapturous grandeur"—the music being provided solely by the voices of the nine Fisk singers. Evaluating the whole concert, the *Gazette* observed the prevalent repetition of passages of religious import by the full chorus such as, "And I hope I'll join the band/And chatter with the angels/Sooner in the morning," and referred repeatedly to the fervor with which the Singers offered their songs, which overrode any deficiencies of training that might have been evident.[15]

Celebratory as the *Cincinnati Gazette* piece was, it also bore witness to the tensions that surrounded the Fisk Singers as they began to build a public profile. The article concluded with an anecdote about how the pastor of the Vine Street Church had approached a rival newspaper, the *Commercial*, to post a short notice about the Singers' forthcoming performances. What resulted read as follows: "A band of negro minstrels will sing in the Vine Street Congregational Church this morning. They are genuine negroes, and call themselves the Colored Christian Singers."[16] According to the *Gazette*, this reference to the Singers as "negro minstrels" gave such offense that it provoked a comment from the Reverend Halley of the Seventh Street church at the evening meeting, who expressed his shock at the "anti-Christian" character of the announcement and the newspaper that issued it. This would hardly be the last time that the Fisk Singers were conflated with minstrelsy.

Shortly after their arrival in New York, the periodical *Day's Doings* featured an unsympathetic cartoon portraying the Singers' appearance at Beecher's Plymouth Church, with a caption that satirically referred to Beecher as "the manager of a Negro minstrel troupe."[17] Ultimately, though, this tendency to view the Jubilee Singers as just another minstrel troupe was far outweighed in the public rhetoric of the time by the effort to differentiate their efforts from their blackfaced counterparts, an effort that was grounded in an emergent discourse of black musical authenticity that gained weight in the years surrounding the Civil War.

Seeking Realness

In the summer of 1851, the New York music publisher Hermann Saroni embarked on a trip from west to east, directing regular letters to the readers of his musical magazine, *Saroni's Musical Times*. His report for the week of July 26 came from Louisville, Kentucky, where he found a veritable "Utopia of musicians" that made him look with regret upon the things lacking in the East's musical metropolis. Concluding his letter, he described how his efforts to sleep the previous night had been interrupted first by the incessant buzz of mosquitoes, and then by a sound far more pleasurable that provided temporary relief: "one of those wild yet pensive strains with which the negroes on Southern plantations while away their time and enliven their task," sung by a "soprano voice... of a most delightful quality, flexible and true, full, ringing and sympathetic." It was Saroni's first direct encounter with such music and its effect on him was indescribable. Lacking words to properly express his response, he reflected: "Is it not strange that our Ethiopian minstrels, instead of giving the wild strains of the Southern negro, and retaining their white faces, will give us distorted, wretched modern melodies, making them Ethiopian merely because they are sung by pseudo negroes."[18]

Twelve years later, in 1863, the Unitarian minister Henry George Spaulding published an article, "Under the Palmetto," describing his experience visiting the Port Royal encampment off the coast of South Carolina. In the midst of the Civil War, Port Royal became the site for a great "experiment" in which Northern missionary abolitionists, with the assistance of Union soldiers, provided education and other services to the large population of freed black slaves on the island.[19] Conveying what he encountered at Port Royal, Spaulding included one of the most detailed accounts to date concerning the distinctive character of black religious song. Spaulding provided lyrics and transcribed melodies for several songs, and placed them in the setting of the "shout," the distinctive form of black religious worship that drew attention from white observers during the years surrounding the Civil War, and has subsequently been interpreted as a formative aspect of African American culture.[20] Offering some general observations on the songs of the South Carolina freedmen, Spaulding noted: "A tinge of sadness pervades all their melodies, which bear as little resemblance to the popular Ethiopian melodies of the day as twilight to noonday. The joyous, merry strains which have been associated in the minds of many with the Southern negro, are never heard on the Sea Islands." He then proceeded to tell a quite peculiar story of seeing a troupe of "genuine" black minstrel performers called the Charleston Minstrels during his sojourn, which presented a reasonably good approximation of the sort of minstrel entertainment more commonly associated with white performers in the North. Although he found the performance to be modestly amusing, in the end he was left to observe: "One could not help feeling that a people, whose very natures are attuned to harmony, are capable of something better than even the most perfect imitation of those who have so grossly caricatured their race."[21]

These two accounts show the existence of a mounting discourse on African American music that began to grow in the years leading up to the Civil War and accumulated momentum during the War, when unprecedented numbers of Northern whites came into contact with Southern blacks and documented their impressions. Although both Saroni and Spaulding display condescension toward their black subjects in a manner characteristic of their time, they are both essentially sympathetic auditors, finding something genuinely moving in the music they encounter and something worthy of reminiscence. Crucially, they both are impelled to make sense of what they've heard through a comparison with blackface minstrelsy. So thoroughly had blackface performance shaped the mid-century perception of black music and culture that it was the inescapable point of reference for any encounters with the "real" thing. Whites in blackface, by Saroni's account, distorted the "wild" and affecting melodies of Southern African Americans and so could only provide "pseudo Negro" music. For Spaulding, the lie of minstrelsy lay in its suggestion that black music making was predominantly fun-spirited, when his experience told him otherwise. Finding the minstrel version of blackness to lack veracity, Saroni, Spaulding, and a select group of their Northern white counterparts generated a new rhetoric of African American authenticity that was an essential precondition for the success of the Fisk Jubilee Singers.

Pivotal to this development was the 1867 publication, *Slave Songs of the United States*, edited by William Francis Allen, Charles Pickard Ware, and Lucy McKim Garrison, the first significant published collection of African American music, most of which was gathered at Port Royal. Following suit from those others seeking the "truth" of black music, the editors open their introduction to the collection with reference to minstrelsy, although in this case their purpose was principally to establish the long-standing popular interest in "negro melodies."[22] More to the point, they stress that the bulk of the songs collected were "taken down by the editors from the lips of the colored people themselves."[23] No "spurious imitations" here, these songs are marked as the real thing—although much to their credit, the editors also acknowledge that Port Royal has not necessarily given them access to the full range of black musical expression. Sacred songs far outnumber secular ones, but the latter are said to arguably retain more "pure" qualities of black expression; and instrumental music is almost entirely lacking even though black slaves were known to commonly use various musical instruments in other areas of the country.[24] Transcribing the songs, moreover, posed unique challenges for the editors, who continually draw attention to those elements that defy conventional notational practices, especially where the rhythmic qualities of the music are concerned. Ultimately, Allen, Ware and Garrison viewed their effort to overcome such difficulties as an urgent one, suggesting that, "these relics of a state of society which has passed away should be preserved while it is still possible."[25] This preservationist impulse complemented the search for accuracy in transcription and authenticity of source material, and marked the text as the product of a distinctly post-Civil War, and post-slavery, sensibility.

Echoes of this sensibility resounded through the public reaction to the Jubilee Singers, nowhere more forcefully than in the vivid letter written by the Reverend Theodore Cuyler to the *New York Tribune* following upon their January 18, 1872, appearance at Cuyler's Lafayette Church in Brooklyn. A Presbyterian minister, Cuyler stood alongside Henry Ward Beecher as one of the most outspoken advocates of the Jubilee Singers during the troupe's early rise to notoriety. By the time the Singers performed at Cuyler's church, they had already made a strong impression upon Beecher's congregation, but had drawn only brief and not always flattering reports from the New York press. Cuyler testified to the emotional power of the Singers upon his own congregation in no uncertain terms, exclaiming: "I never saw a cultivated Brooklyn assemblage so moved and melted under the magnetism of music before. The wild melodies of these emancipated slaves touched the fount of tears, and gray-haired men wept like little children."[26] Like Gustavus Pike in his first encounter with the Fisk Singers, Cuyler and his congregants experienced a potent form of what sociologist Jon Cruz has termed "ethnosympathy," through which white auditors came to acknowledge the distinctive humanity of African American subjects via a type of sympathetic identification that made the difference connoted by race into something strongly felt.[27]

Adding to the emotive force of the Jubilee Singers for Cuyler was the nature of their material. As he reported, their program included not just the best-known slave songs such as "Go Down, Moses" and "Roll, Jordan, Roll," but "a fresh collection of the most weird and plaintive hymns sung in the plantation cabins in the dark days of bondage." One such piece, "I'll Hear de Trumpet Sound in the Morning," Cuyler termed "the very embodiment of African heart-music," while more broadly he claimed that listening to the Singers, "one might imagine himself in the veritable Uncle Tom's cabin of the 'old dispensation.'" The reference to Harriet Beecher Stowe's immensely influential novel suggests the degree to which even sympathetic white listeners such as Cuyler continued to have difficulty separating the impression made by "real" African Americans from that derived from the era's popular culture. Nonetheless, Cuyler insisted that the unadorned pathos of the Jubilee Singers made them into "living representatives of the only true native school of American music. We have long enough had its coarse caricature in corked faces; our people can now listen to the genuine soul music of the slave cabins, before the Lord led his 'children out of the land of Egypt, out of the house of bondage.'"[28] In distinguishing themselves from the blackface performers who had dominated public representations of black music up to that time, then, the Jubilee Singers provided white auditors with a rare sense of direct access to the music and culture found on the Southern slave plantation, something that minstrelsy had often promised but could not deliver in such seemingly unfiltered form.

For all their apparent genuineness, the Jubilee Singers were not entirely thoroughgoing in their performance of "pure" slave culture. Despite Cuyler's enthusiasm for the troupe's singing of spirituals, one of his favorite parts of their concert at Lafayette Church was a rendition of the decidedly secular tune, "Home, Sweet Home," a song established on the formal concert stage by

Jenny Lind and, more recently, Christine Nilsson. Even as spirituals occupied more and more of the troupe's programs, the Jubilee Singers never entirely forsook their efforts to emulate recognized figures of the European tradition, evident in the program reproduced in Figure 2.2.

More to the point, the way in which the Jubilee Singers sang black spirituals itself bore the strong imprint of European musical practices. White's manner of arranging the songs in concert with Sheppard, which was subsequently formalized by the New York-based arranger, Theodore Seward, employed a sort of conventional harmonization of vocal parts that marked a significant departure from the prominent heterophony of the spiritual in its vernacular form. The spiritual as a private manifestation of black slave culture involved multiple voices singing in a kind of rough unison that was organized by a tonal center but allowed considerable room for the individual voices to move freely with the sung melody. As part of the public musical performances staged by the Jubilee Singers, by contrast, the spiritual became subject to a new sort of vocal discipline guided by White's aspiration toward a "homogeneous sound" in which the various registers—soprano, alto, tenor, bass—achieved a seamless blend.[29] Due to the changes wrought by the Jubilee Singers in their rendering of the spiritual, the musicologist Samuel Floyd has charged: "In the Jubilee Singers' renditions, the powerful Negro spiritual had been transformed into a fine imitation of itself."[30]

Not all who heard the Jubilee Singers were so impressed with the refinement of their approach. Writers for some of the era's music journals were especially dubious about the troupe's efforts. For these observers, any interest in the Singers' ability to evoke the truth of the slave experience was trumped by the evolving standard of "high" musical expression that looked to Europe for its measure of artistic success. A critic for *Brainard's Musical World*, based in Cleveland, thus observed: "We like to see the students of Fisk University . . . study and cultivate music . . . but this is not a sufficient reason why we should white wash their performances."[31] More cutting was the commentary in *Loomis' Musical and Masonic Journal*, published out of New Haven, Connecticut. Writing of a recent performance by the Singers at the Music Hall in New Haven, the magazine dubbed the concert "a burlesque on music, and almost on religion. We do not consider it consistent with actual piety to sit and be amused at an imitation of the religious worship formerly engaged in by ignorant but Christian people; and as for calling their effort a concert, it is ridiculously absurd."[32] The race of the singers clearly remained a deterrent for some observers to taking them seriously either as musicians or as representatives of religious devotion.

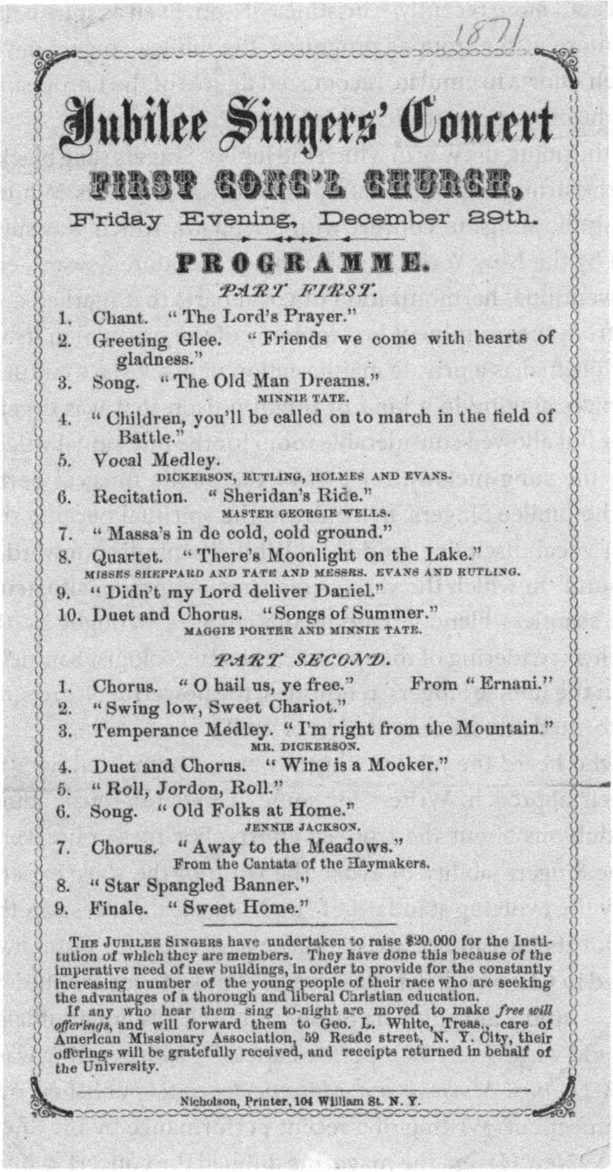

1871

Jubilee Singers' Concert

FIRST CONG'L CHURCH,

Friday Evening, December 29th.

PROGRAMME.

PART FIRST.

1. Chant. "The Lord's Prayer."
2. Greeting Glee. "Friends we come with hearts of gladness."
3. Song. "The Old Man Dreams."
   MINNIE TATE.
4. "Children, you'll be called on to march in the field of Battle."
5. Vocal Medley.
   DICKERSON, RUTLING, HOLMES AND EVANS.
6. Recitation. "Sheridan's Ride."
   MASTER GEORGIE WELLS.
7. "Massa's in de cold, cold ground."
8. Quartet. "There's Moonlight on the Lake."
   MISSES SHEPPARD AND TATE AND MESSRS. EVANS AND RUTLING.
9. "Didn't my Lord deliver Daniel."
10. Duet and Chorus. "Songs of Summer."
    MAGGIE PORTER AND MINNIE TATE.

PART SECOND.

1. Chorus. "O hail us, ye free." From "Ernani."
2. "Swing low, Sweet Chariot."
3. Temperance Medley. "I'm right from the Mountain."
   MR. DICKERSON.
4. Duet and Chorus. "Wine is a Mocker."
5. "Roll, Jordon, Roll."
6. Song. "Old Folks at Home."
   JENNIE JACKSON.
7. Chorus. "Away to the Meadows."
   From the Cantata of the Haymakers.
8. "Star Spangled Banner."
9. Finale. "Sweet Home."

THE JUBILEE SINGERS have undertaken to raise $20,000 for the Institution of which they are members. They have done this because of the imperative need of new buildings, in order to provide for the constantly increasing number of the young people of their race who are seeking the advantages of a thorough and liberal Christian education.

If any who hear them sing to-night are moved to make *free will offerings*, and will forward them to Geo. L. White, Treas., care of American Missionary Association, 59 Reade street, N. Y. City, their offerings will be gratefully received, and receipts returned in behalf of the University.

Nicholson, Printer, 104 William St. N. Y.

Figure 2.2 Concert program for a Fisk Jubilee Singers performance on December 29, 1871. This program documents the mix of religious and secular offerings that the Jubilee Singers included in their earliest concerts, including two selections by Stephen Foster.

In light of these perspectives, two articles that appeared the following year, in April 1873, are especially revealing. By this time, the Jubilee Singers had become an established phenomenon, appearing at the massive World Peace Jubilee in summer 1872—to be detailed below—and touring across much of the Eastern and middle sections of the US. Currently, the troupe was in preparation for its first overseas sojourn to England, which would commence the following month. It also faced its first significant competition in the public singing of spirituals from a rival company arising out of the Hampton Institute, another black educational institution located in Virginia. This expansion of the jubilee-singing fold prompted some observers to comment on the general state of black music making and the impact to date of the Jubilee Singers.

So did the leading highbrow music journal of the day, *Dwight's Journal of Music*, reprint an article from the *New York Weekly Review* on the subject of "Negro Folk Songs." Although noted for his unflinching support of European, and especially Austro-German music as the highest sort of expression, editor John S. Dwight had shown sympathy for the study of the music of black Americans as early as 1862, when he published in his journal two landmark statements on the topic, one by James McKim and the other by his daughter Lucy—one of the future co-editors of *Slave Songs of the United States*—both of whom reported on their observation of the black population at Port Royal.[33] Now, more than ten years later, Dwight republished an article that elaborated upon Theodore Cuyler's foregoing claim that the music of black former slaves was the only true native American music. "It has remained for the obscure and uncultured Negro race in this country to prove that there is an original style of music peculiar to America," asserted the unnamed *Weekly Review* editor, who summarized the career of the Jubilee Singers to date and compared them to the more recently arrived Hampton Singers, whom he termed "less cultured than their predecessors" but "even more characteristic" in their manner of presenting black music before the public.[34] This latter judgment referred to the greater presence of Southern black dialect and the bodily motions characteristic of African American religious worship among the Hampton singers, as compared with the Jubilee Singers who had sought to repress such features in their onstage comportment. Here the refinement of the Jubilee Singers was acknowledged, at least in relative terms, but that quality did not overshadow what the writer heard as the "strikingly wild" elements of black song or the "hearty sincerity" with which they presented the music, which deserved recognition as the "folks-songs of some four millions of the people of the United States."[35]

Cuyler himself took a similar tack in an article that appeared just a few days later in the *New York Evangelist* prompted by the rising profile of the Hampton Singers. As he did with the Fisk Singers, so now with the Hamptons, Cuyler issued a spirited, enthusiastic review of the troupe's recent appearance at his Lafayette Church. Like the *Weekly Review* critic, he portrayed the latter troupe's music as "even more weird and picturesque, if possible, than those sung by the famous 'Jubilee' troop. Their singing is even more characteristically *negro*." What distinguished Cuyler's missive was his impulse to question the values of those who subscribed to a more European-influenced idea of musical quality. "No music rouses and melts an audience like these plantation melodies, sung by rich negro voices," stated Cuyler, who then reflected upon the distinct character of those gathered in his church: "As I looked at that great audience hushed to silence and melted to tears under the music of nature, I thought of some fashionable concerts at which an elegantly dressed crowd were doing their utmost to get their dollar's worth of 'high art.' I did not know which to pity the most—the poor woman who was screeching Italian on the stage, or the audience who were trying so hard to understand and enjoy her outcry."[36] While *Dwight's* had allowed that African American music deserved consideration as uniquely American music, Cuyler here went a step farther in questioning the existing structure of concert life whereby the elevation of European artists had more to do with status than with sheer musical enjoyment. In this instance, the "realness" of the Jubilee Singers and their ilk was not just a product of their differentiation from the field of blackface performance. Instead, it was a mark of their success at providing genuine emotional catharsis via a mode of musical expression deemed "natural" by virtue of its attachment to the black race.

These various pieces of commentary position the Jubilee Singers between some competing and contradictory notions regarding the meaning of their blackness in relation to the music that they sang and their impact upon the audiences that heard them. Most prominently, the Singers were judged to have presented music of great seriousness, capable of prompting visible outpourings of emotion from a predominantly white audience that relished the troupe's enactment of religious devotion and the progress brought by emancipation. At the same time, even sympathetic listeners like Theodore Cuyler had trouble crediting the members of the ensemble for the trained, exacting character of their approach. Although all evidence suggests that the

Jubilee Singers presented a markedly harmonious and polished version of the black spiritual before the public, their critics could not help but refer to the "wild" and "natural" aspects of their artistry, sometimes almost to the exclusion of other factors. This apparent gap between what one imagines was the sound of the Jubilee Singers and the language with which they were described suggests the extent to which the cultural associations surrounding black music in the postbellum era remained powerfully fixed by certain stubborn ideas concerning the character of African American people.[37] One could say that, despite the decorum with which they presented themselves, the sight of the Jubilee Singers on stage constituted a sort of visual noise that compounded and in fundamental ways countered the sound they produced with their voices. Yet, paradoxically, the perceived difference they embodied was integral to their capacity to generate sympathy among their listeners, who were primed to equate the sound of the spiritual with the sensation of unadorned pathos.

At the Jubilee

In the collective memory of African Americans, the Jubilee refers to the widespread outbreak of collective celebration that accompanied emancipation from slavery and Union victory in the Civil War. According to historian Leon Litwack, the notion of the Jubilee is as much myth as historical reality. African American responses to emancipation were varied, and not all faced with the new reality chose to commemorate it in such a boisterous public manner.[38] Nonetheless, Litwack also records evidence of many such occurrences, which were especially likely to happen in the urban centers of the South. Charleston, South Carolina, gave rise to perhaps the largest such public demonstration, in which more than 4,000 black residents marched through the city streets in the spring of 1865. The parade featured a mock slave auction and chain gang followed by "a cart containing a black-draped coffin inscribed with the words, 'Slavery is Dead.'"[39]

This connotation of "jubilee" is curiously downplayed in the lore of the Fisk Jubilee Singers. Those who have written about the troupe have repeatedly told the story of how George White came up with the name, "Jubilee Singers," after a night spent in prayer. White's inspiration for the name was apparently taken from a chapter in the book of Leviticus in the Old Testament wherein the Lord instructed Moses that every fiftieth year should be a Year of Jubilee, during which all Israelites who had been sold into servitude should be released.[40] The designation therefore marked the parallel, as understood by White, between the status of the Jews in biblical times and the status of African Americans in the current moment. White also understood that the term had a particular currency, as he explained in a letter to Erastus Cravath: "The 'Jubilee'—or 'year of the Jubilee' has been talked of and sung so much in connection with this change [emancipation] . . . that I can think of no expression, or word that so nearly gives the idea, as 'the Jubilee Singers,' and submit it as the result of my effort to get a name."[41] White's choice resonated among the members of the Singers, who readily embraced the new name. Ella Sheppard observed that, "the dignity of the name appealed to us. At our usual family worship that morning there was great rejoicing."[42]

Another not unrelated idea of "Jubilee" seems to have informed the bandleader Patrick Gilmore's choice of the term to denote his grand musical affairs of the postbellum era. In 1869, Gilmore orchestrated one of the largest musical gatherings to have taken place in the US until that time, a massive five-day event he called the National Peace Jubilee that was held in Boston on June 15–19, 1869. Dedicated to the commemoration of the restoration of peace in the aftermath of the Civil War, Gilmore plotted an affair whose massive scope was designed to suit what he imagined was its nationally representative character. A chorus of ten thousand voices and an orchestra of one thousand musicians were the basic components around which Gilmore organized the endeavor. Perhaps even more strikingly, he commissioned the construction of a Coliseum specially made for the event that could hold some fifty thousand spectators, a figure that dwarfed the crowds that had come to witness Jenny Lind during her debut concerts in New York almost two decades earlier. Gilmore explained the significance of the sheer scale of the Jubilee in his published history of the festival, in which he described how his initial vision for the event would not escape him (while peculiarly referring to himself in the third person): "Go where he would, that great chorus, with its thousands of voices, kept roaring in his ears, and the crash of a thousand instruments filled the world around him with enchanting harmony. Look where he might, the vision of a magnificent structure, filled with a vast multitude gathered from all parts of the nation, met his gaze. O, how he longed for others to see the grand spectacle as he saw it, to hear the ravishing music as he heard it!"[43] Like many of those who commented on Lind's opening concerts in 1850, Gilmore was compelled by the power of the crowd as a symbol of public will and the ability of music to turn the crowd into a manifestation of collective harmony.

Gilmore's efforts to stage such a grand spectacle bred considerable skepticism, not least for the formidable editor of *Dwight's Journal of Music*, who was immediately suspicious of the size of Gilmore's plan and of his desire to appeal to the broadest mass of music listeners.[44] Others considered the Jubilee a folly in the making; but Gilmore lobbied the business, arts, and political leaders of Boston tirelessly to ensure that his vision would be realized. He also stage-managed the publicity surrounding the festival in expert, Barnum-esque fashion, producing a bulletin that kept interested members of the public apprised of the event's progress and issuing a series of effusive press releases that most of the daily and weekly press circulated in a spirit of cooperation, generating great anticipatory excitement. As to the program, each of the five days of the festival was designed to have a theme. The inaugural day set the tone with a mix of patriotic fanfare and more reflective material; pieces by Wagner and Mozart intermingled with "The Star-Spangled Banner" and a special "Hymn of Peace" specially written for the occasion by Oliver Wendell Holmes. Also introduced that day was the most notoriously overblown spectacle of the whole festival, a rendition of the "Anvil Chorus" from Verdi's *Il Trovatore* that had, in addition to the full roster of chorus and orchestra, one hundred Boston firemen who pounded out their parts on one hundred anvils. Day two featured a "Grand Classical Programme," with music by Handel, Mozart, Mendelssohn, Schubert, and Haydn, among others; while day three marked the anniversary of the Battle of Bunker Hill with a "Patriotic and Military Programme" that was decidedly more popular in orientation. A day devoted to "Oratorio and Symphony" followed, and the final day of the Jubilee spotlighted a massive chorus comprised of children drawn from the Boston public schools.[45] The arrangement of themes and mix of attractions reflected Gilmore's effort to balance the interests of those who saw music as a vehicle for cultural elevation and those who saw it as a medium of amusement. Gilmore himself seemed to subscribe equally to both notions and reserved his greatest criticisms for those "bigoted musical fanatics" who denied the legitimacy of squarely popular fare.[46]

That Gilmore's National Peace Jubilee happened at all made it something of a triumph; that it occurred in a mostly orderly fashion, all the more so. Ever ambitious, he shortly set to work on a sequel, an early formulation of which appeared at the end of his massive, self-published history of the 1869 enterprise. Having first commemorated the onset of peace for the nation, Gilmore now envisioned a celebration of peace on an international scale. The World's Peace Jubilee, which would eventually take place over nearly three weeks beginning on June 17, 1872, was ostensibly motivated by the termination of the Franco-Prussian War in May 1871. However, reading Gilmore's initial prospectus for the event, it is hard not to see it more as an effort to expand upon his earlier achievement and further promote his belief that ever-increasing scale was equivalent with increased artistic and cultural grandeur. Thus, to befit the international character of the second Jubilee, Gilmore forecast that everything would be double what it had been for the first. Not a chorus of ten thousand, but of twenty thousand; not an orchestra of one thousand but of two thousand, would appear at the World's Peace Jubilee. In keeping with this outlook, he also foresaw the construction of a new coliseum twice as large as that for the first, which could seat one hundred thousand people, and which he characterized as "a grand Temple of Music, that shall be . . . the gathering-place of all nations, upon whose sacred altar every people shall lay its gift of song" (see Figure 2.3).[47] Over its duration, Gilmore proclaimed, each day would be dedicated to the music of a different nation, and each honored nation would send one of its native bands to be featured.

One thing notably absent from the first, National Peace Jubilee, was any recognition of the consequence of Emancipation. An ostensibly national celebration of the end of war and the onset of peace, Gilmore's program portrayed reconciliation in a manner that excluded African Americans and overlooked the importance of slavery and its aftermath. Correcting this oversight does not appear to have been at the forefront of Gilmore's plans for the second, World's Peace Jubilee. Nonetheless, whatever the motivation, the program for the latter festival gave the Jubilee Singers a place—indeed, several places, as the ensemble ultimately appeared on three different days. Their inclusion was a milestone in the history of the troupe and, arguably, in the larger history of African American music. Eileen Southern lauded the occasion, saying, "for the first time black singers were included in a big musical production in the United States."[48] Yet one has to wonder why African Americans were excluded from the National Jubilee but included in the World's. One suspects that the rising notoriety of the Jubilee Singers was itself the ultimate cause for their inclusion, along with the other black performers with whom they appeared. The Methodist journal, *Zion's Herald*, made a more forceful argument at the time. In a short announcement, the publication revealed that the Jubilee Singers had "asked a place in the International Jubilee," which the paper strongly endorsed, asserting: "They should be given

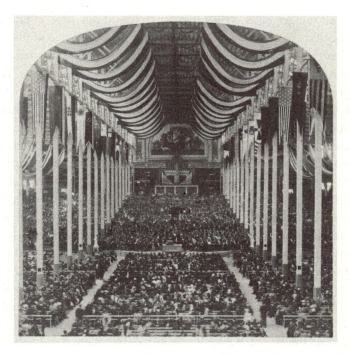

Figure 2.3 A stereoscope image of the interior of the massive coliseum built to house the 1872 World's Peace Jubilee, held in Boston, where the Fisk Jubilee Singers made multiple appearances. Courtesy of the Stereograph Collection, Boston Public Library.

one of the best locations. It cannot be international unless it is first national, and it cannot be national if they and such as they are excluded."[49]

* * *

A reconstituted troupe of Jubilee Singers appeared at Gilmore's second Jubilee. The group had toured tirelessly through New England during the preceding spring. By April they had reached an initial fundraising goal of twenty thousand dollars, which was used to purchase new grounds upon which their home institution of Fisk University would stand. Great an achievement as this was, White and other leaders at Fisk and the AMA viewed it only as a start to the work of the Singers. Returning to Nashville for a brief rest, they were treated to a hero's welcome; but within just a matter of days White resolved to take them out on tour once again. Understandably, not all the Singers were immediately ready to recommence their activity, and one, alto singer Eliza Walker, left the troupe at this time. White, meanwhile, added six new members, partly to offset the exhaustion of the existing Singers, partly out of the desire to be able to field two separate ensembles for this next round of touring, the regular full choir and a select quartet. Walker's replacement Julia Jackson was therefore joined by fellow alto Mabel Lewis, soprano Georgia Gordon, bass Edmund Watkins, tenor Henry Morgan, and new accompanist Josephine Moore.[50]

These extra voices would help being heard amidst the massive undertaking of the World's Peace Jubilee. Indeed, audibility was a core concern for George White in preparing the Singers for their appearance at the festival. Reviews of the first National Peace Jubilee had spent much time commenting on how well particular features could be heard in the vast Coliseum, surrounded by the accompanying sound of several hundred musicians and so many thousands of spectators. Singers suffered particular difficulties on this score. Many who witnessed the event deemed even the lauded voice of the famed soprano Euphrosyne Parepa-Rosa inaudible during portions of her various performances.[51] Although the scale of the World's Peace Jubilee would ultimately not be fully twice that of the earlier event—even Gilmore had to recognize certain limits—such concerns continued to resound through the later festival as well.

Writing many years later, Ella Sheppard testified to the ways in which White adapted his manner of rehearsing the Singers to the unique demands that the setting would place upon their voices, demonstrating in the process considerable understanding of the performance challenges at such a massive event. For their introductory appearance, the ensemble was assigned to sing the "Battle Hymn of the Republic," alternately known as "Mine Eyes Have Seen the Glory"—a song whose Julia Ward Howe-penned lyric was written in 1862 at the behest of a group of abolitionists, the melody borrowed from the popular tune, "John Brown's Body," which heralded the pursuits of the militant abolitionist.[52] White trained the Jubilee Singers in the song for weeks, rightly anticipating that given the enormous size of the orchestra, it would be rendered in the key of E flat, a key that would allow easiest harmonization among the various instruments but would force the singers to carry the tune at a higher pitch than its normal range. Sheppard recounted the circumstances in her valuable sketch of her career with the Singers: "in order to be heard satisfactorily by the vast audience, we must be able to enunciate with perfect accuracy of pitch and purity of tone every word and every part of a word in a key three half steps higher than usual. So, little by little, each day or two going a bit higher, using his violin, [White] trained us on those words from C to E flat until he was satisfied."[53]

White's efforts combined with the Singers' labors paid off. The World's Peace Jubilee was not the immediate sensation of its predecessor—attendance was reported to be almost embarrassingly low for the opening days of the 1872 festival—but interest grew as the affair proceeded. As Gilmore had projected, most days of this second Jubilee were dedicated to a particular nation and featured some exemplar of that country's music. Day one, dubbed the "Grand National Day" and dedicated to the United States, included the US Marine Band playing a selection of "favorite airs of England and America." Other favored guest bands were the Band of the Grenadier Guards of London for day two's "English Day," the Band of Kaiser Franz Grenadier Regiment for day three's "German Day," and the Band of the Guard Republicaine of Paris, for "French Day" on day four. The fifth, "Austrian Day" of the Jubilee featured one of the most popular guests of the whole festival, the composer and conductor Johann Strauss, who led the orchestra in a rendition of his already famed "Beautiful Blue Danube" Waltz. While the national themes were meant to grant the various days of the festival a kind of coherence, Gilmore was far from scrupulous in his application of nationalist logic to the program. Opening day's eclectic potpourri of offerings, from Wagner and Liszt to Rossini and a reprise of Verdi's "Anvil Chorus" from the first Jubilee, might have been justified as an attempt to preview the variety of attractions to come. However, the second, "English Day" was hardly less diverse, featuring selections by Bach, Beethoven, Verdi, Mendelssohn, and Strauss, among others; and other days followed suit, only the "German Day" having anything approaching real consistency across a whole day's offerings.

This general, uneven balance between nationalist integrity and internationalist plurality helps to explain how it was that the Jubilee Singers were scheduled to make their first appearance at the festival on day six, dubbed "Russian Day." Not a single "Russian" attraction appeared on that day's program, which instead presented what was becoming a customary mix of choral, operatic, orchestral, and military band selections, by a broadly European cast of composers. "Mine Eyes Have Seen the Glory of the Coming of the Lord," as the song was listed in the day's program, was a rare American song featured at the festival and clearly meant to be a showcase not only of the Fisk Singers but of the black voices of the nation writ large. Characteristically, Gilmore took the occasion to maximize the potential impact, and so the Singers appeared as part of "a choir of 150 black voices . . . with Grand

Chorus, Organ, Orchestra, Military Bands, and Cannon accompaniment."[54] Joining them onstage were the Hyers Sisters, Anna and Emma, two formally trained black vocalists who, like the Jubilee Singers, were at the start of what would be a long musical career.[55] Ella Sheppard provides a vivid account of what transpired as the singing commenced:

> [The Hyers Sisters] were to sing the first two verses, and we the last, "He hath sounded forth the trumpet." Evidently, the sisters had not anticipated the change of key, and to their chagrin they found themselves obliged greatly to strain their voices and unable to sing their parts satisfactorily. The conductor [Gilmore] told us to sing on the choruses, but we preferred to hold all our force in reserve until the time came for us to sing, though trembling like spirited race horses in our excitement to begin. Then with apparently one voice, pure, clear and distinct, we sang out,
>
> *He hath sounded forth the trumpet,*
> *Which shall never call retreat.*[56]

A reviewer for the *Boston Journal* verified that the Jubilee Singers had no trouble being heard by the audience inside the Coliseum, remarking that the troupe took "the lead with an emphasis which was felt even in the great chorus," and further noting: "There was a tremendous outburst of applause at the end of the song, which would not be stilled until it was seen that a repetition was to be given."[57] More colorful was the account of the crowd's response given by Jubilee Singers chronicler, J.B.T. Marsh: "The great audience were carried away on a whirlwind of delight; the trained musicians in the orchestra bent forward in forgetfulness of their parts; and one old German was conspicuous, holding his violoncello above his head with one hand, and whacking out upon it his applause with the bow held in the other."[58]

Following their success on Saturday, the Jubilee Singers returned the next day for a special Sunday afternoon "Grand Sacred Concert." The day's religious theme was more in keeping with the overall mission of the Singers but was not without its conflicts. Sunday concerts—even sacred ones—remained off limits among the most devout segments of the public. Evening concerts were more readily tolerated but daytime concerts were deemed to pose too direct a conflict with more proper Sunday duties like church attendance. Perhaps for this reason, the attendance at Sunday's concert was considerably diminished from that of the preceding day. The *Boston Globe* characterized those who did attend as "an assemblage who did not know whether they should wear the church-going face or the concert-going one."[59] Whether or not the Jubilee Singers were bothered by this conflict is unknown, but they received considerable plaudits from those who came. Although the day's program only lists them as singing a "hymn," newspapers reported them to have performed two of their best-known spiritual selections, "Swing Low, Sweet Chariot" and "Turn Back Pharaoh's Army," to which they added "Roll, Jordan, Roll" after being called back for an encore by the crowd. For one "lady correspondent" writing for the *Galveston News* of Texas, the Singers' appearance this day was far more satisfying than their inclusion on "Russian Day." She deemed the Saturday concert a "hideous failure" but considered the Jubilee Singers to have been the "great feature of the Sunday Sacred Concert... These sang the old plantation hymns as all have heard them sung at plantation meeting. This was a feature about which there was no humbug"—which for this writer, set it apart from so many other facets of the Jubilee.[60]

The Singers' third and final performance of the festival came on the next Tuesday's program, June 25. There was no special theme for this day's concert but instead a special event: President Ulysses S. Grant was to be in attendance, and Gilmore designed the program to pay tribute to the leader. Grant's visit was the occasion for much excitement and newspapers exclaimed that the day drew the largest audience of the whole second Jubilee, coming close to filling the immense Coliseum with some fifty to seventy-thousand people.[61] The day began with a patriotic flourish, a grand performance of "Hail to the Chief" followed by Handel's "See, the Conquering Hero Comes" and an "Homage to Columbia" that built upon one of the best-known national melodies of the time. The remainder of the program presented something of a "greatest hits" of the festival to date, with return appearances by the French and German military bands, the Austrian composer Strauss, and in the penultimate position of the day, the Jubilee Singers. For the Singers, it was not their first opportunity to sing for the President. They had been invited to a private audience with Grant back in March, the morning after a Washington, DC performance.[62] Neither the day's program nor the resulting news items offer indication of the works they sang. One is left to wonder if they performed "Go Down, Moses," as they had done when they met the President three months before. Nonetheless, the troupe's inclusion at such a concert offers clear indication of the degree to which the Jubilee Singers assumed an impressively representative status over the course of their touring to date, as a group of African American artists who sang not just on behalf of their people but as part of the fabric of voices that comprised the nation at large.

Touring Through Segregation

It would be a mistake to overstate the degree of acceptance achieved by the Jubilee Singers. On stage, they usually met with accolades, all the more so as their profile rose following their appearance at Gilmore's Jubilee. Off stage was a different matter. Tales of African American musicians are rife with accounts of the ways in which segregation impinged upon their mobility, and the Jubilee Singers are no exception. Given the time in which they toured, it could hardly have been otherwise. Refusal of hotel accommodations was especially common during the Singers' travels around the US, and the troupe also faced difficulty at times with rail travel as they moved from place to place. An early, typical episode occurred in Newark, New Jersey, in late February 1872. The troupe was booked into the city's Continental Hotel, but its advance agent failed to specify the race of the singers upon making arrangements. The hotel's proprietor, Captain Gillette, was not present at their arrival and so the members of the ensemble were shown to their rooms. When Gillette later found them gathered in one of the hotel's parlors, he quickly addressed George White, demanding that they leave the premises at once. Described as "a Republican . . . anxious and willing to give the colored man all the privileges he is entitled to" by the *New York Telegram* who reported the story, Gillette claimed that allowing the Jubilee Singers to remain at his hotel would imperil his business since "white and black won't mix in the hotel business no how you can fix it."[63] Left without a hotel, the Singers found shelter with a local Congregationalist clergyman, Reverend Brown, who was invited to make some remarks regarding the incident at the troupe's subsequent concert.

That the Jubilee Singers routinely faced such difficulties is notable but not surprising given what we know of American race relations. More striking is the fact that the Singers addressed the incident at a public appearance and that it was deemed noteworthy enough to have made the news as far away as Cincinnati, Ohio. Acts of racism were a common part of the everyday life of American residents. One effect of the Jubilee Singers' rising celebrity was that such acts became subject to a new sort of publicity. Abolitionists had of course drawn great attention to the wrongs of slavery. In the years after emancipation and the end of the Civil War, though, the social boundaries surrounding race underwent substantial revision as African Americans sought to test and establish the parameters of their new status and the still-dominant white population worked to ensure that its power did not unduly diminish. Among the most visible African American citizens of the era, the Jubilee Singers dramatized the tensions inherent in this changing social landscape as they moved from location to location, and often spoke or acted in protest when faced with clear acts of racial discrimination.

Historian Eric Foner observed of the post-emancipation era: "Among the most resented of slavery's restrictions was the rule, enforced by patrols, that no black could travel without a pass. With emancipation, it seemed that half the South's black population took to the roads."[64] Most of this movement involved the migration of African Americans from rural to urban areas within the South, while those more adventuresome went farther afield to parts of the North or West. Where the Jubilee Singers were concerned, their touring efforts marked a sort of double migration: the black members of the troupe had already moved to attend Fisk or otherwise join the ensemble, and as they embarked on their extensive tours effectively moved away from a place that was already a home away from home. Given the relative rarity and brevity of their return visits to Nashville, the individual members also more or less lived on the road for the duration of their engagement with the Jubilee Singers, much as many popular musicians do today. This intensive commitment to geographic motion can well be deemed an extreme instance of the equation that held strong among many newly emancipated African Americans between freedom and mobility.

Still, the conditions under which the Jubilee Singers toured did not grant them full agency over their efforts. Their needs were met where food and lodging were concerned, as well as their management could arrange, but money was often a source of contention, and sufficient rest was at a premium due to the tireless tour schedule that was set for them.[65] Even in their most apparently resistant moments, the singers were not always in full control. Consider again the refusal of hotel accommodations in Newark recounted above. Protest against the hotel owner's actions was most loudly voiced not by any of the Jubilee Singers but by a white compatriot of higher social standing in the community. This dynamic, in which the Jubilee Singers were spoken for rather than permitted to speak for themselves, was characteristic of the way in which their public appearances were managed. Although one of the troupe's male singers was usually appointed to make an appeal to the audience on any given night—early in their career it was tenor Thomas Rutling, while in later years the baritone Frederic Loudin became the principal spokesperson—much more time tended to be set aside for the appeals of White and AMA liaison Gustavus Pike, sometimes accompanied by a select local dignitary, whether a town or a church leader. The resulting didacticism rubbed some spectators the wrong way, as evinced by a letter published by the *Boston Daily Advertiser*, in which a concertgoer chastised White and an unnamed Pike for the length of their speeches and proclaimed that, "the nine singers told their own story, by their appearance and their songs, far better than anyone else could tell it for them."[66]

Whatever constraints the Jubilee Singers faced from within their own organization were ultimately outweighed by those imposed from outside. Although segregationist practices were not as widespread as they would become at the end of the century, in the era of Jim Crow, the desire to more strictly separate black from white drew strength in the time of Reconstruction from white fears of black freedom. For a group of black touring performers like the Jubilee Singers, hotels and trains became contested sites, but so too did the theaters in which they appeared. Some sense of the general attitudes that prevailed during their career can be drawn from an editorial that appeared in the main theatrical paper of the time, the *New York Clipper*. Responding to the recently passed Civil Rights Bill of 1875, which "made it illegal for places of public accommodation and entertainment to make any distinction between black and white patrons," the *Clipper* reprimanded those African Americans who responded to the new law by asserting their equality too hastily.[67] "We learn that on the day succeeding that on which the bill was signed by the President, several of our newly-baptized brethren sought to manifest their equality by sitting down, socially or otherwise, alongside of the palefaces in the orchestra stalls and other parts of theaters reserve for the latter exclusively," proclaimed the paper disapprovingly.[68] The writer saw no cause to object to African Americans serving in Congress or the military, or even attending church alongside their white counterparts. Moreover, they should not be denied access to proper entertainment; but, asserted the *Clipper*, while black theatergoers may rightfully enjoy themselves in those areas that have been set aside for them, they had no reason to encroach upon the comfort of white patrons who did the same. The segregationist logic of the *Clipper*'s perspective was the outgrowth of a theatrical milieu in which black and white audiences might attend the same performances but did so in decidedly unequal ways, with the best seats in the house always reserved for white spectators alone, and African Americans routinely granted access only to the most distant reaches of the hall, if they were admitted at all.

The Jubilee Singers came face to face with such practices twice in the early months of 1873. For a February concert in Baltimore, Pike and his business associate Isaac Hutchins procured the use of the city's Masonic Hall and arranged for the sale of tickets at a local music shop. The ticket agent then refused to sell reserved seats on the floor of the hall to black concertgoers, while assuring white patrons that African Americans would be kept from the main part of venue. When the Singers arrived, they chafed at the restrictions imposed upon the affair, and refused to sing unless more equitable arrangements were made.[69] Pike took control of the remaining ticket sales and by his own account, "proclaimed that any person wishing a seat in any part of the house could have it by paying the advertised price."[70] A few bold black patrons chose to purchase reserved seats alongside their white counterparts, and the concert otherwise proceeded without further incident. Shortly thereafter, the Singers were invited to give a performance at Princeton University. There, too, they found that only a small corner of the venue was reserved for black auditors, a circumstance made more offensive for the fact that the performance was held in one of the campus houses of worship. In this instance they begrudgingly agreed to go on, but White issued a harsh reprimand to those gathered during the concert.[71]

Reflecting on the unequal status of black and white concertgoers raises the question: did the Jubilee Singers appear before audiences that were exclusively or predominantly comprised of African Americans? They did, although recorded instances are few. Two events stand out, both held at Shiloh Presbyterian Church in New York. Founded in 1822 as the First Colored Presbyterian Church, Shiloh had from its inception been dedicated to antislavery activity and advocacy on behalf of African American civil rights. Its pastor at the time of the Jubilee Singers' appearances, Henry Highland Garnet, was among the most outspoken black critics of American racism; and the troupe's two appearances there had a more marked political tenor than the majority of their public performances.[72] The first, termed a "Freedom's Watch Meeting," was held on New Year's Eve, 1871, in the midst of the ensemble's first run of New York dates. Starting with a regular church service at eight o'clock, the evening was then given over to speeches by Garnet, George White, and others, alternating with songs rendered by the Singers. The *New York Times* wrote of the event: "Every subject of interest to the colored citizens of the land was discoursed on. The labor of educating the emancipated slaves, the necessity, of obtaining the passage of a liquor prohibitory law, the true status of man and other topics found favor with the orators, alternated with pleasant plantation melodies and sacred lyrics until the hands of the clock pointed to the last moment of 1871."[73]

On March 30, 1873, the Jubilee Singers made a return engagement at Shiloh, this time to mark the third anniversary of the ratification of the Fifteenth Amendment, which provided Constitutional guarantee of the right to vote. For this occasion, the *Times* provided more detail regarding the composition of the attending audience, observing: "The congregation was a decidedly mixed one, nearly one-fifth being white people who were drawn to the Shiloh Church out of curiosity or sympathy with the objects of the meeting. In the colored part of the congregation," the article continued, "were men who had been slaves, and whose backs, were they bared, would still show the marks of the lashes of cruel masters," as well as Northern blacks who had not known the tribulations of slavery so directly. George White joined Reverend Garnet in the pulpit, while the Jubilee Singers sat in the pews at the head of the congregation. From their post, they opened the evening's service with the Lord's Prayer, as they also began their own concert performances; following which Garnet read the words to the hymn, "Blow Ye the Trumpet, Blow!" which includes the refrain, "The year of Jubilee is come/The year of Jubilee is come/Return ye ransomed sinners, home." The Singers added their voices, and soon were joined by the congregation, collectively singing "with a vim and fervor which seemed likely to lift the roof from the poor old church."[74] Toward the close of the service the Jubilee Singers again performed, this time singing a hymn to the tune of "John Brown's Body"—likely the same "Battle Hymn of the Republic" they had sung with such fanfare at the World's Peace Jubilee—and once again eliciting the participation of the predominantly black congregation in the singing of the chorus.

Entering the World Stage

This second Jubilee Singers appearance at Shiloh Church was one of their last in the US before setting sail for England. From April 1873 until the troupe's disbandment in summer 1878, the Fisk Jubilee Singers spent far more of their time abroad than they did within the US. Other African American music artists had preceded the Jubilee Singers in this path, such as Frank Johnson, an antebellum composer and bandleader whose 1837 visit to London set an important precedent for black professional musicians.[75] Yet the overseas ventures of the Jubilee Singers far outweighed those of their predecessors in their extent and the amount of notoriety they generated, as well as the legacy they left. W.E.B. DuBois recalled the importance of the example set by the Singers when he was a student at Fisk: "Fisk had the tradition of her Jubilee Singers, who once hid in a Brooklyn organ loft, lest pious congregationalists see their black faces before they heard their heavenly voices . . . then the nation listened and the world opened its arms and The Fisk Jubilee Singers literally sang before Kings."[76] Building on the reflections of DuBois, Paul Gilroy more recently used the Singers as an exemplary instance of the broader historical process through which African American music became subject to a broader kind of "cross-cultural circulation" made possible through the convergence of a globalizing culture industry and the existing channels of black diasporic culture.[77] In England and other parts of Europe, the Singers' stature as representative proponents of black American culture grew, while the members of the troupe assumed new awareness of the discrepancies that resulted from American racism.

The foreign tours of the Jubilee Singers occurred in two phases. Their first such endeavor lasted from April 1873 until May 1874 and concentrated exclusively on the United Kingdom. After a year spent back in the US, during which White brought some key new members into the troupe including alto America Robinson and baritone Frederic Loudin, the Singers returned to England in May 1875. This version of the troupe is pictured in Figure 2.4. Initially retracing and expanding their steps through the U.K., they eventually began to experiment with some concerts for non-English speaking audiences. The first of these came during what was supposed to be a restful sojourn in Geneva, Switzerland, in the fall of 1876. Shortly thereafter, in early 1877, they made a short tour through Holland at the invitation of a Dutch merchant. Later that year, the Jubilee Singers embarked on their most extensive effort on the European continent, a tour of Germany that occupied them from October until the following July. Upon the termination of the German tour, the Singers effectively broke up, with White, Sheppard, and a few others at last returning to the US while some members chose to stay overseas. After that point, another version of the troupe formed the following year under the leadership of Loudin and White, but without the formal affiliation with Fisk University and the AMA. Their return from Europe, then, ultimately marked the end of the career of the original Fisk Jubilee Singers.

Figure 2.4 The Fisk Jubilee Singers in 1875, with the lineup that embarked upon the troupe's second tour of England. From left to right: B.W. Thomas, Julia Jackson, Maggie Porter, Ella Sheppard, Frederick Loudin, Hinton Alexander, Georgia Gordon, Jennie Jackson, America Robinson, and Thomas Rutling. Courtesy of the National Portrait Gallery, Smithsonian Institution.

Many aspects of their European travels mirrored their experiences in the US. In England, as in America, the Jubilee Singers relied on elite patrons to work on their behalf. Their primary benefactor in this regard was Anthony Ashley Cooper, the Earl of Shaftesbury, who lent to the Singers the advantages stemming from his noble position and from his standing as one of England's most visible icons of moral fortitude. At the time of the Singers' arrival in England in April 1873, Lord Shaftesbury was president of the Freedmen's Mission Aid Society, a British partner organization of the American Missionary Society. He was thus a logical ally, and with Pike leading the diplomatic charge, the Earl agreed to serve as chair of the troupe's British debut, a private concert attended by invitation only and held at Willis's Rooms, the location of an elite London social club.[78] This habit of appointing some local dignitary as "chair" of their various appearances became customary throughout the Jubilee Singers' subsequent concertizing in

England and other parts of Europe, and was a key strategy through which they forged connections with local civic leaders and legitimized themselves before prospective audiences who may have had only the barest context for the ensemble and their work. It also helped to mark their performances as something other than strictly profit-generating affairs, and lent weight to the appeals for charity they directed at those who came to hear them sing.

Reviews of the Jubilee Singers' Willis's Room debut also bear striking echoes of the troupe's critical reception in the US. If anything, the treatment of the ensemble as an exotic curiosity was even more pronounced in England, a product no doubt of the relative lack of black British residents, slavery having been outlawed there many decades earlier, in 1807. The most peculiar comments along these lines expressed surprise at the variations in color presented by the members of the Fisk Singers. One writer noted that only one of the Singers appeared a "pure-blooded African"—Jennie Jackson—while observing that the others "varied in shades of darkness . . . until in the case of three of the ladies they approached the standard of the pure white."[79] More characteristic were the comparisons between the Jubilee Singers and their blackface minstrel counterparts, which followed a similar logic to those comparisons made by American observers. That blackface minstrelsy recurred so often as a point of reference was an indication of the extent to which the entertainment form had penetrated British culture by the 1870s. British minstrel troupes began to emerge as early as the 1840s, stimulated by the success of touring American companies such as the Virginia Minstrels and the Christy Minstrels, the latter of whom became so widely imitated in England that "the term Christy Minstrels became generic," according to minstrel historian Michael Pickering.[80] As a result, in England like in the US, public portrayals of black music and culture were most commonly associated with white performers in blackface who tended to exaggerate and fabricate racial characteristics through a mix of comic and sentimental registers.

Typical, then, was the perspective of the London-based *Standard*, which opined: "At last we have a real troupe of negro minstrels in London, who give us not mere burlesque singing nor grin with the dental abandon which is supposed to be peculiar to their race. They have not even a 'bones,' a banjo, or a tambourine among them."[81] The troupe's distinction from the prevalent practices of blackface performance resounded among most British commentators. *The Orchestra*, a London music magazine, stressed the singers' connection to slavery, describing their songs as "veritable melodies which were wont to beguile the labour on the plantation, as distinct from Christy-minstrelism and Cockney niggermongery of all class."[82] Most elaborate were the remarks from the *Tonic Sol-Fa Reporter*, which became a key champion for the Jubilee Singers in their British pursuits. Writing of the ensemble shortly after its London debut, the journal asserted: "No notion can be formed of the style of their singing from the well-known Christy Minstrels . . . The assumption of negro character and the negro *style* of singing by our present Christys is as false as the black on their faces . . . No 'tempered' or more properly 'distempered' chords can ever touch the heart like those which the Jubilee singers gave."[83] Like Theodore Cuyler, the critic for the *Tonic Sol-Fa Reporter* heard the purported authenticity of the Jubilee Singers to be as much a matter of the emotional character of their expression as the melodic and rhythmic content or the sheer color of their skin. Their genuineness lay in their ability to stir the sympathy of their listeners. At the same time, the *Reporter* also offered a more culturally grounded explanation for the distinct character of the singers' music, comparing it to that stemming from "the hills of Wales and Scotland . . . the oldest music of Ireland and England," and so presenting it as a sort of proto-folk music performed with suitable artistry.[84]

Apart from its arguments in support of the genuineness of the Jubilee Singers, the *Tonic Sol-Fa Reporter* review provides us with one of the most detailed accounts of a single performance by the troupe that we have, and so warrants further attention. The concert opened in a manner that had become customary for the Singers at this stage of its career, with a rendition of the spiritual, "Steal Away to Jesus" followed by "The Lord's Prayer." A piece propelled by the repetition of the title phrase, the arrangement of "Steal Away" showcased the ensemble's precise timing and mastery of dynamics, the reviewer especially relishing the "double *pianissimo*" with which the refrain was uttered at the song's conclusion. Next came "Gwine to Ride up in the Chariot," in which a different singer took up the solo for the title line during each verse, answered in a call-response fashion by the "unisonous chorus." For "Nobody Knows the Trouble I See Lord," which followed, the troupe showed its talent for subtle but potent dramatic effects. As the audience waited for the Singers to rise and begin their next piece, a single female voice began to softly sing, soon joined by the whole chorus. Only then did the Singers stand, the lead soprano assuming her position at the head of the group and singing with a power that reminded the critic of none other than Jenny Lind.[85] Similar enthusiasm accompanied subsequent songs such as "Turn Back Pharaoh's Army" and "Didn't My Lord Deliver Daniel." The former offered further proof of the Singers' effective manipulation of their shifts between *piano* and *forte*, the ensemble reserving its greatest *fortissimo* utterance for the final verse celebrating the drowning of Pharaoh's army; and the latter demonstrated their command of rhythmic effects, singing with a rapidity that the critic judged forbidding to anyone who might try to emulate their manner. Overall, the review gives clear evidence that, aside from the exotic allure of their skin color and moral righteousness of their mission, the Jubilee Singers succeeded due to the force of their singing and the cleverness with which they presented themselves to their audiences. In other words, they put on a good show.

The speed with which the Jubilee Singers met with acceptance in England can be garnered from the fact that just a day after their performance at Willis's Rooms, they came face to face with Queen Victoria herself. Argyll Lodge in Kensington was the setting, the occasion being a tea hosted by the Duke and Duchess of Argyll, to whom the Singers had been introduced by Lord Shaftesbury following upon their successful debut. Only after their arrival at the event did the Singers learn that the Queen was expected to appear; her presence could be explained by the fact that the eldest son of the hosting nobleman was married to Victoria's daughter, Louise.[86] Queen Victoria arrived with another of her daughters, Beatrice, in tow, and when told by Lady Argyll of the presence of the Singers, immediately requested that they sing for her.

What next transpired was best captured in a letter written by Maggie Porter, one of the members of the Fisk ensemble:

> "Go Down, Moses" was the Duke's favorite, and "Steal Away to Jesus," so we first sang "Steal Away to Jesus," then chanted the Lord's Prayer, and then sang "Go Down, Moses." [The Queen] was very pleasant, but did not have any conversation with us. She told the Duke loud enough for us to hear, that she "was very much, very much pleased indeed," and as each of us retired she bowed and smiled very sweetly. So did the Princess Beatrice. This is the first concert or singing troupe she [Victoria] has listened to since her husband's death ... So she did us quite a favor, for her subjects think they must do whatever she does.[87]

Mindful of the great privilege it was to appear before the Queen of England, Porter was also confounded by the gap between her expectation of what a royal figure should look like and the appearance of the actual Queen, as the next portion of her letter revealed:

> But you are wondering, perhaps, why I don't tell what kind of a woman the Queen is. Well, it is because I don't just know how to describe her, she being a Queen. But were she any other person ... I should say she is a coarse-featured woman, still not ugly for she has a very pleasant face. She looks like a well-to-do English woman ... Why, I could have taken Lady Churchill or Lady Stanley for Queen much sooner than her, because I expected to see the Queen dressed elegantly.

Porter's account offers great insight into the different social codes at work as the Jubilee Singers entered circumstances far removed from their origins. It also shows a character trait that may well have contributed to the troupe's success: they were not cowed into subservience by their social superiors, but in fact went into such occasions expecting to be treated if not as equals, then at least as people worthy of due consideration. As Porter said to conclude her letter, many British people "seem to think we do not think so much of the privilege [of meeting the Queen] as they would, and I don't know that we do."

Having an audience before the Queen certainly opened many doors for the Singers, who would soon have an impactful encounter with another of England's most prominent figureheads, the Prime Minister William Gladstone.[88] However, for all the positive notice that was generated around the Singers, organizing the British tour was no simple proposition. G.D. Pike's published account of the tour, a strangely self-serving document, nonetheless offers some valuable insight into the mechanics of the troupe's endeavors. In the US the Singers pursued a course whereby appearances in churches regularly alternated with performances in concert halls, which entailed two different ways of generating revenue—the first through donations, the second through paid admission. This approach allowed them to appeal to two different constituencies, one that was primarily religious and generally eschewed public entertainments, the other primarily a music-loving audience that was accustomed to paying for its public leisure. In the untested territory of England and other parts of the United Kingdom, it was unclear if one or the other of these approaches would yield better results, but the group's managers White and Pike tended to favor the more commercial course in their British pursuits. The Willis's Room affair presented a third model, which was used intermittently by the Singers at various points: private concerts for which attendance was by invitation only, that would rely upon donations but from a more select audience.

Writing about one such event, in the seaport town of Hull, Pike remarked on the difficulty he faced as tour manager working within the expectations of the British public. Held at the Hope Street Chapel in Hull, the performance was given to an audience comprised of about fifteen hundred people from the "best of families" who had been invited by the chapel's pastor, Reverend W.C. Preston. After making his appeal to those present, Pike found that the collection was much better than expected, but at slightly more than fifty-two pounds was only about half of what the Singers would have received had they charged admission for the same event. Pike remarked further: "When Mr. White or I said we ought at least to realize £100 per night, they looked upon us with apparent pity. No benevolent enterprise ever had an agency that could raise money like that."[89] Therein lay the rub: the Jubilee Singers was an organization that presented itself to transcend strictly commercial considerations but had financial ambitions in keeping with a more profit-minded sort of concert promotion. To meet such ambitions required that Pike and White scramble to build interest in the troupe at every step along the way; for as Pike explained elsewhere: "though a moderate-sized hall could be filled at low prices with only the ordinary methods of advertising used by persons giving public entertainments, yet in order to sell a large number of reserved seat tickets at 3s. each, a great amount of pressure was needed."[90] Their reputation may have preceded them, but no Jubilee Singers performance was assumed to be able to sell itself. For the troupe's managers, touring—whether in the US or abroad—involved a continual process of thinking ahead to the next location to determine the best methods whereby word could be gotten out.[91]

One difficulty that was significantly diminished in their European travels was the effort to find suitable accommodations. The Jubilee Singers faced little of the overt discrimination from hotel owners that they had in the US and found themselves able to travel and move freely in public without the anxious, watchful eyes upon them to which they had grown accustomed back home. In this, they foreshadowed the experiences of scores of other African American musicians who, having traveled to make music overseas, felt better treated abroad, and whose feelings toward the US transformed accordingly. This shift in perception was powerfully conveyed by one of the troupe's newest members, Frederic Loudin, in an article that appeared some months after the commence of the Jubilee Singers' second British tour, in October 1875. A baritone singer with a commanding stage presence, Loudin had joined the troupe less than a year earlier. Born to free parents and having lived most of his life in Ohio and Pennsylvania, he was already nearly thirty years old at the time that he joined the Fisk Singers, and he did so never having any previous affiliation with the school. Trained as a printer, Loudin was an independent black professional, articulate and outspoken, and he would become a leader among the members of the troupe, eventually reviving the company after its formal association with Fisk University had dissolved.[92]

Loudin began his remarks on the nature of his British experience with the following provocation: "I have never known practically the meaning of the word freedom in its highest sense but three months in my life, and though it is with shame for my own boasted land of freedom I say it, yet it be true that those three months have been spent in Great Britain." His further remarks drove the point home even more forcefully:

> And I now affirm that no black man, born and raised in the United States of America, can realize what it is to be absolutely free. And I further assert that no black man in America can realize what he suffers, and what a depressing and humiliating influence his manhood and higher nature is under until he is able to rise above and breathe an atmosphere untainted by the deadly and polluting poison of American prejudice. Think what it would be to be able to go to any hotel, restaurant or confectionary, or any place of amusement, and not simply to be able to make your way in at the point of some law, but to be absolutely welcomed . . . and then not to be stuck away in some hole or corner, lest some of the other customers will see you and become indignant because a "nigger's" money pays for just the same as his does, and is just as gladly received.[93]

It is difficult to measure the impact of Loudin's statement upon American readers; but the sheer force of his rhetoric has to be considered the equal of other better-remembered spokespersons for black civil rights such as Frederic Douglass and W.E.B. DuBois. Indeed, Loudin could be said to exemplify in this passage DuBois's classic formulation of the African American experience of double-consciousness, the way in which the black American "ever feels his two-ness,—an American, a Negro, two souls, two thoughts, two unreconciled strivings, two warring ideals in one dark body, whose dogged strength alone keeps it from being torn asunder."[94] He further embodies a central insight put forth by Paul Gilroy in his revision of DuBois's concept: that the "two-ness" of African American subjectivity comes into sharpest relief when considered in an international framework. For Loudin as for DuBois, skepticism concerning the promise of freedom tendered by the US was fortified by "experiences of travel both within and away from America."95

However welcoming England proved, it was not beyond reproach on matters of race and social justice, and Loudin and the rest of the Jubilee Singers soon showed themselves ready to take the country to task. At issue was a controversial "Slave Circular" released by the British admiralty in June 1875, which instructed members of the Royal Navy not to accept any fugitive slaves on board their craft, and to return any slaves that did come on board to their masters assuming they were owned legally.96 The order was viewed by many British citizens to violate the country's longstanding opposition to the institution of slavery, and gave rise to an energetic political debate that lasted from the final months of 1875 into the summer of 1876. A second version of the circular put forward in December 1875 made only minor changes and if anything prompted even stronger public outcry than had the first. Not until the following August did the issue run its course, when Prime Minister Benjamin Disraeli and his cabinet offered a third revised circular that took a noncommittal stance regarding the deeper issues raised by public criticism concerning England's support for freedom within its own borders and in its imperial endeavors.

The Jubilee Singers seem to have unveiled their response to the Slave Circular in December 1875, around the time that the second circular was released. At a performance in Lancaster, Loudin sang a solo selection "written especially to commemorate the uprising of the people of this country to put down the recent Admiralty 'Slave Circular.'"97 Reviewing the concert, the *Lancaster Gazette* did not name the song but noted that Loudin sang it "with much feeling" and provided an encore rendition in response to audience demand, at the end of which the rest of the ensemble joined their voices with his to sing the chorus of "Rule Brittania." More details about the song appeared six days later in a review of a concert at Durham. The *Northern Echo* identified the selection as "The Standard of the Free," and provided a significant sample of the song's lyrics, which portrayed the Slave Circular as a "shadow" that fell upon England's political landscape, but then hailed the triumph of the "nation's voice" as it demanded its leaders to "take back the accused word." Here the Singers did not wait for an encore before they joined Loudin in a climactic version of "Rule Brittania" but added their voices the first time around, leading to a great burst of enthusiasm from the Durham audience and a "vociferous" call for the song to be performed again.98

"The Standard of the Free" was a rare song originally composed for the Jubilee Singers, with lyrics by the Welsh-born Congregational minister Llewellyn D. Bevan and music by Theodore Seward, longtime transcriber of Fisk arrangements who accompanied the troupe on its second British tour as musical director. The song was published in an undated edition by J. Curwen and Sons of London, on the cover of which is the note: "Composed for Mr. F.J. Loudin, and sung by him at the concerts of the Jubilee Singers."[99] Given Loudin's willingness to speak on issues of unequal treatment of black subjects, it comes as no surprise that the piece was written specially for him. Although protesting the Slave Circular, the song also praises England and its people for recognizing the error that the policy prescribed by the circular set forth, and so cloaked its social criticism in a strong aura of British patriotism—a crafty strategy, and perhaps a necessary one, for a song meant to be sung by someone whose racial difference was compounded by foreign national status. Yet this effort to temper protest with appeasement was still a somewhat risky proposition and in at least one instance, led to events that did not sit well with all who came to hear the Singers perform.

For the Jubilee Singers concert in Blackburn on Wednesday, February 2, 1876, it is unclear whether or not Loudin sang "The Standard of the Free." The regular review that appeared in the *Blackburn Standard* lacked much detail regarding the evening's program but reproduced some remarks made by Loudin to the audience, to the effect that England's antislavery spirit remained undiminished in the present day. As was customary, further comments followed by various local clergy, one of whom—the Reverend J. McEwen Stott of the Chapel Street Independent Church—appealed to the audience to show its "abhorrence" for such laws as the Slave Circular by rising up as a body in protest.[100] Stott's appeal went unheeded, as the audience refused to stand, and prompted a sharp rebuke in a separate article published in the same issue of the *Standard*. In contrast to the measured tone of the concert review, this second editorial piece accused the Singers of fomenting anti-British sentiment, and chastised the Reverend McEwen Stott for inappropriately seeking to turn a musical event into an occasion for scoring political capital.[101] No other evidence exists to suggest that members of the audience held the Singers responsible for Stott's actions, and other concert reports suggest that in general, the stance of the Jubilee Singers toward the Slave Circular was shared by the vast majority of those who came to hear them. Nonetheless, the incident at Blackburn showed how any given concert by the Singers could be affected by the convergence of local and national political forces, and how the troupe did not just present itself as a neutral party within their host country but aligned itself on one side of a debate that hit close to home.

Voices Carry

While politics was at times explicitly addressed by the Jubilee Singers, the group's primary appeal was of a more sentimental kind. Like Jenny Lind, who in conjunction with P.T. Barnum used her perceived piety and charity to stir the public imagination, the Fisk Jubilee Singers converted religious faith into popular enthusiasm. They did so at a time when the morality of public amusement became increasingly subject to scrutiny and regulation. As we will see in the next chapter, the decade of the 1870s saw the rise of variety entertainment, featuring a mélange of acts that risked crossing the lines of good taste—blackface performance being mixed with a range of other types of ethnic comedy, female impersonation, and multifold physical feats that opened the way toward new manners of exposing the body on stage.[102] Against this backdrop, the Fisk Singers employed some very specific strategies to present the right balance of fun and fortitude, pleasure and piety. They enlisted the assistance of local and national religious leaders, strove as often as possible to appear in houses of worship rather than regular places of amusement, and pursued a course of maximum profit by appealing to the charity, generosity, and sympathy of their audiences.

At times, most notably in their appearances at the World's Peace Jubilee, the Fisk Jubilee Singers performed before crowds of historic scale. Overall, though, the history of the Jubilee Singers is not filled with the epic crowds drawn by Jenny Lind. Although their management, personified by George White and Gustavus Pike among others, had a flair for publicity that bore traces of Barnum's legacy, they never paraded the Singers as mere curiosities. Respectability was the goal, made more paramount by competing and countervailing images of blackness that saturated nineteenth-century American culture and remained dominant into the 1870s and beyond. Partly resulting from the energy with which the Fisk Singers differentiated themselves from their minstrel competitors, the ensemble appeared before more self-selecting audiences than had the Swedish Nightingale. Yet their success also gave rise to a broader popularization of jubilee singing wherein the boundaries between sacred and profane, respectability and ridicule, became far more porous. By the time the Fisk Jubilee Singers ended the first phase of their career in 1878, the numbers of competing jubilee singing troupes had risen into the dozens.[103] Many of these competing ensembles were far less scrupulous in preserving an air of decorum, and some blatantly fabricated academic affiliations or plagiarized endorsements given to the Fisk Singers by the likes of Henry Ward Beecher and even President Grant. The pressures stemming from increased competition contributed to the overall strain that led to the group's break-up and left the Singers having to continually claim their own "originality" against the expanding background of imitators and more legitimate rivals.

Here lay one of the central paradoxes of the Jubilee Singers' legacy: they strove mightily to counter the influence of blackface minstrelsy and provide an alternate model of black musical performance, but minstrelsy remained intact and if anything was strengthened by the incorporation of jubilee singing into its fabric. From this perspective, the achievement of the Fisk Jubilee Singers was decidedly transitional. One would like to think that the sheer force of seeing and hearing a troupe of "real" black performers would have rendered the exaggerated caricatures of minstrelsy obsolete in one fell swoop. Yet minstrelsy, for all that it was presented as a version of black culture, did not rely on authenticity for its appeal, at least not in a straightforward manner. Its success lay in its ability to create a spirit of good times, or to pull at the heartstrings with sentiment. Minstrelsy's pleasures were the pleasures of popular culture, in which "doing good" socially or morally is subordinate to having fun. The Jubilee Singers sought to provide pleasure of a more uplifting sort. They were a part of the popular culture of their time but were also at odds with it, and the success they achieved was attributable to the fact that they appeared during a historical window when the betterment of African Americans was a more widely held goal than it had been before and than it would be again for several decades. Like Patrick Gilmore's two Peace Jubilees, the Jubilee Singers embodied a spirit of optimism that tapped into some deeply held desires in the immediate aftermath of the Civil War, but that would prove much harder to sustain with the passing of time.

For W.E.B. DuBois and many commentators that have followed, the greatest mark of the Fisk Jubilee Singers and their impact resided in the songs they sang, which constituted a living legacy of the African American slave experience and a reminder that the coming of Emancipation did not wipe away the hurts of the recent past. To this should be added the freedom with which the Jubilee Singers moved as they went about their business.

As part of the larger history of American musical performance, the Jubilee Singers showed that the increasingly routine practice of concert touring had implications well beyond the generation of revenue. For a troupe of African American artists like the Jubilee Singers, touring was a way to test and expand the boundaries of their new social situation. On tour, the Jubilee Singers confronted racial discrimination but also brought it to public notice in a new light, leaving audiences and newspaper readers to ponder whether the privileges conferred by celebrity should override the impulse to keep African Americans in their place. Touring also brought the members of the Singers into contact with new ways of being in the world and let them know that the limits imposed by American racism were not universally found. At home and abroad, the Jubilee Singers were the most visible representatives of a mounting debate about black musical authenticity that would shape public perception for years to come. They engendered the first broadly felt stirrings of recognition for what African American music could be if it were unbound from existing constraints, and black artists were given more room to raise their voices and sing on their own behalf, for the world to hear.

3

Economies of Performance

Tony Pastor, Ernest Hogan, and the Emergence of Vaudeville

Interviewed in the summer of 1895, Tony Pastor—then in his thirtieth year as one of New York City's leading theatrical impresarios—was asked to comment on the comic songs that had long been his own performance specialty. Pastor explained that as a songwriter (or song commissioner, a role he more typically held), the newspaper was a continual source of inspiration:

> I believe not only in the power of the public press, but in its utility. It is the most valuable agent the vocalist has ever had for securing subjects for popular songs. The comic vocalist must be quick to perceive the peculiar topic or phase of human life which is liable to interest the amusement-going public, and must be a little ahead of time.[1]

This emphasis upon the topical song was to have great influence in the field of songwriting throughout the last decades of the nineteenth century, as theatrical entertainers sought to find new ways to keep their audiences amused week after week. Indeed, more than topicality, Pastor's concern with novelty signaled a shift in the way that songs, and singers, were put before the public. As the owner and manager of a theater that offered a new program of entertainment each week for a full season, Pastor needed to keep his material fresh and interesting to ensure that audiences would want to return. His perseverance in this enterprise had much to do with his success; so could he claim in 1895: "I've introduced one or two new songs nearly every Monday night during the season for the past thirty years."[2]

That same year, while Tony Pastor reflected upon his long career, an up-and-coming African American artist enjoyed his first significant taste of success. Ernest Hogan was something of a journeyman in 1895, having left his birthplace of Bowling Green, Kentucky several years earlier to lead the life of an itinerant performer. During an extended stay in the state of Kansas,

Hogan happened upon a new dance phenomenon called the "possum a la," the name of which was later shortened to "pas ma la."[3] By one account, Hogan encountered the dance while working as a piano player in Belvidere, Kansas. An African American from New Orleans was the caller for the dance and used the unusual phrase, "pas ma la," as a cue to dancers to change partners and swing in time. Struck by the exotic turn of phrase and the audience's growing enthusiasm for the dance, Hogan used it as the basis for a song.[4] "Pas Ma Las," with words and music by Ernest Hogan, was published by J.R. Bell of Kansas City in 1895, and according to music historians Lynn Abbott and Doug Seroff, constituted one of the first songs to bridge the gap between the vernacular rag dance emerging in the region and popular ragtime song.[5] For Hogan, it laid the groundwork for a career that would see him become one of the most widely recognized performers in the US, and a rare African American artist known as much for his songwriting prowess as for his onstage charisma.

A white ethnic (Italian American) theatrical impresario who used popular song as part of larger strategy to produce a sense of novelty on stage week after week; an African American performer who quickly learned the professional worth of a published song. Tony Pastor and Ernest Hogan had disparate careers, but together they typify a period of major transformation in the history of American entertainment and in the presentation of live music. In the broadest sense, they represent the extended phase during which variety, and then vaudeville, theatrical entertainment supplanted blackface minstrelsy as the dominant form of American public amusement. Pastor was a pivotal transitional figure in this development. He gained ownership of his first theater in 1865, just as the variety theater was coming into its own. By the time he established his third and most enduring venue in 1881, vaudeville was still some years away, but Pastor had already done much to anticipate its arrival; and upon his death in 1908 he was heralded as one of its primary architects. Hogan's career gained momentum in the mid-to-late 1890s, when vaudeville was a recognized phenomenon. He entered the field as one of a wave of talented black artists who were finding new professional opportunities in the theatrical world. Unlike the members of the Fisk Jubilee Singers, however, who strove to educate and elevate public morality as much as to offer amusement, Hogan was an entertainer through and through. Like his more celebrated contemporary, Bert Williams, he struggled to assert his autonomy but never entirely broke from the legacy of blackface performance that continued to loom large.

For all their differences, Pastor and Hogan had a common vocation: both were comic singers. The union of music and comedy was one of the dominant trends of the time and indicated the degree to which music became "theatricalized" in connection with variety and vaudeville performance. Concerts and recitals—dedicated events in which musical performance was the sole featured attraction—were largely the province of high culture in the late nineteenth and early twentieth centuries. The separation of culture into "high" and "low" spheres, which was still in its nascent stages during Jenny Lind's successes of the 1850s, became more fully realized throughout the later part of the century, giving rise to the modern institution of classical music.[6] The Metropolitan Opera House, Carnegie Hall, and Symphony Hall in Boston were among the new spaces constructed between 1880 and 1900 that gave classical music patrons a distinct class of venues they could call their own. During this same time span, vaudeville grew as the principal medium for a style of public amusement that was unquestionably "popular." Vaudeville privileged accessibility over enlightenment; it strove to offer something for everybody while seeking to avoid offending what was perceived to be the average patron. Musical performers gained a vital new platform in vaudeville through which they could reach audiences of unprecedented breadth. Reaching those audiences, though, meant that a singer or instrumentalist was only one part of a larger bill of attractions. Music never existed with any degree of autonomy on the vaudeville stage; and to "sell a song" in vaudeville, the singer or instrumentalist had to invest it with qualities of showmanship that could appeal to the least musically inclined of auditors, a talent that was shared by Pastor and Hogan and other comic singers of their ilk.

Selling songs, as an activity unto itself, assumed new significance during the period when Pastor and Hogan enjoyed their greatest success. Paralleling the rise of vaudeville was the growth of a system of commercial song production the likes of which had never before existed in the US. This development, eventually given the name "Tin Pan Alley," was a major turning point in the history of American popular music. During the Tin Pan Alley era, songwriting became a profession in a more durable way than it had ever been before, while song publishing became truly national in scope. In effect, the writing and publishing of popular song became industrialized during the Tin Pan Alley era in a manner evocatively described by pioneering popular music historian Isaac Goldberg, who characterized Tin Pan Alley as "the Newspaper Row of music. It is a species of song-and-dance journalism."[7] The congruence of Goldberg's description with that of Tony Pastor, casting song production as a kind of daily or weekly journalism, reinforces the new importance assigned to currency in the musical culture of the time. Songs offered by Jenny Lind, or the Fisk Jubilee Singers, often gained value through their association with various traditions—whether a national tradition, like Lind's Swedish or Scottish airs, an ethnic or racial tradition like the spirituals of the Fisk Singers, or a purely popular tradition associated with long-standing favorites like "Home Sweet Home." Tin Pan Alley invested far less importance in the tried and true. The imperative was to create new songs that had an instant air of familiarity even as they came across as something that the audience had not heard before.

If songs constituted a kind of reportage, the vaudeville theater was where audiences went to hear the news. Historians of popular music have noted the integral interrelationship that existed between vaudeville and Tin Pan Alley, stressing the significance of "plugging a song" on the vaudeville stage as a major step in turning songs into hits.[8] Yet vaudeville has routinely been assigned a kind of secondary importance in most histories of popular music and its business—the song has been treated as the thing, with performance considered an adjunct to the real business of selling songs via the medium of published sheet music. Assessing the careers of Tony Pastor and Ernest Hogan in connection with this new economy of popular song production means giving performance the consideration that it deserves in this larger historical process. Selling songs was not just an end in itself. Throughout the vaudeville era, but especially in the early part stretching from the 1880s to the first decade of the twentieth century, it was also a crucial means of selling shows; and for vaudeville artists themselves, the show—not the song—was more often the thing.

Enter Vaudeville

Like Tin Pan Alley, vaudeville represented a new system of combined economic and cultural production. When vaudeville first emerged is a matter of some debate. Traces of the word arise as early as the 1870s. Many sources cite Sargent's Great Vaudeville Company, formed by H.J. Sargent of Louisville, Kentucky, as one of the first to use the term, dating from 1871. By 1875, a theater in Louisville took the name of the Vaudeville Theater although, according to a *New York Clipper* notice, it was not connected to Sargent but was under the management of the Chapman Brothers. That early notice of the

Vaudeville Theater in Louisville, brief as it is, reveals much about the content of vaudeville as well as the general impulses that contributed to vaudeville's rise. On the bill for the week of September 27, 1875 were the Barlow Brothers, song-and-dance men who specialized in "plantation eccentricities"; the Star Sisters, a dancing team; Johnny Murphy, a singer who rendered Irish material; and Worden and Mack, another song-and-dance duo who appeared in blackface. Performances at the theater, according to the *Clipper*, were "devoid of all slang and vulgarism;" and "for the purpose of attracting and pleasing the ladies and children, the Chapmans propose giving a Saturday floral matinee, each lady and child being presented with a floral offering."[9] Many of the qualities that would define vaudeville were already well in place in this 1875 theater: an eclectic array of attractions that are varied according to type of performance specialty (singing, dancing, comedy, or some combination thereof) and spotlight ethnic and racial difference as a point of identification or a source of (racist) humor; an effort to claim moral propriety as a defining feature of the theater's offerings; and a concern with reaching members of the audience—women and children—who were previously considered marginal to the cultivation of a theatrical public, if they were not excluded altogether.

For all that was in place by the 1870s, the vaudeville era proper is usually dated from the later 1880s and early 1890s forward; and even by the 1900s key aspects of vaudeville were still falling into place.[10] The principal changes that brought vaudeville to fruition had less to do with the content of the entertainment than with the institutions supporting it. Starting in the 1880s, theaters began to combine themselves into consolidated circuits, sometimes overseen by a single owner, but increasingly into the 1890s and early 1900s controlled by organized groups of theater owners and managers who came to exert an enormous influence over the character and economy of American popular theater. Turning to the *Clipper* again, one finds ready of evidence of these changes beginning to take hold by 1880. The May 8, 1880, issue contained advertisements by two sets of theater owners who heralded the expanded scope of their operations. Brooks, Dickson, and Hickey announced a "Grand Circuit" for the coming 1880–1881 season, and outlined a set of theater holdings that was remarkable at the time for its geographic breadth and diversity, with separate theatrical divisions in New York, Michigan, Ohio, Indiana, and Illinois, as well as a "Southern" division that included theaters in Louisville, Nashville, and Memphis.[11] J.H. Haverly's Amusement Enterprises could not quite compete with the geographic scope of Brooks, Dickson, and Hickey, but nonetheless claimed ownership over five theaters—three in

Manhattan, one in Brooklyn, and one in Chicago—and several distinct companies, mostly of the minstrel show variety.[12]

The combined investment of the Haverly organization in theaters and theatrical companies indicated the larger implications of this trend: as theater owners built and combined their spheres of influence, performers conducted their careers in a way that increasingly required them to make arrangements with powerfully concentrated interests. Part of the consequence of this development was that theatrical agents assumed greater control as the intermediaries who could bridge the gap between the demands of performers and theater owners and managers. Touring became not only increasingly national in scope but also increasingly rationalized, as performers would often sign contracts for engagements that would take them across a wide geographic range while working within a single circuit or small combination of circuits. When the system was at its height of operations, from the 1890s through the 1910s, profits grew enormously, and the salaries for the biggest star performers became dramatically inflated; accordingly, the gap in pay and recognition between the biggest stars and ordinary working performers also grew precipitously. In effect, as Tin Pan Alley denoted the industrialization of popular song production, so vaudeville came denote the mass production of theatrical entertainment. Together they laid the foundation for the modern "culture industry" that would encompass film, radio, television, and recorded popular music.[13]

Pivotal to the commercial expansion of vaudeville was Benjamin Franklin (B.F.) Keith. In partnership with Edward Franklin (E.F.) Albee, Keith would build the most prominent theatrical empire of the vaudeville era. He began his show business career in the circus, including a stretch working under P.T. Barnum, from whom "he learned about the importance of broad audience appeal."[14] Further following in Barnum's footstep's, Keith's first major foothold as an entertainment entrepreneur came as the proprietor of a Boston dime museum, which he ran with the more seasoned amusement businessman George Batcheller starting in 1884. A key turning point in Keith's career came in 1887: he broke his association with Batcheller in that year while fortifying his partnership with Albee, converted his Gayety Musee and Bijou Theater into a more elegant venue that was focused on offering popular-but-refined entertainment at affordable prices, and opened a second theater in Providence, Rhode Island modeled along similar lines. Keith and Albee added a third theater to their holdings in 1889, set in Philadelphia. The ad reproduced in Figure 3.1 trumpets their expanded holdings, which

Figure 3.1 B.F. Keith advertises his growing vaudeville theater holdings. By the 1890s Keith and his associate, E.F. Albee, exerted significant influence upon the shape of the market for live theatrical entertainment. From the *New York Clipper* (January 17, 1891).

took another step forward in 1893, when they moved into New York City by procuring the Union Square Theater, located proximate to Tony Pastor's namesake theater on Fourteenth Street. From that point forward Keith and Albee continued to increase their theatrical holdings but more importantly, they sought to work in combination with other theater owners to centralize the mechanisms through which artists were hired and paid, theatrical bills were assembled, and tours were organized across the US. Influenced by the 1896 formation of the Theatrical Syndicate, which organized the booking of hundreds of "legitimate" (non-vaudeville) theaters under a single umbrella, Keith and especially Albee took the lead in establishing first the Association of Vaudeville Managers in 1900, and then the United Booking Office or U.B.O. in 1906.[15] With the latter, the evolution of vaudeville into big business was complete, and the American entertainment industry assumed the shape it would retain until modern mass media forms became dominant in the 1920s and 1930s.

The economic imperative that drove vaudeville's growth also reconstituted the connection between music and other cultural forms and the mass audience. As we have seen in previous chapters, the impulse to draw large crowds of concertgoers became one of the driving engines of change during the time of Jenny Lind's concert tours and remained in place through Patrick Gilmore's Peace Jubilees of 1869 and 1872. With Lind, the crowd resulted from Barnum's mastery of national publicity channels combined with a desire to see Lind firsthand that cut across class lines to a significant degree. The assembly of the Peace Jubilee crowds was almost an act of will by Gilmore, who appeared to follow the philosophy, if you build it, they will come. In neither case did these crowds, or the broader phenomenon of the mass audience, become fully routine or systematized. There was no circuit of theaters in place for Lind's tours; Gilmore had to build stadia of sufficient scale to accommodate the crowds of his imagination.

As such, vaudeville represented the first era in which the effort to draw the widest possible audiences became institutionalized as a matter of economic practice—and arguably as an exercise in small-scale cultural democratization. Yet in a material sense, the crowds of vaudeville differed markedly from those that attended Lind's concerts or Gilmore's Jubilees. No crowds of 8,000, let alone 50,000, came to attend a given vaudeville performance. The scale of vaudeville theaters was kept moderate, with between 1,500 and 2,000 seats constituting a common "big time" house and 3,000 existing at the upper limit. Financially, this had the effect that the goal became not just drawing the largest crowd to any one show, but to continuously turn over one large audience after another, giving rise to the policy of "continuous performance" that came to dominate portions of vaudeville by the 1890s. Meanwhile, the moderate scale of vaudeville houses had a different sort of effect as well: even in a full house there was a sense of intimacy between artist and audience, which resulted from the relative proximity that vaudeville audiences had with the artists onstage and from a performance aesthetic in which direct engagement of the audience was fundamental. Vaudeville, then, worked along two distinct but interrelated lines: within each theater, during each performance, there was an "intimate crowd" that was assembled and addressed by the managers and the artists who appeared on the bill; while across the whole circuit of vaudeville there was a much larger audience, what might be called a "dispersed crowd" that was brought into being with an unprecedented scale of coherence as a target of entertainment.

Pastor's Progress

Tony Pastor's biographers have dubbed him the "Dean of the Vaudeville Stage" or alternately the "Father of Vaudeville."[16] His status as a key figure in vaudeville history is widely accepted and almost beyond dispute. Yet these characterizations may distort as much as they reveal about his importance. For instance, upon the death of Tony Pastor in 1908, the *Philadelphia Telegraph* observed:

> Variety's father in the United States lived to see the passing of variety as a form of stage entertainment.
>
> Now they call it "vaudeville." But the late Tony Pastor never accepted the term. He claimed that since he had introduced this form of entertainment, and given it its greatest vogue, he was within his rights in insisting that the English "Variety" rather than the French "Vaudeville" should be the designator.[17]

Pastor explained his dissatisfaction with the term "vaudeville" in his own words in an interview late in his career:

> There is hardly any difference in method between then and now. The modern vaudeville is in no particular dissimilar from the variety shows of the '70s, except in the matter of patronage. Our country has grown larger, our wealth greater and wages are higher, consequently we have larger theatres, most costly appointments, effort increasingly strenuous and more competition.
>
> In this way public attention has been challenged; and presto! a new name—vaudeville—there you are, but the old idea, the variety show is still with us, the old name more comprehensive than the new.[18]

Tony Pastor's career prefigured many of the developments that contributed to the rise of vaudeville, but his biases demonstrate the degree to which he was the product of an earlier moment in the history of American entertainment, when vaudeville was just another, fancier term for variety. As Gillian Rodger observes in her valuable history of the variety theater, the choice of term was not idle. Between variety and vaudeville lay a host of tensions, according to Rodger:

These tensions include those between performing and entrepreneurial managers; between traditionalists, who sought to keep their male audience happy, and innovators and pragmatists, who sought to expand their audience to include women and children and later ethnic populations; and finally between the older generation of managers, who had shaped the development of the genre in its first decades as an independent form, and younger, entrepreneurial managers, who entered the genre during the 1870s, 1880s, and later.[19]

Pastor, seen in Figure 3.2, was one of the veteran managers referred to by Rodger, but he was also one of variety's great innovators. When he entered the ranks of New York City's theatrical managers in 1865, he was on the leading edge of the turn to variety entertainment, a hybrid style of theater that drew upon the varied format of the minstrel show but made racial impersonation just one feature among many (without ever abandoning it entirely). Emerging at the tail end of the Civil War, variety often had an air of scandal about it—it can be seen to have laid the groundwork not only for the polite offerings of vaudeville but also the distinctly more impolite pleasures of burlesque.[20] Pastor staked his future fortune squarely on the side of politeness, but he did so while maintaining a strong populist appeal that contributed to his nearly unprecedented forty-three-year run as a manager-performer. He preserved, but also modified, this appeal as he moved from his initial theatrical home in the Bowery to two subsequent houses further uptown.

* * *

Tony Pastor began his managerial career at 201 Bowery Street in an establishment he named Tony Pastor's Opera House. Although he was a novice theater manager at the time, he was hardly new to the stage. Born in 1833,[21] Pastor often claimed that his performance career began in 1846, when he was reportedly part of a blackface minstrel troupe that also included the famed minstrel performer Billy Whitlock at P.T. Barnum's New York museum.[22] The circus provided the true beginning, though: Pastor and his two brothers, Frank and William, apprenticed with circus manager John Nathans, and throughout the 1850s the young Tony earned a growing reputation as a circus attraction with a gift for comedy and skill for putting over a song. Pastor's shift from the circus to the variety theater came around 1860. In April 1861 he began an extended tenure at the American Concert Hall at 444 Broadway

130   LIVE MUSIC IN AMERICA

Figure 3.2 In this 1879 photo, Tony Pastor strikes a pose befitting one of the leading variety theater impresarios of his time. Courtesy of the Billy Rose Theatre Division, The New York Public Library for the Performing Arts.

in New York, run by Robert Butler. There, Pastor refined his act as a singer of topical comic songs, a specialty that carried over from his circus days. A notice from the *Clipper* during his time at the theater captured the degree to which Pastor had become a crowd favorite, exclaiming, "As a comic vocalist, Tony has no superior in this country . . . [he] can always draw a big crowd wherever he is engaged."[23] By March 1865, Pastor had formed his own traveling company, with which he would tour to various locations around the US in the spring and summer; and his theater at 201 Bowery opened soon thereafter, on July 31 of that year.

That Pastor called his theater an "opera house" was indicative of a time when the boundaries between "high" and "low" culture remained in flux. An opera house was usually a place of general entertainment; even the Astor Place Opera House, site of the infamous 1849 conflict between elite and working-class New Yorkers, was not strictly a place for the performance of opera. Astor Place was, though, very clearly created for an upper-class constituency that had still not fully staked out its cultural interests some two decades later. The location of Tony Pastor's Opera House in the Bowery was an indication of its rather different character. When Pastor opened the theater in 1865, the Bowery had a long-standing reputation as a center of working-class male leisure in New York, typified by the figure of the "Bowery b'hoy" that had been a common feature of the popular discourse about New York and its working class residents since the 1830s and 1840s.[24] It was also an area viewed with moral suspicion, housing one of the city's most recognized vice districts, where intoxicating drink and commercial sex could be readily procured.[25]

Regarding theatrical entertainment, the Bowery had become home by the early 1860s to a novel sort of institution that stirred considerable attention and scandal, the concert saloon. As the name suggests, the concert saloon was essentially a drinking establishment that offered music and other sorts of stage attractions. The patrons of these places—who were by almost all accounts exclusively male—would pay a small admission fee to be entertained while sharing a drink with other men, and to draw the attention of the waiter girls who served drinks and, perhaps, offered sexual favors for additional payment. Whether the waiter girls were in fact prostitutes remains unclear. Theater historian Brooks McNamara suggests that many of these young women had theatrical talents of their own that they would exhibit, and that they likely promised the male clientele of the saloons more than they would actually provide in the way of sexual services so as to better draw attention to themselves.[26] However real the presence of prostitution was, its perceived prevalence made the concert saloons a target for reformers. In April 1862 the New York state legislature passed what became known as the "Anti-Concert Saloon Bill," which specifically prohibited the sale and consumption of alcohol, and the presence of waiter girls, in the same space where a performance took place or in a space that was immediately accessible from the theatrical auditorium or lobby. Following upon the passage of the bill the New York police conducted a series of raids upon many of the city's establishments, leading to a rash of closures.

In the wake of this conflict, the variety theater gained momentum as a more "respectable" alternative to the kind of rough, male-oriented entertainment situated in the concert saloons. This was the breech into which Tony Pastor jumped with his Opera House. Pastor's ability to build an image for himself as a purveyor of respectable entertainment while situated in the Bowery is a testament to his skill at negotiating the social and moral landscape of New York City. Some suggestion as to how he did this can be drawn from an advertisement he placed in the September 6, 1865, edition of the *New York Herald*, which appeared just over a month after he opened the theater. The ad announced the waging of an operatic war that pitted Pastor against Max Maretzek, a concert promoter whose career dated back to the 1840s and who had long been one of New York's leading proponents of high-class opera—indeed, Maretzek was even hired to restore programming at the Astor Place Opera House in the wake of the 1849 riot, without success.[27] At the time, Maretzek was preparing to embark on a new season of Italian opera at the Academy of Music, one of the city's more prominent venues for the continued promotion of music for expressly elite audiences. He also had recently declared a "war" of his own against the *Herald*, which he accused of extorting several thousand dollars in payment from concert managers—in the form of paid advertising—in order to draw positive critical attention in its pages.

Against this backdrop, Pastor's ad for his own Opera House is remarkable along several lines. For one thing, it revealed the opportunism with which Pastor was able to curry favor with one of the most influential newspaper editors in New York, the *Herald*'s James Gordon Bennett. Bennett's paper had been a vocal supporter of "people's" entertainment since the time of Jenny Lind and had championed the cause of the concert saloons against moral reformers, a stance at odds with that taken by more squarely middle-class publications such as the *New York Times* and the *Tribune*. Although Pastor positioned his Opera House as an alternative to the concert saloons, he also sought to appeal to the audiences that patronized such establishments, and the *Herald* was a key vehicle for doing so. Further indicating Pastor's motives was the rhetoric of the ad, which used imagery of a sort of cultural class war that was—intentionally or not—reminiscent of the conflict that had been at work in the Astor Place riot sixteen years earlier. According to the text of Pastor's ad, the "war" between Pastor and Maretzek was also a war between "THE PEOPLE'S OPERA" and "ITALIAN OPERA," involving "ARISTOCRACY, IRISHOCRACY, AND OILOCRACY" and "DEMOCRATS vs. SHODYCRATS."[28] Deploying such populist assertions with full force, Pastor then quoted an extensive, laudatory appraisal of his new Opera House that appeared in the *Clipper*, which suggested that Pastor's brand of entertainment, featuring "singing, dancing, gymnastic, minstrel and various other performances," suited the audience of the lower east side where his theater was located; whereas Maretzek "cannot look for much of this kind of patronage" and so had to rely on "his own set," whose fortunes were reduced by the end of the Civil War.

Pastor aligned himself here, at the start of his career as a theatrical impresario, with the will of a popular audience that was only at a slight remove from the world of the concert saloon, but he also made claims in another competing direction. The same ad stressed the strong moral character of his entertainment by emphasizing his Saturday afternoon matinees, at which ladies and children could safely enjoy the same program that the men of the Bowery patronized at night. That the matinees were considered a novelty and a critical selling point could be seen from the way that the ad concluded: with the notice that Pastor and his "mammoth troupe would APPEAR EVERY NIGHT, AND SATURDAY AFTERNOON"—the final three words repeated eleven times in succession. Here we might recall the notice for Louisville's Vaudeville Theater described above, in which matinees for women and children were similarly highlighted as a special attraction. The growing prevalence of matinees, which Pastor did much to cultivate, was a signal of a larger change that gave the theatrical turn to variety and then vaudeville such a transformative cast. Matinees were an essential means to draw more women to the theater because the social conventions of the time held that only women of ill repute would be seen in public during the evening. To draw women to the theater, in turn, required that the theater be perceived to possess qualities of character that would not tarnish a woman's reputation, whatever the time of day. As managers like Pastor tried to build a female constituency for their theaters, then, they also began to redefine the popular theater as a less rough and masculine, and more respectable, space.[29] In a sense they were following some of the same logic that led P.T. Barnum to invest so much effort in promoting Jenny Lind, but they did so in a way that proved to have a more enduring impact on the subsequent shape of American public life.

* * *

Pastor stayed in his Opera House at 201 Bowery for a decade. By the time he shifted the location of his theater from the Bowery to Broadway in October 1875, his stature—and that of variety entertainment more generally—had risen considerably. Just months earlier, in April, the New York *Morning Telegraph* observed the unique occasion of Pastor presenting his variety troupe at the Academy of Music, the same theater where Max Maretzek had planned a season of Italian opera in 1865, and a venue typically associated with a resolutely middle-class audience. Wrote the paper: "If any manager had sought to give a regular variety entertainment at the Academy of Music five or six years ago, he would have been deemed insane . . . But time, energy, and an elevated class of performers have subdued fashionable prejudice, and on the 20th Tony Pastor and his due company for the first time held undisputed possession of the Academy stage, to an overflowing house."[30] Meanwhile, Pastor's own theater had developed one of the most loyal and demonstrative followings to be found in the city, which according to a vivid account in the *New York Times*, contained a mix of Irish, American, and Italian boys in the cheap seats of the gallery, and an array of "mechanics and others" on the more expensive (but still moderately priced) parquet floor. A night of Italian opera at the Academy might cost $2 or more for admission, but at Pastor's Opera House one could gain entry to the gallery for twenty-five cents (fifteen for boys), while a seat on the parquet cost fifty or seventy-five cents.[31] These prices would remain in place when Pastor moved to his new location.

Pastor's move from 201 Bowery to 585-587 Broadway was, literally and figuratively, a move from the margins closer to (if not quite at) the center of New York's changing entertainment landscape. He took up what had previously been the Metropolitan Theater, a place dating back to the 1850s that had mainly housed minstrel shows. Pastor biographer Parker Zellers said of the new situation in which the enterprising manager found himself: "Pastor's house was in the middle of it all. Directly across the street was the Metropolitan Hotel and Niblo's Garden, a block south the elaborate white-marbled and once-modish St. Nicholas Hotel, and a block north the Grand Central Hotel."[32] Of more immediate concern, competing variety theaters the Theatre Comique, Olympic Theater, and the Globe were all within a couple of blocks. Yet this concentration of activity seemed to have served Pastor well. Moreover, while Broadway was hardly lacking in opportunities for iniquity, Pastor's location on such a central artery—and away from the Bowery—gave his claims of good moral character new credibility. Pastor quickly capitalized on the change of location by issuing a series of advertisements in the *New York Times*, where he called his new theater the "family theater of New York" in the weeks following its opening.[33]

At his Metropolitan Theater, Pastor first laid claim to the new term "vaudeville" as a way to differentiate his offerings from those of his competitors, a maneuver that contributed to the claims that he somehow "fathered" vaudeville.[34] However, his entertainment remained much as it had been for the past decade, featuring several acts over the course of a three-hour show presenting a diverse range of specialties. A comparison of two typical bills of performers appearing at Pastor's Opera House and his new Metropolitan Theater, respectively, can serve to illustrate the basic continuity in the content of his theater's offerings.

The first of these programs, dated April 3, 1871, opens with an overture by the resident orchestra—a standing feature of Pastor's theater from the beginning.[35] Next comes the first proper act of the bill, a series of character songs by the Female Minstrels, a comic singing troupe, followed in turn by a song and dance routine by James Cummings. At this point, Pastor makes his appearance, third on the bill, to offer his own set of comic songs. His turn is succeeded by a dance offering dubbed the "Grand Triple Clog Hornpipe," and then by what is described as an "Ethiopian Extravaganza"—contemporary parlance for a blackface minstrel act—titled, "A Squire for a Day." Ada Wray, having appeared earlier with the Female Minstrels, returns for a set of songs and banjo solos. After Wray come the Kincade Family "in a Grand Parlor Entertainment," and then a suggestively named act, "Golden Showers," by Johnny Wild and Frank Kerns. Two acts featuring Irish songs are to follow: Miss Marie Gorenflo presents what is described on the program as "Hibernian lilt"—presumably songs of a more melodic and sentimental variety—while Miles Morris offers "his famous Irish comic songs." Yet another blackface act, this time termed an "African Interlude," comes next, in the form of a parody of the Italian opera "Il Trovatore." A reprise of the Kincade Family and another overture by the orchestra precede the closing act, a theatrical afterpiece characterized as a "local drama" with the title, "The Segar Girl! or, Life in a Great City," in which several of the performers who appeared earlier in the bill also take part.

For opening night at his Metropolitan Theater, on October 4, 1875, Pastor's program also starts with an orchestral overture.[36] A comic sketch entitled, "The Wrong Man," follows; to be succeeded by a sister act—the Freeman Sisters, Lizzie and Susie—that appears in two short pieces, "The Flirt" and "On Board the Mary Jann." A pair named Venus and Adonis next demonstrate their physical feats on the velocipede (an early type of bicycle), and then Pastor comes out for his usual routine of songs and sketches. The Fieldings bring a mix of Irish comedy and song, while Miss Jennie Morgan offered popular songs and ballads of no particular ethnic association. "Ethiopian" (blackface) specialists Sanford and Wilson present an act called "The Troubadours" that features their musical "eccentricities." More physical attractions—this time in the form of gymnastics—attend the act of the Lenton Brothers; after which the main headliner of the bill (apart from Pastor), Gus Williams, appears. Williams specialized in "Dutch" songs, sayings, and stories, the term "Dutch" being the contemporary theatrical slang for a German characterization, and he was one of the bigger stars to be associated with Pastor's theater during the 1870s. His act is followed by further "eccentricities" of McKee and Rogers; William Carleton in yet more Irish-themed material; and Carrie and Chas. Austin, whom the program describes as "world-renowned Artistes" in the field of military exercises, such as the "Manual of Arms" and "Bayonet Combat," which they demonstrate on the stage. Then, to close the bill, another theatrical afterpiece, which by 1875 had become a customary climax to Pastor's shows: "The Dutchman on a Visit," which brings Gus Williams back to the stage in the role of "Gottholb Krousehorn."

Comparing these two Tony Pastor programs, offered more than four years apart at two different theaters, allows us to see how much the basic form of Pastor's variety theater had attained a kind of standard shape early in his career. Overtures and afterpieces gave a night at Pastor's theater a kind of narrative arc, a clearly designated beginning and end. In between, though, linear continuity was far from the main attraction. Building on the legacy of blackface minstrelsy, the variety theater emphasized spectacle over narrative, to use a distinction drawn by Eric Lott.[37] That spectacle might highlight any number of features: physical strength or agility, whether in the form of dance, gymnastics, or other sorts of bodily feats; spectacles of ethnic and racial difference, which occurred along a kind of continuum with Irish and "Ethiopian" attractions at either end and other kinds of ethnicities such as "Dutch" somewhere in between; and spectacles of gender difference in which women were particularly subject to display for their curious or alluring qualities, most evident in the appearance of the Female Minstrels of 1871, but also apparent in the appeal of sister acts like the Freeman Sisters and later, the Irwin Sisters—May and Flo—who would become among Pastor's most popular artists later in the decade. Compounding this mix of spectacular attractions was an emotional range that swung wildly between the sentimental and the comic from one part of the show to the next. Comedy was Pastor's primary stock in trade, but sentimental songs and sketches were a necessity for an effective variety program, and when mixed with the pull of a lilting woman's voice or the tug of ethnic nostalgia attached to Irish and blackface minstrel songs, served to heighten the affective charge of the material on display.

One phase of Pastor's programming represented a bit of a break with his own established conventions by the late 1870s and marked his effort to bring further distinction to his variety offerings. In 1878, W.S. Gilbert and Arthur Sullivan's breakthrough comic opera, *H.M.S. Pinafore*, first appeared in the US after its original British production. The popularity of the piece spread like wildfire, facilitated by the absence of clear copyright protection for foreign works produced in the US. Dozens of productions were staged in major and minor cities throughout the US, as American audiences responded to the work's mix of wit and social criticism, filtered through a musical style that was, in the words of musicologist Raymond Knapp, deceptively "natural" sounding.[38]

Pastor was just one of many who jumped on the *Pinafore* bandwagon, and he debuted his own parody of the Gilbert and Sullivan piece in March of 1879, titled "T.P.'s Canal Boat Pinafore." This style of comic opera, even done parodically, marked something of a departure for Pastor. Unlike the variety theater, light opera and musical comedy in the manner of Gilbert and Sullivan had dramatic coherence and consistency that made it more like the "legitimate" theater and opera of the time. By the account of the *New York Clipper*, Pastor—and playwright J.F. Poole, to whom the adaptation of *Pinafore* that appeared in Pastor's theater was credited—retained nearly all of the original words and music, and only took great liberties with the non-musical dialogue, a sign that Pastor's goal in presenting the work was not simply to make fun but also to infuse some of the legitimacy attached to the Gilbert and Sullivan work into his own theater.[39] A subsequent notice in the *Clipper* reinforced this impression: "Those who have the idea that 'H.M.S. Pinafore' is so broadly burlesqued as to lose its original character [at Tony Pastor's Theater] are agreeably surprised with a representation of the work which will bear favorable comparison with any we have had. One or two of the characters have been exaggerated in burlesque style, but it is done in a neat and effective way, and the others remain intact."[40] During the next three years Pastor staged two subsequent versions of Gilbert and Sullivan's comic operas, *The Pirates of*

Penzance and *Patience*, and they would provide a singular point of continuity as he moved from his Metropolitan Theater to his next location.

* * *

In 1881, after just six years, Pastor made yet another move—one that would prove to be his last, to a place on 14th Street between 3rd and 4th Avenues that had previously housed the Germania Theater. If Pastor had been "in the middle of it all" on Broadway, his new location was even more central to New York's commercial and cultural life of the time. For one thing, Pastor's 14th Street Theater was situated within the Tammany building, home to Tammany Hall, which was the locus of Democratic Party politics in New York City as well as a long-standing place of well-heeled masculine sociability. More generally, the Union Square district emerged in the 1870s and 1880s as a bustling shopping and entertainment district, and the area running along 14th Street came to be known as the Rialto. Here were located the Academy of Music, Steinway and Chickering Halls—New York's principal venues for classical music performance at the time—along with the Union Square Hotel and Theater and other prominent attractions.[41] A handbill that instructed theatergoers "How to Get to Tony Pastor's" indicates another key feature of the area: this stretch of 14 Street was accessible to a growing array of transportation options—specifically, horse cars and elevated railroad stations—that had developed in Manhattan and gave residents increased mobility to move throughout the city.[42]

An artist's rendering of Pastor's 14th Street Theater, shown in Figure 3.3, portrays the bustle and the gentility associated with it. Striking is the preponderance of signage: "Tony Pastor's," reads a large sign jutting out from the building, while above the entryway another sign—more on the order of a marquee—announces the full name, "Tony Pastor's New 14th Street Theater."[43] On the left, another sign reading "Tony Pastor's" appears above what looks like a ticket window. Away from the building and on curb beside the street, two frontage signs also have Pastor's name on them along with his picture, further identifying the theater with its namesake manager. To certify the visibility of these signs, a set of lights is affixed to each side of the theater's entrance, while a taller set of lights appears on either side of the stairs leading to the entry. Several streetlights also ensure that Pastor's theater will be on display for those denizens of the night who might be seeking an evening's entertainment. In the street itself is a horse car, presumably having deposited some theatergoers at their destination. The sidewalk in front of Pastor's

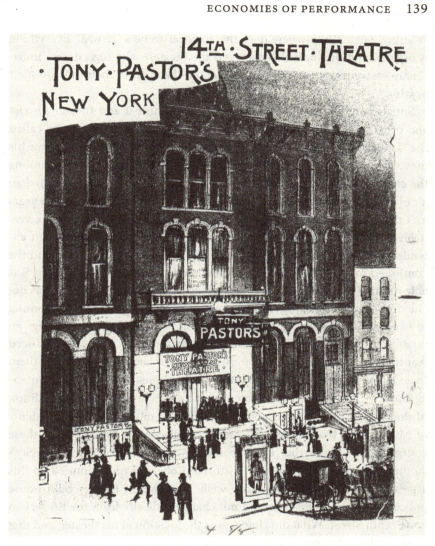

Figure 3.3 Tony Pastor's 14th Street Theater, opened in 1881, was the last and most famous of the succession of variety theaters under his ownership. Courtesy of the Billy Rose Theatre Division, The New York Public Library for the Performing Arts.

theater is full of life, and people: tellingly, many of those depicted are shown in pairs, whether women accompanied by men, or a child accompanied by an adult, reinforcing the long-standing characterization of Pastor's as a "family theater." A more concentrated gathering of people stands by the door, awaiting entry. Yet nowhere does there appear to be a "crowd." Everything is orderly, and the individuals around the theater—although drawn indistinctly—have a clear air of politeness about them, from their dress to their bearing.

Situated in New York City's most vibrant musical and theater district and proximate to the burgeoning shopping district that came to be called the "Ladies Mile," Pastor was well positioned on 14th Street to continue his move to make the variety theater a respectable and popular option among the city's leisure-going residents. Opening night at the new theater had an air of triumph about it and solidified the extent to which after sixteen years as a theatrical manager and performer, Pastor himself had become a veritable New York institution.[44] His matinee policy had long ago been extended to two afternoon shows a week, on Tuesday and Saturday; and the continued impression of the good character of patronage that Pastor was able to draw into his theater came through in an 1884 account: "It was decidedly a 'family' audience, a large number of ladies, many of them coming in twos and threes, without escort, showing that it is politic to manage an establishment of this description in such a manner that no gentleman need fear to bring his wife, sister or mother to 'see the show,' or even allow them to go by themselves. This state of affairs reflects great credit upon the management."[45] Pastor also perpetuated what had become his annual tradition of doing a string of spring appearances at the more highbrow Academy of Music. Now that his own theater was adjacent to the Academy these engagements only further underscored how far he had risen in the city's cultural firmament.[46] Vaudeville historian Robert Snyder summed up this aspect of Pastor's career trajectory well: "The core of Pastor's bills, house policies, ads, and philosophy did not change radically from the Bowery to Fourteenth Street. What did change was the location of his theater, and that made all the difference."[47]

Producing Novelty

Fourteenth Street, where Tony Pastor's new theater was located, would also become the first section of New York to be associated—retrospectively, it should be said—with the reorientation of popular music song production that came to be called Tin Pan Alley.[48] Musicologist Charles Hamm observes that the original location of Tin Pan Alley was in Union Square around East

Fourteenth Street, and further dates the origins of Tin Pan Alley to 1881 with the publication of the song, "Wait Till the Clouds Roll by," written by Charles Pratt and issued by the music publisher T.B. Harms.[49] The coincidence of the year 1881 with the opening of Pastor's 14th Street Theater is far from idle. Music publishers who contributed to the expansion of the market for popular song moved to the Union Square district for the same reasons as did Tony Pastor: because it offered the highest concentration of musical venues and institutions of any part of the city; and because it was a center of leisure, entertainment, and consumption in the evolving metropolis.

The most compelling direct evidence of the allure of the area from the music publishing side comes from Isidore Witmark's memoir of his career with M. Witmark and Sons, one of the most successful and enduring music publishing firms to be associated with Tin Pan Alley. Witmark and Sons began in the mid-1880s out of the Witmark household in the area now known as Hell's Kitchen, at 402 W. 40th Street near Ninth Avenue in New York. By 1888, Isidore and his brothers—Julius, Jay, Eddie, and Frank—determined that they were too far afield from the action. As Witmark and co-author Isaac Goldberg put it: "In 1888, the theatrical Rialto was on Fourteenth Street between Broadway and Fourth Avenue . . . A number of important considerations had convinced the Witmarks that they were too far from the center of operations . . . [so] they had made up their minds to move to 32 East Fourteenth Street."[50] This put them about two blocks from Pastor's Theater, which was at 143 East Fourteenth Street, on the opposite side of Union Square.

Why did it matter for a song publisher to be located near the heart of the city's theatrical life? Because in this era before sound recording had become dominant, selling songs required the promotional exposure offered by the public performance of musical works. The phonograph, it is worth noting, had been invented by the time Tin Pan Alley and Tony Pastor both set up shop on Fourteenth Street in New York. Thomas Edison produced his first working phonograph in 1877 and the device was presented to the American public through a series of news stories and public demonstrations, such as one that occurred at New York's Irving Hall in June 1878.[51] However, it would be more than a decade before the phonograph, and its competitor the gramophone, became anything approaching commonplace in American homes or in public spaces such as phonograph parlors; and only in the 1920s would sound recording truly begin to supplant sheet music as the prevailing commodity form of music.[52]

The transformation of the American music industry associated with Tin Pan Alley was driven by sheet music sales. We have seen in earlier chapters how the selling of published sheet music contributed to the construction of Jenny Lind as an iconic public figure whose image was also turned into a commodity; and how it helped to codify the songs performed by the Fisk Jubilee Singers into a recognized genre called the spiritual. The example of Lind is most germane to the practices of Tin Pan Alley music publishers, for whom the production of popular song became tethered to the production of celebrity. Ultimately, the way to sell the most copies of a given song in sheet music form was to persuade the greatest number of potential music buyers that this was a song they wanted to hear repeatedly, which meant that it was a song they would play, and sing, for themselves. Private, domestic consumption of sheet music was the primary source of profit for music publishers, connected to the growth of the market for musical instruments, most notably the piano but with string instruments like the guitar, banjo, and mandolin also assuming more currency toward century's end.[53] To sell sheet music in sufficient quantities to bring the profits they desired, publishers could not rely on something so ambiguous and unreliable as the "taste" of the public. A song's value had to be asserted, and demonstrated, over and over, preferably by a performer of demonstrated popularity. This emphasis on the "hard sell," and corresponding use of modern techniques of sales and promotion, made Tin Pan Alley so transformative in the history of the American music business; and it was in the variety—or vaudeville—theaters of the 1880s and 1890s that many of these techniques were refined and put to use.[54]

Where the theatrical promotion of popular song was concerned, the most prevalent practice was that of "plugging" a song. Song plugging happened when a music publisher took deliberate steps to ensure that one of its songs would be put before the public in a performance setting. Often this involved arranging with a particular performing artist that the song would feature in her act, usually with the promise that the song would help to "make" the artist's act just as the artist could help to "make" the song a hit. Star artists had important working relationships with music publishers based on these sorts of arrangements, while striving performers could be sold on a song as a vehicle to move further up the ladder of success. There also came to exist a class of quasi-performers who were called "pluggers," and whose job it was to go into any place where music was being performed and get the song they were promoting heard in some fashion—if not by singing it on the stage, then by singing it from the audience. As the pioneering songwriter and music publisher Charles K. Harris put it: "A new song must be sung, played, hummed, and drummed into the ears of the public, not in one city alone, but in every city, town and village, before it ever becomes popular."[55]

Among publishers seeking to plug their songs, Tony Pastor's 14th Street Theater loomed large. This remained true well into the 1890s and early 1900s, after B.F. Keith and other theatrical impresarios had encroached upon Pastor's territory and posed a challenge to his success. Harris, in his autobiography, recalled that in 1898, "Fourteenth Street was then the Mecca of the song pluggers as well as the publishers. As soon as the lamps were lit, the pluggers would cluster around Tony Pastor's, that being their headquarters, where . . . all the singers could usually be found."[56] Music publisher Edward Marks also colorfully paid tribute to Pastor's theater as the place where songs could be made into hits. For Marks, writing about the mid-1890s, Pastor's existed at the top of a sort of food chain of theaters that had at its bottom the kinds of "low dives" that had been subject to the zeal of reformers since the time of the Civil War.[57] Starting in saloons and beer halls, a song might work its way up to Pastor's, which was set apart by its reputation for entertainment that was of high quality and inoffensive moral content. When Marks scored his first successful plug at Pastor's theater, placing the song "Little Lost Child," with the singer Lottie Gilson, his own career in music publishing took a huge step forward.

Reflecting back, Marks observed that what made Pastor's theater such an effective vehicle for song promotion was the peculiar relationship that Pastor and his theater had with its audience. Whereas big-time vaudeville came to be defined by wide-ranging national circuits, theaters like Tony Pastor's remained unique, singular locations: "Variety had been a matter of individual houses. Miner's, Pastor's, Koster and Bial's made up their bills from week to week, dealing directly with the entertainers who played pool and drank beer in the neighborhood. Each proprietor formed a public which had faith in his taste."[58] Perhaps the most trusted theater manager in New York, if not the whole US, Pastor's reputation could be used to bolster the effectiveness of a song plug, just as it could put the stamp of success on given vaudeville act.

* * *

To construe Pastor's role in promoting popular songs as essentially supportive, a service he provided to music publishers, is to misunderstand the historical relationship that existed between variety—and vaudeville—theater and Tin Pan Alley. By the 1890s, it is fair to say, music publishers were setting much of the agenda for these transactions as the business of producing and selling popular songs assumed a new aggressiveness. Before that point though, it was the theater owners like Pastor who had greater influence and more of a controlling interest in featuring new songs. Here I would return to a point I made at the outset of this chapter: from the start of his career as manager Pastor worked to inject his productions with an air of novelty. This could be seen in the mix of stock and rotating cast members that he featured from week to week, the continual pursuit of new personalities to put on stage—many of whom were increasingly drawn from the British music hall and French cabaret from the 1880s forward—and his consistent production of new afterpieces. Most importantly in connection with the history of popular music, this feature of Pastor's programming aesthetic could be seen in the regular turnover of new songs that appeared in his house from week to week, and that was especially apparent during his own turns as one of the leading comic vocalists of his day. Writing of the advent of Tin Pan Alley, David Suisman has observed that producers of popular music in the 1880s and 1890s "had to promote a steady taste for the new among consumers" to create a market for popular song that would remain reliably profitable.[59] Although Pastor never embraced the economies of scale that drove the parallel expansion of Tin Pan Alley and vaudeville, in his use of popular song he anticipated the preference for the novel over the familiar that would be integral to the modern music industry's rise.

Pastor's specialization in the rendering of topical songs has already been noted. Some of these songs had an expressly political cast. Pastor was an avid and virulent supporter of the Union cause during the Civil War, for instance, and singing selections such as "The Union Volunteers," "The March of the Union," and "Uncle Sam is for the Union, and out Against Disunion" —all included in Pastor's *New Union Song Book*, one of several such collections he issued during the early years of his career—contributed significantly to his stature as one of New York's most popular comic vocalists.[60] We should not interpret Pastor as some sort of precursor to Bob Dylan with his concern for topicality, though. Something of the range and character of his musical material can be gathered from the title page of *Tony Pastor's Complete Budget of Comic Songs*, which lists among its contents, "Original Local Lays, Eccentric Lyrics, Comic Songs, Humorous Irish Ballads, Patriotic Vocal Gems, Stump Speeches, and Burlesque Orations." The variety of categories mimics, in a sense, that of the variety theater more broadly. More to the point, a topical song could be about almost anything. Any topic, subject or issue that had an air of currency was fair game, as long as it was something that Pastor thought would resonate with the audience that attended his theater.

"Of novelty this is the age/It matters not what it is." So sang Pastor in the opening lines of a song, "The Carte de Visite Album," that he featured in 1865, the same year that he opened his opera house at 201 Bowery.[61] The song presents a blueprint for the sort of novel effect he pursued in his topical songs. Cartes de visite were small commercial photographs that circulated widely during the Civil War, such that there was contemporary talk of "cartomania."[62] Many of the images distributed as cartes de visite were directly connected to the war—pictures of soldiers, of Lincoln and other political and military leaders, and even pictures of slaves. Also well represented were figures from the world of art and entertainment whereby cartes de visites contributed to the further cultivation of celebrity in the mid-nineteenth-century US. Collecting cartes de visites became a popular pastime and, according to historian of photography Andrea Volpe, the first widespread use of photo albums grew in order to contain them. Singing a song about cartes de visites, then, Tony Pastor was commenting on a distinctly timely topic. Furthermore, the song's subject allowed him to integrate a wide range of political and cultural references into his act. Singing about an album of such images, he identifies a range of current notable persons by name, including actors like Edwin Forrest and Adah Menken, authors like Harriet Beecher Stowe, and newspapermen like Horace Greeley. The last verses of the song turn more toward the war, and Pastor the patriotic Union supporter closes the song with an image of General Sherman exercising the nation's will: "For mighty soon our nation's space/He'll free from rebel thralldom/And traitors then shall have no place/In Uncle Sam's big album."[63]

Also revealing are the few details about the song's creation we are able to know from its published form. "The Carte de Visite Album" is not attributed to Pastor—rather the credit reads, "written *for* Tony Pastor" (emphasis added), with no other attribution, and this in itself carries an important connotation: Pastor was not the author of all, or even most of the songs that he sang, but his multiple roles as manager, theater owner, and performer gave him claim to a peculiar sort of authorship rooted in his power to commission songs. Another key detail appears at the head of the song, with a similar implication: the melody is based on that of another song, "Chanting Beauty." Again, this quality was typical. The lyrics he sang were original, if not written by him then written for him; the melodic content was almost always borrowed from some other source. This might seem to work against the aura of novelty, or originality, that Pastor worked to project; but in another way the very referential character of Pastor's songs accented the novelty of the material by drawing upon music that was recognizable to his audiences but singing these familiar tunes with a clear difference from their original intent.

More illuminating evidence of Pastor's work as a commissioner of songs comes from the letters that Pastor exchanged with professional songwriters. Two personal letters, dated 1889 and 1892, respectively, find the songwriters Felix McGlennon and Matt Woodward granting Pastor exclusive US right to sing their songs in exchange for payment. The first, from McGlennon, reads:

> Memorandum that I Felix McGlennon of 69 Dale St. [illegible] Manchester England have in consideration of the sum of four pounds two shillings and one penny (£4-2-1) receipt of which I hereby acknowledge assigned to Tony Pastor Esq. the sole & exclusive copyright or right of public performance in the United States of America of two dramatic pieces & words of songs written by me & two musical compositions composed by me entitled "Darlings" and "In the Streets of New York Town."[64]

The second letter, by Woodward, announces:

> In consideration of the sum of $25 (Twenty five dollars) to me in hand paid, I do hereby give to Mr. Antonio Pastor the sole and exclusive right to sing my song entitled "She was a simple Country Girl" in the United States, Canada, Great Britain, and Ireland, until November 1st 1892, when I am permitted to publish said song for my own behoof.[65]

These letters show clearly that Pastor's decision to feature certain songs did not just arise from the lobbying efforts of music publishers. Pastor exercised much direct say over the songs that appeared in his theater into the 1890s, when the influence of music publishers was beginning to grow. That he required exclusive right of performance, even to the extent of preventing a song's author—Woodward—from publishing his song on his own behalf makes it clear that for Pastor, the value of a song mattered most for how it fit into a night's entertainment, not whether it would sell to the public as a separate commodity.

Perhaps the most intriguing such document is an 1876 letter written to Pastor by I.F. Farrar of Leeds, England. It is clearly part of an ongoing exchange between the two, and the amount of detail it conveys makes it worth quoting at length:

> Your favour of the 31st duly to hand and many thanks. The terms you name £1-0-0 for every song suiting you will do quite well for us. All songs we send not suiting you if you could sell for us we will allow 5/- to every £1-5-0. Thus if you sell a song for us you charge £1-5-0 keep the five shillings yourself and send the £1-0-0 on to us. I enclose a song entitled "Maw is only Maw" with new and original idea and music. I sent you a song in my last entitled "I could tell it if I felt it in the dark." Kindly say if you like in your next. If you would like a topical song we can send you one entitled "The Doings of the Present Day." Touching on the Philadelphia Exhibition, Captain Boyton, The President, and any other topics you would like specially putting in the song if you describe them we can put them in. Trusting to hear from you soon.[66]

Accompanying this letter was an extensive list of other song titles made available by Farrar, described by song type, and the further promise of "upwards of 150 comic, characteristic, Ladies Serio Comic, Topical, Serio Topical, Motto, Low Comedy, Burlesques, Duetts," and other varieties.

The interconnections between songwriting and song publishing and theatrical presentations of music have long been recognized, but rarely have they been captured so precisely as they are in this transaction. Historians of the music business like David Suisman and Charles Hamm have rightly granted considerable credit to the enterprising song publishers who made the selling of songs into big business, from Charles K. Harris to Isidore Witmark to Harry von Tilzer. Pastor's efforts suggest that, immediately prior to the moment when the market for sheet music truly began to grow, entrepreneurial variety managers not only gave new songs a hearing but stimulated their production in ways that have not been fully understood. Audiences attending Pastor's theater came to expect that Pastor would feature a new "budget" of songs on each week's program, and that the other singing artists who appeared with his company would be similarly outfitted with new material. Often, Pastor's audiences were encouraged to take these songs home with them. In 1862, early in his career as a comic singer at the American theater on Broadway, Pastor published nine song collections—or songsters—assembled from the material he sang onstage, sold for ten cents each.[67] He continued this output throughout the early years of his career as a theater manager, and while his production of songsters diminished over time, souvenir booklets containing a small sample of songs associated with Pastor remained available throughout his career. The 1892 song pamphlet, *Tony Pastor's Music Box*, was one such item available for purchase at his 14th Street Theater, that featured several songs composed by Felix McGlennon and others as sung by Pastor (for only one of which does Pastor receive songwriting credit).[68]

Pastor did not get into the business of publishing songs, just as he did not become the proprietor of a national circuit of theaters—that was left to the likes of Benjamin F. Keith and Edward Albee, whose 1893 acquisition of the lease to the Union Square Theater, across the street from Pastor's, was a milestone in the transition from variety to vaudeville. Although Pastor toured the US with his troupe and hired a wealth of international performers to appear at his theaters, his efforts remained concentrated on New York City and the succession of theaters he managed there. Within those theaters, he effected a significant realignment concerning the performance of popular song in the context of theatrical entertainment.

The setting of Pastor's theater ultimately gave these songs their punch. How Pastor's musical offerings were converted into theatrical currency was evocatively portrayed in an 1875 *New York Times* account, from Pastor's last days at his Bowery opera house. No act drew the allegiance of the theatergoers as much as Pastor's own, and by the account of the *Times*, Pastor's true talent lay in using song to move the crowd toward participation:

> Mr. Pastor then came on the stage and sang three songs. Before beginning the last one he announced that the chorus would be given with great effect, as he observed an unusual number of "the gang" present. The song was, "You'll never miss the water till the well runs dry." At the conclusion of the first verse the boys in the gallery faintly joined in the chorus. Mr. Pastor remarked they would do better next time, as they were merely getting their voices in tune. The next chorus was sung considerably louder and tolerably well. Mr. Pastor said that people might talk of the Italian opera, the German opera, and the opera buffers, but they were not "a marker" to the Bowery buffers. For this graceful compliment to their vocal abilities, Mr. Pastor was loudly applauded by the boot-blacks in the gallery. The boys became very excited, and the chorus of the last verse was given with enthusiastic vim and

genuine vigor. Mr. Pastor signified his approval by saying that it was "solid," and bowed his way off into the wings, smiling contentedly.[69]

Surely there is salesmanship going on—pitching his songs, Pastor also sold himself as the most consistent and reliable presence in an otherwise rotating cast of attractions that appeared at his theater week after week, and year after year. Yet the entrepreneurialism on display should not deafen us to Pastor's skill at navigating the complex and changing interconnections between musical taste and preference and social and economic class after the Civil War. At a time when classical music was being defined as something of proven worth and enduring value, Pastor committed himself to an ethos of novelty and immediacy that left its imprint on the performance and production of popular song.

Circulating the "Coon Song"

Pastor's theater continued to run, with greater or lesser degrees of success, throughout the 1890s and until his death in 1908. Yet the theatrical and musical tides changed significantly as the 1890s progressed. Vaudeville grew further into a fully nationalized phenomenon in ways that left a manager like Pastor, whose career was largely staked on the success of a single theater, at a disadvantage. The market for printed popular songs exploded with the 1892 publication of Charles K. Harris' "After the Ball," which was reputed to have sold two million copies or more by some accounts, setting a new bar for success. Meanwhile, newer stage and song styles arose that displaced some older popular offerings. These changes prompted Maggie Cline, an Irish songstress whose career dated back to the late 1870s, to bemoan her own current lack of work in an 1897 interview. Cline had been a regular feature at Tony Pastor's 14th Street Theater since the early 1880s, enjoying her greatest success with the 1890 song, "Throw Him Down, McCloskey." Now, seven years later, Cline complained:

> I'll tell you why I'm not working. The variety public has degenerated. They've become May Irwinized and Fay Templetonized. They've lost their appreciation of good, old, honest Irish songs. This craze for nigger songs has become a regular black plague. They've thrown down McClusky [sic] in

favor of "All Coons Look Alike to Me" and "I Want You, My Honey." It ain't right, and I don't like it.[70]

Among those subject to Cline's condemnation was a fellow alumna of Tony Pastor's theater, May Irwin. First gaining notice in the 1870s as part of an act with her sister Flo, by the 1890s May Irwin had become one of the earliest and most celebrated of a peculiar sort of female singer then in vogue: the coon shouter. A large woman with a physically imposing stage presence, Irwin was among a group of female vaudeville artists who turned the medium's push for "respectable" entertainment on its head. For some this involved regular appearance in male drag; indeed, this had become a specialty of Irwin's sister Flo.[71] May Irwin's own stage persona often had an air of masculine swagger about it, but she was more renowned in the 1890s for the brash character of her racial impersonations. In the words of vaudeville historian Alison Kibler, Irwin and other "coon shouters" such as Fay Templeton used "racial masquerade to create or augment an unconventional appearance that then became the currency of their comedy."[72] Although her act was a clear outgrowth of the legacy of blackface performance, Irwin did not typically blacken her face on stage. The racially coded qualities of her approach came through in her movements, her use of dialect speech, and in the content of the songs she sang, which constituted a new category, the "coon song." And no coon song had as much impact as one cited by Cline and associated with Irwin, "All Coons Look Alike to Me," with words and music by the African American songwriter and performer Ernest Hogan.

The August 30, 1896 edition of the *Kansas City Star* reported that, "Ernest Hogan, composer of 'Pas Ma-La,' [sic] has written a new song for May Irwin entitled 'All Coons Look Alike to Me.' Miss Irwin expects it to be a great go."[73] By October of that same year, the African American newspaper, the *Indianapolis Freeman*, announced: "A decided success is assured of Hogan's latest song, entitled: 'All Coons Look Alike to Me.'"[74] "All Coons Look Alike to Me" became one of the biggest song hits of the 1890s, the success of which was one sign that the business of popular song production was coming of age. The song also stands as testimony that popular song of the 1890s remained shaped by an unsettling mix of racial desire and disdain toward African Americans. Through "All Coons Look Alike to Me" and other similar songs, the racism that ran through the history of American popular music since the advent of blackface minstrelsy assumed a distinct modern form.[75]

Figure 3.4 Ernest Hogan in a characteristically comedic pose. Courtesy of the Billy Rose Theatre Division, The New York Public Library for the Performing Arts.

Ernest Hogan (see Figure 3.4), the composer of "All Coons Look Alike to Me," was one of the most successful black songwriters and performers of the years surrounding the turn of the twentieth century. "All Coons Look Alike" was the follow-up to his earlier hit, "Pas Ma La," discussed at the beginning of the chapter. The two songs, issued a year apart, opened many professional doors for Hogan that may otherwise have remained locked; and "All Coons Look Alike to Me" especially became his calling card, with which he would remain identified for the remainder of his career, which was cut short by his death from tuberculosis in 1909. However, the song also became something of a burden for Hogan as it quickly was made to stand for the unremitting racism of the era's popular culture. Confounded by the contradictions involved in the fact that one of the most seemingly racist artifacts of early Tin Pan Alley was crafted by an African American songwriter, until recently historians have not given Hogan his due. While his contemporary, Bert

Williams, has undergone a kind of canonization as the key African American artist that managed to subtly subvert the racism of his day, Hogan is still commonly seen as a figure who cooperated with the era's racism more than he undermined it, who pursued professional success at the expense of his own dignity.[76]

Seeking to redress the extent to which Hogan's career has gone largely unexamined, Lynn Abbott and Doug Seroff assign him especial importance in their reconstruction of black popular music in the pre-jazz and blues era, arguing that "there is particular need to reassert Ernest Hogan's place in the pantheon" of influential African American artists.[77] To do so is to recognize that Hogan's achievements cannot be reduced to one infamous song, and to acknowledge that his work as a songwriter cannot be removed from his work as a performer. In a way that parallels the efforts of Tony Pastor, Hogan stands out for his combination of songwriting with other professional pursuits. At a time when the production of popular song was becoming increasingly rationalized—when publishing houses kept songwriters on staff whose business was precisely to craft new songs for sale, which would then be "sold" to performers who would help sell the songs to the public—Hogan stepped onto the stage to sing material of his own creation, along with that composed by others. A study of Hogan's dual career as songwriter and performer offers another distinct perspective on how popular songs entered the field of theatrical entertainment during a time when both Tin Pan Alley and vaudeville were coming into their own, and when black artists faced new opportunities in the entertainment field that brought the prospect of risk and reward in roughly equal measure.

"All Coons Look Alike to Me" remains essential to Hogan's story precisely for the way it signified the risks and rewards that Hogan faced as a black artist of his time. I am less concerned with the song itself than with its reception, and with the various ways in which it appeared before the public. If, as Charles K. Harris observed above, the key to making a song a hit was to ensure that it be heard as widely as possible, then "All Coons Look Alike to Me" can serve as a valuable case study of that process. The questions that I have, in a sense, are basic: Where was the song performed and by whom? Under what circumstances was it most likely to be discussed or invoked by contemporary observers? By concentrating not on the song text of "All Coons Look Alike to Me" but on its circulation, we can better understand the impact it had on the musical practices of its time and the role it played in Hogan's own rising profile as a leading black entertainer of his day. More than that, we can understand how a particular song became subject to public contests over race and representation in which black artists like Hogan figured prominently.

* * *

At the time that Hogan published "All Coons Look Alike to Me," he was touring with a company called the Georgia Graduates, an all-black road show that purveyed a sort of latter-day minstrelsy built around song, dance, and comedy. Hogan, like almost all African American comic performers of the time, would have appeared in the show in blackface, and he already had a growing reputation as one of the best comic singers among black variety artists. The Graduates were one of several similar units that proliferated in the 1890s and 1900s as African American performing artists began to enter the field of professional theatrical work in unprecedented numbers. This trend had been growing since the 1865 founding of the Georgia Minstrels, to which the name of the Georgia Graduates paid tribute.[78] The other half of the troupe's name, though, was an effort to capitalize on the success of the more genteel ensembles such as the Fisk Jubilee Singers and the comparable singing troupes that had come out of the Tuskegee and Hampton Institutes that, as we saw in the last chapter, broke critical new ground in the public performance of African American music. For the Georgia Graduates, as for many similar organizations, the suggested association with an institution of higher learning was completely fabricated, but it was a sign that in black vaudeville as in vaudeville more generally, the appearance of respectability was a crucial selling point.

Hogan issued his first songwriting success, "Pas Mas Las," with a regional music publisher in Kansas City, J.R. Bell. With "All Coons Look Alike to Me," he attracted the support of Witmark and Sons in New York, which gave the song the broader promotional support needed to make it a hit on a national scale. Witmark and Sons' willingness to publish Hogan's song was likely the result of several factors: Hogan's rising profile as a performer and songwriter; the successful pitch of the song to an already established star such as May Irwin; and not least, the deep interest of the Witmark firm in upholding and perpetuating blackface minstrelsy as a performance tradition. In Isidore Witmark's memoir, the author and his collaborator Isaac Goldberg assert: "Minstrelsy was on Isidore's part an obsession which became an integral part of the firm's activities."[79] The House of Witmark supplemented its regular song-publishing endeavors with material meant to appeal to amateur performers who wanted to stage their own minstrel shows, including a mail order service. As late as 1939, when Witmark's book was published, he and Goldberg saw fit to observe hopefully, "it is not without the bounds of reason that the minstrel show, in altered form, will return."[80] Publishing Hogan's modern "coon song" in 1896, then, was part of a larger commitment on the part of Witmark and Sons to reproducing and updating the logic of the established minstrel show.

These trappings of minstrelsy are fully evident on the cover for the main sheet music edition of "All Coons Look Alike to Me." Hogan's name appears prominently on the cover page as the song's writer and composer, and he is also characterized as the "composer of the famous 'Pas-Ma-La' [sic.]." When one considers the history of the music industry and the routine ways in which African American artists were exploited well into the rock 'n' roll era, this clear attribution of authorship is no small thing. Yet it is nearly undone by the surrounding imagery, which portrays a row of black male suitors all vying for the attention of a single black woman on the right of the page. All the figures have absurdly exaggerated features, most prominently bright red, oversized lips that protrude markedly from their black faces. That the various figures all are dressed in a sort of parody of high-fashion clothing, with top hats and tuxedos on the men and a well-fitted dress with billowing sleeves on the woman, only adds to the aura of racial caricature, evoking the dandy figures that had been common in minstrelsy since the 1830s. This in a sense was the cost of doing business for an African American artist as ambitious and entrepreneurial as Ernest Hogan: to gain a mass audience was to subject oneself to the perpetuation of debilitating stereotypes.

As a musical work, "All Coons Look Alike to Me" addressed a thoroughly conventional subject for popular song. Hogan's protagonist is a man bemoaning the fact that the woman he loves has lost her interest in him and turned her attention to another man. Because it is a comic song, Hogan does not treat this subject matter with much sentimentality. Any pathos in the lyric exists to further heighten the satirical intent, which concentrates primarily on the greed and acquisitiveness of his female love object. The other man in this scenario is a "leader" in society and, most importantly, "he spends his money free"; social and economic status therefore becomes the source of the singer's anxiety and the cause of his sorrows. When his paramour says to him, "All Coons Look Alike to Me," it is her way of letting him know that she has moved on, and for her purposes one black man is as good as the next—and one who has more money to spend on her is better. On this point, however, the contradictions of Hogan's song come into focus; because however innocent the song's title phrase may have been within the context of its narrative and chorus, it had a much different and almost unmistakable connotation when considered and heard on its own. African American writer and social critic James Weldon Johnson put the matter succinctly in his 1930 survey of *Black Manhattan*: "The melody of the song was beautiful and the words quite innocuous, but the title became a byword and an epithet of derision."[81] More than the song itself, that title phrase circulated widely and permissively through *fin de siècle* American culture, serving as a lightning rod for racial conflict and a carnival mirror in which the warped character of the country's race relations was reflected and distorted.

One further detail of the published song deserves consideration: the final page offers a "choice chorus" featuring "Negro 'Rag' accompaniment," arranged by Max Hoffman, a staff musical arranger with Witmark and Sons.[82] According to ragtime historians David Jasen and Gene Jones, the song in its published form marked "the first use of the word 'rag' on a song sheet"—Scott Joplin's pivotal "Maple Leaf Rag" was still three years away.[83] How this feature of the song may have affected the way in which it was performed by Hogan and others is nearly impossible to discern. Unlike his counterpart Bert Williams, Hogan left no sound recordings of his own. The two earliest and best-known recordings of Hogan's song that do exist, by George Gaskin in 1896 and Arthur Collins accompanied by banjoist Vess Ossman in 1902 (all white artists) suggest two very different ways of approaching the song. Gaskin sings the song much more "straight," with little exaggeration of vocal effect and little of the heightened sense of syncopation that we might expect from a song attached to the genre of ragtime; and the same can be said about the rather unembellished piano performance that accompanies him. Collins, on the other hand, injects much more energy into his vocal performance, a byproduct of his also pushing the racial caricature suggested by the song's title to an extreme. What most stands out from this latter recording, though, is the sheer virtuosity of Vess Ossman's banjo performance, which moves through rapid and clearly picked arpeggios with a sure hand and a pronounced, syncopated rhythmic attack. Chances are that, instrumentation aside, Hogan's performances at the time of the song's publication in 1896 would have more closely approximated the Gaskin record, but that is an educated guess at best. What is sure is that, between the "rag" designation of "All Coons Look Alike to Me" and the grounding of his earlier song, "Pas Mas La," in an emerging dance culture situated in the state of Kansas in the mid-1890s,

Ernest Hogan contributed significantly to the music that became ragtime, including the extent to which ragtime would be associated in the public imagination with a strong tendency toward racial derogation.

* * *

Witmark may have relied on the popularity of May Irwin—and to a lesser extent, of Hogan himself—to help promote "All Coons Look Alike to Me" to a wider public. Yet the true mark of a song's success was not its association with a single artist but the breadth of occasions in which it would have been performed. We have already seen that, in this age before sound recordings were a dominant medium, songs circulated via performance. Newspaper accounts offer evidence of "All Coons Look Alike to Me" in a range of distinct settings that attest to the song's multifaceted appeal.

Surveying the range of documented performances listed in Table 3.1, certain patterns come to light. First, one might note the geographic range represented by this list of renditions. Urban centers such as New York, Los Angeles, Washington, DC, and Chicago are joined by more provincial locations like Kalamazoo, Michigan, Helena, Montana, and Aberdeen, South Dakota. One gets a sense, then, of the truly national character of the song's reach. This geographic breadth corresponds loosely with a division between professional and amateur performance. Several of the performances listed here—by Clarice Vance, Anna Held, Paola del Monte, Fannie Fields, Billy McClain, and Albert Bailey—occurred in the context of professional vaudeville, the realm also inhabited by May Irwin and by Hogan himself. Among these artists, Vance warrants notice for having been, along with Irwin, one of the earliest female artists to be classified as a "coon shouter."[84] Billie McClain and Albert Bailey, on the other hand, were African American vaudeville artists whose position was very much akin to that of Hogan. Then there are the four separate amateur performances about which I have found evidence, all of which, significantly, are minstrel shows. While the dedicated minstrel show was becoming passé as a feature of the professional theater by the late 1890s, its persistence among amateur troupes provided a ready audience for Hogan's song but also likely invested the song with the most retrogressive kind of significance as a vehicle for reproducing stereotyped portrayals of blackness. This was the audience for which Witmark and Sons was producing its mail order kits and other materials designed to help amateur minstrels stage productions of their own. Given the recurrence of Hogan's song in these settings, we might assume that Witmark was promoting "All

Table 3.1 Performances of "All Coons Look Alike to Me," 1897–1898 (excluding performances by Ernest Hogan himself)

Performer	Theatrical Company and Location	Date	Performance Type
Clarice Vance	Kernan's Lyceum, Washington, DC	February 1897	Professional—vaudeville
I.T. Long	YMCA Minstrel Show, Cleveland, OH	February 1897	Amateur—minstrel show
Anna Held	Great Northern Theater, Chicago, IL	April 1897	Professional—vaudeville
Meine's Orchestra	Westlake Park, Los Angeles, CA	July 1897	Professional—brass band
R. Rau	Native Sons Minstrel Show, Catalina Island, CA	September 1897	Amateur—minstrel show
Paola del Monte	Koster and Bial's, New York City	October 1897	Professional—vaudeville
Fannie Fields (singing in German)	Kalamazoo, MI	November 1897	Professional—vaudeville
Billy McClain (singing in German)	Darkest America company (various locations)	November 1897	Professional—vaudeville
Hungarian Boys' Military Band	Orpheum Theater, Los Angeles, CA	November 1897	Professional—brass band
Albert Bailey	Washburn's Double Minstrels (location unspecified)	December 1897	Professional—vaudeville
Master Hanna	Ming's Opera House, Helena, MT	January 1898	Amateur—minstrel show
Miss Maggie Arntz	Black Belles of Coontown, Aberdeen, SD	February 1898	Amateur—minstrel show

Coons Look Alike to Me" to these same customers as something that could appear as a special feature in their shows.

Maybe the most curious detail in the above table is that two separate performances of Hogan's song were sung in German, one by a white female artist (Fannie Fields) and one by a black male (Billy McClain). Without any further detail about either performance the significance of this gesture is hard to discern. This could have been a way to blend and combine different registers of ethnic mimicry. Ethnic impersonation in vaudeville was hardly limited to that concerning African Americans and, at a time when audiences were ready to laugh at any sign of ethnic or racial difference, the comic effect could well have been compounded if incongruous elements were put together in clever ways. Yet the racial gap between the two "German" renditions of "All Coons Look Alike to Me," and the fact that the two performances were reported during the same month (November 1897), suggests another possibility: that McClain's performance was meant to be a parody of the white singer, Fields. If that were the case, it would begin to suggest how even the most seemingly racist of popular songs could be made to signify something quite different when performed on the stage.

The mutability of "All Coons Look Alike to Me" as a stage vehicle is all the more apparent when considering several alternate versions of the song that emerged within a couple years of its initial publication, compiled in Table 3.2.[85] Here again, we see evidence of the way that racial humor assumed many forms in late nineteenth-century vaudeville, and that a certain strain of ethnic comedy played upon the suggestion of switching one racial category for another. "All Cohens Look Alike to Me," "All Chinks Look Alike to Me," and "All Spaniards Look Alike to Me" represent distinct realms of ethnic

Table 3.2 Alternate versions of "All Coons Look Alike to Me"

Performer	Song Title	Theatrical Company and Location	Date
Frank Finney	"All Cohens Look Alike to Me"	Casino Theater, Anaconda, MT	March 1898
Nat Lucas	"White Folks Every Coon You Meet Don't Look Alike"	Unspecified	April 1898
Unspecified	"All Chinks Look Alike to Me"	*A Trip to Coontown* (location unspecified)	April 1898
Billy Miller	"All Spaniards Look Alike to Me"	Oliver Scott Refined Negro Minstrels (location unspecified)	July 1898
Howard Morton	"White Folks All Coons Don't Look Alike to Me"	Unspecified	October 1898
Chas. Williams	"All Colored Folk Look Like Little Black Gnat to Me"	Belford and Stanley Concert Co. (location unspecified)	November 1898

and racially based performance that were part of the era's theatrical entertainment—the latter may be the most improbable until one recalls that the Spanish-American War was raging at the time. All these iterations of Hogan's song presumably revel in the notion that the same basic joke could be translated into any setting in which race and ethnicity were the focus of attention. As such, they reveal the broader contours of a cultural moment in which racial difference was subjected to various types of intensified scrutiny, of which satire was one prominent way of both coming to terms with difference and keeping it at a safe distance.

That five out of six of these alternate versions of Hogan's song were done by African Americans and reported in the black newspaper, the *Indianapolis Freeman*—the exception is Frank Finney—draws attention to another significant trend: "All Coons Look Alike to Me" did not circulate as an unchallenged statement of racial objectification but generated a substantial response through which the meaning of the song was contested and often subverted. Clearly the most pointed titles along these lines are "White Folks Every Coon You Meet Don't Look Alike" and "White Folks All Coons Don't Look Alike to Me." The addition of "white folks" to these song titles gives them an almost confrontational cast, as if recognizing that the real issue at hand is not the words of a black songwriter but the racist perceptions of white people that Hogan's words might affirm. Then there is "All Colored Folk Look Like Little Black Gnat to Me," which offers no apparent critique of Hogan's song but instead parodies it through exaggeration. What resounds most strongly through these various re-workings of "All Coons Look Alike to Me" is that the song, once in circulation, became part of an active network of intertextual commentary within which its meaning was far from static; and that the connotations of the song were most contested among Hogan's black peers. The effect of these contests could be seen when Hogan changed publishers to release his songs, "I Love My Little Honey Best of All" and "I Don't Like That Face You Wear," leaving Witmark and Sons for Howley, Haviland & Co. Promoting the first of these songs, Hogan's new publisher asserted: "All coons do not look alike to the author of 'All Coons Look Alike to Me.' Read the title again for corroboration."[86] Although Hogan remained a well-liked artist whose profile continued to grow, Howley, Haviland & Co. must have determined that he needed some rehabilitation of his image for his songs to remain sellable—and maybe Hogan had too.

Addressing the black theatrical world during the turn of the twentieth century, historian Karen Sotiropoulos observed:

In a sense, African Americans had turned the world of popular theater into a black public sphere—a social space that facilitated discussion of public concerns. No formal organization underlay this sphere of interaction, but a new black public culture had emerged out of the informal networks sustained by the Marshall [hotel], the theater pages of the black press, and theater companies themselves.[87]

Considering the various ways in which Hogan's song became reworked, I would add popular song and musical performance to the list of features that contributed to the black public sphere of which Sotiropoulos writes. An individual song like "All Coons Look Alike to Me" might appear to leave the racist underpinnings of the period's entertainment industry intact. However, no song—and especially no wildly successful song—existed in a vacuum. Hogan's song certainly offended the sensibilities of many listeners and observers, including many African Americans who, wishing to attain a sort of respectability for themselves that the song seemed to deny them, rejected its value.[88] It gave rise to a prominent discourse on what kinds of representation were acceptable, and appropriate, for an era in which African Americans were becoming a more visible and recognized part of American music and theater. The various re-workings of Hogan's song in performance suggests that its implications were consistently open to reinterpretation. That very openness, the song's contradictory qualities, and the more fundamental contradiction of a black performer and songwriter who produced such a song in the first place, had much to do with its impact. Sung by black and white performers, by professional vaudevillians and amateur minstrels, "All Coons Look Alike to Me" was one of the signal expressions of an era that, according to Elijah Wald, began to see the transition from "white people watching black people to white people trying to liberate or modernize themselves through the adoption of black styles."[89]

Taking It to the Stage

As his most (in)famous songwriting creation moved across American culture, so Ernest Hogan's own mobility grew as well. The documented instances in which Hogan performed "All Coons Look Alike to Me," depicted in Table 3.3, are relatively few, and they only scratch the surface of his career trajectory in the years when the song enjoyed its greatest currency.

Table 3.3 Ernest Hogan's Performances of "All Coons Look Alike to Me"

Theatrical Company and Location	Date
Black Patti Troubadours, Toronto, ON	November 1897
Black Patti Troubadours, Hueck's Opera House, Cincinnati, OH	December 1897
Black Patti Troubadours, Park Theater, Indianapolis, IN	December 1898
Black Patti Troubadours, Marquam Theater, Portland, OR	February 1899
Hogan's Afro-American Minstrels, Orpheum Theater, Honolulu, HI	April 1900
Cherry Blossom Grove Roof Garden, New York City	September 1900

Nonetheless, the sheer fact that Hogan sang the song is notable, and his stature as a performing artist grew dramatically during these same years. In the fall of 1897, following a year during which "All Coons Look Alike to Me" had become a prominent part of national soundscape, Hogan joined the Black Patti Troubadours, then perhaps the most prominent black touring company in the US. An advertisement that appeared in the *New York Clipper* (Figure 3.5), which announced Hogan's membership in the troupe, trumpeted him as the "Author of the World's Famous Coon Songs, 'All Coons Look Alike to Me' and 'The Pas-Ma-La' [sic.]," indicating how much Hogan's reputation preceded him, but also how much his songwriting success and theatrical career were implicated with one another.[90] Most of his known performances of

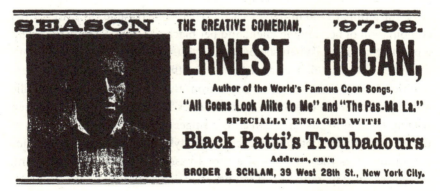

Figure 3.5 Engaged with the Black Patti Troubadors for the 1897–98 touring season, Ernest Hogan announced his association with the organization in this ad that foregrounded his talent and success as a songwriter. From the *New York Clipper* (July 3, 1897)

the song came during his tenure with Black Patti, and evidence suggests that he sang the song if not nightly, then at least regularly as one of the troupe's star attractions. Moreover, those items that mention his singing of the song offer the impression that it brought down the house.

In her own way, the Black Patti—born Matilda Sissieretta Jones—epitomized the struggles and contradictions of this era of black entertainment as powerfully as did Hogan, if not more so. Jones trained as a concert singer in the manner of her African American predecessor Elizabeth Greenfield, who became known as the "Black Swan" during the 1850s and drew comparisons to Jenny Lind. She began her professional performing career in the 1880s, first with a troupe of Jubilee Singers who followed in the wake of the Fisk company, and then seeking to gain recognition as a concert attraction in her own right.[91] She was one of several African American female vocalists who gained a measure of notice at the end of the nineteenth century for their ability to sing concert music in the high European style; and like those others, who included Flora Batson and Marie Selika, Jones faced difficulties breaking through to white audiences and being taken seriously in a realm of musical performance that many observers deemed unsuited for black female talent.

Her name, the Black Patti, was indicative of her divided stature. Meant to pay tribute to her vocal abilities, it cast her as a counterpart to one of the leading white prima donnas of the time, Adelina Patti, suggesting that Jones' talent could only be understood as a reflection of the more "legitimate" world of white European concert music.[92] This is not to say she enjoyed no success. For a time in the mid-1890s she earned considerable celebrity for the combination of her singing talent and her blackness, which made her talent a point of curiosity. When she began her touring company, the Black Patti Troubadours, in 1896, her name guaranteed the company a measure of recognition from the start; but her move from the concert stage to vaudeville also represented capitulation to the difficulties faced by an African American woman seeking to sustain a career as a singer of "serious" music.[93] Even at this stage, Patti did not quit or change her style of singing. Instead, she incorporated it as the final act of a broad-based vaudeville entertainment, presenting an "Operatic Kaleidoscope" in which she earned her own headlining status as the star of a show that bore her name.[94]

Hogan joined the Black Patti Troubadours for the troupe's second season, and he would stay with them for two years, until the spring of 1899. From the start, he established himself as a leading attraction in his own right, rivaling

Patti for audience devotion and critical accolades. Just as his tenure with Black Patti was getting underway, in September 1897, Hogan was profiled at length in the *Indianapolis Freeman*, in a piece that discussed his upbringing in Bowling Green, Kentucky, his decision to leave home at an early age to pursue a theatrical career, and the perseverance that ultimately led to his great success as the author of "All Coons Look Alike to Me."[95] Whatever ambivalence surrounded that particular song, Hogan was here cast as a model of upward mobility that readers of the paper were encouraged to admire, and a figure whose life typified widely held values concerning the importance of racial uplift.[96]

One of the earliest detailed accounts of Hogan's tenure with Black Patti appeared two months later. The *Kalamazoo Gazette* announced the forthcoming appearance of the Black Patti Troubadours to the western Michigan city, and to give readers a preview it reprinted a review of the company's recent show in Toronto. The review offers a clear sense of the multi-faceted nature of the entertainment offered by Black Patti's troupe, which was a full-scale vaudeville show unto itself. Opening the show was "At Jolly Cooney Island," a comic skit that parodied the fabled amusement park and featured Hogan prominently. More comedy followed, as did much singing, by the Troubadour Sextette—a vocal harmony group—and by Black Patti, who offered the audience "Way Down Upon the Swanee River" and "Home, Sweet Home." By the account of the review, Hogan seems to have been one of the last acts to take the stage, and was easily the biggest hit: "Mr. Ernest Hogan, in his original 'Coon' songs, including 'All Coons Look Alike to Me,' 'What Are You Gwine to Tell Massa Peter,' etc., was encored again and again, and had he continued until midnight the house would have still been looking for more."[97] A similar, if more abbreviated, account of Hogan's success with the audiences that came to see the Black Patti Troubadours appeared a month later in the *New York Clipper*, concerning the company's performance at Hueck's Opera House in Cincinnati: "Black Patti's Troubadours did a nice business. Ernest Hogan, the author of 'All Coons Look Alike to Me,' responded to many encores of that most famous of his creations."[98]

Probably the most comprehensive description of a Hogan performance during this time came a year later, in December 1898, when the *Indianapolis Freeman* reviewed the appearance of the Black Patti Troubadours at the city's own Park Theater. The Park was the principal theater in Indianapolis where headlining African American attractions would appear. It was not a "black" theater, but accounts suggest that it was more integrated than most other theaters of the period. Segregated seating was customary throughout vaudeville's history. If theaters admitted African Americans at all, they were typically made to sit in the upper galleries, the same portion of the theater where Tony Pastor's gallery gods held their turf. Theaters set aside for African Americans were few and far between; the establishment of Church's Park and Auditorium in Memphis, Tennessee in 1899 was a crucial milestone, followed by others like the Pekin Theater in Chicago, opened in 1905. For the most part, artists like Hogan and companies like Black Patti's routinely faced audiences that were predominantly white and in which black theatergoers were on the margins. The Park did not marginalize black theatergoers to the degree that was standard, and because it was in Indianapolis, and the *Freeman* had the most comprehensive coverage of black performing arts of any national publication at the time, performances there were often reviewed with greater attention than one would find for performances by black troupes in other settings, including New York.

When the Black Patti Troubadours came to the Park Theater during Thanksgiving week, 1898, the *Freeman* reported that the company "drew the largest audiences ever assembled in this magnificent new theater;" and further proclaimed the Troubadours to be "undoubtedly the best troupe of colored performers ever seen in this city."[99] Ernest Hogan's value to the company was a running theme in the *Freeman* review. He is credited with writing the opening musical skit, "At Jolly Coon-ey Island," and amongst the many new songs introduced during the skit—which appears to be a showcase for novelty—Hogan performs the standout number, "If They'd Only Fought with Razors in the War." His biggest star turn, though, came toward the end: "Ernest Hogan, the 'Black Chevalier,' in his refined monologue, kept the audience in fine humor. He sang songs of his own composition: 'Honey You've Made a Hit with Me,' and 'I Don't Like That Face You Wear.' The audience went wild and they made it impossible for Mr. Hogan to leave the stage until he had sang the song that had made for him a national reputation: 'All Coons Look Alike to Me.'"

"He sang songs of his own composition": this key line makes plain that when Hogan stepped onto the stage, his status as a writer as well as a performer of popular songs followed him and heightened the manner in which audiences responded to his appearance. Those audiences did not just enjoy it when Hogan sang his signature composition: they demanded that he do so, as if a performance by Hogan would have been incomplete without that song. That the song itself, and many others sung by Hogan such as "If They'd

Only Fought with Razors in the War," reinforced some of the most unsavory kinds of stereotypes concerning African Americans, should certainly give us pause. Hogan himself was reported to have regretted the extent to which "All Coons Look Alike to Me" had damaging effects that he did not foresee and could not contain. Most famously, the *New York Age* columnist Lester Walton reported two years after Hogan's death, in 1911, that Hogan repeatedly expressed misgivings about the song:

> Although Ernest Hogan, the late comedian and song writer, first attracted general attention by writing the song, 'All Coons Look Alike to Me,' yet for several years before his death he often expressed regret that he wrote the composition. More than once he declared to me that while the song made him a big sum of money and was instrumental in putting him forward in the theatrical business, he feared that the sentiment expressed in it had done the race a great harm.[100]

Yet Walton's recollection hardly settles the matter. The vaudeville veteran Tom Fletcher, in his valuable historical memoir of a career in black entertainment, offered a very different take on Hogan's views. He too recounts a conversation he had with Hogan about the song, which is certainly not accurate word for word but has as much veracity as does Walton's reflections:

> Son . . . this song caused a lot of trouble in and out of show business, but it was also good for show business because at that time money was short in all walks of life. With the publication of that song, a new musical rhythm was given to the people . . . That one song opened the way for a lot of colored and white songwriters. Finding the rhythm so great, they stuck to it changing the lyrics, and now you get song hits from my creations without the word "coon."[101]

Hogan's peers and contemporaries appear to have sided more with Fletcher's version of this legacy than with Walton's. By the time of his death his accomplishments had long transcended the credit he received for "All Coons Look Alike to Me." In the summer of 1898, when still a member of Black Patti's Troubadours, Hogan was the lead performer in the groundbreaking African American production, "Clorindy, or the Origin of the Cakewalk," the result of a collaboration between the writer Paul Laurence Dunbar and the composer Will Marion Cook. Upon leaving Black Patti in 1899, Hogan joined a company that traveled overseas to perform in Australia and then Hawaii. From there, Hogan appeared in the leading vaudeville halls of the US, including as a regular attraction on the Keith circuit. With Billy McClain, he started one of the longest lasting black vaudeville companies of its time, the Smart Set, in 1902; and three years later, another company that he helped to organize—the Memphis Students—was reputed to have signaled the start of the jazz age by no less an observer than James Weldon Johnson.[102] During the last years of his life Hogan toured tirelessly as the featured performer in two theatrical productions that he had a significant hand in conceiving and producing, "Rufus Rastus" and "The Oysterman."[103] During his run in the latter show, he had to withdraw from the stage due to ill health in February 1908, suffering from tuberculosis, which would take his life in May 1909.

Some months after his withdrawal from the stage, in June 1908, Hogan's professional colleagues held a testimonial benefit in his honor at the West End Theater on 125th Street, in Harlem. Such testimonials were not uncommon and were a holdover from the time when artists routinely held benefit concerts to close out a season in an effort to generate some additional income. At this stage, Hogan, for all his success, was not only physically incapacitated but had fallen into financial hard times and so his peers responded accordingly. Reporting on the event in the days leading up to it, Lester Walton noted, "Never before has the profession responded so willingly to make a testimonial a success. Not only have the colored performers offered their services but many well-known white comedians have notified the management of their desire to appear on the bill."[104] Among those involved in organizing the event was a who's who of the black entertainment field, including Bert Williams and his partner George Walker, Bob Cole, J. Rosamond Johnson, James Reese Europe, and Walton himself. Such broad participation among the professional class of black entertainers gives further evidence of the growth of a black public sphere described above in conjunction with the world of theatrical entertainment.

As such, the evening presented something of a summation of black theatrical talent at the time, combined with an overview of Hogan's highlight-filled career. The mood was mostly lighthearted, with moments of sympathy for Hogan's situation scattered throughout. Williams and Walker, third on the bill, got things "right" with their comedic exchanges, a highlight being Williams' song, "The Right Church, but the Wrong Pew." Various former partners of Hogan appeared throughout the night, including one of his earliest associates, Tom Brown, and John Rucker, who appeared alongside

Hogan in his last show, "The Oysterman." A running comic effect came from a Mr. Gaiten, of the musical group the Five Musical Spillers, who repeatedly came to the stage with a mandolin in hand only to learn that it was not his time to go on. One of the most surprising moments came when an ensemble calling themselves "This Quartette," comprised of Williams, Walker, Bob Cole, and Rosamond Johnson, came on stage to sing only the first line of the song, "I Stood on the Bridge at Midnight"—"That's all, just the first line, and it was a howling success," wrote Lester Walton in his review of the affair.[105] The most telling part of the night, though, came near the beginning, when the orchestra played selections from some of Hogan's best-known songs. By Walton's account, "the applause was vociferous, especially when 'All Coons Look Alike to Me' was rendered." That an audience of his peers would express their appreciation for a song of such compromising character was a mark of Hogan's pioneering combination of song craft and stagecraft, and the ambivalent but crucial role of the coon song in giving rise to a distinctly modern form of black musical and theatrical entertainment.

Two Vaudevilles?

The realm of vaudeville occupied by Ernest Hogan and his African American contemporaries might be viewed as something largely separate from mainstream vaudeville as cultivated by Tony Pastor in prototypical form, and by the likes of B.F. Keith and E.F. Albee in its more "mature" phase. Black vaudeville artists had their own social institutions—the Marshall Hotel of New York being one of them, where black professional entertainers gathered and built a sense of fraternal solidarity that helped them weather the pressures they faced. More to the point, they increasingly worked within their own companies from the 1890s forward, with Black Patti's Troubadours finding its counterpart in the traveling productions of Williams and Walker, Cole and Johnson, and eventually of Ernest Hogan himself in the last years of his career, along with several others that achieved greater or lesser degrees of visibility. Performing artists found their efforts matched by a growing range of creative figures whose accomplishments lay more behind the scenes, whether as dramatists (Paul Laurence Dunbar, Jesse Shipp) or as composers and orchestra leaders (Will Marion Cook, James Reese Europe). While theaters specifically catering to black audiences were few and far between during the era of vaudeville's emergence, black audiences grew along with the new prominence accorded to star black artists; and at times the connection forged between artists and audiences in these settings appears to have opened a space where the usual restrictions upon black participation in American public life were challenged. In this regard Hogan and his peers can be seen to have extended the legacy of the Fisk Jubilee Singers, but they also moved that legacy in a dramatically different direction, their efforts squarely residing in the field of secular popular entertainment.

As with the Fisk Jubilee Singers, one should not overstate the autonomy that African American vaudeville artists enjoyed at this time. White theatrical agents managed nearly all the companies that featured black artists. The music publishers were under white ownership, as were the majority of the theaters where they appeared. Eventually these circumstances would begin to change. In the decade after Hogan's death a circuit of black theaters would begin to grow, eventually named the Theater Owners Booking Association or T.O.B.A. Some of the T.O.B.A. theaters would be owned by African Americans; all catered to black audiences almost exclusively and featured black talent. Building upon the pioneering but short-lived Gotham-Attucks music publishing firm, a black-owned firm founded in 1905 in which Ernest Hogan had a stake, W.C. Handy and his business partner Harry Pace would found the Pace & Handy Music Company in 1913, laying the groundwork for the more widespread circulation of songs composed by African American songwriters, especially in the emerging genre of the blues.

Ernest Hogan and his contemporaries paved the way for these advances, and some of his peers—like Handy, whose own career as a minstrel band musician stretched back to the 1890s[106]—would help to usher in the next era of black musical and theatrical development. For Hogan, Bert Williams, and the other leading black vaudeville artists of the 1890s and early 1900s, though, their careers remained largely ensconced within the larger structures of the American entertainment industry. The institutions of vaudeville and Tin Pan Alley were the vehicles through which they gained national attention, and the demands of working within these institutions required them to develop material and personae that could communicate and entertain across the color line. They had to take the expectations of white audiences into account when putting their acts together; and they had to adopt and project qualities that look deeply discomfiting to us as retrospective observers. Hogan indirectly explained his way of navigating these expectations in an unusual 1903 interview with the *Standard*, the daily newspaper of Anaconda, Montana: "An audience is a plaything. You have to be careful not to let them think you know more than they do. You just coax 'em to laugh sort of gently and let 'em think they know the most for a while. Then you get 'em won and you can do anything with 'em the rest of the evening."[107] Nowhere does Hogan mention race here, but the dynamic he describes between performing artist and audience makes it clear that for Hogan, as for other black artists of the time, managing the audience was a delicate undertaking. His awareness and astute ability to prepare an audience for what he had to offer helps to explain how a song with a racist lyric could be sung in a way that challenged or undermined that lyric's implications; how modern syncopation could inject an air of subversive energy into what might otherwise be merely retrograde material; and how a black artist seeming to engage in self-mockery could also be celebrated for his songwriting wit, accorded the status of being an author and cultural creator in his own right.

Tony Pastor clearly faced a different set of challenges in his more than forty years as a theatrical impresario. For Pastor class rather than race was the most salient boundary. From the start of his career as a manager of his own theater, he worked very deliberately to take a style of popular entertainment that was designated as unquestionably "low" in its appeal to working-class patrons and reinvent it as something more widely perceived as honorable. At times he did this by specifically seeking to align himself with cultural institutions of a "higher" stamp, evident in his near-annual spring performances at New York's Academy of Music. More often though, Pastor did not strive to elevate his brand of variety theater through claims to cultural "distinction." Instead, instilled a sense of respectability into his offerings through consistent appeals to female patrons—who had historically been excluded from more rough, masculine fields of popular culture such as blackface minstrelsy—and, most instrumentally, by strategically relocating his theater to adapt to the evolving character of New York's amusement landscape. From the Bowery to Broadway to Union Square, Pastor's succession of theater locations traced a sort of upward movement of popular theater in New York City as a whole, landing in a spot that was home to the growing consumer culture of a rising middle class, and setting the stage for the transition from the localized world of variety entertainment to the flourishing mass economy of vaudeville.

Respectability was one facet of Pastor's path to success, but so too was novelty, and this latter value was more specifically suited to the needs of the changing cultural economy. Even before he became a theatrical manager in his own right, Pastor the comic singer encouraged audiences to expect something new if not night after night, then at least week after week, as he continually refreshed the "budget" of songs he offered them. This approach anticipated the mode of production attached to the selling of popular songs that music publishers would foster in the guise of what became known as Tin Pan Alley. In Pastor's career, we see that the impulse toward novelty came as much from the imperatives of variety and vaudeville performance as it did from the needs of those who were in the business of producing and promoting popular songs. If audiences were to be expected to return to a favored theater from one week to the next, they needed the assurance that there would be something new for them to see and hear. This demand for novelty was the principal tie that bound together vaudeville and Tin Pan Alley, and it informed the careers of artists like Ernest Hogan as well, whose reputation may have been built on a durable hit song, but who still needed to keep changing with the times and finding new ways to present himself before the public. Indeed, Hogan's career offers a compelling example of how racial difference could itself be exploited for novelty appeal—this is one way to understand the widespread viability of the coon song and its correlate musical style, ragtime, and one facet of popular music at the turn of the twentieth century that remained powerfully in place as the ragtime era turned into the jazz age.

4

Remaking Liveness

The Social Geography of Early Jazz

Few artists in the history of jazz enjoy as controversial a reputation as the Original Dixieland Jazz Band. A group of white musicians from New Orleans, the ODJB made history in 1917 by creating the first recordings to be released and received as "jazz" (or "jass," as it was then often called) for the Victor Recording Company. The whiteness of the ODJB, and the unsettling efforts of the band's leader Nick La Rocca to disclaim any African American influence on his music, has made it a lightning rod concerning the priority it should be assigned as the "first" jazz band to make records and gain a national audience. Music historian Lawrence Gushee has made the case for an alternative view of early jazz history, recovering the career of the Creole Band, an African American group from New Orleans whose national tours across the United States began more than a year before the ODJB left New Orleans for Chicago.[1] Because the Creole Band never made any recordings—and also perhaps because they were of color—they received nothing like the attention granted to the ODJB, and so passed into history as little more than a curiosity until Gushee reconstructed their achievements.

In a sense the debate over how to weigh the efforts of these different jazz pioneers is also an argument over how much we should consider recordings to have greater historical value than live performances. The Creole Band reputedly was given the opportunity to record, also with Victor, in 1916 but either failed or refused to do so for reasons that remain murky at best.[2] Should we question the logic according to which their historical significance hinged on whether they made or released recordings? At the time, few African American artists were making records—the uptick in recordings by black artists would not take hold for another four years, following the crucial efforts of vaudeville blues singer Mamie Smith and her patron, songwriter Perry Bradford.[3] Making a record would have been a breakthrough, but it would also have been something of a novelty, for working bands in 1916 and for many years thereafter mainly earned their money and their reputations through performance.

This was as true for white bands like the ODJB as it was for African American ensembles like the Creole Band. At the time the Dixieland Band's recordings were made, it was playing a historic engagement at Reisenweber's, a restaurant situated at Columbus Circle in Manhattan, where it had begun appearing in late January 1917. While the records the ODJB made for Victor may have begun the process of turning jazz into a globally recognized form, the extended residency they enjoyed at Reisenweber's was a landmark of comparable importance. It consolidated at an early date the geographical path that many subsequent jazz musicians would follow, from New Orleans beginnings, then a move north to Chicago where a broader reputation got made, and then on to New York where they gained further exposure and entered an expanding field of national popular music production.

The ODJB's tenure at Reisenweber's also, crucially, confirmed that jazz quickly earned unique status as a valuable and singular live music attraction. A little-known, or little-discussed, feature of the band's engagement at Reisenweber's is captured in the renewal of its contract to continue performing there, which was signed and ratified on March 25, 1918. The third clause of that contract includes an unusual, and perhaps unprecedented, requirement:

> The "musicians" and each and all of them do hereby agree that the services it is contemplated that they and each of them will render hereunder are of unique and extraordinary nature, and that they render what is commonly known as Jazz music, in like manner which is unique and extraordinary insofar as it pertains to the rhythm and time of their rendition of such music.[4]

It would be near impossible to answer the historical question as to whether this contract makes the Original Dixieland Jazz Band the first group ever to have been specifically hired to play jazz in a public setting. What is clear from the ODJB's contract is that the management of Reisenweber's recognized the value of jazz as a popular attraction that exerted appeal through its novelty, its rhythmic qualities, and, implicitly, its danceability. Rarely has the role played by live music venues in helping to codify and define a genre been illustrated so overtly.

Jazz, then, in the years of its emergence, assumed meaning in large part through the places where it was played.[5] Reisenweber's was one sort of place, and an especially noteworthy type at that: the cabaret, a small-scale public setting where music and other sorts of theatrical attractions were offered alongside fine dining, consumption of alcohol, dancing, and a kind of sociability between men and women (or men and men, or women and women) that was sexualized to a greater or lesser degree, but without the suggestions of sexual commerce that had pervaded earlier institutions like the concert saloon.[6] The cabaret was, in effect, the prototype for the nightclub and ultimately for the jazz club, the performance setting most identified with jazz as a genre throughout its history. Yet that evolution from cabaret to jazz club happened only gradually, from the 1910s to the 1930s; and only constitutes one element in the larger story of how jazz performance entered into American life in the first decades of the twentieth century.

The following is a partial list of the kinds of places where one could expect to find jazz—or proto-jazz—played from the start of the twentieth century until the end of the 1920s, by which time it was a clearly recognized and established genre:

"Low" dives (i.e., Funky Butt Hall in New Orleans)
Public parks
Street parades
Steamships and excursion boats
Trains
Public meeting halls
Dance halls
Cabarets
Vaudeville theaters
Nightclubs (which were not jazz clubs per se)
Speakeasies
Rent parties
Movie theaters
College campuses (dances and fraternity parties)
Roadhouses
Ballrooms
Concert halls

This list may seem unexceptional—is it ever the case that genres of music inhabit only a single kind of performance venue? And yet, writing about popular music genres in his formative 1981 article on the subject, Franco Fabbri posited: "Each genre has its own space set out in a particular way," and went on to elaborate:

> The distance between musicians and audience, between spectator and spectator, the overall dimensions of the event are often fundamental elements to the definition of a genre, and often guide the participants, in the right or wrong way in determining what they should expect about other rules of genre; often "how you are seated" says more about the music that will be performed than a poster does.[7]

Fabbri's observations about the spatial character of genre "events" can be applied to all manner of musical settings, from the classical music concert hall to the juke joint of the blues, the country music honky tonk, or the convergence of heavy metal and arena rock.[8] Yet his comments presume that genres of music are performed and presented in a social environment where dedicated spaces of a sort exist to support them; and this is not always the case, especially when genres or styles of performance are in the early stages of their emergence. Just as Jenny Lind was not able to appear exclusively in concert halls, because there were not enough such venues across the US to support her, so jazz during the first decades of its emergence did not appear in any one sort of space. Instead, jazz inhabited a diverse array of spaces, in each of which the musicians adapted the music to fit the contours of the performance situation and to meet the expectations of the audiences who listened and the people that hired them.[9] This chapter will explore some of the variety of venues and practices through which jazz assumed public prominence from the 1900s to the 1920s, seeking to understand throughout the kinds of larger changes that the music brought to the performance and presentation of live music in the US in these years.

Shadowing this chapter is the fact that jazz emerged at a time when recorded popular music, radio broadcasts, and movies assumed greater currency as part of the fabric of American life. To highlight the significance of jazz as live music should not mean ignoring its value as recorded music or its place in these other areas of modern media. Indeed, part of what gave jazz its transformative impact was precisely the fact that it was reaching audiences through multiple media channels, creating the sense that it was saturating national cultural space. The outcry that surrounded the emergence of jazz—the fears that it would erode the moral fabric of the US while also degrading its taste—was as much a response to the apparent sheer ubiquity of the music as it was an effort to contain the threat posed by jazz to the logic of racial segregation, or the way jazz rhythms were believed to unleash desires that were best held in check. From this vantage point the variety of settings in which jazz appeared was another indication of a changing cultural landscape in which the music became subject to representation on a national scale in ways that were historically new. Vaudeville and Tin Pan Alley foreshadowed this enlarged national field of cultural production and continued to exert a pronounced influence into the era when jazz emerged. However, with the rise of jazz, popular music fully entered the age of mass culture and consumption. Given this was the case, what is striking about jazz as a medium of live performance is that it remained rather small scale throughout these years. Jazz may have been produced nationally but in performance, it was often consumed not just locally but intimately, not among massive crowds but in spaces where the faces of the performers were easily visible and never too far away.

"I Heard Buddy Bolden Say..."

Peter Bocage was a light-skinned Creole from New Orleans who contributed to many notable music ensembles from that city in the early twentieth century, as a violinist and on cornet. Like many Creole musicians of his generation, he was formally trained, and although he collaborated with darker-skinned, non-Creole African American musicians he viewed them with a certain measure of distance stemming from what he understood to be their different musical sensibilities. Interviewed on January 29, 1959, by William Russell, the founder of the Hogan Jazz Archive at Tulane University, and future Archive director Richard Allen, Bocage offered his informed impressions of the New Orleans jazz world of years past. Asked directly by Richard Allen, "Who do you think was the first band to ever play any jazz or ragtime?" Bocage replied with one of the most compelling explanations of jazz origins that has been recorded:

> Well, I attribute it to [Buddy] Bolden, you know ... you see, Bolden was a fellow, he didn't know a note big as this house you understand what I mean; and whatever they played, they caught [learned by hearing] or made up, you see? Say—they made their own music, and they played it their own way, you understand? So that's the way jazz started ... just his, his [improvisation], you see. And then the surroundings—the surrounding at that

time was mostly people of—oh, you might say of a fast type, you know—exciting, you understand? And those old blues and all that stuff, you know just came in there, you see.[10]

Subsequent research has shown that Bolden, an African American cornet player celebrated for the sheer power of his sound, was not so musically uneducated as Bocage suggests.[11] Yet Bocage's basic claim here reflects one of the most potent narratives concerning jazz origins. Jazz, by this account, began in "fast" surroundings, where musicians with little formal training but great facility applied themselves to flexible blues song forms that they used as the basis for imaginative and freewheeling styles of improvisation.

New Orleans looms large over jazz history. Going back to the 1930s, at least, the city's jazz historians have worked to separate history from myth, to discern which stories about the city are mainly apocryphal and which can be substantiated, while also trying to learn from the rich array of legendary tales without dismissing such accounts out of hand.[12] No figure associated with New Orleans jazz is as shrouded in myth as Buddy Bolden, whose performing career lasted for nearly a decade from roughly 1897 to 1906 and stands as one marker of the genesis of jazz at the turn of the twentieth century. Interviews with the earliest African American jazz musicians in New Orleans testify to Bolden's undeniable influence. However, documentary evidence of Bolden's career is scarce, he predated by many years any effort to produce jazz on record, and he spent the last twenty-five years of his life institutionalized, suffering from what was likely to have been schizophrenia. A tragic artist whose sound is lost to history, Bolden's standing as a jazz progenitor depended primarily on the memories of those who encountered him and the rich oral tradition that New Orleans jazz musicians have built and preserved to commemorate their lineage.

If Bolden is the personage most associated with the beginnings of jazz, then Funky Butt Hall is the primary setting where this most potent strain of early jazz germinated. Founded as Union Sons Hall in 1866 by an African American relief organization, it was located at 1319 Perdido Street, just down the street from another key setting for black New Orleans dance music, the Odd Fellows and Masonic Hall. The neighborhood was predominantly African American—but not Creole; these were the "Uptown" blacks, darker skinned and farther removed from the Francophone cultural background of New Orleans than the "Downtown" Creoles.[13] Union Sons Hall was also at a remove from the famed brothels of Storyville, also known as "the District," which were mainly the province of piano players and rarely hosted ensemble performances. By the end of the nineteenth century, Union Sons Hall was regularly used for dances, drawing an audience of working-class African Americans who frequently engaged in rough and rowdy behavior.[14] The hall was dubbed the Funky Butt some time after 1900 through its association with Bolden, whose signature song included the words, "I thought I heard Buddy Bolden say/Funky butt, funky butt, take it away."[15] This was the sort of "fast" environment evoked above by Peter Bocage, a low dive or in the terms of the day, what was often called a honky-tonk. Another Creole musician, the trombonist and bandleader Edward "Kid" Ory, offered probably the most vivid description of the interior of Funky Butt Hall:

> The place was always packed. The dances would be held on Saturday and Monday nights. This amazed me as there were no decorations, the building was just a shell and a honky-tonk if ever I saw one but of fairly good size. It would accommodate about 700 people, the way they jammed themselves into those places in those days. All they wanted to do was move around just a little, rubbing against each other, and they called it dancing.[16]

Louis Armstrong, who grew up in and around the neighborhood where Funky Butt Hall was located, recalled in his autobiography his growing awareness as a young boy of these places of nighttime amusement: "On Liberty, Perdido, Franklin and Poydras there were honky-tonks at every corner and in each one of them musical instruments of all kinds were played. At the corner of the street where I lived was the famous Funky Butt Hall, where I first heard Buddy Bolden play. He was blowing up a storm."[17] That Armstrong, who was no more than five years old when Bolden retired from performing, could have been exposed to such seemingly "adult" recreation says much the striking public availability of music in New Orleans at the time. He further explained: "Of course, we kids were not allowed to go into the Funky Butt, but we could hear the orchestra from the sidewalk. In those days it was the routine when there was a ball for the band to play for at least a half hour in front of the honky-tonk before going back into the hall to play for the dancers."[18] So it was that the music of the honky tonk was brought out onto the street for the enjoyment of those who could not gain admittance. Yet Armstrong's exposure did not end there. He peered into the forbidden environment from outside, where he caught a glimpse of the activities that made it off limits, recalling that as Bolden's band played a tune like "The Bucket's

Got a Hole in It," "some of them chicks would get way down, shake everything, slapping themselves on the cheek of their behind."[19]

In this setting, the dance orientation of Bolden's music was paramount, as it continued to be in the music that became known as jazz for decades to come.[20] At a time when African American music and dance had been placed under greater control by the city of New Orleans—decades after the famous Congo Square dance rituals had passed—this physically expressive, sexually suggestive dance became a means to reclaim public space for the city's black population. Conflicts were sure to arise in such a climate, spurred by the strict efforts to regulate dance events pursued by the city's political leaders. An 1858 city ordinance, revised in 1893, required approval from the mayor's office for any public balls, stipulating that, "immediately after the passage of this resolution it shall be unlawful to establish or set aside any place for public entertainments without the consent of the City Council."[21] As with all such regulations, the ordinance did not bring an immediate stop to all unlicensed activity but it gave the police and city officials greater administrative power to exercise their authority through surveillance and arrests.

Police records collected by Bolden's biographer, Donald Marquis, document the local struggles that resulted from this legislation, often revolving around the efforts of the city's many black social clubs to carve out space for their dance events. In one letter, dated June 3, 1911, Inspector of Police James Reynolds writes to the Mayor, Martin Behrman, informing him of complaints made against a dance hall located at the corner of Seventh and Magazine Streets and explaining: "There is always a policeman detailed at these dances, but I have instructed Sergt. Cearns to have two additional men in that precinct on nights that these dances are going on . . . and if there is any disturbance, the use of obscene language or the commission of a nuisance, to take proper action and to make arrests."[22] Other correspondence shows a consistent concern with the "vulgar dances" on display at these gatherings. One case involved a complaint made against dances held upstairs from a saloon at 240 S. Rampart Street, occupied by an organization called the Red Cross Pleasure Club and, periodically, by a second group named the Chicago Pleasure Club. Described by Captain L.W. Rawlings of the New Orleans police, at these dances "the men and women who attend these receptions engage in vulgar dancing to the discomfort of the white residents living in the immediate vicinity of the place."[23] Supporting Rawlings' account are signed complaints from three white residents, one of which, Joseph Ferrantelli, characterized the scene as follows:

They started at about 8 O'Clock P.M., and kept up piano playing and singing until 1:30 O'Clock A.M., they had also a sign on the sidewalk in front of the saloon marked "Free Dance to night upstairs" from my room I could see into the hall where negroes men and women were engaged in vulgar dancing, this in the presence of wife and family.[24]

The basis for conflict in these instances derived in part from one of the very qualities that also made New Orleans such a rich social and musical environment: residential segregation was not rigidly in place, such that black dances occurred in neighborhoods that were ethnically mixed. While some white residents were—perhaps justifiably—disturbed at the interruption of their sleep by the loud music and "vulgar" dances, others were no doubt drawn to these same sounds and practices, evident in the preponderance of white jazz bands that grew throughout the 1910s.

* * *

Another window into this social world comes from the posters used to promote the dances and events sponsored by the city's black clubs. Here a spirit of fun and, to a degree, social responsibility displaces the preoccupation with vulgarity and disorder that pervades the police reports. Like Louis Armstrong's memory of Funky Butt Hall, the posters reveal a social and musical scene in which dancing was of paramount importance. Yet the occasions they document were not nearly so "low-down." The social clubs who sponsored these various dances, balls and excursions were often comprised of a more respectable class of African Americans.

Traces of this respectability can be found throughout the twenty-two posters housed at Tulane University's Hogan Jazz Archive, starting with the names of the clubs themselves, which include the Young Men's Olympian Benefit Society, the Well-Known Gentlemen, the Lafon Old Folks Home Auxiliary Committee, and the Young Men's High Art Social and Pleasure Club. Many events were benefits of some kind, sometimes for the general fund that these organizations kept on hand for the relief of their members, sometimes for a specific purpose such as the December 19, 1910 ball cosponsored by the Young Men's High Art, Overland and Eclipse Social Clubs to purchase an artificial leg for a young boy named Son Green.[25] Women were commonly given a special invitation to attend these events in a way that evokes a parallel to variety and vaudeville performance, their presence being used to offer some guarantee of a more reputable sort of entertainment. At times this suggestion was made more explicit, as in the poster for another 1910 ball, this one given by the Orleans Athletic Club, that stated: "Through your kind co-operation and patronage our past amusements have met with tremendous success and they have been conducted sociably and morally by us and we promise this affair will be one of the Grandest Events of modern times."[26]

Such injunctions toward morality did not mean that the general atmosphere was austere and forbidding. These were pleasure clubs too, after all, the nocturnal habits of which were routinely made evident with the fact that nearly all events advertised dancing from 8:00 p.m. to 4:00 a.m. Slang and catch phrases peppered these promotional posters, conveying to the potential attendee that a good time would be had by all. Characteristic was the verse atop a poster for a "Grand Lawn Party" hosted by the Queen and Crescent Social Club in cooperation with the Equality Social and Pleasure Club, in August 1909, seen in Figure 4.1: "Pleasure and Frolic are all that you can hear/But times are quite dull for the middle of the year/So don't stop to differ, don't stop to buzz/Come in and join the frolic of the Queen and Crescent S.C."[27]

Among the most common settings for these gatherings was Economy Hall, located at 1422 Ursulines Street in the Treme neighborhood of New Orleans, several blocks to the north of Storyville and the area that housed Funky Butt Hall. Economy Hall was the meeting grounds for the Economy and Mutual Aid Association, founded in 1836, but like many such halls also functioned as something of a general center of community activities.[28] Its importance to the evolution of New Orleans jazz became codified when Kid Ory started to regularly rent the hall in 1912 for weekly Monday night performances. Louis Armstrong recalled in his memoir that his first performance with Ory's band, a major step up in his own career, came during one of those Economy Hall shows in 1918, when he came in to replace his mentor, Joe Oliver.[29] Well before that date, the hall was hosting regular dances, balls, and other events that gave the city's black social clubs an occasion to dress up, fortify their bonds with one another, and raise money to fill their coffers.

Musically the dominant figure in this realm of black social dancing was John Robichaux, a Creole violinist and bandleader that enjoyed a long career spanning from the early 1890s to his death in 1939.[30] Robichaux is not typically accorded the status of jazz pioneer. His band was of a more refined sort, playing strictly arranged versions of popular dance tunes, with no blues and little proclivity toward improvisation. He was said to have the best "reading"

Figure 4.1 This poster for a "Grand Lawn Party" held by the Queen and Crescent Social Club of New Orleans on August 9, 1909, features a characteristically witty verse prompting prospective party goers to attend. Courtesy of the Hogan Archive of New Orleans Music and New Orleans Jazz, Tulane University Special Collections.

band in New Orleans, and his band also had a pronounced versatility that came from being able to take nearly any published song and perform a convincing rendition. Robichaux's presence on so many of these posters is another sign that these balls tended toward a more "respectable" sort of music and dance-based activity. However, like a later proponent of "refined" dance music, Paul Whiteman, Robichaux employed musicians who could play in a more energetic, improvisatory style such as clarinetist George Baquet, and he was said to play a "hotter" sort of dance music when the situation called for it.[31] That he was no stick in the mud can be garnered from the verse used to promoted his appearance at a dance on January 8, 1900: "Kill it kid for it is nothing but a chinch/Walk in to it for it is a lead pipe cinch/ For that 3 o'clock Quadrille it all the go/When ever it is played by the old boy Robichaux."[32]

Robichaux is best remembered as Buddy Bolden's principal foil. The two prominent bandleaders had a celebrated rivalry that manifested itself most publicly when they played across from each other at two parks that were patronized by African American residents of New Orleans in the early twentieth century. Lincoln Park was primarily Robichaux's domain, while Bolden typically held forth at Johnson Park, although would sometimes appear at Lincoln as well. Of the two Lincoln offered a wider range of activities, including balloon ascensions and vaudeville-style entertainment in which the band would be one attraction among others. Johnson Park was mainly known for hosting baseball games, but like Lincoln had a building on its grounds that functioned as a dance hall, where Bolden often appeared.[33] Bolden's most fabled move occurred during those nights when he and Robichaux played opposite each other. As recalled by Louis Jones, a barber who befriended Bolden upon his move to New Orleans in 1894:

> That's where Buddy Bolden used to say to [trombonist Willie] Cornish and them, say, "Cornish, come on, put your . . . hands through the window . . . 'N I'm going to call my children home." He would be at Johnson Park; Robichaux would be at Lincoln Park. Buddy Bolden would start to play too, and all the people at Lincoln Park come on over . . . where Buddy Bolden was.[34]

Jazz historians have interpreted this gesture—Buddy Bolden calling his children home across the park from Lincoln to Johnson—as an early triumph for true, "gut bucket" New Orleans jazz over the more strait-laced society music of Robichaux's band.[35] It is a mistake, though, to draw too strict a divide between these areas of New Orleans's musical life in the years when jazz was coming to light. While Bolden distinguished himself with his low-down approach to the blues, he was also known to play many of the same types of songs as the more refined Robichaux, including waltzes, schottisches, and quadrilles. Bill Matthews, who played drums with Robichaux for a time, recalled: "Buddy was the loudest cornet player we ever had in the city of New Orleans," but he was also "the sweetest trumpet player in the world . . . He could play just as sweet as he could play loud."[36] Respectable and low down, sweet and hot—these competing values were continually in dialogue in New Orleans during the formative years of jazz and would continue to inform the music as it evolved.

Mobile Music

Three of the posters cited above advertise excursions, and specifically railroad excursions. These were trips of short duration—day trips, in effect—on which passengers would travel to some location a few hours away, spend a portion of the day picnicking and enjoying the outdoor setting to which they had been brought, and then re-board the train to return home that night. Bands were commonly hired as entertainment for these excursions, which would typically be provided during the time after arrival at the day's destination where the picnic might also become a dance, or even a battle between competing bands. Such was the case for a 1907 "Grand Excursion Picnic" held at Lincoln Park that was to entertain passengers who had arrived from Shreveport, Louisiana, and other parts of the state. As the poster for the picnic announces in Figure 4.2, the main event was to be "the Grand Band Contest between Prof. Robichaux's Orchestra of New Orleans, La., and Prof. Markham's Orchestra of Shreveport, La."[37] City and regional pride were at stake in these events but just as importantly, the excursions provided a key medium through which jazz music spread outward from New Orleans and other locations where it took root to outlying places and populations.

Fifteen years later, Kid Ory and his Sunshine Orchestra participated in a similar enterprise. At this point in 1922, Ory no longer resided in New Orleans but had relocated to Southern California. The trip for which he played on August 5 of that year took passengers from Los Angeles to San Diego and then Tijuana, Mexico. This train would have a special social car for dancing, although as with other such endeavors, the main entertainment

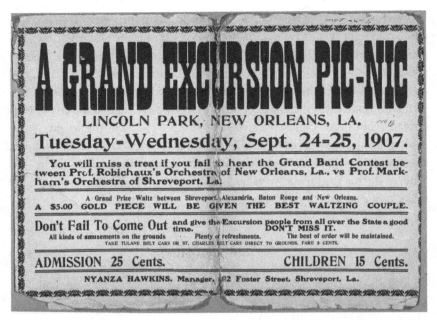

Figure 4.2 Poster for a "Grand Excursion Pic-nic" at New Orleans' Lincoln Park on September 24–25, 1907, highlighted by a musical contest between the orchestras of Professors Robichaux and Markham. Courtesy of the Hogan Archive of New Orleans Music and New Orleans Jazz, Tulane University Special Collections.

would be reserved for the destination where a full cast of black vaudevillians led by comedian Eddie Rucker would be on hand, and Ory's Sunshine Orchestra would play.[38] A photograph of Ory's band appears in the ad, and the band is characterized as "the only race jazz band that has made phonograph records on the coast" —a description that refers to Ory's record of the songs, "Ory's Creole Trombone" and "Society Blues," released just weeks earlier under the auspices of Southern California music entrepreneurs the Spikes Brothers, which is generally considered to have been the first commercial recording released by an African American jazz band playing in the New Orleans style.[39]

Recordings played an enormous role in helping to spread jazz across the US and even overseas. Yet the fact that the first recordings released by an African American band from New Orleans came only after that band had relocated to California tells us that recordings often depended on other, more fundamental kinds of cultural and geographic movement. Jazz was a highly mobile form of music from the moment of its inception, and jazz musicians were always on the move—sometimes moving within a contained regional network of performance opportunities, other times taking great leaps toward parts unknown, to extend their reputations, discover new opportunities, escape racist circumstances, or just to see what they would find. The apparent rapidity with which jazz moved from place to place had its analogue in the use of jazz as a favored entertainment on railroad cars, steamboats, and other modes of transportation. Playing in transit was in many ways like any other experience of being on tour, except that when musicians performed as part of these excursions, the mode of transportation also became a kind of stage, what historian Robin Kelley, addressing a different context, has called "moving theaters."[40] For the African American musicians who participated in these traveling engagements, their state of being on the move was part of the performance.

It is tempting to suggest that all this movement signified the expanding range of freedoms that African Americans enjoyed in the first decades of the twentieth century, and in one sense that would be true. The emergence of jazz, and blues, as significant commercial idioms coincided with the "great migration" through which millions of African Americans transplanted themselves from rural to urban settings, often moving from the South to the North (or, from the East to the West) in the process. Migration, however, was never a simple move toward freedom, and some of the greatest hardships faced by African Americans came during the experience of being in transit, of getting from place to place. The rigid segregationist logic of Jim Crow made transportation into one of the most contested fields of American social life, and those types of transportation that commonly crossed state lines—boats and trains—occupied an especially complex space. Of the three train excursions advertised among the posters held at the Hogan Jazz Archive, two explicitly noted the segregated character of the trips, one promising "separate cars for colored people," the other proclaimed to be a "strictly white excursion."[41] In other instances, such as the excursion that featured Kid Ory, the passengers were all African American.

If anything, the riverboats where jazz appeared on day and evening excursions were even more strictly segregated. Traversing the Mississippi and Ohio Rivers, the steamboats owned and overseen by the Streckfus family repurposed a mode of transportation that had been used primarily to move consumer goods and raw materials into something designed for passenger travel. The purpose of these trips was not typically to get from one place to another, but rather to have time in the boat, on the river, while it moved just far enough to offer a temporary sense of escape from daily circumstances. Having their heyday in the years just after World War I and through the 1920s, steamboat excursions packaged a kind of nostalgia in which the natural power of the river commingled with a vision of an earlier industrial era in which social relations remained harmonious so long as everyone knew their place.[42] Most of these trips catered exclusively to white patrons, although select lines did also hold special excursions on which African American passengers were admitted on board. Pops Foster, the New Orleans bass player who was a member for a time of the leading black riverboat band, described the social patterns that characterized the experience from a musician's perspective:

> The dances on the riverboats were segregated. Monday night out of St. Louis was for the colored. There were as many whites as colored on Monday nights and you could hardly get on the boats that night. In New Orleans no colored were allowed on the boats. In Memphis and Pittsburgh sometimes they had colored on Monday nights. We called Mondays "Getaway Night" because you could get away with anything. The guys in the band would walk around smoking cigarettes and drinking, and come down off the stand.[43]

Music was a central part of these riverboat excursions, provided mainly to accompany dancing. Most of those hired were white and played a sort of society music that was light on syncopation. However, a handful of black bands also appeared, the most successful of which by far was the series of bands led by pianist (and calliope player) Fate Marable. Marable enjoyed one of the longest and most storied careers of any riverboat musician, black or white, spanning the decades from the 1900s to the start of World War II. His greatest talent, according to riverboat jazz chronicler William Kenney, was his eye for talent in others and ability to recruit first-rate musicians into his band. In this connection, the period of Marable's career that is best known is the short span from 1919–1921 during which he drafted some of the most promising players out of the New Orleans jazz scene, including Pops Foster, drummer Warren "Baby" Dodds, trombonist William "Bebe" Ridgley, and Louis Armstrong on cornet. For Armstrong this was a pivotal experience, the transition between his life as a New Orleans musician and his move North to join his mentor, Joe Oliver, in Chicago. Musically, Armstrong and his peers had to work hard to adapt to the format of Marable's band, which like that of Robichaux was predicated on the musicians' ability to read written arrangements and follow them with note-perfect accuracy, at a tempo that was dictated by owner Joseph Streckfus's beliefs about what best suited the white dancers who patronized his boats.[44] Although the discipline would prove more than Armstrong wanted to bear, he credited his time in Marable's band for expanding and refining his musicianship in ways that would have enduring value.[45] The musical and racial order on the steamboats was alternately confining and liberating; but as Pops Foster suggested above, it was perhaps when black passengers were on board that the African American musicians themselves had the greatest sense of "getting away" from the usual constraints they faced, and established the sonic outlines of a migratory experience that had wider repercussions.

Jazz in the Act

Five years before Armstrong and his New Orleans compatriots joined Marable's riverboat ensemble, in 1914, the Creole Band convened in California. They were not the first group of African American musicians from New Orleans to move so far afield but they broke new ground for the scope of their touring, and their brief career dovetailed with the historical moment when jazz began to gain more recognition on a national scale. Bill Johnson, a string bass player, was the principal organizer of the Creole Band, and had already relocated from New Orleans to California when he assembled the band from a group of New Orleans players, some of which had also already moved west and some of whom made the trip to join the group. The most celebrated member of the Creole Band was cornet player Freddie Keppard, while others included violinist James Palao, clarinet player George Baquet— who had previously been a member of John Robichaux's band—trombonist Eddie Vincent, and guitarist Norwood "Gigi" Williams. Singer and dancer Henry Morgan Prince would join shortly after the band's founding and was the only one of the group's members not to hail from New Orleans.[46]

Most significantly, for my purposes, the Creole Band's touring efforts principally came via vaudeville. By summer of 1914 the band had joined the Pantages vaudeville circuit, through which they toured up the west coast to Seattle and then moved into the Midwestern region, reaching Chicago in early 1915. As an attraction designed for appeal on the vaudeville stage, the Creole Band had to cultivate some more theatrical qualities as part of their stage show to meet the expectations of audiences; and all available evidence suggests that they did so in the form of "a traditional plantation darky act."[47] It is not clear that they blacked up, but they had stage props evocative of a Southern plantation, wore clothes similarly evocative of such a setting, and one of the group's set pieces was a version of the Stephen Foster song, "Old Black Joe." An early review of the band, from an appearance in Portland, Oregon, succinctly captured the unruly mix of elements coursing through their act: "No musicians ever got more melody out of ragtime that the Orleans Creole Band. The old plantation songs also are taken care of and few have cut a bigger swath with the local vaudeville fans than the Creole band members."[48] Here and elsewhere, observers noted the distinctive character of the Creole Band's "ragtime" music, since the word "jazz" was still only starting to take hold in the vocabulary of newspaper reviewers during the band's early tours. When the likes of the Original Dixieland Jazz Band began to gain recognition in Chicago in 1916, some acknowledged that this black band from New Orleans had been in the advance guard of the mounting jazz craze.[49]

Appearing in this setting, the Creole Band could be seen to have followed in the footsteps of Ernest Hogan and Bert Williams, as much as Buddy Bolden. Doing so would have been a surer path to success, since black vaudeville artists had gone furthest in establishing the terms according to which African American performing artists might gain recognition among the wider mass audience, and acceptance among white theatergoers in particular. Yet this effort to fit existing black stage roles may also have contributed to the marginal place assigned the Creole Band in the writing of jazz history. Moreover, vaudeville theaters made an uneasy setting for the presentation of jazz. The fixed seats of the theaters ensured that no dancing would take place unless it was on the stage. Jazz historian Bruce Boyd Raeburn has suggested that the general confinement of the Creole Band and other early proto-jazz practitioners to this sort of staged entertainment restricted their influence due to their lack of direct contact with dancing audiences.[50] Despite these limitations, vaudeville was integral for the presentation of jazz from the mid 1910s and throughout the 1920s in ways that have not been fully appreciated. Vaudeville made jazz into a music that was to be watched, and listened to, in a seated and at least semi-attentive manner well before the more celebrated move of jazz into the concert hall that occurred in the 1920s and 1930s. Jazz performers in turn used vaudeville to experiment with qualities of stagecraft that would have seemed out of place in other sorts of performance environments, and took advantage of vaudeville as a medium for expanding their reach beyond the devoted cabaret dwellers.

Take, for example, two of the earliest African American jazz musicians who became recognized for their virtuosity on their respective instruments, clarinetist Wilbur Sweatman and cornet player Johnny Dunn. Sweatman was another figure whose career began well before "jazz" as such was a recognized phenomenon, earning a reputation by 1910 as one of the most accomplished "ragtime" clarinet players to be found. After playing alongside respected African American bandleaders W.C. Handy and P.G. Lowery—the latter of whom worked primarily in the realm of the circus[51]—Sweatman moved into vaudeville, where he gained renown for his talent as a player and composer of such songs as the popular "Down Home Rag." His showpiece was an exhibitionistic display during which he performed on two, and sometimes three, clarinets at once. The maneuver was such a signature part of Sweatman's act that in 1919, when his performing and recording career reached a sort of peak with his Original Jazz Band, he engaged in a debate in the pages of *Variety* magazine on whether he had in fact originated the multi-horn trick. Disputing the claims of a competitor, Sweatman asserted: "I planned and carried out the idea of playing two and three clarinets at once, had never seen or heard of anyone doing it, therefore consider myself the originator, and also started this jazz craze for the clarinet and am the originator of jazzing and slurring on that instrument."[52] His tendency toward showmanship, tailored to the spectacular nature of vaudeville entertainment, has led to his dismissal by many historians of early jazz, but *Chicago Defender* columnist Dave Peyton supported Sweatman's claim toward being a jazz pioneer in a 1925 column, in which he recalled the clarinetist's appearance at Chicago's Grand Theater as early as 1906, where "white players would come from all across the country to hear Sweatman moan on his clarinet."[53]

Like Sweatman, Johnny Dunn spent some of his formative professional years playing under W.C. Handy. His breakthrough, though, came as a member of Mamie Smith's Jazz Hounds. He can be heard on Smith's landmark 1920 recording of "Crazy Blues," the record that opened up the market for "race records" made by African American artists for African American record buyers. Dunn was also part of the touring Jazz Hounds band that accompanied Smith on the road in the early months of 1921, many of whose engagements were in the growing sector of vaudeville-style theaters patronized by black audiences. Smith gained renown as a blues singer, but the fact that her band was called the Jazz Hounds suggests how porous the boundaries between these genres of music were perceived to be at the time.

Dunn was an eminently theatrical and flamboyant musician remembered by his peers for his unique and innovative array of "tricks." In Dunn's case the tricks were not physical—as in playing multiple horns at once—but aural. Garvin Bushell, a clarinetist who played alongside Dunn in Smith's recording band, gave him credit as "the guy that made double-time famous, and he introduced wa-wa effects with the plunger."[54] Fellow cornetist Rex Stewart, who claimed Dunn as his earliest influence, provided a fuller account of his technical achievements:

> I first heard Johnny Dunn play back home in Washington when I was a boy . . . I gaped open-mouthed when I heard the sounds emanating from a long slender contraption played by a tall slender brownskin fellow on the stage. The contraption was a trumpet, a special type which I later found out was called an English coach horn . . . I was just flabbergasted when, later in the program, Dunn picked up another much shorter trumpet and made sounds like a horse whinnying and a rooster crowing! . . . Johnny made sounds on that horn such as I never imagined. He made that horn moan, he made it chitter and wa-wa like a baby's crying. But the greatest effect of all was when he did the flutter tongue. This gimmick broke up the house. Dunn reserved it for special moments like when the band would be playing soft and sweet, with the lights way down low. He'd start on about the twelfth bar of a 16-bar strain and go from a whisper to a roar, flutter tonguing, and the crowd in the dance hall would answer with yells of approval.[55]

Not all who heard Dunn were equally impressed. Pops Foster, for instance, having come up musically amidst the likes of Joe Oliver, Freddy Keppard, and Louis Armstrong in New Orleans, dismissed him for playing in "just a wa-wa-wa style."[56] One gets the sense that Dunn's theatricality, and his affinity for unusual and even radical timbres such as that created with the flutter tongue technique, got in the way of his ability to play solos that had the sort of fluent cohesion that would later be prized as a mark of true jazz artistry. In this vein, it should be remembered that even Joe Oliver was known for his array of "tricks" on the cornet, and that only after the mid-1920s did horn players seem to put particular value on melodic continuity and harmonic advancement in developing their solos.[57] Dunn therefore epitomized a model of jazz virtuosity that was influential in its earliest years and was especially well suited to the demands of adapting jazz to staged theatrical performance.

Mamie Smith, the face and the voice in front of the Jazz Hounds, commands attention in her own right in this connection. Like the Original Dixieland Jazz Band, Smith's achievement is typically defined through her groundbreaking recordings, overseen by African American songwriter and entrepreneur Perry Bradford. However, just as the ODJB solidified the connection between jazz and cabaret entertainment with their 1917 engagement at Reisenweber's, Smith typified the connection between vaudeville, jazz, and blues. By Bradford's account, the song with which Smith became most identified—"Crazy Blues"—began its life under a different title, "Harlem Blues," as part of a black-cast production called *Made in Harlem* that opened at the Lincoln Theater in 1918.[58] When her recordings for the OKeh record company began to hit in 1920, Smith quickly became a headline attraction at the leading black vaudeville theaters. Female blues artists such as Ma Rainey had been touring through the black vaudeville and tent show circuit for years at this point, but Smith's new status as a recording star gave her a level of visibility that was unprecedented among female African American musical artists.

Capturing the enthusiasm that surrounded her, the March 5 edition of the *Chicago Defender* carried two separate reviews of Smith's weeklong engagement at the city's Avenue Theater. Regular theater columnist Tony Langston noted the immense crowds turning out to see Smith and expressed appreciation for the lavishness of her gowns—an indication of the way that Smith and other "blues queens" of the era established a template for black femininity that foregrounded glamour and offered audiences a model of upward mobility.[59] The other, unattributed article dedicated more attention to Smith's singing style, noting with surprise:

> One would imagine from the records that [Smith] was of a rough, coarse shouter. To the contrary, she was a splendid reproduction of May Irwin, who made this class of amusement what it is today and what it will remain ... Her last number, the "Crazy Blues," justly called the King of all Blues, hit the audience in Baby Ruth order and took a real curtain call and would have done honor to any artist in the business.[60]

That the reviewer uses May Irwin as a point of comparison suggests two things: Smith was a more "refined" sort of blues singer than would be customary among African American vocal artists; and the influence of white female "coon shouters" upon perceptions of black song remained pronounced enough by 1921 that an artist like Smith still had to sing in the shadow of her white counterparts. Just as importantly, Smith's "live" act is judged according to the expectations of her recordings, offering a clear indication of how the success of African American artists in the recording field changed the terms under which they appeared, and were received, onstage.

In fact, Smith's extensive touring throughout the year 1921 might be seen as the first instance in which a black musical artist undertook a performance tour that was largely designed to promote the sale of recordings. From our current twenty-first-century perspective this is standard industry practice. During the first decades of the twentieth century, though, it was generally taken as a truism that recordings served to promote an artist's personal appearances, not the other way around. In this light, a full-page ad taken out by OKeh Records in the record industry journal, *Talking Machine World*, to publicize its growing catalog of Mamie Smith titles—shown in Figure 4.3—is striking for the way it asserts the pronounced commercial interrelationship between Smith's records and her touring activity. Under the heading, "Mamie Smith Advertises in Person," and with copy addressed not to regular consumers but to the record dealers whose job it was to sell Smith's recordings to the public, OKeh announced:

> Under the direction of the Standard Amusement Co., Mamie Smith, assisted by her All-Star Revue, a large company of well-trained artists, is giving concerts in all the large cities throughout the country. Due to her popularity, capacity-filled houses are guaranteed. And the enthusiasm created, in turn, has in every instance stimulated the sale of her records . . .
> A CONCERT TOUR OF THIS CHARACTER IS THE VERY BIGGEST THING IN ADVERTISING.[61]

Confirming the promotional strategy laid out by OKeh, Perry Bradford describes in his autobiography an occasion on which a record dealer in Norfolk, Virginia, booked Smith for a one-night performance and proceeded to sell over ten thousand of her records in a single night, claiming: "he had ten helpers handing out the records (at one dollar per copy) so fast during that half-hour intermission . . . that it looked like Barnum & Bailey giving away silver dollars."[62] Bradford's account is likely exaggerated but even so, along with OKeh's advertisement, it suggests that the emergence of the race

Figure 4.3 "Mamie Smith Advertises in Person": Okeh Records' advertisement for blues singer Mamie Smith suggests that the singer's live performances were a means of promoting the sales of her recordings. From *Talking Machine World* (April 15, 1921).

records market in the early 1920s coincided with a new understanding of the interconnections between recordings and live performance that would, over time, reshape the ways in which music was sold, profits were gathered, and musical performances were evaluated.

* * *

The expansion of the black vaudeville and theatrical circuit created a vital new avenue for African American musical artists—and especially blues singers, who came to dominate the circuit throughout the 1920s—to gain exposure. On the mainstream vaudeville stages, those where white patrons were the primary if not exclusive audience, opportunities for black jazz and blues musicians were comparatively far more rare. Mainstream vaudeville complemented the cultural work done by sound recordings in establishing that the most widely recognized and popular sorts of jazz were associated with white performers. The relative success of the Creole Band was something of an anomaly in this sphere, and the band's endeavors largely predated the moment when "jazz" as such began to circulate more widely as an established style. Much more common were white singers, instrumentalists, and bands who invoked jazz to convey a certain spirit of high-energy fun.

Sophie Tucker was perhaps the leading white artist in this vein at the time when jazz first started to have a pronounced presence in vaudeville. That she was also a noted cabaret artist, who both preceded and succeeded the Original Dixieland Jazz Band at Reisenweber's, attests to her remarkable versatility and success at striking an effective and alluring balance between cabaret-style intimacy and vaudeville-style theatricality.[63] Tucker began her performing career as a "coon shouter," very much in the May Irwin mold. She appeared in blackface regularly for a time but came to resent the fact that she was unable to be onstage as "herself." In her autobiography, Tucker describes the moment when she was finally able to perform without being blacked up as transformative, a moment when she embraced not just her whiteness but her working-class Jewish identity as well, which infused her persona for the rest of her career.[64] Still, African American music remained a prominent resource for the singer, as did the racially infused mix of humor and pathos that often went along with it, and like many artists whose careers began in the first decade of the twentieth century, she adapted her musical material to changing tastes and styles as ragtime gave way to jazz.

In the summer of 1916, Tucker and her agent, William Morris, put together the first incarnation of her Five Kings of Syncopation, a group of five instrumentalists who helped the singer navigate her way toward jazz.[65] She would not record with the group for another two years, but as a performing ensemble Tucker and her Kings were among the advance guard of white musicians who brought jazz to the forefront of national entertainment in the US. Although the instrumental lineup of the Five Kings was not always specified, a 1918 review noted that the band included violin, piano, cello, cornet, and drums, suggesting that Tucker's version of jazz was light on horns and more heavy on strings than some comparable ensembles, but in a manner characteristic of white jazz groups at the time.[66] Tucker was already an established vaudeville star when she formed the Kings, and from the start, her appearances with the troupe moved back and forth between cabaret and vaudeville settings. An appearance at the Keith and Albee-owned Colonial Theater in New York in March 1917 drew accolades, and credited Tucker as "the first to show a sign of progressiveness in her particular field," a nod to the bold gesture she made by surrounding herself with a full jazz band.[67]

Three years later, after concluding a successful, months-long run at Reisenweber's, Tucker found herself at the Palace, another Keith theater considered by then the pinnacle of vaudeville establishments. About her band, *Variety* reviewer Jack Lait enthused: "Kings is right. She has the last breath in jazz bands." Tucker remained the main attraction, and the way she moved through her act epitomized some of the wider connotations that jazz assumed on the vaudeville stage:

> She syncopated a ditty, then did a mammy ballad ("Chocolate Drop") in a red baby firelight spot, then her "Wild Women" scream and an old-fashioned Tuckerism by medium of "Alexander's Band Is Home from France." The superlative band played and she returned in the dizzy creation that she used in "Hello Alexander" . . . and knocked the living daylights out of "Nobody Knows," with comedy butt-ins . . . Sophie hit solidly. She is still the foremost syncopator, despite her "refinement," and she can get closer to an audience than any other individual on the stage. Miss Tucker is pure vaudeville—melodious, gaudy, lowbrow, naughty, intimate, punchy and fast.[68]

This final list of superlatives offered by Lait to describe Tucker could just as well be taken as a representative set of descriptive terms for jazz writ large, as it was construed circa 1920. The incorporation of jazz onto the vaudeville stage, as embodied by figures like Tucker, furthered the process through which the boundaries of moral acceptability were stretched in a medium that was designed to provide inoffensive entertainment to the greatest number of people. Jazz fit the pace of vaudeville, its speed an aural and rhythmic complement to the quick changes between acts that were the modus operandi of the format. Tucker's mastery of this ability to shift quickly and seamlessly from one number to the next made her "pure vaudeville," while the skillful accompaniment of the Five Kings of Syncopation heightened the excitement that attended to her presence and also, crucially, allowed her to strike the right, necessary balance between her familiarity as an established star of the stage (known for her "old-fashioned Tuckerisms") and her ability to bring something new to her act with every engagement.

* * *

Well beyond Tucker's appearances there, the Palace allowed jazz artists to claim a sort of "legitimacy" not typically conferred upon jazz when it appeared in other kinds of settings. As Tucker herself observed, "To play the Palace was to American performers what a command performance is to a British actor. Something to live for . . . To go on there was what 'going on at Tony Pastor's' was in the Gay Nineties."[69] Tracking the success of three further artists who played the Palace—Ted Lewis, Paul Whiteman, and Duke Ellington—reveals some of the different inflections that jazz assumed on the vaudeville stage as it moved through different waves of popular acceptance.

Lewis and Whiteman stood at opposite ends of the spectrum where the popularization of jazz was concerned. Lewis, like Tucker, epitomized the convergence of jazz and comedy. A wild-haired elfin figure, Lewis served as something like a clown prince of jazz after gaining attention first as a member of the Earl Fuller Jazz Band in 1917—in which he played clarinet—and then as the leader of his own band. By 1919 he was well established as a cabaret artist and had a regular slot in the "Greenwich Village Follies," a long-running revue at the Greenwich Village Theater that lightly satirized the bohemian habits of the Village's residents. Lewis made his Palace debut during his run with the "Follies," in late August 1919. He appeared at the head of a five-piece band in which he played clarinet and saxophone, accompanied by cornet, trombone, piano, and drums. The band drew strong reviews, but Lewis was unquestionably the star in a manner captured by the *New York Clipper*:

> Versatility is one of [Lewis's] biggest assets and in the short time he was on he exhibited sufficient entertaining ability to promise all sorts of success

in vaudeville. He plays the clarinet and saxophone, recites, sings and does a shimmy dance that makes all the wriggles done by the female specialists in this line look trivial and foolish. There is nothing suggestive in the Lewis dance, just a remarkable exhibition of the new craze which is bound to make the other shimmy experts look to their laurels.[70]

The shimmy was a sexually suggestive dance that, for a moment, was all the rage in the cabarets of New York and entered the field of vaudeville as well. Sophie Tucker even recorded a song about the craze, "Everybody Shimmies Now." As the reviewer notes, it was typically danced by women and so offered a rather clear distillation of the common link between jazz music and sexualized spectacle. Doing his own version of the shimmy, Lewis managed both to neutralize its sexual connotations and to capitalize upon the gender reversal that was involved for a male performer to shake his stuff in the required manner. An example of the lengths to which Lewis was willing to go to please the crowd, such antics—combined with the more than capable musical efforts of his band—would allow Lewis to maintain his status as a leading jazz attraction up to the early 1930s.

Writing about a subsequent Lewis appearance at the Palace five years later, in 1924, *Variety* reviewer Abel Green noted approvingly: "Lewis makes no pretext at symphonized syncopation, nor does he aspire to glorified jazz. His is jazz of the lowest and 'meanest' order, and the reversion to the elementary is all the more refreshing."[71] The contrast Green draws is directed at the growing effort to refine and elevate jazz by presenting it in a more "symphonic" manner, from which Lewis stood apart. Paul Whiteman was the undoubted figurehead of this movement, and his efforts to move jazz into the concert hall will be addressed at greater length in the next chapter. Here I want to look at a transitional moment in Whiteman's early career when he first made the shift from cabaret attraction to big-time vaudeville star.

Whiteman's Palace debut came in October 1921, just over two years after Lewis hit the stage there. At the time he was in the midst of a four-year run at the Palais Royal, a high-class cabaret in New York, where he had been appearing since the previous September. Even before he began his engagement at the Palais Royal, Whiteman had begun working on his distinctively orchestrated and carefully arranged approach to jazz. A native of Denver, Colorado, and a violinist, Whiteman was the son of a man who long served as the superintendent of music education for the Denver school system.[72] His musical career began as section player in symphony orchestras, first in

Denver and then in San Francisco. It was in the latter city that Whiteman came into more regular contact with jazz, where it had been undergoing a vogue for as long as anywhere else in the US.[73] Learning that he could earn more money playing in a jazz band than working in a classical orchestra, Whiteman made the switch and set about the task of applying his formal training to the music, seeking to reproduce the qualities that jazz players achieved by "faking" (or improvising) their parts while translating them into written arrangements.[74] The first version of his band to embody these musical goals came together in Los Angeles at the end of 1919. Within the next year he would make the move east, where his reputation grew and his brand of symphonic jazz gained significant momentum.

Whiteman was no less of an entertainer than Lewis or Tucker, but his brand of showmanship was of a very different sort. For his opening at the Palace, there was no shimmying to be found. Whiteman even eschewed the conventional practice of using title cards to announce the songs as they were played, a device that made it easier for the audience to follow along. Instead, he played a thirty-two-minute set of instrumental music in what was already recognized to be his signature style. *Variety* editor Sime Silverman, who reviewed the performance, noted that Whiteman's distinctive brand of dance music "gave a new tone to New York restaurants, the soft tone. He has muted everything except his salary."[75] That soft tone set him apart from the usual manner in which jazz was presented in cabarets and on the vaudeville stage alike but was quickly becoming a widely imitated standard. For Silverman, the change marked by Whiteman was not only welcome, but it was necessary:

> Vaudeville had to get him, vaudeville needs him, for those who have heard of the Whiteman band but haven't the money or the clothes for the coveur and menu card of the Palais Royal, will get the idea from Whiteman's music on the vaudeville stage . . . It's a new era in dance music. It shows up the blaring blatant jazz band combinations vaudeville has stood so patiently for.[76]

By Silverman's account, the qualities that make Whiteman such a hit on vaudeville—and even more so, such an important addition to the ranks of vaudeville attractions—are twofold, and they might well appear contradictory. On the one hand, Whiteman brings new class and refinement to the presentation of jazz on or off the vaudeville stage. This was Whiteman's motivation all along and it marked a major turning point in the public reception of jazz. Importantly, though, Whiteman's move to make jazz more refined does not necessarily make its appeal more exclusive. This brings us to Silverman's second main assertion, that Whiteman's move into vaudeville makes his sort of jazz more accessible than it would be if it stayed ensconced at the Palais Royal. Indeed, for Silverman, Whiteman's jazz is built for accessibility, its "soft" tones and inviting rhythms suited for all manner of listeners and not just the young enthusiasts who tended to favor jazz in its more "blatant" variations. Vaudeville was in a sense the perfect medium for Whiteman to test the degree to which his experiments with jazz arrangement would find favor with "average" listeners, and his success at the Palace set the stage for his subsequent endeavors.

By the time Duke Ellington reached the Palace, in the spring of 1929, he was already a well-established figure in New York City club life through his performance runs first at the Club Kentucky and, starting in 1927, the Cotton Club. These "black and tan" establishments were a critical medium through which African American jazz artists made their music known, the significance of which will be taken up in greater detail shortly. Although jazz had long been a feature of the Palace's programming by this time, black jazz artists had rarely appeared on the Palace stage. The most significant African American musical artist to have preceded Ellington at the Palace was Ethel Waters, who played there for the first time in 1927 and became, in effect, one of the most successful "crossover" artists of the 1920s, a rare black singer who had made the shift from playing in predominantly black vaudeville houses to predominantly white ones.[77]

Ellington had been playing for white audiences himself in his black and tan shows, but as it did for Whiteman, Lewis, and others, the Palace offered access to a different sort of patronage, not the "night people" who inhabited the cabarets but a broader audience whose acceptance could lead to a larger sort of commercial breakthrough. However, the Palace's allure was not quite what it had been earlier in the decade. Its fortunes were declining, as were those of vaudeville writ large, due to the new array of entertainment options that had become prominent, especially the coming of the sound film signaled by the massive success of the 1927 film, *The Jazz Singer*, featuring Al Jolson. By 1929, vaudeville houses were converting to movie houses by the droves, while existing film theaters were installing the necessary equipment to project films with pre-recorded music and dialogue.

The Palace, as the most illustrious vaudeville house in the country, was able to stem the tide of these innovations to a degree, but the situation was turning even there. By October 1927, *Variety* reported on declining gross earnings at the Palace, a theme it picked up on again in May 1929: "At one time in its career the New York Palace netted as much as $800,000 a year. Now if it nets $300,000, that's top."[78] This decline in the financial strength of vaudeville, and the Palace in particular, was the backdrop for the theater's decision to book more black musical artists, as the potential draw must have outweighed any former opposition to featuring them on the nation's most prestigious vaudeville stage. Whether or not the Palace had lost some of its luster by 1929, Ellington retrospectively recognized the importance of his first appearance there. Asked in 1952 to reflect upon his career highlights in *Down Beat*, Ellington listed his debut at the Palace as his first significant professional milestone after having secured his place at the Cotton Club. He explained: "In those days there were certain things you had heard about that you always wanted to experience, and one of those was playing the Palace Theater on Broadway. It meant reaching the peak for any artist who worked vaudeville, since the Palace was the ultimate in that field."[79]

Proof that a Palace appearance could boost his profile came when the *New York Times* took brief but generally laudatory notice of Ellington's appearance there, his first significant mention in the paper. Although he got nowhere near the column space as the week's headliners, the Marx Brothers, the *Times* characterized Ellington and his orchestra as a "first rate blackamoor band, come down from deepest Harlem to provide a series of specialties that range from tepid to torrid."[80] *Variety* did not wield such racially loaded language in its review of Ellington's Palace act, but expressed reservations about his readiness for vaudeville. Acknowledging that Ellington's band was one of the "hottest" in New York City, it complained that whenever the band moved away from its more up-tempo selections it fell flat and did not hold the attention of the vaudeville audience. Particularly subject to criticism were a "boy soprano" and "girl blues singer," both unnamed, who hit the wrong note with the crowd, the former because he was overcome by stage fright, and the latter because she sang a selection, "Handy Man," deemed too suggestive for the setting.[81] On the other hand, Ellington's regular band members were hailed as exceptional "trick instrumentalists," a turn of phrase reminiscent of the qualities that made Johnny Dunn such a standout attraction earlier in the decade. They soloed with aplomb, played their section parts with stirring vigor, and at their best presented "good music for vaude or anywhere else ... What they can do to the bell of a trumpet or trombone makes anybody's feet move."[82]

In the end, Ellington's Palace engagement may have been but a small step in a large career. Yet his appearance there was followed in short order by several other moves that further heightened his visibility: joining the cast of the Florence Ziegfeld stage production, *Show Girl*; appearing with the French singing sensation Maurice Chevalier at New York's Fulton Theater; a return engagement at the Palace that drew rave reviews; and then his first full-fledged national tour in the summer of 1930 which ultimately brought him to Hollywood, where he appeared in the feature film *Check and Double Check*, supporting radio stars Amos and Andy. Ellington's debut at the Palace was arguably the thing that set this sequence of events in motion and so demonstrated that even in decline, vaudeville could bring jazz to a wider public and make select jazz artists stars of a higher magnitude than they would otherwise be. This was particularly so for an African American performer like Ellington, who may not have been admitted to the Palace stage if the theater's own fortunes had not suffered a downturn.

In Close Quarters

From Tucker to Lewis to Whiteman to Ellington, we have seen throughout the previous section that there was regular and frequent traffic between the vaudeville stage and the cabaret. Until the end of the 1920s, vaudeville, and especially the most high-profile theaters, was where artists turned when they sought to "make it" in broader, show business terms. Making it in vaudeville did not mean escaping the cabaret. It could mean returning to the cabaret at a higher price tag, while opening a wider range of professional opportunities that went beyond stage work, such as recordings or even film. The most successful jazz careers of the 1910s and 1920s, those led by the likes of Whiteman, involved regular movement between the different performance venues and media outlets where jazz might be featured. Even with these varied performance options, though, the cabaret—or some version of it—remained central to the jazz economy. More to the point, the cabaret probably did more to define jazz in this early phase of its history than any competing performance space, with the possible exception of the dance hall or ballroom. While the roots of jazz might be traced to New Orleans honky tonks, public recognition of jazz came with the music's move into the cabaret and the association remained strong for years to come.

The earliest known uses of the word "jazz" in print occurred on the West Coast, in Los Angeles and San Francisco, in the years 1912 and 1913.[83] Oddly, these early appearances of the word occurred in connection with baseball and the link between jazz and music was only hinted at. Two years later, in July 1915, an article in the *Chicago Tribune* put the word in a more recognizable musical setting. At the time, Tom Brown's Ragtime Band, a group of white musicians from New Orleans, was appearing at the city's Lamb's Café and causing a stir. Members of the local musicians' union resented the success of these unruly outsiders and reportedly used the word jazz—or "jass" as it was then commonly cast—to denigrate them.[84] For *Tribune* writer Gordon Seagrove, jazz did not have such damning connotations. Rather, jazz was just the right music to help lifeless married men shake away their inertia and get rid of the emotionally "tired" feeling that was the blues. Titled, "Blues Is Jazz and Jazz Is Blues," Seagrove's article all but conflated these two terms of musical reference, suggesting that blues are the historical music "started in the south half a century ago and are the interpolations of darkies originally. The trade name for them is 'jazz.'"[85] Clearer than the proper designation of this music was its most common setting, for this "blue" music, according to Seagrove, "has become the predominant motif in cabaret offerings; its wailing syncopation is heard in every gin mill where dancing holds sway."[86]

It would take another year for "jazz," the term, to catch on more widely; and when it did, the association with the cabaret remained paramount. *Variety* had a column dedicated to news about cabaret offerings that began in 1912, but only in October 1916 does jazz begin to feature there. The news was coming from Chicago, where in the time since Tom Brown's band had first entered the scene, other white groups—some also from New Orleans, others hailing from points West—had joined the fray and made an impression. Hailing the city's already established reputation as a setting where trends in nightlife gained momentum, *Variety* announced:

> Chicago, the home of "Walkin' the Dog," "Ballin' the Jack" and sundry other cabaret features, has added another innovation to its list of discoveries in the so-called "Jazz Bands." The Jazz Band is composed of three or more instruments and seldom plays regulated music. The College Inn and practically all the other high class places of entertainment have a Jazz Band featured, while the low cost makes it possible for all the smaller places to carry their Jazz orchestra.[87]

Remarkably, only a week after this notice, the same publication issued a follow-up piece in which it refuted the notion that Chicago deserved credit as the starting place for this newly identified style. *Variety* cites the authority of its New Orleans correspondent, unnamed, who posits:

> Little negro tots were "Ballin' the Jack" in New Orleans over ten years ago, and negro roustabouts were "Turkey Trotting" and doing the "Todolo" in New Orleans as far back as 1890 . . . "Jazz Bands" have been popular there for over two years, and Chicago cabaret owners brought entertainers from that city to introduce the idea.[88]

The "discovery" of jazz in Chicago cabarets by one of the leading US entertainment news outlets, then, led to an almost immediate debate over the origins of jazz that encompassed race (assigning priority to black rather than white dancers and musicians) as well as geographical location. In a sense, it would take decades for jazz criticism and historiography to untangle the questions raised in these two *Variety* columns.

Moreover, the second column—while vague about the details—evokes the circumstances that led to the prominence of jazz in Chicago nightlife, which was fostered by a deliberate effort to bring more New Orleans-style music to the city. In particular, a band of New Orleans players, most of whom had come up under the mentorship of influential drummer and bandleader Jack Laine, was imported to Chicago by an enterprising promoter named Harry James and installed in March 1916 at Schiller's Café, a cabaret that according to William Kenney resided "on the southern edge of the Levee vice district and the northern edge of the fast emerging black belt."[89] At first they were called simply Stein's Band from Dixie, named for drummer Johnny Stein, but soon the name had changed to Stein's Dixie Jass Band.[90] Lineup changes led to Stein being replaced by Anthony Sbarbaro, who joined trombonist Eddie Edwards, pianist Henry Ragas, clarinetist Alcide Nunez, and cornet player Dominic "Nick" LaRocca. When Larry Shields replaced Nunez on clarinet later that same year, the lineup of the Original Dixieland Jass Band fell into place, and the rechristened group had moved its quarters from Schiller's to Casino Gardens, where they garnered the attention that led to their invitation to relocate New York and take up residence at Reisenweber's in the first month of 1917.

A publicity postcard from the time of the Dixieland Jass Band's engagement at Casino Gardens gives some indication of the venue and its qualities.[91] The image of the interior of the cabaret is hand-drawn, not a photograph, but nonetheless finely detailed. It shows in the foreground an array of small square tables with white tablecloths, each table surrounded by three or four chairs. Above the floor where the tables are distributed, a low ceiling hangs, decorated with ivy and pinecones, providing some of the "garden" effect in the establishment's name. On the far wall at the back of the space more atmospheric decoration appears in the form of a large mural that features shadowy black figures against a white background. A mix of people and animals, the figures look to be at play and, although they are only shown in outline, give the suggestion of being naked. The connotation is less sexual than exuberant, while also offering some sense of primitive, pre-civilized fun, an association that would run throughout the cabaret's history in the 1910s and 1920s. Near the back wall, at the rear of the floor and to the left sits a piano and accompanying bench, suggesting that this is where the band would play. Strikingly, it is at the same level as the tables and chairs where the patrons would sit. There is no sign of a stage, no sense that the performers would appear at a remove from the patrons sitting around them.

A similar card promoting Reisenweber's, depicted in Figure 4.4, shows a space with many comparable features but also some telling differences. The room shown is the "Four Hundred Club Room," which is the place where the Original Dixieland Jazz Band appeared upon their arrival at Reisenweber's in January 1917, but was only one among several rooms at the establishment that housed evening entertainment.[92] Named for the term used to describe the most select members of New York society—"The Four Hundred" was a term that used since the nineteenth century to describe the wealthiest faction of the city's residents—the "Four Hundred Club Room," and Reisenweber's as a whole, sought to confer a sense of exclusivity upon its patrons that added to the allure of the experience of going there. Here too, the floor is populated with tables covered by white tablecloths. These tables also have place settings on them, suggesting that more than Casino Gardens, Reisenweber's was a place where people came to dine as well as to drink and dance. It is a much bigger room than that shown at Casino Gardens and the decorations, like the name of the room itself, suggest a more "upper crust" atmosphere, with rows of chandeliers hanging from the ceiling and tasteful wallpaper with a hint of classical Grecian motifs supplanting the primitivist murals found at the Chicago cabaret. The performance space at Reisenweber's is also more obviously demarcated than that of Casino Gardens, occupying a clearing in the center of the floor. Yet it too is not elevated and is surrounded on three

Figure 4.4 A postcard shows the interior of the "Four Hundred Club" Room at Reisenweber's establishment in New York City, where the Original Dixieland Jass Band held an extended residency beginning in January 1917. Note the writing on the postcard by bandleader Nick LaRocca that this was the "ODJB Room." Courtesy of the Hogan Archive of New Orleans Music and New Orleans Jazz, Tulane University Special Collections.

sides by the tables where the room's patrons would sit, providing a level of proximity, accessibility and intimacy between audience and performers that was probably the most definitive and singular marker of the cabaret as a performance institution.

Compared to the standard vaudeville theater environment, cabaret spaces such as those at Casino Gardens and Reisenweber's had several distinguishing features. The tables gave patrons a sense that they occupied a space that was on some level, their own.[93] Sitting at their tables, cabaret inhabitants could enjoy the sense of public participation and collective spectacle that came from a night on the town but also felt free to engage in acts—eating, drinking alcohol, sweet talk, kissing, and other sorts of intimate behavior—that would have been considered out of bounds amidst the dense, linear rows of seats that characterized a more conventional theatrical space. The movability of the chairs allowed patrons to control their position relative to the cabaret setting and whatever activities might be happening there. They could sit so that their focus was directed entirely inward, on themselves and whoever accompanied them; or they could angle themselves toward whatever performance might be happening to have a better view.[94]

Such mobility of perspectives was an analogue to the dancing that was central to cabaret nightlife, through which patrons moved their bodies in a more vigorous manner. The Original Dixieland Jazz Band, as a cabaret attraction, exhibited certain commonalities with the vaudeville jazz acts. They engaged in broad comedy while performing such songs as "Livery Stable Blues," whose menagerie of animal sounds enabled some of the "trick" playing that became such a popular feature of the era's music. Their reputation, though, was primarily as a band whose music possessed distinctive rhythmic qualities and was exceptionally well suited for dancing. Recall the terms of their 1918 contract with Reisenweber's, cited at the outset of this chapter, in which they were required to play jazz music "which is unique and extraordinary insofar as it pertains to the rhythm and time of their rendition of such music." According to one review that appeared early in their engagement there, they scored a notable success on these grounds:

> The Jazz Band has hit New York at last, but just how popular it will become here is a matter that is going to be entirely in the hands of certain authorities that look after the public welfare. There is one thing that is certain and that is that the melodies as played by the Jazz organization at Reisenweber's are quite conducive to making the dancers on the floor loosen up and go the limit on their stepping. Last Saturday night the Jazz musicians furnished the bigger part of the music for dancing at the 400 Club and the rather "mixed" crowd that was present seemed to like it, judging from the encores that were demanded and from the manner in which the dancers roughened-up their stepping.[95]

Crucially, dancing patrons occupied the same floor space as did the performers. The clearing in the center of the "Four Hundred Club Room" at Reisenweber's might, at one part of the evening, house a floor show with some singers and other entertainers occupying the spotlight. When the ODJB came onto the floor, they stood at one end of the clear space and the dancers took up the rest. In this way, as cabaret historian Shane Vogel has observed, even the larger cabarets "managed to generate a sense of closeness and intimacy ... through relations of performance that designated the performance space as the domain of the audience."[96] Jazz, in its earliest manifestations, became tethered to the pronounced sense of public intimacy that cabarets encouraged and was the basis of their success. The music became accompaniment not just to dancing but to the varied range of behaviors that came to epitomize the cabaret. Jazz contributed significantly to the status of the cabaret as an "action environment," the term used by Lewis Erenberg in his valuable history of New York nightlife in the early twentieth century.[97] What mattered most was the way in which the different activities of the cabaret blurred together and so crossed and challenged the boundaries that existed between audience and performers, and between public and private notions of acceptable behavior.

* * *

Just two years after the ODJB hit New York, an even more seismic event changed the terms of American nightlife. January 1919 saw the passage of the Eighteenth Amendment, which prohibited the sale of alcohol in the United States. When the legislation, also called the Volstead Act after the Minnesota congressman who drafted the bill, was implemented a year later, on January 17, 1920, it appeared that the age of the American cabaret was at an end. In a sense it was, for the cabaret as it had evolved during the previous decade was no longer tenable. As we know with hindsight, though, Americans showed great resolve and resourcefulness in circumventing the new laws and especially in major urban centers such as New York and Chicago, the infusion of alcoholic beverages into American nightlife hardly faded away.[98] Instead, it went underground; or to put it differently, strategies had to be found to hide the extent to which drinking in public remained common. One strategy already begun before Prohibition was the designation of drinking establishments as private "clubs" that were exempt from some of the municipal restrictions that otherwise applied to such enterprises. Having patrons procure inexpensive memberships created the appearance of a private, relatively exclusive social sphere. Such clubs evaded police harassment for staying open past the citywide curfews that were used to regulate nightlife and, after Prohibition, operated as spaces where "members" could drink from their own alcoholic stash.[99] The nightclub, as an offshoot of the cabaret, was born from these efforts. Speakeasies occupied a similar territory in the new cultural economy of leisure but were a step down on the ladder of legitimacy, avoiding regulation not through the veil of membership but more simply by remaining beneath detection.

In New York, the sheer proliferation of these places provoked efforts on the part of the city government more specifically designed to regulate them.

As legal scholar Paul Chevigny points out, the first of the city's cabaret laws passed in 1926 was already based on an obsolete understanding of the nightlife economy, since it was really "speakeasies" and not "cabarets" that were sparking the greatest concern.[100] Nonetheless, the law put into place a legal definition of a "cabaret" that would remain with minor alterations and exert great influence on the local character of New York's cultural life for six decades. According to the text of the law, a cabaret was "any room, place or space in the city in which any musical entertainment, singing, dancing or other similar amusement is permitted in connection with the restaurant business or the business of directly or indirectly selling the public food or drink."[101] Any place that fit this definition now had obtain a license from the city to operate legally. Places defined as dance halls, a separate category, required a similar license. The new law also imposed a curfew on such establishments of three o'clock in the morning. Together, the new licensing requirements and the curfew were much like the comparable laws operating in the city of New Orleans cited earlier. They created a new system of surveillance to which cabaret owners, patrons, and employees—including musicians—were subjected. Over time, musicians would uniquely suffer from these laws, especially after 1940 when they would be required to carry identification cards to be employed in any place deemed a cabaret. Even in 1926, though, the cabaret law indicated the extent to which public consumption of intoxicants was associated with the conjunction of music and dancing that jazz had fostered; and as a result, jazz became construed as something of a threat to public order in its own right.

Not coincidentally, New York passed its cabaret laws at a time when jazz and nightlife institutions were becoming increasingly associated with the city's predominantly black areas. The Prohibition era saw Harlem rise to become the most visible African American urban district in the United States. As was true for the development of Manhattan more generally, black Manhattan had undergone a process of continual relocation over the course of several decades leading up to the 1920s, following a general trajectory of moving from downtown to uptown. During the earlier part of the twentieth century, the time when Ernest Hogan, Bert Williams, and their compatriots had dominated the world of black entertainment, the center of African American social life had been the Tenderloin, an area stretching from Twenty-third Street to the south and as far north as Fifty-seventh Street, with Sixth Avenue as its central artery.[102] Straddling the neighborhoods currently known as Chelsea and Hell's Kitchen, the Tenderloin was known as one of the city's most active vice districts and also had some of the most significant black cabarets of the pre-jazz era, such as Barron's, owned by African American Barron Wilkins, who eventually moved his club uptown to Harlem as the population tide shifted.[103] The turn uptown began in the 1910s and continued throughout the 1920s, driven by a wide mix of economic, political, and cultural factors: a deliberate effort to encourage African Americans to buy Harlem real estate; a new push for political autonomy among African Americans following the end of World War I, signified by such movements as Marcus Garvey's United Negro Improvement Association, based largely in Harlem; and an enormous influx of southern black migrants into New York which put pressure on existing population centers and further stimulated the search for new areas in which to settle.

As the black population of Harlem grew, the area gave rise to a new array of cabarets that came to define the height of bohemian fashion for a certain segment of the city's residents, white as well as—or perhaps even more than—black. "Black and tans," the name given to the institutions where white and African Americans gathered together, was a holdover from the nineteenth century, when it designated houses of prostitution that served an interracial clientele, where white and black female prostitutes might work side by side.[104] The suggestion of licit or illicit sex remained associated with the black and tans into the 1920s, but the activities were just as likely to revolve around interracial dancing and drinking. Prohibition gave such places a new aura of being at once forbidden and alluring. Combined with the changing demographics of New York City and the rise of new social codes according to which social intercourse with African Americans could be a marker of daring, adventure, and progressive leanings for white club goers, the black and tans of Prohibition-era Harlem assumed a cultural cache that was unusual for such institutions to possess. At the same time, the very popularity of many black and tans was based on a paradox, insofar as the most prestigious among them were also the most exclusionary, allowing white patrons to enter Harlem and watch African American performers in an intimate cabaret setting while keeping all but the most elite black patrons out. The Cotton Club was especially notable in this connection, but was joined by Connie's Inn, Small's Paradise, and the Nest Club, among scores of others.[105]

Stemming from these features, the tenor of Harlem's cabaret culture was strongly split between those places that primarily existed for the entertainment of the local African American residents and those places that catered to white patrons. Surveying Harlem's nightlife as part of a series on "Night

Life of the World," *Variety* editor Sime Silverman denounced the black and tans and all but avoided them, claiming that they existed only to allow their proprietors to "get every dollar he can out of every white who goes into it."[106] One place that made the cut on his Harlem excursion was Small's Paradise (pictured in Figure 4.5), which drew a significant white clientele but did not exclude black patrons in the manner of the Cotton Club or Connie's Inn. Observing the scene there, Silverman was critical of the white "downtowners" that dominated the club, dancing until 3 A.M., but praised the resident band, an African American aggregation led by Charley Johnson, for providing "hot" dance music of a quality rarely to be found downtown and worthy of whatever price the patrons of Small's were charged.

Offering more of an insider's perspective was African American novelist and literary editor Wallace Thurman, who provided some of the most revealing accounts of New York nightlife to come out of the Harlem Renaissance. In a multi-part set of articles on "Negro Life in New York's Harlem," Thurman devoted considerable space to the different layers of the neighborhood's leisure economy and the racial divisions that structured

Figure 4.5 The interior of Small's Paradise, one of the leading Harlem nightclubs of the 1920s, and a place where African American patrons were welcomed to a greater degree than at the likes of the Cotton Club. Courtesy of the Schomburg Center for Research in Black Culture, Photographs and Prints Division, The New York Public Library.

Harlem nightlife. Writing in November 1927, Thurman identified about a dozen Harlem nightclubs that had the status of destinations for those outside the area: Bamville, Connie's Inn, Barron Wilkins, the Nest, Small's Paradise, the Capitol, the Cotton Club, the Green Cat, the Sugar Cane Club, Happy Rhones, the Hoofers Club, and the Little Savoy. About these establishments as a group, he observed: "Most of these generally have from two to ten white patrons for every black one. Only The Hoofers, The Little Savoy, and The Sugar Cane Club seem to cater almost exclusively to the Negro trade." Continuing in this vein, he made a categorical distinction between those clubs that existed mainly for the amusement of white patrons and those oriented more to black attendees:

> Harlem's far-famed night clubs have become merely side shows staged for sensation-seeking whites. Nevertheless, they are still an egregious something to experience... White night clubs are noisy. White night clubs affect weird music, soft light, Negro entertainers and dancing waiters, but, even with all these contributing elements, they cannot approximate the infectious rhythm and joy always found in a Negro cabaret.[107]

Thurman's main example of a more "low-down" and, by implication, genuine African American cabaret was the Sugar Cane Club, which he described as a "subterranean passageway," much longer than it was wide. The Sugar Cane had a "rough" aura and was markedly cramped, with the orchestra stand "jammed" against one wall and about a quarter of the tight space reserved for dancing.[108] Entertainment on the evening recounted by Thurman came from an "unsophisticated Negro jazz orchestra" that accompanied a female blues singer. When the singer's act was over, the dancing began. Notably, Thurman observes that at this point in the night, the lighting of the Sugar Cane changed, the white light used to illuminate the singer dimmed, leaving mood-enhancing red and blue spots to be cast on the dancers themselves who "squeeze out from behind the tables and from against the wall, then finding one another's bodies, sweat gloriously together... animal beings urged on by liquor and music and physical contact."[109] Thurman found a similar atmosphere at the Harlem speakeasies that existed a rung below even such cabarets as the Sugar Cane. Here too, he suggests, there was more "spontaneous joy" and more genuine "thrills" than at the larger, more accessible cabarets. The reason had to do with the heightened intimacy that was the result not just of the smaller size of these settings, but the fact that the patrons of these places were "not subject to be watched by open-mouthed white people from downtown and the Bronx."

Writing in 1931, at the tail end of the Prohibition era, white comedian, musician, and nightclub performer Jimmy Durante said of Harlem:

> Today's Harlem is red-hot and low down, and the tide of colour [sic] isn't all black either... the night loafers who wind up in Harlem don't know there is such a thing as a colour [sic] line. It's a habit to taxi northward along Lenox Avenue when the sin cellars in the paleface sector have shut up. You go sort of primitive up there, with the band moaning blues like nobody's business, slim, bare-thighed brown-skin gals tossing their torsos, and the Negro melody artists bearing down something terrible on the minor notes.[110]

Wallace Thurman's indignation at the white presence in the Harlem black and tans was fueled by these objectifying tendencies, and his rightful anger was directed not just at white money, which kept these institutions afloat, but the gaze of white spectators which exerted control of its own. This was the dynamic involved in "slumming," one of the favored pastimes of early twentieth-century bohemia, through which privileged nightlife dwellers pursued thrill and adventure in urban areas known for some combination of poverty, vice, "unconventional" sexuality, and a racial character that lent itself to a sense of "exotic" encounter on the part of visiting outsiders. As a primary destination for those driven by such desires, the black and tans of Harlem and other similar urban districts succeeded through their "use of black culture to promote intimacy among middle-class whites."[111] For Thurman, this intimacy deprived Harlem's African American residents from inhabiting their own part of the city without being somehow put in the service of white onlookers. The presence and predominance of white spectators made the black and tans a space where any African Americans in attendance could not fully be "themselves," and as a result the intimacy found there was a false intimacy when judged against the more secluded and autonomous spaces of the black cabarets.[112]

Sime Silverman, the white veteran vaudeville critic, essentially shared Thurman's position on this point. Although he demonstrated less knowledge about the inner workings of those Harlem places predominantly patronized by African Americans, he mirrored Thurman's distaste for the effect that moneyed "downtowners" had on the atmosphere in the black and tans. The value judgment that comes into focus here would have a powerful influence and a long legacy in the formation of jazz criticism and the writing of jazz history.[113] Although Silverman and Thurman both treat the music they find in the cabarets as a secondary consideration to a large degree, they make it clear that in the first instance, an African American band (that led by Charley Johnson) has things to offer that a white band cannot do; and in the second instance, that in the right setting an "unsophisticated" black band in combination with an audience of black dancers generates a sort of uninhibited sensuality not to be found anywhere else. The play of oppositions at work in these two commentaries—black vs. white, low down vs. high class, uptown vs. downtown, unrestrained vs. inhibited, and ultimately, authentic vs. artificial—grew from the peculiar social relations of the Harlem cabaret in the Prohibition era. Taken together, they indicate how much the climate of opinion surrounding jazz and its place in the cabaret had evolved in the decade since the Original Dixieland Jazz Band made its way to Reisenweber's. White artists remained the most popular with a general audience, but it was no longer taken for granted that white musicians were the best representatives of jazz or that the tastes of white audiences should determine what jazz should be.

Dance Dance Dance

Cabarets, in Harlem and elsewhere around the US, had much in common with dance halls. Both kinds of institutions fostered levels of public intimacy that challenged the social and moral codes of Progressive reformers and Prohibition advocates. Both also, of course, made social dancing a central feature of urban nightlife. The orchestration of dancing and its coexistence with other attractions was markedly different in the two sorts of establishments, however. In the cabaret, the time given to dancing existed as one part of an evening's entertainment. Cabarets routinely offered a floor show, usually comprised of a combination of singing and dancing, with scantily clad chorus girls as a primary feature, while the house band provided accompaniment. Dance halls, by comparison, mainly existed for the purpose of allowing individuals and couples to dance. There was rarely any other entertainment besides that provided by the band; and in the taxi dance halls that were especially common in San Francisco, Chicago, New York, and other major and minor cities, where customers paid by the dance, both the dancing and the musical performance were strictly regulated to allow for the greatest amount of turnover from one dance to the next. Cabarets operated almost as though they existed out of time, but throughout the 1910s and early 1920s dance halls marked time with a rigidity that had a profound effect on the music that was played there.

Commercial dance halls, like cabarets, predated jazz, and were among the primary kinds of locations out of which jazz emerged in the 1910s. Dances such as the Texas Tommy, the Turkey Trot, and the Shimmy came from the dance halls and set the stage for the shift from ragtime to jazz, as much as the music itself. The experience of playing in these halls was common among the first generation of musicians who contributed to the making of jazz. Unlike the cabarets, though, which tended to have some measure of prestige attached to them, performing in the dance halls brought little glory. These halls were more squarely working-class leisure establishments and the social atmosphere was akin to that found at a place like the Funky Butt, or even the older concert saloons that had in many ways been a precursor to such places. The overlap of dance halls and the sex trade was common, while the musicians who worked there played very much in the service of the patrons and the hall's owners, who set the rules for the pace of the music and types of tunes that were played over the course of an evening.

In San Francisco the importance of the dance halls to the creation of jazz has been especially well documented. That city's Barbary Coast district gave rise to a vibrant dance music scene in the first decade of the twentieth century, and New Orleans string bass player Bill Johnson—later of the Creole Band—spent considerable time there and across the bay in Oakland from 1904 forward.[114] Oakland native and pianist Sid LeProtti recalled the influence of Johnson's string bass style on his own rhythmic conception of four beats to the bar—instead of the more standard two beats of ragtime—which he put into practice in his So Different Orchestra, a pioneering San Francisco ensemble.[115] LeProtti also provided one of the most graphic descriptions we have of the workings of an early twentieth-century dance hall from the musician's perspective. The hall in question was Purcells, a leading dance establishment of the Barbary Coast:

> As you come in on the left was the bar, and on the other side there was a partition. The partition was open, and the girls all stood up there in front behind it. As you went in, you selected your girl to dance with. You bought little copper checks for twenty cents apiece, and then you gave one to the girl every dance. The girls turned the checks in at the end of the night. Ten

cents went to the girls, and ten cents went to the house. You took the girl out and started dancin'. The floor manager come and took your order while they're dancin'. "What do you want to drink?" he'd say. You'd say, "Whiskey," "Wine," "Beer," or "Cigar," and he'd call this out to the bartender. Then the floor manager would blow the whistle, and the minute he blew the whistle, you had to stop the music right now, wherever it was. Then he'd say, "Play a waltz," then fine, you'd play it. They didn't waste any time when business was good...

When business was good, we used to play between twenty-six and thirty dances an hour. It was nothin' for the piano player to have tape on the end of his fingers and wear out a good piano in a year.[116]

Trumpet player Rex Stewart offered a similar, if less detailed, account in his memoir. In this case the hall was in Newark, New Jersey; and while Stewart cannot remember the proper name of the place, he remembers that he and his band mates called it the "Chain Gang" because of the working conditions there:

The unusual experience here was that we started playing at 8:30 sharp and each number had to be precisely one minute long. Sometimes we would get a request for a ballad tune and would get only as far as the middle before the floor man would blow the whistle as a signal for the next dance to begin. The girls were paid two and a half cents a dance and they earned around 40 or 50 dollars a week, which was big money in those days.[117]

These commercial dance halls were not settings where musicians had license to ride a groove for as long as they chose, or where dancers might lose themselves in an extended sensual reverie. Rather, in dance halls of this sort, the fundamental capitalist insight that time equals money was put into practice in a stark manner. Male patrons paid per dance; the women who danced with them were paid according to how many dances they worked in an hour, and during a night; the owners made their money from ensuring the greatest number of dances possible in a night, using the whistle—reminiscent of the time discipline of factory labor—to ensure the requisite amount of turnover. Musicians, though, were not paid by the dance, but only given a lump sum for a night's labor. Without them, in this era before the jukebox, there would have been nothing to accompany the dancing, yet they were treated as a background effect.

One might assume, given the severe restrictions placed upon the musicians working in the commercial dance halls, that they would have rebelled against these settings. Indeed, few musicians of any ambition hoped to spend their careers performing under such conditions. Yet the dance halls were a vital source of income for musicians early in their careers, or those who did not quite have the talent to merit recognition on the sheer strength of their playing alone. For musicians like Rex Stewart, they allowed the development of skills that became crucial to their subsequent careers in jazz. The dance halls were to Stewart what the Streckfus Steamboats were to Louis Armstrong, a site of essential training and onerous discipline. Playing in commercial dance halls required musicians to become alert to the needs of the audience and to those who managed the venues where they played; forced them to develop skills that allowed them to shift direction on the spot; and demanded they cultivate the kind of versatility that would be a key to success in a competitive music industry. All these imperatives encouraged a sort of improvisation but not the sort that is most typically valorized in jazz histories. It is not the improvisation involved when an artist spontaneously develops an idea in a sustained, self-expressive manner; nor is it the sort of improvisation that is built from musicians working collectively to break free from the constraints of rhythmic or harmonic regularity. This mode of improvisation came from musicians having to respond to a confining environment that nonetheless gave them opportunity to make a living through the making of music, so long as they kept the audience—and the exchange of money—moving.

*　*　*

A major change came over the course of the 1920s as commercial dance halls gave way to a higher class of ballroom. Harlem, again, was the seat of this cultural shift, with the Savoy Ballroom marking a new phase in the standing of jazz as dance music. Opened in March 1926, the Savoy was designed to accommodate a mass of dancers with a level of comfort and air of refinement that was unusual, especially in a public setting designed for African American patrons. The manager of the Savoy, Charles Buchanan, announced the difference between the ballroom and the sorts of dance halls with which Harlem residents were more familiar in an ad that appeared a week after the March 12 opening in the *New York Age*. In the ad, the Savoy management offered a $1000 reward for information concerning a "malicious report" that the ballroom was "charging extra for every dance in addition to the regular admission price and that it is quite expensive to come here for an evening's pleasure." Asserting that this report was "absolutely false," the ad outlined the admission price for the Savoy, which was fifty cents Monday through Friday evenings and Sunday afternoons, and seventy-five cents on Saturday and Sunday evenings and holidays. Lest the reader miss the point, the ad further insisted, "There are no other charges whatsoever."[118] The message was clear: not just was the Savoy an affordable option for a night out, but the dance hall policy of paying per dance was becoming an outdated practice, or distinctly déclassé.

Another feature of the Savoy stands out for the way it signals a departure from the established dance halls. Surrounding the enormous dance floor was a lounge where, according to the ad, "there are ample chairs for hundreds of people who can sit idly by and watch the dancers and enjoy the music and the entertainment." An undated reservation guide for the Savoy (Figure 4.6) includes a floor plan for the ballroom that bears out the ad's description.[119] Configured as a rectangle, the bandstand at the Savoy was in the center of one of the room's longer walls, meaning that the depth of the large room was relatively shallow from front to back, with the sides extending farther out from the bandstand in either direction. The dance floor was immediately in front of the bandstand, so that dancers could enjoy greatest proximity to the music. Then, extending out from the dance floor toward the back and on the sides, were a series of boxes that immediate lined the floor, behind which were smaller tables and lounge chairs—the lounge area referred to above. The diverse range of spaces within the Savoy was unusual and especially distinctive was the fact that the ballroom included so many areas that were designated more for sitting, and assuming the role of spectator, rather than being out on the floor dancing. Such comfort would have completely undermined the function of the commercial dance halls, where encouraging patrons to sit and watch the entertainment would result in a significant loss of profit. At the Savoy, dancing was integrated into an evening out that also included dining, drinking, and commiserating; and the bands that appeared there consequently had more freedom with repertory, without the mandate to change songs every minute or two as long as they maintained the interest of the dancers positioned closest to the bandstand.

Just over a year after the opening of the Harlem Savoy, its owners established a counterpart in Chicago. It too promised a more refined sort of jazz entertainment for black patrons and quickly found a significant audience on the city's South Side, already established as one of the nation's centers

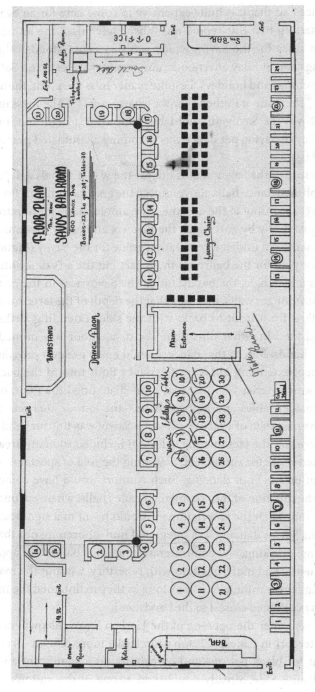

Figure 4.6 Floor plan for the Savoy Ballroom, the leading Harlem dance nightspot opened in 1926. Courtesy of the Manuscripts, Archives and Rare Books Division, Schomburg Center for Research in Black Culture, The New York Public Library.

of jazz activity. An article in *The Light and Heebie Jeebies*, the same African American newspaper that carried Wallace Thurman's foregoing account of Harlem, discussed the unique policy of the Chicago Savoy, which stemmed from the way the place operated as "a combination of theater and ballroom."[120] Central to the ballroom's effort to offer patrons its own version of continuous entertainment was the regular employment of two bands nightly, one more "sweet" and one more "hot," a feature also in place at the Harlem Savoy. For the Chicago Savoy's debut in November 1927 the resident bands were led by Charles Elgar and Clarence Black—with Elgar's band offering the "hotter" style and Black the "sweeter". As a reviewer put it when commenting on the opening night festivities: "The consensus of opinion . . . has it that both orchestras are in a class by themselves . . . The policy of continuous music with hardly a stop as each orchestra takes its turn keeps the dancers in a state of exultation always."[121]

A new hot band took up residence at the Chicago Savoy in April 1928, headed by Carroll Dickerson and featuring Louis Armstrong as soloist. By this time Armstrong's stature had grown enormously through his recordings for Okeh—now heralded as the great "Hot Fives" and "Hot Sevens"—but he was only beginning to make the moves that would turn him into a widely recognized star outside of the black community. His tenure at the Savoy, where he remained with intermittent gaps for nearly a year, was a major step along the way. It gave him exposure to an estimated 15,000 paid customers a week and allowed thousands more to hear him via a nightly radio broadcast transmitted from 11 pm until midnight—a rare opportunity for an African American musician at this time, shared by Duke Ellington from his post at the Cotton Club.[122]

Within the Savoy, the performance conditions that made the venue into a theater as much as a ballroom ensured that when Armstrong stepped up for a solo, he would be listened to. Dave Peyton, in his weekly *Chicago Defender* column, devoted regular space to Armstrong throughout the Savoy engagement, testifying two weeks after the Dickerson band's opening that, "Louis is the only musician I know of who really stops the ball, just as an actor stops the show."[123] A week later, Peyton described the scene when the Savoy's two regular bands, led by Dickerson and Black, were joined by a third "guest" band headed by veteran Erskine Tate. Peyton resorted to some local slang to capture the impact that Armstrong had on the Savoy audience:

> "Pouring oil" is an expression created by the musicians in Chicago. By that they mean some band has played better than the other. Last Saturday

night at the Savoy ballroom in Chicago three orchestras played, Clarence Black and his gang, Carroll Dickerson and his gang, and Erskine Tate and his gang . . . A note was handed to the house orchestras by [Savoy house manager] Mr. Fagin, asking them to join in and play the "Savoy Blues" with the guest orchestra. This was wonderful. The three bands, consisting of 37 players, rocked the beautiful ballroom with their scintillating music. It was Louis Armstrong, a member of Carroll Dickerson's orchestra, whom this writer has termed the "Jazz Master," who saved the hour. As the boys would say, Louis poured plenty of oil and it soaked in too. The crowd gathered around him and wildly cheered for more and more. Louis really poured oil last Saturday night.[124]

"Pouring oil" as he did, Armstrong elicited the excitement of the Savoy through the combination of virtuosic musicianship and charismatic stage presence that would ultimately make him one of the biggest stars to come out of the 1920s jazz age. He was assisted by the properties of the Savoy. The large capacity of some four thousand patrons, and the mix of areas that encouraged different styles of engagement with the music, created an environment where a performer of Armstrong's strength could demonstrate his ability to appeal to a wide constituency. At the same time, unlike that other sphere into which artists moved in order to "make it"—vaudeville—Armstrong maintained his connection to the most visibly active segment of the audience, the dancers, who remained a primary gauge of success in the ballroom setting.

It was at the Savoy that Armstrong developed the set piece that became his most celebrated articulation of the jazz soloist's art, "West End Blues," which he recorded just two months into his tenure there. In its recorded version, "West End Blues" has become as canonized as any single work of jazz, taken as an ultimate example of the way in which an improviser's freedom could give shape to a musical utterance with a composer-ly shape. What significance should we attach to the fact that Armstrong woodshedded the song for weeks at the Savoy before committing it to record? That he did so offers the best indication that the audience at the Savoy was there as much to watch and listen as to dance, for "West End Blues," with its relatively sedate tempo and its breathtaking solo passages, was hardly designed as a song meant primarily to keep the audience moving. George Whettling, a drummer who was part of a noted coterie of white Chicagoans drawn to Armstrong's playing, recalled:

> One of the best summers I ever had was when Louis was at the Savoy Ballroom in Chicago . . . When Louis started blowing the introduction to

"West End Blues" . . . everybody in the ballroom started screaming and whistling, and then Louis lowered the boom and everybody got real groovy when he went into the first strains of "West End."[125]

The boisterousness of the audience response described by Whettling suggests that the terms of musical spectatorship at the Savoy were not those of the concert hall: the audience felt free, and was expected, to express its strong approval for a performance that pleased them. Some of those audience members also, almost certainly, danced as they listened, which did not impair their appreciation of Armstrong's riveting performance but enhanced it. What matters is that, when Armstrong tore into the opening fanfare of "West End Blues," the audience recognized the song and responded to it in kind. It was not just a generic song designed to get them dancing—be it a waltz, a foxtrot, or even a blues—but a specific selection by a recognized artist whose musical mastery was a key component of his growing star power.

Armstrong's approach to "West End Blues" was shaped by another key feature of the Savoy as well. Thomas Brothers points out, in his detailed account of Armstrong's evolution through the 1920s, that the Chicago Savoy was likely the first place where Armstrong performed live before an audience using a microphone.[126] Microphones and amplified public address (p.a.) systems were only beginning to be used in live music performances by the late 1920s; in years to come, of course, this incursion of amplification into the field of live music would have major repercussions. For Armstrong, appearing at the Savoy, it mainly had the effect of allowing him to tone down his vocal presence and sing with a new softness, as it did for other male vocalists like Bing Crosby and Rudy Vallee who were associated with the style of "crooning." While Armstrong's charging trumpet fanfare at the opening of "West End Blues" grew from his exuberant ability to command the attention of a dance hall crowd, his nearly crooning vocal—much changed from earlier stand-out performances such as "Heebie Jeebies"—bears the mark of this new ability to project the most subdued voice to a broad public.

Jazz in Its Place(s)

With its radio hook-up and its p.a. system, the Chicago Savoy exemplified the extent to which musical performance—or the "liveness" of music, to use Philip Auslander's term—was being mediatized in new ways during the early history of jazz. This did not just have to do with the growing prevalence of recorded popular music during the 1910s and 1920s, although recordings were certainly a major part of the larger cultural shift then taking place. Rather, music venues themselves functioned as a kind of media, with each distinct sort of place (honky tonks, public meeting halls, excursion boats and trains, vaudeville theaters, cabarets, dance halls and ballrooms, among many other settings) imposing its own framework on the music that appeared there. Jazz fit into each of these types of places in ways that were unique, and in many cases—perhaps most notably the cabaret—the music affected the space as much as the space affected the music, if not more so.

Writing about jazz at a later point in the music's history, popular music scholar Fabian Holt has observed: "The growing diversification of jazz in the mid twentieth century into cultures of traditional, modern, pop, and art jazz makes it difficult to represent the genre in the singular and increases the need to specify which culture of jazz one refers to."[127] The foregoing survey of jazz performance spaces and conditions should make it apparent that similar complexity characterized the earliest years of jazz's emergence as a recognizable form. Where jazz performance was concerned in the 1910s and 1920s, it was less the case that so many subgenres or subdivisions of the music existed, but rather the way in which the performance conditions themselves varied so widely made the most difference. Whether an event was designed to include dancing or not, whether the audience was sitting or standing (or some combination of both), whether the stage was clearly demarcated from the area occupied by the audience, whether the audience was consuming alcohol—all of these factors had an impact on the performance of the music. So too, of course, did those macro-social factors such as whether a given setting was geared toward black or white audiences, or whether it was positioned as a more refined and respectable environment or one more "suspect" according to prevailing social norms. At times we might hear traces of these elements of performance in the recorded jazz of the era, as we do on "West End Blues"; but much of what constituted jazz in these years never made it onto record or if it did, had negligible impact relative to how the music came across when it was encountered in a live setting.

Considered most broadly, live jazz in the first decades of the twentieth century helped establish the terms for a new sort of public intimacy in which dancing of a more uninhibited character became more widely accepted among diverse classes of Americans, and in which the mixing of white and African Americans in urban settings assumed new fluidity. This is not to say that jazz brought full-scale liberation from older restraints upon the freedom of bodily expression or racial commiseration. Rather, live jazz became a primary medium through which the most public struggles over these issues were waged; and the places where jazz was performed acted as a sort of ground zero for these contests over the appropriate ways to inhabit public space. More than anything though, the very multiplicity of places and meanings attached to jazz, combined with the acknowledged social mobility of the music, were the qualities that made it into the most representative genre of Western modernity as it was articulated in the early twentieth century. Jazz was not only high or low, neither was it only black or white. As a field of practice, jazz was a medium through which these points of cultural distinction and conflict were reconfigured without being reconciled. In the next chapter, we will see further manifestations of the peculiar mobility of jazz as we look more closely at its movement into the concert hall.

5
Culture High and Low
Reinventing Concert Music

What makes music modern? Few aesthetic questions generated more debate in the two decades following the end of the First World War. When the editors for *Musical America* took up the matter in a November 25, 1933, editorial, however, they had a specific concern in mind. The short article, titled "'Modern' and 'Mod'ren' Music," commented on the application of the term "modern music" to popular song and dance tunes, including jazz. Modern music was already a notoriously slippery formulation. It could not just be replaced by seemingly less obtuse phrases like "contemporary music" because the modernity of modern music was not simply a matter of chronology, but also had to do with musical form and compositional methods. "Atonality, polytonality, the new counterpoint and sundry other manifestations of an altered outlook on many basic principles of the art, are signposts but not absolute criteria" of what makes music modern, by the account of *Musical America*. As multifaceted as this understanding of modernity might be, one point remained clear: "the term 'modern music' has to do with art music, not popular music." The editors continued:

> The music of the night clubs, the revues, the musical shows and the dance floors is not "modern music." Alike for those who champion it and those who regard the modern movement as abortive, "modern music" involves questions of serious art . . . The gulf separating art music from popular music is just what it has always been. If there are those who cannot draw the line in dealing with the music of their own day, let them look back and try to reconcile, as one and the same thing, the café, vaudeville, and ballroom tunes of forty years ago with the symphonies of Brahms or the tone-poems of Strauss. This may help them to realize that the music which figures on Paul Whiteman's programs is popular music, not modern music; that, with debatable exceptions, the compositions of George Gershwin and other jazz writers are popular music, not modern music.[1]

Thus was the ideological line drawn in the sand. The boundary between high and low, serious and popular music, needed to be maintained for *Musical America*'s readers. Only serious music with high art intentions earned the label of modern music. Popular music was something else.

Ironically, the journal calling itself *Modern Music* took a very different stance on this same problem. *Modern Music* was the house publication for the League of Composers, an organization that had a major influence on the growth of musical modernism in the US. The composer-critics who were the principal contributors to the journal were not any more at peace with popular music than the editors of *Musical America*; but unlike the latter, they refused to deny its relevance to their own work. Writing in an issue commemorating the tenth anniversary of the organization, in early 1933, the composer Marc Blitzstein offered a survey of the past decade that demonstrated the increased traffic between "art" and "popular" musical worlds. The title of Blitzstein's piece, "Popular Music—An Invasion: 1923–1933," indicated the anxiety that underpinned the subject matter for modern composers of Blitzstein's stripe and conveyed the position from which popular music would be viewed by such artists. Their world of "legitimate" concert music was a realm inside; popular music was outsider music, invading that sphere of legitimacy.

Blitzstein was not just a defensive highbrow commentator, though. An astute social critic, and a musical artist with populist designs of his own, his portrait of this "invasion" was almost sanguine. According to his understanding, what transpired during the past ten years was that, "for the first time, serious composers turn their attention to the field [of popular music], purposefully, with an 'esthetic' in mind." Or, to put it more baldly, "you can say that popular music invaded the concert hall."[2] The evidence was plentiful in the work of George Antheil, Kurt Weill, Louis Gruenberg, and Aaron Copland; and also, crucially, in the work of Gershwin, the man from the other side, whom Blitzstein characterized far more sympathetically than had *Musical America*: "a popular composer, writing what is to a Stadium-full of people important concert music, and writing it to the satisfaction of Mr. Damrosch, Mr. Koussevitzky, and the Committee of the I.S.C.M."[3] Blitzstein understood the engagement with popular music to be part of a larger process through which modern music and modernist composers questioned the "constancy" of musical values, analogous to the neo-primitive rites of early Stravinsky, the machine aesthetic of the Futurists and their disciples, and the taking up of various strands of "folk" music for inspiration. As to the artistic results of this intermingling of "serious" and "popular" approaches, Blitzstein drew mixed conclusions. He acknowledged that even the most accomplished American composers, such as Aaron Copland, could only go so far in approximating the character of "real jazz." On the other hand, he praised popular artists themselves for having resisted the incursion of "serious" composers. "One grows to believe in the real worth, wherever it may be in the scale of values, of the untinkered Tin-Pan-Alley 'number,'" mused Blitzstein, who concluded: "Serious music might even learn a lesson from this persistently 'low' art, in the matter of discovering one's place, and respecting it."[4]

Blitzstein to the contrary, popular music—and jazz in particular—hardly stayed in place during these years. We saw in the last chapter that jazz throughout the 1910s and 1920s was a highly mobile musical form, occupying a diverse range of performance venues that made it into a phenomenon that could not be reduced to a single steady definition. One move still to be examined is the move of jazz into the concert hall. For all intents and purposes, this move began with Paul Whiteman's pivotal—and divisive—1924 concert at Aeolian Hall, which he dubbed an "Experiment in Modern Music" and which is now best remembered as the event where George Gershwin's groundbreaking composition, *Rhapsody in Blue*, received its first performance. Other performances, such as James Reese Europe's series of Carnegie Hall concerts in the early 1910s, importantly prefigured the Whiteman concert; but no previous concert—and few subsequent ones—had the impact of Whiteman's "Experiment" in provoking a reconsideration of where jazz fit into the fabric of American musical life. That Whiteman, moreover, appropriated the phrase "Modern Music" for his 1924 performance at Aeolian Hall puts the perspectives discussed above in a new light. When the editors of *Musical America* objected so strongly to the application of the phrase "modern music" to popular music of the sort associated with Whiteman, they took an expressly reactionary position designed to contain a line of development already several years in the making. Marc Blitzstein recognized as much in his piece for *Modern Music*, but also presented the case that popular music remained strongest when it did not aspire to the condition of concert music. Whiteman, on the other hand, unapologetically sought to elevate jazz by "taming" its wilder properties and refashioning it for what he perceived to be more sophisticated tastes.

The move of jazz into the concert hall was more than an effort to provoke a shift in the music's standing from "low" to "high." Observed over the long term, the period from the mid-1920s to the mid-1940s, from the time of Whiteman's "Experiment" to the further consolidation of the jazz concert with the advent of Norman Granz's Jazz at the Philharmonic, saw substantial reconfiguration of the "highbrow"/"lowbrow" divide in American musical culture. To fully grasp the nature of this historical moment requires a wide-angle lens of the sort that has largely been lacking in scholarship on jazz and American classical music alike, to comprehend how changes in the one area laid the groundwork for changes in the other. During these same years American classical music underwent major transformations of its own, which pointed in two directions at once: on the one hand, the growth of a base of native composers who worked to develop resources and institutions to support the creation of artistically challenging contemporary music; on the other hand, the consolidation of authoritative institutions like the New York Philharmonic that enshrined an increasingly fixed notion of the classical music canon. Connecting these two tendencies was the common goal to build the largest possible audience for American concert music, which was pursued through a variety of methods: increasing the subscriber base for major concert series at venues like Carnegie Hall, but also taking advantage of the mass media forms of sound recordings, movies, and especially radio. When classical music of the time is viewed not through the efforts of major composers and their works but through the efforts of concert promoters, booking agencies, and media outlets seeking to sell the music to the public at large, the separation between art and commerce that "highbrow" musical values have long sought to uphold withers away. For jazz to make its move into the world of concert music then begins to appear as a move toward, not away from, a mass audience. To fully appreciate the significance of this development, we first need to step back in time to explore how the concert hall became the institution that it was by the 1920s.

Concert Halls and Cultural Hierarchy

The process according to which American culture, and music, became stratified according to a rubric of "high" and "low"—or "highbrow" and "lowbrow," in cultural historian Lawrence Levine's influential formulation—was gradual, uneven, and always incomplete. In chapter one, we saw that Jenny Lind's arrival in the US in 1850 coincided with an intensified effort to impose a separation of different cultural spheres in the wake of the Astor Place Riot, which was itself an outgrowth of cultural conflict between distinct classes of theatergoers in New York City. Yet the boundaries between these spheres were not securely in place, and Lind appeared to affect a sort of reunification of the divided cultural fields of the time—in particular, that between middle-class and working-class concertgoers. The decision to stage her American debut at Castle Garden also reflected the conditions surrounding Lind's appearance in the US. There was, effectively, no purpose-built concert hall in New York City at the time of her arrival in 1850, and certainly none that would accommodate the audience that the concert's promoter, P.T. Barnum, hoped to draw. Following an unsuccessful effort to build a venue to house her debut concerts, Lind appeared at Castle Garden, a capacious setting where the spectacle of the crowd nearly overshadowed the singer herself.

By Levine's account, the impetus to construct a stricter hierarchical difference between "highbrow" and "lowbrow" cultural forms grew markedly in the decades after the Civil War. The motivations for this enhanced cultural divide came from the economic elite class of industrial capitalism, which turned to the realm of art and culture as a bulwark against a public sphere that was becoming—from its perspective—disorderly due to waves of new immigrants, the accompanying growth of labor unrest, and continued social uncertainty stemming from the troubled status of African Americans in US social life. In the face of these perceived threats to public order, Levine argues that the capitalist elite assumed a threefold response: there was a retreat from the public to the private sphere; a corresponding effort to transform public space through hierarchized systems of taste and canons of "good behavior;" and a push to convert cultural "strangers" to elite ideals and practices.[5] Deriving from these latter two impulses, a new ideology took root that invested select works of art—whether music, theater, visual art, or literature—with an almost religious kind of significance for their capacity to embody the highest human values. This tendency toward "sacralization" underpinned the definition of "high" art as a realm apart, separated not only from other, "low" cultural forms, but from the pressures and stresses of everyday life in a stratified capitalist society. Public places of culture (museums, libraries, opera houses, and most notably for my purposes, concert halls) proliferated from this moment in the late nineteenth century forward, with the understanding that such places were designed to enhance and codify the individual contemplation of great artistic works.[6]

The building of dedicated concert halls, then, did not just follow from a utilitarian desire to have suitable performance spaces. It derived from a conviction that musical works of the highest character should be listened to in something like an ideal environment, a place that was designed to provide the best conditions for aesthetic experience. Prior to this point in the late nineteenth century, few such dedicated concert halls could be found even in major cities like New York, Philadelphia, Chicago, or Boston; and some that had been created, such as the New York Academy of Music built in 1854, lost ground due to changing tastes and social habits of their core audience. Among these cities, only Philadelphia's Academy of Music, opened in 1857, maintained its standing as the city's leading concert venue beyond the first decade of the twentieth century. Elsewhere, civic leaders took their cue from developments overseas, and the US joined a wave of international concert hall construction that ran from the 1880s to the 1900s. Leipzig, Amsterdam, and Berlin all opened new concert halls during the 1880s; 1891 saw the opening of New York's Carnegie Hall, the first of the American venues to mark this rise of activity. Boston would follow suit in 1900 with the opening of Symphony Hall; and Chicago would see the opening of its Orchestra Hall in 1905.[7] In each of these settings the construction of the concert hall was financed and sponsored by financial and industrial elites of the kind that are central to Levine's account, figures that sociologist Paul DiMaggio has termed "cultural capitalists" for their commitment to the fine arts and cultural philanthropy as a means of solidifying and extending their status as leaders of their respective communities.[8]

In the case of Carnegie Hall, the stimulus for the project came from an alliance of economic and cultural elites. Industrialist Andrew Carnegie stood for the former, conductor Walter Damrosch for the latter. Damrosch's father Leopold exerted significant influence upon the musical life of New York City from the time of his migration from Germany in 1871 until his death in 1885. He spent a year as conductor of the New York Philharmonic Orchestra, but more notably he founded two new musical organizations, the New York Oratorio Society and the New York Symphony. In the last year of his life, the elder Damrosch also forged an important working relationship with the recently built Metropolitan Opera House, where he was hired to conduct a season of Wagnerian opera at a time when the American taste for Wagner was just beginning to take root. Unfortunately, in the midst of his endeavors Leopold Damrosch fell ill from pneumonia and passed away in February 1885. His son Walter, only twenty-three at the time, picked up the baton at both the Met and with the New York Symphony, and from that point forward his own stature as one of the leading lights of the New York musical scene rose significantly.[9]

Carnegie, for his part, adhered to the ideals of social Darwinism espoused by British social theorist Herbert Spencer, which held that differences in wealth resulted from the differential capacity of individuals and groups to compete in the competitive capitalist marketplace.[10] According to Carnegie, the poor could not be trusted to better themselves, which rendered more conventional forms of charity inefficient. As he argued in his influential essay, "The Gospel of Wealth": "Neither the individual nor the race is improved by almsgiving. Those worthy of assistance, except in rare cases, seldom require assistance. The really valuable men of the race never do . . . He is the only true reformer who is as careful and as anxious not to aid the unworthy as to aid the worthy."[11] Philanthropy therefore stood for Carnegie as a form of social engineering, doing a species of good work on behalf of the larger society while ensuring that resources did not fall into undeserving or irresponsible hands. Although he was not especially known to be a devotee of music, Carnegie identified "halls suitable for meetings of all kinds, and for concerts of elevating music," to be one of his recommended categories of philanthropic giving, with the suggestion that such facilities "do much to make the lives of the people happier and their natures better."[12]

The idea for Carnegie Hall arose through chance, when Walter Damrosch and Andrew Carnegie happened to be on the same ship crossing the Atlantic during an 1887 voyage. Carnegie was traveling with his new wife Louise, a devoted singer and patron of the arts who helped to nurture their budding acquaintance.[13] Damrosch was invited to join Carnegie at his castle in Scotland, and there the idea for a new concert hall took root. Two years later, in 1889, Carnegie established a corporation that would oversee the construction of the hall. While his patronage was crucial to the building of the hall, his support had its limits, in keeping with his larger philosophy of philanthropy. Carnegie would not endow the music hall beyond the time of its construction. Once built, it was meant to become a self-supporting entity.

All the appointed directors of the new Carnegie Hall corporation were members of the New York business community save one, the architect William Tuthill, who designed the building. Tuthill had no prior experience with concert hall design but he was a musical enthusiast who sat on the board of the Oratorio Society and had an interest in the science of acoustics.[14] His design for the main concert room of Carnegie Hall departed from what was then becoming the standard rectangular or "shoebox" form, and was most distinguished by the inclusion of four tiered galleries that maximized the seating capacity of the hall—which was, at nearly 3,000, quite a bit larger than its European counterparts—while keeping the overall space relatively compact. Notably, this design also resulted in a refined acoustic environment. As explained by architectural historian Michael Forsyth, the efficient seating layout of Carnegie Hall and other similarly structured venues creates "a relatively small volume for the area of seating and consequently a short reverberation time. The tiers of seats present a large sound-absorptive area to the orchestra, with a smaller area of sound-reflective wall surface than in the traditional rectangular hall, which further increases the clarity of sound because of the absence of the 'masking' effect of reverberation, but at the expense of fullness of tone."[15] This last defect went unnoticed among the auditors in attendance at the ceremonial opening of Carnegie Hall on May 5, 1891, where Damrosch oversaw the first day of a five-day festival of music during which he conducted the Oratorio Society and the New York Symphony, and where the special guest would be Russian composer Pyotr Ilyich Tchaikovsky. The *New York Times* headline conveyed the general reaction to the new hall: "It Stood the Test Well."[16]

While Carnegie Hall was generally regarded as a success in terms of its acoustic properties, the building of Boston's Symphony Hall during the ensuing decade truly made architectural acoustics a primary consideration in concert hall design. Symphony Hall stood as a milestone in the evolution of what science historian Emily Thompson has called the "soundscape of modernity." By Thompson's account, "Symphony Hall was recognized as the first auditorium in the world to be constructed according to laws of modern science. Indeed, it not only embodied, but instigated, the origins of the modern science of acoustics."[17] The key figure in the acoustic design of the hall was a Harvard physicist named Wallace Sabine, who was hired by Henry Higginson, the Boston financier who founded the Boston Symphony Orchestra in 1880 and now sought to provide the organization with an improved performance space.

Sabine's breakthrough came in his work on measuring reverberation time. The appropriate amount of reverberation was one of the most delicate details to be addressed in the design of a concert hall. Too much reverberation and the sound would become muddled; too little and the sound would appear flat and lacking in dimension. Previous concert hall designs, such as Tuthill's for Carnegie Hall, achieved good results but did so according to specifications that were often inexact and difficult to reproduce. Sabine, through extensive experimentation, found a way to measure the potential reverberation time of a given space with a new degree of exactitude. More groundbreaking was that he developed an equation that allowed reverberation time to be predicted prior to the moment of construction, by determining numerically the relationship between the variables that contributed to a room's acoustic qualities: the volume of the room, the surface area of its building materials, and the sound absorption of those materials.[18] With Sabine's formula in hand, the designs of architect Charles McKim were evaluated according to new criteria. The goal was no longer to reproduce the physical layout of existing concert halls of distinction, but to achieve an effective balance of elements according to an abstract set of principles that gave the desired acoustic effect top priority. Upon completion in 1900, Symphony Hall epitomized the union of scientific rationality and aesthetic contemplation, creating a modern listening environment that was predominantly employed to hear and appreciate musical works representing a great tradition of European art music.

By the time jazz came onto the scene as a prominent musical style in the late 1910s and 1920s, classical music had only recently become ensconced in the concert hall. This move was just one manifestation of the growing highbrow/lowbrow divide that took root during the late nineteenth and early twentieth centuries, but its significance cannot be overstated. The emergence of the modern concert hall made that cultural divide into something that had a concrete spatial dimension: classical music more and more happened in one sort of space designed to accommodate habits of listening that had arisen alongside the status that became attached to it. No other musical styles would have spaces they could so securely claim for themselves for many years to come; and when dedicated jazz clubs began to emerge in the 1930s, they were designed according to a very different set of criteria. Nobody was going to hire a Harvard physicist to help design a place meant primarily to house jazz or other forms of popular music. While jazz fans later adopted behaviors that classical music audiences also subscribed to—to prioritize attentive listening above all, to prefer silence while listening, to be seated rather than standing or dancing—they did so in bars and dance halls where the music routinely competed for attention with other features and activities. The paradox, though, is that as jazz gradually moved into the concert hall from the 1920s forward, it did not simply follow a path of refinement. Audiences did not become silent en masse. The music was not "classicized," at least not in consistent or straightforward ways. As jazz was remade through its shift into the concert hall, so it contributed to the remaking of concert music.

An Experiment

Writing about the emergence of the jazz concert in an important 1989 essay, jazz scholar Scott DeVeaux posits that Paul Whiteman's 1924 "Experiment in Modern Music" was a premature effort to bring the music into the concert hall. Although he notes the significance of the event DeVeaux judges its larger impact to have been limited, and charges that Whiteman's "Experiment" was "an attempt to impose a concert form on jazz 'from above.'" For later jazz concerts from the 1930s forward, by contrast, the impetus came "'from below' as an outgrowth of the ordinary situations in which jazz was performed."[19] I would suggest that DeVeaux is wrong on two counts here. To say that Whiteman's 1924 concert was an imposition "from above" misconstrues Whiteman's vast popularity among American music fans. Although the bandleader often aligned himself with elite society, he also showed an ability to straddle "high" and "low" cultural fields that was nearly unparalleled among his contemporaries. His concert at Aeolian Hall reflected more than anything the cultural in-betweenness that Whiteman and his orchestra represented at the time. Meanwhile, DeVeaux is also mistaken to claim that later jazz concerts came "from below." Events such as Benny Goodman's 1938 Carnegie Hall concert and the two "From Spirituals to Swing" concerts held in 1938 and 1939, to be discussed later in this chapter, depended on the patronage of powerful music promoters such as Sol Hurok and John Hammond. Both concerts presented jazz within an evolutionary framework that suggested its progress over time in a manner that was largely borrowed from Whiteman's earlier "Experiment."[20] Whereas DeVeaux believes that the "true" history of the jazz concert only began after 1935, I contend that there was substantial continuity between Whiteman's efforts of the 1920s and the developments of the ensuing decade.

Paul Whiteman, like the Original Dixieland Jazz Band, holds a conflicted place in the writing of jazz history, and for similar reasons. The success of both has been understood to indicate that, in the 1910s and 1920s, white artists were able to capitalize on jazz in a way that their African American counterparts could not. Moreover, both have been charged with deliberately diminishing black contributions to jazz in order to bolster their own perceived achievements. In the case of the ODJB and especially the band's leader, Nick LaRocca, this latter charge is incontestably true. The case against Whiteman is far less clear-cut. Whiteman did not deny the African American basis of jazz, but he did suggest that his own music represented a significant advance from what others, black and white, had achieved. He also showed an unfortunate tendency toward racial stereotyping of African Americans in his stage shows and his broader media presence. Whiteman himself, though, arguably did less to marginalize the efforts of black musicians than did the scores of critics writing in the 1920s that celebrated him as the greatest exponent of jazz to date and showed little recognition of the value of music made by African Americans. A representative instance comes from the noted critic Gilbert Seldes, who was more fair-minded than many of his contemporaries, and yet still offered the following in a survey of jazz: "Nowhere is the failure of the negro to exploit his gifts more obvious than in the use he has made of the jazz orchestra; for although nearly every negro jazz band is better than nearly every white band, no negro band has yet come up to the level of the best white ones, and the leader of the best of all, by a little joke, is called Whiteman."[21]

Where the writing of jazz history has been concerned, perhaps Whiteman's greatest offense is that his music did not "swing" with sufficient heat. In the great divide between "sweet" and "hot" jazz that typified early jazz, Whiteman was incontestably on the "sweet" side—indeed, he all but set the template for it. So, when jazz critics starting in the 1930s invested the "sweet" vs. "hot" division with new significance, and elevated "hot" jazz to a position of unquestioned superiority, Whiteman was rendered an inadequate and, indeed, inauthentic representative of the style—a position from which his reputation never fully recovered.[22] Reasserting Whiteman's importance for twenty-first-century readers, popular music scholar Elijah Wald observes that the bandleader was pivotal for the way he embraced an inclusive definition of jazz. While some of his contemporaries such as the San Francisco bandleader Art Hickman sought to distance themselves from the term even as they employed some of its stylistic markers, Whiteman worked to broaden how jazz might be defined; and against widespread public criticism of the style he remained a staunch if ambivalent defender.[23] The "Experiment in Modern Music" that Whiteman staged at Aeolian Hall was indicative of Whiteman's stance, a self-serving exercise in "elevating" jazz that maintained one foot squarely in the realm of popular entertainment, and that made a case to the general public—and to elite tastemakers—that jazz was music worth taking seriously.

* * *

When we encountered Whiteman in the previous chapter, he had just made his debut at the most prestigious vaudeville theater in the country, New York's

Palace, in October 1921. The qualities according to which Whiteman became the most successful and heralded bandleader of the 1920s were already well in place by then, including a softening of the usual timbre of the jazz band through the use of an expanded orchestra; smoothing out the rhythmic articulation of jazz so that it maintained a suggestion of syncopation but was less enervating than that purveyed by many of his contemporaries; and a deft arranging style that was facilitated by longtime Whiteman associate Ferde Grofé, who joined the band on piano in 1919 and quickly became the leader's favored arranger.[24] Grofé's arrangements meshed with Whiteman's aspirations: the sonorities had a lushness that conferred an air of class, but also deftly exploited the unique talents of band members such as trumpet player Henry Busse and reed player Ross Gorman, and integrated the sound of a wide array of instruments and playing techniques. Over time, the approach taken by Whiteman, Grofé, and the members of the orchestra gave rise to the classification, "symphonic jazz," a term that indicated of the hybrid character of their music, and that had an expanding range of adherents in rival bandleaders such as Vincent Lopez, Ben Bernie, and Paul Specht, who became Whiteman's principal rivals for the jazz spotlight.

By the end of 1922, Whiteman was the leader of a jazz band craze in which he not only set a new stylistic template using what *Variety* described as "crooning" orchestration, but also set a new pace for turning the jazz orchestra into a money-making proposition.[25] His standing as a standard-bearer of sophistication was enhanced by his efforts to "jazz" the classics—that is, to take selected pieces from the repertoire of classical music and arrange them according to the stylistic dictates of jazz. Among his most popular such works was "Song of India," the melody for which was adapted from the Russian composer Nikolay Rimsky-Korsakov's *Chanson Hindoue*. Whiteman's musical mixing of popular and classical styles was not to everyone's taste, to be sure. It was one of the features of his music that made him at times a lightning rod for criticism, and a feature that he worked tirelessly to defend.[26] That it was controversial, though, seemed only to add to the appeal, and Whiteman wielded the ability of his band to shift between different registers of "popular" and "classical" performance almost like a magic trick when he took the stage at Aeolian Hall.

As to Aeolian Hall itself, it was one of a series of buildings occupied by the Aeolian Company, a manufacturer of musical instruments that had enjoyed overwhelming success as the leading US producer of mechanical or "player" pianos. By housing a concert hall in the same building as its sales room,

Aeolian was following an established path whereby piano manufacturers functioned as major patrons of classical music concerts in the not-so-altruistic hope that doing so would stimulate piano sales as well. Steinway Hall in New York and Chickering Hall in Boston were the models for such endeavors, and each enjoyed significant stature for a time. The Aeolian Hall in which Whiteman staged his "Experiment in Modern Music" was constructed in 1912 in a wave of construction on 42nd Street that accompanied a key moment in the growth and consolidation of Times Square.[27] Designed by the architects Whitney Warren and Charles Wetmore, the building was a seventeen-story structure that housed considerable office space along with the Aeolian company's quarters and the concert hall. The latter was much smaller in scale than Carnegie Hall, with a stated capacity of 1,362.[28] Suitably, the opening concert in the Hall was a recital by the Polish pianist Gottfried Galston on November 2, 1912, soon followed by a concert featuring the New York Symphony Orchestra under Walter Damrosch, which took up residency for its concerts in the new hall that fall. In both instances Aeolian Hall was judged a success, although its size and specifications made it generally more advantageous for solo recitals and chamber music than for full orchestral concerts.[29] By the time Whiteman appeared there with his orchestra in 1924 the hall was a well-established concert venue that continued primarily to program classical music. As such it would serve Whiteman well in his plans for his "Experiment." He would later say of his choice of venue: "It started the talk going, at least, and aroused curiosity. 'Jazz in Aeolian Hall!' the conservatives cried incredulously. 'What is the world coming to?' "[30]

Once he had his venue, Whiteman executed a publicity campaign that would have made P.T. Barnum proud. News of the impending concert began to circulate in December, a full two months before the scheduled date. The first, short notice in the *New York Tribune* spelled out the objective of the concert in deliberately provocative terms. Whiteman was planning a concert "with a purely American program" that was meant "to settle the question of what is American music, and whether jazz is music or not."[31] To address the second question, he outlined his design to have a series of public rehearsals in the weeks leading up to the concert at Aeolian Hall for which music professors and recognized critics would be invited to pass judgment. Whiteman also announced his plan to showcase new work by prominent American composers and songwriters, in this instance Irving Berlin and Victor Herbert—the latter a renowned composer, conductor, and cellist who was the leading American exponent of operetta. A more extensive notice about the upcoming concert appeared two days later in *Variety*, in which the most significant new piece of information was the expectation that George Gershwin would contribute music for the occasion. Quoted about his goals for the concert, Whiteman was strangely self-effacing given the grandiose shape of the affair. He explained, "I've been forced to find something new in which to devote my orchestra's talents. The symphonic syncopation we originated is no longer novel because there are others doing it, maybe better than we." Yet *Variety* trumpeted Whiteman's aspirations more loudly, telling readers that, "The jazz leader does not intend to play strictly jazz numbers alone. He will do operatic excerpts legitimately."[32]

All the emphasis laid on soliciting the opinions of established musical experts might seem to confirm Scott DeVeaux's claim cited previously, that Whiteman's Aeolian Hall concert was an effort to place jazz on a pedestal "from above." Undoubtedly, Whiteman pursued an agenda that had cultural elevation as one of its primary goals, and that disowned the value of more "lowly" styles of jazz in the process. However, his aspirations along these lines cut in two directions at once. If he wanted to demonstrate the superiority of his own more refined approach to jazz orchestration, he also sought openly to challenge the presumption of conservative cultural authorities to determine the terms according to which music was assigned artistic value. Whiteman was pointed on the matter in his book, *Jazz*, co-authored with Mary McBride and published two years after the "Experiment in Modern Music." There he offered the following during his reflections on the concert:

> Here's something I have never been able to understand. Why should it be supposed that all the good taste in the world is monopolized by a few people? Isn't it possible that the so-called masses have considerable instinctive good judgment in matters of beauty that they never get credit for? My notion is that beauty is for everybody ... That's why I resent the self-assurance of certain high and mighty art circles.[33]

Whiteman was nothing if not contradictory when addressing these issues and the inconsistencies in his position would persist throughout his career. He was a dedicated popularizer who nonetheless wanted the approval of cultural authorities; he clearly recognized the power that inhered in the sanctum of the concert hall, and he wanted to lay claim to it both to raise his own cultural standing and to poke holes in the process through which some musical styles were granted more legitimacy than others. In effect, he was the very model of middlebrow.

The program for the "Experiment in Modern Music" was built around Whiteman's competing aims. His opening gesture was especially loaded: a quintet drawn from the larger orchestra offered its rendition of "Livery Stable Blues," the first song issued by the Original Dixieland Jazz Band seven years earlier.[34] Whiteman's plan was not to pay tribute to his predecessors, but to use their song as an example of the wild, untrammeled quality of jazz in its formative state to provide a backdrop against which its subsequent evolution could be measured. Framing the concert in such terms was a clear marker of Whiteman's impulse to elevate jazz as a musical form and was a feature of the "Experiment" that would have enduring influence on later efforts to "concertize" jazz. The choice of "Livery Stable Blues" was especially strategic along these lines, as the song's rambunctious style was compounded by the incorporation of animalistic sounds—the clarinet emulating a rooster's crow, the cornet whinnying like a horse.

Whether Whiteman effectively got his point across was unclear. He himself expressed concern in his memoir that the audience's evident enjoyment of the piece might have undercut his intent to use it as a "primitive" counterpart to the more legitimate features to come.[35] *New York Times* critic Olin Downes openly dissented from Whiteman's purpose with the tune, offering in his review of the concert: "Thus the 'Livery Stable Blues' was introduced apologetically as an example of the depraved past from which modern jazz had risen. The apology is herewith indignantly rejected, for this is a gorgeous piece of impudence, much better in its unbuttoned jocosity and Rabelasian [*sic*] laughter than other and more polite compositions that came later."[36] Here, then, Whiteman's own bid for respectability was called into question, his efforts to mobilize the audience's "good taste" being turned against him. This happened in large part because his musicians gave a performance of the tune that was more than merely satirical. It was an expert jazz performance, and so while it may not have fully worked as Whiteman planned, it did demonstrate the capabilities of the members of his band.

Once past the opening song, Whiteman brought out the full orchestra. He appeared at Aeolian Hall with an ensemble that was much expanded from the groups with which he typically recorded and performed. At the time of the "Experiment," Whiteman usually recorded with an orchestra of about twelve musicians including himself; in concert he had an orchestra of fifteen.[37] As a violinist as well as conductor of the group, he was most often the only string player apart from banjoist Mike Pingitore, although at times he used a second violinist. For the Aeolian Hall concert, the string section grew to eight violins and two double basses, with Pingitore still featured on banjo. Elsewhere, he used two trumpets, two trombones, three saxophones, two French horns, and a drummer, bringing the total orchestra to twenty-one members.[38] The increased size of his ensemble, and especially the heightened number of strings, marked Whiteman's goal for the concert to offer music closer to the sonorities of "classical" orchestration than was customary even with his own "symphonic" jazz style. A later, even larger version of Whiteman's orchestra, organized along the same principles, appears in Figure 5.1.

Almost as soon as Whiteman brought out the full orchestra, he veered into territory that went against the grain of concert hall decorum. The next section of the concert offered two comedy selections that were expressly meant to find humor in the fact that some of the era's most popular songs could be heard to have a basis in classical melodies. So did Whiteman seek to demonstrate that "Yes, We Have no Bananas"—one of the greatest song hits of the early 1920s—had its melodic roots in the "Hallelujah" chorus from Handel's *Messiah*. He coupled the song with another adaptation, "So This Is Venice," derived from a nineteenth-century piece, "The Carnival of Venice," that had long served as a showcase for virtuosity by violinists and trumpet players alike.[39] In this instance, Whiteman band member Ross Gorman took the lead, as he also did on the Whiteman recording of the same song made in January 1924, just a month before the concert at Aeolian Hall. On the recording Gorman demonstrated his prowess on three instruments—clarinet, oboe, and alto saxophone—exemplifying the common capability of members of Whiteman's band to perform skillfully on multiple instruments, a talent that expanded the range of timbres available to the band as a whole and was taken to signify the distinct sort of virtuosity that his players possessed. At Aeolian Hall Gorman seems to have played several more instruments than three in a way that indicated his technical and comedic powers in equal measure. Olin Downes dubbed him "that virtuoso and imp of the perverse," while Abel Green observed in his review for the *New York Clipper* that the piece "allowed that versatile reed expert to utilize many, many forms of reed instruments to sensational effect. Each chorus repeat was a novelty in arrangement, Gorman stopping the show completely."[40]

Two points are apparent from the opening sequence of Whiteman's "Experiment in Modern Music." First, while Whiteman entered Aeolian Hall with the intention to demonstrate the legitimacy of his style of music, he did

Figure 5.1 Paul Whiteman and his Orchestra photographed as they appeared at the Hippodrome Theater in 1925, about a year after their groundbreaking "Experiment in Modern Music" at New York's Aeolian Hall. The expanded format of Whiteman's orchestra here is much as it appeared at Aeolian Hall, designed to capture the hybrid effects of the bandleader's symphonic jazz. Courtesy of the Paul Whiteman Collection, Williams College Archives and Special Collections.

not adopt an unremittingly "serious" tone to do so. As John Howland has pointed out, there was a significant residue of vaudeville programming philosophy and performance values at work in Whiteman's "Experiment."[41] The concert grew in seriousness as it proceeded, and the works that dominated the second half of the program—by Victor Herbert, George Gershwin, and Edward Elgar, whose *Pomp and Circumstance* was the closing selection—were invested with an artistic weight the earlier pieces lacked. Still, levity was a notable feature of the concert, and it tempered the pretensions that were evident elsewhere. Second, the apparent discrepancies between Whiteman's recording of "So This Is Venice" and the version offered in concert suggest that contrary to what many jazz historians have presumed, Whiteman and his orchestra did not just play things "straight," as they were composed. In concert, his band extended pieces well beyond the duration that could fit on a side of a record, and a player like Gorman had room to do a sort of improvisation. The playing was highly stylized and exhibitionistic—Gorman's "trick" of moving between one instrument and the next was akin to Wilbur Sweatman's playing of two or three clarinets at once. This again was in keeping with the performance values of early jazz, and especially jazz as it was presented in theatrical settings to seated audiences, when a more spectacular kind of musicianship was often used to enhance the music's entertainment value.

The eclecticism of Whiteman's approach remained in the foreground as the program proceeded. To demonstrate the contrast between "legitimate" approaches to scoring a piece of music and a "jazz" approach, he offered two versions of the song that gave him his first hit recording in 1920, "Whispering," the first played without adornment, and the second of which was "jazzed" to the point where the melody was deliberately made hard to discern. Several sections of the concert, although framed by a similarly pedagogical intent, served mainly to showcase the Whiteman orchestra doing what it did best—playing carefully wrought and imaginatively arranged versions of popular songs. Pianist Zez Confrey took center stage around the mid-section of the concert to play a series of selections that showcased his virtuosic technique, providing a link with Ross Gorman's earlier turn in the spotlight and foreshadowing the later appearance of George Gershwin, who was the featured piano soloist for his own new composition, *Rhapsody in Blue*. In the immediate lead-up to Gershwin's piece, Whiteman presented a set of songs under the heading, "Adaptation of Standard Selections to Dance Rhythm." In effect, this was the part of the concert most oriented toward his well-known practice of "jazzing" the classics, although as Thornton Hagert has pointed out in his overview of Whiteman's concert, none of the pieces in this part of the program—Frederick Logan's *Pale Moon*, Edward MacDowell's *To a Wild Rose*, and *Chansonette*, based on a piano work by Rudolf Friml— could be considered more than light classics.[42]

Whether *Rhapsody in Blue* should be considered more than a "light classic" was far from settled at the time of the concert and for decades after. It was without question the work on the Aeolian Hall program that commanded the most attention and has had the most enduring influence. The story of its creation has been told many times over and need only be recounted here in brief. Whiteman had previously worked with George Gershwin and sensed that they held sympathetic aims. He casually mentioned to Gershwin that he might ask him to write a piece for a special concert he was planning. When news of Gershwin's contribution to the "Experiment in Modern Music" began to circulate, Gershwin had not yet committed to the project and so was suddenly pressed to write a new extended work in a matter of weeks. The final version of *Rhapsody*, as it was played by Whiteman's band at Aeolian Hall, owed nearly as much to Ferde Grofé as it did to Gershwin, for it was Grofé who orchestrated the piece, using his intimate knowledge of the Whiteman band to do so.[43] Members of Whiteman's orchestra also contributed to the piece in substantial ways during the process of preparing the concert, most notably Ross Gorman, who demonstrated for Gershwin how the dramatic opening clarinet glissando could be played.

Rhapsody in Blue embodied many of the central tensions that shaped the entirety of Whiteman's Aeolian Hall concert. Unlike every other selection presented by Whiteman, it was clearly designed as a "concert work" in the usual understanding of that term; and yet as a "rhapsody" it used a form that was not especially distinguished in the classical canon, which opened the way to charges of "formlessness" by unsympathetic critics.[44] *Rhapsody in Blue* made full use of the expanded orchestral ensemble that Whiteman had assembled for the concert but also served as a showcase for Gershwin's own considerable skills as pianist, with the work's sixteen-minute duration split about evenly between solo piano and full orchestra. The conception of the work as it was orchestrated, moreover, was far from the sort of "absolute music" most esteemed by celebrants of classical music as a high art, relying too much on the specific talents and styles of the individual players. Although *Rhapsody in Blue* would eventually be assimilated into the repertory of American symphony orchestras, at Aeolian Hall it was performed as a piece that was nearly inextricable from the particular symphonic jazz vernacular put forth by Whiteman and his musicians. Its successful afterlife is a testament to how much the work, and Whiteman's concert as a whole, shifted the ground on which American concert music stood. Eleven years after its debut, the composer and critic Virgil Thomson said of *Rhapsody in Blue*, in grudging appreciation, "It is the most successful orchestral piece ever launched by any American composer. It is by now standard orchestral repertory all over the world, just like Rimsky's *Scheherazade* and Ravel's *Bolero*."[45]

Writing three-quarters of a century later, Elijah Wald made a new case for the significance of *Rhapsody in Blue*. About Gershwin's work, Wald claims that it "was the *Sgt. Pepper* of the 1920s, the work that forced a dramatic rethinking of what popular music could be."[46] For Wald the comparison is not entirely to the credit of either work. His goal is not to remind us of the greatness of either Gershwin (or Whiteman) or the Beatles but to have us reconsider their cultural impact, and on that score he offers a pointed observation: "it is a profound irony that the attempt to make highbrow art out of jazz in the 1920s (which put white artists at the forefront of the movement) is generally recalled by historians as an embarrassing wrong turn, whereas the attempt to make highbrow art out of rock 'n' roll in the 1960s (again putting white artists in the forefront of the movement) is generally viewed as a step forward for the genre."[47] Wald's stress on the "whiteness" that has typically accompanied claims of "highbrow" cultural value is important to bear in mind. It echoes Lawrence Levine's own explanation for the etymology of the terms "highbrow" and "lowbrow," which he associates with the nineteenth-century field of phrenology wherein the study of the size and shape of the cranium was used to draw inferences about the intelligence and character traits of different racial groups.[48]

While whiteness may bind together the efforts of Whiteman, Gershwin, and the Beatles, there are significant differences to be observed as well, beyond the obvious stylistic distinctions. *Sgt. Pepper's Lonely Hearts Club Band* was issued as an album at a time after the Beatles had retired from playing concerts. *Rhapsody in Blue*, by contrast, was written very much as a concert work to be performed by Whiteman's unit. Indeed, the whole piece could not fit on the records of the day and was shortened significantly by Gershwin, at Whiteman's request, when they joined to create the first recording of the work in June 1924, four months after the concert at Aeolian Hall. This is not just an incidental difference. Wald claims, with justification, that after the Beatles stopped playing concerts, they created music that was increasingly less danceable—a shift that paralleled wider changes taking hold in rock music of the 1960s. One cannot say the same for Whiteman. His performance regimen if anything, intensified in the months and years after the concert at Aeolian Hall. To a degree, that concert provided a new model for his performance career moving forward. Whiteman would restage the "Experiment in Modern Music" twice more in New York in the ensuing months, once again at Aeolian Hall, and then for his first concert at Carnegie Hall on April 21, 1924.[49] He took a version of the concert on the road with him, with Gershwin usually on hand to play his piano parts; and he staged many subsequent "Experiments," holding his eighth and last such concert at Carnegie Hall on Christmas day, 1938.[50]

Whiteman's performance career was not confined to the concert hall after his groundbreaking "Experiment." Just over a year later he did a turn at the New York vaudeville house the Hippodrome, where according to the reviewer for *Variety*, he proved that he could "come back before the $1 and $1.50 public and click with his advanced ideas of syncopation as he has done with the $3 concert crowd."[51] The following summer, Whiteman announced that he would be moving into movie theaters upon accepting a lucrative offer from the Publix theater chain.[52] Whiteman's arrangement with Publix, which guaranteed his band an unprecedented $9,500 weekly pay, came at a time when leading movie theaters were incorporating elaborate stage presentations to solidify their hold on middle-class audiences and eliminate any lingering competition from straight vaudeville. For his performances in these venues Whiteman assumed a concert style of presentation, and used *Rhapsody in Blue* as the climactic number, guaranteed to bring down the house. However, Whiteman's contract for the tour also stipulated that he would appear at a weekly ball in each city, which would be done for the express purpose of allowing the band to play for dancers. In other words, Whiteman's move into the concert hall did not precipitate his turn away from playing dance music.[53] Instead, the Whiteman orchestra's dance-ability became a sort of value-added attraction as its concert career progressed.

The Classical Scene

Two days before Whiteman's first "Experiment in Modern Music," on February 10, 1924, a special lecture-recital on jazz was presented at the Anderson Galleries, an art gallery on 59th Street in New York, by a relatively new organization called the League of Composers. The League was founded the previous year as an offshoot of the International Composers' Guild. Both organizations had the common aim of advocating on behalf of contemporary music and living composers, although the differences—and the rivalry—between the two groups have become the stuff of legend in the chronicle of American musical modernism.[54] In its first season of concerts and public programs, the League—and its manager, Claire Reis, one of a number of influential women working to bring modern music to the American public—saw the current enthusiasm for jazz as a subject that its audience of "serious" music enthusiasts would want to know more about. As announced in the *New York Tribune*, the program presented three perspectives on "the momentous question of 'Jazz,'" by Edward Burlingame Hill, a composer and Harvard professor of music; Gilbert Seldes, the widely known critic who was a prominent advocate for the popular arts; and Vincent Lopez, a pianist and bandleader who was one of Paul Whiteman's chief rivals in presenting music listeners with a more "refined" sort of jazz.[55] Appearing in the company of Hill and Seldes, Lopez read a paper on the virtues of modern dance music and played a brief assortment of pieces with his orchestra, including his own "jazzed" arrangement of selections from *Carmen* and *H.M.S. Pinafore*.[56]

The jazz program offered by the League of Composers was, in effect, a sort of inverse of Whiteman's "Experiment." Both events had an obvious didactic purpose; but Whiteman chose to make whatever case he had to present primarily through his musical program, whereas in the League's presentation the music offered by the Lopez orchestra was almost secondary. As an outsider to the classical establishment, Whiteman's concert at Aeolian Hall was a grand gesture to be let in, at least part of the way, to a place understood to have an air of elite exclusivity. For the League of Composers, ensconced in that world of classical music, their question was whether jazz should in fact be let in, a question that the speakers on that day answered in the affirmative, and that Lopez's presence helped to certify. Whiteman's concert drew an audience in keeping with the hybrid character of the program. As described by Abel Green in the *Clipper*: "The house was sold out twice over, and drew one of the oddest audiences in America. It transplanted 'tin pan alley' with its music publishers and song pluggers to Aeolian Hall, rubbing shoulders with operatic artists, musical critics, and an extremely 'wise' musical contingent."[57] While we have little record of the audience for the League's event, one presumes that it was fairly small and self-selecting; the lack of detailed reviews after the fact suggests the relatively modest impact that it had beyond the inner circle of attendees.

On the other hand, the members of the League of Composers were not necessarily secure in their "insider" status either. As composers and patrons who primarily championed the cause of contemporary art music, they were also in a struggle to gain recognition in the face of musical institutions more likely to welcome the music of the past than the music of today. In this connection the different venues of the two events are telling. Whiteman, after all, appeared in Aeolian Hall, one of the leading concert halls in New York City. The Anderson Galleries, by contrast, were principally designed to present visual art, not music. Although the odd location was due in large part to fact that this was a lecture-recital and not a strictly musical affair, there was more to the story. The League's regular concerts during that first season were held in the Klaw Theater, a Broadway venue that was perfectly respectable, to be sure, but that typically housed plays, not music.[58] Although the League's stature would grow over time, in this early phase the League of Composers had neither the influence nor the constituency to lay claim to New York's more established and "legitimate" concert halls. By the same token, their use of alternate spaces marked their activities as distinctive and governed by a different set of goals than the programs that might appear in Aeolian or Carnegie Hall.

To offer some perspective on how such events as Whiteman's Aeolian Hall concert, or the League of Composers' jazz lecture-recital, fit into the bigger picture of New York concert life at the time, we can use a summary of the 1923–1924 season written by Olin Downes for the *New York Times*. By Downes' account, the New York Philharmonic Orchestra played one-hundred concerts in its season for that year; and the New York Symphony Orchestra, the organization conducted by Walter Damrosch, performed 107 concerts. Other organizations giving orchestral concerts in New York that season were the State Symphony Orchestra, the Society of the Friends of Music, and several visiting orchestras including the Boston Symphony Orchestra, the Philadelphia Orchestra, and the Cleveland Symphony Orchestra. Assessing the overall content of the programs offered by these various orchestral ensembles, Downes enumerated the composers whose works were featured most often during the 1923–1924 season. Leading the pack was Richard Wagner, who had twenty-five different works performed a total of eighty-four times. Beethoven had twenty-four works featured but exceeded Wagner in total performances with eighty-seven. Tchaikovsky placed third as the most oft-played composer, with Brahms fourth, Richard Strauss fifth, then Mozart, Bach, Saint-Saens, Liszt, Johann Strauss, and

Rimsky-Korsakov, the last three of whom were effectively tied for ninth place.[59] This was the substance of the mainstream classical music world as of 1924. Only one of these composers was alive at the time—Richard Strauss—and none would have been considered at the forefront of "modern" music as it was then construed. (Stravinsky was the leading figure on that score, with six works played during the year.) And, notably, none were American.

Neither the League of Composers nor the International Composers' Guild had a primary commitment to American music. Their perspective on contemporary music was decidedly internationalist and cosmopolitan, and their memberships included many European artists or figures recently migrated to the US from overseas. Indeed, as Carol Oja points out, the lecture-recital on jazz sponsored by the League of Composers was the only program given by the association in its first season that accorded any prominence to American music.[60] Nonetheless, as the League in particular evolved it placed more emphasis upon programming American music and even more so, admitted a wide range of American composers into its circle, including Aaron Copland, Virgil Thomson, Roger Sessions, George Antheil, Louis Gruenberg, Roy Harris, Randall Thompson, Marc Blitzstein, and many more. Several of these composers also became contributors to the organization's in-house journal, which began publication in fall 1924 as the *League of Composers' Review* but would in 1925 assume its new title, *Modern Music*. Promoting the interests of American composers became, on some level, a pragmatic matter for an organization based in the US seeking to increase the notoriety of music being made in the present day. Yet the support offered by the League of Composers to music by American composers was more than casual and gained significant momentum through such *Modern Music* essays as Aaron Copland's influential 1926 missive, "America's Young Men of Promise."[61]

The tensions within the classical music world that gave rise to the League of Composers, the International Composers' Guild, and other analogous efforts, do not fit neatly within the breakdown of music and culture into distinct "high" and "low" spheres. Lawrence Levine, for example, presents the rise of classical music and other highbrow forms as the result of a unified front motivated by the shared goal of solidifying the social prestige of an emergent, dominant economic class. However, the classical music world in the US was never so clearly unified; and the years during which jazz began to enter the field of the concert hall coincided with a period when the fault lines within classical music expanded and became newly visible. Advocacy on behalf of American music in the face of Eurocentric cultural values was nothing new and could be dated back to the time of Jenny Lind and even earlier. But only with the firm institutionalization of a classical music canon that was, along with the rise of the concert hall, another effect of "sacralization," and that held to the faith that the greatest music was that which had stood the test of time, did there grow such discernible conflict between the core values of classical music and supporters of the new, the modern, the contemporary.[62]

Whether the latter constituted a sort of avant-garde or not is a difficult question to discern. The avant-garde has historically been defined along multiple lines, including opposition to established art institutions and embrace of popular culture as a strategy for calling into question received ideas about artistic value.[63] Philosopher Bernard Gendron documents the importance that popular music, and jazz in particular, had for avant-garde artists working in Paris, including the composer Darius Milhaud, whose *La Création du Monde* prefigured a series of modernist musical works in which the influence of jazz was clearly audible. American composers such as Aaron Copland and Virgil Thomson were themselves studying in Paris during these years, and both were strongly influenced by Milhaud and the other French composers known collectively as "Les Six."[64] Of the two, Copland was the more struck by the possibilities of jazz as a compositional resource, and while his musical work gave indication of incorporating jazz prior to his stay in Paris, his interest in the music was fortified by the uses to which he saw it being put by his European counterparts.[65] When compared with the marked enthusiasm that the French composer Milhaud had for jazz, though, the efforts even of Copland, and of most American composers of the time save for Gershwin, to engage with jazz appear cautious and full of ambivalence. Jazz provided a vital medium through which American composers could work out some new ways of articulating the "American-ness" of their music; yet few wanted to dissolve the boundaries between "high" and "low" musical cultures, just as they did not want to overturn the dominant musical institutions of their time. In this they were not fully representative of the historical avant-garde. They created their own institutions not to replace existing ones, but to build an infrastructure through which they could begin to cultivate the kinds of reputations that would bring them to greater notice.

Still, there was an oppositional aspect to the stance taken by the young moderns that revolved around the ways in which they understood the music of the present in relation to the music of the past. Certainly, they did not reject the value of the latter. In fact, many of the rising generation of American composers would eventually come to be labeled "neo-classicists" for their efforts to revisit the styles of past composers and classical forms and renew them through modern sensibilities concerning tonality and other fundamental musical properties. It was more a question of balance: should new music be subordinate to older repertory; should works already received into the canon be at the core of concert programming, or should work by living composers be given priority? In this, the tensions that pervaded the classical music world of the 1920s and 1930s, and that particularly attended to matters of musical modernism, exemplified a central facet of music scenes explained by media scholar Will Straw:

> Different cultural spaces are marked by the sorts of temporalities to be found within them—by the prominence of activities of canonization, or by the values accruing to novelty or currency, longevity and "timelessness." In this respect, the "logic" of particular musical cultures is a function of the way in which value is constructed within them relative to the passing of time.[66]

Straw's observation was developed to explain popular music scenes of the late twentieth century, but I think it is fair to say that the American classical music scene of the 1920s worked along similar lines. To go further, I would suggest that the cultural conflicts surrounding the status of new music in the 1920s set the stage for subsequent struggles over whether the music of "then" was of greater value than the music of "now." For rising composers in the 1920s, this was not just an aesthetic question but a professional one: if contemporary music could not find places to be heard or be established as something of clear value, then the vocation of being a composer was rendered ineffective.

* * *

The very organizational names—International Composers' Guild, League of Composers—bespoke the priorities at work in this milieu. As Claire Reis, who had a hand in founding both organizations, wrote in her memoir: "it was made known that the *raison d'etre* for establishing our new group was *the composer*."[67] Such emphasis on the composer as a creative agent in the making of new music contravened the structure of the major symphony orchestras, within which the conductor was the figure invested with the most artistic authority. The role of the conductor in shaping the repertory and the standards of American classical music had been growing consistently since the late nineteenth century, when the German émigré Theodore Thomas cultivated a new aura of seriousness around the performance of concert music.[68] Other conductors had assumed prominence in the years since Thomas's death in 1905, and composer/conductors were not entirely uncommon, with Gustav Mahler's brief tenure at the head of the New York Philharmonic (1909–1911) providing a noteworthy example. The general trend, though, was toward a marked separation of responsibilities that elevated the conductor to a position of unchallenged dominance. By the 1920s this pattern had fully flowered, and the mainstream classical music world was dominated by a coterie of star conductors who worked with the leading symphonies. Longest serving among the major figures of the time was Frederick Stock, who had inherited the mantle of the Chicago Symphony Orchestra from Thomas and would continue in that role until 1942. Leopold Stokowski held his position with the Philadelphia Orchestra since 1912 and remained until 1941. A newer presence was Serge Koussevitzky, who came from Paris in 1924 to begin a twenty-five-year tenure at the head of the Boston Symphony Orchestra.

Then there was Toscanini. Italian conductor Arturo Toscanini first found acclaim at the La Scala opera in Milan.[69] In 1908 he was lured to the US to take up the baton with the Metropolitan Opera, where he alternated leadership with Mahler and ultimately, by some accounts, drove his Viennese counterpart away to his position with the Philharmonic. Returning to Italy in 1915, he was restored at La Scala where he held firm during World War I, but then came into conflict with the Fascist government upon Benito Mussolini's rise to power in 1922. Four years later, in 1926, Toscanini was named co-conductor of the New York Philharmonic, alongside the German Wilhelm Furtwängler. When it was announced the next year that he had been given a five-year contract to be the Philharmonic's principal conductor, the news resonated through the New York musical world.[70] Already an esteemed figure in the US, Toscanini's tenure with the Philharmonic made him a musical celebrity whose fame transcended the boundaries of the classical music audience; and his notoriety grew even further when, after leaving the Philharmonic, he took over the NBC radio network's symphony orchestra in 1937, giving him a broad national platform.

Critical praise for Toscanini could seem boundless. Characteristic of the encomiums that accompanied his performances with the Philharmonic is a 1932 review by A. Walter Kramer, the editor of *Musical America*, of a program in which Toscanini conducted what some classical concertgoers would have considered a sort of platonic ideal of musical works: Beethoven's Third Symphony (the *Eroica*), and excerpts from two operas by Wagner, *Die Walküre* and *Tristan und Isolde*. Kramer enthused:

> Hardly ever in our experience have we listened to a more perfect concert than this one. The great conductor was at his best. His Beethoven was a magnificently conceived and adjusted outpouring of music to which he devotes himself with supreme humility, yet with compelling authority. Of his Wagner, nothing more need be said than that it was a complete realization.[71]

Crucial here is Kramer's description of Toscanini's demeanor as a conductor, combining the features of humility and authority. The humility was expressly held in relation to the musical work. As Joseph Horowitz observes in his elaborate study of the conductor's career in the U.S, one of the qualities for which Toscanini was most celebrated was his commitment to representing the "truth" of the works that he presented with the orchestra.[72] For his celebrants, this characteristic made him uniquely capable of presenting works of the highest esteem to the musical public. Works that were already certified in their supposed greatness, conducted by a figure whose own greatness brought out the best in those works, leading an orchestra whose players were so attuned to the will of the conductor that they could realize his interpretation with near perfection—this was, for perhaps the majority of classical music concertgoers in the 1920s and 1930s (and maybe still today), what a concert was supposed to be.

Of course, there were dissenters. One substantive line of criticism was that Toscanini had a fatal aversion to musical modernism and an accompanying resistance to programming work by American composers. A summary of the 1931–1932 season by the New York Philharmonic-Symphony (so named because it had merged with the Symphony Society in 1928) observed that only five American works had been offered that year, as compared with thirteen German works, eleven Austrian, eight French, seven Russian and seven Italian. Most damning, though, among the various conductors who led the organization for part of the season, Toscanini was one of four that had not programmed a single American work, a pattern already understood to be common practice when he commanded the orchestra.[73] By 1938, after Toscanini assumed his role at NBC, he was taken by the German social theorist Theodor Adorno to stand for the widespread cultural tendency to treat music as a "fetish." In Adorno's understanding, the way that Toscanini was promoted to the public as the great "Maestro" whose musical mastery was beyond question, marked a sort of dissolution of the boundary between "light" and "serious" music. For Adorno this was a threatening development, suggesting that all music was subject to the same process of being rendered into a commodity, packaged for ready consumption, such that the music itself no longer mattered. Whatever pieces were programmed, if Toscanini was the conductor, it was assumed to be good.[74]

Herein lay the paradox embodied in Toscanini's prominence, which was also emblematic of the paradox of American classical music during the period in question. Toscanini personified for many observers the qualities that made classical music into the highest sort of artistic expression. Yet the Toscanini audience was, as Joseph Horowitz points out, a mass audience. This was especially true after he took hold of the NBC Symphony in 1937, but even at the head of the New York Philharmonic, Toscanini's audience was never limited to the patrons that attended his performances in Carnegie Hall. His recordings from these years were not plentiful, but the steady stream of newspaper reviews ensured that his reputation circulated widely, and his appearance on the cover of *Time* magazine in April 1934, upon the occasion of his sixty-seventh birthday, certified his notoriety.[75] Toscanini's supporters invested in him the hope that classical music could expand its audience without compromising its standards. There would be no need to promote artistic intercourse with jazz, no need to admit that canonical works were insufficient to sustain a regimen of elevated musical appreciation. What was lost, for commentators like Adorno and other less academic skeptics, was a critical understanding of the works being performed. Their greatness, like that of Toscanini himself, was assumed at the outset. In this, Toscanini represented another version of middlebrow. As apparently different from Paul Whiteman as one could be, Toscanini and Whiteman contributed to a common cultural goal of taking "highbrow" cultural values and making them more accessible for the consumption of middle-class consumers who lacked the financial and educational resources of the "cultural capitalists" that built institutions like Carnegie Hall, but longed to claim some of the status associated with such institutions and the music that resided there.

A Tale of Two Managers

The growth of the classical music audience into something that had mass dimensions was not simply an organic development, as the music's supporters wanted to believe; and neither was it a straightforward outgrowth of the new media culture that surrounded the music. Rather, to the extent that certain varieties of classical music gained a kind of mainstream cultural appeal in the decades following World War I, they did so due to deliberate efforts made by those working on behalf of the music to promote it to the largest possible audience. In the realm of recordings, the Victor company had made great inroads since the dawn of the twentieth century, when it portrayed the opera singer Enrico Caruso as the greatest star of recorded music in the US and used its Red Seal series of records to lend an aura of prestige and legitimacy to its releases.[76] Toscanini himself recorded for Victor and his radio career happened under the same corporate imprint, given that Victor would be bought by the Radio Corporation of America (RCA), which created the NBC radio network.

Concerning classical music concerts, two parallel lines of development stimulated the growth of audiences during the 1920s and 1930s. On the one hand, civic leaders in cities and towns across the US followed the example of major metropolitan areas and organized the creation of new symphony orchestras, and the construction of new concert halls. On the other hand, a new level of commercial acumen was brought into the field of concert promotion by managers whose commitment to high culture values was coupled to a fierce, business-minded approach that viewed the need to build the classical music audience beyond its elite base as a paramount concern. Two figures in particular stand out on this score: Arthur Judson, who began his career as a music educator and then a journalist before assuming the management of some of the most prominent concert organizations of the era, including the Philadelphia Orchestra and the New York Philharmonic; and Sol Hurok, who made his mark as an artist manager and concert promoter, working with an illustrious array of performers across the fields of music and dance. In many regards they are a study in contrast, Judson the organization man as against Hurok the independent, Judson the agent of consolidation and Hurok the risk-taker. Together they illustrate some of the primary mechanisms through which classical music came to enjoy something like mass acclaim through the decades of the 1920s and 1930s.

* * *

Arthur Judson's first move into music management came in 1915, when he was invited to take on the management of the Philadelphia Orchestra. Leopold Stokowski, a charismatic figure whose esteem would come to rival Toscanini's, had assumed the conductor's role three years earlier; and the two together helped to build the Philadelphia Orchestra into one of the leading concert organizations in the US, considered by many observers to be musically superior to the New York Philharmonic. Meanwhile, Judson quickly began to diversify his interests. He took on the management of individual concert artists as an adjunct to his work as an orchestra manager, and in 1918 he formed Concert Management Arthur Judson—a move that would seem to have created a notable conflict of interest, since Judson was now serving as both a buyer of talent (in his role with the Philadelphia Orchestra) and seller of talent.[77] If there was an ethical conundrum in Judson's combined tasks, it did not give him pause. Instead, the move marked the beginning of a pattern through which Judson accumulated a wide range of institutional commitments and responsibilities, in the process building a sphere of influence that was arguably unrivaled in the realm of musical business.

A major break came in 1920, when Judson was made the manager of a series of outdoor concerts held at Lewisohn Stadium in New York, on the campus of the City College. The Stadium Concerts, as they were called, were part of a growing trend toward summertime concert programming in outdoor settings, also apparent in the creation of the Hollywood Bowl in California.[78] Judson's effectiveness in this new role set the stage for his being hired to manage the New York Philharmonic in 1922. With this appointment Judson now oversaw the affairs of two of the leading symphony orchestras in the US. Between the two his association with the Philharmonic would be the more enduring, but he held onto his post with the Philadelphia Orchestra until 1935, when unresolvable tensions between he and Curtis Bok, chairman of the orchestra's board, led to his resignation.[79] Judson remained with the New York Philharmonic until 1956. He was at the helm during the Toscanini years and for two decades afterwards, and he helped to oversee the significant 1928 merger between the Philharmonic and the New York Symphony Society. Over time his influence upon the organization would be called into question. In the midst of the 1946–1947 season, Artur Rodzinski abruptly resigned from his position as musical director of the Philharmonic, accusing Judson of undue interference with his responsibilities.[80] Ten years later, in 1956, New York music critics Howard Taubman and Paul Henry Lang wrote biting assessments of the Philharmonic's loss of artistic focus and direction, placing no small amount of blame on Judson's various business entanglements—criticisms that seem to have precipitated Judson's resignation.[81]

In the early phase of his appointment though, Judson was rarely censured so publicly. Although his musical tastes were notoriously conservative, Judson's business sense was decidedly modern.[82] The watchword for Judson's managerial philosophy from the early 1920s forward was "cooperation." He pursued it at all levels, developing a set of business alliances with competing managers, with other concert organizations, and ultimately with emerging media corporations to create a field of unified interests such as had not previously existed in the classical music world. An early move in this direction came in 1922, with his involvement in the short-lived Associated Musical Bureaus, a cooperative arrangement among nine music managers and agencies stretching from New York to Chicago, Atlanta to Portland, Oregon. As described by the *New York Times*, "The new organization aims through economies of management on a broad scale to facilitate the bookings of instrumentalists, singers and groups of artists suited to appear publicly."[83] Such practices had previously belonged to the domain of vaudeville, where regional and national cooperation between managers had given rise to the first fully nationalized entertainment industry in the US, as was discussed in Chapter 3. Judson envisioned a similar degree of large-scale economic coordination in the field of classical music concert promotion.

Momentum for pushing this vision forward gathered as the decade progressed. Judson embraced radio as a medium that could offer critical support to the advancement of classical music at a time when many in the music business still looked at radio with suspicion, fearing that it would draw away audiences and cause significant loss of revenues. In 1926, he took a major role in establishing the basis for a national radio network that provided significant competition for NBC, whose dominance at that point was more or less unchallenged. Forging a partnership with the Columbia Phonograph Company in 1927, Judson was on the ground floor of the new CBS radio network; and when the company withdrew its investment, Judson held on until new support could be found in the figure of William Paley, who provided a needed infusion of cash and assumed presidency of the network in late 1928.[84]

Judson's alignment with CBS set the stage for what was probably the biggest move of his professional career: his leadership in the Columbia Concerts Corporation. Established in December 1930, with William Paley as chairman and Judson as president, the Columbia Concerts Corporation was built to capitalize on the potential for synergy that could exist between radio and concert promotion. Under the corporate auspices of CBS, seven major concert management agencies merged their efforts to create the Columbia Concerts Corporation, with Concert Management Arthur Judson at the front of the line.[85] NBC had already established its own concert bureau the previous year, which would continue to expand. Between them, CBS and NBC turned their artist management services into the most powerful agencies of the 1930s. In both cases, the concert management wing was given over to classical music artists predominantly, as can be seen from the list of performers in Figure 5.2; the overall goal was to promote artists who would achieve prominence in the concert field and then be given broadcasting opportunities as well.

Musical America explained the rationale for the Columbia Concerts Corporation in language that was likely scripted by Judson himself, although it went unattributed:

> One of the principal needs of the music industry was coordination. The creation of the Columbia Concerts Corporation substitutes cooperation for competition. The local manager is no longer invited to shop for his talent. Laying out a satisfactory, well-rounded concert course is now a simple matter for the local manager. He has more than 125 artists available to him, and there is a rich variety of talent in every field of music as well as for every budget. Costly and unnecessary competition is a thing of the past. Tours will be concentrated, artists with have better routed bookings, all the various sources of waste which created expenses formerly borne by the ultimate consumer as well as by the New York manager and the artist will be eliminated.[86]

It is important to remember that part of the context for the efforts of both CBS and NBC along these lines was the economic depression that hit in 1929 and was worsening in the early 1930s. Major music organizations ran into considerable financial difficulties during this time. Both the Metropolitan Opera Company and the New York Philharmonic had trouble meeting expenses; there was even talk for a time that Carnegie Hall would be converted into a movie house.[87] Cooperation of the sort described here was designed to be a safeguard against diminishing returns. Yet the logic that underpinned the creation of the Columbia Concerts Corporation was also consistent with longer-standing goals that Judson pursued throughout his career. The rationalization of tour itineraries, the centralization of talent booking—these

Columbia Concerts Corporation

of

Columbia Broadcasting System

Alphabetical Listing of Artists Available for Concerts, Opera, Radio, etc.

SOPRANOS
Josephine Antoine
Rose Bampton
Natalie Bodanya
Charlotte Boerner
Hilda Burke
Winifred Cecil
Agnes Davis
Muriel Dickson
Elen Dosia
Jessica Dragonette
Mafalda Favero
Enya Gonzalez
Helen Jepson
Lotte Lehmann
Hope Manning
Lucy Monroe
Grace Moore
Rose Pauly
Lily Pons
Maria Reining
Bidu Sayao
Rosa Tentoni
Mary Tock
Carolyn Urbanek

MEZZO SOPRANOS
Edwina Eustis
Helen Olheim
Risé Stevens

CONTRALTOS
Bruna Castagna
Anna Kaskas
Kathryn Meisle
Sigrid Onegin
Elizabeth Wysor

'CELLISTS
Gaspar Cassadó
Marcel Hubert
Gregor Piatigorsky
Joseph Schuster

TENORS
Paul Althouse
Michael Bartlett
Joseph Bentonelli
André Burdino
John Carter
Richard Crooks
Beniamino Gigli
Edouard Grobé
Tito Guizar
Charles Hackett
Frederick Jagel
Allan Jones
Charles Kullman
Eyvind Laholm
Ronald Marsilia
Nino Martini
Ernest McChesney
James Melton
Richard Tauber
Alessandro Ziliani

BARITONES
Richard Bonelli
John Brownlee
Norman Cordon
Nelson Eddy
Wilbur Evans
Keith Falkner
Igor Gorin
Lansing Hatfield
Julius Huehn
Ray Middleton
Robert Nicholson
Paul Robeson
Lawrence Tibbett
Robert Weede

BASS
Salvatore Baccaloni

TWO PIANOS
Bartlett and Robertson
Malcolm and Godden
Vronsky and Babin

PIANISTS
Erno Balogh
Simon Barer
Harold Bauer
Emile Baume
Robert Casadesus
Eduardo del Pueyo
José Echaniz
Daniel Ericourt
Dalies Frantz
Boris Golschmann
Vladimir Horowitz
Ernest Hutcheson
Amparo Iturbi
José Iturbi
Julius Katchen
Muriel Kerr
Ida Krehm
Eugene List
Mieczyslaw Münz
Guiomar Novaes
Serge Prokofieff
Ezra Rachlin
Mariana Sarrica
Ernest Schelling
Ruth Slenczynski
Reginald Stewart

VIOLINISTS
Arnold Belnick
Iso Briselli
Marjorie Edwards
Mischa Elman
Zino Francescatti
Jascha Heifetz
Stephan Hero
Joseph Knitzer
Yehudi Menuhin
Toscha Seidel
Albert Spalding
Joseph Szigeti
Patricia Travers
Robert Virovai

SPECIAL ATTRACTIONS
The Mozart Boys' Choir of Vienna
  Dr. Georg Gruber, Conductor
Vandy Cape
  Singing Satires
Dorothy Crawford
  Original Character Sketches
  Assisted by Concert Pianist
Elen Dosia and André Burdino
  Joint Recitals
Ionian Singers
Lotte Lehmann and
Lauritz Melchior
  Joint Recitals
Russian Imperial Singers
Bauer—Spalding—Cassadó
  (Piano, Violin, 'Cello in trio programs)

HARPISTS
Beatrice Burford
Mildred Dilling

FLUTISTS
Georges Barrère
L. D. Callimahos

ENSEMBLES
Barrère-Britt Concertino
Barrère Little Symphony
Coolidge String Quartet
Gordon String Quartet
Kneisel-Alden-Turner
  (Violin, 'Cello, Piano)

DANCERS
Devi Dja and her Bali and Java Dancers
Jooss European Ballet
Carola Goya
La Meri
Angna Enters

HEADQUARTERS: 113 West 57th Street, NEW YORK CITY

CHICAGO OFFICE: 932 Wrigley Building

Los Angeles:
L. E. Behymer, 705 Auditorium Bldg.

Hollywood:
Columbia Management of California, Inc.
Columbia Square

Figure 5.2 This 1939 advertisement for the Columbia Concerts Corporation shows the extensive list of classical music artists represented by the company, an indication of the influence of leading artist manager Arthur Judson. From *Musical America* (February 10, 1939).

were the same goals that had been pursued by vaudeville managers since the 1890s, and with the same end in mind of turning concert booking into an economy of scale on a national level. At a time when vaudeville was in precipitous decline, classical music agents like Judson sought to fill a void, and they built institutions for purposes of concert promotion the likes of which would not be replicated in the popular music realm for years to come.

* * *

Arthur Judson may have been the most influential power broker in the concert field by the early 1930s, but he did not necessarily have the most recognizable name. That honor likely would have gone to Sol Hurok. The difference in styles between the two could be seen in the way they listed themselves when they promoted performances. While managing the New York Philharmonic, Judson's name always appeared in the orchestra's ads, but in small type at the bottom as a subtle reminder of his role. When advertising the solo artists he managed, he was billed at the top, but as Concert Management Arthur Judson—as though his name were inextricable from some larger corporate structure. Later, after the formation of Columbia Concerts Corporation, Judson's name became even more subsidiary. He was the man at the top, but his power was largely under disguise. By contrast, Sol Hurok always put his name first and, especially after he was established, in terms that were unmistakable. Early on, Hurok emulated the practice of other music agents, listing events under the rubric, "S. Hurok's Musical Bureau" or something similar. For a time, he was "S. Hurok, Inc.," but by the late 1920s he devised the designation, "S. Hurok Presents," rendering the act of concert promotion into an assertion of his own will and effort. This simple gesture, conjoined with Hurok's many accomplishments over a long career that lasted from the 1910s into the 1970s, made him into an icon of sorts for a later generation. As legend would have it, when the leading concert promoter of the rock era, Bill Graham, first got his start working with the San Francisco Mime Troupe in the mid-1960s, he had a nameplate on his desk that read, not "Bill Graham," but "Sol Hurok."[88]

Hurok's standing as a role model for Graham was ethnic as well as professional: like Graham, Hurok was an Eastern European Jew who immigrated to the US after experiencing considerable turmoil. In Hurok's case the Russian Revolution of 1905, and the anti-Semitic pogroms that happened in Russia during the early twentieth century, were the stimulus for his decision to come to the US; he arrived the next year at age eighteen, settling first in Philadelphia and then moving to Brooklyn.[89] His earliest efforts at organizing concerts and other cultural events came through his work as a labor organizer on behalf of the Socialist Party. In his memoir, ghostwritten by Ruth Goode, Hurok recalls with pride his success in booking the sensational young violin virtuoso Efrem Zimbalist to perform at a Socialist Party benefit in 1912, and at a reduced rate from his usual performance fee no less.[90] Hurok presented Zimbalist at Carnegie Hall the following year, but the bulk of his activity remained concentrated for a time in Brooklyn, where he took over the management of a Labor Lyceum in the Brownsville neighborhood and oversaw a busy calendar of banquets, lectures, and rallies. Meanwhile, he had his eye set on Manhattan and approached the manager of the immense vaudeville theater the Hippodrome to present a series of Sunday concerts. Hurok's plan to offer classical music in a popular theater was hardly unprecedented, but what was new was his deliberate effort to cultivate an audience for such attractions in a leading Manhattan vaudeville house among the same Jewish immigrant population he served, and lived among, in Brooklyn. He advertised the concerts in foreign-language newspapers and used neighborhood stores to sell tickets: "There was a drug store in Harlem and a drug store in Brooklyn, a jewelry store in the Bronx. In Brownsville there were seats at Levinson's Music Store, 1737 Pitkin Avenue, and on East Broadway it was Katz's Music Store at Number 183."[91] This was not the clientele that comprised the subscriber list to the Philharmonic. It was a new class of "serious" music patrons, and Hurok's success in drawing them to the Hippodrome formed the basis for his own growing notoriety. By his own account, the "Hurok audience" was born.[92]

Cultivating a new demographic for classical music audiences, Hurok gained increasing notoriety for his promotion of European, and especially Russian—or Soviet—artists. Although he had some notable dalliances with American music and American performers, as will be discussed shortly, Hurok was unabashedly Eurocentric in his proclivities. His memoir hinges on his management of a series of high-profile artists who came from Russia, including the operatic baritone Feodor Chaliapin and the ballet dancer Anna Pavlova, with whom he scored some of his first and greatest successes. He remained a special champion of Soviet music and even more so Soviet dance in the US for decades to come, even signing a contract with the Soviet government in 1930 that granted him exclusive right to engage artists from the Communist nation in the United States and UK.[93] In 1932 Hurok successfully managed the Ballet Russe de Monte Carlo, a revival of the esteemed

Ballet Russes company that had visited the US in 1916 under the leadership of choreographer Serge Diaghilev and disbanded upon Diaghilev's death in 1929. Figure 5.3 shows the impresario with Russian dancer and choreographer Leonide Massine, a leading force in the company. Hurok relished the sense of prestige and glamour attached to foreign artists; he exploited their exotic appeal in his promotional approach and sought to embody these qualities for himself in his personal life. As he put it in his memoir, when recalling the regular trips to abroad to scout for new talent: "it was on the originality, the quality, the variety of my importations from Europe that I was to make my name in the next fifteen years."[94]

In this facet of his career Hurok was not so different from Arthur Judson. Hurok, though, was not the institution builder that Judson was, and neither did he hold Judson's faith that "cooperation" between competing interests was the key to success. This is not to say that Hurok completely avoided

Figure 5.3 Sol Hurok, right, with esteemed Soviet dancer and choreographer Leonide Massine, 1938. Hurok's championing of Soviet artists performing in the US was a key to his success as a concert promoter and artist manager. Courtesy of the Jerome Robbins Dance Division, The New York Public Library for the Performing Arts.

any entanglements. When the influence of the Columbia and NBC concert booking agencies became pervasive, Hurok was compelled to align with NBC. He did so, however, under a special arrangement that allowed him to preserve a considerable amount of his independence. Unlike so many other booking agencies that became fully merged with the larger corporations, Hurok made a deal that gave NBC oversight of artists he managed when they toured outside of New York but allowed him to retain control over the promotion of those artists within the city. He also maintained his own publicity staff, which gave him critical resources to continue to operate with relative autonomy. Perhaps most notably, he kept his own brand, so that his imprint of "S. Hurok Presents" would remain in place for all artists who worked under him.[95] The dynamics of the arrangement were readily apparent in an ad that NBC Artists Service placed on the back cover of the January 25, 1932, issue of *Musical America*. Presenting an extensive roster of ninety artists divided into twelve categories for the forthcoming 1932–1933 season, NBC depicted the breadth of its impact on the concert industry. Among those artists, eleven had asterisks beside their names, including six in the top-ranked category of "Special Attractions." These were the artists that NBC booked, according to a small note at the bottom of the ad, "by arrangement with S. Hurok."[96] Even within NBC's own promotional efforts, then, Hurok got special billing.

Despite his Eurocentric leanings, Hurok also selectively put his weight behind American artists as well. Probably his most celebrated such association resulted, somewhat ironically, from his scouting trips to Europe. It was in Paris that Hurok encountered the African American contralto Marian Anderson, in the spring of 1935. At the time Anderson had been working as a professional concert artist for well over a decade. Born in Philadelphia in 1897, Anderson came of age singing in the Union Baptist church attended by her family. Through her church affiliation she made a crucial artistic and professional connection in 1911 with the African American tenor Roland Hayes, who became a lifelong mentor to Anderson.[97] For both singers, African American spirituals—rendered in a refined, formalized style that was indebted to the emergence of the spiritual as a concert form through the career of the Fisk Jubilee Singers—became the key to acceptance. The genre was heard to "naturally" suit their vocal talents by critics and audiences of the time, and the projection of faith and respectability that the spirituals conveyed helped to temper some of the prejudice that kept black artists largely excluded from the sphere of formal concert music. With spirituals as a foundation, Anderson broadened her training throughout the 1910s and 1920s, such that her programs featured work by the likes of Handel and Brahms as prominently as they did works of recognized African American provenance. When she won a vocal competition in 1925 sponsored by the National Music League and held in conjunction with the Stadium Concerts in New York, she caught the attention of Arthur Judson, who managed the concerts; and two years later he signed her to his Concert Management Arthur Judson agency.[98] Yet Judson never put the full weight of his support behind the singer and that combined with the racism she encountered as a touring black concert artist in the US kept her in Europe throughout much of the late 1920s and into the mid-1930s, setting the stage for her encounter with Hurok.

The pride that Hurok took in luring Anderson away from Judson can be garnered from the coy way that he recalled the incident in his memoir—leaving Judson's name unsaid, he writes, "I knew her American manager well. He is still, has been for many many years, one of the most respected names in the music business."[99] Whatever respect Hurok had for Judson, he set about his task of advising Anderson on how to get out of her existing commitment. The contract that Hurok offered to Anderson was modest at the start, with a guarantee of fifteen concerts in the US upon her return. Unlike Judson, though, Hurok brought great care and commitment to his promotion of her appearances and crafted a publicity campaign that projected onto her concerts the aura of a jubilant homecoming. He booked her first concert upon her return at Town Hall, a midtown Manhattan venue that had become one of the city's leading places for the presentation of classical music concerts. In the buildup to her Town Hall concert of December 30, 1935, Hurok placed an ad that announced Anderson to be performing "After the Greatest European Triumph Ever Achieved by an American Singer!"[100] This was clearly ballyhoo, but the reviews that followed upon the concert indicated that Anderson had returned to the US with a new degree of artistic credibility in the ears of her auditors. Writing for the *New York Times*, Howard Taubman sang her praises most loudly in a piece that helped pave the way for the subsequent success of Anderson's American career. "Let it be said at the outset: Marian Anderson has returned to her native land one of the greatest singers of our time," began Taubman's review; and he ended by comparing the singer with another African American figure noted to have succeeded in the face of racial adversity: "If Joe Louis deserves to be an American hero for bowling over a lot of pushovers, then Marian Anderson has the right at least to comparable standing. Handel, Schubert and Sibelius are not pushovers."[101]

Anderson's ascent to the status of culture hero truly took hold just over three years later, when she sang on the steps of the Lincoln Memorial in Washington, DC, on Easter Sunday, April 9, 1939. The event has been enshrined as a signal moment in American musical history and in the history of American race relations, prefiguring the growth of the modern Civil Rights movement after World War II. It came about only after the national women's organization, the Daughters of the American Revolution, refused to allow the singer to appear in Constitution Hall, the Washington, DC auditorium it controlled, due to a policy that excluded black artists from appearing there. Public comment on the action of the DAR grew gradually over the course of January 1939 and became a groundswell in the ensuing weeks, reaching a particular high point when the nation's First Lady, Eleanor Roosevelt, announced her resignation from the DAR at the end of February.[102] Meanwhile, the effort to find an alternative venue for Anderson in one of the city's public schools reached an impasse when the school board ruled against the idea on the grounds that such a move would go against the "dual system" of segregated black and white schools.[103]

Hurok was one of several figures who worked behind the scenes to coordinate a response to Anderson's situation, along with Walter White, head of the National Association for the Advancement of Colored People, and various others. He also took credit, in his memoir, for the idea to have her appear at the Lincoln Memorial, although Hurok's biographer Harlow Robinson suggests that the idea came from someone working in the office of Oscar Chapman, Assistant Secretary of the Interior, who then raised the issue with his boss, Secretary Harold Ickes.[104] Whether or not he procured the use of the Lincoln Memorial, Hurok had done much to support Anderson's fair treatment since he began to manage her career, and was outspoken in his criticism of the racism she faced during the planning of the concert, stating at one point that the performance would be held "as a rebuke to all who have snubbed the Negro singer."[105] It was that, and more. The estimated 75,000 who came to hear Anderson sing that day, captured in Figure 5.4, carried an echo of the tens of thousands that had witnessed the Fisk Jubilee Singers appear at Patrick Gilmore's World's Peace Jubilee nearly seventy years earlier. Anderson's brief program was like a condensation of her regular concert programs of the time, split between European concert works and African American spirituals, the latter of which were featured in the final half of her performance. As to the audience, it was full of dignitaries but also contained a roughly equal number of white and African Americans.[106] For Anderson

Figure 5.4 Marian Anderson, shown on the lower left, singing to an audience of some 75,000 people from the steps of the Lincoln Memorial in Washington, DC, April 9, 1939. Courtesy of Everett Collection Inc./Alamy Stock Photo.

its scale likely reinforced the sense she had that, "my significance as an individual was small in this affair. I had become, whether I liked it or not, a symbol, representing my people."[107] Hurok, for his part, portrayed the crowd as a veritable "sea," the effect of which was "indescribable;" and his account of the concert provides the climax of his autobiography, representing the pinnacle of his personal and professional achievements to date.[108]

The Jazz Concert, Take Two

Another of Hurok's endeavors of the late 1930s does not even get mentioned in that same autobiography—his promotion of Benny Goodman's appearance at Carnegie Hall on January 16, 1938. Perhaps its omission was because Hurok was not the driving force behind the concert. He joined the initiative to stage Goodman's performance after being approached by Wynn Nathanson, a publicist who handled the account for the "Camel Caravan" radio show on the CBS network, on which the bandleader had begun appearing the previous fall.[109] Hurok was valued because of his established authority in the world of classical concert music and his ties to Carnegie Hall, where he had started to present his own concert series in October 1937.[110] According to Irving Kolodin, the music critic who co-authored Goodman's autobiography and was sitting in Hurok's offices at the time that the idea for the concert first arose, the established promoter needed to be convinced that this was a worthy project. Only after attending a Goodman band performance at the Madhattan Room of the Hotel Pennsylvania and seeing "so many well-dressed people spending money on an attraction" was Hurok ready to be brought on board.[111] Even then, the fact that Hurok does not discuss the concert in his memoir suggests that it did not fit neatly with his preferred image of enlightened refinement.

Chroniclers of Goodman's concert, long considered a milestone in jazz history, have accepted this version of Hurok's image, construing his involvement in the Goodman concert as something of a one-off, and Hurok's biographer, Harlow Robinson, conveys the same impression. It is notable, then, that this was not in fact Hurok's first venture into jazz concert promotion. He seems to have presented only one such previous event, but it was a concert of some consequence: the November 1924 appearance of Vincent Lopez and his jazz orchestra at the Metropolitan Opera House that followed Lopez's lecture-performance with the League of Composers earlier that year. In an ad placed in the November 23, 1924, edition of the *New York Herald Tribune*, Lopez's concert—which occurred that day—appears under the heading, "S. Hurok, Inc., Announces," alongside a series of Sunday afternoon concerts presented by Hurok at Aeolian Hall featuring several other upcoming performances more of the sort with which Hurok was usually identified.[112] His involvement with the Lopez concert was also noted in the extensive review that appeared in *Variety*, where Abel Green compared it unfavorably with Whiteman's earlier "Experiment" at Aeolian Hall, but nonetheless judged it significant for further "beating a way for other glorified jazz orchestras ... which refuse to be confined merely to dance engagements at hotels, cafes or passing attention on the stage in vaudeville or production."[113] Among the standout works at the Lopez concert was *Evolution of the Blues*, composed by W.C. Handy in conjunction with Lopez's arranger, Joseph Nussbaum. An extended symphonic reworking of some of Handy's blues themes, it was Lopez's closest counterpart to the centerpiece of Whiteman's concert, *Rhapsody in Blue*, and marked a notable distinction attending to the Lopez performance, foregrounding the work of an African American composer. In this Lopez sought, in the words of jazz historian John Howland, to "out-jazz" Whiteman, and yet in other regards—such as the use of a forty-six-piece orchestra—he also seemed to be trying to "out-classicize" his competitor as well.[114]

Hurok's involvement in promoting Vincent Lopez at the Met and Benny Goodman at Carnegie Hall, nearly fourteen years apart, indicates the continuity between the renewed effort to present jazz in the concert hall from the late 1930s forward and the earlier moment in the mid-1920s when the boundaries between "serious" and "popular" music were reconfigured. And Hurok's successful promotion of such figures as Marian Anderson, combined with the popularity of star conductors like Toscanini and the consolidation of corporate influence in the promotion of classical music concerts, also demonstrates that classical music was not only a repository of elevated values in the 1930s. With the advent of national radio networks, each of which oversaw its own concert booking agency, classical music was part of the musical mass culture that grew from the boom period of the 1920s through the bust of the Depression and into World War II. In this, it paralleled jazz as much as the two musical spheres were set apart from one another. Jazz was inarguably the music that was more widely popular and that coursed through the channels of mass distribution with greater force. The "Swing Era," as it came to be called, was a pivotal moment in the growth of the American music industry, and swing critics came to routinely bemoan the music's commercialization as the audience grew and the style evolved.[115] That criticism, in turn, was part of a wider movement to treat jazz as something that had inherent aesthetic value—not only when it was made into something that sounded like classical music, but when it was played on its own terms.

Benny Goodman's Carnegie Hall concert in early 1938 crystallized these competing tendencies that came to bear upon the cultural position of jazz during the swing era. It was an unmitigated commercial proposition instigated by an adman to further publicize the Goodman band and its radio appearances. Equally it was an effort to borrow the prestige attached to classical music institutions—and to figures like Hurok who worked within those institutions—for the purpose of giving jazz greater legitimacy. To the extent that Goodman's Carnegie Hall concert had the effect of encouraging a more "serious" approach to jazz performance and appreciation, though, the inspiration came as much from developments that had occurred within the jazz world of the time as from without.

Jazz venues in the 1930s, on the cusp of the time when "swing" shifted from verb to noun, were much as they had been in the last half of the preceding decade. Large ballrooms and small cabaret-style settings remained the prevalent settings for jazz performance. By the time the 1930s rolled around, more of these spaces were equipped with radio hook-ups to allow bands to broadcast from the venues where they performed, thus facilitating the rise of a national audience that could listen to the same attractions across a wide geographic expanse. Competition for prized radio dates was intense and drove the swing band economy. There were far more bands than there were choice spots, but smaller regional dance halls across the country emerged and gave rise to a national touring network that outstripped what had existed in the 1920s. Adding to the changed entertainment climate was the epochal end of Prohibition in 1933, with the passage of the Twenty-first Amendment to the Constitution. The nightclub culture of the Prohibition years, never especially hidden from view, now became a sanctioned above ground phenomenon, and jazz in effect moved along with it.

To some degree the convergence of the end of Prohibition and the rise of the jazz club was sheer coincidence. The Onyx Club, located on a section of 52nd Street in midtown Manhattan that would earn the moniker "Swing Street," may be the first venue to have warranted such a title, and it began its life during the tail end of Prohibition. Prior to this time there had been no such thing as a "jazz club" in the way we would think of such a place today. Jazz was a regular feature in clubs and cabarets around the US, but it was only one feature among many, and at spots like the Cotton Club where Duke Ellington's band had held sway since 1927, the floor show, the chorus girls, and the alcohol-soaked atmosphere drew people in as much as the music itself. At the start the Onyx was a speakeasy like many others, but it quickly gained a clientele of working musicians who favored it as an after-hours hangout. According to jazz critic Wilder Hobson, the club relocated to a larger space shortly after the repeal of Prohibition and some time after owner Joe Helbock received his liquor license, the crowds began to come.[116] What drew them was small-group "hot" jazz played by African American musicians such as the Five Spirits of Rhythm, or solo jazz played by the likes of the titanic virtuoso pianist Art Tatum.[117] The musicianship was first-rate, and the setting allowed for a focus on the playing and the players that was, by all accounts, unique. Moreover, the Onyx and other likeminded spots such as the Famous Door and the Jam Club were too small to house dance floors. As a result, observed Abel Green at the start of 1936, "The appeal is all ear;

[the music] may inspire to hoof, or sway, or syncopate, or hotcha... but there isn't room for any hoofing. Therefore, the ear appeal is paramount."[118] Or, as Hobson described when looking back in 1939, "The United States has had good jazz bands in public places for twenty years and suddenly a good-sized portion of the population sat down and listened to them. With the help of liquor, of course."[119]

This last line reminds us of how starkly different jazz clubs were, as places and as institutions, from concert halls, and how different it was to listen with concentration in such a space. Jazz clubs were not built to foster aesthetic contemplation; they were far from being designed as temples of music. Even as audiences turned their attention to the music, they still had occasion to drink and socialize, and the entertainment factor remained paramount. Laughter, talk, the sounds of glasses clinking and drinks being served—these all co-existed with the sounds of the music, constituting another side of the "soundscape of modernity," one that was not governed by scientific acoustics and the fetish of sonic perfection, but that required listening in a multi-sensory environment where distraction was all but inevitable.

* * *

New habits of listening also manifested in other environments where jazz was performed. Much has been made of Benny Goodman's stand at the Palomar Ballroom in Los Angeles during the summer of 1935, as the moment when Goodman's career as a bandleader really took off and, by some accounts, the "swing era" as such truly began. As recounted in Goodman's autobiography, one of the things that signaled his acceptance by the audience at the Palomar was that at a certain point, "half the crowd stopped dancing and came surging around the stand. It was the first experience we had with that kind of attention, and it certainly was a kick."[120] Later that year Goodman's band played an event where the emergent listening culture taking hold among jazz audiences was even more apparent. During a stand at the Joseph Urban Room of the Hotel Congress in Chicago in the late fall of 1935, Goodman was asked to play a special jazz "concert" by a group of dedicated enthusiasts led by Helen Oakley who had formed the Chicago Rhythm Club. For Oakley and other Rhythm Club adherents, the concert would be an occasion to hear jazz be played without all the usual accompanying distractions. Goodman, by his own account, was initially resistant to the notion that his band should be presented in such rarefied fashion, but ultimately consented to the concert, which was held in the Urban Room on December 8.[121] Attendance at the concert—billed as a "Tea Dance"—exceeded all expectations, with some eight hundred people crowding into a room with a capacity of five hundred and fifty. More than the turnout, though, the demeanor of those gathered was the real news. Reporting for *Down Beat*—the Chicago-based jazz magazine that had only begun publication the previous year—Carl Cons observed, "A crowd of society debs, musicians, bookers, etc., were so enthralled with the music of Benny Goodman's band . . . that they positively preferred to listen and watch. In fact," added Cons, "the boys were so enthusiastically received that the only attempt at dancing was instantly booed."[122]

Of course, jazz in the swing era remained dance music, as it had been in years past. Dancing was a preferred activity among a vast majority of swing fans, and as was the case with Paul Whiteman in 1924, no band could afford to turn its back on dancers even when they engendered visibly different kinds of audience response. Goodman's band was as likely to stir comment for prompting vigorous dancing where it was not expected as for encouraging audiences to listen while standing in place. A case in point came during Goodman's stand at New York's Paramount Theater that began on March 3, 1937. Movie theaters had supplanted vaudeville theaters by this point, and many had dispensed with a "live" element, as movies proved to have sufficient drawing power on their own. But the Paramount began a policy of hiring dance bands to accompany its films in the first months of 1936, clearly hoping to take advantage of the swelling popularity of such bands at the time.[123] Prior to booking Goodman most of the bands that appeared there had been decidedly of the "sweet" variety—indeed, the band that initiated the band trend there was Paul Whiteman's, still going strong in 1936. Bringing a more "hot" style of jazz, Goodman also pulled a noticeably different audience to the theater, which was apparent even before the appointed opening time.

When Goodman and his musicians arrived at the Paramount at 7 a.m. for rehearsal they already found hundreds of theatergoers lined up outside, most of them high school aged—what would in a few years be called "teenagers," but were now just viewed as kids. By 10 a.m., two hours after the doors opened, more than four thousand had been admitted to the theater, and the crowds kept rotating throughout the day, building to a total of over twenty thousand as one show ended and the next began. *Variety* reporter Cecelia Ager captured the energy of the crowd in her account, writing from the perspective of the theater's managers:

> For soon they saw enacted in their theater, as Mr. Goodman's program progressed, a demonstration of approval of their talent-booking, tradition-shattering in its spontaneity, its unanimity, its sincerity, its volume, in the

childlike violence of its manifestations. Publicity Manager McInerney, seeing it, was like crazy. He saw a theater alive with ads writing themselves. "They are dancing in the aisles," he saw. "They are leaping from their seats, they are waving their arms . . . " Mr. McInerney saw all this—for once he didn't have to make it up.[124]

Previously, theater engagements had been a time for jazz bands to play to a non-dancing audience; the fixed seats and the rules of decorum dictated as much. Goodman's Paramount stand illustrated that the norms of the ballroom could be moved into another kind of setting. In the force of the young audience's response to Goodman and his orchestra, swing showed itself to have given rise to a youth culture of considerable scope. The cheap ticket prices and around-the-clock shows made Goodman's performances accessible to young theatergoers in a way that his ballroom appearances were not. For the Paramount, this would not be the last time it was the scene of a pop music explosion with adolescent audiences at its center.

Viewed from the perspective of audience response, Goodman's appearance at Carnegie Hall did not approach the effusion that accompanied his Paramount performances. Neither, though, did it seem to evoke the kind of concentrated attention evinced at the Urban Room concert. In part this was because the audience, although predominantly comprised of Goodman devotees, also included a significant proportion of regular Carnegie Hall patrons whose curiosity was laced with a certain amount of skepticism. Whiteman's Aeolian Hall concert drew a similarly varied crowd; but if anything, the mix at Goodman's concert, and the resulting behavior, was even harder to read. *Down Beat* presented two markedly contrasting portraits of the audience in two accounts that appeared in the February 1938 issue. For Annemarie Ewing, who guides the reader through the social trappings of the concert, Goodman exerted a kind of masterful control over those assembled, who ranged from "collegians or their equivalent" to "gray-haired gentlewomen." Acknowledging that the "holy-roller enthusiasm" sometimes generated by Goodman's band was largely lacking, she insisted, "for the most part, the audience did just what the music indicated. When it was noisy, they were noisy . . . And when the music lowered to a quiet passage, folks sat rapt and quiet, too."[125] On the other hand, H.E.P., writing the lead review for the magazine, saw much greater disparity, claiming that the audience contained "adolescent schoolboys attired like misprints in Esquire, who applauded everything" and "baggy-eyed pseudo-sophisticates who applauded nothing."[126]

Where Ewing saw the reconciliation of different audiences, H.E.P. saw constituencies whose different expectations were contradictory in a palpable sense, having an impact not just on the reception of the concert but on the performance itself.

Goodman's performance, and his program, at Carnegie Hall substantially departed from the precedent set by Whiteman in key particulars. H.E.P. complained that it was too much like what Goodman offered in other engagements, but this was in a sense the greatest strength of Goodman's concert and a telling signal of the changes that had taken hold in the status of jazz since 1924. The Carnegie Hall concert was not an exercise in symphonic jazz. Goodman did not augment his band with classical orchestral players or a string section. Those musicians who appeared as guests were there, in effect, to heighten the sense of "swing"—and to signal a level of racial inclusiveness that had been notably lacking from the Whiteman affair. Similarly, there were no special pieces composed for the occasion and nothing on offer that smacked of the effort to mingle jazz and classical music on a formal level. Goodman would show strong leanings toward precisely such moves in the aftermath to the concert, taking on a growing number of collaborations with classical music ensembles and composers.[127] At Carnegie Hall, though, he presented a "straight" jazz program in keeping with the mounting sensibility that construed jazz as "listening" music above all.

In terms of continuity with the Whiteman "Experiment," the linchpin of the proceedings was the segment titled "Twenty Years of Jazz." It was a clear corollary to the gesture with which Whiteman opened his concert, when a small group of his musicians offered a take on the ODJB's "Livery Stable Blues" designed to portray the "primitive" state from which jazz had evolved to its present sophistication. Notably, Goodman does not place his own historical feature at the start of the concert but only after the band have played three numbers in its own style, such that there is a swerve within the concert from the present to the past. Irving Kolodin, the critic who wrote the program notes for Goodman's concert and liner notes for its later release on record, claimed that the "Twenty Years" segment was his idea.[128] He offers little explanation for his motives on this score, but given that Kolodin's main background was as a classical music critic, I would surmise that he did so with two likely objectives: as a way to educate those concertgoers who might have lacked sufficient background in jazz; and as a way to invest jazz with a sense of history that was at least analogous, if not nearly as historically deep, as was found in the classical sphere.

As to the selections, the carryover from Whiteman was further apparent in the inclusion of another ODJB selection as the starting number, "Sensation Rag." It was followed in succession by takes on "I'm Comin' Virginia," played as a tribute to Bix Beiderbecke, with relative unknown Bobby Hackett doing the trumpet part; "When My Baby Smiles at Me," a short excerpt evoking a childhood hero of Goodman, clarinetist Ted Lewis, who is here mainly subjected to satire; "Shine," with rising trumpet star Harry James doing his best impersonation of Louis Armstrong, high spirited almost to the point of exaggeration; and "Blue Reverie," a Duke Ellington tune for which Goodman brought out three of Ellington's star soloists, Johnny Hodges on soprano saxophone, Harry Carney on baritone sax, and Cootie Williams on trumpet (see Figure 5.5). While parts of the "Twenty Years of Jazz" presentation are played for laughs, all told Goodman treats jazz history with far more reverence than did Whiteman—although by casting Ellington in the role of "historical" figure there is also a bit of sleight of hand involved, since Ellington (and Armstrong as well) were still very much active on the contemporary scene.

Figure 5.5 Benny Goodman, left, with trumpeter Cootie Williams, trombonist Vernon Brown, and saxophonist Johnny Hodges, during Goodman's concert at Carnegie Hall, January 16, 1938. Gift of Lawrence Marx, Jr. in memory of his brother, Albert Marx. Courtesy of Carnegie Hall Rose Archives.

The presence of three of Ellington's orchestra members signaled what may, in turn, have been the greatest departure from the precedent set by Whiteman. At Aeolian Hall in 1924, the African American contribution to jazz was rendered all but invisible. Goodman's inclusion of music by two black artists in the "Twenty Years of Jazz" segment suggested a rather different conception of jazz history. That he featured three black musicians as part of the performance went a step further. In this, Goodman consolidated his position as a white bandleader who was willing to challenge the standard separation of jazz groups into all-black or all-white aggregations. Coming of musical age in a Chicago jazz scene where white musicians openly worshipped at the feet of black players such as Armstrong and King Oliver, Goodman's clarinet style had always borne audible traces of African American influence and he had made records with black musicians since the early 1930s, including sessions with Bessie Smith and Billie Holiday produced by John Hammond. As a bandleader, with Hammond's support and coaxing, Goodman began regular collaborations with the black pianist Teddy Wilson in 1935, forming a trio with drummer Gene Krupa. The trio first performed together in public in 1936; the following year Goodman brought another African American musician, vibraphonist and drummer Lionel Hampton, into his group to form the Benny Goodman Quartet.[129] At the Carnegie Hall concert the short sets by the trio and quartet, one during the first half and another during the second, were widely considered as highlights of the whole affair. In these details and others—his indebtedness to the arrangements of African American pianist and bandleader Fletcher Henderson, the long jam session that included members of the Count Basie orchestra—Goodman foregrounded the African American presence in jazz during his concert at Carnegie Hall in a manner that clearly broke with the standards of an earlier era in jazz's elevation.

And yet, Goodman's achievement here needs to be qualified twice over. First, whoever else appeared with Goodman at Carnegie or contributed to the music he played there, it was still his concert in the end. Black artists had performed at Carnegie Hall as feature attractions in the past—the aforementioned James Reese Europe, whose Clef Club concerts in the years from 1912 to 1914 showcased a distinctly African American musical aesthetic that pointed toward the transition from ragtime to jazz; W.C. Handy, whose 1928 concert there was designed as an overview of black musical history, setting his own blues song compositions alongside an array of spirituals, art songs, and jazz, with the "Negro Rhapsody" *Yamekraw*, composed by James P. Johnson and played by Thomas "Fats" Waller, as a sort of centerpiece.[130] Yet no black popular music artist drew the attention that accompanied Whiteman in the 1920s, and Goodman in the 1930s. That Duke Ellington was left to watch members of his own band play alongside Goodman from the audience in a sense indicates the dynamic at play here. So, too, does the fact that none of the black performers who appeared at Carnegie Hall played with the full version of Goodman's orchestra—even the regular members of his organization, Teddy Wilson and Lionel Hampton, whose appearances in person and on record were almost always limited to the trio and quartet formats. Boundaries were being crossed by the late 1930s, but there were still clear limits upon the degree to which the strictures of racial segregation could be challenged, and white musicians remained likely to receive acclaim for their achievements in a way African Americans were not. Goodman's Carnegie Hall concert showed both the advances made and the restraints still in place upon the recognition of black contributions to jazz.

Meanwhile, it is important to view the presence of black musicians at Goodman's Carnegie Hall concert in relation to their appearances on the stage in connection with classical music. This is the second point of qualification: when compared with the visibility that such artists as Marian Anderson and Paul Robeson achieved in the classical music field by the late 1930s, the inclusion of black artists in Goodman's Carnegie Hall concert seems like a half-measure. Certainly, classical music was not the more racially inclusive space. Anderson and Robeson, and those few other black music artists who gained notoriety as "legitimate" concert artists, were exceptional and were treated as such. Both also faced considerable adversity over the course of their concert careers, as evinced by the circumstances surrounding Marian Anderson's performance at the Lincoln Memorial—an artistic triumph that arose out of the deeply embedded, systemic racism that constrained the circumstances under which she could perform. Nonetheless, when one sees reports of the audiences that Anderson and Robeson could draw, and the enthusiasm they generated, the restrictions that existed around black jazz musicians of the era in their efforts to have their work construed as "legitimate" become all the more apparent.

Here we might return one more time to Sol Hurok. His involvement in the Vincent Lopez concert of 1924, where a work of W.C. Handy's was featured, in the revival and flourishing of Marian Anderson's concert career, and in Goodman's Carnegie Hall appearance suggest a point of continuity in the breaking of racial boundaries in the concert hall that has gone largely unacknowledged. Unlike many other analogous figures including the much-heralded John Hammond, Hurok worked both sides of the classical/popular divide, which gave him the cultural authority and the pliability to effect changes that recalibrated the relationship between the two.

* * *

Jazz concert events proliferated significantly in the months and years after Goodman's Carnegie Hall performance; and many of these events pushed the envelope of racial inclusivity and black participation considerably farther. The two "From Spirituals to Swing" concerts organized by John Hammond and staged at Carnegie Hall in December 1938 and December 1939 have drawn much comment from jazz historians for their groundbreaking character. Hammond was one of the great ideologues of the jazz world of the 1930s, a young white man of privileged background who supported a range of leftist causes, at the forefront of which was the push for African American equality. He was also a manic jazz fan who was constantly scouting and had the connections and the resourcefulness to make things happen for his favored artists professionally, through his combined pursuits of music criticism, record production, and concert promotion.[131]

"From Spirituals to Swing" effectively brought Hammond's varied concerns together in a concert package that was designed to elevate "authentic" African American music and demonstrate that jazz was just one stage in a much larger process of artistic evolution. Hammond's political concerns were apparent in the sponsorship of the first concert by the magazine, *New Masses*, a left-wing publication that had grown out of the broad-based movement culture of Depression-era America known as the "Popular Front." At that first 1938 concert in particular, the evocation of black music history was especially pronounced and explicit. Hammond went so far as to begin the evening with recordings of African tribal music to send a message to the audience about where the music being presented had derived. From there the program intermingled performances of a decidedly "folk"-like character—Mitchell's Christian Singers, a gospel singing group from North Carolina; Sonny Terry, playing blues harmonica—with music considered more "up-to-date" including the rough-hewn modern gospel of Sister Rosetta Tharpe, the charging boogie woogie blues piano styles of Albert Ammons, Meade "Lux" Lewis and Pete Johnson, and culminating in the modern swing of the Count Basie Orchestra.[132]

Organized largely by genre—with "Spirituals and Holy Roller Hymns" followed by "Soft Swing" followed by "Harmonica Playing," then by "Blues," and so on up to "Swing"—the program also gave the air of a sort of music-historical pageant, taking the audience on a loosely structured chronological journey through black music. The historical narrative suggested by the concert's structure paralleled the earlier moves by both Paul Whiteman and Benny Goodman in this direction; in all these instances, for jazz to be treated as concert music, it had to be treated as music that had a history—that was not just the music of today. Yet Hammond's use of history also marked a critical break. Much more so even than with Goodman's concert, Hammond placed African American music and culture squarely at the center of whatever historical trajectory jazz was heard to have arisen from. He further offered an evolutionary backdrop that drew a less stark line between the "primitive" past and the "refined" present, suggesting that the music's development was more of a continuum—and so giving greater legitimacy to those styles heard to be rooted in the past.

Duke Ellington pursued a rather different mode of invoking the African American past in his own first Carnegie Hall concert. Of all jazz artists, black or white, Ellington earned a reputation as a composer and bandleader that granted him considerable legitimacy in certain quarters of the "serious" music establishment. As early as 1932, the critic R.D. Darrell subjected Ellington's body of work to the sort of careful overview typically reserved for classical music composers.[133] Writing in *Modern Music*, Aaron Copland said of Ellington when comparing him to other jazz figures, "The others . . . are hardly more than composer-arrangers. Ellington is a composer, by which I mean, he comes nearer to knowing how to make a piece hang together than others."[134] Not all in the jazz world equally appreciated the refinement of Ellington's evolving style. John Hammond, for one, notoriously subjected Ellington to criticism in 1935 upon the release of "Reminiscing in Tempo," one of Ellington's first efforts at extended form composition, charging that the artist was relying on "slick, un-negroid musicians" in his band and losing touch with the "troubles of his people."[135]

Against the arrogant standards of racial authenticity voiced by Hammond, Ellington appeared to hold to the notion that only a long form work in symphonic style would be adequate to the task of representing the sweep and scope of African American history. Since the early 1930s, Ellington had discussed in interviews his conception of such a work. With *Black, Brown, and Beige*, which was debuted at Carnegie Hall on January 23, 1943,

Ellington appropriated the symphonic jazz model and invested it with renewed value, bringing to it a "serious social intent" that had been absent from earlier endeavors in that mode.[136] Although the piece, and the concert overall, generated mixed reviews, Ellington's Carnegie Hall concert broke important ground for foregrounding his role as composer above all. No previous jazz concert—not Whiteman's, nor Goodman's, nor anyone else's—had only featured the work of a single composer. Presenting his music in this way, Ellington refashioned one of the most established conventions of the classical music concert world—the composer's concert—in his own image, staking a unique claim to musical legitimacy as an African American composer whose primary musical language remained couched in jazz and other black vernacular forms.

The Jazz Concert on Tour

A kind of apotheosis of the development of the jazz concert, or at least the phase of its development that started in the mid-1920s, came with the advent of the Jazz at the Philharmonic concert series in 1944. The creation of the Los Angeles-based concert promoter and record producer Norman Granz, Jazz at the Philharmonic (JATP) struck an unusual balance between the effort to elevate jazz into something of higher cultural standing and the effort to present it as a widely popular attraction. Indeed, as Granz built Jazz at the Philharmonic into the basis of a small musical empire, he demonstrated the economic viability of the concert mode of jazz presentation to an unparalleled degree. His biographer Tad Hershorn has argued that Granz was not only in it for the money despite charges to the contrary. Rather, according to Hershorn, Granz pursued three intersecting aims throughout his career that manifested themselves most forcefully through Jazz at the Philharmonic: "presenting good jazz, challenging segregation, and showing that good money could be made by bringing the two together."[137] Granz assembled integrated black and white line-ups of musicians to perform at his JATP concerts in a manner akin to Benny Goodman and John Hammond's efforts, and with a spotlight squarely on African American artists above all. He went beyond these earlier endeavors, though, in his insistence upon integrated audiences. The promotion of Jazz at the Philharmonic as a touring package made this aspect of Granz's work even more difficult and impactful, as he challenged the segregationist practices at concert venues around the

US. It also made the concerts a different kind of economic proposition from their predecessors, a reproducible commodity the reach of which was expanded by Granz's concurrent move into record production, creating what were effectively the first proper "live" recordings.

Jazz at the Philharmonic adopted a different format for the jazz concert from the events staged by Goodman (with Hurok) and Ellington in particular. The latter fell into the category of "concert hall appearances by nationally recognized swing orchestras," in Scott DeVeaux's characterization; while JATP was on the order of "smaller-scale concerts that attempted to reproduce the atmosphere of the jam session in more formal surroundings."[138] Jam sessions became a defining feature of jazz culture throughout the 1930s and 1940s. Initially they were commonly held as private events where musicians challenged each other to demonstrate their inventiveness in a loose format where songs became the vehicle for extended improvisational flights by the soloists. This feature of the jam session has remained a powerful alternative institution in the jazz world, providing a setting where musicians could test the limits of technique and musical vocabulary while not having to worry about pleasing an audience.[139] By the mid-1930s, though, a version of the jam session also started to be presented as a public attraction, offering audiences the opportunity to hear musicians perform with an informality that was perceived to be lacking, or to have been lost, amidst the carefully orchestrated arrangements of the large swing bands like those led by Goodman and Ellington. The jazz clubs along 52nd Street were among the places where jam sessions began to attract an audience, drawing both diehard jazz devotees and curious onlookers who caught onto the larger swing phenomenon.[140] Goodman's inclusion of a "jam session" feature in his Carnegie Hall concert was a sign of the rising profile of this mode of jazz performance. Four years later, the white Chicago-born guitarist Eddie Condon staged the first of what became a long-running series of concerts at Town Hall in New York that featured a collection of star players taking turns playing in various small-group or solo spots and climaxing with all the assembled players joining in a large-group improvised jam for which Condon served as "conductor."[141]

Norman Granz's first forays into concert promotion came in connection with the promotion of jam sessions as public events in Los Angeles. Of Russian Jewish heritage like Sol Hurok—but a child of immigrants rather than an immigrant himself—Granz grew up in a predominantly Jewish section of L.A. that was adjacent to the city's burgeoning area of African American nightlife along Central Avenue in the downtown district. By the early 1940s, when he was moving between studies at U.C.L.A. and enlistment in the military as US involvement in World War II heightened, Granz became a regular patron at clubs such as the Capri, owned by Billy Berg, where artists like Nat Cole, Lee Young and his more famous brother Lester were regular performers.[142] Drawn in by the competitive dynamic and the rich virtuosity of the playing he heard at jam sessions around Central Avenue, he also became acutely aware of the racial inequities faced by African American artists who worked in the clubs. In 1942, Granz approached Berg—who had moved from the Capri to another club called the Trouville—with a proposition, motivated by an exchange he had with Billie Holiday in which the singer complained that her black friends had not been admitted to a show she had performed. Recalled Granz:

> I proposed to [Billy Berg] that he give me Sundays, when he was ordinarily closed, to put on jam sessions, but under very fixed conditions. The first, obviously, was that he had to completely mix the public . . . Secondly, he had to pay the musicians. I didn't want them jamming for nothing . . . I also insisted that he put tables on the dance floor, so people would have to listen. And the hook to the whole thing was, that if it worked . . . that he would promise to do it the rest of the week. And, of course, he made more bread that day than he ever made in his life.[143]

For Granz, from the start of his concert promoting career, the motivations that would carry into his staging of Jazz at the Philharmonic were already in place: a commitment to desegregating the jazz audience; an insistence that jazz be treated as listening music above all; and a concern with the financial bottom line.

After nearly two years of presenting jam sessions in this manner, Granz began to look for opportunities to move out of the nightclubs and into a venue where the music might be heard to greater advantage. His first such venture took him to the Music Town, a small rehearsal hall on the south side of Los Angeles where he presented a series of Sunday afternoon sessions that featured performers such as Nat Cole and saxophonist Illinois Jacquet.[144] Granz set his sights, though, on a larger and much more prestigious setting: Philharmonic Auditorium. Built in 1906, the building—initially called Temple Auditorium—was not a purpose-built concert hall in the manner of New York's Carnegie Hall or Boston's Symphony Hall but was a multi-purpose space designed to hold the church services of the L.A. Baptist congregation along with a variety of performing arts endeavors.[145] Only in 1920 did it assume the name Philharmonic Auditorium, when the L.A. Philharmonic Orchestra—established in 1919—took up residency there. From that point forward, Philharmonic Auditorium became the leading classical music concert hall in L.A., a position it retained until the 1960s.

Granz brought his first jazz concert package to the Philharmonic Auditorium on July 2, 1944. Organized as a benefit for the Sleepy Lagoon Defense Fund, the event appeared to put Granz's political sympathies in the foreground. The Sleepy Lagoon case, which had occurred in 1942, involved the arrest of hundreds of young Latinos in connection with a murder case where the evidence was incomplete and circumstantial. Nearly two dozen of those arrested were tried, with three convicted of first-degree murder and several more convicted and imprisoned for lesser offenses. The perception of unfair handling and racist motivation against Latinos in the case led to the formation of the Sleepy Lagoon Defense Fund among local California activists, and Granz joined with the organization in sponsoring his first Philharmonic concert.[146] Advertising the concert, Granz made the political motives clear but also evoked what by 1944 was a growing tradition of jazz concert performances within which he clearly wanted to include his new venture. "They Jumped at Carnegie Hall! They Tore the Roof Off at the Metropolitan! And Now . . . ! Jazz at the Philharmonic!" declared a newspaper ad in the lead-up to the event, which also promised an array of star performers headed by the King Cole Trio and Meade Lux Lewis—the latter a carryover from John Hammond's "From Spirituals to Swing" concert.[147] Granz's rhetoric was telling: he was not promoting an air of unspoiled refinement, but sought to build interest by playing upon what in 1944 was still perceived to be the novelty and incongruity of jazz being presented in a formal concert setting.

The format of that first "Jazz at the Philharmonic" concert gave further indication that Granz was not seeking to present jazz in an unusually "serious" manner. Previous jazz concerts dispensed with the classical trappings that had infused the experiments of the 1920s. Granz abandoned even the historical angle that had in different ways informed the efforts of Goodman, Hammond, and Ellington. Some of the selections played by the JATP musicians had already attained the status of recognized standards, such as "Lester Leaps In," which served as a solo vehicle for Lester Young during his tenure with Count Basie, or "Body and Soul," which became a signature tune of Benny Goodman and his trio and was also turned into a major set piece by saxophonist Coleman Hawkins on a landmark 1939 recording.[148] In later years, when both Young and Hawkins joined the "Jazz at the Philharmonic" concerts, these songs became a way of testifying to the legacy of the two musicians while also demonstrating their continued virtuosity in the present. Neither played at the first of Granz's Philharmonic concerts though, and the familiarity of these tunes and others on the "Jazz at the Philharmonic" stage was meant not to invest the music with historical associations, but to give the musicians a shared platform for improvisation that would also stir recognition by the audience.

Spontaneous exchange between the musicians was the favored mode in Granz's productions, as it was in the jam session ethos more generally. This also seems to have been why he preferred to hire musicians as solo artists who would be joined in groups that were largely assembled just for the concerts, rather than hire whole existing bands or small groups to comprise the program. Even the one cohesive group hired for the first JATP concert, the Nat Cole Trio, was affected by a last-minute line-up change when guitarist Oscar Moore became unavailable and Cole called upon a substitute, Les Paul. The interplay between the black pianist Cole and white guitarist Paul generated some of the highest points of that first concert, in terms of heated audience response competing with the effusive playing of tenor saxophonist Illinois Jacquet, a veteran of the Lionel Hampton band who became one of the longest-serving members of Granz's JATP aggregation.

All could be heard to stirring effect on a number simply titled "Blues," on which the rhythm section of Cole, Paul, bassist Johnny Miller, and drummer Lee Young accompanied a front line of Jacquet, fellow tenor sax player Jack McVea, and trombonist J.J. Johnson. Jacquet's solo followed those by Cole, McVea, and Johnson; after playing a chorus of solid but rather conventional swinging blues, he tilted abruptly into the highest registers of his instrument, pushing well beyond the standard tenor sax scale into a realm of screeching high notes filled with overtones that signaled the seeming abandonment of refined technique in favor of sheer sound. Coming on the heels of Jacquet, Les Paul began to solo in a fairly subdued fashion. A pioneer in the use of the electric guitar, Paul was a few years away from becoming a full-on star in his own right. Playing as part of JATP, he showcased considerable technical skill on his instrument combined with equally sharp showmanship. As his solo proceeded, he began to trade lines with Cole, Paul feeding single-note bursts to Cole of an increasing degree of difficulty to emulate, and Cole playing them back with facility and much good humor. Paul later described their dynamic: "I threw out one of my easiest runs and Nat picked up the bait. I threw out a tougher one, and Nat climbed on my back again. He didn't know I was walking him into the center of the ring . . . Well, I had a few runs that I knew would kill him. I waited until I got everyone on the edge of their seat, then I let Nat have it with both barrels, and the whole place went crazy."[149] On the recording of the piece that was later issued as one of Granz's series of JATP releases, the audience response is strong and audible throughout the exchange, with the crowd sometimes laughing at a particularly clever turn of musical phrase, and other times expressing surprise when Cole was able to match Paul's provocations to the note.

Reviewing Granz's first Philharmonic concert, *Down Beat* noted Granz's success in drawing more than two thousand people to the auditorium despite a relative minimum of advance publicity. The magazine also set the crowd-pleasing elements of Granz's promotional efforts in opposition to the perceived artistry on display. *Down Beat*'s reviewer conveyed the excitement demonstrated by the audience: "The kids went wild over the screaming harmonics . . . produced by Illinois Jacquet. They squirmed with glee as Guitarist Les Paul produced novelty sound effects on his electric guitar." Yet the report further asserted, "it was agreed by everyone having any familiarity with the idiom that the musical fare at L.A.'s first jazz concert savored more of night club entertainment than serious jazz."[150] Musicians Meade Lux Lewis and Barney Bigard were singled out for their contributions; the review carried traces of the "moldy fig" mentality that held a preference for hot jazz as it was played in the pre-swing idiom of the 1920s over more modern stylistic directions. Still, the suggestion that for all their elevated trappings, Granz's concerts fell short of the expectations that attended to jazz as a concert hall attraction would follow the promoter in the years to come, as would the notion that his productions elicited a response from the audience that went against the grain of concert hall decorum.

* * *

Granz's first concert at the Philharmonic was recorded due to an arrangement that he made with Armed Forces Radio Services whereby they recorded the show for later broadcast and he would keep the master recordings.[151] During the next year, as he arranged further concerts in Los Angeles under the "Jazz at the Philharmonic" banner, Granz looked for opportunities to release the recordings made from that first concert and later ones that he recorded himself. Previous concert events such as Goodman's Carnegie Hall concert and the "From Spirituals to Swing" affairs had been recorded but remained unreleased until many years after they occurred. The notion that recordings made from a "live" event could be suitable for commercial distribution significantly broke with the assumptions of the music industry at the time that only in the isolated space of the studio could music be recorded with sufficient clarity to meet the standards for release. By Granz's recollection he faced resistance along these lines when he took the recordings from the first "Jazz at the Philharmonic" concert to RCA-Victor executive Mannie Sachs, who rejected them for including mistakes and crowd noise. For Granz, such qualities gave the recordings a special aura that made them more, not less desirable: "I said, 'But you don't understand. That's exactly the reason you should put it out. You don't want a retouched photograph if it's a documentary.'"[152]

Failing to sell his concept of documentary-like "live" recordings to RCA or any other major record labels of the time, Granz turned to an independent. By summer 1945, Granz reached an agreement with Moe Asch, then at the start of a career that would turn him into a major figure in the history of American folk music recordings. Asch's Folkways record label was established in 1948; in 1945 he ran a small label called Disc. In a handwritten letter on hotel stationery dated on a Friday in August 1945, Norman Granz conveyed to Asch: "Pursuant the deal you offered me yesterday about my Jazz at the Philharmonic record, namely—$2000 to cover costs and 15 c per record royalty—I accept. However, in view of your cooperation during this deal, I think it only fair that I knock off my commission so that you only pay me $1850 plus the royalty."[153] Some time later a press release issued by Granz under the "Jazz at the Philharmonic" heading announced the agreement and explained the unique nature of the releases that would follow: "THE JAZZ AT THE PHILHARMONIC recordings were made under unusual conditions. Neither the musicians participating in the philharmonic concert nor the audiences were aware of the fact that they were being recorded. The result is a spontaneous, whole hearted performance, completely uninhibited."[154] For Granz, the projection of a certain sense of "liveness" associated with the concerts was of paramount concern and also had major promotional value. That quality would distinguish his JATP recordings from others on the market, and further served to cement the sense that his work as a concert promoter was inextricable from his work as a producer of recordings.

The first recording under the "Jazz at the Philharmonic" name came out in October 1945. It consisted of two songs, "How High the Moon" and "Lady Be Good," from a concert that Granz had staged at L.A.'s Philharmonic

Auditorium earlier in the year, on February 12. Issued as an "album" at a time when 78-RPM records were still the norm, each of the extended cuts—more than ten minutes long apiece—took up three sides, thus making it into a three-disc set overall.[155] For the next two years, Granz released his JATP recordings with Asch's Disc company, which put out four further installments all recorded "live" at Granz's concerts. By 1947, though, Granz took up the notion that he might oversee the release of the recordings himself, a move that was in keeping with his drive toward self-direction but also in line with the historical moment, when independent record labels proliferated as the majors struggled to adjust to a market for recordings that had been severely disrupted by the Second World War. *Variety* announced the news in June 1947 that Granz would be setting up his own recording company, to be called Clef.[156] His first release with the new label followed in September, constituting Volume Six in the ongoing "Jazz at the Philharmonic" series, and promoted as the first recorded pairing of Coleman Hawkins and Lester Young.[157] With the formation of Clef Records, Granz expanded his mark as a leading impresario of the post-War jazz world and laid the foundation for his work as a record producer that would lead to landmark recordings by Charlie Parker, Billie Holiday and Ella Fitzgerald.

* * *

Fall 1945, when the first of Granz's "Jazz at the Philharmonic" records was released with Moe Asch's Disc label, was also when Granz took his first JATP unit on tour. The moment was marked by an announcement coming from a new L.A.-based enterprise, *Jazz Tempo*, a newsletter published out of the city's Tempo Music Shop by owner Ross Russell.[158] Dated December 1945, the first issue of *Jazz Tempo* screamed with the headline, "Be-bop Invades the West!" Russell enthusiastically noted the imminent arrival of Dizzy Gillespie's sextet, featuring Charlie Parker, in what would be a historic stand at the latest nightclub run by Billy Berg—at whose earlier clubs Norman Granz had begun his career in concert booking.[159] Elsewhere in the two-page issue, Russell gave a strong plug for Granz's first tour, just getting off the ground:

> Norm Granz began what looks to be a successful touring jam session ... here in Los Angeles November 26. Personnel included the Hawk, Roy, Lux and a flock of other big-draw jazz names. Granz ... is scheduled to hit all major coast cities before swinging through mountain states and the east, and

expects to slug Jim Crow hard at every stop with a bid for mixed audiences. Around half of crowd at Philharmonic was Negro.[160]

That Granz's first JATP tour coincided so exactly with the arrival of bebop on the West Coast helps to situate the aesthetic that drove the promoter's efforts. Most of the musicians he featured were already well-established stars of the swing movement, but Granz was attuned to current directions in jazz as well, and both Parker and Gillespie would make appearances with the tour in years to come. Meanwhile, Russell's notice also spotlighted Granz's continued concentration upon race relations in his endeavors. His concerts at the Philharmonic drew a significant proportion of African Americans; taking his show on tour, he ran up against segregationist norms at many points along the way.

Granz included a clause in his contracts with concert venues that prohibited any efforts to segregate black and white concertgoers. He insisted not only that African Americans should be allowed to enter the hall, but that they should be admitted under the same terms as white patrons—no separate seating area, as was customary in many venues around the US. If a venue or a promoter refused to accommodate his requirements then Granz did not book a show there. The non-segregation clause was so vital to the concerts that he foregrounded it in the concert programs he produced for JATP performances, informing those in attendance: "Granz includes an anti-discrimination clause in all his contracts, forbidding segregated seating, a practice which he hopes more bands and other musical units will adopt."[161] When his touring unit rolled into Jackson, Michigan, and faced discrimination at a local eatery that refused service to the party because it included several African Americans, Granz showed that his willingness to stand up to racism was more than just talk. He and his musicians stayed at the restaurant, called the Regent, for two hours requesting service to no avail. At the time when the evening's concert was to start, Granz went to the hall and explained the situation to the audience, offering refunds to those in attendance and then returning to the Regent with the city's police chief. Regent owner Angelo Johnson held his ground and would not take orders from Granz and the musicians—who included Howard McGhee, J.C. Heard, Helen Humes, Hank Jones, and Flip Phillips. The party left to play their scheduled concert, and then Granz and the five musicians all filed a civil rights discrimination suit against Johnson, who ultimately opted to pay fines rather than change his restaurant's policy.[162]

Touring with JATP gave wider exposure to Granz's efforts as an advocate for racial justice, but in keeping with his larger approach, it also generated greater revenue. The two went hand in hand by Granz's account, for the demonstrated commercial success of concerts that were integrated both on the stage and in the audience would convince others to follow suit. His first tour in fall 1945 was uneven financially, but his second tour the following spring had a much wider impact, generating news reports at many stops along the way that alternately commented on his push for racial integration, the artistic success of the performances, and the great audience turnout. Not all the reviews were raves: Granz drew especially sharp criticism from a *Chicago Tribune* critic who complained that the JATP concert presented at the city's Civic Opera House was an "anachronism" that lacked both the planning and the spontaneity to have made it compelling.[163] Yet the same review observed that the concert was a "financial wow," with the audience overflowing into the surrounding streets. By the time the tour reached Carnegie Hall for a climactic series of four concerts as part of the Carnegie "Pop" series, the commercial success of the venture as a concert hall attraction on a national scale was well established. At Detroit's Masonic Temple Auditorium, JATP drew a standing-room-only crowd of over 4,600, with gross receipts of $9,260.40, more than three times what Eddie Condon's touring aggregation had earned at the same venue.[164] The final Carnegie Hall "Pop" concert was a sell-out, with *Down Beat* reporting that the show earned "the largest gross ever registered by a series jazz concert in Carnegie Hall."[165]

In the midst of it all, Granz and his booking agent, the Gale Agency, placed a large, two-page display ad in *Variety* magazine that effectively encapsulated his achievements to date, reproduced in Figure 5.6.[166] The ad appeared during the run of JATP concerts at Carnegie Hall, and characteristic of Granz's approach, it gave him top billing—his name in giant letters above the "Jazz at the Philharmonic" title and dwarfing the names of his featured artists, who included Coleman Hawkins, Lester Young, Meade Lux Lewis, and Helen Humes, all perennial players with the tour. A photo on the right side of the ad showed a packed auditorium, likely the Chicago Civic Opera House; another photo beside it showed hundreds of fans being turned away at the door for the same performance. Telegrams from auditorium managers in Chicago and Detroit to the Gale Agency testified to the success of the JATP concerts and the desire to book further shows in the future. Most suggestive though was the caption that appeared twice, with different inflections. "A New Kind of $howbu$ine$$: Look at These Reviews," headed a selection of excerpts from reviews in New York, Seattle, and Chicago, providing eyewitness accounts of the large audiences that accompanied the tour at many stops along the way. "A New Kind of $howbu$ine$$: Look at These Grosses," in turn, appeared over a report of gross receipts from concerts in Chicago, Detroit, Los Angeles, and many other points concluding with New York's Carnegie Hall. Granz had demonstrated his capacity to turn Jazz at the Philharmonic into a reproducible concert experience, and so to make the jazz concert into a commodity on a national scale.

The crowds, the boisterous audience behavior, and the money: these were not the qualities around which to build an appeal to elevated high culture values. Granz, however, never relinquished his efforts to cast JATP as a more refined sort of jazz concert presentation, even when reviews and details of the performances suggested otherwise. A statement in the concert program for the third national JATP tour, in Fall 1946, offered a perspective that would not have been out of place in the symphonic jazz era twenty years earlier: "JAZZ AT THE PHILHARMONIC, according to Granz, represents a trend which jazz is likely to take in coming years, when . . . the concert stage will attract thousands of people who will have a good time, whose listening standards will be raised, and jazz, which heretofore has been an italicized art, will attain capital definition and stature."[167]

A decade later, in the mid-1950s, Granz took measures to contain the audience's tendency to respond vocally and, by some measures, inappropriately at various points during the concerts. He recalled that he circulated handbills to concertgoers titled, "How to Act at a Jazz Concert," prompted by the frequent interruptions faced by the figure that had become the tour's biggest star by that time, Ella Fitzgerald.[168] One such notice appeared in a Fall 1956 concert program, and found Granz exhorting his audience to adopt standards of behavior that had become enshrined through the decades as suitable to the concert hall:

> You know it's becoming quite a problem to put on a good Jazz Concert today. It isn't the musicians, because they play the best way they know how. And, it isn't 99% of the audience . . . No, it's a handful of exhibitionists who see fit to spoil the Concert for everyone else, both the musicians as well as the rest of the audience . . . Sure, it's O.K. to get excited and applaud and even cheer your favorite tenor man, or your favorite trumpeter, on "Perdido" or "Cottontail" or "Flying Home," but why not keep quiet when these same artists play "Body and Soul" or some other beautiful ballad? After all, a

Figure 5.6 "A New Kind of Showbu$ine$$": This two-page ad trumpeted Norman Granz's success in taking his Jazz at the Philharmonic concerts on the road as a touring aggregation. From *Variety* (June 5, 1946).

Z' — *(Director Of The Academy Award Winning Short—'JAMMIN' THE BLUES')*

JAZZ AT THE PHILHARMONIC

JAZZ IN CONCERT STYLE

Featuring **COLEMAN HAWKINS, LESTER YOUNG, MEADE LUX LEWIS, HELEN HUMES, BUCK CLAYTON AND OTHERS**

Currently Appearing At Carnegie Hall, New York With the "Pops" Series For 4 Weeks

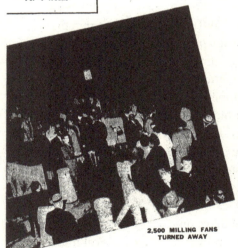

2,500 MILLING FANS TURNED AWAY

A NEW KIND OF $HOWBU$INE$$
Look At These Reviews

"Not since I was 17 and got caught in one of those stumpedes for Benny Goodman have I seen such an ardent, frantic audience as greeted The Jazz at the Philharmonic concert staged at Carnegie Hall, Monday night by Norman Granz."—New York PM.

"The Moore Theatre last night turned away hundreds of swing disciples after the stage was packed with fans and every nook and cranny of the theatre held a happy addict...."—Seattle Times.

"Jazz Biz a Whiz.... A milling crowd, policemen, and attendants shouting "Sold Out" one-half hour after the start of a concert is a strange sight at any musical event in Chicago.

For the first time in my experience, stub seekers were still at the door and lining the sidewalks when I left near the end of last night's organized jam session at the Opera House where Norman Granz put on his "Jazz at the Philharmonic" with an orchestra of top name jazz men."
—Chicago Herald-American.

"Twenty-five hundred milling fans turned away.... Jazz concert packed Civic Opera House...."
—Chicago Daily News.

"The customers squealed like Sinatra fans at the heated improvisations of their favorite performers and every one got their money's worth."—Chicago Sun.

"Jazz at the Philharmonic is a financial Wow!"
—Chicago Tribune.

A NEW KIND OF $HOWBU$INE$$
Look At These Grosses

CHICAGO	$12,000	(Per Night)
DETROIT	$11,500	(Per Night)
LOS ANGELES	$ 6,500	(Per Night)
SAN FRANCISCO	$ 5,200	(Per Night)
SEATTLE	$ 4,800	(Per Night)
DAYTON	$ 3,700	(Per Night)
MINNEAPOLIS	$ 5,000	(Per Night)
DENVER	$ 4,600	(Per Night)
N. Y. CARNEGIE HALL	$ 4,200	(Per Night)

Selected as the Best Record Album of the Month by Esquire Mag. Exclusively recorded by Disc Record Co.

ENCY, Inc., 48 West 48th Street, New York —— LO-3-0350

Jazz Concert could become pretty boring if all you'd hear would be the up-tempo, loud numbers . . . It isn't good manners to be shouting or talking when Ella is singing a ballad or when Oscar [Peterson, pianist] is playing something very pretty. After all . . . you'll enjoy Ella, Oscar, and the MJQ more if you listen quietly.[169]

The presence of the Modern Jazz Quartet—MJQ—on this installment of the JATP tour was a sign that much had changed by 1956. Jazz and classical music had entered a new phase of rapprochement and cross-fertilization that would be fitted with the designation "Third Stream" music. At the same time, rock 'n' roll emerged as a new attraction, giving rise to its own brand of musical excitement and social unrest, to be detailed in the next chapter. Granz's message to audiences about "how to act" was caught in between these divergent trends. He was not counseling complete silence but was suggesting that the audience respond to the performances in a manner consistent with the music itself. Still, his insistence on "good manners," and more so his suggestion that "quiet and pretty" music should be accompanied by quiet attentive listening, suggest that even in its most aggressively commercial form, the production of jazz concerts also entailed the effort to infuse jazz with the values of art music. What had changed most, from the time of Paul Whiteman to the time of Jazz at the Philharmonic, was that the music in question was no longer expected to take on different formal qualities to justify this different sort of treatment. Jazz was to be treated as art music unto itself, and the audience, not the artist, was made into the primary subject of cultural elevation.

* * *

For the 1950 installment of Jazz at the Philharmonic, Granz was touted in the concert program: "What Sol Hurok has proven to be for classical music and ballet, Norman Granz has become for jazz." He, or his copywriter, elaborated on the comparison six years later: "Granz has earned a reputation as 'the Sol Hurok of Jazz,' a fitting and yet not altogether accurate description. For all his brilliance as a promoter of ballet and classical music, Hurok was not concerned in his concerts with fighting racial discrimination. Granz most definitely has been."[170] Granz had in fact broken important ground for making the racial integration of audiences a key principle behind his concert promotion efforts. Then again, while Hurok was nowhere near as thoroughgoing in his pursuit of similar goals, the two had more in common along these lines than Granz wanted to admit. More than their efforts to combat racial discrimination, though, Granz and Hurok shared the conviction that "good music," however defined, could be popularized through effective salesmanship, and that the concert hall was the venue best suited to achieve such ends. That belief was the outgrowth of a period extending from the mid-1920s to the mid-1940s when the boundary between "high" and "low" cultural spheres in the US grew uniquely permeable due to the emergence of new media forms and the resulting push to bring certain styles of classical music to the widest possible audience. As the postwar era progressed, many in the classical music establishment recoiled from such initiatives, and the pursuit of a sort of strenuous modernism removed from the imperative to court popular audiences would increasingly gain ground. In this sense it was jazz, not classical music, that most typified the mingling of populist and highbrow impulses moving forward—all the more so after the rise of rock 'n' roll introduced a new embodiment of "low," popular music against which the standing of jazz as art music might appear more convincing.

6

The Perfect Package

Rock 'n' Roll Concerts in the 1950s

Prelude: "Rock and Roll Dem"

Willis P. "Billy" Sweatnam was a leading light of the blackface minstrel stage, coming out of Philadelphia. His career belonged to that post-Civil War moment in the history of blackface minstrelsy when it was still a major form of US entertainment but was losing ground to new styles of variety and vaudeville theater, a shift that was detailed in Chapter 3. Like the best minstrel performers, Sweatnam was celebrated for his versatility. His specialties were many: he could act the "wench" (minstrelsy's distinctive form of female impersonation); he had excellent comic timing; he was a solid character actor; and his singing voice was strong.[1] In 1878, Sweatnam brought his talents to New York, where he appeared with Bryant's Minstrels at the Grand Opera House. According to the account of the *New York Clipper*: "He displayed his versatility by appearing on the bone-end and singing 'Rock and Roll Dem' in the first part, and by singing a number of his own comic ditties and acting Alexander in his own sketch of 'Blue Glass' in the olio."[2]

Let me repeat: in 1878, a blackface minstrel artist named Billy Sweatnam appeared on a New York stage and sang a number titled "Rock and Roll Dem." The *Clipper* does not suggest that this number was a particular sensation, and there is no more information about the song in the brief review. However, another item published four years later in a Toronto humor magazine, *Grip*, offers some further spare but tantalizing details. Now, in 1882, Sweatnam appears in a minstrel troupe that also includes the veteran performer Charlie Backus. Again, Sweatnam occupies the bone end, while Backus stands opposite him on the "tambo" (or tambourine) end of the minstrel line. After some comic repartee between Sweatnam and the company's interlocutor, and a ballad sung in falsetto by troupe member Stanley Grey, Sweatnam offers up "Rock and Roll Dem," which the report describes as a "plantation ditty," and further characterizes in the following terms: "It has the regular negro swing, and the feet of the audience keep involuntary time with it."[3] Thus, by the early 1880s, Billy Sweatnam had been featuring a song at least periodically in his minstrel show appearances for four years or more with the phrase "rock and roll" in its title, and that song—an adaptation of the familiar "plantation" idiom dating back to Stephen Foster—was noted for its "negro swing" and ability to make audiences move their feet.

Connections between the historical form of blackface minstrelsy and rock 'n' roll have been drawn frequently. Often the goal of such observations is to question the terms according to which the currency of "black music" and culture was converted into something more accessible to white listeners through rock 'n' roll. The infamous line attributed to Sun Records founder Sam Phillips—which was recalled by his former assistant Marion Keisker— that, "If I could find a white man with the Negro sound and the Negro feel, I could make a million dollars," has been invoked to similar ends. In either case there is an argument about exploitation, and also about imitation: the dual trope that Eric Lott termed "love and theft" in which white artists or music entrepreneurs appropriated elements of African American culture because of their genuine attraction to it, and for the way it suited their own cultural need to break free of Victorian restrictions; and then turned their version of "blackness" into the most recognizable, visible, and profitable one.[4] To find evidence that the term "rock and roll" has some basis in minstrel performance, then, might be seen as further instantiation of this pattern of racial expropriation.

Even if we interpret Billy Sweatnam's song "Rock and Roll Dem" in this light, the sheer fact of its existence—which has never before been documented as far as I know—offers more concrete evidence of a historical link between the phrase "rock and roll" and the musical and performance practices of nineteenth century minstrelsy than has been previously shown. It would be drastically overstating the case to suggest that the history of rock 'n' roll begins here. The phrase itself only means so much, after all; and too much about Sweatnam's song, "Rock and Roll Dem," remains unknown. For me, the most compelling unanswered question remains: what is the "dem" that is referred to in the song's title? My first assumption, when I found the article in the *Clipper*, was that it might be a reference to the bones, the instrument that Sweatnam held on his end of the minstrel line. To "rock and roll" the bones would be to shake and rattle one of the primary sources of percussive energy in minstrel music. Yet this was probably wishful thinking. The evidence gleaned from the *Grip* account suggests that, if this was a plantation song, "dem" might well be the inhabitants of the plantation—an intriguing possibility as well. Speculation aside, Sweatnam's rendition of "Rock and Roll Dem" in 1878 indicates how much we still have to learn about the evolution of American music and indicates how many layers of historical sediment accumulated between the emergence of a phrase like "rock and roll" in one context and its reappearance, decades later, in another.

After the Ball

Much ink has been spilled on the question, "What was the first rock 'n' roll record?" Far less has been said concerning a parallel question, "What was the first rock 'n' roll concert?" However, an answer to the latter does seem to be accepted: the Moondog Coronation Ball, held at the Cleveland Arena on March 21, 1952, and organized by disc jockey Alan Freed in association with promoter Lew Platt and record store owner Leo Mintz (Figure 6.1). The Moondog Ball is almost too fitting as a starting point for "live" rock 'n' roll. It was not much of a concert—only one artist, the black saxophonist Paul Williams, best known for his 1949 rhythm and blues hit, "The Hucklebuck," performed a single song before it was called off.[5] What made the Moondog Coronation Ball such an event was the crowd. The arena had a capacity of nearly 10,000, but the *Cleveland Plain Dealer* estimated that some six thousand concertgoers stood outside the venue without tickets; later reports increased the overall size of the crowd to some 25,000 inside and outside the arena.[6] When the thousands who could not gain admittance to the show tried to crash the gate, chaos ensued, and the performance ended on the order of the police. Live rock 'n' roll, then, was born with a riot that foreshadowed the music's status as a lightning rod for controversy in the years ahead.

A white photographer on the scene named Peter Hastings took the photos that offer the best visual record of the Moondog Coronation Ball. He later said to Cleveland music journalist Jane Scott: "I can still see that crowd below us. It was getting bigger all the time. It was frightening. I took the picture. Then we got out of there as fast as we could."[7] Hastings' awe at the sight of the crowd comes through in the images he captured. The most famous shot, an aerial view taken from up in the stands, shows the crowd in a blur of constant motion. Almost all traces of the specificity of the event are drowned in a sea of bodies that appear to be excited by the sheer fact that they are surrounded by other bodies in an equal state of excitement.

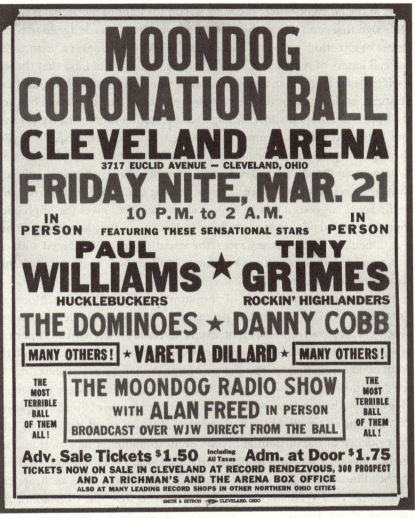

Figure 6.1 The poster for the Moondog Coronation Ball, held at the Cleveland Arena on March 21, 1952, and organized by Alan Freed in association with Lew Platt and Leo Mintz. Of the announced performers, only Paul Williams performed briefly before the event was halted due to the efforts of thousands of people outside the arena to gatecrash. Courtesy of the Terry Stewart Collection, Library and Archives, Rock and Roll Hall of Fame and Museum.

Only at the far right, where the stage sits on the floor of the arena, is there a clear sign that something other than the crowd itself was designed to be the center of attention: a placard that reads, "WJW Moondoggers," associating the call letters of Alan Freed's radio station with the fan base that showed itself to be far larger than anyone had anticipated. A second photo, taken by Hastings at closer to ground level, shows the same blur of motion but now the bodies are more distinct. Young men dressed in their most stylish suits and hats, and their accompanying young women in their equally stylish dresses, some talking, some holding each other, some looking like they are dancing even though the music had presumably already stopped. Although there were reports of violence at the Moondog Ball, and Hastings' reaction to the scene suggests a reason to be scared, the photo gives the impression more of a crowd of people out to have the best time they know how. While it is difficult to make out any faces, the visual evidence combined with existing oral testimony confirms one further salient fact: nearly all in attendance were African American.

The race and youthfulness of the crowd that attended the Moondog Coronation Ball enhanced the perception of public disorder that many observers projected onto the event. Even Cleveland's main African American newspaper, the *Call and Post*, expressed dismay at the gathering, although the point of objection for reporter Valena Minor Williams was less the crowd itself than the way the concert was an instance of exploiting "Negro teensters."[8] This exploitative tendency was displayed in the response of Freed's employer, WJW. In the aftermath of the Ball, the station issued an advertisement used the evidence of the turnout at Freed's event to highlight its power and influence among Cleveland listeners. "Radio Alone Pulled 25,000!" shouted the headline, which floated above photos of Freed and African American performers Paul Williams and Tiny Grimes who were due to headline the canceled show. The ad's copy continued: "Using WJW **only**, Alan Freed, emcee of 'The Moondog House,' pulled an overwhelming 25,000 to the Moondog Coronation Ball. Here's proof that Cleveland's Chief Station is still Cleveland's best buy."[9] Using the Moondog crowd to appeal to prospective advertisers, WJW—and Freed himself—played upon an association that had been circulating since the time of Jenny Lind. Crowds may appear threatening and present the possibility of social unrest; but crowds, properly managed and controlled, could also mean markets, and money. In this case, what was historically new was the way that the crowd on display at the Moondog Coronation Ball reinforced Freed's, and the station's, growing awareness that black audiences and the music they preferred had hitherto unrecognized profit potential.

More than any figure of his time, Alan Freed exemplified the crucial synergy that existed between radio broadcasting and concert promotion, which figured prominently in the emergence of rock 'n' roll. Disc jockeys across the US saw their influence grow substantially during these years, in conjunction with the playing of records issued by the swelling ranks of independent record labels dedicated to the promotion of rhythm and blues and new strains of country music in which the African American influence was more pronounced than it had been for some time. For DJs such as Tommy "Dr. Jive" Smalls in New York, Al Benson in Chicago, Tommy Edwards in Cleveland, and Georgie Woods in Philadelphia, among many others, the promotion of live shows became an integral way to extend their influence beyond the airwaves.[10] Through staging concerts these DJs were able to build audience loyalty and develop a lucrative new revenue stream for themselves and their employers. In the process, they also made a significant contribution to the racial integration of musical entertainment. Black and white artists nearly always appeared alongside one another in the package shows assembled by Freed and his peers; just as crucially, audiences were also often integrated to greater or lesser degrees, which posed a challenge to the segregationist practices that remained in place in many parts of the US. Similarly to jazz in the 1910s and 1920s, rock 'n' roll concerts did not sweep away the barriers to racial integration but instead became one of the primary sites in the culture of the 1950s where the boundaries drawn around race in the public sphere were contested and revised.

Rock 'n' roll concerts, also like the jazz concerts of an earlier era, played a vital role throughout the 1950s in defining the genre. Alan Freed's concert promotion activities were especially significant in this light. There was arguably no other place in American culture where the phrase "rock 'n' roll"—which he began applying to his concerts in 1955—appeared with such visibility and such consistency, and the artists who played on the package bills assembled by Freed served as an index for the emergent genre, marking its changes and continuities as it evolved. Of course, Freed's radio work was also crucial for developing and disseminating an ongoing discourse about rock 'n' roll, as was his broader multimedia career, which included film, television, and regular appearances in print media. Among his varied activities, though, Freed's work as a concert promoter drew the most public notice—at least, until he became embroiled in the notorious "payola" scandal starting in late 1959—and the crowds that came to his shows served as evidence of the tangible force and character of the rock 'n' roll audience in ways that his radio listenership never did.

Chitlin's and Honky Tonks

The sheer scale of the Moondog Coronation Ball and many comparable events of the early rock 'n' roll era confounds some of the most familiar and established narratives of rock history. Typically, the rise of rock 'n' roll is told through the chronicle of the release of specific records—the starting point is variable, but it is not unusual to trace a line from Roy Brown's "Good Rockin' Tonight" (1947) to Wynonie Harris' cover of the same song released in 1948, to "Rocket 88" by Jackie Brenston and his Delta Cats (1951, the band led by Ike Turner), and then perhaps to "Shake, Rattle and Roll" as done first by Joe Turner, soon thereafter by Bill Haley (both 1954). From here, we enter the fold of rock 'n' roll proper, since 1954 is also the year that Elvis Presley issues his first single, "That's All Right" coupled with "Blue Moon of Kentucky." The labels that put out these records get nearly as much priority as the artists. For the songs listed above they are DeLuxe, King, Chess, Atlantic, Decca, and Sun—all but one (Decca) an independent label of the sort heralded as principal patrons of innovation in post-World War II recorded popular music.

How did these songs gain the exposure they needed to become cultural touchstones? Radio was of paramount importance, creating something like a secret society of listeners that delved into musically unknown territory, with the DJs as their guides. Yet for the artists that had the biggest commercial breakthroughs—Bill Haley, and of course Elvis—radio was just the starting point. Film appearances pushed Haley to the next level of stardom, first with the use of his song, "Rock Around the Clock," in the soundtrack to the movie, *Blackboard Jungle* (1955); and then with Haley's appearance in one of the earliest films that sought to exploit rock 'n' roll's appeal to the burgeoning teen audience, *Rock Around the Clock*, titled after his hit song (1956)—also, not coincidentally, the first of several films to feature Alan Freed in a prominent role. For Elvis Presley, television brought the biggest initial breakthrough. The impact of Presley's succession of television appearances throughout the early months of 1956 has been well documented, from his earliest foray on *Stage Show* hosted by the Dorsey Brothers, to his shattering enactment of "Hound Dog" on Milton Berle's variety show, and then to the censored Elvis that appeared first on Steve Allen's show and finally on Ed Sullivan's, where he proved that his charisma and talent could show through even if he were only filmed from the waist up. Presley's film career upped the ante on the notion that the biggest stars were figures who managed to package their appeal across all the available media of the time—a model of stardom that Alan Freed himself embodied for a time as successfully as any single figure apart from Elvis.

Given the expansive range of media outlets that coexisted with and facilitated the commercial rise of rock 'n' roll, live performance has generally been accorded secondary importance by historians and critics of the music. This tendency has given rise to a growing critical orthodoxy in some quarters that the essence of rock 'n' roll, the aesthetic basis of the music, lies in the recorded work. Theodore Gracyk's influential study, *Rhythm and Noise*, took what had been implicit in much rock historical writing—that recordings formed the foundation for rock 'n' roll's emergence as a distinct sort of musical and cultural practice—and made it explicit. His fundamental assertion, "Rock is a tradition of popular music whose creation and dissemination centers on recording technology," is argued with nuance and complexity; and it has helped to spur a major move in popular music studies toward the analysis of recording technology and record production techniques as fundamental parts of the creative process behind the music.[11] Gracyk does not dismiss live performance as a medium, but he argues—convincingly—that in the rock era there is no clear, one-to-one relationship between what happens when musicians play "live" and what happens when they gather to produce music in the recording studio. When an artist such as Elvis Presley entered Sam Phillips' Sun studio, by this understanding, he was not seeking to capture on record a sound and style he had already developed as a performing artist. Made through the collaboration of Elvis, his fellow musicians Scotty Moore and Bill Black, and producer Phillips, the record itself became the work, a self-standing creative statement whose power stood apart from any prior or subsequent re-creation of the same song in a live performance setting.[12]

Elvis offers what is in many ways a singular instance of the rock 'n' roll star as recording artist. Unlike many of his contemporaries, his career as a performer really began, for all intents and purposes, in the recording studio; and after he came under the management of Colonel Tom Parker in 1956, his career was increasingly steered away from concert appearances due to Parker's belief that to make Presley a star of the broadest, most profitable sort, movies were the most effective medium.[13] Yet this facet of Presley's career can be overstated. Once his recording career was under way, live performance was an essential means by which Presley built a connection to his expanding audience, at least until his induction into the Army. When asked in 1957, while working on his third film, *Jailhouse Rock*, which medium he preferred between movies, television, and personal appearances, Presley did not hesitate to reply: "Live audiences are my favorite. Pictures are next and then television. When I go on stage before thousands of kids I'm like any performer. I feel good. People say I inspire the riots that go on when I sing. That's not true, but there ain't a performer alive who doesn't like that wild acceptance."[14] To use Presley as an example of the ways in which recording superseded live performance in the creation, and definition, of rock 'n' roll is therefore to misrepresent many facets of his early career. It is not necessary to claim that live performance should take priority over recordings to suggest that, concerning Elvis Presley and more broadly, the role of live performance in the making of rock 'n' roll has not been adequately explained.

* * *

As was true during the early jazz era, many competing strains of live music presentation coexisted in the years when rock 'n' roll emerged. For African American artists in particular, the hub of activity was the network of bars, dining establishments, and small theaters across the US that earned the sobriquet, "the chitlin' circuit." According to journalist and social historian Preston Lauterbach, the origins of the "chitlin' circuit" can be traced back to the 1930s, when the T.O.B.A. circuit—the leading black theatrical network of the 1920s—became defunct. Trailblazing figures such as musician and journalist Walter Barnes of Chicago and booking agent Denver Ferguson of Indianapolis sought to fill the void left in the world of black entertainment, developing new venues in urban areas where none existed, or opening paths for touring musicians into hitherto untapped markets.[15] By the late 1940s, when changes in black popular music had given rise to the newly coined "rhythm and blues," African American live music entrepreneurs such as Don Robey in Houston and Sunbeam Mitchell in Memphis arose in parallel with a new crop of artists whose incessant touring was a necessary complement to the release of records and pursuit of radio airplay.

For Lauterbach, a key moment in the evolution of the circuit was the tour of New Orleans-based singer Roy Brown following the release of his pivotal 1947 record, "Good Rockin' Tonight." Booked by Ben Bart, head of the

Universal Attractions talent agency, Brown embarked on a tour in late 1948 that, according to Lauterbach's account,

> would spread chitlin' circuit rock 'n' roll coast to coast, from the ballrooms Walter Barnes had played, up to big-capacity theaters in New York, Chicago, and Los Angeles. Bart sold blocks of Brown dates to the chitlin' circuits most powerful promoters—Howard Lewis in Dallas, B.B. Beamon in Atlanta, Ralph Weinberg and Don Robey—and booked Roy "Around the World," as the upper-echelon Northern black theaters, Harlem's Apollo, Baltimore's Royal, Washington's Howard, the Paradise in Detroit, and the Regal in Chicago, were collectively known.[16]

By 1948 and 1949, then, one of the principal currents of music that contributed to the rise of rock 'n' roll was coursing through a live music circuit that looked informal and ramshackle at ground level, but that was connected by an increasingly sophisticated infrastructure through which regional promoters participated in a national market.

White artists, and specifically white Southern artists, who participated in the side of rock 'n' roll linked more to country music, found a parallel set of performance opportunities in the "honky tonk" bars and saloons that spread across the American South and Southwest starting in the post-Prohibition years of the 1930s. The term "honky tonk" was not new at the time—we have seen it applied earlier to the kinds of "low" working class establishments that were one setting out of which jazz emerged, in connection with Buddy Bolden and New Orleans. It assumed new currency in the context of a booming leisure economy that was driven first by oil refineries in the Southwest and then by war production throughout the South as the US entered World War II.[17] By the end of the war, honky tonk had emerged as a new popular style of country music, epitomizing the tendency toward what Richard Peterson has termed "hard shell" country in which a strong sense of urban Southern regional identity combined with coarse emotional songs of loss, heartbreak and romantic conflict.[18] The honky tonks remained vital performance venues at this time as well, and figured prominently in the early careers of key rock 'n' roll figures such as Scotty Moore—Elvis Presley's long-time accomplice on guitar—and Carl Perkins. Perkins, for example, began playing in the "tonks" around his Tennessee home as a young teenager in combination first with his older brother Jay, and then with younger brother Clayton added on stand-up bass. As a duo, Carl and Jay made their debut at the Cotton Boll, owned by Hubert Miller, in 1946. By the early 1950s, with Clayton in tow, they had graduated to the El Rancho, described by Perkins' biographer David McGee as a "classier breed of honky-tonk," distinguished by the fact that it had a small stage to set the performers apart, and cloths draped over the tables.[19] Although the violence and drunkenness of the honky tonk settings could be overbearing, Perkins had fond recollections of the audiences he encountered there and the way they provided a testing ground for his early ventures into songwriting: "The tonks is where I got a reading on a lot of my stuff; I'd just try writing it raw in the clubs, and if they jumped out there and kicked and got to rockin', I'd remember the titles and very little else. And that's the way I'd write my songs. But if they kept sittin' there I'd cut it pretty short."[20]

Honky tonks never seem to have been stitched together into a national circuit in the manner of the African American establishments that comprised the chitlin' circuit. Most likely this is because white artists had more opportunities open to them when they began to advance in their careers. In country music, radio programming and live performance had forged important interrelationships well before rock 'n' roll was on the horizon. The Grand Ole Opry, the leading country music broadcast emanating out of Nashville, was as much a weekly live music event as a radio show from early in its history; and its importance as such was consolidated with the 1943 move into the Ryman Auditorium in downtown Nashville. By the time rock 'n' roll artists came onto the margins of the commercial country music scene in the mid-1950s, the Opry conducted itself as a standard-bearer of the genre and did not exactly welcome the new artists with open arms; Elvis Presley's only appearance on the Opry in October 1954 drew a notably cool reception.[21]

He fared much better, though, during a series of appearances on the *Louisiana Hayride*, based in Shreveport, Louisiana, one of which is pictured in Figure 6.2. The *Hayride* was broadcast from a theater that held nearly four thousand people, and audience response within the venue was an important gauge of whether an artist was right for the show. Scotty Moore recalled that the band's first set on the *Hayride* was tentative, not least because the musicians could barely hear each other. By the time they returned for a second set on the same night's broadcast, though, they were more attuned to the setting, and the audience had turned over so that there were more young people in the crowd. Presley and his band connected with the audience this time around and would become a regular feature on the show for months to come.[22] Presley's appearances on the *Hayride* marked a milestone in his career for two reasons: it was a moment when he proved that his appeal as

Figure 6.2 Elvis Presley, center, flanked by guitarist Scotty Moore (left) and bassist Bill Black (right) during an appearance on the Louisiana Hayride. Courtesy of Michael Ochs Archives/Getty Images.

a performing artist extended beyond Memphis, where he had started out, and it marked the first occasion that he, Scotty Moore, and bassist Bill Black played with the drummer who would become the band's fourth member, D.J. Fontana. In the recording studio Presley's band had been a three-piece; only on stage did they become a quartet.

* * *

The discrete sectors of live music that took shape in the post-World War II era—the chitlin' circuit and the honky tonks, respectively—reflected the racial segregation that still held sway through most of the US at the time. Challenges to segregation also grew substantially in this period, with the mounting Civil Rights movement changing the terms according to which Americans construed race relations in the abstract and on a day-to-day level. Where rock 'n' roll is concerned, much has been made of the ways in which records and radio functioned as media that facilitated the crossing of the color line. Young white listeners whose own identities were in flux could explore African American music via mass media channels that allowed them to connect with the sounds of black America even if they remained at a remove from the material realities of African American life. Much of the music created at this time was characterized by what music critic Greil Marcus termed "racial confusion," as the lines drawn between "black" and "white" styles grew indeterminate in a setting where the logic of racial segregation was increasingly subject to question.[23] On the radio, this impulse toward "confusion" further derived from white disc jockeys such as Alan Freed at WJW in Cleveland and then WINS in New York; John Richbourg, Gene Nobles, and Hoss Allen at WLAC in Nashville; and Hunter Hancock at WPOP in Los Angeles. The sheer enthusiasm with which these deejays and scores of others promoted African American rhythm and blues led many listeners to presume that they were themselves African American, all the more so when white radio personalities assumed black speech patterns and mannerisms, presenting a sort of "racial ventriloquy" that was a spoken analogue to the mixed signals heard in the music itself.[24]

Programming black music, made by black artists, carried risks for broadcasters—especially on television where the race of the performers was more difficult to disguise, but even on radio, where listeners had been socialized to hear certain sounds as "black." Southern audiences and even more so Southern politicians and news media were often suspicious of anything that connoted bringing black and white together, and so broadcasters (especially those networks whose reach was national in scope) often used their need to preserve their Southern audiences as a justification for exercising caution and avoiding African American content.[25] In the realm of live performance, these risks were more direct and potentially more inflammatory. Especially but not exclusively in Southern states, it was still very much the norm in the postwar era for African American music artists to appear before African American audiences; this was the logic that made the chitlin' circuit into a necessary and profitable phenomenon. White artists tended to face the same restrictions in reverse although in this case it was less often treated as a prohibition, and more as a matter of common sense. In many states practices implemented during the time of vaudeville remained in place: rather than have racially mixed audiences occupy theaters at the same time, African American artists might play a segregated show in the early evening for their primary black audience, and then another later show, also segregated, at which white audiences would be admitted. In other instances, balconies were used to enforce segregation, with one racial group occupying the floor of the theater and the other the upstairs section.

Segregation, it is important to remember, is ultimately a means to regulate access to public space. There are a host of distinct but interrelated practices that are designed to define and confer rights of privacy; but in general, it is public not private spaces that are subject to segregation along racial or other lines. The logic behind racial segregation as it was practiced in the United States was designed to limit the extent to which African Americans might be included in the regular public life of the nation, the individual states, and local municipalities. Segregation, in other words, was predicated not only on the avoidance of integration or contact between whites and African Americans, but upon the denial of a legitimate place for African Americans in the public sphere. Understanding this facet of segregation, whether it is carried out legally or through extra-legal means, is crucial for understanding why, even when certain events were mainly or exclusively designed to appeal to black audiences—as the Moondog Coronation Ball in Cleveland was, along with many music events organized throughout the 1940s and 1950s—they could be perceived to pose a threat to public order. A large crowd of African Americans raised a particular sort of anxiety, deriving from the normative assumption that public space was meant for white bodies, not black ones. An integrated crowd that included both whites and African Americans provoked a more acute sort of anxiety, because from a segregationist standpoint racial intermixture was something to be avoided at all costs. In both instances, rock 'n' roll concerts during the 1950s challenged established norms, but that challenge was limited and took hold gradually across the nation as a whole.

Artists both white and black experienced the contradictions that could come to the surface when they presented themselves before the public in circumstances where racial sensitivity was heightened. African American rock 'n' roll pioneer Chuck Berry recounts an incident in his autobiography in which he was contracted to play a show in Knoxville, Tennessee, following the success of his first single for Chess records, "Maybellene." Berry's song was itself representative of the "racial confusion" so pervasive at the time, an up-tempo number that had a rhythm and lyrical cadence more evocative of country music than contemporary blues or rhythm and blues. Often construed as a "black hillbilly," Berry was apparently hired in this instance on the presumption that someone who sounded so "country" on record must be white; consequently, when he appeared to perform in Knoxville, he was turned away from his own gig with the explanation, "It's a country dance and we had no idea that 'Maybellene' was recorded by a niggra man."[26] Berry further explained that he was forbidden from playing at the club due to a city ordinance. He later learned that in such incidents he would be paid regardless of whether or not he was in fact allowed to perform, but he was nonetheless forced into the degrading position of "hearing my song played by the band they had hired to replace me."[27]

For white rockabilly artist Carl Perkins, one of his most difficult encounters came when he was booked onto the Top Record Stars of 1956 tour in the summer of that year. The show featured a line-up of mostly African American artists, including Berry, Frankie Lymon and the Teenagers, and singing group the Spaniels. Perkins was one of three white artists on the bill, and the tour manager warned him before the opening appearance in Columbia, South Carolina, that the audience could get rowdy being exposed to such an exciting batch of black and white performers in a state where segregation remained securely in place. Sure enough, when Perkins and his band took the stage, they were immediately struck by the spectacle of young audience members being crushed toward the front of the crowd. Sensing that things were about to get out of control, the African American tour manager—who is only named "Charlie" in Perkins' recollection of the event—waved the band off the stage and into the wings before their set was over, and the stage was immediately overtaken by members of the audience.[28] Perkins was so shaken by the unrest of the crowd that he temporarily left the tour, and only returned after much persuasion on the part of Sun Records label head Sam Phillips.

Perkins' story has an important flip side: the concert where he appeared clearly went against the grain of segregation by presenting black and white performers side by side. Another stop on this same tour brought the challenge more to the surface. At a performance in Houston, Texas, wrote *Pittsburgh Courier* journalist Cliff Richardson, "For the first time in history Negro and white couples danced on the same floor here."[29] Perkins himself was given credit for encouraging the racial lines drawn at the event to be crossed. The emcee for the event, African American disc jockey Hotsy Totsy (Chester

McDowell) of KYOK, announced that the dancing portion of the entertainment would commence after an intermission, but police who were present sought to prevent the dancing, presumably out of fear that white and black concertgoers would intermingle more than they judged to be appropriate. Despite the police order, white attendees joined their black counterparts on the dance floor, encouraged by Perkins who reportedly said from the stage, "Let's everybody in here rock and roll." According to Richardson's article in the *Courier*, "What happened then must have sent the Citizens Councils members home with the shakes." The audience danced without restraint, but the police remained watchful and forced the music to stop thirty minutes before the scheduled close of the performance.[30] Such episodes, which were not isolated occurrences, instantiate the claim made by saxophonist H.B. Barnum, who toured with Little Richard: "When I first went on the road there were many segregated audiences. With Richard, although they still had the audiences segregated in the building, they were *there* together. And most times, before the end of the night, they would all be mixed together."[31]

Booking Rhythm and Blues

The Top Record Stars of 1956 was one of the many "package" shows that were organized throughout the early rock 'n' roll era. If the shows that coursed through the chitlin' circuit and the honky tonks represented the ways in which black and white artists traveled different channels, in the package shows the different streams of American popular music met.[32] This is not to say that package shows were always integrated affairs. Country music and rhythm and blues each gave rise to their own versions of these packages in the years leading up to rock 'n' roll's emergence and the logic whereby white country artists would appear with other white country artists, or black rhythm and blues artists with others of the same description, carried into the rock 'n' roll era and beyond. Increasingly though, starting around 1955, shows that featured white and black artists in combination became more common, and the mix of artists on the stage was an important strategy to draw mixed audiences as well. The most important precedent here came from neither country nor R&B but from jazz: Norman Granz's Jazz at the Philharmonic concerts, discussed in the previous chapter, provided a powerful model for the integrated package show in which the showcase of black and white artists onstage was designed for venues where black and white audiences would be in attendance. Jazz at the Philharmonic—which was still very much a going concern when rock 'n' roll was getting underway—also provided an important example of how the "package" style of live music presentation could be the basis of a profitable and sustainable business model. By the time rock 'n' roll proper became a widely recognized phenomenon in the mid-1950s, a burgeoning live music industry was falling into place with package shows as the most visible and lucrative product.

Race was only one of the considerations that went into the assembly of a package show, and not necessarily the most important factor. The key principle behind these shows was to present a cross-section of artists diverse enough to make the audience feel like it was getting a varied night of entertainment but still connected to a field of music that was coherent to a greater or lesser degree. Probably the most salient distinction between performers on a package bill was between those artists who were dominated by a single personality (Fats Domino, Carl Perkins, Jerry Lee Lewis, Chuck Berry) and those who appeared as groups, and singing groups in particular (the Teenagers, the Drifters, the Moonglows, the Dominos). Typically, there was some effort to have a mix of male and female artists as well. The former were far more prevalent, but promoters often used the latter to add an air of sex appeal for young male concertgoers—although some female performers such as Lavern Baker and Ruth Brown had a stature comparable to any male artist on the bill. Nearly all artists, male or female, black or white, booked onto a package show had current records out, and some also appeared in the rock-oriented films that began to proliferate after 1956. Cross-promotion was thus critical to the success of these shows, and so it was also considered good practice to include a mix of artists who had already achieved some significant level of name recognition and artists who were just getting off the ground. To a degree this mix anticipated the later organization of lesser known "opening bands" and better-known "headliners" that became standardized in the 1960s and 1970s. However, with so many artists appearing in a given package, the pacing of an evening's entertainment owed as much to older notions of "live" entertainment inherited from vaudeville and variety theater as it did to the strict linear progression of openers and headliners that took root in later years.

Standing behind the production of these shows were the industry players who pulled all the pieces together, among whom the booking agencies and promoters figured most prominently. We saw earlier how R&B singer Roy Brown's touring activities were coordinated through the cooperation between these interested parties, in his case between booking agent Ben Bart of Universal Attractions and various regional promoters who had established relationships with performance venues in particular territories around the US. As the package tours grew in scale and potential profitability, the influence of these figures within the industry grew as well.

Billboard, by the 1950s the leading music industry publication of record, followed the growth of the package shows within the rhythm and blues sector of popular music carefully throughout the early and middle years of the 1950s. The first significant show of this kind to capture the magazine's attention was a 1953 package put together by the Gale Agency under the title, "The Rhythm and Blues Show." Featured on the bill was a strong mix of African American R&B artists including Ruth Brown, Wynonie Harris, and the Clovers, along with jazz saxophonist Lester Young, comedian Dusty Fletcher, and boxing legend Joe Louis, who was at the time seeking to capitalize on his stature in the black community by becoming a stage attraction.[33] The success of the Gale Agency's debut R&B package led to the production of a second, competing venture announced toward the end of 1954, the "Top Ten R&B Show," which was assembled by Shaw Artists Agency in partnership with Lou Krefetz, manager for the singing group the Clovers. Top artists for the "Top Ten" show were the Clovers (unsurprisingly), Fats Domino, Joe Turner, the Moonglows, Faye Adams, and Paul Williams and his orchestra—the same Williams who had put in the only stage appearance at Alan Freed's Moondog Coronation Ball nearly three years earlier.[34] Indicating the emerging structure through which booking agents and promoters worked together to carve out the circuits through which these touring packages moved, *Billboard* also listed the various promoters who would handle the show in different parts of the country: Irvin Feld on the East Coast down to Virginia (more about whom will be said shortly); the Weinberg Office in the South; Howard Lewis in Texas and the Southwest; and unnamed promoters who would handle the show in the Midwest.

By the beginning of 1955, when the "Top Ten R&B Show" was preparing to hit the road, *Billboard* reporter Bob Rolontz identified the R&B packages as a major rising trend. According to Rolontz, the previous year had seen two successful packages across the music spectrum, Granz's "Jazz at the Philharmonic" and the Gale Agency's "Rhythm and Blues Show," but the year ahead was poised to see many other similar shows take the stage around the US. The success of this model of live music presentation was, for Rolontz, above all a sign of "the hard work of the various r.&b. agencies in putting together smart packages and booking them at the right spots and at the right price so that all parties—the artist, the promoter and the agency—can earn some money."[35] Continuing to extoll the virtues of booking agencies as primary innovators within the R&B market, Rolontz offered a revealing analysis of the singular conditions that prevailed in the R&B concert world:

> The relationship between artist and agency in the r.&b. field has always been different than it is in other spheres of the business world. First of all, no one knocks off early in the r.&b. field, neither the booker nor the artist. Any artist who wants to work every day in the year can do so in the r.&b. field, and any booker will stay at his job all night to get his talent all the dates they deserve. It is this relationship that has helped to bring about the new giant r.&b. shows, which bid fair to turn into one of the most profitable angles of the business for some of these agencies.[36]

Rolontz's portrayal of the business relationship that existed between R&B artists and their booking agencies is undoubtedly too rosy, as is his celebration of the work ethic that artists and agents alike exhibited. One could just as well say that in many instances, the artists were tirelessly put to work by booking agencies to maximize financial return. Yet the artists cooperated with these arrangements because, for all the risks that African American artists assumed in being on the road, their performances remained a more sure and reliable way to earn money from their talents than the records they made, since the recording industry had patterns of exploitation in place that were more entrenched and easier to hide than the live music sector.

However much Rolontz overstated the benevolence of the booking agencies toward the artists with whom they worked, he was right to assign them a lead role in shaping the changing live music landscape of the time. As one former booking agent, Dick Alen, said when looking back at his career, "That generation of record men invented the business, same as the early rhythm and blues agents are the ones who invented the rock 'n' roll business of *how* to tour."[37] When *Billboard* spotlighted the growth of the rhythm and blues market in its issue of February 4, 1956, it placed the emphasis squarely on the promotion of R&B shows over the production of R&B recordings—a surprising move for a magazine long known for its charts of best-selling records. Representative of this accent on live music was a list of "Major Agencies Booking Rhythm & Blues Talent." The list included ten agencies, most of which had their affiliated artists highlighted: Associated Booking Corporation, Buffalo Booking Agency, Milton Deutsch Agency, Gale Agency, Herald Attractions, Reg Marshall Agency, Johnny Robinson Agency, Shaw Artists Corp., and Universal Attractions. All were based in either New York or Los Angeles except the Buffalo Booking Agency, which was in Houston. Among them Gale, Shaw, and Universal were the biggest, with Buffalo a competitive fourth place. Between them, the four biggest agencies managed the touring activities of nearly two hundred individual artists and bands, including: B.B King, Junior Parker, and Willie Mae (Big Mama) Thornton at Buffalo; Lavern Baker, the Drifters, Screaming Jay Hawkins, and Chuck Berry at Gale; Ruth Brown, Ray Charles, Bo Diddley, Fats Domino, and the Moonglows at Shaw; and the Five Royales, the Penguins, the Midnighters, and Roy Brown at Universal.[38] With so many artists working under their oversight, the booking agencies were in the strongest position to pull together the package shows that became the common currency of the era's live music offerings, and any promoter seeking to produce a show on his own had to deal with the agencies to get access to top performers.

Super Attractions

This is not to say that promoters were in an entirely secondary position. Without the knowledge of specific territories and venues that promoters had, booking agencies would have faced much more difficulty orchestrating tours of sufficient scope to keep their artists on the road for more than a few days at a time. More to the point, the balance of power between booking agencies and promoters was always in flux. Promoters attached their names to the events they produced in a more public way: a promoter's reputation could help to sell an event, especially when that promoter—as in the case of Alan Freed and the many other disc jockeys who entered the promotional field—was already a known figure. Even those promoters who were not also entertainment personalities often developed names that became a recognized part of the shows they staged, a pattern that would continue into the later rock era with the prominence accorded to the likes of Bill Graham. And as much as promoters depended upon the booking agencies to secure talent, they often took the lead in assembling whole packages and tours that had the scale and variety to match what the agencies were putting on the road.

Among the promoters of the early rock 'n' roll era, one name stands out: Irvin Feld. Feld's name appears in many a rock 'n' roll history, but he is rarely assigned more than passing importance. Even during the 1950s when he produced some of the most successful rock 'n' roll package tours in the US, he was routinely misidentified in the pages of *Billboard* magazine as "Irving," a mistake that has made its way into many subsequent works. Yet with his brother Israel (or Izzy), he built a live music empire from his base in Washington, DC, that would not really be paralleled until the rise of Bill Graham more than a decade later. Rick Coleman, in his authoritative biography of Fats Domino, calls Feld with some justification "the first super concert promoter of rock 'n' roll."[39] In comparison to Alan Freed, Coleman emphasizes that Feld undertook wide-ranging tours at an earlier date and thus arguably did more to make the rock 'n' roll concert a truly national phenomenon. Feld's support for African American artists was at least as deep-rooted as was Freed's and he reserved top billing for black performers like Fats Domino well into the time when white rock 'n' roll stars were gaining more prominence. By the end of the 1950s, Feld and Freed were competing head-to-head for audiences, and while Freed ultimately lost his standing due to a host of controversies surrounding him starting in 1958, Feld maintained his credibility until he left the concert business in 1967 upon purchasing the biggest circus organization in the US, the Ringling Brothers Barnum and Bailey Circus.

The Feld brothers entered the music business through the drug trade—but not illicitly. Their first joint operation was a drug store in the heart of black Washington on 7th Street NW. Opened in 1940, the store included a section dedicated to selling records, and that parcel of music-related enterprise set the stage for the future direction of their careers. Sociologist and rock historian Philip Ennis shared a unique reminiscence of the Feld brothers' store in the opening pages of his book, *The Seventh Stream*. Ennis grew up in Baltimore and claimed that he was entirely unaware of African American popular music until he was hired to work at the Felds' drug store as a high school student. In his recollection:

> It was a new world, Seventh Street, one of the main drags in black Washington. At the drugstore's doorway was stationed a dried up little man with a "pet" gila monster selling "Nature Tonic." Into the street blared the latest race records. Enough street traffic was lured into the store to fill half its interior with cartons of those records, all 78s and simply wonderful.[40]

When the Felds noticed that more customers were coming to their store for the records than for the pharmaceutical products on sale they adapted their business accordingly, and opened two subsequent "Super Music" stores in other parts of the city in 1944 and 1946.[41] Following from their experience in record sales, their first efforts to branch out beyond retail came with a record label, Super Disc, on which they issued Arthur Smith's "Guitar Boogie," a major country crossover hit released in 1945 that anticipated some of the characteristic moves of rockabilly.[42] By 1950 the Felds and their Super Music and Drug Stores received notice in *Billboard* for their sponsorship of a radio show hosted by African American disc jockey Jon Massey on station WWDC, a move that the magazine suggested went against the grain of the pervasive "Jim Crowism" of the DC area.[43]

That same year the brothers entered the field of concert promotion, with their initial efforts concentrated in the area of African American gospel music. Gospel, like blues, was undergoing a major phase of revitalization in the post-World War II period as the boundaries between sacred and secular African American music were redrawn. The Felds had some of their biggest early successes aligning themselves with one of the most forward-thinking artists in the gospel field, Sister Rosetta Tharpe. Tharpe was an extroverted performer and a groundbreaking female musician who relished the capacity of her electric guitar to generate a joyfully discordant noise. Recognizing Tharpe's broad appeal among Washington's southern migrant population and her ability to project her big sound and personality, Irvin and Israel Feld staged a concert on July 2, 1950, featuring the gospel star in an ambitiously staged "spiritual concert" at the city's Griffith Stadium that also featured the Golden Gate Quartette, the Harmonizing Four, the Sunset Harmonizers, and a reunion between Tharpe and her former singing partner Madame Marie Knight.[44]

The success of that show—which drew more than 20,000 people with a top price of three dollars per ticket—prompted Irvin to pursue an even more audacious plan for the following year. At his urging, the unmarried (and twice divorced) Tharpe agreed to find a husband within the next several months, so that her wedding could be held at the same Griffith Stadium and combined with another large-scale concert. With her husband-to-be Russell Morrison in tow, Tharpe was married on July 3, 1951, before an audience that was variously estimated to be between 20,000 and 30,000, and then was the featured artist in a post-wedding concert during which she sang and played electric guitar while still wearing her wedding dress. Her biographer, Gayle Wald, has called Tharpe the first female "stadium rocker" due to her two Griffith Stadium concerts, presaging the more widely recognized achievements of Janis Joplin by more than a decade. Meanwhile, Shirley Feld—wife of Israel, and an instrumental part of the Feld music organization in her own right— recalled that the wedding concert was their greatest success to date, leading the way toward the brothers' expanded scale of operations.[45]

Through such events Irvin and Israel Feld created the basis for Super Attractions, their concert promotion venture. Tracking their progress through the first half of the 1950s, several features of their career are striking. First, the Felds were not single-minded in their allegiance to any single style or genre of music. They moved from gospel to rhythm and blues promotion quite seamlessly by all appearances; but they also supported whatever music suited the opportunities that presented themselves, including classical music, jazz, and the more mainstream "adult" pop of the era. Second, the Felds did not simply promote shows on an ad hoc basis. They forged deals with venues that gave them privileged if not exclusive right to promote shows in those spaces, which made their concert promotion business more stable and sustainable than most of their competitors. Both qualities of their career were evident in the deal they struck to promote shows at the Carter Barron Amphitheater in Washington, DC, a government-owned performance venue with whom they won a contract starting in 1954, after an earlier failed bid.[46] Presenting a summer concert series at Carter Barron for several years running, the Felds pitched their entertainment to middle-class family audiences. Their first season featured the National Symphony Orchestra, and in later years the star attractions would include the likes of Danny Kaye and Harry Belafonte.

Crucially, the Felds never limited their field of operations to Washington, DC By the time they formed their deal with Carter Barron, *Billboard* reported that they already had comparable arrangements in Philadelphia, Pittsburgh, and the Virginia cities of Norfolk and Richmond; soon they would also add Winston-Salem, North Carolina, to the list.[47] These associations again gave them a competitive advantage when they started arranging touring package shows, as they already worked with a host of venues distributed through a broad area. Meanwhile, within the city of Washington, the Felds' combination of interests yielded its own advantages. What had become four Super Music retail outlets by 1954 served as ticket outlets for the pair's local promotions, and as *Billboard* described, "queues of ticket purchasers frequently represent buyers of disks as well... As customers line up for tickets, salesmen discreetly distribute circulars showing the latest disk releases. [Irvin] Feld said this has resulted in 'tremendous impulse buying.'"[48] The ability of the Felds to exploit the cross-promotional potential of this setup was further demonstrated in a display ad run by the Felds in the *Washington Post* (shown in Figure 6.3) in connection with the March 1956 opening of the film, *Rock Around the Clock*, which featured performances by Bill Haley and the Comets and the Platters. The ad invited readers to a "Rock 'n' Roll Jamboree" organized by the Super Music Stores, which included personal appearances by Haley and his Comets, and the Platters at two Washington Theaters where the film would be playing, with free records and pictures of the artists given to the first several hundred people in attendance.[49] Readers were further implored to buy all the Haley and Platters records they might want at the four Super Music stores, and were informed of an upcoming concert featuring the two artists along with several other top rock 'n' roll stars to be held at the National Guard Armory on June 3, tickets for which were already on sale at those same record shops—and the show, of course was also produced by the Felds and their Super Attractions promotional company.

That June 3 show was part of the first major touring package pulled together by Super Attractions. Previously the Felds had played the role of regional promoter for packages that were assembled by the big booking agencies. The Biggest Rock 'n' Roll Show of 1956, though, was a Feld production from start to finish. Bill Haley, the white singer and bandleader who was still riding high on his hit song "Rock Around the Clock" was the linchpin of the Felds' talent package but the lineup of artists ran deep. Accompanying Haley and the Platters were Clyde McPhatter—for whom Irvin Feld would also become personal manager—Lavern Baker, Joe Turner, the Teenagers, the Teen Queens, Bo Diddley, the Drifters, the Flamingos, the Colts, and Red Prysock and his Rock 'n' Roll Orchestra, who would provide accompaniment for the headline artists. Opening on April 20 with a show in Hershey, Pennsylvania, the Biggest Rock 'n' Roll Show of 1956 consisted of forty-eight concert dates in total and would run into the early part of summer.[50] It was one of the most ambitious package tours planned to date, not least due to Feld's use of the phrase "rock 'n' roll" as part of the tour's title. As we will see, "rock 'n' roll" entered the field of live music promotion through the efforts of Alan Freed; but at the time that the Felds took the Biggest Rock 'n' Roll Show on tour, Freed was concentrating his own live promotion efforts on New York

Figure 6.3 Advertisement for a "Rock 'n' Roll Jamboree" sponsored by Washington, DC-based concert promoter Irvin Feld and his Super Music record shops. The ad shows the power of cross-promotion, with Bill Haley and His Comets and the Platters making personal appearances on behalf of a new movie, *Rock Around the Clock*, that would be accompanied by giveaways of both artists' records, and then a return appearance for two concerts as part of the Biggest Rock 'n' Roll Show of '56, a package tour assembled by Feld and his brother Izzy. From the *Washington Post* (March 13, 1956).

City and some surrounding urban centers. It would be two more years before Freed would try to mount a touring package with the scope of what the Felds put on the road in 1956. The Biggest Rock 'n' Roll Show of 1956, then, was the first package show that brought the phrase "rock 'n' roll" on the road on something approaching a national scale.

* * *

Taking their operations on tour as they did, the Felds made the risky decision to concentrate much of their activity in Southern states. Given their base in Washington, DC, and their strong ties to venues in Virginia and North Carolina this was a sensible move, but it nonetheless meant that they needed to be mindful of the potential for conflict as they brought their combinations of white and African American artists into areas where segregation was still strongly observed. Indeed, the racial climate surrounding popular music at the time that the Biggest Rock 'n' Roll Show of 1956 began its tour could not have been more tense. The early months of 1956 had seen rock 'n' roll become the target of racist attacks by segregationists, most vocal among whom was Asa Carter of the North Alabama Citizens Council, who portrayed the music as part of a conspiracy designed to lower the moral character of Southern white youth.[51] On April 10 of that year—only ten days before the Biggest Rock 'n' Roll Show was set to begin—a group of white men attacked the popular African American singer Nat "King" Cole while he was onstage performing in Birmingham, Alabama, as part of an integrated package show (but one that was decidedly not of the "rock 'n' roll" variety). The attack on Cole caused reverberations around the US. Most observers were shocked at the action taken against Cole, which was unquestionably motivated by racism and resistance to desegregation.[52] Yet Cole himself also became a target for criticism among some African American commentators for agreeing to appear in a segregated venue—for the show where he was attacked was one held for whites only, while a separate show reserved for African American concertgoers was to be held later that same night.[53]

In the wake of the attack on Cole, *Billboard* asked whether concert promoters would change any of the plans they had for shows booked in the Southern region. The magazine speculated that one of the package shows currently on tour—the Shaw Agency's "Top 10 R&B Show"—might only play to black audiences and also suggested that Bill Haley, the lone white star on the Feld brothers' package, might be pulled from some locations to minimize the risk of conflict.[54] Overall, though, the general message was, the show must go on, and Irvin Feld denied that any changes had been made to the itinerary for "The Biggest Rock 'n' Roll Show of '56." The Southeast was Feld territory, and whatever difficulties went along with promoting package shows in the area were outweighed by the potential profits to be made. More to the point, despite the resistance against rock 'n' roll that existed among certain segments of Southern society, the music had a strong Southern audience that was eager for opportunities to see the music performed live and was willing to go against the norms of racial segregation to do so.

Still, it would be wrong to overstate the status of Irvin and Israel Feld as civil rights pioneers. Like most who worked in the music industry, they were pragmatists, always ready to adjust their strategy to circumstance or based on the lessons of experience. For example, the brothers did not withdraw Bill Haley from any portions of the Biggest Rock 'n' Show of '56 tour. When they reached Birmingham, Alabama, on May 20, however—where Cole had been attacked just over a month earlier—they encountered picket lines by members of the North Alabama Citizens Council, despite the fact that the concert was reserved for an exclusively white audience as Cole's had been.[55] The following year, when Super Attractions put together its biggest touring package to date, the "Biggest Show of Stars for 1957," the Felds adopted a different approach. Beginning with a performance in Pittsburgh, Pennsylvania, the "Biggest Show of Stars" was planned to run for eighty shows, with a lineup that included Fats Domino, Clyde McPhatter, Lavern Baker, Frankie Lymon, Chuck Berry, the Crickets (with Buddy Holly), Paul Anka, the Everly Brothers, the Spaniels, the Bobbettes, Johnny and Joe, the Drifters, Tommy Brown, and Paul Williams and his band.[56] However, when the show swung to the South about a month after the tour began, the white artists on the bill—the Crickets, Paul Anka and the Everly Brothers—were dropped for appearances in Chattanooga, Birmingham, New Orleans, Memphis, and Columbus, Georgia. The African American newspaper, the *Pittsburgh Courier*, accused the Felds of "bowing to Jim Crow" with their decision and called for performers and promoters to take a stronger stand in combating segregationist practices, charging that "the Feld troupe is not in line with the latest in thinking!"[57] Ultimately, the Felds and other promoters of the era walked a difficult line, at times testing the limits of what might be allowable, at other times holding back to avoid disruption. Taking such an ambivalent approach they widened the market for live rock 'n' roll considerably, but also contributed to the factors that made the music such a volatile commodity.

The DJ Arrives

Few promoters, or even performers, associated with rock 'n' roll in the 1950s were as caught up in its volatility as Alan Freed. In a sense, concert promotion could be seen as but a sidebar for Freed when compared to someone like Irvin Feld. His primary occupation was as a disc jockey, which itself was a fairly new designation marking a significant change in the character of radio programming. More generally, he was a broadcast and media personality whose efforts reached into television, film, and even recordings, through a deal he made with the independent Coral record label. Freed became a larger-than-life figure by pursuing every avenue of exposure that he possibly could. Within the panoply of outlets where he appeared, the promotion of live performances might seem almost anachronistic, an effort to hold onto an older mode of cultural presentation amidst the transformed media environment of the 1950s, in which television, radio and sound recordings combined to make the home into a sphere of cultural consumption to an unprecedented degree.

As we have already seen, though, live music was itself undergoing significant changes during the time when rock 'n' roll started circulating through American culture. These changes were partly demographic: African American audiences were targeted in ways that posed a threat to the established racial order, all the more so when they were part of a larger, integrated audience. Of equal importance, young audiences—bearing the imprint of "teenagers," another term that momentously gained currency in these years—were coming out in droves, a circumstance that created new opportunities and posed new challenges for those in the business of concert promotion. The combination of racial integration and an appeal to young people made rock 'n' roll concerts into a potentially explosive property. Even the North Alabama Citizens Council reserved its greatest condemnation for the possibility that *young* white southerners would be led down the precipitous path toward integration by the music. Meanwhile, the economic features of the live music industry underwent innovation as well. Booking agents and promoters created an infrastructure for live music promotion and production that paralleled the spread of independent record labels that sprouted throughout the US in the years following World War II, in each case pursuing opportunity where larger, established corporate players were slow to move. The package shows that surfaced in these years were forged through cooperation between record labels, promoters, and booking agencies, as artists with current releases were the bread and butter of the packages and an artist with a hit record (or several) was the best guarantee of a good crowd.

Radio, by the 1950s, played a much-enhanced role in the process of making records into hits. The very prominence accorded to disc jockeys in this era reflected of dramatic changes in radio programming where music was concerned. Prior to 1945, when music appeared on the radio it was usually under the guise of a "live" broadcast. From Louis Armstrong at the Savoy Ballroom in Chicago to Benny Goodman at the Hotel Pennsylvania, from the Grand Ole Opry at its various Nashville homes to Arturo Toscanini at NBC Studio 8H, radio audiences had come to expect that when they heard music on the air they were listening a performance, something that was being played as it was being heard. This is not to say that recorded music never had a place on radio during this time. It was widely broadcast but was much more common during the midday hours than the mornings or evenings when listenership was at its highest; and it was much more likely to be heard on local or regional stations that did not have a wide broadcast range than on the major national networks.

With the realignment of the music and media industries that occurred during and after World War II, new space opened for sound recordings to become a more predominant feature of radio programming. In a sense, the most important factor was the rise of television, which happened with great force in the early 1950s. When the same national networks that dominated radio redirected much of their capital and production efforts into the new medium, the type of programming that the radio networks had promoted—comedic and dramatic serial narratives, newscasts, and remote broadcasts of live music performances, all arranged in blocks that were anywhere from fifteen minutes to several hours in length—started to recede, largely because it was expensive to maintain. Independent radio stations entered to fill the void left by the declining stature of the national networks, and they found the use of recorded music as the basis for programming to be cost-effective while also proving immensely popular among listeners.

Disc jockeys grew as a presence on the airwaves alongside the new preponderance of recorded music. In one sense they stood in for the absent musicians who were displaced by recordings; they were there to guarantee that some quality of "liveness" remained in place if not in the performance of the music, then surrounding what listeners heard. On another level, though, the disc jockey was as much a surrogate listener as a replacement performer. Much of the responsibility for choosing the music to be played on the air in the new radio climate fell to the DJ, and this control remained an essential part of the DJ's role until the Top 40 format began to proliferate later in the 1950s, through which program managers worked to impose a more uniform character on the playlists featured on their stations.[58] Until that time, DJs worked to balance their own taste with what they assumed their listeners wanted to hear, and what they presumed would help their sponsors to best promote the products they sought to advertise.

The best DJs were known for their taste and the mix of music they played, but they were also known for their personalities. To sell the music they played, to sell the advertisements that kept their shows on the air, DJs also sold themselves. Some were soft-spoken, mellow guides to musical enjoyment. Some were storytellers. Some were proto-political community activists who linked music to a broader sort of social awareness. And some were wild-eyed enthusiasts who channeled an out-of-control spirit meant to push their listeners to the edge of excitement. Alan Freed, seen in Figure 6.4, was among this latter camp. His on-air persona was boisterous, vigorous, and uncontained. Freed would routinely shout words of encouragement—"Ohh! Yeah Yeah! Hey!"—over the swinging rhythm and blues songs that were the heart of his show through the early and middle years of the 1950s, almost as though he was egging on the performers.[59] He brought the same verve to his reading of advertisements by his sponsors, such as *Erin Brew*, a locally made beer in Cleveland. In both cases, Freed projected manic energy, but more than that, he cultivated an air of authenticity. He implored his listeners to believe that he meant what he said, that he could be trusted, that he knew their tastes and did his best to bring them what they wanted. One could say that Freed, like all the best DJs, was a pioneer in a powerful form of direct address marketing. Yet in his case, as with many other white and African American DJs around the US, his skills at salesmanship changed the market in which he worked. Along with the efforts of independent record labels, booking agents and concert promoters, disc jockeys like Freed built a demand for rhythm and blues, and rock 'n' roll, that shifted the terms according to which African American music was sold to white audiences in the mid twentieth century. As Arnold Shaw wrote in his pivotal history of rhythm and blues, "Although other white disk jockeys may have devoted full shows to R&B disks, Freed performed the feat of building a large white audience for records that had previously been of interest only to blacks."[60]

It is a striking fact of radio, and rock 'n' roll, history, that the moment at which radio programming began to place less emphasis on airing "live"

Figure 6.4 Alan Freed at the microphone during a New York radio broadcast on September 6, 1955. Photo by Popsie Randolph. Courtesy of Michael Ochs Archives/Getty Images.

musical performances and more emphasis on the playing of records was also a moment when disc jockeys—as a sidebar to their work on the air—entered the realm of live concert promotion. As was noted at the opening of this chapter, Freed was only the most prominent of the DJs who made concert promotion into a major secondary focus of their activities. The rhythm and blues field was especially notable in this regard and many African American DJs played a major role in conjunction with the new booking agencies in the promotion of African American R&B artists in leading black urban theaters such as the Regal in Chicago and the Apollo in Harlem. For DJs like Freed, Chicago's Al Benson, and New York's Tommy "Dr. Jive" Smalls, concert promotion provided a substantial source of additional income, and just as crucially it gave them an important field in which to extend their influence and demonstrate the power of their draw among listeners. We saw in conjunction with Freed's Moondog Coronation Ball that for DJs and stations alike, the ability to draw a large, physical crowd to an event had a selling power that went beyond any single concert. Radio's audiences, although quantifiable to a degree, were invisible. Concert promotions offered a means to turn the broad but abstract mass audience into something concrete and tangible. Doing so, however, also required that DJs enter the same conflict-ridden field of social relations that was faced by promoters like Irvin Feld. Alan Freed never took his promotions down South in the manner of Feld but he faced comparable challenges in the urban North, demonstrating that rock 'n' roll's dual capacity to bring young audiences together and divide public opinion was at work in all parts of the US.

Promoting Rock 'n' Roll

Following the original Moondog Coronation Ball, Freed continued promoting his events under the "Moondog" name from spring 1952 until fall 1954. His promotional activities did not slow down following the tumult of the Coronation Ball, but he took a more cautionary approach to the events he organized subsequently. A short notice in *Billboard* observed of the Moondog Maytime Ball, held in May 1952, that extra police were on hand to "avoid a repetition of a situation when a similar show was staged in March."[61] For that show and others he organized in the months ahead, he offered reserved seats—a measure that helped with security issues, but no doubt also was meant to counter charges that he and his partners Leo Mintz and Lew Platt had deliberately oversold tickets to the Moondog Coronation Ball to generate more profit for themselves.[62]

To avoid conflict with Cleveland city officials, who remained wary of Freed's efforts, he took his shows to other locations removed from the city proper. An advertisement that appeared in the June 21, 1952 edition of the *Call and Post*, the African American newspaper that previously criticized Freed for his exploitation of black youth, announced the program for Freed's Moondog Moonlight Ball, which consisted of "3 Big Dances, 3 Consecutive Nights, 3 Different Cities." Thursday, June 19, saw a performance at the Crystal Beach Ballroom in Vermilion on Lake Erie; Friday, June 20, featured a dance at the Summit Beach Ballroom in Akron; and on Saturday, June 21, the Avon Oaks Ballroom in Girard, Ohio, would host the night's entertainment. Performers included singing group the Swallows—noted as King Records recording artists—as well as singer Edna McGriff and a band headed by Buddy Lucas, all African American performers. Pictured in the ad, Freed would appear at each performance in person and broadcast live on WLW from each event.[63] Freed's presence at these events was a key factor in motivating concertgoers to attend them, while their presence in turn certified his status as someone who did more than just play records—he created opportunities for young music fans to see their favorite artists in person.

Eventually, Freed began to test the waters farther afield. The syndication of his radio show on stations outside of Ohio provided him with the impetus to do so. One of those stations, WNJR of Newark, New Jersey, gave him entry into the New York metropolitan radio market. The station was the first in the greater New York area to adopt a format designed to appeal to African American listeners around the clock, with rhythm and blues and gospel as the primary styles. Along with Freed, two other white DJs known for their promotion of African American music—Zenas Sears from Atlanta and Hunter Hancock from Los Angeles—taped shows for WNJR, making the station something of a conduit for national trends.[64]

Sensing opportunity, Freed staged a pair of May 1954 shows at the Newark Armory, which he dubbed the "Moondog Coronation Ball," harking back to his first, news-making promotion of two years ago. Reporting on the event in *Billboard*, Bob Rolontz remarked with some amount of wonder that the crowd of over 10,000 was the largest Freed had drawn since his first Coronation. More notably, claimed Rolontz, "Not since the hey-dey of the swing bands has a dance in the East created such excitement or pulled so strongly."[65] A solid lineup of African American artists including the Clovers, the Harptones, Muddy Waters, Charles Brown, and the Buddy Johnson orchestra with singer Ella Johnson, had much to do with the draw, but some of the success had to be attributed to the popularity of Freed's radio show as well. And, if the demographics of the concert were indicative of Freed's listenership, his audience remained overwhelmingly young and predominantly African American. Rolontz characterized the crowd at the Armory as being mostly comprised of "youngsters from 15 to 20, and about 20 per cent of the crowd was made up of white youngsters"—a higher percentage of white concertgoers than had attended Freed's Ohio promotions, but still with a clear black majority.[66] Supporting this assessment, an article in the African American magazine, *Our World*, offered portraits of several Freed fans that attended the Newark show, all of them young African Americans that the publication termed "Moondoggies" after Freed's own nickname.[67]

The Newark engagement was, in a sense, a preview of Freed's own move east, which happened later that summer. In July 1954, Freed was lured away from his Cleveland position by WINS in New York City. Freed's salary of $75,000 would make him among the highest-paid disc jockeys in the country, and was the highest salary ever paid for an R&B disc jockey working for an independent (non-network) station.[68] Significantly, that salary would only be the base of Freed's compensation. WINS also had an ambitious plan to syndicate Freed's show well beyond the New York area, for which the DJ would earn that much more. A letter of agreement between Freed and WINS station manager Bob Leder, dated August 10, 1954, outlined the terms of this portion of Freed's contract, stipulating that Freed would receive $5,200 to cover the production expenses for his show, and would be paid fifty percent of all net income generated by selling the syndication rights.[69] By late August, before Freed's show had even begun to air on WINS, *Billboard* reported that the station had already sold the rights to Freed's show in five markets outside of New York, and had the goal of placing him in sixty markets overall.[70]

Lucrative as Freed's contract with WINS had the potential to be, the move to New York was not without its difficulties. Within the first few months of his going on the air in his new post, Freed became embroiled in two controversies that signaled the scrutiny that came with his move into the largest media market in the US. The first brush-up stemmed from Freed's status as a white DJ who was gaining notoriety through his promotion of African American music. Writing in the *Pittsburgh Courier*, George Brown reported that the success of white disc jockeys like Freed was taking opportunity away from their black counterparts. By his account, white DJs were less likely than their African American peers to exercise discerning judgment in selecting what to play; they capitalized on the most sensationalist qualities of the music to better excite their listenership. Yet Willie Bryant, a popular Harlem-based black DJ, stated the real crux of the matter as quoted by Brown:

> The Negro in radio will be pushed out of the field if the outfit that backs the white disc jockey Moondog [Freed] is allowed to get away with what it is doing. The man apes Negroes on a 50,000 watt stations here in New York [sic.]. They intend to network the show to sixty stations and that means that sixty Negroes will not get jobs... If the show ever gets network coverage, we are dead in radio.[71]

Freed's entry into the New York market, then, was seen by Brown, Bryant, and other interested observers to grant white disc jockeys undue authority in presenting black popular music to the public at large—all the more so given the stated plans that WINS had for syndicating Freed's show.

A second controversy seemed, on the surface, more trivial than the conflict surrounding Freed's standing as a white DJ whose success was built on the promotion of African American music. Yet it would prove to have more lasting repercussions. In November 1954, the blind New York street musician Louis Thomas Hardin, better known by the name "Moondog," sued Alan Freed for infringing on the use of his chosen title. There is no evidence to suggest that Freed directly lifted his own use of the "Moondog" name from Hardin, but the musician had an earlier claim and a New York judge found in Hardin's favor.[72] Forbidden from using the tag that had been his main point of identification to the public, Freed began to place greater accent on a secondary phrase that had been part of the title of his radio show. According to Freed biographer John Jackson, the DJ began referring to his show as the "Moondog Rock 'n' Roll Party" while still in Cleveland, but he did not seem to invest any particular significance in the phrase "rock 'n' roll" as a term that referred to a particular style of music—at the time it seemed to connote something more like the spirit or energy that the music was believed to engender.[73] His concert promotions throughout his Cleveland career always carried the "Moondog" name and never applied the phrase "rock 'n' roll." This was all about to change.

When *Billboard* announced the decision in Freed's court case with Hardin, it observed: "Freed is now calling his program the 'Rock and Roll Show.'"[74] The name would in fact be "Rock 'n' Roll Party," but the point was the same: with "Moondog" now unavailable, "rock and roll" (or, "rock 'n' roll") would become the primary term used to classify Freed's endeavors. Significantly, the time of the court ruling coincided with Freed's plans to stage his first New York City concert; and in his live promotions as on the radio, Freed now favored his new "rock and roll" title. *Variety* thus reported, in the lead-up to that first show: "The jamboree will be tagged 'Rock and Roll Ball.' Freed previously had promoted similar affairs in Cleveland and Newark under the Moondog Ball monicker but he recently lost the title to the original Moondog, Louis Hardin."[75] And so, Alan Freed's career as a "rock and roll" concert promoter was officially set to begin.

* * *

That first New York production would eventually be promoted under the title of "Alan Freed's 'Rock 'n' Roll' Jubilee Ball." It was held in the St. Nicholas

Arena, a venue typically used for boxing matches with a seating capacity of about six thousand. Because the arena held fewer people than the show was expected to draw, Freed and his co-organizers made it into a two-day event, on Friday and Saturday nights, January 14–15, 1955. As he had done with earlier promotions, Freed announced the show tirelessly over the air from his perch at WINS. He also used other promotion and sales techniques that reflected his growing stature and popularity. In the lead-up to the concert Freed sent a direct mail plea to listeners who had written him cards and letters in the time since he had moved to New York. Informing them that their names had been placed on a "Rock 'n' Roll" preferred mailing list, he explained that they were being given "advance information about the first big ALAN FREED 'ROCK 'N' ROLL' JUBILEE BALL as well as the opportunity of ordering your tickets for this great event, prior to the opening of the ticket sale to the general public." A mail-order coupon appeared at the bottom of the page, and Freed assured readers that the advance sale price of two dollars per ticket represented a savings of fifty cents off the door price, which would be two dollars and fifty cents. Crucially, Freed announced the roster of performers that would appear at the shows—a strong mix of African American artists that included Fats Domino, Clyde McPhatter, Joe Turner, the Clovers, and the Moonglows—and characterized the whole list as a group of "sensational 'ROCK 'N' ROLL' ARTISTS," making it clear that at this stage, he was using the term not just as a general descriptor but as a reference to a new stylistic category.[76]

Offering a different window into the background behind Freed's first New York show is a letter spelling out the terms according to which Freed's concert promotion work would be tied to his position with WINS. The letter was designed to ensure that Freed's endeavors in the live music realm would not clash with the terms of his contract with the station. It came not from Freed himself but from the Seig Music Corporation, a newly established entity that the DJ formed in partnership with his old Cleveland associate Lew Platt and with a new acquaintance he had made since arriving in New York, Morris Levy, to represent his non-radio promotional work. Levy had one of the most fabled careers of any mid-century figure: his reputed ties to organized crime made him the subject of decades worth of rumors and, in the 1980s, the target of an FBI investigation.[77] Owner of the famed Birdland nightclub, Levy knew the lay of the land in Freed's new center of activity and the two collaborated to put the DJ's stamp on New York live music.

The letter that Levy, as the president of Seig Music Corporation, addressed to WINS on Freed's behalf, offered the station ten percent of the gross profits that would be earned from all "theater, dance and concert promotions" produced under Freed's name for a period of ten years. There is no evidence to suggest that any similar agreement existed with Freed's former employer, WJW in Cleveland, so these terms likely reflect the stricter language of his WINS contract with regard to his exclusive commitment to the station. Yet the letter makes it clear that more than Freed's name and presence are at issue. In a pivotal clause, Seig "admits, recognizes and acknowledges that the GOTHAM BROADCASTING CORPORATION"—the parent company of WINS—"has the exclusive right to the name and/or title 'ROCK 'N ROLL', 'ROCK 'N ROLL PARTY' and/or similar names and/or titles." The offer of payment made to WINS, then, is for the use of these terms—"ROCK 'N ROLL" and "ROCK 'N ROLL PARTY"—in connection with Freed's promotional efforts.[78] This remarkable document shows just how valuable the phrase "rock 'n' roll" had become in a short time to Freed and his employer; and further demonstrates that live music was a central medium through which the "rock 'n' roll" title became affixed to the music it came to represent.

That Freed was ahead of the curve in latching onto the "rock 'n' roll" label at this time is clear from the fact that all the major trade papers—Bi*ll*board, *Cash Box* and *Variety*—characterized the music presented at Freed's Rock 'n' Roll Jubilee Ball as rhythm and blues, not rock 'n' roll, a classification that also reflected the fact that all the artists on the bill were African American. *Billboard*'s focus was squarely on the bottom line, noting the $24,000 gross for the two shows and the fact that Freed had sold out tickets for both St. Nicholas appearances before the doors had opened for the first night.[79] *Cash Box* waxed more enthusiastically about the show itself and was especially struck by the size and character of the crowd that attended the event. The anonymous *Cash Box* writer observed:

> A total of about 12,000 people jammed the hall on both nights. When we say jammed we must add that the word hardly describes the solid mass that stood for five hours to see the wonderful r & b show that Freed had arranged. Seen from above, the enthusiastic teeners seemed to be jelled into one swaying body with thousands of heads.[80]

Strikingly, given the uproar over the racially mixed character of concert audiences throughout the 1950s, there is no mention of the racial breakdown of the crowd. For *Cash Box* the defining element was not race but youth and, joined by their age and their excitement for the music on display, the teenage crowd appears as a single unified mass.

In other instances such an undifferentiated mass audience might appear threatening; indeed, the rock 'n' roll audience was often held up as an example of the most negative aspects of mass culture, which many observers in the 1950s took to be a force for cultural decline.[81] Here though it is a cause for celebration, as the crowd's main characteristics appear to be their enthusiasm and adoration for Freed and the many performers who took the stage. That enthusiasm in turn got passed along to the artists themselves, leading to a final number that "lasted about half an hour" and "was rocked in the atmosphere of a revival meeting." Continued the *Cash Box* account:

> With Joe Turner at the mike and Fats Domino at the piano, the entire troupe returned to the stage for a closing that was without parallel. Singers and instrumentalists danced, dancers and singers grabbed instruments and instrumentalists, and dancers sang. Alan Freed and his lovely wife, Jackie, jitterbugged and the kids went wild. An exhausting but thrilling experience.[82]

Even Morris Levy was swept up with the excitement of the evening. In his recollection, "The ceiling was actually dripping from the moisture. It was *raining* inside the St. Nicholas Arena. I'm not exaggerating."[83]

Writing in *Variety*, Herm Schoenfeld also avoided any direct mention of the racial composition of the audience at the St. Nicholas Arena. However, the tenor of his article made it clear that Freed's debut as a New York dance and concert promoter had the impact it did not just because of the size of the crowd but because of its character—later estimated to have been split almost evenly between black and white concertgoers.[84] Under the headline, "R&B Big Beat in Pop Music," Schoenfeld took the success of Freed's shows as an indication of a larger sea change: "Once limited to the Negro market, the r&b influence has now crossed all color lines to the general pop market."[85] That it was a concert event, and not the crossover success of a particular record or set of record releases, that prompted such a proclamation further certifies that developments in the live music realm were critical in pushing rock 'n' roll forward to broader public attention.

Otherwise Schoenfeld's account reinforced that of the *Cash Box* report. The audience was identified above all by its youth, as "kids" who not only seem to appreciate the "noise" generated by the performers but take the music as a cue to make noise of their own "with a shattering repertoire of whistles, hoots and mitt-pounding." When Schoenfeld says of the dynamic at work in the relationship between the music and the fans, that "the combos based their arrangements on a bedrock repetitive rhythm that seemed to hypnotize kids into one swaying, screaming mass," there is an undertone of anxiety at the specter of mass culture missing from the *Cash Box* communiqué.[86] Nonetheless, Schoenfeld ultimately comes away from the event struck by the sheer energy on display in the music, the "frantic hoofing" of the dancers, and from Freed himself, whom he characterized as "a rhythm & blues evangelist" whose dedication was evident in the fact that on the radio, he routinely favored records by black artists and generally ignored covers of r&b records by white pop stars, judging them pale imitations of the "real" thing.[87]

If the Moondog Coronation Ball might be considered the live music event that kicked off the rock 'n' roll era and anticipated much that would follow, Freed's "Rock 'n' Roll" Jubilee Ball was the first rock 'n' roll show as such, or least the first for which we have such clear documentation. Each show, in a sense, was a sort of debut for Freed, and each served to further advance his notoriety as one of the most savvy and extroverted promoters to have arisen in conjunction with new musical trends. Both events also shone an exclusive spotlight on African American artists who remained at the heart of Freed's radio and concert programming alike. The two performances diverged significantly, though, in the racial composition of their audiences, and not coincidentally also in the way those audiences were represented to the public through corresponding media accounts. In 1952, the almost exclusively African American audience for the Moondog Coronation Ball sent shockwaves through the local Cleveland press that resonated nationally as well. Rarely had such a large crowd of African Americans turned out for such an event, and the unrest that attended the show can be taken as an index of the uncertainty and excitement that resulted when a mass of young people asserted their prerogative to take up space in public. Observers also stressed the charge of enthusiasm that audiences brought to the "Rock 'n' Roll" Jubilee Ball, but nowhere was there the suggestion that these crowds were out of control. The mix of white and black concertgoers in the latter instance contributed to the high pitch of excitement at the show without subsuming or overwhelming the performance, and commentators treated the audience more squarely as a sign that a new market was opening, with Freed leading the way toward capitalizing on the opportunities it might offer. Yet the fear that the rock 'n' roll crowds drawn by Freed could tilt toward disorder never disappeared, and as his concert promotion career progressed his ability, and willingness, to control the audiences that attended his shows became increasingly subject to question.

The Big Beat

Following upon the success of the St. Nicholas shows, Freed's promotional endeavors assumed a predictable pattern. Holidays became points on the calendar when Freed would stage a series of shows in succession, usually lasting for about a week, sometimes two. In February there were the birthdays of Washington and Lincoln; in March or April there was Easter; in July there was Independence Day; in September there was Labor Day; and then at the end of the year there was the Christmas and New Year's holiday. Tying his shows to times of the year already set aside for festivity enhanced the sense that each Freed show was a special occasion, but it had practical value as well, since each of these points on the calendar coincided with a time when young people would have a break from school and were more available to partake of Freed's offerings. The rhythm of Freed's concert calendar was shaped by the life patterns of his target demographic in an unusually pronounced way.

For venues Freed began concentrating more on movie theaters, starting with his first promotion after the St. Nicholas performances, which took place at the Paramount Theater in Brooklyn. Theater managers, who had been losing audiences to the new entertainment technology of television, saw that staging shows of the likes put on by Freed was a crucial way to bring young audiences back into the theaters. Meanwhile, the theaters offered the advantages of a ready-made infrastructure for putting on a show; as the British tour manager Jef Hanlon explained, in a comment that could also apply to the US context, "The outlook was the cinema circuits 'cause they had seats, they had box offices, they had a stage, they had stage lighting, they had stage lighting switchboards . . . So they were equipped and that's where they went."[88] Once Freed began a film career of his own, with the 1956 release of *Rock Around the Clock*, movie theaters fulfilled an additional purpose of allowing tie-ins between his personal appearances and live music promotions and his larger media presence. Interestingly, Freed did not typically harness his live promotions to the films in which he appeared—when movies accompanied his package shows they were typically B-movie dramatic fare that served largely as filler on the program. Most likely this was because the double attraction of a Freed movie and a Freed show would have cut down overall revenue since the films could draw audiences without the musical performances and vice versa. Still, Freed did organize personal appearances at several New York theaters for the opening of the movie, *Rock, Rock, Rock!* in December 1956, bringing Chuck Berry and singer Connie Francis along to meet fans and help plug the attraction.[89]

More to the point, with the release of four films between December 1956 and April 1958, playing at theaters in New York and around the US, movie theaters became a primary space through which Freed's standing as the leading rock 'n' roll impresario of his day assumed national proportions well before he organized a tour on anything like a national scale. This was even more the case because each of Freed's four main starring vehicles—*Rock, Rock, Rock!*; *Don't Knock the Rock*; *Mr. Rock and Roll*; and *Go, Johnny, Go!*— effectively featured him emceeing a cinematic package show. The plots for each of these films were notoriously threadbare, usually revolving around some sort of manufactured conflict between parents or town elders and "the kids" over the latter's choice of music, which was always rock 'n' roll. To the extent that these films held together it was through the sheer force of the performances offered by the likes of Chuck Berry, Frankie Lymon and the Teenagers, Little Richard, and the many others that lip-synched their way through their hit selections, in many cases demonstrating surprising charisma before the camera while giving moviegoers an energetic visual complement to the pre-recorded songs.

The location of the New York theaters where Freed held his package shows alternated between Brooklyn and midtown Manhattan. One area that remained off-limits where concert promotions were concerned was Harlem. We have already seen that Harlem DJ Willie Bryant expressed consternation at Freed's entry into the New York radio market. In the live music realm, another African American DJ based in Harlem—Tommy "Dr. Jive" Smalls, who appeared on the air on WWRL—staked the strongest claim to Harlem as a territory for promoting R&B package shows and for a time presented significant competition to Freed's own endeavors. Smalls arrived in New York in the early 1950s after getting his start in radio on a small station in Savannah, Georgia; and upon arriving up North, was mentored by the veteran African American DJ Douglas "Jocko" Henderson, who built a significant reputation as a live music emcee and promoter in his own right.[90] On the night that Freed opened his first engagement at the Brooklyn

Paramount Theater, April 10, 1955, Smalls held his own "Dr. Jive Ball" at Harlem's Rockland Palace featuring a roster of artists that included Roy Hamilton, the Buddy Johnson orchestra with Ella Johnson, the Cadillacs, and according to *Billboard*, a surprise appearance by Billie Holiday.[91] It would not be the last time that Smalls and Freed would have competing shows at the same time and while Freed's shows typically garnered the larger share of the grosses and publicity, Smalls made it clear that his white counterpart did not have a monopoly on the New York market for R&B and rock 'n' roll performances.

Smalls gained his greatest notoriety in connection with the Apollo Theater, the historic venue that by the 1950s stood at the top of the crop of urban black theaters that existed as a higher-class complement to the more modest bars and restaurants that comprised the chitlin' circuit. At the time that Smalls began to promote shows at the Apollo, R&B artists had already begun to make their way onto the theater's programs. In fact, the overwhelming success of R&B acts brought about a major change in the way the theater assembled its bills. From the time of its christening in 1934 until the early 1950s, the Apollo retained a variety show format that was a holdover from vaudeville. A turning point came with the August 1949 engagement at the theater by an up-and-coming African American singing group called the Orioles, led by the talented vocalist Sonny Till. Although they were not the headliner but only listed as an "extra attraction" on the week's bill, by the second day of their engagement lines to see the Orioles overwhelmed the theater's capacity.[92] From that time forward, Apollo owner Frank Schiffman and his son Bobby came to realize that the appeal of singing acts like the Orioles justified eliminating the other kinds of acts that comprised the typical variety bills; and with the promotional help of Smalls, the theater began a policy of featuring R&B revues modeled after the package shows that had been gaining ground nationally.[93] By the fall of 1956 the elder Schiffman acknowledged Smalls' impressive success with the R&B packages he brought to the Apollo, telling the *Chicago Defender* that the DJ had "drawn $35,000 worth of admissions each of the 10 times he [had] appeared there during the past 18 months."[94] Although Smalls' career, like Freed's, would be curtailed by allegations brought against him in the payola investigations of 1959–1960, the work he did in building the Apollo as a primary venue for rhythm and blues would deeply influence the theater's subsequent history.

* * *

February 1957 saw the greatest convergence of combined rock 'n' roll promotional activities in New York City and in many regards marked the high point of Freed's own concert-giving career. During a stretch beginning on February 19th, New York would see Jocko Henderson host a rock 'n' roll stage show at the Loew's State Theater on Broadway, the first such show held at that venue; Tommy Smalls bring another of his R&B revues to the Apollo; and Alan Freed oversee a week-long stint at the Paramount Theater in Times Square.[95] Freed, in this instance, presented a live package in conjunction with the newly released film in which he starred, *Don't Knock the Rock*; and the double attraction drew record-breaking box office to the Paramount despite the competition he faced from Henderson and Smalls.

Headlines appearing in major urban newspapers captured the sensational attention given to Freed's engagement at the Paramount: "Times Sq. Rock 'n' Rolls to Wild Teenage Beat," said the *Boston Globe*; "Rock 'n' Roll Addicts Take Over Times Sq.," noted the *Chicago Tribune*; "Rock-Roll Fans Mob Paramount, Set off Bedlam," exclaimed the *New York Herald Tribune*; while the *New York Times* observed, "Rock 'n' Roll Teen-Agers Tie up the Times Square Area."[96] Although Freed had drawn substantial crowds to his shows many times previously, the sheer fact that he had such success in Times Square—the nerve center of American entertainment and media—made his engagement a national news item in a way that had never quite happened before. Yet the crowds were also large and very visible, extending well beyond the confines of the theater and taking up several blocks in one of the most densely traveled urban settings in the country.

Photos in the *Chicago Tribune*, the *New York Herald Tribune*, and the *New York Times* portrayed the crowds on the street, with the *Times* presenting a dramatic aerial shot and the other two papers favoring a more on-the-ground approach. In all cases the most striking detail was the police barricades being used to keep the members of the crowd in order, and the accompanying reports of police presence in and outside the theater, as can be seen in Figure 6.5, with the *Times* estimating that some one-hundred seventy-five New York police officers were brought in to contain the threat of any possible disruption that a mass of young people was believed to pose. Also visible from these photos, and others showing the action in the theater, was just how much the character and complexion of Freed's audiences had changed by 1957. In the *Chicago Tribune* photo, one black face stands out amidst a sea of white concertgoers standing in line. An interior shot

Figure 6.5 Young fans line the streets of midtown Manhattan awaiting the chance to see the movie, *Don't Knock the Rock*, accompanied by a live rock 'n' roll presentation promoted by Alan Freed at the Paramount Theater, February 23, 1957. Courtesy of Underwood Archives/Getty Images.

published by the *New York Herald Tribune* showed a few more black faces scattered among a predominantly white crowd near the Paramount stage, including two standing at the front. Freed's selection of artists remained strongly tilted toward African American performers at the time—the lineup at the Paramount for the week featured a predominantly black cast of musicians with Ruth Brown, Frankie Lymon and the Teenagers, the Cadillacs, and the Platters as the lead attractions.[97] Yet the growth of his audience was clearly fed by the swelling ranks of white teenagers who were drawn to rock 'n' roll as the style assumed greater presence on a local and national scale. This in a sense was the real subject of the various news stories that covered the event of Freed's opening at the New York Paramount, for as he had before, Freed's ability to draw a crowd made the scope of rock 'n' roll 's appeal concrete in a way that mounting record sales and radio audiences had not.

Edith Evans Asbury, writing in the *New York Times*, best conveyed the scene at the Paramount, with a focus squarely on the audience:

They began lining up at 4 A.M. to see the show at the Paramount Theater. It wasn't until eighteen and a half hours later—at 10:30 P.M.—that the last of the line entered the theater. Late arrivals continued buying tickets, however, until the box office closed shortly after 1 A.M ... A theater spokesman said that 15,220 patrons had attended the six stage and seven movie shows between 8 A.M. and 1 A.M. The attendance figure and receipts of $29,000 set opening day records for the thirty-one-year-old theater, the spokesman said.[98]

The Paramount had a history of hosting performances that were retrospectively seen as turning points in the history of popular music and youth culture: Benny Goodman in 1937, Frank Sinatra in the early 1940s. Freed's opening there joined this longer history and, at least in terms of sheer numbers, superseded it. The fact that throughout the day of February 22, while some 3,600 might be admitted into the Paramount for a single show, another several thousand young people stood their ground outside the theater on the city's sidewalks for hours on end waiting their turn, was taken by reporters as a sign of the powerful, almost disturbing dedication that these young fans had toward rock 'n' roll and toward Freed in particular. Adding to the imperative that the crowd be kept under close watch was the rhythm of the day's entertainment, whereby shows were held sequentially in roughly two-and-a-half to three-hour intervals from morning until late at night. Although separate admission was charged for each show, many in the audience chose to stay in the theater from one performance to the next, a problem that was only resolved when Freed told the crowd that if they went outside they would be greeted by the show's stars, who did in fact wave to the audience from windows above the street while dropping pieces of paper with their autographs on them.[99]

Readers looking for details concerning the musical side of the day's performances would be searching in vain. The absence of any but the most cursory discussion of the music that drew these masses of young fans is striking and, as John Jackson notes, was an index of just how much the major news media failed to understand the core appeal of rock 'n' roll.[100] Still, curious elements of the performances do come through: that the Paramount, for example, had a distinctive stage that would rise from underground when the "live" portion of the show was about to begin, and would then sink back down when transitioning to the showing of the film, *Don't Knock the Rock*.[101] Other qualities resonated with the earlier reports that had emanated from Freed's stand at the St. Nicholas Arena two years before, such as the general excitability of the audience, whose persistent screaming, hand clapping, foot stamping, and whistling added a participatory dimension to the performances that was clearly part of the appeal for the young people in attendance.[102]

Dancing became another means for the members of the audience to become part of the action themselves and served as way to break free of the constraints imposed by the fixed seats and aisles of the theater's layout. Standing on seats and dancing in the aisles was widespread and became a particular target of police efforts to exert control over concertgoers. Reporting on day two of the Paramount engagement, *New York Times* reporter Edith Evans Asbury noted that police turned flashlights on theater patrons who stood on their seats and repeatedly ushered dancers out of the aisles. However, members of the audience persisted in their efforts to enjoy themselves in ways they saw fit. By Asbury's description: "After each stage show, as Mr. Freed and the orchestra dropped slowly from view on the sinking stage, the audience burst into the aisles and surged forward. A line of shoulder-to-shoulder policemen along the front of the stage restrained the boys and girls from leaping into the pit and onto the descending stage."[103] A year previous, white audience members in Birmingham, Alabama, had breeched the boundary between the stage and the floor to wage an assault on the black pop star Nat "King" Cole. At the Paramount in New York, the stakes were not so starkly defined. Audience members certainly showed no signs of antagonism toward the artists. Instead, the police themselves became a target of resistance for the simple fact that they sought to impose their own idea of order upon a music event designed to accommodate a different standard of conduct. That Freed himself deliberately cultivated, and catered to, this different standard could be garnered from his statements made when interviewed backstage: "I see those scrubbed faces looking up at me from the orchestra, and I know they are like my own kids. If they want to jump and clap hands, that's all right. If the theater gets a few broken seats, that's their problem."[104]

* * *

Freed's flippancy in the face of public concern was laudable to a good degree. He refused to back down when facing pressure, and he often appeared as a nearly tireless advocate for the music he promoted and the fans who flocked to it. Profiled in *Pageant* magazine in 1957, just months after his stand at the New York Paramount, Freed came across as a thoughtful populist who was concerned above all with defending the ability of young people to pursue their musical tastes as they saw fit. The writer, Theodore Irwin, captured something essential in the opening to the story, observing, "A noisy crowd is just a crowd... unless it's composed of adolescents and then it's labeled a 'riot.'"[105] Against this tendency to look with suspicion upon teenage behavior, Freed justified the appeal of rock 'n' roll to its young audience along various lines. He held that any music should be considered a positive influence and rejected the suggestion that rock 'n' roll had a morally negative impact: "Whether he's playing a ukulele or listening to rock 'n' roll records, a child is cutting his teeth on music, and I say he's on the path to finer music."

Yet the main value of rock 'n' roll was more basic according to Freed: it was music that young people discovered for themselves and made into their own. His concerts, in turn, provided the space where those same young people could enact their devotion in a way that connected them to others who felt the same in an atmosphere that was—ideally, at least—free of inhibition:

> Our in-person shows... are a wonderful outlet. When performers come on stage, the children jump and scream, drowning out the entertainers. Why? Because the kids have listened to records of those songs and know every note and word, so they do the performing. The show is in the audience, not on the stage... Their exuberance is rock 'n' roll jubilation... Yet our critics call rock 'n' roll madness. Is it madness for kids to enjoy themselves?[106]

There is no doubt that remarks such as these were largely self-serving. Suggesting that rock 'n' roll was something the kids found for themselves, Freed diminished his own influence upon their taste, thus seeking to remove himself as a target of criticism while explaining his success as a mere side effect of the authentic longings of contemporary youth. Nonetheless, Freed also recognized in important ways that the key to a good rock 'n' roll show was creating a setting in which the audience felt like it was contributing to the action—that it *was* the show. Freed may have profited from their enthusiasm, but he did not encourage passivity.

Many, however, distrusted Freed and feared what would happen if young people exercised too much autonomy. Since the time of the first Moondog Coronation Ball, confidence in Freed's concern for public safety and his capacity for successful crowd control had often wavered. His mounting success throughout the middle and later years of the 1950s only heightened these anxieties and followed him as he put together his first major touring package for the spring of 1958. Prior to this point, Freed had taken his shows beyond New York to nearby settings such as Boston and Providence, but he had never undertaken a full-fledged tour on the order of those organized by Irvin Feld. Now, he would be going head-to-head with Feld, who took his own latest package on tour concurrently. From the moment the two tours were announced, commentators envisioned a sort of battle of the titans of rock concert promotion. Ren Grevatt, reporting for *Billboard*, suggested that the competing demand for top artists could cause difficulties for Feld and Freed in booking the shows, and predicted that the artists would come out ahead for the ability to play one opportunity against the other to receive top pay.[107] Writing in the same publication a month later, Bob Rolontz confirmed that talent costs were inflated by as much as 20 percent due to the direct competition between the two promoters, and stressed the high financial stakes at issue, which indicated the overall growth of the rock 'n' roll concert field: "A tour that goes well can gross from $10,000 to $15,000 per night on the average, and more on two-a-night stands at the large arenas that the shows play today. This means that if all goes well, the two rock 'n' roll shows could each gross well over $500,000, and the Feld show [which was due to be on the road for several weeks longer] . . . could conceivably hit $1,000,000."[108]

Freed's tour, which would be conducted in partnership with the Shaw Artists Corporation booking agency, would go out under the heading, "The Big Beat."[109] "The Big Beat," like "rock 'n' roll," was a phrase that Freed had been using on-air and in published statements for some time. At a moment when controversy surrounding "rock 'n' roll" and Freed's place in promoting it had grown, his adoption of the phrase seemed like a move to distance himself from the more widely known term—something that *Billboard* suggested later in the year.[110] Opening at the Brooklyn Paramount on March 28, 1958, the tour concentrated heavily on dates in the Northeast and Midwest, scheduled to hit various cities in Connecticut and Pennsylvania, going as far south as Baltimore; then move through Ohio, Michigan, southern Canada, Illinois, and Wisconsin; and further west to Iowa, Nebraska, Kansas, and Oklahoma, before returning to the Northeast for shows in Massachusetts, Connecticut, Rhode Island, and upstate New York. The South, then, remained largely outside the orbit of Freed's efforts, as did the West Coast. As for the tour's lineup, it was one of the strongest Freed had ever fielded as well as one of the most diverse. There were effectively three headliners on the tour: Jerry Lee Lewis, Chuck Berry, and Buddy Holly and the Crickets. The talent was hardly all concentrated at the top, though. Frankie Lymon, Screamin' Jay Hawkins, Larry Williams, and black female singing group the Chantels also appeared on the bill, along with a preponderance of white male singing groups—Danny and the Juniors, Billy Ford and the Thunderbirds, Dickey Doo and the Don'ts. Rounding out the lineup were Jo-Ann Campbell, the Pastels, Ed Townsend, and the ever-present Alan Freed Rock 'n' Roll Orchestra.[111]

For the first several weeks of the tour, two stories dominated media reports. First was the usual accent on the boisterous character of the performances and the corresponding enthusiasm of the audiences in attendance. Jerry Lee Lewis, who at the time was riding high with a string of recent hit records released by the Sun label, was most often spotlighted as the artist who stirred the greatest response among concertgoers, as in the colorful account of a Dayton, Ohio, reporter:

> The most thunderous applause, of course, came when the show's top star, Jerry Lee Lewis, swung into action, this consisting largely of swinging his thick mane of yellow hair in a peculiar backward all-shook-up motion and gyrating his limbs. And the crowd went wild, letting loose with piercing screams, shouts and whistles, actually dancing in the aisles where possible and standing on the seats and yelling and clapping hands to a fare you well.[112]

Lewis' presence on the tour was not without its complications. Always a brash personality, he continually jockeyed for position with the other artists on the bill and, by many accounts, had a particularly fierce rivalry with Chuck Berry that turned ugly when Lewis directed a racial slur against his African American counterpart.[113] Such behind-the-scenes tensions compounded the difficult financial reality that became apparent as the tour proceeded, which was the second major news thread to emerge. After a month of being on the road in competition with Irvin Feld's "Biggest Show of Stars for 1958" tour, spokespersons for both tours admitted that earnings had been below expectations. A representative for Feld said you "could flip a coin" as to whether the tour would turn a profit, while the Freed enterprise was said to be "maybe a few dollars in front." A third tour, called the "Rhythm and Blues Cavalcade of '58," was pulled from the road entirely.[114] It appeared that, for the time being at least, the market for rock 'n' roll package shows had reached a saturation point.

A different sort of trouble came to the surface when the "Big Beat" tour came to Boston on Saturday, May 3. Boston had been a site of conflict for Freed in the past; city authorities had often wielded a heavy hand in seeking to control youth culture, and a stabbing incident that followed a Freed-sponsored concert there a year earlier, in April 1957, had led to crackdown against rock 'n' roll shows that was only recently lifted at the time of the "Big Beat" appearance.[115] Police presence in and outside of Boston was prominent at Freed's shows from early on, and grew along with the size of the crowds he drew as happened during his February 1957 engagement in New York's Times Square; but Boston police used particular force in seeking to contain the behavior of the audiences that attended Freed's shows. The stage was thus set for a confrontation that would have wide-ranging repercussions for Freed's career and for rock 'n' roll as a medium of live performance.

That night, several thousand young concertgoers packed into the Boston Arena, where they stood on seats, danced in the aisles, and issued all manner of exclamations to enact their involvement in the music emanating from the stage. According to John Jackson, some who were in attendance sensed an undercurrent of tension within the audience that was stronger than usual and possibly stemmed from the presence of some of the city's neighborhood gangs.[116] By the account of the *Boston Globe*, though, Boston Arena manager Paul Brown became aggravated not because of any unusual threat but due to the typical behavior exhibited by rock 'n' roll concert audiences. Annoyed that the crowd ignored orders to step off their seats and move out of the aisles as soon as the police turned their backs, Brown claimed that he ordered the house lights to be turned on against Freed's wishes—a maneuver meant to make the crowd more easily subject to surveillance. Brown described Freed's response with frustration: "So what did Freed do but apologize over the microphone for the bright lights and added, 'It looks like the police in Boston don't want you kids to have any fun.'"[117] According to Brown, Boston Mayor John Hynes, and members of the city's police department, this statement had the effect of fomenting an increase in the crowd's unruliness, which then spilled outside the Arena upon the conclusion of the show. In the aftermath, a wave of violent crime was said to have occurred, perpetrated by "satin-jacketed" gangs who had been in attendance; one young man, Albert Reggianni, was hospitalized with multiple stab wounds to the chest.[118]

What ensued was a classic example of a moral panic. Freed was indicted by the City of Boston on charges of inciting a riot, and secondary charges of promoting anarchy in violation of a Suffolk County statute.[119] Subsequent Freed appearances in Troy, New York, New Haven and New Britain, Connecticut, and Newark, New Jersey, were canceled; a show in Providence was allowed to take place but Freed himself did not take part.[120] Even Irvin Feld suffered as a result, as city officials in his home base of Washington, DC, denied his request to bring his "Biggest Show of Stars for 1958" to Griffith Stadium.[121] While the controversy swelled, Freed unexpectedly resigned from his position at WINS, claiming that the station did not adequately stand in his defense. He also categorically denied making the statement that was attributed to him and rejected the suggestion that he had explicitly spoken against the police to the audience gathered at the Boston Arena—a claim that was supported by several eyewitnesses, although not without some dispute as to his culpability. Explaining his actions to the *Boston Globe*, he said: "These kids in Boston were the greatest . . . But the police were terrible. They were brutal. They grabbed kids and shoved them back . . . I was shocked. After all, I've got teenagers myself."[122] As he did so frequently, Freed assumed a paternalistic posture, portraying himself as a defender of the young people in his audience, someone who did what he could to ensure that their right to a good time would not be unduly restrained by adult authority. In the end, Freed would be exonerated of all charges against him in the Boston episode. By then, however, the damage had been done to his credibility, and the payola investigation that led to the final decline of his career was already underway.

Trying to make sense of the events that took place in Boston, *Billboard* writer Ren Grevatt acknowledged Freed's irresponsibility in handling the situation, but also noted that the police contributed to the hostile tone of the proceedings. Grevatt quoted Freed's longtime business associate, Jack Hooke, who said that before any trouble had started during the Boston performance, a policeman on the scene approached Freed brusquely and told him, "We don't like your kind of music here." Grevatt further posited, "Some have called the whole episode a type of witch hunt in which an individual became a symbol and a target," anticipating the manner in which Freed would serve as an all-too-ready target when the payola hearings got underway a year later.[123] Offering another perspective was concert attendee Wallace

Vaine, an adult rock 'n' roll fan who had been at the Boston Arena show and wrote to the *Boston Globe* to dispute the most common account of the night's happenings. Vaine rejected the suggestion that Freed was responsible for whatever violence or disorder had occurred, claiming that the source of trouble was primarily a small group of "hoodlums" who were acting out of a basic impulse to sow conflict. Much of the blame, for Vaine, also lay with the venue, which he found unsuitable to the nature of the music and spirit of the audience. As he explained: "Mayor Hynes constantly referred to Alan Freed's show as a dance although it was actually more of a concert with dancing forbidden. This is ridiculous. You would not expect people to sit quietly for 2 ½ hours listening to tangoes, rumbas, or foxtrots. Why should you expect them to for rock 'n' roll, which is much more animated?"[124]

The underlying confusion in Vaine's observations speaks to a source of tension that has rarely been acknowledged when considering the conflict and controversy that surrounded rock 'n' roll during the mid- to late 1950s. Was Freed's show a dance or a concert, and what difference did it make to construe it as one or the other? Certainly, there were many instances when rock 'n' roll performances challenged the social and political imperative to maintain racial segregation and restrict African American access to public space. Compounding this challenge along racial lines was the threat perceived to accompany the occupation of public settings by masses of young people who appeared to be acting with undue autonomy and without proper adult supervision. These two points of tension, taken together, created a widely felt need among civic authorities and venue managers alike to maintain order at all costs, which meant in practice that efforts to police audience behavior at rock 'n' roll shows such as those promoted by Freed became fundamental and at times, threatened to overwhelm the entertainment value of the shows.

Meanwhile, audiences continued to grow, and to accommodate them Freed and fellow promoters like Irvin Feld sought larger venues to maximize their returns. A decade before became a recognized phenomenon, "arena rock" or something like it had already become an entrenched phenomenon in the most profitable field of rock 'n' roll concert promotion. Yet this move into the arena happened, in effect, too early. Arenas often lacked the infrastructure to properly stage such events, arena managers were just as often socially uncomfortable with the nature of the events and the crowds they drew, and audiences demanded a degree of freedom of movement that these arenas—and analogous spaces such as movie theaters—were not built to allow. The implosion of Alan Freed's career as concert promoter resulted from all these factors, but the heart of the problem laid in the gulf that existed between how the crowds that attended Freed's shows wanted to experience them and what the venues themselves would accommodate, as physical spaces and as enterprises governed by a particular set of controls and expectations about how audiences should behave.

7

Crowds, Chaos, and Community

Music Festivals from Newport to New Orleans

Five people signed the founding articles of association of the Newport Jazz Festival, or "The Jazz Festival of Newport, R.I., Inc." as it was called in the document dated April 28, 1954. Three of them—William P. Sheffield, J. Russell Haire, and W. Ward Harvey—were lawyers who presumably lent their names out of support for a worthy cause. Two, Louis Lorillard and his wife Elaine, were the primary protagonists behind the instigation of the festival, Newport residents who felt the need to enliven the resort town's cultural offerings. One name notably absent was that of George Wein, the jazz musician turned impresario who had been planning with the Lorillards to produce the festival, but whose name would not appear on any official documents until the minutes of the first board meeting held on May 10, 1954, when he was voted a place on the organization's board of directors.[1] Wein would become perhaps the single most significant figure in the history of American music festivals from the staging of the first Newport Jazz Festival later that summer throughout much of the latter twentieth century and continues to be active at this writing. Yet he did not work singlehandedly and the vision that informed the founding of the Newport Jazz Festival—the event that set the modern evolution of US music festivals in motion—was a shared one.

That vision was spelled out in the third article of the document, which read:

> Said corporation is constituted for the purpose of promoting an interest in music; conducting and holding music festivals, jazz band festivals, band concerts and other musical concerts and other entertainments, for the entertainment, amusement, recreation and pleasure of the public; conducting and holding musical competitions and other musical festivals and generally promoting the interest of the public in music; raising funds for the establishment of scholarships for the assistance of talented persons interested in music; and generally conducting and promoting various functions, fetes, fairs, festivals and concerts, without profit, for charitable purposes.[2]

The corporation established to produce the Newport Jazz Festival was therefore a nonprofit entity. Its status as such was telling. Among other things, it suggests that the principals did not need to reap profit from their endeavors. (This would not apply to Wein, though, who struggled throughout his concert promoting career with the tensions between the nonprofit structures in which he often worked and his need, and desire, to earn money for himself.) As it was first imagined, and to a degree as it was carried out in its early years, the Newport Jazz Festival was at root a philanthropic enterprise.

For the festival and its founders to make jazz into the object of philanthropy was a significant innovation. Jazz throughout most of its history had been viewed as commercial music, not needing the kind of patronage bestowed upon classical music and other forms of "high art." However, circumstances had changed by the mid-1950s. We have seen that jazz, by the mid-twentieth century, was established as a form of concert music. It retained a significant commercial foothold, but by 1954 the contemporary tide was beginning to turn, with rock 'n' roll just over the horizon. The Newport Jazz Festival marked a new phase in seeking to bestow upon jazz a kind of cultural legitimacy. Using the structure of a festival had a very different resonance than the move of jazz into the concert hall. The festival format was less codified than concert presentations and gave more room for artists and especially for audiences to make their own meanings out of the event. When in 1960 the Newport Jazz Festival had its own version of the disruptions that had characterized the Moondog Coronation Ball, Alan Freed's Boston concert, and many other events of the past decade, it became clear that festivals were not a medium in which a strict division between cultural spheres or music genres and their audiences could be upheld.

That a non-classical music festival might be organized as a nonprofit undertaking was an idea that gained wider currency. Another of Wein's enterprises, the Newport Folk Festival, assumed a similar shape and pursued its mission with decided rigor. Even in rock, the pivotal 1967 Monterey Pop Festival was established as a nonprofit foundation with objectives resembling those announced by Newport Jazz, seeking to promote "any project which would 'tend to further national interest in and knowledge and enjoyment of popular music.'"[3] Yet the rock festival, overall, would follow a different template. More often than not, the profit motive was operative with rock festivals. More to the point, rock festivals generally did not stake their claims to significance in the language of cultural elevation that music festivals built on the model of Newport had employed. Rock festivals of the late 1960s and early

1970s developed a different vocabulary infused by the burgeoning countercultural sensibilities of the era, which at its most idealistic cast rock not as a refined art but as an integral component of a whole, alternative way of life. Festivals, by this logic, were instantiations of a sort of ideal community—a perspective that rock fans, artists, and critics (and to a degree, promoters as well) inherited from the realm of folk festivals where a parallel notion that music was of, for, and by the people had taken hold.

In all the major realms in which music festivals took root during these years—jazz, folk, and rock—idealism mixed uneasily with the practical realities of presenting music on such a large scale, not to mention presenting it outdoors. The outdoor setting—whether in a park, a sports field, a patch of farmland, or an island—came to be a nearly taken-for-granted feature of music festivals as they evolved from the 1950s forward, and it mattered in two distinct ways. Festivals sought to bring musical forms typically experienced indoors into the open, and so retained and built upon a Romantic belief that encounters with nature could heighten aesthetic experience. The places where musical festivals happened, however, were hardly natural in any strict sense of the term. Jazz, folk, and rock all had significant technical requirements needed to make the outdoor locations where they were presented into settings where music could be heard and seen by the multitudes of fans who would be in attendance. In effect, the staging and sound reinforcement materials needed to produce music festivals on a scale of the Newport Jazz and Folk Festivals, the Atlanta Pop Festival, Woodstock, and New Orleans Jazz and Heritage Festival, along with scores of others, represented an updated case of what cultural historian Leo Marx called "the machine in the garden," technology in this case not intruding upon the natural environment but co-existing with it in apparent non-contradiction to make it more habitable.[4] More materially, festivals became a locus of technical innovation due to the heightened challenges involved in creating the conditions to put on a large-scale music event outdoors. Figures such as lighting and stage design specialist Chip Monck and sound engineer Bill Hanley played an integral role in establishing the specifications according to which festivals could succeed in holding audience attention through the combined effects of sound and spectacle. Hanley particularly personifies a kind of through-line of festival history unto himself, having produced the sound at one time or another at all of the above-named festivals.

Music festivals mattered to the larger development of American live music along multiple fronts in the two decades following the founding of the

Newport Jazz Festival. Most saliently, festivals helped to push the business of live music more and more toward large-scale production, laying the groundwork for the arena and stadium rock economy that is the subject of the following chapter. Because they so often had an aura of idealism surrounding them, however, music festivals could never be reduced to strictly commercial ventures. There is a definite line to be drawn between the festivals of the mid-twentieth century and the capital-intensive modes of live music production that followed, but these festivals represented a very different template for building an economy of scale based on singular events in a set location rather than the staging of shows that could be moved from one city to the next in rapid succession. The combination of scale and singularity gave festivals the aura they would come to possess and made them flash points for contests over cultural values that coursed through the musical styles put on stage.

What values were at stake in the major music festivals of the era? Reflecting on the riots that broke out at the 1960 Newport Jazz Festival, Scott Saul noted two prominent ways in which they were understood: "for musicians and music critics, it was a case study in the decadence that threatened jazz if its entrepreneurs pandered to the profit motive; and for other editorialists largely outside the jazz press, it was proof of the younger generation's inane, dangerous combustibility."[5] Writing about a very different instance of cultural conflict—the moment when Bob Dylan "went electric" at the 1965 Newport Folk Festival—Elijah Wald argued: "If there was tension on the grounds that weekend, it was not so much between acoustic tradition and electric modernity as between people excited to be part of that kind of huge sensational event [overall attendance at the festival had been more than 74,000] and people worried that their pilgrimage site was being overrun by pop fans and money-changers."[6] In jazz and folk alike—and in rock, where the influence of both would loom large—festivals came to stand for a host of tensions that characterized the social role of popular music in the post-war era.

Some of those tensions concerned the music itself. Should the music presented at festivals be of a more refined character or should it spotlight more untutored sorts of artists who represented a common and arguably more democratic sort of cultural practice? Should the more traditional or more modern elements of a given branch of music be most highlighted? Both questions resonated especially strongly in the fields of jazz and folk but for different reasons. Many of the tensions coursing through music festivals concerned the audience. What was the mix of older and younger segments of the listening public and how much should the festival cater to one or the other?

To what degree could festivals promote social heterogeneity at a time when struggles over racial inequality and the desegregation of public space were paramount? Should the crowds attending music festivals be treated mainly as spectators, there to listen and watch with attention, or should they be encouraged to take an active, participatory role in the proceedings? Underpinning these various layers of concern, as both Wald and Saul suggest, was the matter of money. How much should it determine the shape of the popular arts? Even when they were staged as nonprofit enterprises, festivals generated concern about the influence of financial motives, whether in connection with wealthy benefactors or corporate interests. That these conflicts were experienced so profoundly before rock festivals as such became a phenomenon unsettles the most widely held perceptions of music festivals within which events like Monterey Pop and Woodstock have tended to overshadow all that came before. This chapter builds on the work of Saul, Wald, and others who have made the case that the music festival as a cultural phenomenon had been gathering force from the mid-1950s forward, and to argue for the importance of understanding that jazz, folk, and rock festivals are part of a common history.

What Makes a Festival?

Festivals, of course, were not new to the American musical landscape in the 1950s. Recall Patrick Gilmore's two massive Peace Jubilees of 1869 and 1872, discussed in chapter two. Neither was billed as a festival per se but both events had many of the aspects we associate with festivals: multiple days of music programmed as part of a single event; a unique musical setting (albeit in this case, not one situated outdoors); an emphasis on diversity of musical offerings that are nonetheless bound together under some unifying rubric; and an effort to stage an event of uncommon scale, in terms of both the number of performers on display and the number of audience members in attendance.[7] More generally, the US in the second half of the nineteenth century saw a mounting succession of music festivals. Choral festivals that gathered together regional singing societies at a common location became something of an institution by the early 1850s, enough to draw comment from John S. Dwight in an 1853 article whose simple title—"Musical Festivals"—belies its historically valuable content.[8] The previous year, 1852, saw the first substantial festival devoted to military brass bands held at Castle

Garden in New York City, where Jenny Lind had debuted to the American public only two years before.[9] Festivals dedicated to symphonic and orchestral music emerged more gradually but were given a significant boost by the Cincinnati May Festival inaugurated in 1873 under the music direction of the eminent German-American conductor Theodore Thomas, which historian Robert Vitz claims to have played a major role in building a wider audience for the Germanic symphonic tradition that was enshrined as the crux of the classical music canon in the later decades of the nineteenth century.[10]

One of the most influential nineteenth-century models for the long-term evolution of American music festivals came from abroad. Richard Wagner's establishment of the German town of Bayreuth as an outpost for the concentrated performance of his operatic works, first staged in 1876, offered a powerful instance of a music festival driven by intensive shared involvement in a discrete repertoire. Much of the commentary on Wagner's project in developing the Bayreuth opera house and accompanying festival has stressed his idea of the *Gesamtkunstwerk*, a vision of the artwork as an all-consuming blend of elements drawn from music, drama, dance, and poetry.[11] The setting of Bayreuth contributed significantly to the appeal that Wagner's long-running operatic festival came to exert as well. In his historical study of the Bayreuth Festival, Frederic Spotts remarked: "One of Wagner's shrewdest decisions was insisting that the Festival should be held in relative isolation. 'Island' is a word recurring again and again when artists try to explain Bayreuth's singular atmosphere. The seclusion has a remarkable psychological effect, not only encouraging total concentration on work but creating a remarkable familial spirit."[12] One might consider how much Spotts' observations about Bayreuth can be applied as well to a place like Newport, Rhode Island, and many other locations chosen to house American music festivals over time. Wagner in Bayreuth aspired to create a festival that was almost a world unto itself, and its relative remoteness combined with its annual, recurring character made it into a site of pilgrimage, someplace that Wagner devotees would want to return to year after year.[13]

Moving into the twentieth century, festivals devoted to art music remained among the most prominent such undertakings. In Europe, the Austrian town of Salzburg gave rise to two festivals in the early 1920s that represented the competing currents of early twentieth century musical culture. The Salzburg Festival, established in 1920, commemorated the town as the home of Mozart and sought to create a musical medium for enacting a conservative notion of cultural unification following the ravages of World War I. As detailed by music historian Michael Steinberg, "The Salzburg Festival and the cultural program it embodied were thus Austro-German . . . Catholic, and conservative," and the repertory was "grounded in a classical literary and aesthetic pantheon" that encompassed Mozart, Goethe, and festival founder, poet, and playwright Hugo von Hofmannsthal.[14] A chamber music festival held as part of the 1922 Salzburg Festival was the stimulus for the creation of the International Society for Contemporary Music, or ISCM, which held the first of what would become an annual series of festivals devoted to contemporary art music in Salzburg in 1923. Against the classicism of the principal Salzburg Festival, the ISCM festivals were aggressively focused on the new and the modern, and against the conservative nationalism that motivated Salzburg, the ISCM as an organization was motivated by an internationalist, cosmopolitan vision.[15] These competing tendencies—between local, national, and cosmopolitan; between tradition and modernity—would surface repeatedly as music festivals entered the era of mass participation in Europe and the US alike.

American modernists took inspiration from the ISCM festivals and other events in Europe to create the Yaddo festival, held on a secluded estate in Saratoga Springs, New York, that has become a celebrated artists' retreat. First held on April 30 and May 1, 1932, the Yaddo Music Festival would be presented several more times throughout the 1930s and intermittently until 1952. First programmed entirely by composer Aaron Copland, Yaddo eventually took in a broader range of perspectives in its repertoire choices, but especially at the outset the emphasis was on the work of living composers, with Copland's own music being featured alongside that of Charles Ives, Virgil Thomson, Roger Sessions, Roy Harris, and several others.[16] As at Bayreuth, the setting accounted for much of the special character and appeal. Music critic Irving Kolodin, reviewing the first Yaddo festival, stressed that the audience "heard these works under ideal circumstances; through the windows one could see a vast expanse of wooded hills beyond the even lawns that fringe the house. Here the doctrine of American music was preached, in sonatas and string quartets, to a group of listeners singularly engrossed and responsive."[17] Yaddo was a decidedly *un*-mass festival, catering to an elite and exclusive audience of composers, critics and new music enthusiasts who were part of an inner circle. It stood as an alternative to the large-scale outdoor classical music concerts presented at Lewisohn Stadium in New York, the Hollywood Bowl in Los Angeles, and several other major cities around the US that arose throughout the 1920s and 1930s where the programming philosophies of the major symphony orchestras and their musical directors held sway. Both settings—the popular, outdoor classical music concert and the exclusive rural retreat to showcase more select styles of American music making—influenced the shape of American festivals to come.

* * *

Music of a more vernacular sort was the focus of a different strain of festival development that grew during the first decades of the twentieth century. Folk music scholar Ronald Cohen locates the emergence of folk festivals in ethnic singing festivals among German and other immigrant communities in northern US cities from the 1850s forward.[18] A more self-conscious effort to present what was understood as folk music in a festival setting took hold in the Southern US some decades later. The Georgia Old-Time Fiddlers Convention, first held in Atlanta in 1913, built on a long-standing tradition of fiddling contests; but by framing fiddling as the embodiment of "old-time" traditional values, it situated this music as part of a historic cultural lineage that allowed white residents of the burgeoning New South metropolis to construct a shared past in the face of modernity. It was the first of several public Southern musical enterprises that portrayed traditional music—especially that associated with the region's Appalachian mountain residents—as the repository of an unvarnished Anglo-Saxon whiteness, the desire for which grew in a cultural and political atmosphere oriented toward the reinstatement of white supremacy and legal segregation.[19] Similar impulses underlay the Mountain Dance and Folk Festival founded by Bascom Lamar Lunsford in 1928 in Asheville, North Carolina; and the American Folk Song Festival created by Jean Thomas in Ashland, Kentucky, in 1930, which might stand as the first proper "folk" music festivals in the US that were named as such.[20] Crucially, both festivals expanded the range of music that was offered under the folk music heading beyond the confines of the fiddling convention, with considerable emphasis on ballad singing and string band performance as well as varieties of rural Southern dancing.

Following on the heels of the festivals in Asheville and Ashland was the White Top Folk Festival, first held in its Virginia mountain setting in 1931. White Top was formed out of the cooperation of folk music patron Annabel Morris Buchanan, businessman John Blakemore, and composer John Powell. Folklorist David Whisnant's account of the festival's history suggests that it was motivated by an impulse that was common to the festivals of the time, to find a medium beyond scholarly books and commercial recordings to publicize traditional music and culture. Observed Whisnant:

> A public festival . . . would bring the performers out of their isolated surroundings and place them before an appreciative audience. That approval would heighten the performers' sense of self-worth and pride in their imperiled culture. Confronted by the beauty and authenticity of the "real thing," the audience would be moved to forsake vulgar commercial imitations. If such an event were repeated enough times, the public would be reeducated and its taste refined and elevated.[21]

Elite patronage infused White Top with a set of values not far removed from those of the classical music concert hall. Evidence that the White Top festival presented folk music in a manner that was sympathetic with the aims of cultural elevation can be found in the enthusiastic reports about the festival's first years that appeared in *Musical America*, a publication that was almost exclusively oriented toward news of the classical music world. Buchanan herself filed the first such report in 1931, recounting a mix of musical contests in various styles of instrumental and vocal performance and lectures by recognized authorities including Powell and folklorist and Vanderbilt University professor George Pullen Jackson.[22] By the third year, 1933, attendance had grown to nearly twenty thousand, and among the guests was the first lady, Eleanor Roosevelt, whose appearance further legitimated the festival's mission. Jackson, writing that year's festival report, emphasized that the music on display represented a distinctly local, non-commercial set of traditional practices that could be traced back to "the cultural mists of the Anglos, Saxons, and Celts," further asserting how much folk festivals of the period placed primacy on the search for a purified form of cultural whiteness.[23]

A more broadly inclusive folk festival came about with Sarah Gertrude Knott's establishment of the National Folk Festival, first produced in April 1934. Knott, a native of Kentucky, was strongly influenced by her predecessors, especially Lunsford and his Mountain Dance and Folk Festival. More than those of the preceding festivals, however, Knott's approach was multi-ethnic, including Native Americans, European immigrant and laboring communities who were not of the South, and African Americans. Among the folklorists who took part in the early festivals was Zora Neale Hurston, and among the performers were the Fisk Jubilee Singers.[24] Compared to the other folk festivals that emerged in the late 1920s and early

1930s, the National Folk Festival treated folk performance as more of a theatrical endeavor, and Knott did not draw such strict lines between the traditional artists that appeared at the festival and the kind of rural Southern music that was released on commercial recordings. As a result, the festival was sometimes the target of criticism by figures such as Alan Lomax, who thought that Knott's conception of folk art was too inclusive, not in terms of the range of ethnic and racial groups featured but in terms of the quality of the artists and the degree to which they represented "authentic" regional cultures.[25] Nonetheless, Knott put forth an enduring folk festival model further distinguished by the fact that it did not occur in the same location year after year but regularly moved around, with the first festival in St. Louis, the second in Chattanooga, the third in Dallas, and so forth, this regional diversity compounding the relative diversity of the festival participants.

* * *

Certain elements were shared across the classical and folk music festivals that took root in the early twentieth century. In some cases—the Salzburg Festival, and all the folk festivals held in the US—music festivals functioned as vehicles for cultural preservation. The desire to preserve and maintain past cultural forms was, as many have observed, a distinctly modern impulse, shaped on both sides of the Atlantic by the destructive and socially unsettling impact exerted by World War I and later, the onset of the Great Depression. The latter phenomenon created the social conditions in which the first wave of widespread popular interest in folksong developed, which the folk festivals of the time anticipated and from which they benefited. All of these festivals worked to sanction, on some level, elite perspectives on cultural value. In the sphere of classical music this took shape through engagement with the question of whether the more historical or the more contemporary manifestations of music as art should be given greater support. In the folk music realm, as we have seen, elite patrons and "experts" in the form of academically trained folklorists or art music composers were invested with curatorial power to make choices about what elements of folk music should be represented in a given setting.[26] As disparate as the music presented at classical and folk music festivals may have been, their shared commitment to affirming the aesthetic value of white-identified musical forms and traditions was a manifestation of the degree to which they were shaped by socially dominant values. Yet the folk festivals still, crucially, built a new medium for the widespread appreciation of vernacular music made by non-professional artists and, in the

National Folk Festival especially, created a platform for representing some of the multiplicity of American regional and ethnic cultures that would be expanded upon by future festival producers.

New Thing at Newport

The elite patronage of early festivals carried over to the Newport Jazz Festival upon its founding in 1954. To set the festival in Newport situated it in a place best known as a resort for the very wealthy, where historic mansions stood as monuments to the acquisitiveness of the Gilded Age. Not that Newport was an entirely homogeneous community. Its year-round residents were more likely to be tied to the large US Navy base or to work in the shipbuilding industry that flourished there, and included a downwardly mobile working class. The wealthiest residents were those who came during the summer months, and the notion that Newport should host a summer music festival was largely designed for their benefit even though, as circumstances would show, the festival audience drew upon a far wider range of jazz fans and other tourists in search of a destination for summer recreation.

More telling than the demographics behind the Newport Jazz Festival were the comments attributed to the festival's founders that their primary inspiration came from the realm of classical music. *Down Beat*, reporting on preparations for the first festival, offered the following account: "The basic goal of the festival, according to the committee, is to establish jazz as an art form in the eyes of the American public . . . The idea of the festival is to make it an annual affair that will compare with different classical festivals that are presented throughout the country, similar to Tanglewood."[27] A nearly identical statement appeared in the program for the first festival: "The far-reaching objective of the jazz festival is to make Newport to jazz what Tanglewood is to classical music. The festival can and should become a focal point, an actual physical setting, in which jazz can flourish in its finest form."[28] Tanglewood was a likely point of reference. Motivated by the desire to create "an American Salzburg," it was an established New England music festival that catered to a similar population of wealthy summer residents in a relatively secluded setting.[29] Tanglewood also represented something of a synthesis of the two competing models of classical music festival or outdoor concert that had emerged in the early twentieth century: the concerts presented in the famous Shed were designed to have broad appeal and regularly drew four thousand or more listeners; but the instruction in composition, conducting, and performance offered through the Berkshire Music Center (opened in 1940) involved the participation of a far more select and exclusive group of master teachers and gifted students who constituted something of an inner circle.[30] To use Tanglewood as a model, then, suggested that the jazz festival at Newport was to be a place where putting the best of jazz on stage would coincide with serious jazz study.

This latter aspiration never fully took hold. Indeed, the environs of Tanglewood gave rise to something much closer to the kind of jazz education envisioned by the founders of the Newport Jazz Festival with the short-lived Lenox School of Jazz.[31] Still, it is important to note the contours of the vision that governed the Newport festival at its outset. Tanglewood and other classical music festivals were a primary point of reference because there was no real corollary in jazz to the kind of festival the Newport organizers sought to produce. Jazz concerts, although they were governed by similar objectives, were far more contained spatially and temporally, their programs limited to a single afternoon or evening in a fixed, enclosed setting. The Lorillards and George Wein—the key players in staging the festival—had something else in mind.

In his autobiography, Wein claims that his inspiration for programming the festival arose from the nights he spent hopping from one jazz club to another around Manhattan in the years after his discharge from the army in 1946: "I remembered my nights in New York City when I had started off in Greenwich Village at 8 P.M., gone to Harlem, and ended up seven hours later at 52nd Street . . . I heard Dixieland, big bands, swing, unique singers, and modern jazz . . . I'm sure that was what directed my concept of the first Newport Jazz Festival."[32] Wein, though, had also been promoting jazz shows in his own right since the late 1940s, had owned a popular Boston jazz nightclub since 1950, and in recent years had even taught a course on jazz history at Boston University. As a jazz-musician-turned-businessman, his vision of jazz was upwardly mobile, joining the pursuit of cultural legitimation to the pursuit of profit in a manner very much akin to that of his rival promoter, Norman Granz.

Like Granz, Sol Hurok, Alan Freed, and many of the promoters who would go on to reconfigure the live music economy in the arena rock era, Wein was a Jewish American who found the entertainment business to be a field of opportunity. Born in Lynn, Massachusetts, in 1925, and raised in the relatively affluent suburb of Newton, his father a physician, Wein admits that his life path was not especially marked by Alger-esque struggle.[33] He began playing piano at a young age and was leading his own jazz band by the time he was a teenager, a dedicated devotee of swing. Drafted into the army in 1944, upon his discharge he came to realize the difficulties of the working musician's life. Already committed to jazz, he saw that concert promotion might be a way to turn his musical enthusiasm into a source of livelihood. In 1949 he produced his first jazz concert in partnership with musician Edmond Hall. Presented at Jordan Hall, an auditorium at Boston's prestigious New England Conservatory, the program titled "From Brass Bands to Bebop" traced the historical evolution of jazz, by then a conventional framework for jazz concerts.[34] The evening was a sell-out and steeled Wein's resolve to continue along the concert promotion path.

Storyville, Wein's Boston nightclub, opened the following year, in 1950. Named after the fabled red-light district of New Orleans, it tapped into the popular mythology of the music's history, as would a second club he opened, Mahogany Hall. Yet Wein otherwise worked diligently to erase any associations between jazz and the underworld economy. Wein said of Storyville that it was "never a joint. We had no floor show, no drug dealers or resident hookers. We kept things clean."[35] He elaborated on the point in a 1957 profile authored by Nat Hentoff, the influential Boston jazz critic. Of Storyville, Wein claimed:

> At base, we are trying to break the distasteful reputation the term "night club" itself has to many people in Boston. I help do it by writing on jazz for the Boston *Herald*, by conducting a credit course in jazz at Boston university ... Another way we help dispel the unfavorable connotation of a "night club" is not to allow any concessions ... We also allow no unescorted women at the bar. We do not require a particular standard of dress by our patrons, but the tone of the room is such that a person feels out of place if he's not dressed properly.[36]

Wein's remarks are almost a blueprint for the ethos that had infused so much of the institutional culture of jazz by the mid-twentieth century, seeking to claim that the music deserved to be listened to with the respect and attentiveness that had historically been reserved for classical art music. His emphatic tone also stresses, though, that this effort remained a work in progress. Storyville was still a nightclub and audiences were disposed to want to order their drinks and talk through performances. Thus did Wein acknowledge,

"We do try to keep our audience quiet . . . But we also realize that if the performer himself can't basically hold the crowd, we can't hold it for him."[37] A similar balance of pragmatism and idealism would be necessary in his work with the Newport Jazz Festival, where the competing tendencies toward elevation and celebration (and intoxication) would also be in play.

Paying tribute to his collaborators, Louis and Elaine Lorillard, in the program for the 1958 Newport Jazz Festival, Wein called the couple "the first patrons of jazz." The three can be see together in Figure 7.1. He expanded on the significance of their support: "Jazz, like any art form, has need for patrons. Whether it be kings of old, vying with each other to have the greatest artists in their personal courts, or the friends of the Boston Symphony orchestra, or governmental subsidization of cultural activities, patrons are essential to artistic progress."[38] More than a source of financial support, the whole idea for the festival began with the Lorillards, and it was they who hired Wein as producer, on the strength of his reputation and advice they received from friends and associates including John Hammond. The Lorillards were, moreover, the

Figure 7.1 George Wein (left) with Elaine Lorillard (center) and Louis Lorillard, at the first Newport Jazz Festival in 1954. Courtesy of the *Newport Daily News*—USA Today Network.

reason why the festival was in Newport, and their social connections enabled the use of the elite Newport Casino tennis facility to host the festival the first year. Elaine Lorillard especially became an outspoken advocate for the festival and her perspective very much complemented that of Wein; both, from their different vantage points, had a vested interest in seeing jazz move up the ladder of social respectability. Mrs. Lorillard, as she was most often called in festival publicity, became an object of curiosity in her own right, the seeming incongruity of her support for jazz as a wealthy socialite in effect standing in for the paradoxes surrounding the festival at large. A description in a 1956 profile was typical: "Mrs. Lorillard... is both social and sociable but she is far from a rebel"; and yet having become drawn to jazz as a college student, she "embarked on a crusade to prove that jazz deserved something better than smoke-filled dives and zoot-suited patrons."[39]

* * *

It is worth pausing for a moment in recounting the history of the Newport Jazz Festival to consider its parallels with developments overseas. British scholar George McKay has located the emergence of modern UK festival culture in the decade of the 1950s. Jazz especially provided the soundtrack for the early British festival movement and the Beaulieu Jazz Festival, first staged in 1956, was an event of particular prominence. McKay's reconstruction of the early years of the Beaulieu Jazz Festival emphasizes its strongly pastoral elements and the way it gave rise to a "carnivalesque" atmosphere that allowed young participants to temporarily inhabit a sphere where the norms of everyday life were replaced by a more fluid set of social relationships. By his account: "Wild, pastoral living, self-policing, DIY music making, and a non-commercial economy—many of the ingredients of the free festival movement are glimpsed here up to a decade before its popularization in Britain."[40] Like Newport, the Beaulieu festival was created in large part due to elite patronage. The festival was held on the estate of Lord Montagu of Beaulieu, a young noble who had previously achieved notoriety during two widely publicized trials on charges of homosexuality. Beaulieu's motto for its 1957 festival drew attention to the alliance of privilege and popular music: "A combination of blue blood and the blues."[41]

Newport, too, would see a certain degree of carnivalesque activity as it evolved, especially by decade's end. More so than at Beaulieu, though, the wilder aspects of the festival existed in tension with the push toward order and respectability. Often, the two elements of the festival seemed almost to exist in separate spheres, the Apollonian and the Dionysian at times co-existing with relative equilibrium, at other times coming into direct conflict. The programming of the first 1954 festival exemplified the mix of impulses at work.

As was customary at jazz concerts designed to shroud the music in an aura of legitimacy, the selection of artists at the first Newport Jazz Festival was designed to present in microcosm some sense of the historical evolution of the music. Opening night featured, in succession: a set of "traditional," 1920s-style jazz played by an ensemble led by guitarist Eddie Condon; a selection of songs featuring vocalist Lee Wiley backed by an ensemble comprised of the same musicians that opened the show; and then a free-wheeling, Dixieland-style jam session. After an intermission, the focus shifted to jazz of a more modern stripe. An early version of the Modern Jazz Quartet took the stage, led by vibraphonist Milt Jackson and including Horace Silver on piano. Following them was a series of small groups playing in the modern style, led respectively by trumpeter Dizzy Gillespie, pianist Oscar Peterson, and saxophone players Lee Konitz and Gerry Mulligan. Bringing the night to a musical close was vocalist Ella Fitzgerald, by then an established star whose notoriety was bolstered in recent years by her regular appearance on Granz's Jazz at the Philharmonic programs.[42]

Stitching this sequence of musical performances together was Stan Kenton, who served as emcee for both nights of the festival. Kenton was himself an icon of modern jazz, but of a very particular stripe. A white bandleader whose modernistic arrangements were constructed to foreground musical complexity and signal progress, Kenton was something of a self-styled jazz intellectual. During both nights of the festival, Kenton did more than offer brief introductions to the musical acts. He delivered a detailed narrative in which the biographies of the individual musicians were tied to the larger contours of jazz history. Moreover, he followed a script that was carefully composed and extensively detailed. The script for opening night alone was twenty-pages-long, and its author was the critic Nat Hentoff.[43] In substance it reiterated a message in keeping with the advance publicity surrounding the festival: jazz had evolved to the point where it was a highly sophisticated art form, but public perception of jazz in the US had not yet recognized the full value of the music. The Newport Jazz Festival, in words delivered by Kenton, was one significant step toward remedying that situation: "Setting up a jazz festival at the same time of year as the many excellent classical music festivals around the country serves to symbolize the fact that jazz has indeed achieved maturity as an art form that makes it varied and vital enough to be the subject of a festival."[44] Moving from these opening remarks to characterization of Dixieland jazz, swing, and modern jazz styles, building up each performing artist as a living embodiment of a segment of an evolving jazz canon, Kenton's work as emcee was designed to offer a small course in jazz history as a complement to the night's music. That Wein and the other festival organizers thought it was necessary reflected their deep desire to impose order on the proceedings.

From the start, this effort to control the festival experience met with resistance. Reporter Gardner Dunton, writing for the *Providence Journal*, observed that the audience—estimated at some seven thousand, which far exceeded the expectations of the festival organizers—was impatient with the excessive formality. When Newport mayor John Sullivan came to the stage to welcome the audience at the opening of the evening concert, the crowd, according to Dunton, "interrupted constantly, with applause indicating they were getting more restless." They did a version of the same when Kenton stepped to the microphone to deliver the first part of his narration, with members of the crowd shouting, "Let's have music!"[45] The sheer size of the crowd, and the way that it tested the capacity of the Casino, ensured that the evening would not be a fully buttoned-down affair. More than that, the social mix evident in the audience drew comment, much as it did for Jenny Lind in 1850, or Paul Whiteman in 1924. Dunton provided the following portrait: "Dowagers and debutantes, sailors and their gals, and couples from many places mingled with thousands of hepcats under a starlit sky . . . Never before has there been such an assemblage in Newport, not even for the famous America's Cup races of two decades ago."[46]

Echoing his impressions were the reviewers from the major metropolitan centers of Boston and New York. *Boston Globe* critic Cyrus Durgin was impressed by the responsiveness of the audience as well as its mix of fashion sensibilities: "To judge by the applause, whistles, yells, shouts, and what-not, jazz is the great democratic leveler of music. This was evident, too, in the appearance of the crowd tonight, which turned out in all styles of raiment from black ties and dinner jackets to sport shirts of wild patterns and colorings."[47] Writing for the *New York Times*, Howard Taubman colorfully evoked the way members of audience filled a venue that was not prepared to seat so many of them: "People stood all over the outdoor arena where tennis matches normally are played. Some sat on the ground, and a few wild young 'uns took posts on the roof of a two-story building. On this precarious perch several of the lads stood and dipped and swayed when the music pulse grew so warm that there was no remaining still."[48] And so, the carnivalesque was part of the Newport Jazz Festival from the beginning, but it was on the outskirts, inhering in qualities imported by the audience against the producers' design.

* * *

Taubman's report carried a headline that is highly suggestive in retrospect: "Newport Rocked by Jazz Festival." When the first Newport festival was produced in July 1954, rock 'n' roll was still just a nascent phenomenon. In the concert realm, Alan Freed's Moondog Coronation Ball was two years past. Freed made the move to the New York radio market in the same summer of 1954 when the Newport Jazz Festival debuted, but his use of the phrase "rock 'n' roll" in connection with his concert promotion activities would not come until the start of 1955. Nonetheless, "rock" was already in the air in the years leading up to the emergence of rock 'n' roll proper, and its association with a burgeoning youth culture that was drawn to the rhythmically propulsive dance music performed by black and white artists would continue to grow during the very years when the Newport festival established itself. George Wein and other Newport organizers were concerned to contain the impulses of the crowds that attended the festival in part because they did not want their events confused with the growing stream of package tour productions that presented R&B and rock 'n' roll, to large audiences of young people.[49]

In light of these matters, dancing at the festival became charged with significance. Jazz concerts had demonstrated increasing concern with encouraging the "right" kind of behavior, as we saw with Jazz at the Philharmonic, which tended to favor audiences remaining seated rather than being on their feet, and jazz historians have commonly judged the suppression of dance to be integral to the treatment of jazz as a more "serious" type of music.[50] At Newport, dancing was never expressly forbidden, but neither was it especially encouraged. Tellingly, there was no effort to create a specific place at the festival set aside for dancers. When festivalgoers danced in place at their seats, it was tolerated, but when they spilled into the aisles, festival security was not always so hands-off.

These conditions were the backdrop to one of the most fabled moments in the early history of the festival, the 1956 appearance by Duke Ellington and his Orchestra, highlighted by a forceful, nearly fifteen-minute-long version of "Diminuendo and Crescendo in Blue" on which saxophonist Paul Gonsalves improvised twenty-seven choruses of blues-based virtuosity. Ellington's set that night has been widely celebrated and memorialized for several reasons. First and foremost, it was seen as a major moment of professional and artistic rebirth for the veteran bandleader. Only six weeks after the performance, an extensive profile of Ellington in *Time* magazine enthused: "The event last month marked not only the turning point in one concert; it confirmed a turning point in a career. The big news was something that the whole jazz world had long hoped to hear: the Ellington band was once again the most exciting thing in the business."[51] Ellington's resurgence coincided with his having signed a new record contract with Columbia Records, who had reached an agreement with festival organizers to record several of their acts during the 1956 affair, including Ellington's. The resulting album, *Ellington at Newport*, became the best-selling record of Ellington's career and allowed the performance to circulate widely beyond those who were present on the night of Saturday, July 7.[52] In this regard, "Diminuendo and Crescendo in Blue" was the first in a series of festival performances that gathered cultural influence through the combined impact of in-the-moment intensity and mass-mediated replay, setting the stage for subsequent turns such as Jimi Hendrix's "Wild Thing" at the Monterey Pop Festival, or Santana's "Soul Sacrifice" at Woodstock.

Just as crucially, Ellington's performance that night and the excitement generated by the orchestra stretching out in such dramatic fashion was taken as a moment when the Newport Jazz Festival came into its own. 1956 was the second the year the festival was held at Freebody Park, after the proprietors of the Casino denied the use of the venue for 1955. Freebody Park had a larger capacity than the Casino, capable of holding crowds of ten thousand or more. Opening night of the 1956 festival, though, was a rain-soaked evening that drew only 3,500 to hear the likes of Count Basie and Sarah Vaughan. Attendance surged on subsequent nights, with Dave Brubeck, Ella Fitzgerald, and Louis Armstrong the featured performers on Friday, and Ellington's orchestra headlining the Saturday concert. Attendance that night was reported to be over eleven thousand and the audience was primed for Ellington's band, which played a short set to open the concert, and then returned to close the show, performing until nearly 1 AM. The excitement that broke out when Gonsalves and the orchestra blew their way through "Diminuendo and Crescendo in Blue" was captured in a photo essay by Bob Parent in *Down Beat*, where an image of Gonsalves playing his saxophone (Figure 7.2) appeared below a blurred picture of dancers in motion. The caption filled in

Figure 7.2 Saxophonist Paul Gonsalves in the midst of the propulsive extended solo he played during the Duke Ellington Orchestra's performance of "Diminuendo and Crescendo in Blue" at the 1956 Newport Jazz Festival. Photograph by Bob Parent. Courtesy of Getty Images.

the details of the scene: "when Duke and his men roared across the Sunday night horizon, the audience suddenly fused into a heatedly unified pulsating congregation. Sporadic dancing broke out all over Freebody park and continued to spread in wide varieties of happily improvised choreography. Most of those who weren't dancing stood on chairs, cheering or wide-mouthed in silent, graphic pleasure."[53] Here was evidence that the Newport Jazz Festival, for all the trappings of formality, could give rise to moments of genuine, unrepressed spontaneity, shared by an audience of thousands and prompted by one of jazz history's towering figures.

One figure seemed to personify this rush of dance ecstasy: a woman later identified as Elaine Anderson, a socialite from New Bedford, Massachusetts, whose exuberant dancing from the expensive boxes near the front of the stage drew considerable attention from photographers, other audience members, and even the band. On the back cover of the original *Ellington at*

Newport album, she appears anonymously, her hands raised above her blond hair, a caption calling her "the girl who launched 7000 cheers." Her dancing helped to spark the sense that something special was happening during "Diminuendo and Crescendo in Blue." For George Wein, however, the figure of a woman dancing so uninhibitedly in the visible, exclusive box section of the crowd generated anxious concern. As recounted by John Fass Morton, previously "Newport had seen dancing only at the margins . . . Tonight, the young at the head of the aisles were spilling into the photography pit and into those boxes that had emptied earlier in the evening. As more and more pressed forward, the last vestige of order collapsed . . . Wein now worried about injuries."[54] With the Pinkerton guards who served as festival security in tow, Wein tried to stop Anderson's dancing and even to have her ejected from the grounds—a move that Elaine Lorillard fiercely resisted. Anderson was ultimately allowed to stay, and continue dancing, but Wein remained on edge, coaxing Ellington to end as it got later into the night. Ellington himself, in his memoir, captured the tension that emanated from the impresario, describing how Wein was "walking in time to the music, with his face serious on the police side and smiling on our side."[55]

The dynamic set in motion as Wein tried to contain the unfolding events of Ellington's performance epitomized the interplay between order and spontaneity that gave the Newport Jazz Festival its distinctive character. Wein's description of the crowd's reaction nearly fifty years later remains telling, his anxiety palpable decades after the fact: "The power of that beat, and the ferocity of Paul's solo, is what stirred the crowd to those heights. Duke himself was totally caught up in the moment. The audience was swelling up like a dangerous tide."[56] Elsewhere, Wein captures the degree to which Ellington's performance at Newport 1956 represented a rich transitional moment: "That sort of audience response would become more common in the soon-to-come rock-and-roll era . . . But no one had ever witnessed anything like it in 1956, and no one could have predicted or expected it."[57] Of course, the rock 'n' roll era had already effectively come by then, and such audience enthusiasm had been witnessed at many concerts throughout 1956. What was unexpected was that a *jazz* audience would respond as they did, in 1956. That they did so despite Wein's effort to manage the crowd suggested something of the unique power that the festival setting had as a vehicle for generating public enthusiasm on a massive scale.

* * *

During the ensuing four years, the Newport Jazz Festival became a broadly popular phenomenon. Headlines for the 1957 Newport Jazz Festival trumpeted "record" attendance day after day. "Jazz Festival Record Crowd Honors Louis Armstrong," announced the *Newport Daily News* in its report on opening day; while day two brought, "Jazz Festival Again Breaks Mark at Gate with 11,500."[58] By the end of the four-day festival, overall attendance was said to have been around fifty thousand, nearly twice what the 1956 event had drawn, and for the first time the Newport Jazz Festival ended with a sizable profit.[59] *Billboard* magazine used the festival's success that year as an index of the growing market value of jazz, especially in the sphere of concert presentation. Calling the 1957 Newport festival "what must have been the biggest and most successful jazz presentation of all time," journalist Bill Simon focused on the audience: a mix of "adults this side of the half-century mark," mainly visible in the expensive box seats, and young "pilgrims" that "pooled travel facilities, slept in cars and subsisted on hot dogs. But," observed Simon, "the majority must have come fairly well-heeled" given that ticket prices started at $3 and accommodations were no bargain. Crucially, "the crowds demonstrated intense interest in all of the happenings," and "top jazz performers were treated as national heroes."[60] Newport, from this vantage point, seemed to strike the perfect balance between mass adulation and dedication to the finer elements of jazz artistry.

Not all were so quick to approve the broad success, and the wide net, of the festival. Several critics directed their discontent at Wein's programming philosophy. Richard Gehman, writing in the *Boston Advertiser*, asserted that the festival was being run "like a vaudeville show: George Shearing was put on and taken off; Stan Kenton was put on and taken off; Ella Fitzgerald was put on and taken off; and so on," which precluded any performer from building the sort of momentum that Ellington's orchestra had developed the preceding year.[61] Whitney Balliett, jazz critic for the *New Yorker*, saw the sheer scale of the enterprise as a problem unto itself. Channeling the mid-twentieth century suspicion of mass culture that had taken root among intellectuals of the era, Balliett characterized the festival as being of "bulging, General Motors proportions," with seven long concerts (afternoon and evening), more than forty groups, and the enormous audience suggesting a musical version of a factory assembly line.[62] Balliett reiterated his criticism the next year, calling the 1958 Newport Jazz Festival "a statistician's dream: There were seven concerts . . . and two musically illustrated morning lectures, all of which amounted to over thirty-five solid hours of music and talk; approximately two-hundred and fifty musicians . . . and a total attendance of sixty thousand . . . But bigness is more partial to flabbiness than muscle, and the bigger the Newport convention has grown, the softer it has got."[63]

Wein pushed back against the critics, using his regular column in the *Boston Herald* to defend the festival.[64] Maybe the most intriguing line he took was his effort to explain what, exactly, the nonprofit status of the Newport Jazz Festival meant in practice. In a column that appeared just a week after the conclusion of the 1957 festival, Wein wrote: "First, 'non-profit' does not mean that the festival does not want to make money." The Lorillards, in their role as patrons, had not endowed the festival with funds to sustain it, but they had guaranteed to underwrite possible losses. Now that Newport had earned a significant financial surplus for the first time, the festival could use the available funds to support its mission, "the furtherance of jazz as an American art form." Concluded Wein, "So I hope it is now clear with respect to the Newport Jazz Festival, 'non-profit' means, that while the festival must be self-sustaining, any excess income must be used for the cultural promotion of jazz."[65]

The compulsion to offer this explanation came because, to all appearances, the maximization of crowds and revenues looked a lot like music industry business as usual. *Billboard* continued to report on the Newport Jazz Festival as though its primary significance was the revitalization of the market for jazz, on record as well as in performance. That the festival had arranged specific deals with Columbia Records in 1956, and with Norman Granz's Verve label in 1957, only bolstered the sense that Newport was not just a potentially lucrative weekend of jazz in concert, but an event that affected the larger jazz economy. Wein, meanwhile, undoubtedly saw the building of the Newport brand as a means of building his own career as a concert promoter. His activities grew dramatically throughout the later years of the 1950s. In late 1957, Wein announced the creation of a new company, Concert Jazz Productions, which promoted concert tours by jazz artists independently of the Newport enterprise, starting with a tour by Dave Brubeck.[66] The following year, Wein opened a branch of his Storyville club in the Cape Cod town of Harwich.

Also in 1958, Wein stretched the bounds of his work with the Newport festival itself in two directions: he assembled a lineup of Newport-associated performers to appear at that year's World's Fair in Brussels, Belgium; and he worked in partnership with the Sheraton Hotel corporation to present a scaled-down jazz festival in French Lick, Indiana. The former endeavor, arranged with the full participation of Louis Lorillard as president of the Newport Jazz Festival board, indicated the growing prominence of jazz as a tool of Cold War diplomacy, which informed festival programming from the start.[67] As for the French Lick festival, it was a significant move by Wein to forge a partnership with a major private corporation, foreshadowing later sponsorship deals he would pursue under the auspices of Newport. A Sheraton representative, Al Banks, reached out to Wein with the desire to use a jazz festival to breathe new life into one of the company's properties in an isolated corner of Indiana. For Sheraton the jazz festival was one part of a multi-pronged strategy to use cultural programs as a way of building business. During the month of August 1958, the same property would host a choral festival, a Country Music Jamboree, and a program called "Classical Galaxy" that presented orchestral concerts.[68] For Wein it was a major opportunity to see if the festival model he had developed at Newport during the past four years could be exported to a different setting.[69] Its success was shown by the fact that the following year, 1959, Wein continued the Sheraton partnership and added festivals in Toronto and Boston to the event in French Lick. A press release issued by the Newport Jazz Festival board emphasized that in expanding its activities, the organization had also "voted to retain the exclusive services of Boston's George Wein on an annual basis," a move that signaled its concern "with the promotion of many and varied activities throughout the year."[70]

Explaining the expansion of activities, Wein stressed that the mission and objectives of the Newport organization had not changed. Moreover, he rejected any suggestion that the extension of the Newport model of festival production to other settings represented some sort of one-size-fits-all approach to jazz presentation. Interviewed by Bob Rolontz of *Billboard*, Wein emphasized that "each of the festivals, Newport, French Lick, Toronto and Boston, would be an individually staged show, altho a number of artists are expected to be featured at two or three of the festivals."[71] Despite these assurances, the move to make the Newport Jazz Festival organization into such a multifaceted enterprise inalterably shifted the terms under which Wein worked. Newport was no longer simply the name attached to the setting of a popular jazz festival. It was becoming an exportable brand that allowed Wein to oversee the production of live jazz in any number of alternative locations. As things turned out, the new ventures were not a resounding success—the Toronto and Boston festivals lost considerable money, and the Newport Jazz Festival board withdrew its involvement, which did not preclude Wein from pursuing such initiatives under his own name. Meanwhile, though, the organization branched out in another direction that involved not a geographic move but a change of stylistic orientation. Newport was about to become associated with something other than jazz.

Folk Festival Revival

"A Folk Music Festival." That heading appeared in the minutes to the March 20, 1959, meeting of the board of directors of the Newport Jazz Festival, which offered the following account of the board's discussion:

> Mr. Wein strongly advocated The Newport Jazz Festival starting a Folk Music Festival at Newport this year and there was general discussion as to whether it was advisable to have such a festival prior to or after the Newport Jazz Festival, or whether it should be merely one afternoon's program during the Jazz Festival. A motion was made, seconded, and, on a majority vote, adopted that The Newport Jazz Festival present a Folk Music Festival at Newport.[72]

Wein's suggestion was hardly out of the blue. Evidence of the movement that came to be known as the folk revival had been mounting for the better part of a decade by 1959. The massive popular success of the singing group the Weavers—featuring Pete Seeger, Ronnie Gilbert, Lee Hays, and Fred Hellerman—at the turn of the 1950s was one mobilizing factor. A more underground current had been set in motion by the 1952 release of the *Anthology of American Folk Music*, compiled by maverick artist/intellectual Harry Smith and released on the Folkways label formed by Moe Asch (who, years earlier, had released the first live recordings made at Norman Granz's Jazz at the Philharmonic concerts).[73] Folk music, like jazz, was taking shape as a sort of popular music for a sector of the public that did not like to admit that it consumed what was "popular"—bohemians and intellectuals who sought cultural alternatives but who themselves constituted a wide base, especially when joined with the growing mass of young college students whose tastes were similarly oriented. Wein had even been programming folk acts on occasion at his Storyville club, booking the black folksinger Josh White as early as 1952 and later bringing in artists such as the African American singer Odetta—through whom he formed an acquaintance with Albert Grossman, her manager.[74]

Journalist and Rhode Island native Rick Massimo, in his history of the Newport Folk Festival, identifies Grossman as the first of four figures with whom George Wein would align himself, who served as "native guides to the world of folk music."[75] Of the four—who also include Pete Seeger, Bob Jones, and Jay Sweet—Grossman had the most surface similarities to Wein. Both were Jews born in the 1920s (Grossman was two years younger), in major cities that were not New York (Grossman was a Chicago native) who moved into the nightclub business in the 1950s. That Wein ran a jazz nightclub and Grossman a folk nightclub, Chicago's Gate of Horn, was in some ways a circumstantial distinction. A more fundamental difference was that Wein was bent primarily on making jazz respectable, and Grossman mainly wanted to make folk popular without losing its aura of authenticity. Using the four categories that Elijah Wald devises to characterize the folk revival—community music making, preservation of ethnic and regional traditions, "people's music" as proletarian enterprise, and a professional folk performance scene—Grossman was strongly oriented toward the latter.[76] Over the years Grossman became a music industry giant as he moved into the world of artist management, earning reverence and fear for his business acumen as he oversaw the careers of Joan Baez, Peter, Paul and Mary, the Butterfield Blues Band, Janis Joplin, the Band, and most famously, Bob Dylan. In 1959, his artistic and commercial vision merged with Wein's and together they shaped the program for the debut Newport Folk Festival.

Unlike the jazz festival, for which the primary models came from the world of classical music, there was plenty of precedent and to a degree, competition, in the field of folk music festivals. Many of the earlier generation of festivals—the Mountain Dance and Folk Festival, the American Song Festival, the National Folk Festival—were still running. Joining the established festivals was a widening range of newer events prompted by the folk revival. Compared to the first wave of folk festivals, far more of the current wave were based in the Northeast, and many were housed at colleges and universities. Swarthmore College in Pennsylvania gave rise to the first significant college folk festival in 1945 and had a significant influence on future folk festival producer Ralph Rinzler, a student there in the late 1950s.[77] Oberlin College in Ohio began its folk festival in 1957, while one of the largest collegiate festivals started out west in 1958, a year before Newport began its folk festival, at the University of California at Berkeley. Organized by

Barry Olivier, a young Bay Area concert promoter and radio personality, the Berkeley Folk Festival employed a format of concerts and workshops that would also characterize the Newport festival, and featured artists such as Pete Seeger, Jean Ritchie, and Billy Faire who would be spotlighted at Newport as well.[78]

Less groundbreaking in its initial incarnation than the jazz festival, the Newport Folk Festival that debuted on July 11 and 12, 1959, marked a consolidation of the folk revival as a burgeoning cultural phenomenon and of Newport as the most visible festival setting in the US. The program lacked the scope and diversity that the festival would later assume but was far from homogeneous. Grossman's grounding in the contemporary folk club scene was obvious in the choice of artists. Odetta, the Clancy Brothers, Bob Gibson, Barbara Dane, Leon Bibb, and Cynthia Gooding, among several others, came to the festival from the professional folk scene, as did the most widely popular of the performers at the 1959 festival, the Kingston Trio. The New Lost City Ramblers—a group that played a galvanizing role in the folk revival and the longer history of the Newport festival, consisting of Mike Seeger, John Cohen, and Tom Paley—also belonged in this category, although their style was more rough and rustic than that of most of their urban folk peers. They were joined by an older generation of folk artists whose careers stretched back to the pre-revival era but remained prominent: Josh White, Pete Seeger, and African American blues artists Sonny Terry and Brownie McGhee. Blues was further represented by the Reverend Gary Davis and pianist Memphis Slim. Chicago rock 'n' roll pioneer Bo Diddley, perhaps the most unlikely participant in the festival, was described in the program book as a "folk singer who has become the rage of the rhythm and blues fields." Earl Scruggs and the Stanley Brothers brought bluegrass to the first Newport festival, a key moment in the convergence of the genre with the folk revival that gathered momentum in the ensuing decade.[79]

Headlines appearing on the same page of the July 13, 1959, issue of *Billboard* captured the somewhat measured, and paradoxical impact of that first Newport Folk Festival. "Folk Music Becomes Big Business in Pop Field," asserted a story that offered a broad overview of the current success enjoyed by folk singers, defining the field broadly to include the likes of the Kingston Trio and Johnny Cash. Just a column over, though, another story informed, "Lagging B.O. Dims Newport Folk Fiesta."[80] Total attendance at the festival was estimated to have been around fifteen thousand, far below the jazz festival attendance, which had run near fifty thousand. In other regards too, the first folk festival was a scaled down affair—only two days as compared with the jazz festival's four. Three concerts, one on Saturday evening, and then afternoon and evening sessions on Sunday, comprised the heart of the first festival, along with a Saturday afternoon workshop led by Frank Hamilton, founder of the Old Town School of Folk Music in Chicago, and a Sunday morning panel discussion on the state of folk music organized by jazz historian Marshall Stearns that featured Folkways Records founder Moe Asch and folklorist Alan Lomax, among others. The workshop and panel discussion were a carry-over from the jazz festival and from the earlier folk festival model of the 1930s, when academic folklorists had appeared alongside the artists on display. These features assumed their own life in the next decade when the workshops became adapted to the distinctive impulses that ran through the folk festival, encouraging active participation of audiences and allowing festival goers to come into closer contact with performers.

Two moments, in effect, encapsulated the strengths and weaknesses of the first Newport Folk Festival. The first was the unannounced appearance of Joan Baez, then an up-and-coming singer in the scene that had grown around Harvard Square in Cambridge, Massachusetts, who joined Bob Gibson onstage for two songs. Baez's performance became a widely remembered part of festival folklore, commemorated in the program book for the second festival in 1960: "Few moments are more exciting or more memorable for an audience than to be in on the discovery of a new and exciting talent. Certainly, the Sunday evening audience at the 1959 Newport Folk Festival lived through such a moment when they heard Joan Baez for the first time . . . Joan Baez," the program copy continued, "returns to Newport this year, not a 'discovery,' but one of the most exciting young folk performers in the country."[81] In its first year, the Newport Folk Festival had a hand in creating one of the most visible stars of the folk revival. Her rising stature, in turn, testified to Albert Grossman's influence. Gibson invited Baez to join him after the two had met at Grossman's Gate of Horn club in Chicago; and following her appearance, Grossman became involved in managing her, landing her a deal with Vanguard Records, also the label contracted to record the festival for a series of "live" releases.[82]

Stardom, however, fit uneasily with the folk revival. Ardent folk enthusiasts believed that the focus should be not on a few select individuals, but on the best exponents of regional styles from across the US who operated beyond the purview of the mainstream music industry. In the Newport Folk Festival's first year, that tension most came to a head in a programming decision made by George Wein in consultation with Louis Lorillard. For the closing Sunday night concert, Wein had bluegrass banjo virtuoso Earl Scruggs scheduled to appear immediately before the closing act, the Kingston Trio. Scruggs was no unknown—he was well established as one of the great instrumentalists of bluegrass—but his recognition at the time was largely limited to fans of the style. The Kingston Trio on the other hand were probably the single most popular folk singing group in the US in 1959. Lorillard pressured Wein to switch the order of the two acts to satisfy members of the audience who did not want to stay so late to see the Kingston Trio, and Wein succumbed. The result was an embarrassment for all involved: the audience would not let the Kingston Trio leave the stage after their set, requiring Trio member Dave Guard to plead with them to give Scruggs a hearing, after which the folk-pop favorites would return for an encore. John Cohen, of the New Lost City Ramblers, said of the episode, "It was bizarre; it was painful."[83] Wein recalled, "I lost a lot of friends in the folk world because of that slipup. It was an insult to Earl Scruggs... For some folk purists, it would take years for me to achieve redemption."[84]

Folk purists may have resented Wein for the maneuver, but the overall assessment of the first Newport Folk Festival was less biting. Writing in *Sing Out*, one of the more exacting vehicles of folk opinion, Irwin Silber and David Gahr offered a moderate assessment: "If the program seemed to be dominated by the 'city' folk-singer with the traditional performer getting only an occasional look-in, this was an accurate reflection of the current folk song 'boom' and the personalities who are dominating it."[85] Putting the scale of the festival in perspective, critic Robert Shelton wrote in the *New York Times* that while attendance figures may have fallen below expectation, "the total is the impressive equivalent of between four and five sell-out concerts at Carnegie Hall."[86] Indeed, the size of the audience over the two days was nearly identical to that which attended the first Newport Jazz Festival in 1954. That an audience of nearly fifteen thousand was now considered grounds for disappointment was a mark of how much had changed during the intervening years. Wein, for his part, expressed satisfaction with the turnout and commented, with a certain degree of prescience, that folk festivals could likely grow to "fantastic proportions." He would prove to be right, but only after recovering from a disruption that nearly ended Newport's status as host for the jazz and folk festivals alike.

Riot and Repercussions

From its 1959 inception until 1970, after which it went on a fifteen-year hiatus, the Newport Folk Festival was always scheduled to occur a week or so after that year's Jazz Festival—with one exception. In 1960, for the only time in its early history, the Folk Festival came first. This detail may be little more than a historical footnote. However, given the events that transpired at the Jazz Festival that year, it was of no small consequence. If the 1960 Newport Folk Festival had been scheduled after the Jazz Festival as it had been the previous year, it would probably not have been held at all, given that the latter was interrupted by a level of unrest that led the city of Newport to revoke the license of the Newport Jazz Festival corporation to produce events in the city. Another possibility is also worth considering, which no published account of the 1960 riot at Newport has raised: the creation of the Folk Festival may have been one of the preconditions for the riot. To be sure, the swelling population of young vacationers at the riot's center was already a visible part of the Newport scene before the Folk Festival came about and had generated disturbances in years past. Photojournalist Burt Goldblatt, in his idiosyncratic narrative history of the Newport Jazz Festival, reproduces several news clippings covering the years 1954–1959 that offer evidence of how the factors that led to the riots of 1960 had been brewing for some time.[87] Nonetheless, as of 1959, Newport was home to not one festival, but two. The next year, the Folk Festival served as a sort of warm-up event, and at the Jazz Festival—still by far the larger of the two—things got beyond the control of the organizers and town officials alike.

Conflict surrounded the 1960 Newport Jazz Festival as soon as it began, although the tension that accompanied the start of the festival was rather different from what prompted its cancellation days later. A group of jazz musicians led by Charles Mingus and Max Roach broke off from the main Newport festival to organize their own, autonomous festival at the nearby Cliff Walk Manor. Support for their efforts came from Elaine Lorillard, by that time separated from her husband Louis who continued to serve as president of the Newport Jazz Festival board. The counter-festival at Cliff Walk was a move by artists who felt as though their contributions had been marginalized by the larger festival to gain more control over the terms under which they were presented. Many of the artists at the Cliff Walk event—Mingus, Roach, Ornette Coleman—dwelled in the realm of modern and avant-garde jazz that was assigned lesser priority in programming the Newport Jazz Festival, where the likes of Louis Armstrong, Duke Ellington, and Ella Fitzgerald continued to be marquee artists.

The bulk of artists involved in planning the Cliff Walk festival were also African American. Although black musicians were prevalent at the Newport Jazz Festival from its inception, poet Langston Hughes was the only African American board member and a recent addition at that, and treatment of black musicians and festivalgoers in the town of Newport had often carried a whiff of segregationist sentiment. The racial divide at work in the counter-festival was evident in the coverage it drew from two very different newspapers. The *Boston Globe* insisted that there was no "bad blood" between the two undertakings, quoting veteran drummer Jo Jones, who explained that it was meant to "further the art of pure jazz and give unknowns a chance to be heard before a knowing audience."[88] By contrast, the Harlem-based *New York Amsterdam News*, targeting a black readership, bluntly characterized the music at Cliff Walk Manor as a series of "Protest Concerts" and cited an anonymous "disgruntled" musician who remarked of the main Newport Jazz Festival, "They're capitalizing on our efforts and not paying us any money."[89]

Audacious as the counter-festival was for challenging the Newport Jazz Festival on its own turf, it was not an isolated event. Newport had stimulated a proliferating range of jazz festivals since its inception in 1954. Several of them sought to compete with Newport on its own terms, featuring a wide-ranging roster of top talent designed to draw large crowds—most prominently the Monterey Jazz Festival in California and the Playboy Jazz Festival in Chicago. Some sought a very different scale of success, however. A case in point was the Bard College Jazz Festival, organized at the esteemed liberal arts college by a group of students led by Ran Blake, a pianist who would become an influential educator and avant-garde musician. The program book for the Bard festival included a long essay that condemned mass culture for its "corrupting influence" that destroyed the singularity of the individual artist. Continued the program note, "Only when some art-form has been able to develop and keep a relatively small, non-mass audience has it shown staying power. Jazz is a rare example of this." The Bard College Jazz Festival was, accordingly, designed to resist the model that had been built by the likes of Newport: "This festival . . . is not the circus-like spectacular which has been presented throughout the country in the past. This festival is approaching the subject in a serious, scholarly, and constructive manner. Instead of catering to the public, or the financial interest of certain producers, the festival will cater to the advancement of America's greatest art."[90] Of course, Wein had professed similar goals himself, but he saw the mass audience as a potential vehicle for advancing jazz. At Bard a more self-selecting audience was prized, and the primary goal—as it was for Mingus, Roach, and the other participants at the Newport counter-festival—was to give the musicians a collective space in which to do their thing.

* * *

Fault lines more immediately tied to the cause of the riot came to light in the program book for the 1960 Newport Jazz Festival. Noted jazz critic Ira Gitler, in a piece reflecting on the festival's history to date, announced his own "schizophrenic" feelings about it. Newport certainly had its share of great moments from one year to the next, acknowledged Gitler, but there were also running issues with programming acts that did not fit with his own conception of jazz—whether that be dancer Eartha Kitt, who performed with Dizzy Gillespie in 1957; rock 'n' roll figurehead Chuck Berry, who played the festival in 1958; or the Kingston Trio, who previewed the first Newport Folk Festival with a set at the Jazz Festival that year as well. This year, 1960, promised a corrective, but other sources of tension remained for Gitler. Most prominently, he asserted, "I dislike big crowds . . . I really don't mind that portion of the crowd that conduct themselves like human beings. Of course, I mean *you*. It's those *other* people. Then again, if I was a teenager, I'd probably get to feeling pretty good on beer. It's just that I hold it better now."[91]

For the middle-aged Gitler, the teenage set was the true source of consternation. He described a scene from the 1958 festival, where young visitors "who hadn't even *been* to the festival" wrecked the lobby of the hotel where he had stayed. Considering the implications, Gitler observed, "Let's face it. Even if there is no rock-and-roll, youth will be served (underage or not) by the very existence of a festival in town. Newport (the festival) can do its part but it cannot play chaperone. Newport (the town) has enough of a problem in the mass of people that gluts the streets."[92] This was the problem, in a nutshell: the festival exerted an appeal that transcended the pull of jazz as a genre or the performers on stage. The festival was, in a sense, the thing, but it also made Newport the town a zone of carnivalesque release in a way that spilled beyond the boundaries of the festival proper.

Indeed, one of the more striking features of the riot that materialized on the night of Saturday, July 2, was that by all accounts it involved not the audience inside the festival gates, but a large crowd—estimated in the thousands—outside the gates. Earlier nights of the festival had not been so well attended.

Rain kept the opening Thursday night concert attendance to just a shade over four thousand, and Friday increased slightly to around seven thousand, five hundred. On Saturday, though, a near-capacity audience of some fifteen thousand filled Freebody Park. The rise was not mysterious—it was a holiday weekend and starting Friday night and throughout the day on Saturday collegiate vacationers streamed into the town. A *Billboard* report, filed before the riot had occurred, captured the scene as one of free-spirited fun:

> As usual, the rooming houses were full to overflowing, and the landladies, having experienced a good weekend just seven days before with the good attendance at the Newport Folk Festival, were brimming with good will. Sports cars of every type and description were on view all over town, and the license plates showed the owners came from as far away as Texas and Maine. Youngsters slept on beaches, on lawns and in their cars and a beer can in the hand still appeared to be a status symbol.[93]

A widely reproduced photo that appeared in news reports after the riot offers a hint of how this scene of jubilation turned: cars full of young men cruising the streets of Newport on Saturday afternoon, with police cars to the side seeking to monitor what was perceived to be disorderly behavior. Tellingly, one of the men depicted in the photo wears an Ithaca College t-shirt, indicating the age and character of those gathered. All of those pictured are white. The scene, hardly ominous on its surface, gained new meaning in the aftermath of the night's events as indicated by the caption used by the *Boston Globe*: "Omen of Things to Come."[94]

After a day full of similar scenes, things came to a head during the evening concert, when a large crowd stood outside the gates of Freebody Park, unable to gain admission. Inside the park, the audience heard high-energy sets by Ray Charles and Horace Silver, but nowhere was there the suggestion that the music itself spurred the conflict. Rather, a segment of those at the gate tried to storm their way in, and the police pushed back. A Rhode Island state trooper can be seen in Figure 7.3 checking one of the gates. The crowd, rather than ceding ground, resisted the police and the confrontation grew from there. A particularly vivid eyewitness account appeared in the *Globe*, provided by Jerry Taylor, a freelance journalist from Newport. According to Taylor, the initial crowd that caused the disturbance probably numbered about a thousand. However, after the police responded, the size of the crowd grew dramatically and "the beer cans and the bottles started flying." State

Figure 7.3 A Rhode Island state trooper checks the gate at the 1960 Newport Jazz Festival on July 3, 1960, the night when rioters outside the festival gates led to the event's cancellation and threatened the future of music festivals in the Rhode Island town. Photograph by Joe Dennehy. Courtesy of the *Boston Globe*/Getty Images.

troopers were called in, and later the National Guard. Police used tear gas to try to disperse the crowd but at first the wind blew it back on them. With reinforcements and more tear gas the combined forces of local and state police and national guardsmen eventually pushed the crowd away from the festival site, while bottles and cans continued to be thrown and the windows of police cruisers were shattered. Said Taylor, surveying the aftermath, "The streets were littered with broken glass, cans, and bottles. Cars were overturned. Store windows were smashed."[95] Before the night was through, nearly two hundred people would be arrested, and fifty hospitalized. The next morning, the Newport town council voted, four to three, to revoke the festival's license. An afternoon blues session curated by Langston Hughes became the closing event—where Muddy Waters recorded his pivotal live album, *At Newport 1960*. Concerts on Sunday night and the afternoon and evening of Monday, July 4 were canceled, and the future of the Newport Jazz and Folk Festivals both hung in the balance.

Efforts to make sense of the riot and understand its causes and implications proliferated in the days and weeks that followed. For many commentators the most obvious source of the conflict was the young people themselves. Press accounts recited the same sort of "moral panic" rhetoric that had proliferated around rock 'n' roll concerts. A *New York Herald Tribune* editorial epitomized the moralistic stance taken by many observers, asserting that the "young Americans" at Newport "were rioting for nothing but the perverse pleasure of violence. Theirs was a hedonism gone wild, an irresponsible animal self-indulgence that reflects discredit on their generation."[96] If this was a cross-section of young people acting out, though, it appeared to be a different demographic than that which had spurred unrest at rock 'n' roll shows. Accurately or not, the rock 'n' roll audience was construed as a more working-class audience, and in settings like Boston and Cleveland more racially mixed as well. That the Newport audience was so visibly collegiate made their actions resonate differently, as though the youth rebellion was now growing beyond its customary base. While Newport audiences included a fair proportion of African Americans, meanwhile, the riots were almost entirely associated with white youth. The *New York Amsterdam News* noted this detail with no small amount of sarcasm and a touch of pride: "Of the two hundred or more jailed in the Newport affair, there were no Negroes, only rich little 'chalks.' And there were plenty of us there."[97] Langston Hughes echoed the observation in a more elegiac piece published in the *Chicago Defender*, saying of the rioters, "Incidentally according to the police records there was not a single Negro among them; and the riots had no racial angles."[98]

Others were not so quick to blame the masses of youth that made Newport their destination. The *Herald Tribune* editorial cited above drew a sharp and articulate rejoinder from a reader named Shirley Baty, who redirected responsibility onto the town of Newport itself. In her account of the scene, Baty claimed: "There is not room to house a third of the people who attend, so they sleep in the beach and on yards. For this they are called 'bums.' They were all college kids who had spent a considerable amount of money to get there, only to be thrown out when they failed to conform to Newport's idea of decorum."[99] *New York Times* jazz critic John Wilson similarly accused town officials and businessmen of having "condoned a lax atmosphere in the town," tolerating the scores of partying young people because of "the shot in the arm they give to Newport's economy."[100] Nat Hentoff, on the other hand, laid principle responsibility onto the festival organizers themselves in a scathing assessment:

> The Festival . . . was largely to blame for its own cancellation because in grabbing for more and more receipts each year, it had encouraged the conviction among thousands of teenagers that Newport had become a carnival town over the July 4 weekend. Neither the beer-drinkers nor the musicians had any illusions left that the NJF had anything basically to do with "art." It had become a money-grubbing enterprise of the same category as any giant midway staffed with shell games, taffy candy, freak shows, and thrill rides.[101]

For Wein and other allies of the festival, it was imperative to assert a distinction between the rioters and the festival's core constituency. Wein was quick to make this point in public statements following the riot, suggesting that the riots were mainly due to the "presence of a lot of kids who know nothing about jazz. It's a shame if jazz has to suffer because of trouble started by people outside of the park."[102] This tendency to draw a firm line between real jazz fans and rioting youth gained considerable traction. Bill Coss, an editor at the jazz magazine *Metronome*, insisted: "'Jazz fans' did not riot at Newport. Enforcement agencies did not battle with 'Thousands of Jazz Buffs.' What did happen was that youngsters, who had been openly and unlawfully drinking on Newport streets all day . . . became disorderly and dangerous by evening."[103] Also putting forth this view was Father Norman O'Connor, a Catholic priest from Boston who was a long-standing jazz partisan and close compatriot of Wein's. In a detailed post-riot commentary, O'Connor observed: "First to remember is that the young men and women who made the riot had nothing to do with the jazz audience or jazz . . . It was a crowd of equal proportions of boys and girls. All were dressed in sports clothes, and all carried liquor, and all had no interest in the festival. All wanted to have a good time."[104] Even Hentoff affirmed this line of argument, suggesting that the mistake of the festival was to create conditions that drew thousands to Newport whose interest lay not in the music but in the surrounding revelry.

Countering these contemporary perspectives, cultural historian Scott Saul has argued that the youthful vacationers that made Newport their destination during festival time, and those who rioted, should be understood as connected to jazz, not apart from it. In Saul's provocative formulation, "the Newport riot was one of the most striking expressions of the greater youth audience in the postwar period, the larger circle of fans that radiated out from the inner circle of gigging jazz artists, critics, nightclub stalwarts and amateur musicians."[105] From this vantage point, the riot and the more general appeal of the Newport Jazz Festival to young audiences of the time reveal something crucial about the cultural position of jazz at the turn of the 1960s. Having risen in cultural stature, jazz remained *popular* music as well, music that could prompt a good time, but more critically, music the meaning of which remained contested and unsettled.

I agree with Saul about what the 1960 riot at Newport tells us about the state of jazz. For my purposes, though, the riot at Newport was most important as a turning point in the larger history of US festival culture. Previous festivals, and especially those events like Tanglewood, had primarily been designed to appeal to an adult leisure class. This was the audience that Wein and the Lorillards targeted when the jazz festival began. In the six years since its inception though, and culminating in the riot of 1960, the Newport Jazz Festival demonstrated an appeal to young audiences that defied expectations and to a large extent came to define its image. The riot at Newport encapsulated this larger tension in the underlying conception of the festival and whom it was meant to serve. After the riot, festivals continued to attract multiple audiences, connected to a variety of genres, and assumed many shapes and sizes. But the largest festivals, and the ones that served as bellwethers of the era, would be those where young people gathered in greatest numbers. The Newport Jazz Festival ushered in an era when festivals would be defined through their connection to youth culture.

Festival Reformation

The riot at the 1960 Newport Jazz Festival was to the festival culture of its time what Altamont became almost ten years later—an event that seemed to stop the momentum of popular music festivals in its tracks. For a time, it was unclear whether either the jazz festival or the folk festival would ever continue in Newport. In fact, both festivals would have a flourishing and sometimes tumultuous history through the next decade, but the riot did prompt a serious interruption of activity. A jazz festival happened in Newport in 1961, but without George Wein's involvement. The promoter, Sid Bernstein, gained notoriety a few years hence for producing the two Beatles concerts at Shea Stadium in 1965 and 1966, chronicled in the next chapter. As producer of the

1961 jazz festival in Newport—to be distinguished from the Newport Jazz Festival proper—he presented an event that had its musical high points but ended with a significant financial deficit.[106]

Wein, meanwhile, regrouped and eventually regained control of both the jazz and folk festivals. As he did so, however, the two events assumed a very different relationship to one another. Restaging the Newport Jazz Festival in 1962, Wein no longer worked with the nonprofit corporation that had been so instrumental in founding and supporting the enterprise. He recalled in his memoir that after the riot of 1960, only a single member of the previous board had any interest to continue working with the festival. Wein then made the decision to abandon the nonprofit structure entirely and create in its place a for-profit corporation of which he would be clearly in charge. The new company, called Festival Productions, Inc., signaled another moment of transformation in the history of US festival culture. From this point forward, Wein approached festival production with a level of expressly commercial interest that had formerly been downplayed and suppressed.

Doing so, Wein learned that the shift from nonprofit to for-profit had little bearing on the perceived legitimacy of his efforts. He observed later, "It made no difference to the public that the festival was no longer a nonprofit event. This was an intriguing discovery. People pay attention to what you accomplish. If your work is important, and good for the community, they'll support you; if it isn't, they won't."[107] These comments bear out that Wein never fully abandoned the notion that his work in festival production had artistic and cultural benefits that transcended strict commercial considerations. For the 1962 festival he rededicated his efforts to the promotion of "pure" jazz, judging some of his earlier attempts to cast a broad net with the festival in a negative light. About his larger aspirations for the festival, he told one interviewer, "I want to keep the tone and prestige and importance of the festival . . . This is part of the image I'm trying to create. I'm not cut out to be a one-night promoter; I like to be associated with permanent events."[108]

Unlike the jazz festival, the Newport Folk Festival remained a nonprofit event. Nonetheless, it underwent changes in organization that, if anything, were even more profound. Prior to the riot, the same corporation that presented the jazz festival also produced the folk festival in Newport. Albert Grossman was the only person from the folk music world assigned an official role in connection with the first years of the festival. Following the riot, the Newport Folk Festival was not restored until 1963. In the interim, Wein assembled a completely new, autonomous board of directors that would essentially reinvent the Newport Folk Festival and its mission. Grossman withdrew from the event to concentrate on his managerial work, and Pete Seeger took his place as Wein's primary guide to the folk music world, with Seeger's wife Toshi also contributing significantly. Wein evocatively described the input he received from the Seegers in reimagining what the Newport Folk Festival could be:

> Pete recognized the value of Newport. He agreed to work on reviving the festival. "But I would like to do it differently," he said. Pete and Toshi then explained their idea for a nonprofit, musician-run folk festival. In choosing the content and format of each program, this foundation would consider not only the best interests of the festival itself, but also those of the entire folk world. And under this system, Pete emphasized, all festival performers . . . would receive the same fee of fifty dollars, plus travel expenses, housing, and food.[109]

The Certificate of Incorporation for the Newport Folk Foundation, Inc., dated March 8, 1963, echoed the language used to create the Jazz Festival nine years earlier, defining the purpose of the organization in part to be "to foster the development everywhere of an understanding and appreciation of the folk arts, with particular emphasis on folk music, by promoting and causing to be produced, musical productions, seminars and entertainments."[110]

More visionary was a document that Wein and Seeger coauthored with Theodore Bikel, a widely popular Jewish folk singer, actor, and political activist who joined Seeger as a board member for the newly launched enterprise. Over five pages, the trio provided an outline of every facet of the Newport Folk Festival in its reformed state. Describing the organizational structure of the festival, they stipulated that it should be comprised of a board consisting of seven members drawn directly from the folk music scene. All seven of the original board members—Seeger, Bikel, Bill Clifton, Clarence Cooper, Erik Darling, Jean Ritchie, and Peter Yarrow—were performers of some note, but the document advised that future board members did not have to be: "There are many people who have devoted their lives to folk music who are not known as performers. They have a right to be represented on this committee."[111] With regard to finances, they imagined that a properly produced festival could earn between $30,000 and $50,000 per year and expressed the hope that this money could be used to "underwrite research of ethnic material," which they called "the life blood of folk music." They assigned the tasks relating to the technical side of the festival to Wein's Festival Productions staff and posited the hope that financially the Folk Festival would become "self-sustaining from its inception." Wein, it should be noted, was not to be one of the members of the festival board but instead would occupy one of three "officer" positions, holding the role of Chairman, while his lawyer Elliot Hoffman served as Secretary and accountant Arnold London as Treasurer. The officers would manage the technical and financial details of the Newport Folk Festival but ultimately answered to the board.

Turning their attention to the programming side of the festival, Wein, Seeger, and Bikel proposed a format indebted to that used at the earlier Folk Festivals and adapted from the Jazz Festival, but expanded and recalibrated. There were to be three big evening concerts that would feature a mix of "stars" and unknowns. Daytime activities would consist of a substantially enlarged array of smaller workshop sessions that would concentrate on a single type of music, with sample themes offered such as "Banjoes and Fiddles," "Ballads," "Blues," and "International Folk Music." In their description the workshops would "be opportunity for fans of one particular performer or idiom to really soak up all they want, and for the performer to really give more than a superficial glance at what they can do." And, importantly, these workshops were not to be held on the main stage of the festival but to be presented more informally "under awnings, or tents." Summarizing their vision, Wein, Seeger, and Bikel put forward a broad suggestion about the ideal breakdown of the program. Seventy-five percent, they say, should consist of "country string music, old fashioned and new singing in English of old and new ballads and folk-songs, blues, gospel music. 25% remaining, at least two items of some American traditional music," selected from a wide range of different ethnic traditions among which they included American Indian, Louisiana French, Pennsylvania Dutch, Jewish, Syrian, Puerto Rican, and Asian. This was the folk festival conceived as a living representation of American pluralism, with a nod to global inclusiveness, on a scale hitherto unrealized.

The reformation of the Newport Folk Festival, prompted in part by the disruption occasioned by the Newport riot, reflected the continuing momentum of the folk revival. While the Newport festival was in remission, festivals in Berkeley and elsewhere still flourished and were joined by several new undertakings. Among the most influential festivals to emerge in these years was that held at the University of Chicago, another in a long line of college-based events. Started by students who were part of the school's Folklore Society, the first University of Chicago festival occurred in February 1961. Its timing—several months after the second Newport festival—was no coincidence, for it was motivated by dissatisfaction with the commercial character of the earlier Newport productions, much as the organizers of the Bard College Jazz Festival had been in a parallel realm.[112] Reviewing the 1963 Chicago Folk Festival, John Cohen and Ralph Rinzler noted its success and celebrated its achievement as a festival that was part of a trend "which is being followed at UCLA, Berkeley, Cornell, Queens College and hopefully at Newport this summer . . . bringing the folk back into the folk music revival."[113] The University of Chicago Folk Festival and others like it provided an alternative blueprint for what a folk festival might be—one that George Wein, Pete Seeger, and others involved in the re-launched Newport festival attended to closely.

Another developing stream that shaped the reformed Newport Folk Festival concerned the intersection of the folk revival with political activism. Folk music in the US became strongly aligned with leftist politics during the Popular Front era of the 1930s and the connection remained intact to a degree into the early years of the folk revival, despite efforts during the height of McCarthyism to blacklist Pete Seeger and others for their purported Communist sympathies. The first years of the 1960s saw substantial rejuvenation and realignment of the political priorities of the folk revival in connection with two mounting areas of concern: the escalation of Cold War aggression and the persistence of racial segregation and inequality. Civil rights organizers working in the Southern states increasingly used traditional African American music as an organizing tool, while young singer songwriters including Bob Dylan adopted a "topical" approach that offered commentary on the most pressing issues of the time. *Broadside* magazine, which began publication in February 1962, signaled the heightened significance attached to topical folk songs and importantly documented their uses in the field of activism. At first almost entirely given to the reprinting of song lyrics, *Broadside* began including reports from the field, alternating festival reviews with accounts of civil rights gatherings as though they were two sides of the same coin. Certain events such as the "Sing for Freedom" gathering held in Atlanta, Georgia, in May 1964, which brought together singers of the civil rights movement for a series of concerts and workshops, fused folk singing and political organizing into a vibrant synthesis.[114]

Under its reconfigured leadership, the Newport Folk Festival would not be as directly politicized as other branches of the folk revival, and neither would it be as purist in its motives as rival festivals like that in Chicago. Rather, as John Cohen explained in an appraisal of the folk festival scene that appeared in the 1964 program book: "At Newport, R.I., in the middle of the summer, there is the festival that combines all the good and also the bad aspects of all the festivals, along with many other factors, as well as what seems like the combined number of audience and performers of all the others."[115] Like the Jazz Festival did with regard to jazz in the late 1950s, the sheer scale of the reformed Newport Folk Festival changed the stakes for determining the proper role and function that a festival should play in representing the larger field of "folk music."

Scale in this case referred both to the size of the audiences that attended the Folk Festival and the contents of the program. For the first time, in 1963, the Folk Festival outdrew the Jazz Festival, and by a considerable proportion—an estimated forty-six thousand saw the Folk Festival that year, whereas Jazz Festival attendance had been a still-strong thirty-six thousand. This pattern remained in place for the rest of the decade. Regarding the program, at the 1963 Folk Festival eighteen daytime programs supplemented the three evening concerts. These included a Bluegrass workshop that brought Bill Monroe together with Mike Seeger, Mac Wiseman, and Monroe's manager, Ralph Rinzler; a Ballads workshop that gathered board member Jean Ritchie, Joan Baez, Doc Watson, Judy Collins, rediscovered Southern folk singer Clarence Ashley, and Bob Dylan; and a Blues workshop that introduced Mississippi John Hurt to northern folk audiences some thirty-five years after he made his only recorded work to date. Also on the program were two Children's Concerts; two movie screenings hosted by John Cohen; and a Sunday afternoon "Topical Songs and New Song Writers" workshop that placed rising star Dylan alongside Pete Seeger, folksong activist Guy Carawan, blues veteran John Lee Hooker, and civil rights standard-bearers the Freedom Singers.[116]

Dylan and the Freedom Singers also both performed at the opening Friday evening concert, where they together participated in one of the most iconic moments of the folk revival. *Billboard* provided a vivid account of the scene that transpired during Dylan's short set that night:

Reaching close to his finish of the closing spot on the bill, Dylan called to the stage Peter, Paul and Mary, Pete Seeger, Theo Bikel, Joan Baez and the Freedom Singers from Albany, Ga., all of whom lent a choral backup to Dylan's rendition of "Blowing in the Wind" . . . Following this, Dylan stepped back into the semi-circle of celebrated performers and joined them in an inspiring reading of "We Shall Overcome," which has come to be a sort of national anthem of the integration movement. In this rendition, Cordell Reagon, of the Freedom Singers, lined out the lyrics.[117]

Dylan, in 1963, was not "undiscovered" as Joan Baez had been prior to her appearance at the first Newport Folk Festival in 1959. He even had a long, two-page poem included in the program book for the 1963 festival, a clear sign that he was very much familiar to the organizers and to folk audiences of the time.[118] Still, his performance at the Friday concert and his other appearances on the program that year consolidated his rise as the most lauded young voice of the contemporary folk revival. It also did something more. The image of a line of artists clasping hands that had, from left to right, Peter, Paul, and Mary, Baez, Dylan (just off center), Bernice Johnson (who was on Dylan's left) and the rest of the Freedom Singers, Pete Seeger, and Theodore Bikel—captured in a photograph by John Byrne Cooke—became symbolic of the capacity that the Newport Folk Festival might possess to take all the disparate, competing facets of the folk scene and instill in them a sense of common bond and purpose. Young stood beside old, black beside white, stars shared the stage with those lesser known, and politics in effect was merged with pop.

* * *

Following upon the success of the 1963 festival, the Newport Folk Foundation set about putting its stated commitment to support and nurture folk music research into practice. A wide array of individuals and programs were selected by a special committee to receive financial support. These included the Council of the Southern Mountains in Berea, Kentucky, which had ties to board member Jean Ritchie; folk music magazines *Broadside* and *The Little Sandy Review*; WGBH public television station in Boston; and the Old Town School of Folk Music in Chicago. The Foundation also purchased tape recorders that it would lend for use to musicians Dorsey Dixon and Mike Seeger (also a board member).[119]

Most significantly, in early 1964, board members Alan Lomax and Mike Seeger drafted a proposal for a new position that would work in conjunction with the festival as a sort of in-house traveling folklorist. Their justification for the position read in part:

> There is general agreement that the traditional performers added greatly to the success and to the cultural value of the last festival. The board also seems to agree that we need more performers of this type on the program, and that they should be the best, the most representative and the most exciting that can be found... After considerable discussion it was agreed that someone be employed to help find these performers.[120]

The person hired as a scout for the festival would have a wide range of responsibilities. He would travel around the US and North America to find traditional performers that could be featured at the festival and make connections with already-known regional performers for the same purpose. He would help to coordinate travel and care for these artists at the festival and instruct them in how best to present their work in a festival setting. Furthermore, the scout would "find places where local festivals are needed, where there is a good local base for them and people to run them," an indication of how much the Newport Folk Foundation saw its mission in terms that were much broader than the Newport Folk Festival itself. Closing their memo, Lomax and Seeger recommended that the Foundation hire Ralph Rinzler into this new position. Rinzler, already mentioned several times, was an energetic and multifaceted figure who had attained great influence in the folk music scene as a musician with his bluegrass group the Greenbriar Boys, as someone who had "rediscovered" old-time musician Clarence Ashley and brought Doc Watson to wider attention, and as the manager for bluegrass figurehead Bill Monroe. He was readily accepted as the scout and coordinator for traditional performers and began to work for the Newport Folk Foundation in February 1964.

The fruits of Rinzler's fieldwork were readily apparent at the 1964 Newport Folk Festival. In the program book for that year, Rinzler wrote a detailed article explaining his endeavors: "Using a Nagra tape-recorder, newly purchased by the Foundation for collecting use, I traveled some 12,000 miles, visited and recorded more than 30 musicians and groups in eight States in addition to Nova Scotia and French Canada."[121] Among the artists who attended the festival as a result of Rinzler's scouting work were a group of

Cajun musician from Mamou, Louisiana, marking the first time such a group had performed outside their native region and launching a revival of interest in Cajun music. Others included blues performers Robert Pete Williams and Fred and Annie Mae McDowell; Arkansas singer-songwriter Jimmy Driftwood who had a 1960 hit with his recording of "The Battle of New Orleans"; Frank Proffitt, whose version of "Tom Dooley" had provided the blueprint for the widely popular rendition by the Kingston Trio; and Clayton McMichen, a country music pioneer that Rinzler helped to bring out of retirement. Supplementing the performers recruited by Rinzler were other celebrated representatives of "traditional" music such as Elizabeth "Libba" Cotton, an African American singer and guitarist from North Carolina who came to wider attention through her association with the Seeger family; and in a major act of rediscovery, Son House, the Mississippi bluesman and contemporary of Robert Johnson, making his first public appearance after being located by blues collectors Dick Waterman and Phil Spiro earlier that year. The prevalence of an older generation of musicians, many of whom had been thought dead or at least long removed from any capacity to perform, gave the festival of these years an almost surreal quality, past and present seeming to collapse together. As Robert Cantwell observed, the festival now played a central role in "introducing northeastern urban audiences to the mountain music and traditional blues styles formerly confined to particular regions and communities, decommercializing formerly commercial forms, [and] reinventing cultural categories derived from race and region long axiomatic in folksong scholarship and presentation."[122]

Enhanced dedication to the most "traditional" elements of folk music was only one part of the story of the festival in its new incarnation. The sheer number and range of artists presented at the 1964 Newport Folk Festival was nearly overwhelming. At the opening Thursday evening concert, billed a "Concert of Traditional Music" and hosted by Alan Lomax, the Cajun Band, Elizabeth Cotton, Jimmie Driftwood, Clayton McMichen, Fred and Annie Mae McDowell, and Robert Pete Williams all appeared, as if to announce to the festival audience, look what we went out and found for you. Joining them were Mississippi John Hurt, Bessie Jones and the Georgia Sea Island Singers, the Stanley Brothers, Muddy Waters, Doc Watson and the Watson Family, and sixteen other performers, making for a total count of twenty-seven artists in all—just for opening night. As the weekend proceeded, moving through daytime workshops such as "Broadsides (Topical Songs)" (where Dylan made his first appearance of the year's festival) and the

Saturday afternoon "Blues" workshop where Son House performed in the company of younger blues revivalists Koerner, Ray, and Glover, and Dave Van Ronk, to the capacious evening concerts and Sunday morning Concert of Religious Music, the juxtaposition of older artists with younger ones, of more traditional and more contemporary styles of folk, assumed an accumulated impact. Meanwhile the crowds expanded accordingly, swelling from an opening night attendance of just over four thousand on a characteristically drizzly Newport evening to three consecutive evening concerts from Friday to Sunday that drew more than three times that figure. Overall attendance, reported to have surpassed seventy thousand for the four days, eclipsed the previous high for any Newport festival, jazz or folk.[123] The era of the mass festival had taken another major step forward, fed by a musical style and subculture where mass success was often regarded with suspicion.

Much of the resulting commentary was celebratory, indicated by the summary offered by *Broadside* magazine: "Overall impression of the 1964 Newport Folk Festival: simply great, wonderful, historic."[124] For some observers, however, the very breadth of the 1964 Newport festival caused concern—as had the parallel growth of the jazz festival in the preceding decade. Most articulate in this connection was Paul Nelson, a co-founder of the *Little Sandy Review* and an influential voice among the younger guard of folk music critics. Echoing jazz writer Whitney Balliett's characterization of the Newport Jazz Festival as a "statistician's dream" six years earlier, Nelson observed in *Sing Out* that the 1964 Newport Folk Festival "was finally one of numbers: a struggling, basically honest giant caught in the snare of its own popularity and nearly smothered by the sheer love and admiration of its many fans." Nelson elaborated: "Nearly twice as many people attended this year as last, and attendance records were broken every night of the Festival . . . Nearly 3,000 people attended the Blues Workshop Saturday afternoon, as compared to around 600 at the largest workshop last year," and by his count there had been two hundred twenty-eight artists performing at the festival in all.[125] Figure 7.4 portrays singer Barbara Dane performing at the blues workshop, surrounded by the festival crowd.

Nelson's overall assessment of the Festival was more positive than negative and he praised the opening Concert of Traditional Music as a particular high point, "breathtaking" in its presentation of "active traditional American folk music." Yet he worried, as did many other attendees, that the size of the festival swamped the potential for intimacy that was one of the most valued aspects of the folk music scene. That Nelson's perceptions struck a chord

Figure 7.4 Singer Barbara Dane performs at the Blues Workshop during the 1964 Newport Folk Festival. The workshops were intended to allow for intimacy between artists and audience members, but as crowds swelled, some feared that the intent of the festival would get lost. Photograph by David Gahr. Courtesy of the Estate of David Gahr.

could be seen in the fact that for the next year's program book, in 1965, he contributed an essay in which he diagnosed some of the problems of the previous year and offered a set of remedies.[126] The Festival's board and its producers were listening, a sign of how much the Newport Folk Festival in effect embodied a kind of living dialogue on the current state of folk music and the capacity for a large-scale music gathering to strike an effective balance between spectacle and social engagement.

A Soundman's Journey

Then, in 1965, came the maelstrom generated by Bob Dylan's Newport Folk Festival performance. The story of Dylan's act of "going electric" at Newport has been taken as an emblematic turning point in the intersecting histories of the folk revival and the evolution of rock. Exact details remain highly contested, to the point that Newport Folk Festival historian Rick Massimo devotes a chapter to the episode comprised of a broad patchwork of competing perspectives from dozens of participants and observers, none of which offers a definitive account.[127] I previously wrote of the performance, "If Dylan, by incorporating the electric guitar, gestured toward a new hybrid of folk and rock sensibilities, the controversy stirred by his use of the instrument also indicated the extent to which the electric guitar by 1965 had become an object invested with deep significance among certain segments of the pop audience."[128] On the other hand, Elijah Wald, whose version of the event is as close to definitive as we are likely to get, stresses that the true source of conflict was not Dylan's use of the electric guitar as such, but the way his appearance made manifest tensions that were building in the folk revival for some years and that had marked the commentary on the Newport festival since its inception. Observes Wald of the impact of Dylan's appearance: "It was not Dylan who was transformed by that weekend; it was Newport and the delicate balance of alliances that had formed the folk revival."[129]

One figure at the center of Dylan's epochal performance, but rarely acknowledged for his role in what transpired, was sound engineer Bill Hanley. As Wald rightly notes, it was not just the electric guitar as icon or symbol that caused the disturbance that resulted. Rather, the *sound* of Dylan's band—louder than many had experienced before and marked by considerable distortion—led some members of the Newport Folk Foundation board and the audience to express their disappointment, anger, and even sense of betrayal. That sound was projected through the festival's sound system, which was designed by Hanley, who had worked with the Newport Folk and Jazz Festivals for the better part of a decade at that point. Whether Hanley was himself at the soundboard during Dylan's set is itself one of many uncertainties that surround Dylan's performance, along with such questions as, just how much of the audience booed during his set, or, whether Pete Seeger did in fact try to cut the electrical cord with an ax (the consensus is, he did not). Esteemed producer Joe Boyd offers a vivid recollection of Dylan's set in his memoir, where he claims that he was primarily responsible for adjusting the levels of the mix during sound check along with his friend, Paul Rothchild. According to Boyd, when board members Alan Lomax, Theodore Bikel, and Pete Seeger were storming around backstage demanding that the sound be turned down during Dylan's performance, he was the one that conveyed the message to Rothchild, who by then was working the sound accompanied by Peter Yarrow—also a Newport board member—and Albert Grossman, then serving as Dylan's manager. Yarrow reportedly refused to turn the music down, claiming that "the board is adequately represented at the sound controls and the board member here thinks the sound level is just right."[130] He added a raised middle finger for emphasis.

Hanley, who appears nowhere in Boyd's narration, has his own story to tell. In Hanley's account, he was mixing the sound with Yarrow. They were taking direction from Dylan as to how he wanted the sound levels to be set, and Hanley grew worried: "everything was right at the edge of, before they would self-destruct, the speakers would, and you're in real trouble, when the speakers go out! . . . When Dylan went distorted, that's usually an indication that the speakers are close to their limits." Asked if he thought that Dylan was seeking to distort his sound on purpose, Hanley answered affirmatively but noted that it was still difficult to tell whether the distortion was ultimately coming from the amps of the musicians or from those Hanley had set up for the p.a. system. Although Hanley's system was state-of-the-art for its time, the speakers did not have modern capabilities to handle high output levels without causing a certain measure of sonic distress. This was, according to the sound engineer, the real cause of Pete Seeger's consternation: "Pete was upset that the distortion was messing up the folk movement."[131]

Leaving aside the question of who, exactly, was responsible for engineering the sound during Dylan's set, there is no uncertainty about Hanley's importance to the production of a string of major live music events stretching from the late 1950s through the early 1970s. In this capacity, Hanley was one of a few key figures who established the terms of live sound production in an era marked by growing crowds and commensurately expanding technical systems for projecting the music to those gathered. Others who contributed to this development included the Clair Brothers—Gene and Roy—of Lancaster, Pennsylvania, who began providing their p.a. system for regional events in the early 1960s and then moved on to the national level; and a little later, Augustus Owsley Stanley III, also known as Bear, who designed the sound systems used by the Grateful Dead during the early years of their career along with manufacturing what was known as the most potent LSD then distributed in the US.[132] No sound engineer of the era had a career whose reach expanded further than Hanley's, however. That he remains largely unknown outside the realm of audio engineering, where he is revered as the "Father of Festival Sound," is a mark of how much the technical apparatus required to produce live sound events has gone unexamined.[133] The simple fact is, the modern music festival as it evolved from Newport to Woodstock and up to the present day would not exist without the capability to allow amplified sound to be heard by a huge, dispersed audience in the tens if not hundreds of thousands, with sufficient volume and clarity. Hanley was a primary architect of this capability, and his career makes evident the interconnections that existed at the production level between musical events that have been treated as distinct and disparate undertakings.

* * *

When, exactly, Hanley began working for Wein on the Newport festivals is hard to pin down. He does not appear in any program books until the Jazz Festival of 1962, when Wein re-assumed control after the riot; and after that point his Medford, Massachusetts-based company Hanley Sound, which also included his brother Terry, was routinely listed as the primary sound provider for both the Jazz and Folk Festivals for several years running, until 1967. According to Hanley, however, he first approached Wein about working the Jazz Festival in 1957, when the sound was handled by another New England company, Faircast Systems; and then worked alongside a sound engineer named Myles Rosenthal who was hired by Wein in 1958.[134] Rosenthal had produced the sound for performances at the Forest Hills Stadium in Queens, and a 1958 article on the Jazz Festival effusively described the sound system he had designed, crediting him with overcoming many of the obstacles that had routinely plagued sound production in outdoor venues:

> As tested last night in Freebody Park, the system appears to have a good deal of fidelity and no lack of power ... the "Rosenthal method" appears to have licked some of the bugs in previous amplification of the festivals ... Rosenthal points out that current "public address" equipment is designed only for voice frequencies, about 150 to 5,000 cycles per second, whereas good musical reproduction calls for a range of 50 to 15,000 cycles. Four huge clusters of speakers, including two bass speakers and a treble "driver" with a baffle like an auto grille, have been erected at Freebody.[135]

Rosenthal may well have deserved credit for building the sound system that year, but Hanley claims it was he who did the actual mixing during most of the performances. Recalled Hanley: "A very important part of the sound system is the guy who's controlling the level of the microphones. But [Rosenthal] could care less about that ... So for three years I did that, and then in 1960, George took over down there, and I got to be the prime man."[136]

As Hanley's observations suggest, the work of the live sound engineer involves multiple layers of expertise. One layer, perhaps the most fundamental, involved providing the equipment necessary to make the sound audible within the performance space. This was no straightforward task. P.A. systems had been commercially available for some three decades at the time that Hanley began his career, but the most dedicated professional sound engineers would not simply buy a prefabricated system out of a catalogue and put it to work. Building a high-grade system required exacting knowledge of the product lines of multiple audio component manufacturers; and it also was all but a given that the sound engineer would have considerable electronics knowledge, such that he might customize certain parts or even build them himself. Early in his time working with Wein on the Newport Jazz Festival, Hanley constructed his own speakers, commissioning the cabinet from a contractor who worked across the street from his own shop and installing a set of JBL D130 loudspeakers, a pioneering loudspeaker design first issued in 1948. Soon thereafter he began using McIntosh power amplifiers, expressing a particular affinity for the MC-75, a seventy-five-watt amplifier first made available in 1961.[137] Audio components such as these were produced as much if not more for home audiophiles as for live music production. It was left to Hanley and other sound engineers to determine how they could be best adapted to the demands of a concert or festival setting.

Having the right equipment was just a starting point. Live sound engineering required attention to the quality of the sound as the performance happened. The sound had to be mixed on the spot to ensure that the different frequencies were sufficiently audible, that the lows did not drown out the highs or vice versa. When Hanley's career started the tools available to allow significant adjustment of sound and frequency levels were fairly limited. Mixing consoles had nowhere near the sophistication they would possess by the late 1960s or early 1970s, and so much depended on the ears of the sound engineer and the ability to create the right balance through the proper set-up of microphones, amplifiers, and speakers.

Hanley's attunement to these details was at work in one of the most significant innovations that he had a hand in implementing, the movement of the sound engineer to a "front of house" position so that the mixing of the sound would happen from the vantage point of the listening audience. This aspect of live sound engineering has become such a staple of the field that it is hard to imagine a time when it was not the prevailing convention. Yet as Hanley explains, "Up until that time [around 1960], sound systems were controlled backstage, or like at Carnegie Hall, when you walk in the back door, then the sound system was inside a closet!" Hanley recognized the inadequacy of this setup, and as he tells it, "I demanded we go out in the audience so I could hear what was coming from the stage. And I really invented the front of house positions for the smaller shows, so that you could control everything."[138] To do this effectively, he had to design a way to place the mixing console farther from the installed sound system than was customary, which carried the risk that the strength of the audio signal would be diminished. Over time, he developed what became called a "snake," a chain of cable with transformers at the end that preserved signal strength.[139] Hanley credits George Wein with having grasped the advantages of his method: "Well, it made sense to George, as a musician, to be able to hear what was going on, because he really taught me to listen to music better. He was such a good musician."[140]

Wein returned the favor in his memoir, where he noted that one of the things that gave him confidence when he re-assumed control of the Newport Jazz Festival in 1962 was that he had, in Hanley and lighting technician Chip Monck, "the best in the business."[141] While Wein developed his Festival Productions company and increased the geographical reach of his promotional efforts, Hanley was right alongside him as his favored sound engineer. A 1966 ad that Hanley Sound placed in *Billboard* captured something of the expanding range of his pursuits. Advertising "complete sound systems temporarily installed for your concert or festival," Hanley listed among his credits both Newport festivals—Jazz and Folk—along with festivals in Chicago, Philadelphia, Ohio Valley, Cincinnati, and Detroit. Also telling of the growth of Hanley's enterprise was that he had three office locations by then, one in New York City and one in Washington, DC, along with the home base in Medford.[142] All told, the ad stands as a valuable index of the professionalization of live sound production by the middle years of the 1960s and of the vital role that music festivals played in that development.

* * *

Another sign of Hanley's evolving reputation came in his involvement with the Beatles' 1966 concert at Shea Stadium. Here, Hanley moved more squarely outside of Wein's orbit into the world of rock. This was the Beatles' second Shea Stadium concert and was neither the cultural landmark nor the financial success that had been the previous year's event.[143] Still, in one significant area the 1966 concert marked a major advance on the 1965 show, that of sound production. Promoter Sid Bernstein—who had taken over the production of the jazz festival in Newport in 1961, the year after the riot—recalled, "At the first Shea concert, the screaming kids had overwhelmed the sound system so that no one could really hear the music. I called Bill Hanley, an audio genius who worked out of Boston. Bill set up a sound system that proved to be a vast improvement over the first Shea concert."[144] Hanley offered his impressions of working the concert in a 1989 interview:

> I got to the Beatles when electricity became an extension of the musician. I had learned about and put together an enormous amount of gear. I had four RCA 600W amps that came off of a battleship. They weighed two or three hundred pounds each . . . but it was not enough. When those boys came out on stage, it was absolute pandemonium: you couldn't hear the sound system, you couldn't hear yourself think.[145]

Hanley assembled a uniquely designed and unusually powerful system for the concert that included a custom-built mixing console. He construed his work on the 1966 Shea Stadium concert as a turning point in his own career and in the larger culture of live sound production: "Sound changed from being high-fidelity . . . since the Beatles, it's become a battle of levels. With the Beatles, the on-stage levels were getting higher and higher, and the supporting sound system had to grow just to keep up."[146] Through his involvement in the event, Hanley helped to usher in the age of stadium rock as he had the era of the mass music festival.

Not all of Hanley's work was on such a massive scale, though. He became one of the principal sound engineers associated with the rise of rock ballroom scene that began to take shape after 1965 with the advent of the Fillmore Auditorium in San Francisco. When the Fillmore's storied proprietor Bill Graham decided to open an East Coast venue, he turned to Hanley to install a sound system in what became called the Fillmore East. To have a state-of-the-art system built into the hall was an innovation in itself. Throughout most of the ballroom era, venues provided minimal sound support and it was left to the artists to carry their own sound people on tour. Graham biographer John Glatt observes that the impresario wanted to have a strong in-house system to streamline the staging of shows at the hall. Described by Glatt, the resulting Hanley Sound System "cost $35,000, and Graham only leased it from Hanley, who retained ownership. It consisted of twenty-six speakers... strategically placed around the theater with a total power source of 35,000 watts," and included a cluster of speakers in the center that were suspended over the stage using a unique system of weighted supports.[147] Having put his sonic imprint on one of the leading rock ballrooms of the Northeast, Hanley established his versatility twice over, extending his efforts in the rock realm and demonstrating his ability to work in contained, indoor spaces just as well as open outdoor ones.

Hanley's association with Graham and the Fillmore East, more probably than his long-standing work with the Newport festivals, brought him to the attention of Michael Lang, one of the primary architects of the Woodstock Music and Art Fair (as it was officially titled). By this time, in early 1969 when the plans for Woodstock first generated, rock festivals were assuming momentum of their own apart from the many jazz and folk festivals that had preceded them. The Monterey International Pop Festival, a landmark event held in June 1967, had been preceded by a week by another festival in the Northern California Bay Area, the Magic Mountain Music Festival staged on Mount Tamalpais in Mill Valley.[148] Lang himself staged one of the most ambitious events to date in Miami, Florida, in May 1968; and now wanted to apply the lessons he had learned elsewhere. He partnered with record executive Artie Kornfeld and together they approached a duo of young venture capitalists, John Roberts and Joel Rosenman. The collaboration between the four principals—Lang and Kornfeld representing the dedicated counterculturalists and Roberts and Rosenman the more "straight" businessmen—was famously contentious.[149] Yet there is little dispute that Lang provided the primary creative vision for Woodstock and recruited a production staff that was picked to carry out that vision.

Among those who oversaw the technical details of Woodstock, Hanley was one of several tied to the Fillmore East, along with production coordinator John Morris and technical director Chris Langhart. Also involved was Hanley's long-time associate from the Newport festivals, Chip Monck, who held primary responsibility for stage and lighting design and construction and served as one of the festival's principle masters of ceremonies. Tasked to approach Hanley about the job was Stanley Goldstein, who was a sort of all-purpose deputy working with Woodstock Ventures, the production company that managed the festival. Goldstein himself had a background in sound engineering and was in a good position to recognize the unique value that Hanley would bring to the enterprise. Commenting on the state of live sound production at the time, Goldstein observed:

What people were using were Altec Voice of the Theater speaker cabinets. Not the small Voice of the Theater, the enormous Voice of the Theater cabinets—nine feet tall, four feet wide . . . They were enormous, they weighed a lot but they could not take the power . . . P.A. was really in its infancy, and Hanley was capable of putting together a large system. Maybe not large by today's standards, but at that time, Hanley was—there was nobody else.[150]

This is not to say that working with Hanley was without pitfalls. Goldstein noted that Hanley's equipment was advanced but worn from excessive use. Hanley worked a tireless schedule by 1969, taking one gig after the next, not allowing time to take stock and maintain what he had. On some level, for him, Woodstock was just another job, as he explained with characteristic equanimity later on: "Woodstock didn't feel like a historic moment . . . You're busy making everything work, making it sound good . . . Being a technocrat as I am, I was shut out of the political and historical significance."[151]

Once on board, Hanley grasped the technical requirements of the undertaking. By this time the audio manufacturing sector had adapted to the increasing demand for high-output systems. Earlier in the decade, Hanley relied on seventy-five-watt McIntosh amplifiers. Now the company made an amplifier, the MC3500, that issued three hundred and fifty watts. Another advance was the Crown DC300 amplifier, which put out three hundred watts while using solid-state circuitry that allowed for a significant reduction in size, enhancing transportability while maximizing power. The system Hanley assembled for Woodstock was comprised of multiple McIntosh and Crown amps—he recalls having used nearly twenty of the McIntosh units alone—for a total output of around 10,000 watts, Hanley's best estimate of the strength required to project to the expected audience of around 100,000 people.[152] When it became clear that the audience was far larger than anticipated, numbering several hundred thousand, Hanley had to make quick adjustments as he explained to jazz journalist Marc Myers: "On the first day, I went under the stage to the amplifiers and changed the compressors. These controlled how much information was being sent to the amplifiers. My change brought up the lower levels of the music but also made sure the higher levels didn't distort . . . The music could be heard loud and clear across the entire property."[153] In Figure 7.5, Hanley works the mixing board that shaped the sound from all these amps into something clear and powerful.

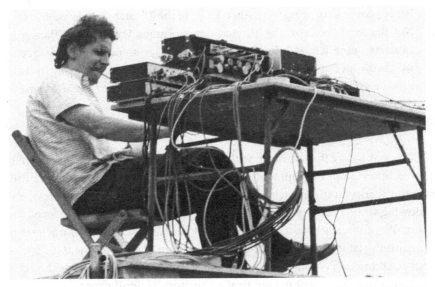

Figure 7.5 Sound engineer Bill Hanley works the mixing board at Woodstock while seated on a platform above the crowd. Hanley's audio ingenuity was one of key factors that enabled the rise of mass music festivals. Photograph by David Marks—3rd Ear Music. Courtesy of David Marks/Hidden Years Music Archive.

Especially groundbreaking was the speaker formation that Hanley and his team built for the festival. Projecting sound across such a large open-air expanse required methods that were largely untested. Hanley oversaw the construction of two speaker towers, each seventy feet high, so as to carry up the slope of the hill that ran from the stage and rose up through the field where the audience was encamped. He assembled the speakers himself, using an array of Altec and JBL components to achieve a desired balance of high, low, and midrange frequencies in cabinets that were eight feet high. The most innovative feature of the design was the arrangement of two levels of speakers, one at the top of the tower and one several rungs below. Hanley said of the setup, "The top section featured full-range speakers focused on the back of the property—which was the highest point on the hill. The bottom speaker sections had to be designed to reach everyone else who was seated on the ground level."[154] Like his earlier adoption of the front-of-house mixing position, Hanley and his crew again intuited that the system had to be adjusted to the needs of the listening audience, recognizing that in such a large festival setting those occupying space near the stage would have a very different experience than those farther away. Their success was acknowledged by Greil Marcus, reviewing the festival for *Rolling Stone*, who wrote: "The music became something that was going on there, and it was terrific, but it was by no means the whole show. The magnificent sound system was clear and audible long past the point at which one could no longer see the bands."[155]

Woodstock marked something of a culmination of a series of milestones in Hanley's career that mapped onto the larger evolution of live music production in the US during a fruitful decade. He later he acknowledged its importance as a turning point: "Volume without distortion raised the stakes and made rock more spectacular ... From a sound perspective, I had never before designed anything nearly as large as I had for Woodstock—or as powerful."[156] Hanley's ultimate understanding of his work on the festival was far from triumphant, though. Reflecting on the longer-term repercussions of Woodstock upon his own career, Hanley noted somewhat bitterly, "It was my downfall, really."[157] He elaborated elsewhere: "After Woodstock, the festival markets dried up. I lost a quarter of a million bucks worth of business in three weeks, and I was already three or four hundred thousand dollars in debt."[158] Part of the problem stemmed from increased police and community scrutiny of music festivals in the aftermath of Woodstock, which was compounded by the turn of events during the Rolling Stones' epochal performance at the Altamont Speedway in December of that year. Hanley also faced mounting pressure from competing sound producers such as the Clair Brothers, who more successfully adapted their business model to the emerging arena rock economy. Still, Hanley remained active well into the 1970s and beyond, and played a major supporting role in several other festivals that helped to define the emergent form of the rock festival and the continuing history of the jazz festival alike.

Festivals, Free and Unfree

The food stands were up on the hill. Below the hill was the stage. Ringing the stage was a sea of people. Ringing the sea of people was a column of movement—people moving—and that column never stopped during the entire festival. There was constant traffic in both directions: people going to the bathroom, people going out to their campsites, people going to get food, people going who-knows-where. Some people were just wandering. So there were stationary people almost as far as you could see in front of the stage, and ringing them was an endless procession of people walking and moving.[159]

Woodstock, as captured in this evocative description by festival attendee and Food for Love worker Peter Beren, magnified the crowd-generating power of festivals by several degrees. It figures as a generational touchstone and provides probably the single most influential image of a music festival to the public at large. Bill Hanley's ambivalent recollections of Woodstock suggest, though, that the sheer scale of the festival was a double-edged sword. Earlier critics expressed worry over how the Newport Jazz and Folk Festivals, as they grew larger, lost touch with core aspects of their avowed mission to serve a particular musical community and celebrate its values. Woodstock generated a parallel set of concerns amidst the largely celebratory rhetoric. Rock journalist Jerry Hopkins asserted, in what was likely the first book-length work dedicated to rock festivals, that in the aftermath of Woodstock, "Festivals had become a part of the 'numbers game,' and the American public, along with Festival promoters, began to accept, however carefully, the fact that the pop, folk or rock festival meant if not big money, certainly big crowds."[160] Much ambiguity dwelled in the relationship between those two measures of scale, money and crowds, all the more so in the case of Woodstock, the model of a "free festival" that was never intended to be free. John Roberts, one of the two principal financial backers of Woodstock, put the matter well: "On August 13 I was still under the illusion that gates could be erected, tickets sold, attendance controlled, food dispersed, and an over-all profit made. By August 14 I knew better. I understood that we were engaged in a last-ditch holding operation."[161]

Both the enthusiasm that attached itself to Woodstock and the ambivalence that it stirred indicated a wider cynicism that settled around the rock or pop festival phenomenon in the two years since Monterey Pop. *Rolling Stone* magazine began publication on November 9, 1967, with a cover story by Michael Lydon asking where the money from the nonprofit festival had gone; and that tenor of suspicion remained prevalent in the magazine's coverage of music festivals throughout the next few years.[162] To no small degree, the skepticism that rock journalists brought to festival commentary was an extension of the disposition that jazz and folk critics had long articulated, and the issues of concern evinced the continuity. Yet there was a mounting sense that the profit motive was even starker in the emergent pop festival field than it had been with festivals past. Promoters were drawn by the lure of staging such a big event successfully, sensing that a new economy of scale was emerging in the field of rock and pop concert presentation. Many of these nascent promoters lacked the experience and preparation required to do the necessary work, and so news of festivals throughout 1968 and 1969 was as often about failed efforts as it was about those that were successfully launched. Jerry Hopkins, again, summed up the prevailing sentiment in June 1969, warning prospective festivalgoers of the need to be cautious of the "inept and/or greedy promoters who've been leaping for the festival bandwagon the past year or so. Especially in recent months, increasing numbers of artists and groups haven't shown up for festivals, because their names were advertised long before deals were made . . . The first pop festival, that held in Monterey two years ago, was by far the best . . . Since then, according to [Monterey Pop producer] Lou Adler . . . 'the music industry has prostituted Monterey . . . now it's a hype. It's become a promoter's tool.' "[163]

Rolling Stone brought these concerns to light on a national level, but they were also prevalent amidst the widening range of underground news publications that circulated in mostly urban settings where the counterculture had gained a significant foothold. An especially trenchant example appeared in the Atlanta underground newspaper, *The Great Speckled Bird*, in association with the Atlanta Pop Festival, held over the July 4th holiday in 1969—about six weeks before Woodstock. The week before the festival, regular contributor Miller Francis, Jr. referenced the Hopkins article cited above to open an extensive critique of the mission of the event, about which he raised several concerns. The sheer expense of it gave him pause, as he noted that its budget had risen dramatically from an earlier announcement of around $40,000 to well over $100,000. More troubling was the apparent cooperation between festival organizers and Atlanta officials in conjunction with annual Fourth of July celebrations. Francis claimed that the alliance suggested at least tacit support for a sort of virulent patriotic nationalism that was at odds with the ostensible values of the festival, signified by the producers' choice of an enlarged hand flashing a peace symbol as the event's trademark, seen in Figure 7.6. Criticizing the plan to produce a huge event at a raceway twenty miles outside of the city featuring predominantly national talent, Francis advised that the organizers of the Atlanta Pop Festival would make a more positive contribution if they did more to support music on the local level, in the city's parks and public spaces. Summing up the contradictions he perceived in the design of the festival, Francis concluded: "The size of the game

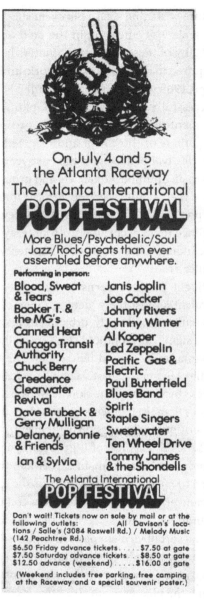

Figure 7.6 Advertisement for the Atlanta Pop Festival, July 4–5, 1969. The festival's peace sign logo became a point of contention for commentators who distrusted the profit motive behind the event. From *The Great Speckled Bird* (July 7, 1969).

has changed all right. The V-sign and a $12.50 ticket to a pop festival are not peacefully coexistent."[164]

Reading through these criticisms, it is easy to draw the conclusion that a fundamental antagonism existed between the money lust of festival promoters and the critics and journalists who set themselves up as the watchdogs and surrogate moral conscience of the festival scene. What this ignores is how much festival producers were themselves beset by the tension between the pursuit of profit and the efforts to build a platform for community expression of shared values through music. The rift between the two factions of the Woodstock production team was the most widely publicized such conflict, but it was far from isolated. Similar tensions ran through the team of people that produced the Atlanta Pop Festival, according to co-producer and longtime concert promoter Alex Cooley. An Atlanta-born entrepreneur who got into the business of festival production after attending the Miami Pop Festival of December 1968 (not the festival produced by Michael Lang, but a different Miami Pop Festival held seven months later that was more successfully staged), Cooley was one of seventeen people that comprised the investors and producers of the 1969 Atlanta festival. Describing his work on the enterprise years later, he characterized it as a "horse put together by committee," but also explained that there were so many principals because that was the only way they could raise the necessary funds. Among the several figures that put in money, there was marked disagreement as to how much of a priority it was to make a profit. Said Cooley: "There were some amongst us who felt like making money off of music was evil and bad. I have to admit, I was wavering on that myself. I later decided that wasn't true, but we made $15,000. That's after we all got our money back that we initially put in."[165] To turn any kind of profit on a rock festival in 1969 was something of an accomplishment, but $15,000 divided among several investors was relatively small return on an event that drew an estimated 100,000 over two days and featured the likes of Janis Joplin, Creedence Clearwater Revival, Blood, Sweat, and Tears, Johnny Winter, Booker T. and the MGs, and two bands that would become major arena rock attractions in the coming decade, Led Zeppelin and Grand Funk Railroad.

An internal production document circulated in connection with the Atlanta Pop Festival offers even stronger evidence that at least the most responsible promoters were mindful of the challenges they faced. Titled "Production and Crowd Communication," the two-page memo typed on the letterhead of the corporation formed to produce Atlanta Pop—International

Pop Festivals, Inc.—is like a condensed crystallization of the producers' ideology of festival organization. The opening sentence laid the matter bare: "Reaching fifty thousand people can be as easy as reaching a thousand if the presentation is not hampered by needless and instantly fabricated paranoias of the promoter."[166] Among these sources of paranoia, the first was the youth audience, which the memo charged was "arrogant enough to feel that their music is rightfully theirs." Mounting calls for festivals to be free because music was a resource of, by and for "the people," had characterized the late 1960s festival scene, extending and elaborating on the impulses evident in the Newport riot that started the decade.

According to the Atlanta Pop producers, these expectations and gestures of resistance could be tempered with the right sort of advance planning. They observe, in language that could be excerpted from a *Rolling Stone* report, "In the past year too many productions have faced veritable distruction [sic] because of senseless fences; because the site was ill chosen; because music had to be turned down and sometimes off; and because the promoter was more interested in getting the crowd in, and not caring whether they leave happy or not." Promoters, the memo continued, needed to recognize that if they planned to expect a crowd to "sit for seven hours with no hint of restlessness," they had to "make concessions to them that would have been unheard of two or three years ago." With that, the producers outlined the key areas that required suitable thought, effort, and planning to present a performance that was not just good but would effectively hold the crowd captive. These included: size and decoration of the stage; proximity of the stage to the audience; quality of sound, asserting that "a great sound system is the most important aspect of production" (and they hired Bill Hanley to provide the sound); effectiveness of good lighting; group set-up, concerning the efficiency of getting artists on and off the stage; and producing a happy group, having to do with the backstage provisions that made performers feel comfortable before and after their appearances. Concluding the memo was the suggestion, "Producing an exceptional show is not hard if the producer can keep himself in the mind of the listener *and* performer at the same time."

Taking the time to enumerate these guidelines to festival production, the producers of the Atlanta Pop Festival demonstrated their commitment to putting on the best show possible and also their interest in finding a formula for festival success that could be replicated. In this they had much in common with George Wein. However, the participating members of International Pop

Festivals, Inc., gave no indication of sharing the other motivations behind the Newport Jazz and Folk Festivals. Nowhere in the corporate minutes or other files preserved by Alex Cooley—who functioned primarily as the talent buyer for the organization—does one find the suggestion of nonprofit status, or a commitment to demonstrating that rock was an art form on par with classical music (or jazz or folk), or a desire to foster educational initiatives through the music. One could take this as another sign that rock, more than the musical styles that previously gave rise to a prominent festival culture, was in the end more dedicated to filthy lucre. Just as consequentially, the magnification of music festivals that took root with Newport Folk further intensified with the advent of rock and pop festivals required the bulk of the organizers' attention to be fixed on pragmatic concerns. How could you provide for the needs of tens if not hundreds of thousands of people over a two- or three-day period while ensuring that the musical performances that comprised the heart of the festival receive the production support necessary to provide a satisfying event, and staying within a designated budget and maybe even generating a profit? Based on the discussions held by the organizers of the Atlanta Pop Festival during the planning phases of the event, these were the driving concerns of their enterprise.

Immediately upon the completion of the Atlanta Pop Festival, several of the producers that comprised International Pop Festivals, Inc., set about organizing a second festival to be held outside Dallas, Texas, in cooperation with local producers Austin Wynne and Jack Calmes of the nascent concert production company Showco.[167] Having demonstrated that the Southeast could support a substantial festival, they now wanted to break ground in the Southwest. The Texas Pop Festival would be held over Labor Day weekend, only two months after the Atlanta affair and a couple of weeks after Woodstock. A handwritten note held in the files of the corporation offered an enthusiastic summary of the rationale for mounting this second festival. Under the heading, "Why Dallas?" appeared the following:

1. No large Pop Festival *ever* in the largest state (Alaska doesn't count).
2. Three day holiday weekend.
3. No conflicting entertainment events of equal size or drawing capacity.
4. Large youth market in immediate Dallas-Ft. Worth area.
5. Dallas central location for a six state area. (500 mile radius)
6. Dallas will follow on the coat-tails of the 2nd most successful festival EVER!

7. The biggest state should and can produce the most successful festival ever bar none.
8. Texas is ready![168]

The optimism and the expansionist vision outlined here offer telling insight into the minds of a group of mostly twenty-something men convinced that they could parlay one success into another. By certain measures, they accomplished their goal, as the Texas Pop Festival drew an audience of around 150,000 over its three days and presented another stellar lineup of performers including many who also appeared in Atlanta—among them native Texans Johnny Winter and Janis Joplin. Yet as reported by *Rolling Stone*, the crowd, large as it was, was smaller than anticipated because of bad publicity and overwhelmingly hot temperatures. Noted John Zeh writing for the magazine, "Much money, time and energy had been spent to take care of an anticipated onslaught that didn't materialize."[169] Alex Cooley recalled that Texas Pop, like Woodstock, became a free festival but not by design, because the ticket takers lost their nerve at the sheer numbers of people seeking admission.[170] And so, big crowds did not equal big money. The promoters took a financial bath, and International Pop Festivals, Inc., effectively dissolved in the festival's aftermath.

Alex Cooley forged on. He produced the second (and last) Atlanta Pop Festival with two partners from the previous year—Richard Bryan and Chris Cowing—and a new collaborator, Stephen Kapelow; all the remaining investors and members of the corporation withdrew. For the second year the festival was moved to a larger site, a raceway in Byron, Georgia, and was extended from two days to three, also during the July 4 holiday. The promoters added something they called a "Symposium on Awareness" to more explicitly integrate discussion of current socio-political concerns into the structure of the festival itself, promising to address issues ranging from drug abuse and ecology to civil rights and "alternatives to war."[171]

Once again, the promoters succeeded in drawing a large crowd, in this case more than 200,000 people, and presented some excellent music including the Allman Brothers, who both opened and closed the festival. And once again, they lost thousands of dollars because so many who attended refused to pay or otherwise got in for free. Commenting on the second Atlanta festival, the *Great Speckled Bird* accused the performers and promoters alike of being "pigs" for putting their desire for financial gain ahead of other priorities, writer Michael Hill wrongly conflating the size of the crowd with the size of the profit.[172] *Rolling Stone* made the dramatic suggestion that, as the summer's biggest festival, the second Atlanta Pop Festival could also be the last of its kind: "Fact is, when 100,000 people start gathering around a fence demanding to be let in free, there's little that anyone can or wants to do to stop them. Since all indications are that any big festival with much advance publicity is going to face this situation, it seems likely that few promoters ... will ever take the chance again."[173]

Cooley, for his part, left the festival field after one further effort in Puerto Rico, the 1972 Mar y Sol Festival, that was his biggest financial loss yet. For the rest of the decade, he committed himself to developing venues in Atlanta, most famously the Electric Ballroom opened in 1974, and became the go-to promoter for arena rock shows in the city and the surrounding region. Indeed, if there is a direct line of connection to be drawn between the advent of the rock festival and the emergence of arena rock as a dominant mode of concert production, it runs straight through Alex Cooley, the only one of the major arena concert promoters to get his start in festival production.

Festival Fusion

Bill Hanley and Alex Cooley both, from their different vantage points, were subject to the larger exhaustion of festival culture that seemed to be setting in by the time 1970 rolled around. Although Altamont has regularly been taken as the end point for a certain period in the evolution of mass music festivals, the challenges and difficulties of producing large-scale music festivals were widely apparent even prior to Woodstock. As a further case in point, consider the 1969 Newport Jazz Festival, held July 3–6 of that year (coinciding with the first Atlanta Pop Festival). George Wein, long resistant to rock music, made the decision to bring rock artists more into the fold of the long-running festival. Explained Wein in his notes for the 1969 Jazz Festival program, his stimulus for pursuing this direction came from a recent Boston *Globe* Jazz Festival where Roland Kirk joined Frank Zappa and the Mothers of Invention on stage: "This was communication with honesty at its highest level with the kids crowding around the bandstand like we used to for Benny and Duke in the ballroom days. This told me something! The kids will go for good music if they hear it."[174] So emboldened, Wein booked a broad cross-section of popular music talent for the festival, including Blood, Sweat, and Tears—whom he termed "the most important group to emerge from the youth music as far as jazz is concerned"—James Brown, Ray Charles, Buddy Guy, Jethro Tull, Led Zeppelin, The Mothers of Invention, and Sly and the Family Stone.

Jazz and rock were already poised in 1969 to have more fruitful, if sometimes fraught, interactions. Miles Davis, another featured performer at the 1969 Newport Jazz Festival, had already released his first tentative foray into electric music, *Filles de Kilimanjaro*, and his landmark *In a Silent Way* and *Bitches Brew* albums would soon follow. Bill Graham commonly booked jazz and rock artists on the same bills at his Fillmore West and East ballrooms. As popular music historian Matt Brennan observes, however, "It was one thing for jazz acts to be included at rock venues, and quite another for rock to be openly welcomed by a jazz festival."[175] At Newport Jazz in 1969, the dissonance between the aesthetics and even more so, the audience expectations of jazz and rock undercut what was, on the surface, a rousingly successful undertaking. Attendance that year set a record for either of the major Newport festivals, surpassing 85,000. The large youth audience attracted by the presence of the rock bands on the bill unsettled the proceedings in a way that evoked the earlier riot of 1960 and the unrest that had accompanied Duke Ellington's performance in 1956.

For the Friday night concert featuring Ten Years After and Jethro Tull, some 22,000 filled the festival venue (now moved to a setting called Festival Field), while another ten thousand perched on a hill beyond the gates. When a section of the fence came down, many onlookers rushed in; police maintained calm, according to *Rolling Stone*, but Wein, as he had done during Ellington's performance thirteen years earlier, projected a sense of unease from his position on the stage that was palpable. The next night, a version of the same scenario repeated during a performance by Sly and the Family Stone, and Wein was even more up in arms, imploring the audience to maintain their cool and restricting Stone and his band from offering an encore.[176] Although no riot ensued either night, Wein was shaken by the experience in a way that was irrevocable. Describing the festival later, Wein called it "four of the worst days of my life. Jazz—the music I loved—was being poisoned and stamped out, and I had served as an unwitting, but willing accomplice to the murder. The rock bands that played the festival were in another league and another world, and their scene had nothing to do with my passion as a promoter or musician."[177]

The events at the 1969 Newport Jazz Festival were one in a series of precipitating occurrences that ultimately severed the bond between Wein's now-historic festivals and the host city. That same year, the Newport Folk Festival lost more than $56,000 due to overspending on talent.[178] Meanwhile, the influx of young rock fans provoked the City of Newport to impose more rigid security restrictions on the production of the festivals, which entailed rising costs and greater logistical challenges for Wein and his production staff. An effort to move the Folk Festival out of Newport in 1970 did not come to pass and so no festival was held that year. The Jazz Festival occurred as scheduled in 1970, its more traditionalist impulses restored and reinforced with an opening night tribute to Louis Armstrong.

In 1971, however, chaos once again descended upon the Newport Jazz Festival. This time it was a product of the basic fact that post-Woodstock and post-Altamont, communities around the US had become far more cautionary about allowing rock festivals to occur in their midst. In the absence of much competing activity, the youth audience came to Newport seeking a festival experience. During a set by Dionne Warwick, the crowd gathered outside the festival gates began to tear down the fence keeping them out and crashed into the venue. Unlike in 1969, a full-scale riot ensued. Following the night's unrest, the City of Newport forced the cancellation of the rest of the Festival and subsequently revoked the license for Wein's Festival Productions to present any further festivals in the city. Wein, overcome by disappointment, complained after the fact: "The free music philosophy is the single most destructive thing to music in America. And that's got nothing to do with business. Free music means one of two things—either a tightly controlled government structure . . . or a bunch of idiots taking over the stage. Either way, artistry goes out the window."[179] There would be no further jazz or folk festivals in Newport for a decade. The Jazz Festival would relocate to New York City for several years, returning to Newport in 1981; and the Folk Festival went into remission even longer, until its revival in 1985.

* * *

That both Newport festivals were forced either to move or to cease activity entirely by 1972 might suggest that the early 1970s marked the termination of the festival impulse that had gained momentum in the US starting in the mid-1950s. This perception ignores the many signs of renewal that emerged during the same stretch of time, however. Rock festivals, to be sure, faced severe challenges and would not be fully reawakened for many years to come. In other musical realms, though, the period did not see a withering of activity. In folk music, the Festival of American Folklife, started by Ralph

Rinzler in 1967 under the auspices of the Smithsonian Institution, became a major summertime attraction that continues to draw tens of thousands of participants to the National Mall each year. The Ann Arbor Blues Festival, later renamed the Ann Arbor Blues and Jazz Festival, struggled financially and politically during its short and checkered history from 1969 to 1974 but provided a model for presenting African American music and musicians in a setting where they were the center of the activity and not a token presence as they were in many other contexts. Michigan was furthermore host to the Michigan Womyn's Music Festival, started in 1976, the most visible of several festivals that were motivated by the convergence of a separatist form of lesbian feminism with the emergence of a "women's music" genre largely oriented toward folk-tinged, self-revelatory work.

Also created during this time frame was the New Orleans Jazz and Heritage Festival, maybe the most enduring and impactful festival to arise out of a moment that has typically been understood as a period of rapid decline. The Jazz and Heritage Festival was yet another production by George Wein, a testament to the veteran promoter's persistence, resourcefulness, and tenacity in pursuing new opportunities. In effect, the festival in New Orleans was something of a fusion of his previous efforts, signified by the dual terms of the title: jazz *and* heritage. Wein explained in a 2008 interview: "I'd produced both the Jazz Festival and the Folk Festival in Newport, and I realized we'd brought a lot of southern people to the Folk Festival, a lot of New Orleans people to the Folk Festival, and I knew quite a few of them . . . The Folk Festival and the Jazz Festival, really combining the two was the inspiration for the New Orleans Jazz & Heritage Festival."[180] At the same time, more so than with the Newport festivals, Wein relied on a base of local collaborators that enabled the New Orleans festival to take root, ultimately giving it a level of support within the host city deeper and stronger than he had cultivated during his often-contentious sixteen years in Newport. The New Orleans Jazz and Heritage Festival, as it evolved from its inception in 1970 forward, became a potent model for a version of "festivalization" that, as sociologist Jonathan Wynn has examined, has characterized a deliberate strategy of urban revitalization in recent decades in such cities as Nashville, Austin, and even Newport upon the reclamation of its namesake festivals.[181]

The idea for a jazz festival in New Orleans long predated Wein's involvement. In fact, it predated the launching of the Newport Jazz Festival by four years. Behind the plan was the New Orleans Jazz Club (NOJC), a group of well-to-do, well-connected (and exclusively white) local enthusiasts in the city who were dedicated to the revival of interest in traditional New Orleans jazz. The organization prefigured many revivalist or preservationist activities in New Orleans, including the founding of Preservation Hall, the establishment of the Hogan Jazz Archives at Tulane University, and the creation of a Jazz Museum. Presenting jazz concerts was part of the organization's plan as well, as jazz scholar Bruce Boyd Raeburn observes, less to earn money for the club than to spark interest and enhance membership.[182] In the May 1950 issue of the NOJC newsletter, *The Second Line*, club president Edmond Souchon authored an editorial that announced as one of the group's goals the following:

> To organize a "National Jazz Festival" of all the hot clubs in America (and foreign lands) to be held in New Orleans. The Festival would last three days, would include marching bands, street parades, tailgate wagons, a concert, a dance . . . It is understood that the first festival would be presented entirely by New Orleans musicians and would not include out-of-town guest artists.[183]

This was a very different vision of a jazz festival than that instituted in Newport four years later along several fronts. It was meant to take place in the streets of the city and not just in a bounded space. Aesthetically it was more oriented toward a revivalist ethos favoring the jazz style of the 1910s and 1920s, with more modern jazz elements left to the side. And this concept of a jazz festival was more aggressively localized, designed to put New Orleans musicians—who at the time often struggled to find engagements—to work and to use jazz as a medium for generating civic pride.

For the next two decades, the NOJC sponsored a running series of live music performances spotlighting local talent including several events that were billed as festivals. These were relatively modest productions, but they found an audience beyond the club's membership and kept the idea of a jazz festival in the city alive. Heightened momentum behind the concept of a jazz festival in New Orleans grew in 1967, when the two hundred and fiftieth anniversary of the founding of the city approached (to be celebrated in 1968). Durel Black, a local businessman who by then had assumed a leadership position in the NOJC, headed the initiative to produce a jazz festival in conjunction with the city's planned commemorative activities. Enlisting the support of Mayor Victor Schiro and state governmental officials, as well as a wide array of local business representatives—many from the hotel and tourist industry—Black and the newly incorporated New Orleans International Jazz Festival, Inc. produced the first New Orleans Jazzfest during the week of May 12–19, 1968.

That first festival fulfilled and expanded on much of the vision outlined by Edmond Souchon eighteen years earlier, opening on Sunday, May 12, with a Jazz Mass honoring deceased musicians and a concert featuring four brass bands—the Olympia, Young Tuxedos, Crawford-Ferguson, and Frank Frederico—in the open air of Jackson Square. Festivities resumed on Wednesday, May 15, with a Parade near historic Congo Square—then officially named Beauregard Square after a general of the Confederacy—through the French Quarter, followed by an evening concert on the Steamboat President. On successive nights, concerts were held at Municipal Auditorium, one of the city's largest public halls located adjacent to Congo Square. The music was not strictly local in its orientation, nor was it singularly traditional. Several New Orleans jazz artists played during the evening concerts including Pete Fountain, Louis Cottrell, Paul Barbarin, Danny Barker, Armand Hug, and Al Belletto, but they were programmed alongside the likes of Duke Ellington (who headlined the concert on Thursday, May 16), Cannonball Adderley, Dave Brubeck, Ramsey Lewis, Gary Burton, and Woody Herman.[184] The event retained much of the character of existing jazz festivals at Newport and elsewhere, with a pronounced New Orleans accent, and it was repeated the following year, in 1969, by the same general organization but at a loss of several thousand dollars.

George Wein assumed production of the New Orleans Jazzfest—renamed the Jazz and Heritage Festival under his supervision—in 1970. However, he had first been approached about the prospect of staging a jazz festival in the city as far back as 1962. At that time, he recalls that a representative from the Royal Orleans Hotel named Olaf Lambert approached him and arranged a meeting between Wein and several members of the city's power elite. In 1962, the negotiations ground to a halt over the matter of segregation. Newport had never been fully welcoming of the African American musicians and festivalgoers that visited the city during the Jazz and Folk Festivals. In New Orleans, racial segregation was far more entrenched. Wein pointed out that many jazz musicians would refuse to play in segregated venues, and expected first-class treatment in hotels, neither of which the city's representatives could guarantee.[185] That Wein was himself married to an African American woman further complicated matters, especially since his wife Joyce played an active role in his concert production endeavors. Conversations between

Wein and city representatives continued intermittently over the ensuing years. In 1968, when the first New Orleans Jazzfest became a more tangible reality, Wein's marriage to Joyce remained a sticking point for the potential public image problem it would present, and so the first two Jazzfests were produced by Willis Conover, a radio announcer who had a long-standing association with Wein's Newport Jazz Festival.[186] Only after the financial failure of the 1968 and 1969 editions of Jazzfest were city leaders ready to adapt their expectations sufficiently to procure Wein's participation.

Once involved, Wein set about applying the lessons he had drawn from the Newport festivals, including those stemming most immediately from his experience at the 1969 Jazz Festival. The producer remembered: "After Woodstock, it had become clear to me that young people would no longer sit in reserved seats at an outdoor concert event ... My first job, then, was to convince the board of directors in New Orleans that the Newport Jazz Festival model was no longer valid. We needed a different approach to presentation and format.[187] The primary innovation divided the Jazz and Heritage Festival into two main constituent components: a series of evening concerts following the design of those that had characterized the first two Jazzfests; and an outdoor fair held in Beauregard (formerly Congo) Square. The Heritage Fair, as it became called, had a certain similarity to the workshops that were such a defining aspect of the Newport Folk Festival throughout the 1960s and would be the primary locus of the festival's presentation of Louisiana music and culture beyond the sphere of jazz. At the same time, it offered a markedly different version of regional traditions from Newport. Local specificity was paramount, there was an overarching emphasis on black music making, and the featured styles were at once traditional and up-to-date, with separate stages dedicated to Blues, Cajun, and Gospel music, and "Street" performances by a range of the city's brass bands. Another layer of local performance came through the inclusion of a troupe of Mardi Gras Indians led by Bo Dollis, African Americans who dressed in elaborate, self-fashioned "Indian" garb and represented a compelling instantiation of black New Orleans street culture. Also featuring twenty regional food vendors and a three-dollar admission charge (as compared with evening concert prices ranging from $3.50 to $6.50), the Heritage Fair constituted a sort of festival within the festival, more inclusive, wide-ranging, and representative of the event's regional base than the formal evening concerts.[188]

Serving as guides to local musical and cultural life were two young music fans and organizers who came to Wein's attention through the curator of

Tulane's Hogan Jazz Archive, Richard Allen. Quint Davis and Allison Miner became Wein's feet on the ground, exerting an especially pronounced influence upon the shape of the Heritage Fair. Davis, a New Orleans native, was the son of local businessman Arthur Davis, who was on the Festival board. Within a matter of time, he became the de facto producer of the Festival, assembling a local crew that provided a ready infrastructure for putting on the event from year to year. Said Wein, revealing what he had learned from years in the festival production trenches: "slowly but surely Quint's organization was taking over completely . . . Which is the only way you can create a great festival is to make it local. Otherwise you have this outside influence. It's a different thing."[189] Miner, who moved to New Orleans from Daytona Beach, Florida in 1967, was just as essential to the Festival's running. Together with Davis, she combed the city's nightclubs, making an especial effort to visit venues in the African American neighborhoods of New Orleans, seeking contemporary blues, funk, and gospel musicians. The first musician that she and Davis booked for the 1970 festival, Snooks Eaglin, was a fiery African American guitarist and street singer who, according to Miner, "didn't play in any club, just for neighborhood groups and churches."[190] To book gospel, they followed leads from listening to the radio, showing up at churches where programs of gospel music were announced. To secure the appearance of the Mardi Gras Indians, they met with Bo Dollis and thirty of his peers at a favorite drinking spot. In effect, they were to the Jazz and Heritage Festival what Ralph Rinzler had been to the Newport Folk Festival, energetic figures who scouted out local talent wherever they could find it, allowing Wein to focus on the bigger picture.

That first year, the Heritage Fair barely drew any crowd at all. Miner described the scene wistfully, saying: "Nobody came. There were about three hundred musicians and volunteers and only about fifty people in the audience . . . Then when the music started, the people in the neighborhood just took pocketknives and slit the thin canvas fence that we had put up. We didn't even care; at least there were people."[191] The New Orleans Jazz and Heritage Festival was not an immediate hit, and the Heritage Fair was decidedly second fiddle to the evening concerts in the audiences it drew and the attention it received. Over time the situation would reverse itself, the Heritage Fair eventually *becoming* the Festival, a shift that was facilitated by the move of the Fair in 1972 to the much larger setting of the New Orleans Fair Ground Racetrack. It took some years for the Jazz and Heritage Festival to turn a profit, but Wein used his business connections to secure sponsorship money from the Miller Brewing Company that helped to offset the losses during the crucial formative years. Rejecting the suggestion that reliance on sponsors tarnished the cultural mission of the Festival, Wein articulated an ethos he called "Commercialism with Credibility" that grew from his pragmatism as a producer but was also undoubtedly sharpened by his antipathy toward those younger music fans whose clamor for music to be "free" had forced him to abandon Newport for other environs.[192]

The crowds would come as the scale and scope of the Jazz and Heritage Festival grew, reaching a peak of 664,000 over two long weekends in April and May 2001.[193] Yet the very intimacy of those first years allowed for moments of musical discovery that had a unique power, foremost among which was the 1971 appearance of Henry Roeland Byrd, otherwise known by his stage name of Professor Longhair. A pianist and primary architect of New Orleans rhythm and blues who recorded a series of classic sides for Atlantic Records in the 1940s and 1950s, Fess (as he was called) had withdrawn from the stage several years earlier, and at the time of his debut at the Jazz and Heritage Festival worked as a custodian at a record shop. Video footage shot by the artist Hudson Marquez captured the scene: a sparse audience that consisted of a high proportion of African Americans gathered around the stage to witness Professor Longhair's return.[194] There was little sense of fanfare, and the music was far from ossified. Accompanied at first only by drummer Edmund Kimbro, the pianist was soon joined by Snooks Eaglin on electric guitar, and the trio generated a loosely rocking noise, with Fess's alternately driving and lilting piano rhythms setting the pace.[195] In many of its particulars the moment paralleled the rediscovery of a host of long-forgotten artists at the Newport Folk Festival from Mississippi John Hurt to Son House, except that Professor Longhair was a figure from the more recent past, his music not so readily sequestered behind the barrier of remote folk authenticity. This was traditional New Orleans music, and it was rock 'n' roll—the two were one and the same, signifying the fluid synthesis of styles that carried the Jazz and Heritage Festival forward.

8

The Politics of Scale

Arenas, Stadiums, and the Industrialization of Liveness

Led Zeppelin began its 1977 tour of the US in Dallas, Texas, with a concert on April 1 at the city's Memorial Auditorium. Compared to many of the venues where the band appeared over the course of its tour, Memorial Auditorium was rather modest, with a capacity of just under 10,000. By contrast, the first leg of the tour would conclude with an April 30 show at the Pontiac Silverdome just outside Detroit that would draw over 76,000, a record at the time for a concert featuring a single artist. The band played in a mix of arenas and stadiums over the three-month tour, with multi-night stands at the two most fabled US arenas, Madison Square Garden in New York City and the Forum in Los Angeles, each of which hosted six consecutive performances. Other shows took the band from the Midwest (Chicago, St. Paul, Indianapolis, Cincinnati) through the South (Atlanta, Birmingham, Baton Rouge, Landover), before culminating on the West Coast with two concerts at Oakland's Alameda County Coliseum.[1] Led Zeppelin's movement from Dallas to Oakland involved more than geography. Dallas was the starting point because it housed Showco, one of the biggest concert production companies in the US that handled Zeppelin's sound and staging, and was home to the corporate headquarters of Concerts West, a leading concert promotion company headed by music industry magnate Jerry Weintraub. Concerts West promoted every one of Led Zeppelin's shows on the 1977 tour except for the two last performances in Oakland, which were handled by FM Productions, under the auspices of Bill Graham, a legendary promoter in his own right who continued to wield great influence in a changing industry.

A year later, the Rolling Stones embarked on a US tour of their own. It was smaller in scale than the Zeppelin tour, with twenty-four concerts during the months of June and July 1978; Led Zeppelin by comparison played forty-four shows on its tour, stretching from April to July, and was scheduled to play more before several dates had to be canceled due to the sudden, tragic

Live Music in America. Steve Waksman, Oxford University Press. © Oxford University Press 2022.
DOI: 10.1093/oso/9780197570531.003.0009

death of Robert Plant's son. The Stones also adopted a different strategy by playing a mix of smaller theaters and large stadiums, rather than adhering to a typical itinerary of arenas and stadiums expected for a band of its stature. Opening shows on the tour were at the Lakeland Civic Center, with a capacity of just over 8,000; and then the Fox Theater in Atlanta, which seats around 4,600. Not until the fifth concert of the tour did the Stones play in a larger-capacity stadium, John F. Kennedy Stadium in Philadelphia, and even after that show they continued to alternate between moderate and large-scale venues throughout the tour.[2] For their July 13 concert at the Superdome in New Orleans, the band broke the record set by Led Zeppelin the previous year for attendance at a concert featuring a single artist, drawing over 80,000.

One detail above all captures the different character of the Stones tour from a production standpoint. The Stones employed a different promoter at every stop along the tour, much in contrast to Led Zeppelin's near-exclusive use of Concerts West. A list of promoters involved in the Stones' 1978 tour offers a concise snapshot of the field of concert promotion in the late 1970s, after a decade of expansion had given the American live music industry a distinctive shape:

> Lakeland, FL: Jack Boyle, Cellar Door Concerts, and Joe Lambusta, Beach Club Booking
> Atlanta: Alex Cooley
> Passaic, NJ: John Scher, Monarch Entertainment
> Washington, DC: Sam L'Hommedieu, Cellar Door
> Philadelphia: Larry Magid
> New York: Ron Delsener, Ardee Productions
> Boston: Don Law, New England Promotion
> Lexington, KY: Phil Lashinsky, Eantam, and Joe Holderman, Sunshine Productions
> Cleveland: Jules Belkin
> Buffalo: Harvey & Corky, John Wolf
> Detroit: Bob Bageris, Bamboo Productions
> Chicago: Jerry Mickelson, Jam Productions
> St. Paul, MN: Randy Levy, Schon Productions
> St. Louis: Irv Zuckerman
> New Orleans: Neil Gunn
> Boulder: Barry Fey, Feyline
> Ft. Worth: Don Law, New England Promotion

Houston: Louis Messina, Pace Management
Anaheim: Larry Vallon, Wolf & Rissmiller
Tucson, AZ: Dan Spellen, Caravan Concerts, and Ron Delsener, Ardee Productions
Oakland: Peter Barsoti, FM Productions

Many of the names on this list—Jack Boyle, Alex Cooley, Larry Magid, Ron Delsener, Don Law, Jules Belkin, Barry Fey—were primary architects of the live music industry as it had evolved from the mid-1960s forward. Others such as John Scher were just on the rise but would have considerable impact in years to come. They wielded great influence, but they also worked within a field of operation that was limited by design, divided into territories that allowed profits to be distributed across a wider range of stakeholders while still facilitating large-scale tours undertaken by Led Zeppelin, the Rolling Stones, and a host of other top acts to be produced as cross-country endeavors. Weintraub's Concerts West, in turn, used a single company to effectively eliminate the middleman and so generate a greater concentration of profits for the band and promoter alike.

Throughout the 1970s and into the decades that followed, the tension between these competing tendencies in the live music industry would be definitive. Ultimately, the push toward centralization prevailed at the highest levels of the industry. Most of the regional promoters with any substantial power—including Concerts West—would be bought out by much larger multinational companies in the 1990s and 2000s, a development that will be detailed in this book's conclusion. That later stage of consolidation was prefigured by the trends that took hold in the fifteen years following the Beatles first appearance at Shea Stadium in 1965. The upscaling of the live music business that occurred during this period unquestionably owed much to the rise of music festivals addressed in the preceding chapter. Yet the momentum surrounding music festivals halted just as the growth of arena and stadium concerts truly took hold. This was no idle coincidence. Festivals, while generating great publicity and at times appearing to encapsulate the spirit of the historical moment, were rarely lucrative and often volatile. The economy that grew around arena and stadium concerts sought to impose a level of predictability upon the staging of large-attendance music events that was lacking in the festival economy as it existed in the early 1970s. Arena rock was the cornerstone of a move to industrialize the production of live music that was unprecedented in its scope.

That move toward profit and predictability has long made arena rock a symptom for many commentators of what went wrong with rock and popular music during the 1970s. Reebee Garofalo and Steve Chapple, in their 1977 critique of the popular music industry, addressed the trend toward monopoly in the live music business, accusing promoters and artists alike of leaving the interests of concertgoers behind.[3] Rock critic Robert Duncan, describing the alignment between arena rock and the genre of heavy metal, termed the phenomenon "the paradigm of the counterculture into the mainstream," a judgment that has remained largely intact in the ensuing decades.[4] Even Bill Graham decried the move into arenas and stadiums, despite his having spent the majority of his career promoting such concerts. For Graham, stadium concerts resulted from the desire among performers to make more money for less work, and marked a clear decline in quality of experience from the smaller ballrooms such as the Fillmore and later, the Fillmore West and Fillmore East, where he had built his career.[5] I questioned the basis of these concerns in my previous work on heavy metal and punk, demonstrating that the rise of a paradigmatic "arena rock" band like Grand Funk Railroad in the early 1970s was not an instance of cultural decline or economic cooptation, but rather instigated a wide-ranging debate over the meaning of live rock and the terms according to which the relationship between rock and its audience was being redefined in the aftermath of the 1960s.[6]

Here I continue and extend that line of inquiry. I am not concerned with mounting a defense of arena rock. Indeed, it is critical to be aware of all the music that was not included under the banner of "arena rock," and the difficulty that black artists and even more so, black promoters had in establishing a foothold in the expanding live music economy will be part of my focus in what follows. My goal is more basic, if far from simple: I want to understand how arena and stadium concerts worked, how such events were produced and how they exemplify a crucially important stage in the evolution of live music in the US.[7]

One can readily connect facets of arena rock to earlier phases in the history of live music: the creation of a national touring network dates back at least to vaudeville, while the expanded scale of concerts from the 1960s forward was the latest in a long line of efforts to channel the cultural and economic force of the audience-as-crowd toward particular ends. And yet arena and stadium concerts are also distinctly of their time. In part this was a matter of money: the sheer dollar amounts at stake in arena concerts of this era far surpassed anything that been generated before, one result of which was a particular set of entangling relationships within which promoters, artists, managers, agents, and other figures all negotiated to gain what they believed to be their fair share. If money was at the root of a charged mode of competitive enterprise, it also underpinned peculiar efforts to give the "people"—that is, the audience—a performance that somehow matched the value of a ticket price. Thus, the imperative to put on a "show" intensified throughout the 1970s and forward, which manifested in a whole other set of complex relationships between sound engineers, stage designers, and others who worked in collaboration with the artists to make concerts that were visually and sonically compelling but could also be transported and re-created at every stop along the way. In conjunction with arena rock, the "live album" truly became codified as a key commodity, and so the interrelationship between live and recorded music was also importantly reconfigured in this era. In all of these dimensions—the need to keep profits stable from one night to the next, the need to get the show on the road, the effort to create the same performance conditions in one venue after another, the selling of a recording of the live event—what stands out is a tendency toward repeatability that is not at odds with the "liveness" of the concert but that is in fact essential to it, and that gave arena rock its singular significance in the historical staging of live music.

Thinking Big

On September 1, 1850, Jenny Lind arrived in New York harbor on a steamship that had embarked from Liverpool and was met by a crowd that numbered anywhere from 10,000 to 30,000, based on published reports. On February 7, 1964, the Beatles—a Liverpool rock 'n' roll band—arrived in New York's Kennedy International Airport on a flight from London to the accompaniment of an estimated 3,000 to 5,000 young fans. Leaving aside that Lind seems to have drawn more of a crowd in her day than the Beatles did in theirs, a historical fact that might occasion some reassessment of certain cherished myths, the rhymes between these two scenes are striking. Accounts characterized Lind's crowd as bursting with enthusiasm, almost animalistic in their passion for contact with the esteemed singer, and only her noble bearing could have a calming effect. As to the crowd that came to meet the Beatles, the *New York Times* cast them in the following terms: "There were girls, girls, and more girls. Whistling girls. Screaming girls. Singing girls.

They held 'Beatles, we love you' and 'WELCOME' signs. When the Beatles's plane touched down at 1:20 P.M. the girls chanted 'We want Beatles.'"[8] Writing in the *Boston Globe*, Tom Wolfe described a mass of girls *and* boys who participated in a "wild" spectacle, "some of them carrying each other on their shoulders, piled in around the plate glass windows around the customs section to watch the Beatles go through. They began stomping on the floor in unison, and the ones who couldn't reach the floor kept time by bouncing off the plate glass."[9] Police were out in full force and exclaimed to the press that they had never seen anything like this. Yet the Beatles were ultimately shielded, according to news coverage, as much by their good humor as by the effectiveness of the security forces at work.

Several key players worked behind the scenes to lay the groundwork for the Beatles' US arrival. Brian Epstein has received the lion's share of attention for his stewardship of the band's early career, and his role in orchestrating the Beatles' first visit to the US was substantial. Television host Ed Sullivan gave the band a highly visible public platform of the sort that was not available in Lind's time or indeed, arguably at any time before World War II, making the Beatles tour of the US a very different sort of media event from those that preceded it. Less heralded but no less instrumental was Sid Bernstein, the promoter who presented the Beatles' first New York concert (and second American performance) at Carnegie Hall and would subsequently organize both of the band's appearances at New York's Shea Stadium, in 1965 and 1966. When the Beatles arrived in New York in February 1964, Bernstein's name rarely appeared in publicity surrounding the band. He had to cloak his involvement with them because he worked for one of New York's top talent agencies, GAC (General Artists Corporation), and for him to be promoting a show on his own would have appeared as a conflict of interest. By Bernstein's own account, he set the process of bringing the Beatles to the US in motion by reaching out to Epstein and booking the date in Carnegie Hall, only after which Sullivan made his fateful decision to invite the band onto his highly rated television show.[10]

Bernstein's decision to stage the Beatles at Carnegie Hall did not have quite the same transgressive weight that surrounded Benny Goodman's appearance at the same venue nearly thirty years earlier. Any notion that Carnegie Hall was exclusively devoted to classical music had long since passed. What had not passed was the still-powerful standing of the hall. It was a place to present an act if you wanted to claim a certain measure of distinction and legitimation. While commentators on the Beatles have generally observed that it was not until the sound of their music began to broaden and diversify from *Rubber Soul* (1965) forward that the Beatles began to be treated as "artists" in the discourse of the day, their appearance at Carnegie Hall laid the groundwork for such judgments and attested to Bernstein's shrewdness as a promoter.

Meanwhile, the scene at Carnegie was evocative of that which accompanied Goodman at the Paramount in 1937, or Alan Freed's Paramount presentations in the 1950s. Tickets went on sale on the morning of January 26, some two weeks before the scheduled February 12 concert. When Bernstein checked in at noon, Nat Posnick—who managed the Carnegie box office—vented: "Sid, what just happened here has never happened in the seventy-four year history of Carnegie Hall . . . Some of the kids camped out all night waiting to buy tickets. When we opened, the line stretched all the way around the block . . . We sold out in forty minutes flat . . . and they're still coming!"[11] Interviewed about the crowd of some five thousand teenagers standing outside the hall in the hours leading up to the show, Bernstein fended off the suggestion that it was a claque brought in for appearances: "Sure the kids are here. It's a status symbol for them to be here, just as it's a status symbol for the 300 adults who are in the house tonight. You don't need a claque in a situation like that."[12] That attending a rock 'n' roll show should confer status upon the audience—this was something new.

The overwhelming demand for tickets to the Carnegie Hall concert prompted Bernstein to consider presenting the Beatles in a much larger venue, as did the success they had playing in larger, arena-sized venues when the band returned to the US for a tour in the fall 1964. Indeed, Bernstein was not the first to present the Beatles in a stadium setting. By the time he contacted New York Mets vice president Jim Thompson in October 1964 about scheduling a concert at Shea Stadium, the Beatles had already appeared at two stadium venues: Empire Stadium in Vancouver, British Columbia, and the Gator Bowl in Jacksonville, Florida. Neither of these concerts drew a capacity audience, though, and in Vancouver, the lack of adequate security led to a near-riot when several thousand spectators left their seats and rushed onto the field to get closer to the stage and the band.[13] Presenting the Beatles in such a space carried substantial risk of the sort that would always, on some level, shadow the business of live music promotion. Adding to that risk were the financial details worked out between Bernstein and Brian Epstein. According to their agreement, Bernstein paid the Beatles a guaranteed $100,000 against 60 percent of the gross box office receipts. Most audaciously though, Bernstein promised that he would pay Epstein ten dollars for every seat that went unsold—nearly twice the top ticket price of $5.65.[14] He was, in effect, gambling on a sell-out in a venue that held over 55,000 people.

About the venue itself, Shea Stadium was as new as the phenomenon of the Beatles. It officially opened to the public on April 17, 1964, two months after the Beatles first visited the US. The opening of Shea Stadium was part of a much larger boom in arena and stadium construction. As noted by architectural historian Howard Shubert, between 1960 and 1985 the four major North American sports leagues—the National Hockey League, the National Basketball Association, the National Football League, and Major League Baseball—sponsored the construction of fifty-seven new buildings, arenas and stadiums combined.[15] Shea Stadium's novelty was further enhanced by its design as a multi-use facility, built to house not only the Mets baseball team but also the New York Jets football organization. This combined function partly accounted for the large size of the stadium, which had a capacity nearly twice that of the previous home of the Mets, the Polo Grounds. Shea and other new sports facilities were not specifically designed to house music events and as they became more commonly used for such purposes, their shortcomings would become clear. Nonetheless, their construction was a precondition to the growth of arena and stadium rock. Shubert provides statistics that capture the change. On the Beatles' North American tours in 1964 and 1965, twelve out of thirty-four venues played by the band were built after World War II. When the Rolling Stones toured the US in 1969, out of fifteen venues where the band appeared, "only three had been built before the Second World War and more than half had not existed when the Beatles had visited North America just four years earlier."[16]

Having procured a newly built large stadium in the biggest media market in the US, Bernstein faced the task of trying to sell enough tickets so that his $100,000 guarantee to Epstein would not leave him in the red. For security purposes, no seats were placed on the stadium field, so only the regular seats in the stands would be used. Bernstein came up with a price range of $4.50, $5.10, and $5.65 based on what section of the stadium the seats were located. Figure 8.1 shows one of the higher-priced tickets. Meanwhile, the terms he negotiated with Epstein presented an immediate challenge. He was to pay the Beatles half of their guaranteed fee up front but did not have the cash available to do so, and Epstein did not want Bernstein to advertise the concert until the guarantee had been paid. Unable to place any print or radio ads, Bernstein began a word-of-mouth campaign, telling kids he met on the

Figure 8.1 "Sid Bernstein Presents": A concert ticket from the Beatles concert at Shea Stadium, August 15, 1965. Courtesy of MediaPunch Inc./Alamy Stock Photo.

street about the upcoming concert. He then distributed instructions for how to order tickets through the mail, using as an address a P.O. Box at the Old Chelsea Post Office. After about three weeks, he went to check the P.O. Box, and was met by two incredulous mail clerks and three large duffel bags full of ticket order requests.

In an age of mass media, Bernstein used old-school sales techniques to engineer his particular promotional coup. As he responded to orders, he circulated letters with instructions for attending the concerts—offering such advice as to bring binoculars—that also let people know that tickets were still available for purchase.[17] Using these methods he managed to sell a reported 55,600 tickets, earning gross receipts of $304,000, of which $160,000 would be paid to the Beatles. Much of the rest went toward the various expenses Bernstein incurred to produce the show, including the rental of Shea Stadium and the construction of a stage suitable for presenting the band, each of which cost about $25,000.[18]

While much about the Beatles appearance at Shea Stadium had an air of novelty about it, the format of the concert was not far removed from the package style of presentation employed by rock 'n' roll promoters of a previous decade, which remained the industry standard. For the August 15, 1965, concert, a string of radio disc jockeys, headed by Bruce "Cousin Brucie" Morrow, emceed different parts of the event. Following a performance of the US national anthem, a group called the Discotheque Dancers demonstrated some of the latest dance steps to a recorded medley of Beatles songs.

Succeeding them were the King Curtis band, Cannibal and the Headhunters, the singer Brenda Holloway (accompanied by Curtis's band), and Sounds Inc., a British instrumental rock ensemble that was also managed by Brian Epstein.[19] The intermingling of African American rhythm and blues with white rock artists was another indication of 1950s programming strategy at work. Each of these artists played very short sets; the whole run of them began performing at 8:00 P.M. and were concluded by 9:14, when Bernstein himself came to the stage to introduce Ed Sullivan, who then introduced the Beatles.[20] Their own set lasted for thirty-five minutes and consisted of twelve songs. This was long by the standards of a package performance and certainly confirmed their status as the star attraction of the concert. However, it was this feature of the Beatles performance—the relative brevity of their performance, and the conciseness of their songs onstage—that would be most subject to change as the expanded rock concert format took hold in the years to come.

For however long the Beatles played, the sound of their music was by almost all accounts barely audible over the screams of the audience. Newspaper reports at the time dwelled on this facet of the concert above all. The Associated Press story printed in the *Los Angeles Times* claimed that after an announcer informed the audience of the arrival of the Beatles, "nothing could be heard but the uninterrupted shrieking of the 50,000 Beatle admirers."[21] In a strikingly similar vein, the *New York Times* described the scene for its readers: "But their fans did little more than see the Beatles as they strummed their guitars, moved their lips, waved their hands, tapped their feet and beat a drum. For in the piercing shrill acclamation, the fans drowned out almost all the singing."[22] Two predominant features can be seen to intersect in these depictions. First, there is the prevalent tendency of public media to reduce the audience for popular music concerts to a mass of raving, irrational creatures. *New York Times* reporter Murray Schumach goes so far as to cast the audience as a crowd of hysterics, almost "demonic" in the force of their enthusiasm. That the audience was also said to be predominantly female was not incidental on this score, for it made their passionate responses that much easier to caricature and regard with a measure of ridicule and contempt.[23] This had long been the ground according to which popular music was rendered unfit for "serious" appreciation, and one could well say that the Beatles could not fully establish themselves as a more "respectable" sort of popular music act until they escaped the scenes of such demonstrations.

Secondarily, the published descriptions of the Beatles performance at Shea Stadium, and the many stories that have circulated afterward, testify to the purported inadequacy of the technical side of the concert and specifically the sound system. The most compact account of sound production at the concert comes from Dave Schwensen's extensive reconstruction of the event:

> For fans to have a chance to hear The Beatles, microphones were placed in front of their 100-watt Vox guitar amplifiers and Ringo's drums. Together with audio from the vocal microphones, the sound was wired to the stadium's public address system and played through small speakers hung from steel support girders in the various seating levels that were basically designed for announcements during sporting events. The performance was also carried through tall, thin yellow speakers lined up along the first and third base lines of the baseball field.[24]

Several facets of this description stand out. The 100-watt amplifiers described by Schwensen were markedly bigger than was customary circa 1965 and were specially built for the Beatles. Yet the amps attached to the electric guitars and bass played by the band were not sufficient to project to such a cavernous space as Shea Stadium. A professional quality p.a. system was required, but this was one technical detail that neither Bernstein nor the Beatles considered essential. A year later, when the Beatles returned to Shea Stadium, Bernstein hired Bill Hanley—already known for his work with the Newport Folk and Jazz Festivals—to handle the sound. In 1965, however, the stadium's house p.a. was left to do the lion's share of the work and was found to be wanting.

Still, the characterization of the experience as one where the Beatles were inaudible should not stand unchallenged. Hearing the Beatles was not just a matter of volume levels or sound quality but of perception and attention, and with more than 55,000 in attendance, there was little chance that all heard the Beatles in the same way. On this score, one fan named Debbie Stern provided an especially rich account: "We were breathing the same air, occupying the same space; albeit several thousand feet away, and screaming our little teenage heads off. People always ask me, 'Did you even hear them?' And my standard answer is, 'You had to scream to hear them.' There was something magical in the way their voices transcended those high pitched screams."[25] In years to come, the volume at rock concerts would increase to the point where members of the audience would barely be able to hear themselves scream. While the lack of suitable volume at Shea Stadium may not have provided a peak aural experience, it fostered a participatory atmosphere in which the audience could feel as though their voices were joined with the performers.

The Promoters

Sid Bernstein's work in presenting the Beatles to the American public, first at Carnegie Hall and then at Shea Stadium (twice), helped to jump start a new phase in the evolution of the American concert business that also redefined what a rock concert might be. Yet Bernstein hardly worked in isolation. Apart from the Beatles manager, Brian Epstein, he relied on the help of a range of associates: his friends and financial backers Abe Margolies and Walter Hyman, who helped him stage the Beatles appearance at Carnegie Hall; Carnegie Hall booker Iona Satescu and ticket agent Nat Posnick; New York Mets official Jim Thompson; and a host of others that helped him tend to the details of concert production. The promoter's role in all this was essentially that of the event coordinator. He helped to tie the various components of the concert together. Crucially, he also funded the event and made sure that all costs were covered. All money, whether due to the artists, the venue, security personnel, or the stage crew, ultimately went through the promoter's hands. Of course, the promoter also stood to profit if the event were a success; but profit would only come after all expenses had been handled. In this regard, the promoter had much to gain but also, potentially, much to lose. The Beatles had their guarantee. Bernstein had none.

Promoting live music has long been an exercise in speculation. Recall Barnum's comments on his work with Jenny Lind—"I risked much but I made more."[26] From Barnum to Sol Hurok to George Wein and forward, promoters have foregrounded the risks they take to justify their endeavors. Bernstein was one in a long line, but he was also part of a new generation of promoters who, individually and collectively, saw themselves as the makers of a new industry. The proof is in the growing body of memoirs left by these figures. Bill Graham, easily the best known of this group of promoters, led the way with his posthumous autobiography, co-authored by Robert Greenfield.[27] Bernstein followed, along with Seattle promoter and radio personality Pat O'Day, Denver promoter Barry Fey, Larry Magid of Philadelphia, Pittsburgh promoter Pat DiCesare, and Jerry Weintraub, who presided over the aforementioned Concerts West.[28] These seven promoter-memoirists are inheritors of Barnum's legacy as an entertainment promoter of enduring influence and as the narrator of show business life and livelihood. Their stories and others combine to make a case for concert promotion as one of the most significant and under-appreciated areas of the modern music industry, and the concert promoter as a figure who has exerted a peculiar sort of agency over the unpredictability of the rock concert economy in the era of arena and stadium rock.[29]

A handful of these promoters had careers that stretched back to the first rock 'n' roll era of the 1950s. Pat O'Day especially stands out in this regard. As a radio DJ, O'Day followed the most well trodden way into rock 'n' roll concert promotion in the 1950s, famously set by Alan Freed. Starting with record hops where he spun platters for the entertainment of teen dancers around the Pacific Northwest, O'Day moved into concert promotion after learning firsthand from the music stars of the late 1950s of the difficulties they faced on the road. In 1959 he began promoting regular Friday night events at the Spanish Castle roadhouse stationed between Seattle and Tacoma featuring a regional band named the Wailers. By 1964 O'Day was booking shows at an additional three venues and staging as many as twenty shows a week. This schedule allowed him to draw his pick of national touring acts, which he presented in combination with local bands emerging out of what was by then a thriving regional rock 'n' roll scene. From a failed effort to promote a standard package show featuring eight performers of middling success, he came to the realization that, "a show with many small acts doesn't add up to a big show. It's still just a show with many small acts."[30] When the city of Seattle opened a new 15,000-seat arena—the Seattle Center Coliseum—in 1964, O'Day brought the Beatles, in what was the third date of their first full-fledged American tour. The experience instilled in him several further lessons: "(1) We could raise our prices; (2) A coliseum-type building was acceptable, and the energy of the larger crowd became a significant part of the show; and (3) Something had to be done about sound systems."[31] Arena rock would gain momentum from such insights.

Pat DiCesare's career in the music industry also began in the 1950s, but atypically, he moved into concert promotion after time spent as a "record man," working as a songwriter and later as a distributor who serviced jukeboxes in the mid-Atlantic region. In 1962, he promoted his first concert as a student at Youngstown State University in Ohio, by the Four Freshmen. Around that same time, DiCesare's mentor in the record business, Tim Tormey, also moved into concert promotion, collaborating with Pittsburgh radio DJ Porky Chedwick to produce the first big musical event at the newly opened Pittsburgh Civic Arena. Featuring twenty-four artists with Jackie Wilson as headliner, Porky Chedwick's Groove Spectacular was a great success and led Tormey to shift his efforts from record distribution to concert promotion. DiCesare joined him in his new pursuits; and they solidified their partnership by presenting the first Pittsburgh concert appearance by the Beatles at the Civic Arena in September 1964—a later stop on the same tour that saw O'Day present the band in Seattle. About the details of the concert, DiCesare recalled: "The setup for The Beatles was amazingly simple. All their equipment arrived in a Ford Econoline van . . . In 1964, we used the same sound system the arena used for sporting events for concerts. The hockey team's locker room served as a dressing room."[32] According to DiCesare, they negotiated to pay the Beatles a $20,000 guarantee against 60 percent of gross ticket sales, an arrangement that allowed the Beatles to earn $37,000 and left DiCesare with a healthy profit of $4,400 (his share of the take after splitting the earnings with Tormey).[33] The following year his efforts took another step forward when he and Tormey presented the Beach Boys at the same Civic Arena, yielding another big payday. Tormey subsequently took a job in entertainment producer Dick Clark's organization and DiCesare staked out an independent path as Pittsburgh's leading promoter for arena and stadium-sized concerts.

Then there was Jerry Weintraub, whose career trajectory suggested a different sort of continuity between the rock 'n' roll era of the 1950s and the rock era of the mid-1960s forward. Like Sid Bernstein, Weintraub began his entertainment career as an agent, hired in the early 1960s by MCA (the Music Corporation of America). A self-styled acolyte of P.T. Barnum—he even titled one of the chapters of his memoir, "Being P.T. Barnum"—Weintraub claimed that as early as 1963 he had visions of filling Yankee Stadium, his vivid imagery (with prose surely crafted by co-author Rich Cohen) painting an evocative picture of the desires that arena rock emerged to fulfill:

> Have you ever stood in an empty baseball stadium? It's unbelievable, all those seats, each representing a person who has to be reached, marketed to, convinced, sold. It was intimidating, and it stayed with me. Whenever I am considering an idea I picture the seats rising from second base at Yankee Stadium. Can I sell that many tickets? Half that many? Twice that many?[34]

Performers such as Steven Tyler of Aerosmith had similar visions of an arena or stadium full of seats as an index of success.[35] For the artist, such a fantasy carried the strong connotation of ego gratification, marking the realization of a certain standard of rock stardom. For Weintraub the fantasy also had much ego involved, but it was the ego of the salesman making the perfect pitch. On a fundamental level, arena rock was generated at the point where these two complementary fantasies converged.

After starting his own management company in 1963, Weintraub relocated from New York to Los Angeles. A few years later he had a big idea: he would endeavor to take Elvis Presley out on tour. Presley had effectively retired from the concert stage following his 1957 induction into the army, since which time he had only performed two isolated concerts in 1961. Bringing him back to a regular performing career was a bold gesture. Weintraub says that he first contacted Presley's infamously difficult manager, Colonel Tom Parker, in the mid-1960s to broach this particular subject, before Elvis had appeared in his widely celebrated 1968 televised "comeback" special, and was flatly refused. He kept appealing to Parker, and in the meantime came to look upon the older man as a mentor. Against the many portrayals of Colonel Tom as a thief and exploiter of Presley's talent, Weintraub asserts that he attended "the school of Colonel Tom Parker, who taught me how to hawk my wares in every part of America."[36] Parker arranged for Presley's return to the concert stage to occur at the International Hotel in Las Vegas during the summer of 1969, without Weintraub's involvement; but in the time leading up to the Vegas engagement, the two men discussed a possible tour, and just a matter of days before Presley gave his first performance in eight years on the stage of the International, they confirmed the deal.[37] To produce the tour, Weintraub partnered with Tom Hulett, then representing a Seattle-based concert promotion company named Concerts West. So it was that, in the fall of 1970, Weintraub's move into arena concert promotion came from working with the biggest rock 'n' roll star of the 1950s.

* * *

A significant cohort of the promoters who dominated the arena rock industry built their early careers around venue management and ownership. The venues they owned were not arenas but smaller theaters that came to be called "ballrooms." Bill Graham's Fillmore Auditorium in San Francisco was the model for such a hall, succeeded by the twin Fillmore East and Fillmore West theaters in New York and San Francisco respectively, and Graham's trajectory exemplifies the pattern whereby promoters used their oversight of local music institutions as a base from which they extended their influence over a city or regional scene. Others who followed a similar route included Don Law, working with the Tea Party in Boston; Larry Magid, a partner in the Electric Factory ballroom in Philadelphia; and Barry Fey with the Family Dog in Denver, an adjunct to San Francisco's Family Dog productions. Jack Boyle's Cellar Door—a Washington, DC venue operated with partner Sam L'Hommedieu—was more an old-style music club than a ballroom, with a smaller capacity and more modest production values, but nonetheless served as a base of operations out of which he built a wide-ranging concert promotion empire.

The rock ballrooms were immensely influential for a short window of time, roughly 1966 until 1971. Graham's Fillmore started in earnest in February 1966. He closed the original location at Fillmore and Geary Streets in San Francisco in July 1968, and the next day opened the newly christened Fillmore West—where he can be seen working in Figure 8.2—in the former Carousel Ballroom on Market Street and Van Ness, just past the point where Market intersected with Haight Street. In the interim, Graham had opened the Fillmore East on Second Avenue in New York City's Lower East Side, which began operations in March 1968.[38] With the Fillmore East and West, Graham extended the geographic range of his influence and converted the Fillmore name from one tied to a specific location to a mobile designation that became part of his personal brand. Even more redolent of Graham's flair for self-promotion was his use of the heading, "Bill Graham Presents," on all the posters and print ads used to publicize his events—the phrase evocative of the promotional methods of Graham's personal hero, Sol Hurok, whose similar "S. Hurok Presents" made a great imprint on the younger promoter when he was growing up in New York. Speaking of Hurok in an obituary that appeared in *Rolling Stone*, Graham exclaimed, "He was my Joe DiMaggio, a hero ... There was really only one."[39]

A defining moment in Graham's career and the evolution of the ballroom scene in San Francisco came early in his tenure at the original Fillmore. For the first weeks that he produced shows at the Fillmore, Graham worked alongside the Family Dog, a collective led by Chet Helms that shared Graham's goal of building a stronger base for presenting live music in San Francisco but was run according to a different set of values. Helms and fellow Family Dog member John Carpenter successfully presented the Butterfield Blues Band at the Fillmore in partnership with Graham, but they clashed over

Figure 8.2 Ever the dealmaker, promoter Bill Graham as he appeared in his Fillmore West office in 1969, with posters of past Fillmore concerts lining the walls. Photograph by Jon Brenneis. Courtesy of Getty Images.

some of the hall's policies such as tolerance of open pot smoking (Graham was more cautious than Helms and Carpenter), and Graham saw the potential to yield more profit without their participation. When the band's run was over, Graham called their manager Albert Grossman the next morning and booked them for a return engagement solely under his auspices, without the involvement of the Family Dog. Helms, learning of Graham's shady dealings, confronted him, and Graham defended himself in terms vividly recalled in his memoir:

[Helms] said, "You booked Butterfield behind our backs."

Somehow, something came out of me and I said, "Chet, you're gonna be in this business and I'm gonna be in this business. And I'll tell you, there's only one suggestion I can make to you. *Get up early.*"

He never forgot that. I never forgot it. Chet *never* got up early. And what I really meant had nothing to do with *when* you got up. It really meant, no matter what time you get up, use your time to work.[40]

Helms viewed Graham's actions as a simple breech of trust. From that point forward he saw that further cooperation with Graham was impossible, and the Family Dog went on to establish the Avalon Ballroom. For Graham, a different principle was at work. Cooperation was fine when it achieved a desired goal, but success in business—and especially in the concert business, where every show was a risk against the odds—required ruthless self-interest. "Get up early": Graham's admonishment has the air of Benjamin Franklin or Horatio Alger about it, tying his success to virtue and hard work. But really, the message was, don't ever let the other guy get ahead of you.

Graham's machinations may have gone against the grain of counterculture etiquette, but the impact of having two leading rock ballrooms co-existing in one city was salutary. Writing of the history of the Haight-Ashbury scene, journalist Charles Perry captured the dynamic generated by the contrasting styles of Graham, Helms, and their respective venues:

> Helms was the artist creating an event . . . Graham spoke only of "creating a situation in which each individual can create his own atmosphere." Helms . . . would sometimes greet newcomers by saying, "Welcome to our church." Over at the Fillmore, Graham would be running around with his clipboard making sure everything happened on time. Whole communes had complimentary passes to the Avalon, while Graham waged perpetual war against extending comp lists . . . The difference was even carried down to the style of lighting. Where at the Avalon the musicians were half-invisible in the murk at the bottom of the light show screen, just like the dancers, at the Fillmore there was always a spotlight on the lead musician, making the band the center of the event.[41]

This last observation was crucial. Both the Fillmore and Avalon put into place a style of presentation that influenced rock ballrooms across the US, through which the music was accompanied by elaborately produced light shows, and the bills moved decisively away from the polyglot programming philosophy of the package tours to settle into a new kind of formula concentrated upon one headlining artist and one or two support artists.

Perhaps the biggest shift was the move to make the music, and the artists, more squarely the focus of audience attention, which transformed events that through 1966 and 1967 were still being called "dance concerts" into events at which the audience was expected primarily to watch and listen with attention. As jazz had done with its move into the concert hall starting in the 1930s and 1940s, rock's move into the ballroom had the effect of making it music for listening to the relative exclusion of being music for dancing. Graham himself said of the change, "The music is more important but because it's important, they're not dancing anymore—they're listening. The world has been told that rock is an art form. You don't dance to art. You should, but this one, you don't."[42] Graham was not just an observer of this change, he was an agent of it; in this as in so many aspects of his career, his influence was much contested.

A rare, illuminating glimpse into how a portion of the audience experienced the transformed culture of ballroom concerts in late 1960s San Francisco comes from a private letter sent by David A. Wiles to Ralph Gleason, music critic for the *San Francisco Chronicle*, who played a key role in the founding of *Rolling Stone* magazine. Wiles's letter is dated October 23, 1968, just a few months after Graham had moved his base of operations from the original Fillmore to the Fillmore West. He starts the letter by praising Graham for the excellence of the shows he has presented at both the old and new Fillmores, but then moves into a complaint that the quality of the concerts has recently begun to suffer. Appealing to Gleason directly, he observes:

> As you yourself mentioned quite a long time ago, the dance-concerts were changing into "concerts" with everyone plopped down in front of the bandstand—which is groovy with me. But does the Fillmore West have to pack people in so tightly that it is impossible to even have a good time anymore—where a person cannot stand if he wants to without being shouted at by rude, obnoxious people—"SIT DOWN." Time was when Bill Graham made a pronouncement from the stage "this is a dance-concert—if someone wants to stand, or dance, or sit—they can" ... What happened to this attitude? It seems that just packing them in for what it's worth is the

complete antithesis of what S.F. and its ballroom scene has meant to many for a long time.[43]

Wiles proceeds to recount his recent experience at a Jimi Hendrix show at Fillmore West, where so many people were "packed in like pigs," leading him to ask, "Must so many tickets be sold that it becomes a matter of survival to see the show?" By Wiles's understanding, crowding had the effect of increasing the tension among concertgoers and the loss of comfort affected the overall vibe. As a result, asserted Wiles, Fillmore West concerts were "not even worth getting dressed up for anymore . . . People still dress beautifully for the Avalon. Why can't the Fillmore retain some of the gentleness and beauty of its past?"[44]

When Bill Graham announced in the spring of 1971 that he would be closing both Fillmores, East and West, he presented as the first of his reasons, "the unreasonable and totally destructive inflation of the live concert scene . . . I continue to deplore the exploitation of the gigantic hall concerts, many of them with high-priced tickets. The sole incentive of too many has become money."[45] Over the long term, these words resonate with irony. Graham moved readily into the realm of arena and stadium concert promotion. He worked with nearly all the major touring acts of the 1970s and 1980s and oversaw one of the country's biggest ongoing exercises in stadium rock promotion, the "Day on the Green" shows that he began presenting at the Oakland-Alameda County Coliseum in 1973, and that became an annual event until the year after his death in 1991. In the short term, Graham's observations suggest that he lacked the willingness or the ability to recognize the degree to which his own career in concert promotion with the Fillmores paved the way for the emergence of the arena concert economy. More than any single figure, Graham retooled the terms of rock concert presentation in the late 1960s, in large part because he figured out how to produce shows with a high level of reliability night after night for several hundred people at a time. Graham always asserted—sometimes with near ferocity—that he was not only in it for the money, and he may well have been sincere. Nonetheless, he tirelessly pursued profit, could be merciless to his competitors, and developed an attention to detail that ensured that every paid customer be counted, and every band should come on stage as close to the scheduled time as possible. These qualities were eminently transferable from the ballroom to the arena. In fact, the shift from the one to the other could not have taken root so successfully without them.

The Agent and the Outlier

Influential as promoters like Graham and his cohort were, their efforts were only one part of the larger system of concert production being put into place. Artists rarely worked directly with the promoters, except in those cases where promoters also took on some of the responsibilities of artist management—something pursued to a degree by Graham and Jerry Weintraub, among others. More typically, booking agents made the deals with promoters that were necessary to build a concert tour. During the years when the arena concert economy was coming to fruition, one agent above all assumed a position of dominance, working to orchestrate the system of territorial sovereignty described in the introduction to this chapter, which most major promoters observed. By the early 1970s, that agent—Frank Barsalona—had become what journalist Fred Goodman called "the true kingmaker of the underground."[46]

Barsalona started his Premier Talent agency in 1964 after a short stint working with GAC, also Sid Bernstein's place of employment when he presented the Beatles at Carnegie Hall. His decision to leave GAC was sparked by the recognition that the established talent agencies were not well suited to represent rock artists. In organizations like GAC, rock performers were lumped in with an older guard of celebrity talent, and the agents—most of whom were older themselves—lacked primary knowledge of the live rock scene. Barsalona created Premier to represent rock and soul artists exclusively and create an agency in which they were treated as a top priority. A 1965 ad appearing in *Billboard* magazine spotlighted the Premier artist list, headed by three British acts—Herman's Hermits, Freddie and the Dreamers, and Wayne Fontana and the Mindbenders—and also including Little Anthony and the Imperials, the Shangri Las, Del Shannon, the Yardbirds, Gary U.S. Bonds, Little Eva, and the Chantels.[47] For its singular emphasis on youth-oriented, rock-based talent, Premier was touted by *Billboard* three years later. Premier invested in the theory "that booking agents should be able to relate to young talent" by hiring an entire staff whose ages were under thirty. As Barsalona explained, this was key to their success because "many of the young performers have managers who are themselves under 30" and who better related to agents their own age.[48] (Barsalona himself was born in 1938, and so was on the cusp of turning thirty when the article appeared.) In an era of "hip capitalism," Barsalona exploited the generation gap to gain a competitive advantage, and in so doing significantly enhanced the bargaining position of rock artists in the emerging live music economy.

As Premier evolved, Barsalona refined a secondary focus that compounded his industry influence: he made a point of becoming the booking agent for British bands looking to tour the US Premier's 1965 roster already showed evidence of Barsalona's preoccupation on this score, but within a few years the British artists he represented came more to define his agency. A 1969 ad declaring that Premier represented "the Talent of the Seventies" captured the change of emphasis. The list of artists represented by Premier now included such British acts as Led Zeppelin, the Who, Ten Years After, Joe Cocker, Jethro Tull, the Jeff Beck Group, Fairport Convention, King Crimson, and Brian Auger, along with a smaller proportion of US bands including Blood, Sweat and Tears, Grand Funk Railroad, and the MC5.[49] By 1971, he had added to this list Yes, Traffic, Black Sabbath, Emerson, Lake, and Palmer, and Humble Pie, as shown in Figure 8.3.[50] Asked about his agency's success in working with these groups, Barsalona observed: "The British groups are only allowed to play in this country slightly less than six months out of one year [due to work visa restrictions]. Consequently, we have to book them in perhaps 26 or 27 markets for a one-month tour. An American group can cover that same ground in four months. We went to England to establish ourselves because we knew that we would be on the same footing as the larger agencies."[51] For British and US groups alike, Barsalona proved himself an able strategist whose work was driven by the assumption that tireless touring was a way to build a level of steady fan support that would be stronger and more enduring than an isolated hit record.

Reporting in 1974 on the growing success of one of Barsalona's acts, the British boogie band Foghat, Loraine Alterman observed in *Rolling Stone*:

> There are two ways an act can make it into the big-time, $20,000-$30,000-plus-box-office-percentages category that can add up to as much as $70,000 a night. One is to have a smash hit (Number One) single and acquire an instant audience . . . The other is to build up a solid audience for live performances that multiplies with each show and insures steady album sales. Foghat is doing it the second way and that's exactly how their agent, Premier Talent president Frank Barsalona, the king of rock & roll agents, built acts like the Who, Ten Years After, Humble Pie and the J. Geils Band.[52]

Figure 8.3 Advertisement for Frank Barsalona's Premier Talent Associates from 1971. The ad highlights the agency's strengths in hard rock and the preponderance of British acts that it represented including the Who, Led Zeppelin, Black Sabbath, Jethro Tull, and Emerson, Lake, and Palmer. From *Billboard* (November 6, 1971).

Alterman effectively channels Barsalona's professional philosophy with her account, and her article provides a revealing view into the priorities that governed the powerful agent's career. Interviewed by the reporter, Barsalona makes it plain that he had an aesthetic that guided his decisions about which bands he should represent. As he put it:

> What I try to look for is an act like Foghat that is a terribly uncomplicated act, a high-energy act . . . There is no way that Foghat can antagonize anybody in the audience. There are people who might not like them, but they cannot bomb. So Foghat should play for as many people as possible. If they play for 10,000 people, they've got to have 2,000 like them and 200–300 who are fans. I think nothing of a new act, a good act, taking a good year-and-a-half to break.[53]

Complementing Barsalona's ideas about touring as the key to long-term success, then, was a vision of the rock audience and of rock as a medium. The audience, as he depicted it, values uncomplicated high-energy fun. If they get it, they will remain loyal. This is nothing less than a description of the new rock mainstream as constituted by the confluence of arena concerts, FM AOR radio, and major record labels who relied upon concert and radio networks to build audience support. Meanwhile, Barsalona's preference for rock of the sort purveyed by the likes of Foghat, Humble Pie, and Ten Years After helps to explain how it was that the arena and stadium concert industry came to be identified with the term "arena rock." Rock was not the only genre that could be adapted to such venues. Rather, Barsalona and others who built the economic framework for presenting these events heard a certain kind of basic, driving hard rock as having the right elements to appeal to a broad mass of listeners without turning too many away. This was the formula according to which, for Barsalona, careers could be built around touring, not recording, as the primary activity.

While Barsalona helped steer the careers of the artists that he represented, he also worked the other side of the professional line. The relationships he cultivated with promoters around the US became integral to his burgeoning agency, arguably more important than his illustrious stable of performers. Agents and promoters were historically antagonists more than partners. Barsalona, going against the grain of this received pattern, determined that building cooperation in this domain was the primary means toward building a reliable, lucrative touring network that took full advantage of the scale of the US concert market.

A window into how Barsalona assembled such a network comes through his association with one of the most prominent rock ballrooms on the East Coast, the Boston Tea Party. According to Don Law, manager of the Tea Party—later to become the most powerful concert promoter in New England—Barsalona came to Boston seeking a venue where he could promote his acts, recognizing that it was a ready market waiting to be tapped.[54] He first approached a rival promoter named George Papadopoulos who ran a small folk-oriented coffeehouse called the Unicorn and a larger rock venue, the Psychedelic Supermarket. Papadopoulos, however, gave Barsalona attitude, acting as though the agent should defer to him. Barsalona went looking elsewhere and found the Tea Party, owned by a Harvard law graduate named Ray Riepen. Law, who had just begun to work at the Tea Party at the time, quickly hit it off with Barsalona, in part because of the young promoter's own music industry lineage—his father, also Don Law, was an esteemed producer and record industry executive. A partnership quickly formed, through which Barsalona brought such acts as Procol Harum, the Jeff Beck Group, Traffic, and Led Zeppelin to the Tea Party, making it into a primary destination for his roster of touring British acts.

What struck Law most about Barsalona as their working relationship evolved was the scrutiny with which the agent learned the internal dynamics of the local rock scene. As Law recalled:

> When Frank would come up to Boston, and he would do this elsewhere, he wouldn't just talk to me. He would talk to somebody at the concessions stand, he would talk to somebody in the box office, he would talk to somebody working for the newspaper. I mean he would really want to know what was going on in the city. And he was very good at picking up what was working and what wasn't working. And his attitude was, I'm going to work with you as long as you're doing something that's helping to break my act, if you're really adding something to this equation.[55]

Law describes a system of relationships that combined sociality with practical concerns. Barsalona befriended Law and many other of the promoters with whom he worked. Yet as a business relationship, their association was based on a series of conditions. A promoter could not just presume that the shows he presented would sell themselves. He had to work actively on behalf of the acts that Barsalona gave him and demonstrate that he could continue to sell tickets in sufficient numbers to allow all parties to earn a suitable profit. If a promoter or a venue fell down on their responsibilities, Barsalona would find another partner.

Other promoters who worked closely with Barsalona confirmed and expanded upon the terms of the partnership. Alex Cooley, based in Atlanta, said of Barsalona:

> He was the first man in this business that had a cogent plan. A thought-out, logical progression of what we should do, of how we could be businesslike but not crazed, and he had certain promoters he worked with and I'm very happy to say I was one of them, and he expected a lot of us. He expected when he called, and he said do this thing, you would do it, and I always did.[56]

Philadelphia promoter Larry Magid specified that Barsalona's expectations concerned promoting artists that he represented who were at different stages of their careers, from top-tier headliners to less established artists who might appear as opening acts on an arena concert bill or as feature attractions in a smaller venue:

> Frank's idea was, one person, one promoter, one city, and you would play Frank's A act, and he'd have a little farm system like the minor leagues, and he'd find a place for his B or C act, and that promoter would work that farm system and help to get that to the A act, would work with the radio station, work with the record company... You would do anything that you can, and you spent your time working on those acts because there was somebody that had your back that was going to replenish the system. And the more he did this, the more acts he got.[57]

Magid's remarks clarify what Barsalona offered to the artists with whom he worked: a promise that he would build their careers from the ground up and had the connections to place them on concert bills around the country in venues that suited their stature. Where the promoters were concerned, the system favored those who had a range of local outlets that would help them effectively corner the market in their respective home bases. While Philadelphia's Electric Factory ballroom closed in 1971, Magid retained the Electric Factory name for his promotion company, through which he presented shows at the city's principal sports arena, the Spectrum; operated a small nightclub, the Bijou; and, by the later 1970s, used the massive John F. Kennedy Stadium for concerts as well. This pattern of diversification became the rule from place to place and enabled Barsalona to streamline his efforts in the manner described by Magid: one person, one promoter, one city.

Accumulating these relationships one city at a time, Barsalona assembled a circuit that was uniquely adapted to the expansionist imperatives of arena rock. By the account of Peter Rudge, the tour manager for the Who, the Rolling Stones, and Lynyrd Skynyrd, "A tour is more than one gig. And [Barsalona] developed that circuit." Rudge represented yet another facet of the rock concert economy of the time, working closely with artists to plan the logistics of their touring endeavors. When he began his tenure with the Who, the band's contract with Barsalona was about to expire. Rudge recalls visiting Barsalona during a trip to New York, and staying out with the agent until 4 a.m. The camaraderie sealed their professional alliance, but like so many other of Barsalona's associates, Rudge remained loyal because of how much he respected the agent's power, ethics, and vision. He portrayed the results of Barsalona's endeavors in vivid terms:

> So rock and roll grew . . . out of the Northeast, the Lakes, and the West Coast . . . You draw a line from Chicago, maybe Minneapolis, but essentially Chicago down, you could include Atlanta, it was the first of the Southern places that meant anything . . . but basically down to Washington, DC . . . Then you take, around the lakes, you could go . . . from Toronto along to Chicago, so you've got Cleveland, Detroit. Right? And then, you're west of the Rockies. Maybe Denver when [Barry] Fey came in and started the Zephyr Ballroom and those things, but that was the circuit. And what Frank did was appoint, as it were, a promoter, and it was for them to lose, you know.[58]

One could say that Frank Barsalona was the B.F. Keith of the rock era, but you would have to add two qualifications. Unlike Keith, vaudeville's primary impresario and circuit builder, he did not seize hold of the "real estate"—Barsalona never moved into venue ownership or management. Also unlike Keith, Barsalona was widely perceived in the industry as an ally to performers, not an antagonist. His ability to win the trust of both the newly christened cultural heroes of rock stardom and the behind-the-scenes figures who promoted their shows made Barsalona into a power broker of nearly unmatched influence throughout the 1970s.

This is not to say that his system was without its downside. For one thing, it encouraged a network of local monopolies. Rival promoters who were not among Barsalona's chosen few were at a competitive disadvantage. At times this even led to legal challenges in places like Philadelphia, where Larry Magid was seen to have squeezed other promoters out of the market. The exclusivity that Barsalona relied upon did not operate equally in all circumstances. New York City, for instance, was too large to be a one-promoter location, and so Barsalona's alliances there fluctuated more than in other areas. Meanwhile, the system decidedly favored promoters who worked principally with white rock artists whose audiences were also predominantly white. The question of how actively African American promoters were discouraged from participating in the network assembled by Barsalona is near impossible to determine, but the fact remains that no African American promoters were part of the circuit, and women were also scarce. Barsalona's circle of promoters was a brotherhood, and many of its members likely bonded over a shared sense of ethnic whiteness—the Italian American Barsalona bringing together a mix of mostly Jewish promoters (Graham, Fey, Magid, Belkin, Delsener—who was Italian and Jewish) in a formation not unlike that in early Hollywood, or in Tin Pan Alley, where Jewish studio magnates and song publishers built the systems on which the film and sheet music industries were founded.

* * *

Another Jewish promoter and self-styled outlier, Jerry Weintraub, refused to cooperate with Barsalona's network, and in so doing revealed its biggest vulnerability. For the system to work, every promoter had to observe the boundaries of their assigned territories. This went against the basic capitalist impulse to expand one's sphere of influence and the potential profits that went along with it. A promoter only had so many ways to increase revenue. The two most straightforward were to raise ticket prices and to present more shows. Ticket prices, it was thought, had a built-in limit beyond which audiences would stop paying—an assumption that would be shattered after TicketMaster, Live Nation, and secondary ticket outlets like StubHub assumed dominance in later decades, but that held fast throughout the 1970s. Territorial expansion therefore appeared the surest route to increase the number of shows that a promoter could offer without oversaturating the local market in which they worked. Barsalona essentially asked the promoters with whom he partnered to give up their most self-serving plans for growth. In return, he offered them reliable, guaranteed access to many of the biggest touring acts appearing in the US at any given time. This is not to say that promoters only operated in a single city. Regional influence could be widespread: Don Law promoted throughout the Northeast, Barry Fey from the Rockies down to the Southwest, Jack Boyle extended his Cellar Door footprint from Washington, DC, down to Florida, and so on. The key was that a promoter would not step into an area that was already acknowledged to belong to a fellow promoter who was also part of Barsalona's network.

Weintraub, however, pursued a national imprint on his own. He began to undertake this strategy when promoting Elvis Presley. Rather than make deals with the individual promoters who served a given region, he sought to work directly with the venue operators, effectively cutting out the "middleman"—the position that promoters historically had held.[59] This approach allowed Weintraub to keep a greater share of revenues in the hands of Presley and Colonel Tom Parker and gave him greater bargaining power by working on a nationalized scale. Weintraub parlayed this approach into the guiding business model of Concerts West, the concert promotion company with which he partnered when his relationship with Presley began, and that he later took over.[60] As long as Weintraub's artist roster remained small, the impact he had upon other promoters was relatively contained. Yet his approach proved appealing to some of the biggest touring rock artists of the 1970s, and by the middle of the decade he was working with Led Zeppelin and Bob Dylan, as well as non-rock superstars such as Frank Sinatra and John Denver. Adding to the sense of encroachment he engendered among his rivals was his aggressive attitude, which remained years later when he wrote his memoir:

> We were remaking the concert business in those years. Starting with Elvis, we took an industry that had been regional . . . and made it national . . . It was just me and the artist, working as partners, cutting deals directly with the owners of concert halls. Costs fell, everyone was enriched . . . Well, that is not exactly true. The fact is, when my business took off, the men who ran the old system, the promoters and operators, first got squeezed, then went under. In the academy, they call it creative destruction. I had invented a newer, more efficient model, which meant the old model was doomed. On the street, they call it pain.[61]

Weintraub almost certainly gives himself too much credit here. During the time when his career in concert promotion was most active, he never truly unmade the existing concert promotion structure put into place by Barsalona and his partners. He did substantially unsettle that structure, though, and created an alternative model that successfully co-existed with it for years and prefigured the more intensive forms of oligopoly and vertical integration to come.

Tensions between Weintraub's way of doing business and the one prevailing among the majority of promoters led to one of the most fabled behind-the-scenes episodes in live music history. On April 23, 1974, thirty-two top concert promoters and a smaller number of agents including Frank Barsalona met for a retreat in Glen Cove on New York's Long Island.[62] The goal of the meeting was to determine what to do about the practice of booking national tours that circumvented local and regional promoters. Weintraub—who did not attend the meeting—was not the only culprit. Bill Graham had overseen successful national tours by Bob Dylan and the Band, and Crosby, Stills, Nash, and Young in recent months that followed a similar template to Weintraub's approach. In fact, Graham later claimed that he was the primary target of the meeting and that his fellow promoters exerted considerable pressure on him to comply with a directive to avoid promoting tours in such a fashion moving forward, something he agreed to do only grudgingly.[63] Graham also inserted some dark humor into the proceedings by hiring a cast of actors to storm into the retreat dressed like characters out of *The Godfather* and carrying musical instrument cases (meant to suggest they actually had guns). The men—twenty in all—addressed Graham, asking him, "Is everything satisfactory?" and then disrobed to reveal shirts emblazoned with the slogan, "Bill Graham Presents."[64]

Graham's power play aside, Barry Fey—another of the promoters present—suggests that Weintraub was the main subject of the meeting from the outset. He was not invited because the others were there to discuss the problem, "What do we do about Jerry Weintraub?"[65] Weintraub not only threatened to take their business away, but he was undermining a system that allowed new acts to develop and build a following. Only after they were successful would Weintraub swoop in and offer them a larger share of a bigger pie, while others had done the work of getting them off the ground. Weintraub himself did not refute this accusation but treated the charges as disingenuous when he addressed them in his memoir, answering back, "Well, hell yes, of course that's what I do. It's called business. Why do you think I'm successful?"[66] Fey, for his part, did not demonize Weintraub as much as some of his peers. According to Fey, the way for promoters as a group to undercut Weintraub was not to pass a resolution, as they did at Glen Cove, but to resort to more hands-on measures—maybe slashing the tires of a tour truck, or arranging for the lights at a Weintraub show to mysteriously turn on and off.[67] For Fey, working as one of Barsalona's appointed promoters, territory was everything. For Weintraub, the market was national, not local or regional. Together, these competing systems worked toward the same goal, to maximize profit by building a network of regional markets held together by intensive national tours.

Production Codes

"Clark Moves Rock," reads the cover of a brief sales brochure. Turning the page, the pitch continues, "And Guarantees to Get It There on Time!"[68] Clark Transfer is a trucking company still in operation as of 2021, which has long specialized in entertainment-related transportation jobs. The brochure, dating from the mid-1970s, highlights the company's then twenty-five-year history, its national reach, and efficiency and reliability in carrying large loads of scenery, lighting, and sound systems from one tour stop to the next. When Clark began working in the theatrical field in 1949, it marked an innovation, replacing the historic reliance on train transportation to move traveling shows from place to place.[69] Rock concerts became part of Clark's itinerary in the early 1970s, and the back page of the brochure announces some of the acts that used Clark to support their travels: the Rolling Stones, Jethro Tull, the Who, Emerson, Lake, and Palmer, Pink Floyd, the Eagles, David Bowie, and Led Zeppelin, among several others. Describing their services, Clark stresses that their enormous stock of vehicles gives them great flexibility in a wide range of needs: "CLARK'S modern fleet of 100 tractors, 40 trucks and 125 air-ride trailers gives us the unlimited capability to handle tours requiring anywhere from a single 20 foot truck up to multiple trailer load tours like Emerson, Lake & Palmer with 7 units, and the Metropolitan Opera with 25 trailers. The fleet of equipment is mated with logistic cargo handling systems, pads, racks and magnesium ramps to transport your electronic synthesizers, delicate sound systems, lighting and expensive musical instruments with CARE and SAFETY!"

Read nearly any account of the largest concert tours of the 1970s and you are likely to come across some mention of how many trucks were required to carry all the materials to mount the production. Two trucks, three trucks, six trucks, and more—the escalating numbers were taken as a visible index of the ways in which, with arena concerts, the proportions of a show were growing not just in terms of attendance, but in terms of production values. Again, the ballrooms laid some of the groundwork here, where more attention was devoted to details of sound and lighting than had been typical in presenting rock concerts up to that time. However, the ballrooms were founded on a different understanding of the relationship between the venue and the technical features of the production. When the ballrooms were dominant, the assumption reigned that the venue provided the primary elements—its sound system would be used, and it contracted for the elaborate light shows that accompanied psychedelic rock performances of the time, with such pioneer organizations as the Joshua Light Show on the East Coast and the Holy See out West. Arenas and stadiums, however, would not be designed with music presentation in mind until many years hence. The Beatles learned that lesson fast and when they withdrew from live performance entirely after their August 29, 1966, performance at Candlestick Park in San Francisco, the decision was partly motivated by the persistent inconsistencies they faced in making themselves adequately heard and seen. Three years later, when the Rolling Stones embarked on the epochal 1969 arena tour that culminated in their infamous appearance at the Altamont Speedway, the band for the first time carried their own p.a. system as well as their own carpet that would be used at each show to dress the stage.[70] From that point forward, mounting a tour became for top artists not just a matter of getting the band from one place to the next, but of transporting the *show*.

That Clark Transfer had established itself carrying Broadway show productions like *Oklahoma* and *Guys and Dolls* on tour is far from incidental. The 1970s has been acknowledged as a time when rock became more "theatrical," a term often invested with metaphorical significance to connote a greater emphasis on artifice over authenticity, and used to draw attention to the ways in which a rock concert was construed more as self-conscious act of performance rather than a medium of raw self-expression.[71] Rock and pop theatricality during the time also had a more material basis to it. Theater became a point of reference for what artists presented in concert, and theatrical professionals exerted increasingly direct influence upon the staging of rock that infiltrated not just design elements—how lighting and stage sets should be conceived—but also more fundamental features such as how to move a show on the road that required a substantial load of equipment.

Rolling Stones tour manager Peter Rudge offers a telling account of how the expertise needed to produce arena-sized concerts had to be found outside the sphere of popular music proper. Rudge began working with the Stones for their 1972 US tour, their first in the country after Altamont. His charge, as recounted by Robert Greenfield in his book-length report on the tour, was to further push the move toward "professionalization" of the band's touring infrastructure that had begun to take root in 1969, despite the surface chaos of that earlier undertaking.[72] Rudge previously worked with the Who and had helped to stage their 1969 *Tommy* tour, which included performances at the Metropolitan Opera House, so he knew well the challenges of mounting a rock show that was designed for theatrical effect. For Rudge this meant making the Stones as much of a self-contained touring unit as possible, carrying all the technical equipment needed to mount their concerts wherever they appeared to a degree that was not yet standard.

Looking for expertise that he could draw upon, he turned to an unlikely source: the traveling ice shows. Rudge consulted with Tommy Collins, a Minneapolis ice skating performer-turned-impresario who managed the long-running Holiday on Ice; and Don Watson, who worked alongside Collins in various endeavors and others including the Ice Capades. Collins in particular helped Rudge decipher the best ways to negotiate the layers of union employees and security staff that worked at arenas scattered across the US. Following the advice he got from both men, Rudge hired union staff to help mount the show, including a cast of riggers—whose job was to hang the stage scaffolding and sound equipment—he recruited from Disney on Ice, and brought Clark Transfer in to handle transportation needs.[73] The staffing of the Rolling Stones 1972 tour also included many road crewmembers—most prominently production manager Chip Monck—with backgrounds in rock performance, but the integration of union professionals from the world of touring ice shows was a notable innovation and a sign that production standards were undergoing a change.

These efforts were integral not only to the behind-the-scenes staging of the Stones' 1972 tour, but to the narrative spun around the tour by the band and its publicists. An extensive press package put together by the Gibson & Stromberg publicity agency credited Rudge with coordinating the conditions that allowed "as many Rolling Stones fans as possible to see and hear the group in a comfortable, non-violent atmosphere."[74] Trying their best to squash any notion that the current tour would give rise to another Altamont,

Gibson & Stromberg included a special section of the press packet with the title, "'72 Stones Tour Highlights New Concepts in Production and Security." Here Rudge was said to have implemented "innovations in booking, consumer protection, security and staging never before used for rock concerts." One line of Rudge's efforts concerned containing the threat of scalpers, a growing phenomenon in the lucrative new arena concert economy. Regarding the staging, Chip Monck and his crew were were credited with a design that provided all the requisite technical features needed to present the Stones with minimal obstruction of sightlines for the audience—an advance on the band's 1969 tour where complaints about the visibility of the stage followed them throughout. "Among the methods for doing this," continued the release, "are towers which hold all sound equipment, except the group's amplifiers, above the sightlines of the viewers."[75] Such an approach depended on the work of the experienced riggers that Rudge had hired from Disney on Ice. The looming shadow of Altamont was no doubt behind this effort by the band's publicists to insist on the expert assembly of the Stones tour, but to emphasize these details also showed just how much, by the early 1970s, an arena concert tour was expected to be a production of unprecedented scale.

Three years later, when the Stones next returned to the US, the stakes were raised even higher. Just looking at the roster of production staff carried on their 1975 tour indicates that for a band like the Rolling Stones, each tour had to be packaged as a unique blockbuster undertaking. A page in the official tour program lists the tour credits. Rudge remained in charge of marshaling the Stones forth on the road and is cheekily listed as "Commander" of the road troops. Beneath him on the roster of tour staff were more than thirty names, ranging in function from his "Admiral" Mike Crowley, to Production Manager (Patrick Stansfield), Stage Manager (Brian Croft), Photographers (Annie Liebovitz and Ken Regan), a range of carpenters and electricians, two Advance Riggers (Joe Branam and Mike Grassley), and specified roles for Amplifier Maintenance, Special Instrument Maintenance, and Hospitality Arrangements.[76] This does not include Rudge's own staff of four assistants, and the principal designers of the tour's lighting, wardrobe, and sound. More than just equipment, a Stones tour—and any comparable concert tour of the time—involved moving an entire production crew from place to place whose collective job it was to ensure that when the band hit the stage, everything required for them to play a show that would transmit to an arena-sized audience was there.

* * *

Maybe the most important addition to the Stones' entourage in 1975 was Jules Fisher. A veteran Broadway lighting designer and producer, Fisher had worked on such groundbreaking shows as *Hair*, *Jesus Christ Superstar*, and *Pippin*, for the latter of which he won the first of eight Tony Awards.[77] In 1974, Fisher moved into rock concert production as well, another indication of how the worlds of professional theater and rock performance were becoming intertwined. His first major undertaking in this sphere was David Bowie's Diamond Dogs tour; the engagement with the Stones came next. For the 1975 Stones Tour of the Americas, Fisher served in the dual roles of production supervisor and lighting director. In the former capacity he took the place of Chip Monck who oversaw the Stones' stage productions in 1969 and 1972. With Fisher in tow, the band's stage presentation became more overtly geared toward spectacular display. The Stones 1975 tour has not gone down in history as one of the band's strongest musically, but it was a milestone for production values. It featured a stage with a distinctive lotus petal design, created by another recruit from the theatrical world, scenic designer Robin Wagner, a blueprint for which appears in Figure 8.4. For tour stops in New York and Los Angeles, the stage was given an extra flourish with hydraulic lifts on the petals that allowed them to be raised and lowered. Accompanying this feature were several others, most notoriously a giant phallus that would unveil itself and stand erect during the band's performance of the song "Star Star," an ode to a groupie that appeared on *Goat's Head Soup*.[78] Such lowbrow humor allowed the Stones to keep their "earthy" image intact but the overall scale of the display indicated they were a band that spared no expense to produce a show fitted to the outsized arena setting.

The phallus became something of a *cause celebre* when, during the second stop of the tour, police and local officials in San Antonio, Texas, threatened to take action against the Stones if they unveiled the inflatable cock. Chet Flippo's report on the opening of the tour for *Rolling Stone* gave priority to the controversy surrounding the Stones' swollen member, but Jules Fisher made a cameo appearance in Flippo's account of the San Antonio concert.

> The cry was deafening when the ten Super Trouper arc lights around the hall stabbed through the darkness to pinion Jagger and Richard in a blinding white circle at a tip of the star. In the lighting box, Jules Fisher, who was imported from Broadway to do the Stones' lights, pointed proudly at his work. Seen from on high, the stage was spectacular—a delicately lit flower that seemed to be suspended and surrounded by what resembled a

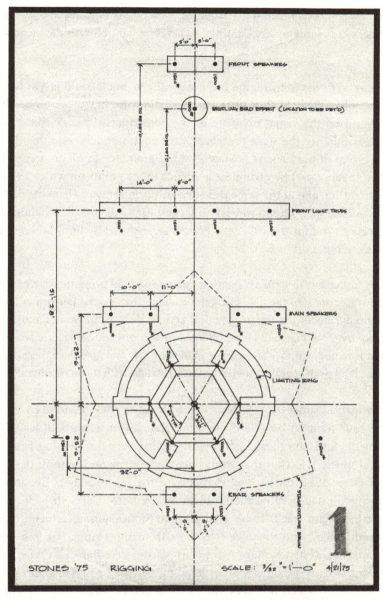

Figure 8.4 This production sketch shows the outline of the elaborate lotus petal stage design used by the Rolling Stones on their 1975 U.S. tour. Drawing by Robert Davis. Courtesy of Jules Fisher/Robert Davis/Library and Archives, Rock and Roll Hall of Fame and Museum.

sea of waving eels which were, of course, arms held overhead and clapping. Fisher's color mixes threw purple, red, yellow and blue simultaneously around the star.[79]

"The star" referred to by Flippo is the stage shape, but it could just as well be Jagger. Unlike the light shows used in rock ballrooms like the Avalon, which often dwarfed the visual presence of the performers, Fisher's effects were meant to enhance the stage presence of the rock star, to create the illusion that a group of performers onstage had the grandeur to fill an arena. This worked in large part by giving the audience many points on which to focus their attention, and at the same time designing an array of elements that ultimately drew their attention back to Jagger, Richard, and their bandmates. The press packet for the 1975 tour, this time prepared by Jim Mahoney and Associates, put it this way:

> Jules Fisher has designed a lighting system that will bring the size of the performer out into the hall, bring the audience toward the performer and communicate all the power, emotion and rhythm of the Stones' musical creativity. The stage will be illuminated in sections so that as one area of light is fading, another area can be made brighter and give the appearance of the light itself actually moving around the stage with the performers.[80]

As production supervisor, Fisher's involvement in the preparations for the Stones tour went far beyond his lighting plan, as impactful as it was. Tour documents find him participating in decisions about everything from the classical music selection that would play before the Stones took the stage to the fabric used on various elements of the stage design. Concerning the former, a handwritten memo includes the note: "Mick to pick one of these triumphant tracks to be used prior to Stones announcement 'Ladies and Gentlemen,'" and includes selections from the Hungarian folk opera *Háry János* by Zoltán Kodály, two excerpts from Béla Bartók's *Concerto for Orchestra*, and several other works including Aaron Copland's *Fanfare for the Common Man*, which would be the eventual choice. Regarding the latter, a sheet with fabric samples attached includes five options: an aqua green to be used for "tarp," bright pink to be used for "dragon tongue"—one of the other elaborate props built for the tour—metallic gold to be used for amp and speaker covers, a white fabric speckled with silver to be used for a shroud, and last but not least, a flesh colored fabric designated with a single word: "cock."[81] The phallus again rears its head.

Other documents from the tour provide a view into the evolution of Fisher's lighting design work from conception to execution. A memo from Fisher to Mick Jagger, dated March 10, 1975—nearly three months before the start of the tour—gave the Stones singer an extensive outline of the various effects that Fisher planned to use. Fisher's description of the basic lighting setup for the tour is worth quoting at length:

> The basic lighting will be provided by a hexagonal or geometric shaped light ring suspended over the stage between 28 feet and 35 feet. This will contain a mammoth amount of equipment to provide back light on all the band members in three or four colors ... In addition, there will be similar backlight arrangements but not as great that will cover the petals and the area upstage of the band for those moments when you are facing the back of the arena. In front of the stage on a straight line bar with the very minimal dimensions is mounted a battery of high intensity, very deep colored lamps to light the forestage.

Compounding this elaborate main lighting scheme was an array of sixteen special effects outlined by Fisher, including "ankle lights" that would project from the base of the backline through the ankles of the performers; a deep blue light field that Fisher says "will have a kind of shimmering ultraviolet effect"; and two separate projectors that will transmit light onto the audience, one using bat or butterfly shapes and the other just using primary colors. Most dramatically, Fisher describes "A huge 'war' type or Hollywood-premier type searchlight mounted at the rear of the auditorium that during the course of the event for one moment might hit a large mirror device in the ceiling and then tilt down until it ends up shooting a six foot diameter beam straight from the rear of the auditorium right on to you." Rounding out the memo, Fisher explains to Jagger what might be considered his philosophy of lighting design: "We will have enough stage lighting alone without the special effects to make a very impressive surround to your performance and the use of the special effects should be with discretion to only add points of glitter or punctuation to what you are doing."[82] All told, the memo provides a rare glimpse into the creative decision making required to make the arena concert experience into a visually stimulating exercise in sensory overload.

Having described the conception for the lighting design to Jagger, Fisher began putting the different production components of the tour together in practice. Three key items let us see some of the negotiations needed to bring such a massive show together. The first: a memo dated March 20, 1975, from Stephen Bickford of Phoebus lighting company, presenting to Fisher a plan to provide searchlights for the extent of the Stones' 1975 tour. Bickford offers suggestions for where to place the searchlights for maximum impact and quotes a price of $1500 a week that he says can be reduced if Fisher also arranges for round trip transportation from the company's San Francisco home base to the first show. The package provided by Phoebus would include four portable searchlights; DC power generators; a three hundred foot power cable for each searchlight; and miscellaneous other elements and parts.[83] The second: a letter from Michael Crowley—Peter Rudge's "Admiral" or second-in-command on the tour—to Tim Mahoney of Tom Fields Associates, contracting Mahoney to provide the lighting truss for the Rolling Stones tour, and also to install all necessary lighting equipment, which would be leased to the band for the duration of the tour. Cost of the truss—the metal scaffolding that would frame the stage and hold all the lighting for the main part of the production—was $66,800. Cost to rent the lighting equipment for the tour was an additional $77,000.[84]

Finally, item three: a memo from Fisher to Robin Wagner, the scenic designer who conceived the lotus petal stage. Fisher instructs Wagner to prepare some information about the construction of the stage and advises him: "The drawings for the stage as presented to the shops were sufficient for theatrical purposes but are too loose for rock and roll touring purposes." He elaborates:

> It is necessary that items meant to tour on one nighters be extremely sophisticated in their method of assembly, weight, means of connection and means to transport and to store.
>
> Sometimes theatrical scenic shops have a tendency to build things that might go together fast with little consideration of how they will stack in the truck or with much consideration as to how they will stack in the truck but not enough consideration of how much time it will take to assembly [sic] all the components in the arena.
>
> I bring this up now because the scenic shop bids might be different when they realize the degree of sophistication required for rock and roll tours.[85]

Fisher, with one major rock tour under his belt but also years of working with traveling theatrical road shows, conveys what is undoubtedly hard-won wisdom about a fundamental fact. However much rock concert production of the 1970s imported techniques and expertise drawn from theater proper, theatrical knowledge had to be revised and transformed to accommodate the demands of a touring rock show. It was up to Fisher and others in his position to determine how best to balance the technical requirements of putting on the best show possible with the logistical requirements that allowed the production elements to go on the road. In the end, it was all about those trucks: building adjustable designs that could be efficiently broken down, stored for transport, and reassembled all over again to project something sensational. That was the lifeblood of the arena concert.

Mothership Disconnections

Following his work with the Rolling Stones, Jules Fisher supervised production on two further tours that pushed the envelope of rock concert staging: the Kiss Destroyer tour and the Parliament-Funkadelic Earth Tour, both undertaken in 1976 (although the P-Funk tour extended into 1977). The latter was especially notable as one of the most elaborate concert tours of the 1970s by an African American band. Documentation of Fisher's work with P-Funk is scarcer than for the other major tours he oversaw but includes one major piece of ephemera: the original drawings used to design the infamous Mothership. Based upon the album cover design of Parliament's 1975 release, *Mothership Connection*, the Mothership was a stage prop of epic proportions, a full-sized mock spaceship that would descend from the ceiling of the arenas where P-Funk appeared down to the stage, releasing the group's charismatic figurehead, George Clinton. In fact, the Mothership was two ships, as Clinton explains in his autobiography: a smaller ship that flew over the audience, and a larger one that descended to the stage. Clinton credits Fisher with the idea to build two separate ships, one smaller and one larger, which greatly facilitated the execution of the bandleader's concept.[86]

In the cosmology of P-Funk, the Mothership is a rich and suggestive symbol of the Afro-futurist vision behind so much of George Clinton's music. The Mothership was a space-aged vehicle, but the song that invoked it on the band's 1975 album also echoed the words of the historic African American spiritual, "Swing Low, Sweet Chariot." Past, present, and future were intertwined in such an image, with Clinton harking back to the Fisk Jubilee Singers and their ilk and carrying forward their efforts to take black voices into the world at large. Like other major figures of African American music including Sun Ra and Jimi Hendrix, Clinton used outer space as a metaphor for the alienation of African Americans and a vehicle for imagining their potential liberation. Funk historian Rickey Vincent explained of the incorporation of the Mothership into the P-Funk stage show: "the landing of the Mothership serves as a metaphor for the 'chariot' responsible for bringing 'the chosen' to the Promised Land. The 'chariot' was a myth, yet this chariot was *real* . . . P-Funk attempted to bring meaning and catharsis to that paradoxical realization of freedom. The Mothership was a celebration of the infinities of which blacks were now capable."[87] Or as Clinton put it, more playfully, "To me it was pimps in outer space, the spaceship as a kind of high-tech Cadillac. Space was a place but it was also a concept, and metaphor for being way out there the way that Jimi Hendrix had been."[88]

Redolent of African American tradition and futuristic fantasy, the Mothership was also a material object that embodied Clinton's desire to approximate and surpass the spectacle of the arena concerts produced by his white rocker counterparts. Hiring Jules Fisher was integral to his goals. Fisher and his associates built the Mothership from the ground up, and the designs used to construct it offer suggestive indications of just how much work was required to bring the idea to fruition. The first page of drawings (Figure 8.5) breaks the spaceship down into component parts, with the main section of the capsule occupying one part of the page, the blasting legs of the ship on another, with detail drawings along the page to specify the structure. Handwritten notes accompany many of the drawings, the most telling of which reads simply, "800 lbs. of lights." A second page illustrates the stairway that would allow Clinton to descend from the Mothership, while a third demonstrates where various lighting elements would be placed upon the ship. A last page offers the richest image of the full Mothership, with markings indicating how it would descend from above and vibrant lines that give the effect that it is moving on the page.[89] Here we see, in four pages of hand-drawn figures, how the Mothership undertook the journey through the design process, comprising a disparate conglomeration of parts that added up to an elaborate piece of funk-rock stagecraft.

When the Mothership was finished, George Clinton was overjoyed with the results. He recalled, "It looked like some kind of unholy cross between an American car from the late fifties and early sixties, a piece of equipment from

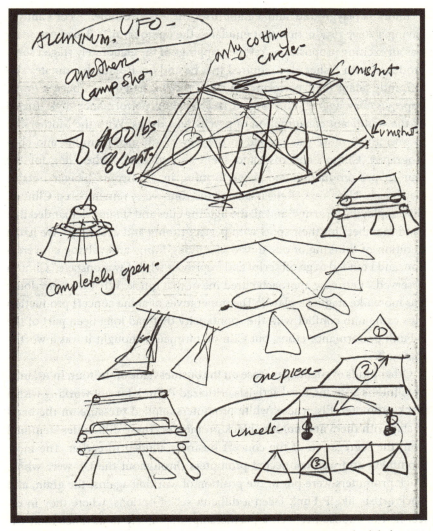

Figure 8.5 "800 pounds of light." The set piece of Parliament-Funkadelic's 1976 Mothership Connection tour, the Mothership stage prop is here shown at the design stage. Drawing by Peter Larkin. Courtesy of Jules Fisher/the Estate of Peter Larkin/Library and Archives, Rock and Roll Hall of Fame and Museum.

a children's playground, and a giant insect. It was awesome."[90] For Clinton, having a stage production that emulated the contours of a Broadway show was an exciting proposition. Yet the trappings of the elaborately staged show produced with Fisher also required that he and his P-Funk bandmates significantly adapt their performance style. P-Funk had always been a loose, improvisatory aggregation with a freewheeling performance style fueled by the significant consumption of psychedelic drugs. With the Mothership in tow, much more was needed in the way of advance planning and choreography. Clinton and his band spent several weeks rehearsing for the tour in pre-production mode, performing in an airport hangar outside Newburgh, New York. Rehearsals for the tour were, remembered Clinton, "like deploying an army," and all the lighting cues and staging demanded that band members hit their spots with perfect timing and accuracy. "We had a tradition of thinking of our music as a living thing, an evolving conversation, and I tended to go off script and improvise while I was onstage," Clinton observed. "Our new approach cured me of that quick. What we were doing was more like staging a play."[91] The imperatives of arena concert production thus came into conflict with the spontaneity that had long been part of the P-Funk performance ethos, but Clinton ultimately thought it was a worthy trade-off.

Other kinds of challenges arose on the business side of the tour. In Atlanta, by Clinton's account, local activists criticized P-Funk for not working with a black promoter. Elsewhere, white promoters applied pressure on the band to stay with them and *not* hire black promoters. These difficulties stemmed from the segregation of the concert business alluded to earlier. The most prominent and well-connected promoters throughout the US were white. Black promoters were put in the position of working against the grain, and black artists like P-Funk faced a difficult set of options, where they in effect had to choose between a partnership most likely to advance their career interests and one that would help to support black business interests and be taken as a sign of racial solidarity. Clinton resolved this contradiction for the Earth tour by forging an association with a Washington, DC, based concert promotion company called Tiger Flower that was built out of a partnership between a white woman, Carol Kirkendall, and a black man, Darryll Brooks.[92] By the time Tiger Flower was profiled by *Billboard* a few years later, in 1980, the company had grown to have four co-owners. While they were not part of the Barsalona-led trust, the company made significant inroads working with a wide range of top-tier African American soul, funk, and jazz acts who did not typically find favor among the dominant concert promotion channels, among whom were the Jacksons, Chic, Weather Report, Tavares, Sister Sledge, and Larry Graham.[93]

With the support of Tiger Flower and other promoters who worked with them throughout the tour, P-Funk held its own as an arena concert attraction. According to John Rockwell, writing in the *New York Times*, their arena-sized success did not grant them full entry into the front ranks of national popularity, however. Rockwell praised the band for artfully mixing theatrical effects with musical substance and offering a performance that did not sacrifice fun for the obviously careful execution. With stage props that were "as lavish as any in recent rock-show memory," and music delivered "with a virtuosity and flair that are almost irresistible if you're there," Rockwell wondered, "Why isn't Parliament-Funkadelic more popular?" His answer had multiple parts, but the crux of the matter lay in a telling observation that sheds light on why black acts were handled so differently than their white peers:

> Above all, P-Funk isn't a real mass success yet because whites have grown afraid of black concerts in general. In some parts of the country, P-Funk audiences are reportedly as much as 25 percent white (some Southern cities) or even 50 percent (the Pacific Northwest). But in the big urban centers it's mostly a black crowd, and whether it's realistic or not, whites seem to be scared: there have been too many reports of black gangs terrorizing isolated whites at black concerts. Only if P-Funk could sell their records to a mass pop audience, and thus encourage whites to attend their concerts in force, would whites feel safe. But since their dazzling stage show helps sell the records, they have a self-perpetuating problem.[94]

Rockwell's observations should not be taken at face value, anecdotal as they are. Nonetheless, they stand as evidence of a perception that was likely widespread if often unspoken. Arena concerts grew during an age of white flight, and so white safety—and black threat—hovered around the phenomenon. As was the case in the 1950s, when Alan Freed and others challenged the norms of racial mixing in public settings, the prospect of an interracial audience, or even a predominantly black crowd of more than a certain size, provoked fear in some quarters, and created the conditions wherein a concert by a popular black artist was treated as an inherently risky proposition.

Evidence of the inequality that resulted from these circumstances was both implicit and direct. Reporting on the success of the Commodores, a Motown group whose "crossover" success was more notable than that of P-Funk, Mikal Gilmore stressed in *Rolling Stone* that the band had always set its sights on "stadiums and coliseums," that selling hit records and playing in nightclubs was not sufficient. Tracing their path from the founding of the band in 1968, Gilmore observed: "Nine years later, the Commodores have met their goal, playing before 600,000 people during their thirty-two city 1977 American tour. According to Motown, thirty-one of those dates were sellouts." What appears like an unfettered success story is qualified, though, by Gilmore's subsequent turn: "Their total audience this year is expected to be about 900,000, modest by today's tour standards, but unusually large for a black act."[95] And therein lay the rub. It was not that African American artists could not succeed in the arena concert economy, but that there was a ceiling to their success due to a variety of structural factors compounded by persistent cultural anxieties surrounding race in the public sphere.

In a series of "Talent Forums" sponsored by *Billboard* magazine that served as a meeting ground for promoters, agents, and others who comprised the business of live music, the issue of promoting black talent became a topic of regular concern. The 1977 Talent Forum held a panel on "Black Live Music Crossover" that reached no clear conclusions, with some celebrating the capacity of black artists to move between different audiences and others suggesting the "crossover" was an outdated concept.[96] A year later, the designated crossover panel presented a more divided picture. R&B promoter Renny Roker emphasized that "audiences have not crossed over," and Cecil Hale of Phonogram/Mercury Records explained that there remained considerable resistance to playing records by African American artists on rock-oriented radio stations, which limited the extent to which white audiences would be willing to see these artists live—essentially the same argument that John Rockwell had offered in his review of P-Funk.[97]

If black artists faced distinct obstacles to enjoying the full fruits of their success in the arena concert economy, then black promoters were at a more marked disadvantage. A 1979 *Billboard* article put the matter starkly with the headline, "Bleak Future for Black Concert Promoters." There, Teddy Powell, a long-established African American promoter who had successfully transitioned into the new economy of live music claimed that white promoters had effectively pushed their black competitors out of the market.

"I don't know why," observed Powell, "We all book into the same auditoriums, we advertise with the same newspapers and radio stations and we're selling tickets to the same people for the same amount of money. But the entertainers still seem to think it's better with the white promoters."[98] Both Powell, who worked out of New York, and fellow African American promoter Joe Meachum who was based in Savannah, Georgia, recognized that cooperation between white promoters, agents, and managers was likely behind the difficulties they faced and yet did not spell out the details. For these promoters, crossover was a mixed blessing at best. Under the more strictly segregated conditions of the chitlin' circuit, black concert promoters had established a substantial amount of independence and relative autonomy; but as Nelson George observed in his late 1980s jeremiad, *The Death of Rhythm & Blues*, the push to crossover forced them to compete in an uneven field where the relationships they had built with artists, venues, and managers no longer held sway. As one anonymous promoter quoted by George asserted, "Your white boys look out for your white boys. Since most of the booking agencies are white they go to the white promoters first."[99] Given what we know about the relationship between power agent Barsalona and the promoters with whom he worked, this is likely not far from the truth.

* * *

No artist typifies the racial discontent of the arena rock economy more than Sly Stone. During the height of his stardom in the late 1960s and early 1970s, Stone embodied the promise of a form of crossover that was not just driven by market considerations. Like Jimi Hendrix did with the Experience, Stone played in a racially integrated band. Whereas the Hendrix Experience seemed to wear its manufactured quality on its sleeve—the two white men joined with Hendrix in a way that drew attention to the guitarist's "otherness"—the Family Stone had the air of a more organic aggregation, bringing together not just black and white players but also men and women into a tight-knit group that left room for each to let their individuality shine through. In the words of Rickey Vincent, "Sly's band didn't just cross racial boundaries, they *obliterated* them . . . The women played instruments, the men sang, and blacks were running the show."[100] This inclusive aura gained force from many of the band's best-known songs and biggest hits, including party anthems like "Dance to the Music" and "I Want to Take You Higher" and instances of social commentary such as "Everyday People" where racism and discrimination were acknowledged and rebuked.

Stone was no simple utopian even in his hit-making phase, as the inclusion of the sharp-tongued track, "Don't Call Me Nigger, Whitey," on his massively successful 1969 album *Stand!* would attest. That deeper, darker strain of his music came more to the surface as he moved into the 1970s, reportedly due to the ways in which his mounting addiction to cocaine and profligate use of other hard drugs intersected with the pressures of being a black rock star at a time when that role could be deemed a contradiction in terms. The first Sly and the Family Stone song of the new decade, "Thank You (Falettinme Be Mice Elf Again)," signaled the turn, the song's message of gratitude upended by the misspellings in the title, suggesting that Sly's "self" was not something he could simply "be." As critic Dalton Anthony observed, "Thank You" was "a brilliant musical and lyrical exposition of the effects of a free-base cocaine high mingled with the rising doubts and contradictions [Stone] was having about his mission as a cultural unifier and rock star."[101] *There's a Riot Goin' on*, released in 1971, pushed the sense of withdrawal even further. It was Stone's highest charting album, reaching number one on the *Billboard* sales charts, but featured the band abandoning the deceptive lightheartedness of their earlier material for a sound that projected the feelings of a bad trip that was part drug haze and part hangover spurred by the trauma of American racism.

The title phrase of Stone's 1971 album could be heard as an echo of the many instances of racially motivated unrest and rebellion that had marked American cities since the mid-1960s. Given Stone's performance record of the time, however, the suggestion that "there's a riot goin' on" could also be taken as a description of many of the appearances that the artist made—or failed to make. During the summer of 1969 Stone gained a national reputation as one of the most electrifying live performers in popular music, and his appearance at Woodstock was widely hailed as a high point of the festival. In the months that followed, though, Stone became increasingly erratic and unreliable. The problem, at least at first, had little to do with what happened on stage, where Stone's presence usually remained compelling and energizing. At issue instead was the difficulty of getting Stone to the stage, or to the gig, in the first place. Drummer Greg Errico recalled of the time,

> The not showing up stuff kind of snuck up, slipped in . . . Sly would always take an experience and, if he could do something with the experience or get something out of it, manipulate it in a different way, he would. We were late and it would create a tension. The promoter would be nervous. The audience would be nervous . . . that tension that was created by being late and

nobody knew what was going to happen, created a thing that once you were there and did your thing, you got off a little more. After all was said and done and we played, it was cool.[102]

Others who worked with Stone have reinforced Errico's provocative suggestion that this tension was something that the bandleader deliberately cultivated. The resulting stress affected all who were involved and created circumstances in which the behavior of the audience could become unpredictable.

A flash point occurred during the summer of 1970 in Chicago. Sly and the Family Stone had canceled a concert in the city and wanted to make up the date by playing a free show. The band was added to the schedule for a free concert series sponsored by the Chicago Park District and held at the Grant Park bandshell. Two other bands were also on the bill, Fat Water and the Flying Burrito Brothers, but their participation was apparently not well publicized. When the appointed start time of 4 P.M. came and not Sly and the Family Stone but Fat Water went onstage to perform, many in the audience of an estimated 50,000–75,000 were confused and upset; as *Rolling Stone*'s Marshall Rosenthal reported, members of the crowd could be heard complaining, "Where's Sly, I bet that motherfucker ain't gonna show." Some audience members—a mix of black and white concertgoers—began to storm the stage, and when police charged the crowd to try to exert control over the situation, things devolved. Bottles were thrown from all directions, and the police responded with teargas. By Rosenthal's account, "It was a riot. Pure and simple. No willful intent, forethought or planning. A bottle-throwing fest growing out of the heat, the crowded conditions, the long hours of waiting without a calming word or chord from the stage."[103] Whether Sly and his band were to be faulted for the turn of events was far from clear. Many blamed him for his late arrival, but the concert organizers fostered considerable uncertainty and discomfort and did not seem to have carefully explained the plan for the day's events to Sly and his management. Still, Sly's track record was already such that the pervading sentiment of "that motherfucker ain't gonna show" was hard to shake.

Promoter Pat DiCesare gave his own firsthand account of booking Stone in his memoir, where it figures as one of his more nerve-wracking experiences. DiCesare engaged Sly and the Family Stone a day after they were scheduled to perform at Madison Square Garden, in November 1970. Stone's reputation already preceded him, and so as soon as the engagement was put on the calendar, DiCesare got a call from Pittsburgh Civic Arena manager Charlie Strong expressing his reservations and informing the promoter that the Mayor of Pittsburgh had voiced his concern as well, fearing that a no-show by Stone could lead to a riot. DiCesare, intent on presenting Sly, came up with a plan: he would travel to New York to see the band play their Madison Square Garden date, and then would personally accompany the bandleader on his journey to Pittsburgh. The Madison Square Garden show turned out surprisingly smoothly, with only slight delays; but the next morning when they were due to leave, Stone excused himself and disappeared. Members of his entourage—including his father—told DiCesare to let it go, and the promoter had no choice.

When show time approached the following night, Sly was still nowhere to be seen. DiCesare had to make the decision that few promoters want to make: should he cancel the concert, or proceed as planned and hope that Stone would show? He decided on the latter course. The Family Stone began playing instrumental versions of their greatest hits to bide the time, and DiCesare waited anxiously. After forty-five minutes, Sly appeared. He was so high it looked to DiCesare that he could barely walk, and did not seem to know what city he was in. The promoter shouted to Sly, "You're in Pittsburgh," and pointed him toward the stage. Once in front of the audience, Stone transformed, and the outcome of the show took DiCesare completely by surprise: "I stayed on the side of the stage to watch him perform and I never saw anything like it! He was more powerful than the night before in New York. He and his band put out more energy than I had ever witnessed in my life with any act, bar none. He completely won over that audience."[104] For all that the show proved an ultimate success, the experience left its mark, and DiCesare resolved that he would "never again expose myself to such an enormous potential risk for the sake of a drug-addled rock star."[105]

A year later, Stone's struggles had progressed that much farther. While recording *There's a Riot Goin' on*, he could barely find a promoter willing to take the necessary chance to present him in concert. Meanwhile, he was engaged in a financial tug-of-war with his long-time manager, David Kapralik, who fronted significant amounts of money to Stone during the years of their involvement and now wanted repayment. Into the breech stepped a veteran promoter named Ken Roberts, whose attitude toward working with Sly indicated that for some in the concert business, the potential for payout would always justify the risk:

I looked at this like the Lloyd's of London theory—the higher the risk, the higher the reward. I said to David "Right now, you are making twenty percent of nothing and William Morris is making ten percent of nothing. If I put up the money for the auditoriums and the guarantees and all of that stuff, then I want a certain percentage of the gross of the concerts because I am the one taking all the risk." I had to put up a lot of notary credits in case he didn't show up. The band didn't have any money. I had to advance some of the money for the different people. Advance it to Sly, then he would give it to his musicians. I did everything through the proper channels. I put everything up. I would get my end from the top and all the expenses would come out and anything that was left would be Sly's and the group.[106]

Taking control of Sly's concert bookings, Roberts arranged for a big gesture: presenting Sly and the Family Stone for three consecutive nights at Madison Square Garden. *Rolling Stone*, in its coverage of the concerts, offered a headline that captured the stakes of Roberts' gamble with overstated flair: "The Struggle for Sly's Soul at the Garden." Timothy Crouse set the stage by observing: "Sly has managed rack up the most erratic performance record since Judy Garland. According to his agent, he cancelled 26 of the 80 engagements scheduled for him in 1970 . . . This year Sly has cancelled 12 shows out of 40."[107]

As the day of the first Madison Square Garden concert arrived, it looked like Stone would be up to his old tricks. He missed six straight flights out of Los Angeles, but finally managed to arrive in New York at 4:30 that afternoon. Further delays prevented Stone from taking the stage until nearly 11 P.M. His performance that night was erratic, with Sly singing off pitch, mumbling near-inaudible comments to the audience between songs, and the band wandering into loose jams that took some of the momentum away from their strongest material. On night two, by Crouse's account, Sly was an entirely different performer: "No mumbling rap, no jams, just one unbroken, hysterical climb. Sly guided the group with microscopic signals—a look, a twist of the back, a telling change of key."[108] Night three was somewhat unsteady but generally continued the high. The band's three-night stand broke a Garden house record, demonstrating that Sly's fans were not put off by his unpredictability. Yet any note of triumph was soured by an episode that happened part way through the show, when someone in the crowd informed a member of Stone's road crew that a person in the audience had a shotgun aimed at the star. Crouse's account of what happened next offers a striking example of how good Stone was at thinking on his feet in front of an arena full of fans: "Sly returned and did a neat bit of crowd engineering. 'Look around you,' he said, 'and make sure the person next to you doesn't have a shotgun. We just want to play for you.' With one stroke, Sly had acquired 24,999 bodyguards."[109] Even at what should have been a high point, a moment of rejuvenation, it seemed that Sly Stone could not shake the sense that things might fall apart at any moment. And somehow, the chaos was there almost by intention.

Writing about the refusal to comply with expectations audible on *There's a Riot Goin' on*, Greil Marcus suggested:

> With *Riot*, Sly gave his audience—particularly his white audience—exactly what it didn't want . . . One gets the feeling, listening, that the disastrous concerts that preceded and followed this record were not so much a matter of Sly insulting his audience as they were of Sly attacking the audience because of what the demands of the audience had forced him to produce. The concerts were an attack on himself as well, for having gone along with those demands and for having believed in them.[110]

What are these demands of which Marcus writes? The suggestion is that Sly resisted expectations on multiple levels: as a black star whose white fans wanted him to stand for unity and not draw attention to racial division; more generally, as a star whose audience wanted him to consistently affirm their vision of him and of the society in which they lived. Sly countered the persistent demand that he provide "good times" with a willful push to confront people with his own bad trip, which he suggested was their trip too. To this I would add: Sly's unwillingness to be on time, to follow instructions, to make each performance as predictable and seamless as possible, exposed the inner workings of arena rock, the preconditions on which it depended and without which it could not keep functioning. Sly was not exceptional in this. The plethora of stories about rock stars and their uncontrollable behavior on the road suggest that this tension between time discipline and hedonistic autonomy was built into the arena concert economy from the start.

One might well ask: was Sly Stone really more wild and harder to manage than Keith Richards? And the answer, I believe, would be no. But Richards, as the 1970s wore on, had a structure surrounding him constructed by Mick Jagger and Peter Rudge that was designed to safeguard against his unpredictability. For a complex set of reasons—which may include his struggles with bipolar disorder—Sly Stone never had that level of security around him.

The Rolling Stones, like the big banks of the twenty-first-century finance economy, were too big to fail. Sly Stone, by contrast, was allowed to gradually push himself toward oblivion. Finally, we should hear the phrase, "there's a riot goin' on" as a commentary on the social perception of Sly Stone and his public impact. Rock audiences were routinely perceived as a threat to social order, something that had been consistent since the 1950s. But they were especially viewed as such when they were comprised of black and white youth together. If the specter of rioting followed Sly throughout his performance career, it was not just because of his disregard for being on time. It was due to his blackness, and the high proportion of African Americans *and* whites together that came to see him do his thing.

Live Record Redux

Given Sly Stone's unpredictability in performance, it is not surprising that he released no live albums during the core years of his career. Just as it became risky for promoters to present Stone in concert, it would have been risky to try to capture his live act on record—unless the goal was to issue an aural documentary with little regard for musical sanctity, a model that very few live recordings of the time followed (but a select few did). The brief excerpts included on the three-album live record of the Woodstock festival remained for years the best opportunity for listeners to hear a slice of live Sly without attending a concert themselves; and as captivating as that performance was, it was better appreciated in the documentary film of the same event.

Other black artists did get their act on record. James Brown, whose epochal *Live at the Apollo* (1963) preceded the arena concert era and anticipated the growing wave of live album releases to come, continued to update his live album catalogue throughout the late 1960s and early 1970s, with a second *Live at the Apollo* volume issued in 1968, the live *Sex Machine* released in 1970, and a third Apollo collection, titled *Revolution of the Mind*, in 1971. Aretha Franklin issued three live albums in the span of four years, all markedly different: *Aretha in Paris* (1968), *Live at Fillmore West* (1971), and most celebrated, *Amazing Grace* (1972), recorded at the New Temple Missionary Baptist Church in Los Angeles. Jimi Hendrix put out his *Band of Gypsys* album, recorded on New Year's Eve 1969 at Bill Graham's Fillmore East, in 1970; many live collections followed his death later that year, including *Hendrix in the West* (1972), *The Jimi Hendrix Concerts* (1982), and complete recordings of his sets at the Monterey Pop Festival and Woodstock. P-Funk issued a live album of their Earth tour, complete with a track titled "The Landing (of the Holy Mothership)," that did not actually document said landing but instead consisted of a montage of Parliament and Funkadelic recordings meant to comically represent members of the band's audience.

Within this lineage, Earth, Wind & Fire (EWF)'s *Gratitude* stands out. Released at the end of 1975, *Gratitude* captured EWF at a moment when they were at their commercial and creative peak, purveying a style of funk that was less infused with rock, as was the case with George Clinton's Funkadelic, and instead bore strong traces of jazz and mainstream pop influence. It was the product of an African American band that had, along with Clinton's P-Funk organization, done the most to adapt both their stage performances and their business practices to the arena concert format. Maurice White, the leader of EWF, had not yet gone the route of full-on stage spectacle. That would come with the band's next tour, in support of their album, *Spirit*, for which White would have a trio of pyramids constructed for the band's stage set that were a sort of analogue to the P-Funk Mothership and a mark of his Afrocentric philosophy. Already, though, EWF had reached a level of relative parity with the touring rock bands of the era that was unusual for an African American funk/R&B combination. White recounted in his posthumously published memoir that that he had worked with Frank Barsalona's Premier Talent agency but left because Premier refused to work with black promoters. Although he did not work with black promoters exclusively after that point, he wanted to ensure that the option was open both to support black initiatives in the music industry and to maintain a more direct relationship with black colleges and other venues where a core African American audience was to be found.[111] Having positioned themselves as a live attraction that maintained a strong appeal to black concertgoers while also reaching into crossover markets, EWF produced a record with *Gratitude* that achieved a rare distinction: a double live album (actually three sides live, and one of studio tracks) that went to number one on the *Billboard* album charts, where it stayed for three weeks in January 1976, three months before another double-live album—Peter Frampton's *Frampton Comes Alive*—achieved the same feat to greater renown.

By the time the arena concert became standard, concert recordings had gained significant currency within the record industry. This trend dovetailed with two parallel developments, the growth of music festivals and the rise of the long-playing album as a dominant sound recording medium.

Throughout the 1950s and 1960s, live albums fulfilled a variety of functions, many of them defined by the genre to which they were attached. In jazz, they documented the capacity of improvising musicians to truly create music in the moment of performance. In folk music, live recordings exhibited a rapport between audience and artist that was rooted in the mix of understated manner and shared sense of political purpose or social vision. Blues and soul recordings also foregrounded the artist-audience relationship but to different effect, commonly presenting the dynamic as highly charged ritual, the performer's expenditure of energy growing with each forceful burst of acknowledgment from the audience, which also was meant to solidify a sense of racial and cultural solidarity.

Tying together these various strains of live music on record was a general understanding that what was being represented was a singular event. From Benny Goodman at Carnegie Hall to Ellington at Newport to the Weavers at Carnegie Hall to James Brown at the Apollo, the majority of early live albums possessed a site specificity that aligned with the suggestion that the listener was hearing one distinct performance. This quality carried into the rock and soul era of the late 1960s and early 1970s, in festival albums such as the three-LP *Woodstock* set released in 1970, and in the many albums recorded at notable rock ballrooms of the era, especially the Fillmore East and West but also others like the Grande Ballroom in Detroit (the setting for the MC5's 1969 *Kick out the Jams*). When the ballroom era gave way to the arena concert, though, something shifted. The later 1970s saw a building wave of live albums that continued into the early 1980s; and the trend, more and more, was to represent not a single concert but a concert tour. Although many of the live albums of this period give the aural impression of a continuous listening experience, they are commonly recorded in multiple locations, and the liner notes and other trappings draw attention to the ways in which they capture a band on the road. This shift is emblematic of the larger imperatives of the arena concert economy, where the goal was not just to present concerts of a certain scale but to reproduce them again and again, from one stop to the next. Live albums of this era stand as a sort of ultimate objectification of the arena concert phenomenon.

Whatever the circumstances, the spread of live recording in these years was facilitated by an innovation that complemented the more general need for mobility in arena concert production. Remote recording had distinct challenges attached to it, not least being the simple need to ensure that adequate recording equipment was available. The solution to this matter was the advent of the remote recording truck, a vehicle fitted with all the requisite equipment to make high-quality audio recordings that could then be transported to a more standard recording studio for final mixing and mastering. When the first fully fitted remote recording trucks were in operation is not well documented. However, the pioneers of the practice are generally acknowledged to be Wally Heider and Reice Hamel. Interviewed by *Billboard* in 1971, Hamel claimed that his efforts at remote recording dated back to the late 1950s, and that by 1965 he had an integrated three-track mobile system, which had expanded to eight tracks by 1971.[112] Heider's efforts are the better known, and he is often credited as the principal pioneer in this area. In the late 1950s, Heider worked as a recording engineer for United Recording Studios in Hollywood. He soon set up a studio of his own, followed by another in San Francisco. Throughout, he was doing remote recordings for a wide range of artists, mostly in the jazz field. Heider had a truck in which he carried his equipment as far back as 1958, but he did not build his first fully equipped remote truck until 1971.[113] By that time he had already recorded the Monterey Pop Festival, portions of the Doors album, *Absolutely Live*, and the 1969 Madison Square Garden concerts that comprised the pivotal Rolling Stones live album, *Get Your Ya-Yas Out*, and his list of credits would swell as the decade proceeded.

Absolutely Live by the Doors and *Get Your Ya-Yas Out* by the Stones represent two distinct sides of the early live rock album of the time. They contrast along several lines: *Absolutely Live* is a "double live" album, a format that provided listeners with extended play length that allowed them to have the sense that they were hearing something approximating the duration of a full concert. *Get Your Ya-Yas Out* offers a single disc of the Stones in performance, the more compact length conveying something of the "no frills" character of the Stones as a live band. While certain Stones tracks such as "Midnight Rambler" and "Sympathy for the Devil" are stretched out a bit from their album length, there is nothing on *Get Your Ya-Yas Out* to compare with the Doors' proclivity for extended performances, evident on "When the Music's Over" and "The Celebration of the Lizard," a poetic incantation by Jim Morrison that moves toward the fifteen-minute mark. *Absolutely Live* is an early example of a composite live album, with tracks culled from several Doors shows. *Ya-Yas* only includes material from a single stop on the Stones' 1969 tour, and so has a more ostensibly "documentary" quality to it. Yet *Ya-Yas* too is a highly edited affair, excluding several songs played by the Stones during their sets at Madison Square Garden and sequencing the selected songs in a way that, while roughly representative of the progress of a Stones live set, was also designed to have maximum impact as an album. *Absolutely Live*, in turn, includes a note to album buyers on the inside sleeve that stresses its authenticity despite the obvious work required to produce the album: "This album was compiled from live performances recorded in cities throughout the United States between August 1969 and June 1970. Aside from the editing necessary to assemble the music into album form, the recording is an organic documentary and absolutely live!"[114]

The almost apologetic tone of this album note suggests how much it was expected that a "live album" have a sense of integrity to it, and how *Absolutely Live* went against the grain. That it was the product of a band on tour, and not a documentation of a single performance, was not something the producers wanted to foreground. An important turning point along these lines was the Grateful Dead's 1972 release, *Europe '72*. The Dead, of course, would eventually become possibly the most oft-recorded live band ever due to their decision later in the 1970s to allow taping of their concerts by fans. Even in 1972, Grateful Dead bootlegs were circulating widely, but this did not prevent the band from issuing their third "official" live album. *Live Dead* (1970), the first of the band's live releases, set an early standard for the "double live" album, with each side given over to only one or two selections, effectively capturing the Dead's capacity for free-ranging group improvisation in a way their studio recordings never quite achieved. With tracks recorded at the Fillmore West and the Avalon Ballroom in San Francisco, it was decidedly an instance of the "ballroom" album, and one that emphasized the band's connection to its hometown audience.

Europe '72, issued immediately following another double live album of Dead material, was a different proposition entirely. The album's title signaled one key point of distinction: this was a record of the band's first full-scale European concert tour and billed itself as such. An entire class of live albums would come to consist of artists recording their concerts abroad, with one set comprised of European locations (Jethro Tull's *Live: Bursting Out*, Queen's *Live Killers*, Santana's *Moonflower*, Supertramp's *Paris*) and others highlighting Japan (Deep Purple's *Made in Japan*, Cheap Trick's *Live at Budokan*, Judas Priest's *Unleashed in the East*, the Scorpions' *Tokyo Tapes*). *Europe '72* was one of the albums that led the way toward this trend, indicating the degree to which the rock concert industry was increasingly global in its reach. A sprawling, three-LP set, the album's seventeen tracks were recorded in five locations, including the Empire Pool in Wembley, London, the Lyceum in London, the Olympia Theater in Paris, the Concertgebouw in Amsterdam, and the Tivoli Concert Hall in Copenhagen. The Dead made no apologies for the scattered source material and offered no explanations to affirm the authenticity of the performances in question. This was a record of the Dead on tour, playing in unfamiliar settings and providing US audiences with a document of their overseas endeavors.

Liner notes for many live albums issued throughout the 1970s and early 1980s included extensive information about tour production details. Providing a list of touring personnel became a commonplace gesture on many live albums. The progressive rock band Yes, on their own three-LP live set *Yessongs* (1973), went one step further. Like a select number of live albums, *Yessongs* included a booklet of photos taken during the band's tour, offering album buyers a kind of souvenir analogous to the concert programs that would be on sale at the band's concerts. Each member of the band— Steve Howe, Jon Anderson, Alan White, Chris Squire, and Rick Wakeman— received their own two-page photo spread in the booklet. The last page, though, was reserved for select members of the tour production staff, including lighting director Mike Tait and a full roster of equipment managers, along with the producer of the album Eddie Offord.[115] This gesture marked an unusual instance of recognition concerning the labor required to mount a tour of arena-sized proportions.

British heavy metal band Rainbow added to their enumeration of tour personnel a detailed list of all the equipment used for the tour that formed the basis for their 1977 album, *On Stage*. The level of specification in Rainbow's liner note list suggests a combination of gear fetishism with the desire to impress upon fans just how large of an undertaking a modern concert tour had become. Not only the general categories of equipment but the particular brands and model names appear in a list that runs down the right side of the album's back cover: 6 Crown DC300A Power Amps, 4 JBL 2300 Horn Boxes 2482 Drivers, and so on. Much of the space depicts the band's instrumentation, and the keyboard and drum configurations contain elaborate detail, every keyboard stand and crash cymbal receiving its due. The standout of the whole list, though, is "The Rainbow," the principal stage prop used by the band throughout their tour. A lighting effect that was designed to give literal presence to the band's name, The Rainbow framed the stage in a half circle, as is shown on the front cover of *On Stage*. The text used to describe the effect in the liner notes is like a little prose poem dedicated to the arena rock imperative toward spectacle, scale, and technical achievement (and is formatted as shown below):

> 40 ft. span across the stage
> 29 ft. high (in the middle)
> Made from 4 sections
> 4 ft. wide x 4 ft. deep x 15 ft. long
> 3000 light bulbs are used
> Each color band is 1 ft. across
> Operated by a portable digital computer
> The first one of its kind in the world[116]

Live albums of the arena concert era tacitly narrated the prevailing mode of production. Concurrently, they told a story about the relationship between performers and their fans. Audience noise is one of the defining features of live albums over time. On Jazz at the Philharmonic recordings of the 1940s and 1950s, the audience was heard to provide aural evidence that a particular improvised instance captured the enthusiasm of the crowd; the sound of the audience in a sense validated the spontaneity of the performance being given. Arena concert albums rarely feature such in-the-moment audience outbursts. Instead, the crowd is heard as a voluminous mass, mainly audible in the space between the tracks to mark the continuity between one song and the next. The sheer presence of the audience on record was assigned value. Foghat went so far as to include a note on their 1977 live album: "Applause: Audience."[117] Participation, when it happens, tends to be highly ritualized, a kind of staged call and response that dramatizes one of the defining features of arena rock writ large: that it afforded the audience a sense of freedom within constraint, the tightly bounded space of the arena or stadium providing the framework within which the audience could raise its voice but not necessarily lose control.

A paradigmatic instance of this dynamic appears on Kiss's 1975 album, *Alive!*[118] The episode appears on track two of side three, "100,000 Years." At nearly twelve minutes, "100,000 Years" is by far the longest cut on *Alive!* Much of the length is devoted to an extensive solo by drummer Peter Criss—unaccompanied drum and guitar solos having become a staple of arena concerts, instances of technical display that allowed individual members of the band to establish a more direct relationship with the gathered crowd.

After some three minutes of Criss playing on his own, singer and guitarist Paul Stanley returns to the microphone and begins to address the audience. "Alright!" Stanley shouts, "I got a question for you!" He then directs a series of questions to different segments of the crowd, whom he names by their location—"over here." For the first group of "over here" people, Stanley asks, "How many people over here like to party?" and elicits what sounds like a suitably boisterous response. Then he turns his attention to the "wild people over here" whom he asks, "How many people over here like to get high?" Criss's drums continue to gallop as Stanley talks to the audience, letting them know he hasn't forgotten about the "people upstairs"—meaning those in the upper sections of the arena, farthest from the stage.

At this point Stanley directs his question to everyone: "I wanna know how many people here tonight [at this point there is a slight pause, and Stanley's voice raises notably for what comes next] BELIEVE IN ROCK 'N' ROLL?" The audience cheers loudly once again, and Stanley prompts them further, saying that if they believe in rock 'n' roll, they have to shout along. One burst of "rock 'n' roll" follows but it is not enough for Stanley, and he tells the audience they can do better. After a second time that is louder but still not sufficient, he pushes further: "I know if you really wanted to, you could bring the roof down." A third cry of "ROCK 'N' ROLL" finally seems to satiate Stanley, and he leads them to clap their hands along with the beat that Criss has never stopped laying down, and then to "stand up for what you believe in," at which point the audience presumably stands and the band charges back in while Stanley sings to those now standing, "Do you feel alright?"

Like Grand Funk Railroad before them, Kiss generated intense enthusiasm among a young cohort of rock fans who were generally considered beneath the dictates of good rock taste as had been established in the pages of *Rolling Stone* and other organs of popular music opinion. This was, in a sense, the "meat and potatoes" audience of the arena concert phenomenon, whose exuberant presence was also heard on live albums by Aerosmith, Black Oak Arkansas, Blue Öyster Cult, Foghat, Journey, Mahogany Rush, and UFO, among many others. A visual corollary to the sound of this mass of young fans letting themselves go appears on the back cover of *Alive!* (reproduced in Figure 8.6). Photographer Fin Costello depicts Detroit's Cobo Hall from a position on the floor near the front of the arena and pointed outward at the audience. Two young male fans stand immediately in the foreground holding a hand-drawn poster showing the faces of the four members of

Figure 8.6 The back cover photo from the 1975 Kiss album, *Alive!* There may be no better image to capture the fantasy of belonging fueled by the phenomenon of arena rock and the way that fantasy helped to build a live music industry unprecedented in scale. Photograph by Fin Costello. Courtesy of Kiss Catalog, Ltd.

Kiss in all their make-up. One of the fans raises his fist in a salute, as though physically testifying to the solidarity in rock that Paul Stanley would later ask the audience to demonstrate. They are surrounded on all sides by a sea of concertgoers seated in folding chairs on the arena floor, while above, the upper tiers of the arena are just as densely packed. This image stands for the fantasy that the arena concert offered to the rock consumer: to attend a concert was to join a community of like-minded fans who were dedicated above all to rock as a style of music and a lifestyle commodity, who liked to party, who liked to get high. And here we should remember what Jerry Weintraub saw when he looked out at Yankee Stadium: "all those seats, each representing a person who has to be reached, marketed to, convinced, sold." As a mode of production, the arena concert industry presented shows, yes, but what it really generated were audiences, whose willingness and desire to be part of a rock crowd kept the engines of the Clark Transfer trucking company moving to the next tour stop.

9

Staging Hip-Hop

Race, Rap, and the Remapping of Musical Performance

Jay-Z, like many of the most successful hip-hop artists, is a master of self-mythology. His up-from-the-projects narrative runs throughout his lyrics, his interviews, and the rhetoric that has accompanied a career that has involved as much engagement with branding and business success as with making music as such. Among the rapper's many achievements, one of the most unsung is his unusual success in the sphere of live performance. Although it is difficult to make the case using hard numbers, Jay-Z is likely the single most successful touring hip-hop artist in the history of the medium—challenged only by his wife and occasional touring partner Beyoncé. His 1999 "Hard Knock Life" tour was the highest grossing hip-hop tour of all time up to that point. Since then, he has continued to stage some of the most lucrative tours of any artist, regardless of genre, and his joint tour with Beyoncé in 2018 ranks as one of the top thirty highest grossing tours ever, and the second highest by an African American artist, topped as of this writing only by Beyoncé's own 2016 "Formation" tour.[1]

At a key point in Jay-Z's memoir-cum-lyrical-exegesis, *Decoded*, he recounts the excitement he experienced when, for the final show of his 2003 tour supporting *The Black Album*—an album that was supposed to mark his retirement from performing, although that would change—he appeared for the first time as a headlining artist at New York's most storied arena, Madison Square Garden. A native New Yorker, the appearance held special significance for Jay-Z, who recalled: "Playing Madison Square Garden by myself had been a fantasy of mine since I was a kid watching Knicks games with my father in Marcy," Marcy referring to the Brooklyn projects where he was raised.[2] Arriving at the arena on the night of the concert, Jay-Z continues, "the sight of my name in lights on the marquee got me in the right frame of mind. I began to visualize the whole show from beginning to end; in my mind it was flawless . . . Michael Buffer, who announces all the boxing matches in the Garden, announced me, and I did my signature ad-libs. The crowd went bananas . . . I ended the concert by 'retiring' myself, sending a giant jersey with my name on it up to the rafters."[3] Casting himself as a sports champion celebrating a storied career, Jay-Z put on a concert that was part charity benefit, with checks presented to the mothers of deceased rappers Tupac Shakur and Biggie Smalls for their respective foundations; part hip-hop variety show, with the roster of guest stars encompassing Missy Elliott, Foxy Brown, Mary J. Blige (shown with Jay-Z in Figure 9.1), Ghostface Killah, Pharrell, R. Kelly, and of course Beyoncé, among others; and part autobiographical narrative, the song selection ranging widely across Jay-Z's career and including a number of early tracks.[4]

Having showcased so many guests throughout, Jay-Z closed the show alone. Wearing a New Jersey Nets jersey (the team for which he was part-owner) and baseball cap, he tells the crowd he "doesn't want to party with y'all, I want to vibe with y'all." The audience hears a voiceover of Jay-Z's mother, Gloria Carter, that announces one of his most poignant autobiographical

Figure 9.1 Jay-Z (right) with Mary J. Blige at the rapper's 2003 concert at Madison Square Garden, a stop on what was then said to be Jay-Z's farewell tour in support of his release, *The Black Album*. The many guest appearances gave the concert the aura of a special event. Photograph by KMazur. Courtesy of WireImage/Getty Images.

tracks, "December 4th," the opening cut from *The Black Album*. As the song starts, the rapper continues to ask the audience, "Can I vibe with y'all?" He works the stage from side to side, and literally and figuratively strips down over the course of the song, throwing his cap into the crowd during verse two, and relinquishing his jersey prior to embarking on the song's third and final verse. Left in a plain white t-shirt and jeans, a single spot illuminating him, Jay-Z recites a lyrical request for forgiveness before landing on the song's final gesture of self-justification, "This is the life I chose or rather the life that chose me/If you can't respect that you're whole perspective is wack/Maybe you'll love me when I fade to black." Asking the audience to "give him some light" during this last passage, the crowd responds in classic arena concert fashion (re-styled for the twenty-first century), holding up a mix of lighters and cell phones. Onstage, with his left arm held high, Jay-Z is shrouded in a cascade of falling lights before he does in fact fade to black, his life story and career trajectory having reached a momentary climax.[5]

Jay-Z's portrayal of this moment as a high point in a career full of them is telling. Live hip-hop is typically treated as an afterthought. Hip-hop histories rarely give concert performances or tours more than passing attention. More so than other twentieth-century genres such as jazz, country, and rock that developed alongside the growth of the recording industry, hip-hop has been considered a medium in which the record is the thing above all. The exception, and it is an important one, concerns the discussion of early hip-hop when the DJ, not the MC, ruled the scene and hip-hop existed primarily as a live medium, albeit one in which the spinning and mixing of records was the primary activity.[6] Tracking the evolution of hip-hop from street and club culture to broad-based popular culture, though, has typically meant highlighting the transition from a live medium to a recorded one. In this light, Jay-Z's choice to recall so vividly his Madison Square Garden "retirement" concert goes against the grain of the received history of the genre. It is a reminder that live music matters in hip-hop, but more to the point, that there is a history of hip-hop as a live medium that extends well beyond the genre's founding years and has yet to be properly told.

This final chapter is an effort to begin to tell that history, guided by the understanding that hip-hop has much to say about the larger state of American live music in the last decades of the twentieth century and the early years of the twenty-first. During these years, hip-hop challenged and perhaps supplanted rock for dominance as the most widely representative form of youth-oriented popular music. In strictly commercial terms, however, the success of hip-hop on the record charts has never fully been matched by its success as a concert medium. Well into the 1990s, it was rare to find any major hip-hop concert tours that could compete with the most successful touring artists in rock and country; among black touring artists, pop R&B artists such as Michael Jackson and Whitney Houston held far more drawing power. Hip-hop's move into the concert industry was thus tentative and was, moreover, met with considerable resistance from a range of figures from concert promoters to venue operators to insurance providers and local authorities, many of whom perceived the principal appeal of hip-hop to young black audiences—or to audiences of black and white youth combined—to present a threat to public order much as early rock 'n' roll concerts had been cast thirty years earlier. The very difficulties that hip-hop faced in becoming established as a broad-based concert medium, then, reveal the degree to which the upper ranks of the live music industry remained uniquely exclusionary regarding black music artists. Jay-Z's insistent celebration of his Madison Square Garden appearance assumes a different kind of significance when viewed against this backdrop: for a black hip-hop artist to get to hold court at such a venue is to defy enduring limits on the public presentation of black popular music.

Despite the anxieties that surrounded live hip-hop in large venues, something like "arena rap" did become an established reality by the mid-1980s. Prefigured by early tours where the likes of the Sugarhill Gang and Kurtis Blow appeared as opening acts for more established R&B artists, the 1984 Fresh Fest tour and its successors, in the words of hip-hop scholar Murray Forman, "introduced the genre in a new, professionalized context, lifting it out of the narrowly defined ghetto terrains with which it was still predominantly associated."[7] Subsequent tours by Run-DMC, the Beastie Boys, LL Cool J, Public Enemy, and N.W.A., among others, expanded the reach of hip-hop as a concert attraction even as public reaction to the music treated it as a cause for alarm. Meanwhile, starting in the early 1990s with the Lollapalooza tours, hip-hop figured significantly in the rejuvenation of the American music festival that gained further momentum with the founding of the Coachella and Bonnaroo festivals in 1999 and 2002, respectively. If anything, the festival scene even more than the arena concert realm exemplified the paradoxes of live hip-hop into the twenty-first century: at once central and peripheral, the presence of hip-hop was considered integral to the staging of a successful event but dedicated hip-hop festivals could hardly be found.

One could say that over time, arena rap and festival culture normalized hip-hop, making it into a commercial genre like any other. Yet the emergence of hip-hop as a distinct performance culture also posed a challenge to the aesthetics of live performance as they existed in rock and other established genres of the time. Here it is important to return to hip-hop's founding moment, and to observe that, even in its original incarnation as locally rooted live music, it was also always already recorded music. In this, it shared a disposition with disco, a movement with which hip-hop grew in parallel. A transformation had taken shape through which DJs emerged as practitioners of a refashioned form of liveness in which the programming of records accompanied public gatherings where audiences acted on their desires to dance, socialize, fight, take drugs, and search for sexual partners. That hip-hop's early history is largely told through the trajectories of a trio of founding DJs—DJ Kool Herc, Afrika Bambaataa, and Grandmaster Flash—is indicative of the music's unusual consistency. More than that, it represents the extent to which hip-hop, disco, and other forms of dance music recast the relationship between "live" and "recorded" music more dramatically than at any time since the popularization of sound recordings during the early jazz age. Live hip-hop is from this perspective a complex phenomenon unto itself, and the choices that hip-hop artists have made about how to present themselves—whether to appear with a DJ onstage or a full band, whether or not to rely on prerecorded tracks for accompaniment—have consequences for understanding the changing consistency of live music writ large.

On the Record

Kool DJ Rock was the stage name of Rocky Bucano, a young protégé of the veteran Bronx club DJ Pete "DJ" Jones, who established himself as the house DJ at an upscale Bronx disco called the Stardust Room. Supplementing his DJ work, Bucano also started a party promotion company called DRB Productions, through which he organized parties around New York City drawing upon a range of DJ talent including Grandmaster Flash, who not incidentally had also spent time apprenticing with Pete "DJ" Jones.[8] Indicative of the events put on by Bucano under the DRB title was a June 30, 1978 "Disco Extravaganza" that featured himself with his "Come Off Crew" alongside Brooklyn DJ Grand Master Flowers, Bronx spinner Kool DJ Dee, pioneering Harlem DJ Eddie Cheeba (spelled "Cheba" on the flyer), and Pete "DJ" Jones himself, said to be "Back by Popular Demand." Like any good disco event, it was to be a very late-night affair, starting at 10 p.m. and lasting "until . . ."—the stop time remaining unspecified. The venue, the Stardust Room, was said to be "new and improved . . . now with three floors of disco party." Prospective party goers were encouraged, "Come be the First to Dance Your Ass Off on All Three Floors!"[9] This was a disco party, much like those that were hosted regularly in New York's downtown districts but with a collection of black DJs who represented some of the city's most concentrated African American neighborhoods.

A different sensibility could be found in the promotional flyers for two events held three years later, in April and July 1981. The name of the production company behind the events itself signaled a contrast: Nubian Productions, a joint venture of influential DJs Afrika Bambaataa and Kool Herc, indicative of Bambaataa's strongly Afrocentric impulse.[10] Bambaataa was a featured DJ at both events along with other members of his Soul Sonic and Cosmic Force crew, which included DJ Jazzy Jay, Kool DJ Red Alert, and MCs Ice Ice, Lisa Lee, Ikey C, and Chubby Chubb. Others appearing on the bill for the two shows included the Cold Crush Brothers, DJ Theodore and the Fantastic Five, and the Funky Four + 1.[11] The designation of the latter as "Sugar Hill Recording Artists" on the flyer for the July 3 event evinced a shift that had taken hold since the disco party of 1978: artists associated with the growing scene in the South Bronx had now been making records for two years, and the designation of "recording artist" brought new status to the performers. The venues for the two events also held significance. T-Connection, host of the April 4 production, was a Bronx club that became a significant sponsor of early hip-hop culture, where Bambaataa and his crew regularly appeared. On July 3 the show was held at the Roller World Skating Rink, one of many instances in New York and locations around the country where a skating rink was repurposed into a music venue—something that provided public space for black popular culture that was otherwise hard to obtain, and that was especially geared toward an audience of under-twenty-one black youth. In the Bronx, high schools, community and athletic centers, and spaces controlled by the Police Athletic League served a similar function.

Notably, the two events of April 4 and July 3, 1981, were billed as "The Hip-Hop Family Reunion Jam" and "The Hip-Hop Family Reunion Jam Pt. 2." While the phrase "hip-hop" had been coursing through the vernacular for some time—audible in the breakthrough 1979 Sugarhill Gang recording, "Rapper's Delight"—it only gradually assumed definition as a term used to identify the music and culture that evolved around DJs, MCs, breakdancers, and graffiti writers. That it was being used by Bambaataa and his associates as something like a genre category can be gleaned from another phrase found on the flyer for the first Hip-Hop Reunion, noting that the show was "dedicated to the hip-hop music of the world!"

Writing about the earliest phase of hip-hop business and promotion, Dan Charnas has observed that the term "hip-hop" gained currency as figures like Bambaataa and his sometime running mate Fred Brathwaite—aka Fab Five Freddy—sought a name to encompass the breadth and uniqueness of the culture they saw emerging in the early 1980s. According to Charnas,

> Soon, figures like Bambaataa and Brathwaite began using the term "hip-hop" to distinguish themselves from disco and to name an entire street culture that had, until then, been nameless . . . "Hip-hop" was purist terminology . . . an endeavor to claim a real musical and cultural distinction between disco and the park jams, between processed music and raw funk, between grown folk and kids, between conformists and rebels, between people who saw themselves as the lubricant for partygoers and other who saw themselves as serious artists.[12]

Deploying the term "hip-hop" as a marker of distinction, then, the "Hip-Hop Family Reunion" shows promoted by Bambaataa in 1981 set themselves up in opposition to precisely the sort of DJ-centered events that had been happening in settings like the Stardust Room for some years. Disco became a term of disrepute, emblematic of a dated sensibility that did not sufficiently acknowledge what was new and singular about the developing movement to which Bambaataa and his cohort belonged. Charnas suggests that a key marker of this shift was the release of the 1982 film *Wild Style*, in which Brathwaite appeared and which was promoted as a "hip-hop movie" showcasing the full range of elements associated with the style. Bambaataa's "Hip-Hop Family Reunion" shows pre-date this milestone by more than a year, demonstrating once again that—as with jazz, as with rock 'n' roll—live performances and the language used to sell them played a major role in defining a musical movement as it was just assuming coherence.

It is a mistake, though, to exaggerate the extent to which hip-hop and disco were antithetical to each other. After all, the flyer for the Hip-Hop Family Reunion Jam, Pt. 2, emphasized that despite the location at a skating rink, there would be "no skating, only dancing." More to the point, disco remained a word that circulated freely into the early 1980s with regard to the promotion of hip-hop events. As music historian Amanda Lalonde noted in connection with the work of hip-hop flyer artist Buddy Esquire—who did the artwork for the first Hip-Hop Family Reunion—"in the late 1970s and early 1980s hip hop was far more interwoven with disco and its suave brand of showmanship" than would be the case just a few years hence.[13] Above all, disco and hip-hop intersected at the point where DJs became central figures within an evolving performance culture that revolved around the playing of records. The rise of what Mark Katz calls the "performative DJ" took root to a significant degree in both styles, evident in common techniques of mixing records and in the songs that DJs chose to play.[14] Where live music was concerned, the parallel emergence of hip-hop and disco had another, broader kind of significance as well, having to do with a recalibration of the interrelationship between live and recorded music, and the spaces where they were enjoyed.

* * *

Sound recordings had long been a feature of public space. Early coin-operated phonographs created in the late nineteenth century were a sort of prototype for the jukebox, which became commonplace in a range of public leisure spaces by the early 1940s. When recordings became a more regular presence on the radio airwaves, the DJs whose job it was to play them often moved into the realm of live music promotion as a way to supplement their income and enhance their name recognition, a phenomenon discussed in Chapter 6. These same DJs also did a host of public appearances including record hops, a key institution of 1950s youth culture wherein a DJ would appear to play records for teenaged audiences at many of the same kinds of settings that, years later, would host early hip-hop performances: high schools or junior highs, and public community and youth centers. There is no evidence to suggest that DJs of this era developed any unusual techniques in the playing of records. As was the case on the air, they presented themselves as attractions on the basis of their strong personalities and their selection of songs—the latter of which would remain a staple of the art of the DJ.

A turning point in US record culture came in the mid-1960s with the advent of the discotheque. The French term connoted a space that was dedicated to the shared public enjoyment of recordings. To have such dedicated spaces rather than the ad hoc settings employed by 1950s DJs during their record hopping activities was a major shift. The function of early discotheques was uncertain, as was the manner in which the records would be played. A 1960 notice in *Billboard* about the "Discotheque de France" described it as a lending library for recordings, not a place to gather and listen (let alone dance).[15] Only a year later, *Variety* observed in a report on Paris nightlife, "Various discotheques spin platters. (Etoile, La Licorne, Epi Club, St. Germaine, Discotheque, Whiskey a Gogo, others.)"[16]

New York's first dedicated discotheque establishment seems to have been Le Club, characterized in a 1962 account as a "snooty membership 'discotheque'... where they dance to canned music."[17] A somewhat more inclusive setting, though one still geared toward an upper crust of nightlife patrons, was Shepheard's, opened at the end of 1963 in the Drake Hotel. The club employed a trio of musicians but was most noted for featuring a DJ named George "Slim" Hyatt, who had previously filled the same role at Le Club and so deserves credit as perhaps the founding DJ of the new discotheque phenomenon in the US. Profiled in *Variety* in 1964, Hyatt was said to have 2,000 records upon which he drew for his nightly, six-to-seven-hour sets. Veteran columnist Abel Green captured Hyatt's skill in choreographing the flow of recordings:

> His extra-sensory perception via the three turntables, on which he seems to magically mix the waddle, the frug, the madison, the mashed potato, in alteration [sic] with anything and everything from conventional foxtrotology to a Charleston, a Viennese Waltz to a tango, and then back to a paso doble, merengue, tamure or a pot-pourri of Brazilian mardi gras songs and the inevitable bossa nova makes him the monarch nightly for several hours of marathon dancing.[18]

Hyatt's skillful ability to navigate between genres that were, in turn, linked to popular dance styles prefigured the work that disco and hip-hop DJs would do in years to come. The key difference was that, at this stage, the DJ remained all but invisible to the dancers, tucked away in a room with his three turntables, and able to watch the action of the dancers only through a small slit in the door.[19]

While DJs such as Hyatt and Terry Noel, who spun records at the hip New York nightspot Arthur starting in 1965, achieved a certain measure of prominence, their presence in the discotheques of the era was not assured. Jukeboxes remained a persistent feature in many of the rising discotheques, and the Seeburg Corporation adopted an especially aggressive marketing campaign to promote a ready-made "discotheque package" that consisted of a jukebox console, two large floor speakers, and décor to convert a space into a suitable dance environment.[20] Many discotheques also continued to employ live entertainment. Although Shepheard's eventually abandoned the trios that would alternate with Hyatt's DJ work, other spots regularly hired singers or bands, including many that catered to the young rock audience. These included the Los Angeles nightspot the Whisky a Go Go, named after one of the early wave of Paris discotheques, where Johnny Rivers was a main attraction on opening night and remained a fixture; and the Phone Booth in New York, where the Rascals made an early impression, bringing in "long haired boys and longer haired girls."[21] Although *Billboard* reported in 1965 that disc jockeys or "spinners" were displacing the use of coin-operated jukeboxes in Chicago clubs—especially those clubs that catered to African American patrons—the matter was far from settled, and the supremacy of the DJ continued to vie with mechanized record players and live performing artists over the next few years.[22]

Whatever was the manner in which the records were played—by a DJ or by a coin-op machine—the discotheque provoked a crisis around the place of live performance in the sphere of public entertainment. The situation was akin to that described by Sarah Thornton in her account of the rise of British dance club culture. In the UK, the Musicians Union began organizing against the public use of recorded music in the 1950s, decrying records for their lack of authenticity and upholding the "live" presence of working musicians as the only proper path to musical enjoyment. Indeed, Thornton goes farther, suggesting that it was only at this moment in the 1950s that for the first time, "the term 'live' entered the lexicon of musical appreciation."[23] I've demonstrated that in the US context at least, the term "live" begins to circulate far earlier. Nonetheless, discussions of live music assumed a new weight in connection with the advent of the discotheque as competing interests vied for influence over how music should be presented and experienced before the public.

A headline in *Variety* captured the mounting tension: "Discotheque: Foe of Talent."[24] Before long, the American Federation of Musicians jumped into the fray just as its counterpart Musicians Union did in the UK. *Variety*, again, put the matter most starkly: "The struggle for survival of live musicians against the seemingly inexorable advance of canned music has flared up again against the discotheques."[25] Members of AFM local chapters in Chicago, Los Angeles, and New York all took particular offense against the policy pursued in some discotheques of hiring "live" musicians to effectively play over or along with records, seeking to offer customers a sense that they were watching performing musicians even as they were listening primarily to the music on record.[26] The concern was in line with AFM policy going back to the 1930s, which had consistently guarded against the potential loss of jobs held by union musicians in the face of technological and cultural change. Union policy evolved over the course of the flare-up, at first prohibiting all union musicians from working in locations where they were hired to perform along with records, then applying pressure on discotheques to hire live musicians to play in alternation with recordings.[27] At no point did union officials acknowledge that DJs might themselves qualify as adequate performing talent or working musicians in their own right.

* * *

Reflecting on the broad transition whereby records became the primary accompaniment to dancing, Thornton draws attention to the evolving terminology used to refer to the venues where dance music grew to prominence. She observes: "The *record hops, disc sessions* and *discotheques* of the 1950s and 1960s specifically refer to the recorded nature of their entertainment. In the 1970s, transition is signaled with the shortened, familiar *disco*. In the 1980s, with *clubs* and *raves*, enculturation is complete and it is 'live' venues that must announce their difference."[28] Hip-hop was very much a part of this process of adaptation, its emergence coinciding with and contributing to the process through which playing records in public lost its aberrant status. And disco, in turn, has gained greater recognition as a sphere in which DJs exerted influence through more than masterful song selection, developing techniques that paralleled and prefigured the work that hip-hop DJs did in repurposing already recorded music.

Frances Grasso was one such DJ. Working at the Lower Manhattan club the Sanctuary, he began to layer records on top of one another, creating on-the-spot remixes from unlikely sources. Dance music historian Tim Lawrence conveys the process that Grasso used to achieve his mixes: "Using his headphones to his full potential, the DJ started to use his left ear to listen to the incoming selection and his right ear to hear the amplified sound in order to forge an imaginary amalgam that . . . could be transformed into sonic reality," an effect he generated most powerfully by placing "the Latin beats of Chicago's 'I'm a Man' over the erotic groans of the vocal break in Led Zeppelin's 'Whole Lotta Love.'"[29] Nicky Siano, who in 1973 assumed the

DJ post at another downtown club, the Gallery, pushed these practices further, cultivating a method of repeating an isolated part of a song by using two copies of the same record that anticipated the looping efforts that became central to remix culture. Siano recalled: "I used two copies with 'I Got It' by Gloria Spencer ... It starts, 'Dnn dnn, yeah yeah, dnn dnn, yeah yeah, dnn dnn, yeah yeah,' and then she goes, 'I got it.' I would play the beginning part over and over and over and over, and then finally bring in the rest of the song. I built my own records."[30]

The same year that Siano began working at the Gallery, Bronx DJ Clive Campbell—aka DJ Kool Herc—started attracting notice as the result of a now-legendary party thrown by his sister, Cindy, on August 11, 1973.[31] That the party was held in the rec room at the apartment building where they lived, 1520 Sedgwick Avenue, suggests the different circumstances in which Herc and his peers developed their craft relative to their downtown counterparts. While the Bronx had its nightclubs and discos, much of the emerging youth culture that became called hip-hop was taking shape in less formal settings, from house parties to public parks. An immigrant from Jamaica, Herc was influenced by the sound system culture that had arisen there, and as his reputation grew, he distinguished himself in part by having a sound system that could overpower his competitors with pounding volume and pulsing bass frequencies. His primary innovation was what he called his "Merry-Go-Round" technique. In one sense, Herc's DJ style resembled that of Siano: he began using two copies of the same record simultaneously to extend certain parts indefinitely, creating loops in the moment of performance. For Herc, though, the segments of the record that he chose to isolate and extend were of a very particular sort, stimulated by his observation of the dancers who moved to his selections. Relaying Herc's fundamental insight, Jeff Chang wrote: "The moment when the dancers really got wild was in a song's short instrumental break, when the band would drop out and the rhythm section would get elemental. Forget melody, chorus, songs—it was all about the groove ... Herc zeroed in on the fundamental vibrating loop at the heart of the record, the break."[32]

Word of Herc's approach began to spread. One of the first to get the news was another young aspiring Bronx DJ named Joseph Saddler, who overheard a conversation between two talented dancers that had attended Cindy Campbell's party and talked enthusiastically about how Herc's concentration upon percussive beats was an incredible spur to movement.[33] Saddler soon checked out Herc for himself and was deeply impressed by the older

DJ's ability to isolate and maneuver between break beats. After seeing Herc at work, Saddler also claims to have noticed a tear in the fabric: Herc did not create an especially seamless flow between the different breaks that he played. Saddler tried to emulate Herc's approach to the DJ set as a "continuous piece of music," but he also dedicated himself to mastering the transition between one break beat and the next so that, as he explained to a friend, "you, the listener, can't tell where one stops and the next one starts."[34] The pivotal insight came to Saddler through much trial and error, that he could achieve the desired level of precision in matching the beats only by breaking a cardinal rule of DJing. He would have to use his hands to hold the records in place until the moment when he was ready to spin it. Using a grease pen to mark the exact spot where he wanted a record to begin to play, Saddler's theory of beat matching found realization.[35] By the time he assumed the name Grandmaster Flash, he had already gained renown as one of the most technically refined DJs working the South Bronx territory.

Hip-hop culture was comprised of much more than DJing, of course—the storied four elements all followed parallel paths of evolution. For my purposes, though, DJing stands out for the way it played upon the boundary between live and recorded music. At a moment when the rock concert economy was dominated by arena concerts, disco and hip-hop DJs alike brought audiences into clubs and other neighborhood spaces where a DJ's performance might draw attention to itself, but was also designed to motivate dancers, such that the audience was as integral to the show as the performer. The Bronx DJs who contributed to this emerging scene distinguished their efforts from the downtown disco DJs and also from DJs working in other boroughs and neighborhoods where black audiences predominated—a difference that was articulated at the opening of this section in the contrasting fliers of the Disco Extravaganza and the Hip-Hop Family Reunion. Joseph Ewoodzie defined five areas of distinction between the DJing scene in the South Bronx and that found in other parts of New York, within which the uniqueness of the break-centered DJ style cultivated by DJ Kool Herc, Grandmaster Flash, Afrika Bambaataa, and others was complemented by a trend toward competitive breakdancing, the use of smaller and less lucrative venues, a prevalence of under-twenty-one audiences, and a tendency toward casual rather than formal attire.[36] These other factors helped to frame the work of the DJs and contributed to the impression that hip-hop was more than a discrete musical style but represented a larger cultural movement. Within that movement, the use of the turntable as a musical instrument in the manner fostered by

Grandmaster Flash and other innovators such as Theodore Livingston, also known as Grand Wizard Theodore, was an integral founding component.[37] Over time, the tools evolved, such that turntables were largely supplanted by digital samplers that offered more flexibility in the manipulation of recorded sound. The preference to use already-recorded sound as the basis for new musical works remained intact for years to come, however, and had particular implications when hip-hop performers began to expand their reach away from their communities of origin to play in front of other audiences that were less familiar with hip-hop aesthetics.

Hip-Hop Under and Overground

By 1981, when Afrika Bambaataa and his cohort were throwing the two Hip-Hop Family Reunion shows, rap music had achieved expanded visibility due to a string of successful recordings, most prominently the Sugarhill Gang's "Rapper's Delight" but also the Fatback Band's "King Tim III," Kurtis Blow's "Christmas Rappin'" and "The Breaks," and the early recordings of Grandmaster Flash and the Furious Five. It was not just through recordings, though, that hip-hop diffused into the culture at large. Live hip-hop performances played a pivotal but underappreciated role in broadening exposure to the elements. Many of the most storied such episodes occurred in spaces that remained decidedly underground and involved the relocation of hip-hop from the Bronx and other outer boroughs into the downtown Manhattan scene. Of comparable significance—but far less often given consideration—were the first stirrings of arena rap evident in the early touring endeavors of Kurtis Blow and the Sugarhill Gang, who provoked curiosity and critical dismissal as they brought a nascent form of live hip-hop performance into the larger concert field.

A signal of the new field of underground relations in which hip-hop was operating could be found on another flyer from the summer of 1981, reproduced in Figure 9.2. Although the venue remained in the Bronx, the rhetoric used to promote the two events on August 22 and August 29 featuring Afrika Bambaataa and his Soul Sonic Force crew indicated that new subcultural connections were being forged. "Punkin' to the Funk Rock," read the heading to the flyer, while a sidebar further specified: "It's not Punk Rock, It's Funk Rock."[38] In fact, the August 29 performance at the Bronx River Houses was attended by downtown scene maker Michael

Figure 9.2 "Punkin' to the Funk Rock": A flyer advertises two appearances by Afrika Bambaataa and his Soul Sonic Force on August 22 and 29, 1981. The juxtaposition of "punk rock" and "funk rock" suggests the intermingling of distinct subcultures that accompanied the move of hip-hop toward wider visibility in New York. Courtesy of the Cornell Hip Hop Collection.

Holman and Malcolm McLaren, former manager of the Sex Pistols, who was in New York to promote his new group Bow Wow Wow. McLaren was at once overwhelmed by what he encountered at the Bronx River Houses and deeply impressed, and he commissioned Holman to invite Bambaataa and his crew to appear with Bow Wow Wow at the downtown club the Ritz. The resulting show on September 15, 1981, which also featured a short film shot by Holman about breakdancing, a graffiti artist at work, and Bambaataa and the Soul Sonic Force accompanied by the Rock Steady Crew of breakdancers, was "the first hip hop show with all the elements put together," with DJs and MCs appearing alongside breakers and graffiti writers, all as part of a shared performance.[39] There is no evidence that Bambaataa knew about McLaren's appearance in time for the event flyer to acknowledge his presence, but it is nonetheless tempting to see the flyer's references to "punk rock" and "funk rock" as a supreme act of signifying upon the infamous producer and his past. More likely, it was a mark of the growing familiarity developing between the uptown and downtown scenes, wherein influences were being absorbed in both directions and hip-hop was gaining definition as a discrete phenomenon.

The Ritz show was not Bambaataa's first incursion downtown, let alone the first moment that hip-hop artists had appeared in venues there. In April of that year he had accepted the invitation of close associate Fab Five Freddy to perform at the opening of an exhibition of graffiti art at the Mudd Club, another club that like the Ritz served as the meeting ground for some of the city's disparate movements. According to *Village Voice* writer Steven Hager, the experience and especially the enthusiasm with which he was received influenced the direction Bambaataa would take with his next recording, the breakthrough "Planet Rock."[40] A month earlier, in March 1981, Sugar Hill Records—the independent label that had issued "Rapper's Delight" and broken the market for rap records open—moved into downtown with its own showcase at the Ritz featuring the Sugarhill Gang, Grandmaster Flash and the Furious Five, and the Funky Four + 1. Although that show did not include all the hip-hop elements as would Bambaataa's appearance at the same club five months later, it provided an occasion for a downtown audience to observe the force of the DJ and MC skills that had come to define rap music by that time. Reviewing the show in the *New York Times*—in the first *Times* review of a dedicated rap concert—Robert Palmer observed the marked difference between the onstage approaches of the Sugarhill Gang and Grandmaster Flash. The former trio of MCs exchanged rhymes to the accompaniment of a tight funk band, likely the same group of studio musicians that played on their records. Grandmaster Flash, by contrast, accompanied his quintet of MCs only with two turntables and an assistant who provided extra hands on the deck. Palmer conveyed the drama and novelty of Flash's approach: "Flash constructed bass and drum parts by repeatedly playing the first few bars of records by Queen and Chic; he created extravagant special effects by stopping records with his hand while they were playing . . . a technique that resulted in a regular, percussive skidding sound"—what would come to be called scratching. He quoted one of the Furious Five MCs, who announced to the predominantly white audience: "What you've just beared witness to is seven men and two turntables . . . Think about it."[41]

Although the venues—the Ritz, the Mudd Club, and others like Danceteria and the Roxy—were on the more experimental or avant-garde end of the spectrum in terms of audience appeal, their location in downtown New York ensured that hip-hop would draw more media attention than it had previously. Much has been made of Sally Banes's influential April 1981 article on breakdancing that appeared in the *Village Voice*, the first detailed story on the dance style that also drew connections with graffiti, rapping, and DJing.[42] More telling in a sense, if ultimately less insightful, was a March 1981 article in *Variety* magazine—as mainstream an entertainment industry publication as could be found—reporting on the increased interpenetration of rock music in dance clubs and black dance styles in rock clubs, which included the Ritz and Mudd Club among the venues where the trend could be observed, and made special mention of rap as part of the phenomenon.[43] Robert Palmer described the continued momentum of the move of hip-hop downtown in September 1982, in yet another article for the *New York Times*, explaining: "Rapping and the associated turntable legerdemain of resourceful disk jockeys like Grand Master Flash have recently become a leading attraction in such downtown rock clubs as the Roxy, Danceteria and the Kitchen." As Banes had the preceding year, Palmer made note of the combination of elements on display, expressing fascination with the work of DJs, rappers, and breakdancers that appeared during the Roxy's Friday night sessions, and calling the whole scene more vital "than anything else in the world of pop today."[44]

Among those participating in the scene of the time who shared Palmer's judgment that hip-hop was the most vital thing happening were the members of the Beastie Boys. At the time the group's members were still teenagers and were mainly committed to the hardcore punk style associated with Bad Brains, the African American punk/reggae band that was their main source of inspiration. A turning point in their evolution, recalled Michael Diamond (Mike D), came with the hip-hop nights held every Thursday by East Village venue Club Negril, where Afrika Bambaataa, DJ Jazzy Jay, and the Rock Steady Crew became ensconced in the aftermath of their successful showing at the Ritz. Diamond said of the scene at Negril that it was "a convergence of cultures—a funny and amazing blend of downtown characters, hip hop pioneers, and curious musicians," and he and his band mates were especially taken with the DJ style of Bambaataa, who was "the first guy we'd seen who took small parts of a bunch of different records and mixed them together into an entirely new song."[45] Even more transformative was an encounter with the Treacherous Three, a trio of MCs comprised of Kool Moe Dee, LA Sunshine, and Special K whose manner of fast-paced routines and clever freestyles would exert a strong influence over the Beastie Boys' formative attempts at rapping. After witnessing the group twice in succession, Mike D claims that their aspirations quickly shifted: "Rap, in all its far-reaching ambition, was now It. Our hardcore punk world simply couldn't compete anymore... So much of hardcore is about limits—shorter, simpler, more speed, more volume—whereas breakbeats and hip hop are all about the limitless—limitless possibilities, limitless imagination... Now all we wanted was to be our own version of the Treacherous Three."[46]

* * *

Another sort of breakthrough was happening before hip-hop artists began to enter into the eclectic and experimental world of the downtown club scene. As early as April 1980, *Billboard* magazine's list of top grossing concerts for the preceding week included three separate shows by a touring package of funk standard-bearers War, new-school funk group the Gap Band, and the Sugarhill Gang, with reported attendance between seven thousand, nine hundred and nine thousand, two hundred for the three shows.[47] Over the next several months, the Sugarhill Gang, the Fatback Band, and Kurtis Blow—three of the earliest rap artists to issue successful records—would move into the arena and large theater touring circuit, producing an overground path to crossover that paralleled the underground path happening in the smaller clubs. Of the three, Blow would gain the greatest notoriety and generate the most comment as the first hip-hop artist touring on a wider scale who appeared on stage not with full band behind him, but with a single DJ, Davey D, thus bringing something approximating the hip-hop club aesthetic to larger venues.

Pictured in Figure 9.3, Blow, born in Harlem as Curtis Walker, was part of the early wave of "rapping deejays," figures who played records and talked over them as a way to build rapport with their audiences. He was especially influenced by the popular DJ Hollywood, who held forth at such venues as Club 371 in the Bronx and the Apollo Theater in Harlem, and who inspired

Figure 9.3 Kurtis Blow in performance, circa 1983, flaunting the physicality that made him a leading live hip-hop performer. Courtesy of Michael Ochs Archives/Getty Images.

Blow to become what he called a "coordinated rapper" whose flow was more deliberately shaped by the rhythm of the music and was designed to elicit audience response.[48] Blow began his performing career in 1976 and quickly formed an association with an upwardly mobile events promoter who was also one of his classmates at City College of New York, Russell Simmons. With Simmons' promotional help, Blow began appearing at venues around the city—he performed at the Hotel Diplomat near Times Square as early as 1977 and had even played at the Mudd Club in 1980, shortly after the release of his debut record, "Christmas Rappin," at the end of 1979.

For Simmons, Blow was the first artist of note that he managed. He credited the success of Blow with helping him build his budding Rush Artist Management business. Simmons hustled to get Blow on record, building on a connection he had made with *Billboard* magazine writer and aspiring record producer Robert "Rocky" Ford who co-produced "Christmas Rappin'" and Blow's next record, "The Breaks," with another *Billboard* staffer, J.B. Moore.[49] The ties between Blow and Simmons were such that the artist, as he transitioned from being a "rapping deejay" to a dedicated MC, even used his manager's younger teen brother Joseph as a DJ for a while—the same Joseph

Simmons who shortly became the Run of Run-DMC, but who for a while was appearing as "DJ Run, Son of Kurtis Blow."[50]

To help broaden Blow's touring base, Simmons turned to a veteran booking agent, Norby Walters. At a time when black artists continued to struggle to gain a foothold in the arena touring economy, Walters was perhaps the most well-positioned white agent who specialized in working with African American performers. He started his agency, Norby Walters Associates, in 1968 after owning a succession of nightclubs in Brooklyn, Queens, and Manhattan; and after mainly representing lounge acts, he turned his attention to disco after one of his artists, Gloria Gaynor, had a breakout hit with "Never Can Say Goodbye."[51] By the late 1970s Walters' agency was strongly geared toward the Urban Contemporary market, in which connection he came to represent several of the earliest rap artists who began to tour outside of New York, including Kurtis Blow, the Sugarhill Gang, Grandmaster Flash and the Furious Five, and, slightly later, Run-DMC, LL Cool J, and Whodini. By January 1981, according to *Billboard*, Walters represented "eight of the top 20, and 24 of the top 100 r&b charted artists," and was managing to place them in venues that had historically been less open to African American talent.[52] Unlike many white agents, Walters and his associates also built up strong alliances with black promoters around the US such as Simmons and used their local knowledge to help build and expand a touring circuit for their artists.[53]

Walters' impact on Blow's performing career could be seen in the bookings that the MC had from late 1979 into 1980. Before his first recording had even been released, Blow scored an opening slot for the funk band Cameo at New York's Beacon Theater in November 1979.[54] The real boost in Blow's concert calendar came the following summer, after the release of his second record, "The Breaks." He was the only rap artist featured among an array of funk and R&B talent in a Summer Festival package at New York's Felt Forum, where he was credited with sparking the crowd's excitement and displaying "acrobatic" dance moves along with his fluent rapping.[55] Later that summer he appeared with disco luminaries Chic on a bill that also included the proto-rap Fatback Band at Nashville's Municipal Auditorium, and on a bill headed by R&B veterans the Isley Brothers at McNichols Arena in Denver.[56] This run of activity culminated with Blow being added as an opening act to the fall tour of the Commodores, one of the most successful touring black pop acts of the era. That the tour also included the Fatback Band was a sign of how rap music was impacting the field of black popular music. Commodores manager Benny Ashburn explained his philosophy behind booking the two acts with regard to the changing demographics of his client's concert audience. As reported by *Billboard*, "The Commodores' latest tour opened with the group playing to 80% white audiences ... In order to insure [sic] that the group would draw more of the traditional black audience [Ashburn] later selected the Fatback Band and Kurtis Blow for openers. 'They're helping us get back our audience,' he said."[57]

Whether or not Blow helped to recalibrate the racial balance of the Commodores audience is unclear, but his presence on the tour elicited some of the earliest detailed critical commentary on hip-hop among national publications. The tour's September 19, 1980, date at Madison Square Garden stirred particular attention by adding reggae superstars Bob Marley and the Wailers to the bill. With the combination of the Commodores and Marley, it would have been easy for Blow's appearance to be overlooked, but the novelty of his performance approach nonetheless captured the interest of reviewers. Writing for the *New York Times*, Robert Palmer offered some suggestive remarks that prefigured his later observations concerning Grandmaster Flash. Terming Blow a "'rapper' with a line of fast-talking rhythmic jive," Palmer noted the connection of rapping to Jamaican music culture—a nod to Marley's presence on the bill—and opined, "Mr. Blow, who is from New York, isn't one of the best talkers on record, but he makes up for it by dancing, prancing and self-delectating, and the disk jockey who manipulated his prerecorded accompaniment was first-rate."[58]

Blow's unique set-up, with DJ Davey D as his only accompanist, also drew comment in *Variety* and *Billboard*, both of which observed that he generated a strong and positive reaction from an audience that was not there specifically to see him. Roman Kozak of *Billboard* best captured the mix of enthusiasm and uncertainty that accompanied Blow's performance:

> Opening the show was Kurtis Blow, who faced a one-third empty house when he started. He had virtually everybody dancing when he ended a half-hour later ... Blow performed with only a disk jockey spinning backup platters but that was enough. The strong r&b and disco dance rhythms were there and Blow added the rest, pacing, jumping, dancing and exploring the audience to a good time. Blow's performance was one long continuous rap into which he incorporated his two singles, "Christmas Rapping" and "The Breaks." It was an unusual performance but certainly not an unpleasant one.[59]

Several qualities marked Blow's stage presence as distinctive, by the accounts of Kozak and Palmer: his intensive physicality, which offset the absence of other musicians; the unusual pacing characterized by a continuous stream of music, as though Blow were rapping over a short uninterrupted DJ club set; and the effectiveness with which Blow and his DJ engaged the audience, getting them up and dancing in an arena that was not an especially suitable dance venue. By this measure, hip-hop's first move into the arena was a raging success.

Not all who saw Blow at this time were so accepting. Philip Harrigan, a reviewer for the African American newspaper, the *Pittsburgh Courier*, took strong exception to Blow's presence, comparing him unfavorably to both star attraction Commodores and the Fatback Band. According to Harrigan, Blow's performance did not "lend itself well to presentation in an auditorium the size of the [Pittsburgh] Civic Arena and not to an adult audience that came out to see the Commodores." Harrigan proceeded to offer an unflattering description of Blow's set: "Blow came onstage with a disc jockey and a sound system. While the DJ played instrumental backing tracks from his two turntables, Blow rapped to the music. And rapped ... and rapped ... and rapped ... much to the delight of the screaming 15 year olds and under in the audience, but dulling to the senses of anyone wanting a little more musical substance."[60] The terms of Harrigan's dismissal were telling. Rap was, in his estimation, only suited to the tastes of teens who lacked musical sophistication and involved an amateurish display that did not earn its place alongside the technical skill and professionalism of a band like the Commodores. In this instance and others, the combination of DJ and MC had something of a polarizing effect as rap artists entered the wider concert field.

* * *

Harrigan's ambivalence toward rap on stage surfaced again in a review of a concert headlined by the Sugarhill Gang, that also featured Grandmaster Flash, the Funky Four + 1, and female rap group Sequence—the same lineup that played at the Ritz in New York the following month. Watching the rap artists perform at the February 7, 1981, concert at Pittsburgh's Stanley Theater, Harrigan's position was more even-handed. He admitted that "there's a real art to rapping," and that many of the songs featured over the course of the evening's show could "hold their own alongside any other pop/funk offerings on the market today." Still, he continued to stress that rap did not belong in a concert hall setting and proclaimed "for shame" regarding the reliance of the Funky Four and Grandmaster Flash on DJs rather than bands for accompaniment. "Put these folks in a club where there's a dance floor and you're in business; put them in the Stanley and you're in for boredom."[61]

What Harrigan failed to remark upon in his rush to judgment was that this package featuring the Sugarhill Gang and an array of other artists who recorded for Sugar Hill Records was likely the first full-fledged touring rap aggregation. Kurtis Blow never ascended to headline status in his career as a large-venue act, but here was a tour where rap artists had top billing and occupied all the support slots as well. The Sugar Hill "Rappers Convention" 1981 tour visited a mix of theaters and arenas, and most of the shows seem to have been in venues like the Stanley, which had a capacity of around 3800. At least one date, though, at the Civic Center in Baltimore, drew more than 11,000 and grossed more than $80,000.[62] More so even than the early tours of Blow, the Sugar Hill Rappers Convention ushered in the era of arena rap, albeit still in provisional form. It would be another three years before the move of rap into the arena concert economy would fully gain momentum.

Arena Rap's Golden Age

Hip-hop historiography has long been governed by the notion of a "golden age" that reached, according to conventional wisdom, from the late 1980s into the early 1990s. Yet the high point of live hip-hop as a large-scale enterprise arguably pre-dated this broader golden age, which has been defined more through the release of key albums than the staging of key performances. If there was a golden age of arena rap, it would have been the short window of time between 1984 and 1988, coinciding with the period when Run-DMC emerged as the leading hip-hop group and when Def Jam Records displaced Sugar Hill as the leading independent rap record label. Case in point: when *The Source* magazine—the debut of which in 1988 was one sign that hip-hop had gained a new measure of prestige and credibility—surveyed hip-hop history in commemoration of its one-hundredth issue in January 1998, the choice for "Most Memorable Hip-Hop Tour" was the 1984 Fresh Fest, which according to the editors "proved the national power of hip-hop music and entertained crowds from state to state."[63] Fresh Fest—or as it was officially named, the Swatch Watch New York City Fresh Festival—was a pivotal event in the history of hip-hop as a live medium, and opened the way toward a new scale of hip-hop concert promotion in which

Run-DMC, the Beastie Boys, LL Cool J, and Public Enemy among others featured most prominently.

Fresh Fest appears to have taken root gradually over the summer and fall of 1984. Although most accounts cite a concert in Greensboro, North Carolina, on August 31 of that year as the first Fresh Fest performance, *Billboard* listed a concert dubbed "A Fresh Festival" in its concert box office report of August 11, 1984. That earlier July 27 concert at Baltimore's Civic Center featured some but not all of the artists who would be part of the Fresh Fest—most notably Run-DMC and the electro hip-hop group Newcleus, along with several breakdancing crews.[64] What is beyond dispute is that the idea for the Fresh Festival came from veteran black promoter Cedric "Ricky" Walker, who saw in 1984 that rap music had untapped potential as a concert attraction. In a mark of the changing of rap's commercial guard, Walker first approached Sylvia Robinson of Sugar Hill Records with the suggestion that he build a tour around her stable of artists—a suggestion she flatly refused.[65] Walker then turned to Russell Simmons, whose Rush Artist Management company had grown substantially due to the mounting success of Run-DMC Working in conjunction with Norby Walters Associates and the Texas-based Pace Concerts, Walker and Simmons assembled a lineup that consisted of Rush-managed artists Run-DMC, Kurtis Blow, Whodini, and Newcleus, along with breakdancing crews the Dynamic Breakers, the Mag Force Breakers and Uptown Express. A single non-Rush musical artist, the Fat Boys, were also part of the tour at Walker's request, and it was their manager Charles Stettler who arranged for the corporate sponsorship of the Swatch Watch company, which infused the production with a needed $350,000 of capital.[66]

Fresh Fest concerts in Greensboro and Atlanta over Labor Day weekend still had an exploratory element to them. Previewing the Atlanta concert, which occurred on Sunday, September 2, 1984, the *Atlanta Constitution* noted the uniqueness of the event for showcasing rapping and breakdancing in roughly equal measure and observed that the Omni—a sports arena that hosted the NBA team Atlanta Hawks games—would leave the floor of the venue clear of seats to allow the audience to dance. Promoter Ricky Walker optimistically projected that having sold three thousand seats already, he would sell "more than 10,000" by showtime.[67] As it turned out, the Fresh Fest drew more than 14,000 to the Omni, prompting Walker to plan a larger and more ambitious undertaking for the touring package.[68] The plan for the tour was soon outlined in *Billboard*, which characterized the Fresh Festival as the "first organized effort to bring [hip-hop] to the country via major performing venues."⁶⁹ This next and primary leg of the tour began with an October 5 concert in Cincinnati and would visit twenty-seven locations across the Northeast, the South, and the Midwest before reaching Long Beach and Oakland, California in December.

As an effort to adapt hip-hop to the arena concert format, the Fresh Fest tour stood apart from its predecessors and also from much that would follow. Reviewers in Providence and Pittsburgh highlighted the diverse character of the audiences who came to the concerts: in Providence there was "a remarkably mixed crowd (black and white, young and old)," while in Pittsburgh "the bulk of the crowd were black teens, with younger ones chaperoned by their parents. White youths were well represented and obviously were just as enthused about the whole darn deal."⁷⁰ What these audiences heard and saw was a dynamic, well-organized, and tightly choreographed show that used the juxtaposition of musical artists and breakdancers to stirring effect. As described by Timothy Cox, reviewing the Pittsburgh performance: "The concert started promptly enough and interestingly, the lights would never be turned on again until it was over . . . The show was non-stop, with two stages; rappers on one, breakers on another. After each act, a dynamic NYC-styled emcee came out and kept the intensity level at its highest."⁷¹ Terry Atkinson similarly portrayed the energy of the Long Beach Arena show in his review for the *Los Angeles Times*: "The program was set up like a two-ring circus. The rappers and their deejays performed on the main stage; in between sets, on another stage set up in the middle of the floor, break-dance groups, including the Magnificent Force, did their generally amazing thing." Atkinson added the telling detail: "All around the floor, informal break-dance circles formed as some of the local best put on some dazzling demonstrations of their own."⁷² The Fresh Festival used the mix of music and dance to create an uninterrupted flow of stimulation suited to the young audiences, black and white, that were its primary target. Even more so, in at least some locations it was designed to allow audience members to participate directly, to display their own dance moves and emulate—or reinvent—what they saw the performers do on stage.

Critical opinion about the musical side of Fresh Fest was divided. *Boston Globe* critic Lou Papineau repeated the biases of earlier rap reviewers by stating his preference for Newcleus, whom he pointedly characterized as "the only outfit to use instruments . . . The spark provided by the human interaction was invigorating." He also expressed his admiration for tour headliners Run-DMC—seen in Figure 9.4—who closed the show with a set that

Figure 9.4 MCs Run (Joseph Simmons, left) and DMC (Darryl McDaniels, right) of Run-DMC perform at the U.I.C. Pavilion, Chicago, during the Fresh Fest tour, October 1984. DJ Jam Master Jay is at the turntables but largely hidden behind Simmons. Note the Keith Haring-designed stage backdrop. Photograph by Raymond Boyd. Courtesy of Michael Ochs Archives/Getty Images.

"provided a stark contrast to the party anthems of the other participants."[73] Atkinson gave the highest praise to Run-DMC, who had "the rhythms of rap down," citing "Rock Box" as a particularly effective piece, "rap at its most stirringly musical."[74] Yet Pittsburgh reviewer Timothy Cox claimed that the Hollis, Queens, rappers could not maintain peak intensity for a full set, preferring the Fat Boys, who displayed impressive stage presence and generated excitement among the crowd.[75] If Run-DMC was not unanimously celebrated, they at least acted as though they owned the stage. A key piece of theater evolved during the Fresh Fest tour, when Run would take the stage praising the other acts that preceded him only to announce: "But I want y'all to know one goddamn thing. This is my motherfucking house!" He would then lean toward the audience with a hand cupped to his ear and yell, "Whose house?"[76] This was hip-hop stagecraft at its finest, by equal turns egotistical, playful, and confrontational.

The Fresh Festival tour's overall gross of $3.5 million far outstripped any preceding efforts to mount a hip-hop tour. That was just one measure of its success. Tellingly, the first published mention of the formation of Def Jam

Records, the independent label jointly formed by Russell Simmons and NYU student-cum-hip-hop aficionado Rick Rubin, came in the midst of the tour, indicating the interconnections between the touring and recording sectors of the still nascent hip-hop industry.[77] When *Billboard* dedicated a special advertorial section to Simmons' various enterprises a few months after the conclusion of the tour, Fresh Fest figured prominently in their coverage. Celebrating the tour, Simmons articulated one of its signal achievements, that it demonstrated the existence of a truly national market for hip-hop: "For example, we get to, say, Chicago, where almost none of our records are playing, and we sell out 20,000 seats. And in cities like Philadelphia, where rap *is* played on the radio, an arena like the 20,000-seat Spectrum not only sold out, the demand was such that another show was added the next day, to which an additional 10,000 tickets were sold."[78] Looking back on the tour years later, Simmons credited it with furthering his own skills in navigating the vicissitudes of the music industry:

> Once on the road, you meet all the record retailers and learn their business when your act stops by to sign autographs. When the act does radio interviews in cities they perform in, you meet all the radio programmers. So on tour you learn retail, radio, marketing and promotion ... All that stuff can't be learned inside a building, because when you work at a label you can only do one job at a time. The 1984 Fresh Fest tour was a triumph of being locked outside the building.[79]

Maybe the best indication of the success of the Fresh Festival tour was that it gave rise to not one but several sequels. Fresh Fest Two retained the structure of the first tour, and all of the main rap artists remained except for Kurtis Blow, whose place was taken by Grandmaster Flash. The scale of the tour grew substantially, visiting some fifty cities, and the overall gross earnings also doubled to $7 million. Swatch was no longer a sponsor, but the final concert of the tour at Nassau Coliseum in Long Island was sponsored by Sprite and to open their set, the members of Whodini rode out on two Honda motorcycles gifted to the rappers for having done some radio spots. Remarked Nelson George, "The involvement of both Sprite and Honda is part of Madison Avenue's ongoing use of hip-hop culture to reach the youth market."[80] A different register of the changing status of hip-hop came with the recollection of Run-DMC's Daryl McDaniels (D.M.C.) that the audience for the second Fresh Fest tour was "maybe 80 per cent white."[81] Some of the change in audience was due to Run-DMC's own increasing stature as the heralds of rap-rock interchange, their second album having made an appeal to white rock audiences with the provocative title, *King of Rock*, and the song of the same name. Hip-hop had also gained greater media exposure across a range of outlets in the months since the first Fresh Fest concluded, with two hip-hop-infused films—*Breakin'* and *Krush Groove*, the latter featuring Fresh Fest artists Run-DMC and the Fat Boys—generating expanded interest.

Fresh Fest appeared poised to become a lasting franchise in the hip-hop concert field, but the third installment in 1986 did not have the impact of the first two. Run-DMC had by then outgrown the package tour format and ascended to proper headliner status for their own "Raising Hell" tour that same summer, mounting the most successful hip-hop tour of the year. The contrasting lineups of the two tours were like an index of the changing tenor of hip-hop by 1986. Headlined by the Fat Boys and also including Kurtis Blow, the Force M.D.'s, and the Jets, Fresh Fest Three struck an uneasy balance between old and new styles and artists. On the other hand, Run-DMC's summer tour joined the group with their Fresh Fest tour mates Whodini and two up-and-coming acts: the Beastie Boys and LL Cool J. Evidence of the differential success of the two tours was plain to see in the *Billboard* "Boxscore" column, where the Run-DMC tour placed five and then six separate shows among the top grossing concerts of the preceding week at different times.[82] Fresh Fest Three did not place a single show on the "Boxscore" list during its run. There would be a Fresh Fest Four in 1987, again headlined by the Fat Boys, but that would be the last.

* * *

Because there is really no such thing as a golden age, the period when hip-hop concerts were ascending gave rise to conflicts that would slow the momentum of hip-hop's move into the arena concert field. Reports of violence at hip-hop concerts began to proliferate in the mid-1980s and gained increasing force over the remainder of the decade. Hip-hop scholars Tricia Rose and Murray Forman have both emphasized the significance of this phenomenon in the evolution of the medium and stressed that it was not the sheer fact that violence occurred at hip-hop shows, but the ways in which those facts were reported—and given exaggerated or misleading importance—that had such detrimental effects. Rose portrays media coverage of the September 10, 1988, concert at Nassau Coliseum in Long Island, where at a "Rap Jam" concert headlined by Eric B and Rakim a nineteen-year-old man was stabbed to death, as a major flash point in this trajectory. For Rose, the panic surrounding the event derived from "a preexisting anxiety regarding rap's core audience—black working-class youths—the growing popularity of rap music, and the media's interpretation of the incident, which fed directly into those preexisting anxieties."[83] Forman judges the August 17, 1986, concert featuring Run-DMC at the Long Beach Arena—part of their hugely successful "Raising Hell" tour—as a more prominent turning point. The violence at the Long Beach show exceeded that at other comparable events, with more than forty people injured by members of Los Angeles gangs inside the arena. Calling the episode "rap music's Altamont," Forman further suggests: "The positive growth that the earlier Fresh Fest tours had engendered as the music expanded geographically was suddenly tainted by an image of ghetto ferocity."[84]

Predating either of these events was the Krush Groove Christmas Party held on December 27, 1985, the first major rap concert that drew national attention for reports of violence. Seeking to capitalize on the wave of publicity surrounding the *Krush Groove* movie released that summer, the Krush Groove Christmas Party was a landmark for other reasons than violence. It was the first dedicated rap concert held in Madison Square Garden. Like Fresh Fest, the concert featured a package of artists managed by Russell Simmons' Rush Artist Management company—Kurtis Blow, Whodini, LL Cool J, Doug E. Fresh, and Dr. Jeckyll and Mr. Hyde. (Run-DMC were scheduled to perform but had to withdraw.) Anticipating the concert, LL Cool J foreshadowed the enthusiasm that Jay-Z experienced nearly twenty years later in talking about his own Garden appearance: "You gotta think big to get big. When you're starting out, you dream about a block party. Then you dream about clubs, then the Beacon, and now we're in Madison Square Garden. I'd like to play the Meadowlands on a stage that's three stories high. Or the Superdome. Look out Bruce!"[85] The closing nod to Bruce Springsteen was recognition that rock remained the dominant mode of arena concert entertainment, representing a horizon of aspiration for ambitious hip-hop artists.

In the same interview, LL Cool J voiced his hope that the Krush Groove concert would help to dispel the negative associations that had attached itself to rap. "There'll be tight security for the Garden show, hopefully, and nothing will happen. Maybe that will show some of the skeptics."[86] Unfortunately, the opposite proved to be the case. The *New York Times* took the lead with its coverage, headlining its account "7 Youths Injured in Concert Fights." The subheading of the article was more telling though: "Roving Groups Flow Through Midtown After 'Rap' Music Show at the 'Garden.'" The article signaled how much the anxieties surrounding hip-hop's move into the mainstream echoed those expressed three decades earlier in association with rock 'n' roll: that black youths would step out from their contained space and move with new mobility through the public at large. Of the reported victims, most were injured after the concert when the crowd dispersed onto the street and made their way toward a nearby theater where the film *Krush Groove* was playing. Police even admitted that they could not clearly attribute all the violence to the concert. Yet the presiding image was nonetheless of young black people who were let loose into the world to run wild, conveyed by the manager of the Rialto Theater where the movie was being shown: "It sounded like thunder . . . They came roaring through here. They were screaming, no words, just noise."[87]

Within two days after the concert the news had spread to the *Washington Post*, and *Variety* picked it up in its next issue, adding the detail that one cause for the unrest of the crowd was the closing of a subway stop at 42nd Street, leaving thousands of people to have to walk to their next destination.[88] More ominously, the entertainment paper noted that officials at Madison Square Garden were considering a ban on future rap concerts—a tactic that many other venues around the country would adopt in the ensuing years. All but lost in the reporting on the concert was the performance itself, or the fact that the majority of those in attendance did not encounter violence or feel threatened. Writing for the *New York Amsterdam News*, columnist Charles Rogers offered a sharp rebuke to the media coverage of the Krush Groove concert, charging that it was motivated by racial bias and quoting the rapper Doug E. Fresh, who said of the evening, "All during the ['Krush Groove'] concert I saw the people having a good time. There was no sense of violence and for the most part it seemed everybody was just there to have fun."[89] Rogers' article was accompanied by a photo of Kurtis Blow on stage alongside a jolly-looking Santa Claus and three women in elf costumes, giving the only hint of the festive atmosphere at the show to appear anywhere in print. Also overlooked in the reporting was the fact that the Krush Groove Christmas Party was a sellout, drawing over nineteen thousand people to Madison Square Garden and grossing $324,000, making it one of the most lucrative rap concerts held to date.[90] What endured was the image of rap-related violence that would place constraints on the staging of live rap performances in years to come.

*   *   *

The aforementioned 1986 Raising Hell tour brought these competing tendencies—the capacity of rap artists to successfully tour arena-sized venues, and the resulting concerns about violence and social unrest—into sharp relief. Run-DMC was riding high on the success of their *Raising Hell* album and even more so, their version of "Walk This Way," done in collaboration with Steve Tyler and Joe Perry of rock veterans Aerosmith and produced by Rick Rubin, Russell Simmons' white partner in Def Jam Records. The Beastie Boys had yet to release their first album, *Licensed to Ill*, which would come out at the end of the year; but the group had previously drawn attention, and stirred controversy, as the opening act for Madonna's "Like a Virgin" tour where they deliberately antagonized the singer's young audience. Existing somewhere between the two was LL Cool J, whose spare, hard-hitting rap style exerted an appeal similar to that of Run-DMC but was tempered over time by a tendency toward hybrid rap/R&B love ballads. If, as Jeff Chang has said, the interracial staff of Rush Artists Management and Def Jam Records "was uniquely suited and highly motivated to pull off a racial crossover of historic proportions," then the Raising Hell tour was the best instantiation of that impulse in the form of a concert tour.[91]

Starting with a May 28, 1986, date in Albuquerque, New Mexico, the tour made its way through the Southeast, into the Northeast and Midwest, and then back again, taking a circuitous route before a concluding performance on August 31 in Norfolk, Virginia.[92] Enthusiasm for the concerts was there from the beginning but the momentum shifted several weeks into the tour when "Walk This Way" was released as a single from the *Raising Hell* album. At that point, recalled Daryl McDaniels aka DMC, "Motherfuckers in the front row started looking like the Ramones and Cyndi Lauper . . . We got a bunch of Madonnas asking for autographs."[93]

Even before then, Run-DMC was working toward another sort of breakthrough achievement with the help of Russell Simmons' right-hand man at Rush Artists Management, Lyor Cohen. Using the song "My Adidas" as a prompt, Run appealed to a sold-out crowd at Philadelphia's Spectrum arena to take off one of their Adidas shoes and wave it in the air. When some five thousand people followed his directive, it set in motion a series of events that led to a groundbreaking sponsorship deal for the group. Cohen reached out to Adidas marketing director Angelo Anastasio, letting him know about Run-DMC's use of the brand's shoes as a way to pump up the crowd. When Anastasio attended the Madison Square Garden date of the Raising Hell tour on July 19 at Cohen's invitation, he witnessed nearly twenty-thousand fans respond to Run's call, "Hold your Adidas in the air!" A one-million-dollar endorsement deal with Adidas followed, what Dan Charnas calls "the first of its kind for a rap group," built on the strength of a gesture used to hype up a concert audience.[94]

That same Madison Square Garden show drew notice on different grounds as well. Echoing the circumstances surrounding the Krush Groove Christmas Party, the *New York Times* and other media outlets picked up the story that there were several arrests during and after the concert on charges of robbery. *Variety* noted that similar trouble arose at an earlier tour stop in Pittsburgh despite the fact that Raising Hell tour promoter Stageright Productions had taken significant security precautions, including the use of metal detectors at the door and increased police presence.[95] This time around, push back against the charges of violence came from several quarters: from Jeff Sharp of Stageright, from Bill Adler, who handled publicity for Rush Productions, from the *New York Amsterdam News*—which questioned the biased reporting much as they had regarding the Krush Groove concert—and from Nelson George at *Billboard*, who pointed out that many of the reported arrests following the Madison Square Garden show happened several blocks from the venue and the link to the concert was speculation at best.[96]

By the time the Raising Hell tour reached Long Beach, it had become a staging ground for a debate about whether rap concerts were safe or whether they provoked violence and criminality. The events at the Long Beach Arena on August 17, 1986, intensified the debate and generated nationwide scrutiny. On one level the Long Beach episode lacked the ambiguity of the earlier instances of rap concert unrest. The reported violence was more widespread and happened almost entirely inside the venue. Greg Mack, a pioneering Los Angeles program director with radio station KDAY, offered a vivid account of the scene inside the arena:

> That was the worst I've ever seen in my life, it was bad. I was MCing it, and what had happened was, they let a lot of gangs in from different areas. Security isn't hip to colors, there were little fights in the beginning. Then this guy threw this other guy right over the balcony on to the stage while Whodini was performing, so they got up on the stage trying to talk to the

guy, next thing you know a whole section was running, gangs were hittin' people, grabbing gold chains, beating people.[97]

Long Beach, the setting of the riot, later gained renown as the home of Snoop Dogg, who made its connection to the burgeoning Southern California gang culture more widely known. In 1986, the parceling of territory between the rival Crips and Bloods was less recognized outside the region. Gang members seem to have used the Raising Hell tour's stop at the Long Beach Arena as an occasion to announce themselves and assert their claims to occupy any space they chose. Run-DMC biographer Ronin Ro recounts a telling detail of the show, when a few gang members approached the stage during LL Cool J's performance, flashed gang signs and then jumped onto the stage.[98] Concert security contained that particular incident but the unrest only grew from there. In the end, the situation became so uncontrollable that the show had to be stopped before Run-DMC ever took the stage.

Nobody could dispute that violence had broken out at the Long Beach concert. Sparking controversy was whether rap music was responsible for the outbreak of violence, and whether the artists—and especially Run-DMC— should be held accountable. Pittsburgh commissioner of public safety John Norton outspokenly condemned the group and rap music more generally, exclaiming in the *Washington Post*, "I feel that when you mix alcohol, drugs, youth, provocative and pornographic music, and then superenergize these kids, you're going to have a problem."[99] George Matson, general manager of the Long Beach facility, took a similar stance, announcing in the days following the concert that the arena would no longer book "any attraction whose patrons have cause or who have a propensity to create situations likely to cause injury to other patrons."[100] Further fanning the controversy was Tipper Gore, speaking for the advocacy group the Parents Music Resource Center, who issued a statement that "angry, disillusioned, unloved kids unite behind heavy metal and rap music, and the music says it's okay to beat people."[101] Run-DMC and their representatives responded by charging that it was the venue that was to blame. Run offered his views in a press conference after the concert, where he explained, "There was a bunch of kids, gang members, and wherever they walked the crowd would move out of their way. They just took over and security was soft," later adding, "These kids have nothing to do with Run-DMC . . . They are against everything I'm for."[102] The question of security loomed large over the concert, with Matson explaining to Long Beach City Council members that they had no way to anticipate the number of gang members that would be in attendance.[103] While there were many security guards present at the arena, uniformed police officers only entered well after the violence had broken out.

In the short term, the impact of the violence at Long Beach was fairly contained. Run-DMC canceled a concert that was scheduled for the following day at the Hollywood Palladium while announcing that they would not play Los Angeles again until they could be assured of better security.[104] Officials at the Providence Civic Center canceled the tour's upcoming appearance there as well due to fears about crowd safety. Yet the tour continued for two more weeks with successful stops in a number of locations including Washington, DC. The real repercussions would take hold in the months and years that followed. One story on the concert noted almost as an afterthought that "the insurance rate paid by Facility Management [at the Long Beach Arena] will be raised at concerts to 20 cents per patron instead of 15 cents."[105] This apparently small detail would come to have considerable impact as venues and insurers weighed what they perceived to be the potential risks of hosting rap shows. By late September, *Billboard* was quoting Raising Hell tour promoter Jeff Sharp on the topic: "Three years ago, I was paying roughly 2 ½ cents per spectator . . . Today I'm paying 26 cents a head. That, in my opinion, is an incredible hike. When you add this to the formidable expenses promoters incur—my company's overhead is about $25,000 a month . . . That makes for a tight situation."[106] It would only get tighter as insurers became reticent to provide coverage for rap shows at any price, and venue managers responded in kind.

One other short-term result of the episode at Long Beach stands as a fitting coda to the whole affair. At the end of January 1987, the Beastie Boys embarked on their first headlining tour supporting their now-released debut album and building on the momentum of their Raising Hell tour appearances. For the group's February 7 show at the Hollywood Palladium, they were joined by New York hardcore punk band Murphy's Law and Southern California ska-punks Fishbone, making plain the effort to join rap and rock audiences that underpinned the Beastie Boys' appeal. Richard Cromelin, reviewing the concert for the *Los Angeles Times*, observed that while the group put on a strong show, "the performance itself wasn't as remarkable as the overall atmosphere and the intensity of the response from a strikingly diverse audience." The scene inside the Palladium led Cromelin to further assert that it "definitely marked a new mutation, or a turn of the corner. It confirmed rap's adoption as the teen-ager's weapon of choice in the perpetual struggle with authority figures. Finishing with a flourish the pop breakthrough by their mentors Run-DMC, the Beastie Boys have yanked rebellion from its heavy-metal and punk ghettos and returned it to the mainstream."[107]

As if to dramatize the transformation that Cromelin identified, when the Beastie Boys finished their set that night, rather than come out for the standard encore, their place on stage was taken by Run-DMC The group's appearance was completely unannounced and by all accounts was a surprise to the Palladium audience. It carried all the more weight because when they had last been scheduled to perform in the L.A. area, Run-DMC was prevented from performing due to the violence at Long Beach and their subsequent concert at the very same Hollywood Palladium had been canceled. They took the stage with a sense of purpose, offering three songs and climaxing with their rendition of "Walk This Way" which got the audience worked into a frenzy. As another reviewer put it, "When they performed ["Walk This Way"] at the Palladium, the ground trembled for blocks around."[108] Closing the concert, the Beastie Boys joined Run-DMC for a version of their own rap-rock anthem, "(You Gotta) Fight for Your Right (to Party)," the hedonistic message conveying an extra measure of resistance in light of the manner in which Run-DMC's appearance at the concert circumvented the efforts of local authorities to prevent them from performing. It was a moment of triumph, but also a measure of the complicated terms according to which rap had achieved crossover success in the 1980s: the white group, no strangers to controversy themselves, still possessed the ability to give their black counterparts a platform they might otherwise not have had.

Concerts in Crisis

Introducing the July 1991 issue of *The Source*, founding editor Jon Shecter offered an autobiographical reflection on his early experiences with hip-hop. Live concerts were at the heart of Shecter's developing relationship with the music growing up as a white Jewish kid in Philadelphia. He recalled with especial fondness the many shows he saw at the Spectrum, Philadelphia's primary arena venue. About these concerts, Shecter claimed, "These big shows were the first evidence that rap had 'made it,' and for those of us outside New York, it was the first chance to see our favorite stars in action."[109] He proceeded to describe a litany of past concerts, from the first Fresh Fest to "several epiphanic Public Enemy performances," to Too Short responding to a booing Philadelphia audience by telling them to "suck his dick," to Salt & Pepa leaving an audience "stunned" when they barely had any records out, and local phenoms Jazzy Jeff and the Fresh Prince "rocking live freestyles." All these memories were now tinged with regret, however, as Shecter contemplated the current state of live hip-hop: "Now I live in New York, and it's '91, and things are too different. I end up seeing all my live rap shows at small downtown clubs... Nowhere is it more evident than in New York that the age of the big hip-hop arena show is dead."[110] Shecter offered little in the way of explanation for the decline in arena rap except to say, "Most blame insurance rates," which had continued to rise to near-unaffordable proportions in the years since the Raising Hell tour. Instead the dominant tone was of nostalgia, loss, and resignation, with Shecter concluding: "For now, I'm stuck sifting through that old shoe box of ticket stubs, reliving past memories of hip-hop greatness."

Shecter's piece was one of several that observed a marked decline in support for hip-hop concerts during the 1990s. His thoughts were prompted in part by a *New York Times* article that portrayed New York City as uniquely inhospitable to performances by hip-hop artists. As proof the article presented information about eight representative venues in and around the city and how many rap concerts they had hosted during the preceding year, 1990. The smallest of the venues, S.O.B.'s, located just south of the West Village, hosted by far the most shows at ten. Next was the Apollo, the fabled Harlem nightspot with a capacity of fifteen hundred, which presented six rap concerts during the year. Of the remaining venues listed, which held between 2,600 and more than twenty thousand people, none had offered more than one hip-hop concert in all of 1990, and four presented none, including Madison Square Garden and the Nassau Coliseum. The author, Rob Tannenbaum, further noted that the Garden had not featured a rap concert in almost four years, while the Coliseum had not held one since the 1988 show where an audience member was stabbed.[111] By these numbers, rap concerts—at least those drawing more than two thousand people—had indeed been all but shut out of the New York area during a time when hip-hop recordings attained widespread success.

The problem was not limited to New York. A few months prior to Shecter's editorial, *The Source* ran a short article by Bay Area writer Danyel Smith on the same phenomenon. Smith started her piece with an account of a Boogie Down Productions show at the Berkeley Community Theater where two young men were stabbed early in the group's set. Following the concert, the

Berkeley Police Chief asked for a ban on future rap shows at the venue, which was agreed upon until protesters showed up in sufficient force at a public hearing to overturn the decision.[112] Smith noted that the incident was part of a national pattern—one that could be traced back to the response to previous events such as the Krush Groove Christmas Party and the Raising Hell concert in Long Beach, wherein public officials used violence as an occasion to prohibit rap performances rather than taking measures to improve or increase safety at these events. Carol Kirkendall of G Street Productions, a leading promoter of hip-hop concerts, made the point that New York and Southern California remained the hardest settings to present rap shows because of gang activity, and reiterated the near-impossibility of working with Madison Square Garden: "I don't want to do another concert there until I sense a different climate on the streets." Leading artist manager Phil Casey once again raised the issue of insurance, offering an indication of how much things had worsened in the five years since the Long Beach incident: "At a rock concert, or a country concert, the normal cost of insurance is 22 to 30 cents a head... At a comparable sized rap concert, the cost is 50 cents to $1 a head."[113] Although some places such as the Henry J. Kaiser Arena in Oakland made efforts to create the conditions where rap concerts could continue to be presented safely and profitably, the national trend toward placing severe constraints on the production of rap concerts appeared clear.

Moreover, the trend did not only involve arena-sized events. The Berkeley Community Theater was a fifteen-hundred seat venue. In Philadelphia, city officials targeted the After Midnight club, one of the most prominent hip-hop clubs in the US during the 1980s. At its height, After Midnight occupied "a 27,000 square foot building with an enormous dance floor that could hold 3,000 people," and was perhaps most famous for a 1985 appearance by LL Cool J at a time when his profile was just beginning to rise. As so often happens in cases where crowds of black youth congregate, the club became subject to routine police harassment and was hampered by a city ordinance that placed restrictions on dance clubs remaining open after 1:00 A.M. Finally, in 1989, the city refused After Midnight a dance license, forcing its closure. The club mounted a legal appeal that appeared successful, with the club owners awarded $3 million dollars in damages, but it was never able to reopen.[114]

By 1997, the situation was so chronic that *The Source* offered another report titled, "Fear of a Rap Concert." Author Lee Copeland highlighted the discrepancy between the success of rap artists in the realm of record sales and the relative lack of success they faced in the concert world. According to SoundScan data from 1996, two of the ten top-selling albums of the year were by hip-hop artists: The Fugees' *The Score* and Tupac Shakur's *All Eyez on Me*.[115] During the same period, according to data from *Pollstar*, the leading source for information about the US concert industry, no hip-hop artists appeared among the top ten concert attractions of the year. The only African American artist who placed in the top ten was Darius Rucker of Hootie and the Blowfish. R&B singer R. Kelly had the thirty-fourth highest grossing tour of the year, and the only tour that included a significant representation of hip-hop to appear in the top fifty was the Smokin' Grooves tour—featuring Ziggy Marley, Spearhead, Cypress Hill, A Tribe Called Quest, Busta Rhymes, and the Fugees—which placed at number forty-seven. Its gross revenue of six million dollars was a fraction of that generated by the top tour of the year by veteran rockers Kiss, which had grossed $43.6 million.[116] Analyzing the phenomenon, Copeland offered much the same explanations that had circulated for a decade, best expressed in the opinion of *Pollstar* editor Gary Bongiovanni: "Rap simply isn't a fixture on the concert scene . . . There are lots of concerns on the part of facility managers and promoters, not because of the music, but because of past problems with shows and because of what might happen outside the show. They have difficulty obtaining liability insurance."[117] Where the concert economy was concerned, rap was trapped in a vicious cycle. The association between rap concerts and violence had assumed the status of common sense.

Rap and Rock Revisited

Amidst this restrictive environment for staging live hip-hop, the intersection of rap and rock assumed new salience. In the early 1980s, underground clubs that mixed the two genres became a key vehicle for promoting a kind of subterranean crossover that foreshadowed the larger mainstream crossover to come. The mid-1980s saw the flourishing of the latter phenomenon through the efforts of Run-DMC and the Beastie Boys, among others, and it was no accident that the heyday of arena rap coincided with a period when rock and rap seemed to enjoy an especially close relationship. Now, in the early 1990s, for rap artists to align themselves with rock presented itself as a strategy to get concert bookings during a time when they were otherwise relatively scarce. While the rap/rock nexus continued to be heard in the music of a select number of artists—most prominently that of L.A. gangster rapper Ice-T and his group Body Count—the issue was more one of programming, of combining rap and rock acts on a single bill that might give hip-hop artists a place on the stage while allowing rock artists the opportunity to capitalize on both the commercial success and the cultural capital that attached itself to hip-hop, which arguably had exceeded rock in its "outlaw" status.

No hip-hop group exploited the rock/rap nexus during this era as bluntly as Public Enemy. Following on the heels of Run-DMC and the Beastie Boys, Public Enemy were similarly shaped by the aesthetic that defined Def Jam Records and Rush Productions, using elements of rock to add sonic heft to the sound of hip-hop and as a means to attract the ears of young white listeners. The group's approach was markedly more confrontational and expressly political than that of the earlier Def Jam artists, however. When the Beastie Boys had Kerry King of Slayer play a solo on their track, "No Sleep Till Brooklyn," it had the air of comedy, like they were sneaking something forbidden into their music and were basking in the incongruity. When Public Enemy sampled a riff from Slayer's "Angel of Death" for their song, "She Watch Channel Zero," on the other hand, it was a perfect synthesis of black and white rage, the thrash metal track enhancing the tension emitted by Chuck D's voice. If this was the sound of crossover, it was predicated on white fascination with African American anger and political disaffection.

Coming up as part of the Def Jam and Rush stable of artists, Public Enemy gained early exposure as touring artists performing alongside Run-DMC, the Beastie Boys, Whodini, and LL Cool J before headlining in their own right. By the summer of 1990, at a time when hip-hop artists were finding it increasingly difficult to get booked, Public Enemy mounted their biggest tour to date in support of their album, *Fear of a Black Planet*. For nearly a year leading up to the tour, Public Enemy had been mired in controversy stemming from anti-Semitic remarks made by Professor Griff, who served at the time as the "Minister of Information" within a group structure that mimicked some of the properties of political organizations such as the Black Panther Party. As a central figure within the S1W security organization that was part of Public Enemy's operations, Griff had been integral to shaping the group's image. In the words of critic John Leland, "the S1Ws gave Public Enemy its identity as forcefully as Chuck D's lyrics or logo . . . The S1Ws . . . militant black men armed with machine guns, unity and information—spoke a simple visual message that any black kid could understand . . . [and] also gave the group an element of rock 'n' roll theater that set it apart from other rap crews."[118] When Professor Griff gave voice to discredited conspiracy theories about Jewish influence on the world economic order, it nearly tore the group apart. The 1990 Tour of a Black Planet found Public Enemy reasserting its integrity, not transcending the controversy but internalizing it and using it as an occasion to rearticulate its core concerns.

Kicking off with a June 27 concert at the Coliseum in Richmond, VA, the Tour of a Black Planet was a full-fledged arena rap tour, keeping Public Enemy and tour mates Kid 'n Play and Heavy D and the Boyz on the road until the first days of September, with several appearances also featuring Digital Underground, Chill Rob G, and Queen Latifah.[119] The lineup suggested an effort to incorporate more pop-oriented rap and R&B acts to add a degree of accessibility in combination with the hard-edged approach of Public Enemy, something that Chuck D confirmed in an interview: "You grab people that can cover your weaknesses. The combination of Heavy D and Kid 'n Play—the sex symbols, the movie stars—they'll bring in a lot more females into the audience."[120] This remark was just one of many indications that Chuck D invested a level of consideration and planning into the live music performances of Public Enemy that was unusual in the world of hip-hop. In the same interview he elaborated on the group's onstage dynamic: "The whole Public Enemy show works on hand-eye coordination between me and [DJ] Terminator X. Then the S1Ws feed off of Terminator, and Flavor [Flav, the second MC and comic foil of the group] feeds off all of us and freestyles."[121] Profiled the following year by *The Source*, Chuck D expanded on his view of the importance of presenting a live show that was tailored to the arena setting: "When I came along I said Public Enemy has to fatten that arena up visually. I designed the show with the S1s covering the side of the arena and Flavor going back and forth like a maniac, me goin off and Terminator perched up."[122] The resulting concerts blended political oratory, dense assemblages of beats and riffs, black nationalist iconography, and the dizzying interplay between Chuck D and Flavor Flav—seen together in Figure 9.5—to stirring effect, leading *Rolling Stone* critic Alan Light to pronounce Public Enemy "as powerful onstage as any group today."[123]

Over the next year, Public Enemy's touring strategies more fully reflected their connection to the world of rock. As Chuck D explained in his memoir-cum-political treatise, *Fight the Power*:

> In 1991 we went on three entirely different tours, playing in front of three entirely different audiences in order to expand our audience without

Figure 9.5 Flavor Flav (left) and Chuck D (right) of Public Enemy work the crowd from the stage of the Joe Louis Arena in Detroit during a stop on the group's 1990 Tour of a Black Planet. DJ Terminator X can be seen in the background, far right. Photograph by Raymond Boyd. Courtesy of Michael Ochs Archives/Getty Images.

alienating any of them. In the span of six months we knocked out an Alternative tour with the Sisters of Mercy, a Thrash Metal tour with Anthrax and Primus, and from December to January we did "The World's Greatest Rap Tour," which featured Queen Latifah, Naughty by Nature, Geto Boys, A Tribe Called Quest, Jazzy Jeff and the Fresh Prince, and the Leaders of the New School.[124]

There was fairly little precedent for this sort of cross-genre touring between rap and rock artists up to that point, with the exception of the Beastie Boys who, as a white rap act with strong rock overtones, had appeared with bands more affiliated with punk and independent rock music with little fanfare. Back in the early 1980s, when hip-hop artists were making their presence felt in downtown New York clubs like the Ritz, touring British punk heroes the Clash tried to showcase rap artists Grandmaster Flash and the Furious Five and Kurtis Blow during multi-day stands in the city and found their audiences far from ready to accept that rap artists belonged with them on the same stage. The appearance of Grandmaster Flash in 1981 was especially notable for the virulence with which he and the group were booed off the stage. Although Kurtis Blow met with a slightly less hostile reaction the following year, it still appeared to be the case that the merging of rap and rock in a live music setting had its limits.[125]

When Public Enemy toured with British goth band Sisters of Mercy ten years later, the tables had turned. The tour also included another British post-punk band, Gang of Four, as well as hard rock band Warrior Soul and hip-hop novelty act the Young Black Teenagers (who were all white); but it was clear from the start that Public Enemy were the principal attraction, even if Sisters of Mercy were the nominal headliners. Sisters of Mercy singer Andrew Eldritch admitted the benefits of touring with Public Enemy, noting that the combination allowed his band to play bigger halls than they would otherwise: "We can bring in all our gear like we do on the European shows and it is good for them [Public Enemy] because they are reaching parts of America they otherwise wouldn't be able to play in."[126] Reporting on the tour, *The Source* explicitly connected the strategy of mixing rap and rock artists to the difficulties of mounting a rap-only tour, and cited booking agent John Marx who supported the views of Eldritch: "I think you're gonna see Public Enemy fans that are white that would not go to see them under normal circumstances ... It's a safer environment for these fans."[127] Of course, the unspoken element here was that the tour might prove less appealing to black fans of the band. The merging of rock and rap on stage may give rap artists a larger forum in which to perform, but it continued the concert industry's tendency to treat young black audiences as a secondary priority. Knowledge of this fact led Public Enemy to stage three different tours in 1991, so that their black fans would not be shut out by their efforts to reach the white rock audience.

Discussing his rationale for joining the "Tune in, Turn on, Burn out" tour—as the Sisters of Mercy venture was named—Chuck D later declared, "I agreed to be on the tour because to me concert tours, whether they were all-rock bills or all-Rap bills, were becoming too predictable. Everything was sectioned off into neat categories and the audiences already knew what they were going to get before the show began."[128] This optimistic gloss was given a more pragmatic read by *New York Times* critic Jon Pareles, who identified both idealistic and practical motives behind what he called the "mix-and-match" approach to concert programming. Noted Pareles: "The ideal is to convene a post-punk community from factionalized rock audiences. The practicality is that because insurers are so leery of violence at rap shows, promoters rarely book all-rap bills; joining rock bands on the road helps rappers to get out and perform."[129]

Based on the evidence of the tour's July 24, 1991 stop at Radio City Music Hall, the practical goals were met more successfully than the idealistic hopes. Given that Public Enemy skipped New York entirely on its "Tour of a Black Planet," the Radio City appearance was something of a landmark occasion for the band and its fans. *Spin* magazine critic Scott Poulson-Bryant observed of the group's performance at the July 24, 1991, show: "There are so many Public Enemy shirts in the audience and this duo [Chuck D and Flavor Flav] plays right to them, running up the elevated side ramps like they were made for rap—or rock 'n' roll."[130] More tellingly, significant portions of the audience left following Public Enemy's penultimate set and prior to the performance of Sisters of Mercy. That reaction might have undermined the notion that this was a breakthrough exercise in merging music across genres, but it validated the suggestion that Public Enemy's fans would turn out in force. As to their performance, the group demonstrated that they were able to command the attention of an audience that was comprised of rap and rock fans. Gene Santoro conveyed the energy of Public Enemy's set in his *Billboard* review: "The diverse audience didn't sit down or stop moving until PE had finished tearing into favorites like 'Bring the Noise' and 'Fight the Power.' The group's rich, dense sonics, Chuck D's resonant, incantatory raps, and Flavor Flav's comic-relief schtick and interaction with the crowd powered a nonstop energy explosion with a socially conscious edge."[131]

More balance characterized the tour that combined Public Enemy with Anthrax and alternative prog-funk-rock tricksters Primus. Because Public Enemy and Anthrax collaborated on a thrash metal remake of the rap group's epochal song, "Bring the Noise," there was also more of a built-in rationale for putting them on the same bill. Reviewing the tour's New York stop—at the Ritz—*Billboard* writer Victoria Starr pointed out that, "unlike this past summer's mixed bills, the crowd seemed equally enthusiastic toward each of the bands," a clear dig at the Public Enemy/Sisters of Mercy tour.[132] Reporting on a concert at the Irvine Meadows Amphitheater in California nearly a month later, in October, Jonathan Gold detected similar excitement even though, by his account, the crowd was "virtually all white."[133] Playing in support of their newly released album, *Apocalypse 91: The Enemy Strikes Black*, and with the controversy over Professor Griff behind them, Gold suggested that Public Enemy "played the show you may have always wanted to see them do, free of ex-member Professor Griff's Anglo-baiting and lead rapper Chuck D's long-winded speeches about flag and country... The goal here, one suspects, was less to challenge the audience with rap than to help them *like* it—on Public Enemy's own terms."[134] Gold perceived that Chuck D seemed genuinely excited at playing to such a large crowd of white metal fans, a notion supported by the rapper's later recollection about the tour: "The audiences were mostly white, but it was a different type of white audience, it was a collaborative white audience. It wasn't a straight-metal audience, the audience knew both groups and both groups' songs."[135] When the two bands joined for a climactic version of "Bring the Noise," according to Gold, "metal and rap at last [fused] into a seamless whole."[136]

Ultimate proof that Public Enemy's multi-pronged tour strategy achieved its goal of opening new space for the band to perform was that, when they finally embarked on their own headlining tour late in the year exclusively featuring hip-hop artists, they were booked to play at Madison Square Garden. At that point, the Garden hadn't hosted a rap show of this kind in four years. The stakes were especially high because the weekend prior to the show, a charity basketball game organized by budding hip-hop entrepreneur Sean "Puff Daddy" Combs at New York's City College resulted in a stampede that left eight people dead. Yet a spokesperson for the Garden downplayed the potential risk of the Public Enemy show, stressing that the venue was far better equipped to handle the entrance and exit of large crowds of people than the City College gymnasium had been. The security details for the concert were indicative of the new reality at hip-hop concerts, and to some degree within the arena concert world more generally: twelve metal detectors were placed at the Garden's entrances, and there would be more than one-hundred uniformed guards inside the arena and many more police officers outside to oversee crowd control.[137]

That the concert occurred without incident was treated as major news by nearly every daily New York newspaper—*Newsday*, the *Daily News*, the *New York Post*, and the *Times* all reported on the event, highlighting that the *absence* of violence at a major hip-hop show was now considered to be noteworthy.[138] The lineup was like a cross-section of the state of rap circa early 1992, with the Geto Boys and A Tribe Called Quest representing the very different directions that hip-hop had moved toward. Still, this was Public Enemy's show. Playing in front of a predominantly black audience, the group foregrounded political confrontation, going so far as to feature as one of its set pieces the mock-hanging of a figure dressed in a Ku Klux Klan robe—repurposing the shock tactics of pioneering arena rock artist Alice Cooper toward anti-racist ends. Some questioned whether arena concerts remained the best way to present hip-hop artists. Frank Owen, writing for *Newsday*, posited that "the unofficial boycott of rap by Manhattan nightclubs over the past couple of years has been more detrimental to the hip-hop scene" than its exclusion from Madison Square Garden.[139] By Chuck D's account, though, arena concerts remained an important sign of equity as well as success. Responding to critics who charged him of artistic compromise for the decision to tour with white artists, which by 1992 included a European tour in support of rock megastars U2, the rapper asserted: "Why did I do tours with U2 and Anthrax? So I could learn what I'm missing. If rock exists for 20 years, how come rap got severe problems now? . . . In this country, there's no such thing as a 100 percent autonomous black situation."[140]

The Festival Revival

From Fresh Fest to the Def Jam artist tours to Public Enemy's World's Greatest Rap Tour, the preference shown in hip-hop concert promotion for package bills featuring four or more artists seemed strangely out of sync with the times. It could be seen as the residue of a still-underdeveloped black concert industry that had never fully reassembled itself in the wake of the chitlin circuit, and that held on to an older way of presenting entertainment. Alternately, the hip-hop package tour was a measure of a genre that was still creating its own format and that always had a somewhat uneasy presence on the concert stage. There was a lingering anxiety among hip-hop promoters and performers alike that a more standard concert bill, featuring a lone headliner and an opening act, would not be enough to hold an audience's attention. Packages provided insurance against this eventuality but also brought their own difficulties that sometimes contributed to the unrest that was so widely associated with hip-hop performances.

As the 1990s wore on though, the hip-hop package tour seemed less obsolete than prophetic. Public Enemy's 1991 tour itinerary, with two of the band's three tours undertaken in conjunction with white rock bands, was a sign that something was shifting beyond the realm of hip-hop. An early gesture toward the evolving syncretism emerging at the time was the Gathering of the Tribes, two day-long concerts held in Southern and Northern California on October 6 and 7, 1990, that were envisioned by Ian Astbury, lead singer for the British rock band the Cult. Astbury's ideals for the concert were decidedly nostalgic, holding up the Monterey Pop Festival as a model, but he also wanted it to reflect a 1990s musical sensibility. For that, he believed the inclusion of rap artists was instrumental to his cause, and so recruited Queen Latifah and Ice T to join the likes of Iggy Pop, the Cramps, the Indigo Girls, Michelle Shocked, former Sex Pistol Steve Jones, and the Charlatans UK.[141] Supported by veteran promoter Bill Graham, whose Shoreline Amphitheater hosted the Northern California show, Gathering of the Tribes was a modest success in commercial terms—the Southern California concert at the Pacific Amphitheater in Costa Mesa drew nearly ten thousand people.[142] Its ethos was more influential than the numbers suggested, though, positing that an idea of diversity encompassing artists of different races and genres could somehow draw a representative generational crowd, producing profit and engendering a sense of collective goodwill.

In effect, Gathering of the Tribes provided a template for reimagining an American rock festival, the model for which would be expanded and refined the following year with the advent of the Lollapalooza touring festival by another retro-minded rock artist, Perry Farrell of Jane's Addiction. Rock festivals had largely gone into remission from the mid-1970s forward, for reasons explored in Chapter 7, even as festivals grew and sometimes flourished in other genres—blues, bluegrass, folk, and jazz among them. Efforts toward a revival had occasionally emerged such as the much-publicized US Festivals of 1982 and 1983, created from the enthusiasm of Apple computers co-founder Steve Wozniak, yet no festival of the era had much long-term impact or drew the attention of a comparable media mega-event such as 1985's Live Aid (which featured a single hip-hop artist, Run-DMC). A variety of factors made the 1990s a more propitious time to seek to revive the rock festival. Popular culture of the 1990s carried a strong tinge of nostalgia for the 1960s and early 1970s that was rooted in a rejection of the pervasive materialism of the 1980s. There was a mounting discourse of generational identification that cohered around the notion of Generation X, which was defined in large part through positive and negative associations with the Baby Boomers that comprised the Sixties youth culture. Not least, a slumping early 1990s concert industry motivated a search for any new idea that could draw audiences, maybe especially if that new idea was also an old idea.

Ian Astbury's most important contribution to this development may have been his insight that a rock festival restyled for the 1990s would have to include rap. In a sense, this too was as much a conservative move as a progressive one. Ice T and Queen Latifah occupied a place at Gathering of the Tribes analogous to that of Jimi Hendrix and Otis Redding at Monterey Pop, or Hendrix and Sly Stone at Woodstock. All of these cases fit a pattern best described by Gina Arnold, who has observed, "At most festivals, black artists have always been more than welcome to play to predominantly white audiences, although black audiences were (and still are) essentially prevented" from attending such events.[143] Lollapalooza institutionalized this dynamic during its initial run from 1991 to 1997, nearly always ensuring the presence of a select hip-hop artist or two on the bill, but never including more than that select few among the main stage artists so that rap would always be in a clearly supportive and subordinate role to rock. One 1990s festival, Smokin' Grooves, broke the pattern by programming primarily black artists and putting hip-hop at its center. A mixed success, it opened new space for the programming of live hip-hop while demonstrating that the creation of a self-standing and durable "hip-hop festival" remained elusive.

* * *

"Concert Business Faces a Bleak Summer," was the headline opening *Pollstar* magazine's "Concert Hotwire" column of May 27, 1991. A mild but still palpable economic recession drove down ticket sales for the season and sent promoters scurrying for solutions. In this environment, package tours of the sort that had been common in hip-hop for the better part of a decade assumed broader currency. Continued the *Pollstar* commentary, "This season we are seeing more three and four act packages with what on paper looks like a stronger bill as artists fight to offer fans the most enticing avenue for them to spend their discretionary dollars."[144] What worked on paper did not necessarily result in box office success in practice, however. For all the media attention that the Sisters of Mercy/Public Enemy "Tune in, Turn on, Burn out" tour attracted, the last several dates had to be canceled due to low ticket sales. A second run of "Gathering of the Tribes" fared no better. Only 4,200 concertgoers attended the show at the Pacific Amphitheater, less than half of the previous year's attendance and nowhere near the capacity of nineteen thousand; and a projected sixteen tour dates had to be scaled back to three.[145] These numbers, and the general trend of the time, made the success of the Lollapalooza touring festival stand out all the more. Its twenty-three 1991 shows grossed $9 million and sold more than 90 percent of available tickets.

When the second installment in 1992 did even better, grossing $19.1 million over thirty-six shows at near 100 percent capacity, the festival sealed its status as one of the major live music success stories of the 1990s.[146]

Nostalgia pervaded talk of Lollapalooza, with invocations of Woodstock a standard part of any press account. However, given its size and status as a touring festival, a more apt comparison would have been the Newport Jazz and Folk Festivals, and more particularly George Wein's early efforts to convert the Newport Jazz Festival into a portable enterprise. Two more contemporary sources of inspiration also loomed large. For one, rock and pop festivals had grown into a major part of the summer entertainment spectrum in the United Kingdom and continental Europe. Marc Geiger, a booking agent who played an instrumental role in planning and producing Lollapalooza, stressed that the example of the European festival scene was pivotal. Interviewed by the *Detroit Free Press*, Geiger explained of the concept behind Lollapalooza: "We just copied it off the Europeans... I was there last summer at the Reading Festival, watching 40,000 kids hanging out, listening to all these great bands in a field in England. I thought, 'This is stupid. In America, we've got all these great outdoor places. We should do something about this.'"[147]

Geiger's comments allude to the second major factor that determined the shape of Lollapalooza. The "great outdoor places" to which he refers were not, on the whole, the kind of wide-open space that housed Woodstock. Rather, they were a proliferating breed of outdoor amphitheater that had arisen as a major venue type in the live music industry. Such venues had been in place for decades, from the Greek Theater in Berkeley, California, to the Hollywood Bowl, and in a different vein, the famous Shed at Tanglewood. With the growth of the concert industry in the 1970s, new economic possibilities evolved for profiting from medium and large capacity spaces that could house rock and pop concerts, and amphitheaters presented some unique advantages to the arenas and stadiums that had become standard. According to concert industry historians Dean Budnick and Josh Baron, when compared to arenas, "Amphitheaters... were far less expensive to build, didn't necessarily use union labor [which kept labor costs down], didn't have sports teams [which made scheduling events easier] and could often hold more people. Moreover, they were designed for live entertainment, which meant that key elements like sight lines and sound amplification were far better than those in arenas."[148] Parallel to the wave of arena and stadium construction that occurred between the 1960s and the 1980s, a wave of amphitheater construction reshaped the live music field, with twenty-nine new outdoor theaters being opened between 1980 and 1998.[149] Gathering of the Tribes reflected this trend, with its two 1990 shows happening in two recently constructed California amphitheaters, the Pacific (opened in 1983) and the Shoreline (opened in 1986). Lollapalooza pursued the amphitheater circuit on a national scale, taking advantage of the outdoor setting and the summertime weather to build the sense of a festival in spaces that typically housed more conventionally produced concerts.

Another difference between amphitheaters and arenas had to do with location. The Forum in Los Angeles, the Long Beach Arena, Madison Square Garden, the Philadelphia Spectrum, Joe Louis Arena in Detroit—these and many other of the most oft-used arenas for pop and rock concerts were situated squarely in urban areas. By contrast, outdoor amphitheaters—and especially those built during the wave of construction starting in 1980—were much more likely to be placed away from urban centers, in decidedly suburban settings. Indeed, it may not be a stretch to suggest that the proliferation of amphitheaters across the US during this era was part of a broader suburbanization of live music entertainment. When considering how a genre like hip-hop might be impacted by such a shift, the implications are clear. Arenas may never have been the most apt setting for presenting live hip-hop, but the venues had the advantage of being proximate to the urban black populations that represented a core hip-hop audience. Presenting hip-hop artists in a suburban amphitheater, by contrast, was akin to making literal the cultural move through which white suburban audiences became an expanding base of hip-hop consumption. William "Upski" Wimsatt addressed the changing constitution of the hip-hop audience in a pointed article for *The Source* that foreshadowed his 1994 book, *Bomb the Suburbs*:

> Industry experts estimate that once a record reaches gold . . . whites constitute at least 60% of the market . . . But the white audience doesn't just consume rap. It shapes rap also . . . Increasingly, rappers address their white audience, either directly, by accommodating its perceived tastes . . . or indirectly, by shunning the white audience, retreating into Blacker, realer, more hardcore stances—all the more titillating for their inaccessibility.[150]

With this in mind, it was almost overdetermined that the rap artists Ice-T and Ice Cube, who would be featured at the first two installments of the Lollapalooza tour—the traveling alternative rock suburban amphitheater festival—were representative of that most "hardcore" of hip-hop subgenres, gangsta rap.

Ice-T brought the added value of using the tour to debut his new thrash metal project, Body Count. Over the next year, Ice-T would become embroiled in one of the defining hip-hop controversies of the era when his song, "Cop Killer"—recorded with Body Count—would generate significant blowback from police organizations and politicians around the US, ultimately leading to the rapper's decision to remove the song from Body Count's self-titled debut album under pressure from his record label, Warner Brothers. That the release of the song coincided with the urban uprising in Los Angeles that followed the announcement of the verdict in the Rodney King trial, where police officers who had mercilessly beaten the African American King were found not guilty, only added to the intensity of the public debate. Lost in the furor generated by "Cop Killer" was the fact that it was not, properly speaking, a rap song. Public commentators could not make sense of a metal song by an all-black band from L.A. that declared open hostility to the police. As a result, claims popular music scholar Barry Shank, "Represented as a rap song capable of inciting its listeners to violence, the attack on 'Cop Killer' stood in for an indictment of black culture itself."[151]

"Cop Killer" was part of the set that Ice-T played with Body Count throughout the 1991 Lollapalooza tour. At the time, the song stirred minimal controversy, prior to the Rodney King verdict and resulting unrest. Instead, it was one of many factors that contributed to the sense that Ice-T was a black hip-hop artist with a unique capacity to crossover, pushing the rap/rock nexus several steps ahead of where it had been. Interviewed while the tour was running, he played up his connections to rock, seeking to counter suggestions that his presence on the Lollapalooza bill was anomalous: "I'm not a traditional black rapper, because I'm too hard for most black audiences . . . I feel perfect out there with the Butthole Surfers, because I know where they're coming from. I know where Henry Rollins is coming from because I used to watch . . . Black Flag back in the punk and hard-core days."[152] Although some reviewers took mild offense at the baldness of Ice-T's anti-police rhetoric during his performances, such concerns were overshadowed by his sheer ability to get what appeared at times to be an indifferent crowd excited and involved with his music, and by his open appeals to unity. At the Pine Knob amphitheater outside of Detroit, he proclaimed from the stage at one point, "Lollapalooza . . . is a chance for all of us to get a look at each other . . . Finally we get to meet each other, and we find out we're not that different from each other."[153] During his set at Lake Fairfax Park, in northern Virginia and near Washington, DC, he said to the audience, "I'm not here to party for you, I'm here to party with y'all," before concluding his set by getting the crowd to join him in a chant of "Fuck the Police."[154]

If there was tension surrounding Ice-T's presence on the Lollapalooza tour, it was less about his provocations aimed toward cops and more about his blunt use of a certain racial epithet, the "N word." His most recent album, *O.G. Original Gangster*, featured liberal use of the word as was characteristic of much gangsta rap, and included an explicit defense of such usage on the track, "Straight up Nigga." On record, the song was framed by a spoken introduction in which Ice-T upholds his right to claim the term, and a postlude where the rapper draws a contrast between the use of the word as a symbol of alliance between fellow African Americans and its use as a term of derision by white racists, which he denounces in no uncertain terms (by having a white-voiced male who utters the insult get shot). Playing before the crowd at Lollapalooza, the latter message may have been harder to discern as Ice-T announced to the audience, "People get on me because I use the word 'nigger' . . . In my category, all of yous are my niggers." As reported by *Rolling Stone*, his pronouncement caused the predominantly white crowd to "go bananas." It also provoked a bitter response from the other African American band on the bill, Living Colour, whose guitarist Vernon Reid asserted before one of the group's songs, "I will die before I become a nigger for your entertainment."[155]

The last word on the matter, in a sense, was had by Ice-T, who joined Lollapalooza headliner Jane's Addiction for a charged rendition of the Sly and the Family Stone song, "Don't Call Me Nigger, Whitey." This song was one of those representing the bleak underside of Stone's more uplifting aesthetic vision, explored in the last chapter. On the original studio version, Sly Stone sang the refrain as a call and response to himself, enacting a racist dialogue meant to highlight the difficulty of communicating across differences, as the song's title line would be answered by its inverse, "don't call me whitey . . ." Rendered at Lollapalooza, Ice-T and Jane's Addiction frontman (and festival organizer) Perry Farrell exchanged the epithets in a more literal call and response between black and white, interspersed with outbursts of jamming by the band. The song's intention as a statement of anti-racism, and in support of unity, was signaled by the song's climax where Farrell and Ice-T would dance across the stage while Jane's Addiction guitarist Dave Navarro and Body Count guitarist Ernie C traded solos.[156] However, as cultural studies scholar Jennifer Stoever astutely observes, the exchange between the white singer and the black rapper exaggerated the aggression contained in Sly Stone's words and established something of a false equivalency between the use of racist language directed against African Americans and whites, respectively. The audience, meanwhile, responded with a level of excitement and anticipation toward each utterance of the "N word" that suggested "a mixture of shock, desensitization *and* titillation."[157] These were the terms according to which hip-hop was integrated into the fabric of Lollapalooza, its presence marking a desire to overturn racial divisions while spotlighting the continued fascination that hypermasculine blackness generated for white audiences.

* * *

Over the ensuing six years, until the first wave of Lollapalooza tours ran aground after the 1997 installment, the preferred style of hip-hop presented at the festival changed by degrees. Ice Cube's presence in 1992 reproduced the same measure of gangsta rap outrage that Ice-T had brought in year one, but the newly added second stage broadened the presence of rap, including Cypress Hill and white rap artists House of Pain. 1993 signaled a bigger shift with the move of Southern "alternative" hip-hop artists Arrested Development to the main stage. The following year, 1994, may have been the most hip-hop intensive of all Lollapalooza tours during the 1990s, as the main stage featured the Beastie Boys and A Tribe Called Quest—both groups consolidating the turn toward a less confrontational but still streetwise approach—while second stage groups included L.A. rap tricksters the Pharcyde and, again, Cypress Hill. Indeed, Cypress Hill's move from second stage attraction to main stage act in 1995 may have been the biggest hip-hop "story" of the whole Lollapalooza enterprise, as it contributed to the group's rise to being arguably the most festival-oriented hip-hop act of the 1990s. Hip-hop nearly disappeared from the 1996 installment of Lollapalooza, though, when the festival organizers significantly asserted a "rock"-based aesthetic that foregrounded metal (Metallica), punk (the Ramones), and their offshoots (Soundgarden, Rancid, Screaming Trees), with the only hip-hop presence being the inclusion of the Wu-Tang Clan on a few select dates. The genre returned in greater force in 1997 with Snoop Dogg as a main stage headliner, but by then the festival had run its course, and after a stillborn effort to revive a touring Lollapalooza festival in the early 2000s, it was revived in 2005 as a standalone, multi-day event held each summer in Chicago.

Writing in *Spin*, Eric Weisbard reflected on the demise of Lollapalooza 1.0 by noting that over the course of its run, the festival's polyglot approach to programming gave way to a series of "subspecies" festivals that were significantly more niche-oriented—updated 1990s women's music (Lilith Fair), jam bands (H.O.R.D.E. and Furthur festivals), metal (Ozzfest), punk and hardcore (Vans Warped Tour).[158] Amidst this wave of genre-specific touring festivals, the Smokin' Grooves festival emerged as the closest approximation of a dedicated hip-hop affair. Started in the summer of 1996, it ran for three years in its original incarnation, and has been intermittently revived in the twenty-first century. Behind the enterprise were two key industry figures: booking agent Cara Lewis, a one-time Norby Walters associate who had moved to the William Morris Agency to become a leading representative of rap and R&B artists on a national scale; and Kevin Morrow of House of Blues, the nightclub chain that was moving into larger-scale concert promotion.

Commonly referred to as the "black Lollapalooza" in media accounts, Smokin' Grooves used the established touring festival as a model for creating an event that had hip-hop at its core but would reach audiences that were not exclusively committed to the genre. Lewis explained in a 2018 interview:

> The first Smokin' Grooves was created as a response to Lollapalooza . . . I wanted to create a tour that could act as a conduit for soul, hip-hop, funk, R&B, and reggae to come together. Kevin understood the change we could create by putting a festival on tour that would combat any fears of this genre of music [hip-hop] and play venues with capacities of 12,000-plus.[159]

Two of the acts on the bill for the first 1996 installment—Cypress Hill and A Tribe Called Quest—were Lollapalooza veterans, while the Fugees, Busta Rhymes, and Spearhead were artists whose approach to hip-hop encompassed other genres such as reggae and soul, and avoided the aggressive ethos of gangsta rap. Topping the bill was Ziggy Marley and the Melody Makers, chosen because they were a more established concert draw but also to confirm the air of a more inclusive setting where rap would not be the only attraction. 1997 headliner George Clinton and the P-Funk All-Stars fulfilled a similar function (see Figure 9.6). The mixing of different black music genres on the same bill was a novel take on the hybrid aesthetic of Lollapalooza but also served as a sign of the continued unease that surrounded the presentation of hip-hop concerts in unfettered form.

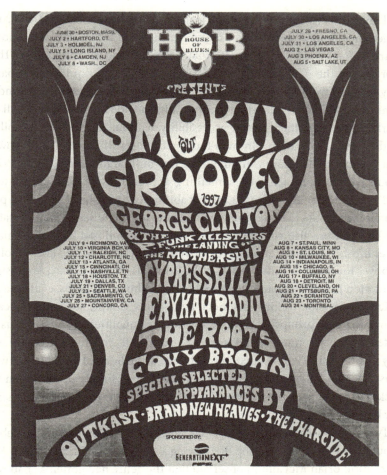

Figure 9.6 Advertisement for the 1997 installment of the Smokin' Grooves tour, a breakthrough effort to present live hip-hop in the style of a touring festival. Placing the likes of George Clinton and the P-Funk All-Stars at the top of the bill was a strategy designed to broaden the tour's reach and avoid some of the stigma attached to hip-hop concerts. From *Vibe* (June 1997).

Smokin' Grooves' debut coincided with the rise to prominence of the Fugees, whose album *The Score* went on to sell over six million copies in the US and many millions more worldwide. Although they only had third top billing on the Smokin' Grooves lineup behind Ziggy Marley and Cypress Hill, it became clear as the tour progressed that they were the primary attraction. Comprised of singer and rapper Lauryn Hill, Haitian born rapper and multi-instrumentalist Wyclef Jean, and his cousin Pras Michel, the Fugees personified the qualities that were designed to set Smokin' Grooves apart from the hip-hop concerts that preceded and surrounded it. They represented the new primacy of a form of "conscious" rap that was markedly set apart from the gangsta rap style, and their music remained grounded in hip-hop fundamentals while incorporating a wide range of other stylistic markers that lent their sound accessibility without sacrificing credibility. In the words of Smokin' Grooves tour mate Busta Rhymes, "They showed that you can be hardcore without killing one million motherfuckers."[160] The group furthermore achieved something approaching gender parity, with Hill's vocal talent and songwriting capabilities making her a standout personality who more than held her own with her two male bandmates. Notably, the Fugees were also something more like a conventional band than many other hip-hop artists, a quality they shared with Spearhead and later Smokin' Grooves touring performers such as the Roots. The trend toward live instrumentation in hip-hop had been growing throughout the 1990s, evident even in Ice-T's decision to form his metal band Body Count, but more typically associated with groups who wanted to capture qualities of "liveness" associated with black musical styles such as jazz, soul, and funk. Onstage, the way that Smokin' Grooves juxtaposed bands using live instrumentation with those such as A Tribe Called Quest who continued to rely primarily on the backing of a DJ made the festival an embodiment of the evolving aesthetics of live hip-hop performance.

Two reviews capture the way that Smokin' Grooves generated debate about the value of live hip-hop. Reviewing a show at Pine Knob, *Detroit Free Press* critic Brian McCollum observed that the genre had gotten a "bad rap" (pun presumably intended) as a concert attraction. He recognized that the Smokin' Grooves tour was "out to reinvent live rap," and suggested that it did so most successfully with the inclusion of the Fugees, who "delivered a melodic, thumping mix of cerebral hip-hop, musically quoting Kenny Rogers as easily as it did Grandmaster Flash." Crucially McCollum credited much of the group's success to their use of live instruments, with which they worked the "near-sellout crowd into a sea of dancing bodies."[161] By contrast, *Indianapolis Star* critic Marc Allan viewed the Smokin' Grooves tour stop at the Deer Creek Music Center outside Indianapolis as a less successful venture. Like McCollum, Allan championed those artists who used live instruments, giving special praise to Spearhead for transcending the genre's purported limitations as a live attraction. Yet most of the show remained constrained by those same limitations in Allan's assessment, as he put forth at the start of his review: "Awkward pacing, listless performances, heavy reliance on prerecorded tracks and repetitive orders from the performers to 'make some noise'—these things kill live rap shows. The Smokin' Grooves tour . . . had many of those problems."[162]

Ultimately, it is impossible to separate the quality of the performances on the Smokin' Grooves tour from the conditions of its production. On this score, the most insightful comment on the tour came from *Cincinnati Enquirer* critic Larry Nager, who remarked of the concert at the Riverbend Amphitheater: "The area's most suburban concert venue presented the summer's most urban tour."[163] This was just one of many paradoxes that surrounded the venture. Reviewing the tour stop at the Garden State Arts Center in New Jersey, Jon Pareles witnessed the disconnect between the apparent good vibes of the concert—and the promotion of marijuana smoking by many artists including Cypress Hill—and the heavy handed security employed by the venue: "Ticket-holders faced frisking and metal detectors; security guards also searched some cigarette packages, and if marijuana was found, they called state troopers, who handcuffed and arrested concertgoers for drug possession."[164] Dream Hampton highlighted a different sort of rigidity that infused the tour: the use of "an ominous digital clock that counts down each act's allotted time, just offstage. If a band is late or exceeds their limit, there are fined."[165] Designed to ensure that the pacing of the shows remained consistent and did not run over time, such measures also imposed an intense sort of discipline on the artists that went against the grain of the loose, spontaneous ethos projected by the tour and its hippie-infused title.

The most pernicious such tensions surrounded the matter of how the Smokin' Grooves tour was promoted. Year two of Smokin' Grooves in 1997 coincided with a story in *Billboard* reporting on the ongoing difficulties that black concert promoters faced within the larger live music industry. Members of the Black Promoters Association of America charged that they were systematically excluded from being able to bid on tours by major African American artists including Luther Vandross, Diana Ross, Sade, and Tina Turner. Also included in their complaint was the Smokin' Grooves tour, which was unrepresented by black promoters.[166] A subsequent story on the situation in *Pollstar* directed some of the blame for the inequities at Cara Lewis, the booking agent who had devised Smokin' Grooves. By this time, in late 1998, a group of five black concert promoters had filed a lawsuit charging discrimination against forty major talent agencies and promotion companies. As part of the suit, African American promoter Jesse Boseman recounted an incident wherein he had contacted Lewis to inquire about promoting two concerts by neo-soul singer Erykah Badu in the New York area. Lewis told Boseman that she was not scheduling concerts for Badu at the time, but when the white concert promoter Ron Delsener called to ask about the same dates, Lewis confirmed that she was scheduling and gave him the rights to one of Badu's concerts.[167] Although her previous employer Norby Walters developed a reputation for working cooperatively with black promoters, that reputation does not appear to have carried forward with Lewis as she became one of the most powerful representatives of black music artists in the industry. As such, any credit given to Smokin' Grooves as a breakthrough hip-hop festival has to be qualified for the way it perpetuated business-as-usual by keeping African American promoters from reaping the benefits of black musical success.

How much of a breakthrough Smokin' Grooves represented, apart from potentially questionable business practices, is debatable in itself. As noted above, the festival's first 1996 installment grossed a respectable $6 million, edging into the top fifty grossing tours of the year. Subsequent installments performed less well, with 1997 pulling $4.6 million and ranking number sixty-seven among the year's top tours, and 1998 earning $4 million and ranking number seventy-five.[168] That these grosses made the tour into one of the top-earning live hip-hop shows of the era says as much about the limitations that the genre continued to face on the road as it does the success of Lewis and Morrow's efforts to devise a black Lollapalooza with hip-hop at its core. That said, Smokin' Grooves did coincide with a broader revival of large-scale rap tours. Looking back, Chuck D—who, with Public Enemy, headlined the third and last installment of Smokin' Grooves in 1998—claimed that it "opened the gates" for the very successful tours undertaken by Jay-Z and DMX in 1999 (the Hard Knock Life tour) and Dr. Dre and Eminem in 2000 (the Up in Smoke tour), both of which were more standard arena tours and far surpassed Smokin' Grooves in earnings.[169] While Smokin' Grooves no doubt played a part in restoring the viability of hip-hop as a live, large-venue attraction, arena rap as such proved to be the more successful commodity. Where festivals were concerned, the legacy of Lollapalooza would be carried on in the likes of Coachella, established in 1999, where until the last decade at least, hip-hop contributed to the composition of a diverse and eclectic festival program but remained a largely subordinate part of the overall experience. Even as hip-hop headliners like Jay-Z, Kanye West, and Beyoncé have grown in stature in recent years, a thriving and sustainable festival in which hip-hop is central and not peripheral has not yet materialized.

Preserving the Elements

In an influential formulation, Nelson George wrote in 1988: "Rap's gone national and is in the process of going regional. That seems like a contradiction, but it's actually easily explained. Rap spread out from New York to attract a loyal, national audience. New York rapped and America listened. Now America is rhyming back."[170] One of the primary engines of rap's regional spread, according to George, were the early tours of Kurtis Blow and Grandmaster Flash; while the principle evidence of the genre's geographic expansion was the growth of independent record labels such as Rap-a-Lot in Houston and Luke Skyywalker in Miami, and the accompanying talent that filled out the rosters of these labels. This simultaneous national growth and localization of hip-hop could further be witnessed in early issues of *The Source*, which included regular scene reports not only from New York and Los Angeles but also from settings as disparate as Seattle, Chicago, Houston, Philadelphia, and Milwaukee and fell under the heading, "The Hip-Hop Nation: Regional Rap Reports."[171]

Across these varied settings, while arena concerts may have been a key medium for spreading the music, hip-hop remained a club culture on the ground. Indeed, embattled as they were, hip-hop clubs became key repositories for those guarding what they understood to be the genre's true definition, and where core elements of the hip-hop aesthetic could be found in revitalized and refashioned form. Over time, a subset of these clubs became the staging ground for the rise of "underground" hip-hop. Hip-hop scholar Mickey Hess explains that a transformation took shape in the early and mid-1990s, when the term "hardcore" that had previously been applied to "hip-hop that stayed true to its musical origins" instead came to denote "a harder gangsta style." "Underground" became the new preferred term for hip-hop that remained committed to maintaining and extending the values attached to the original four elements and often set itself in opposition to the trends attached to the expanding commercial hip-hop industry.[172] Marcyliena Morgan adds, in her study of the Los Angeles hip-hop underground, that the term refers to "a place where truths can be told, and where people can remove their veil to expose their spirits and thoughts without fear for their life."[173]

It is also a space founded upon "hiphop's persistent focus on skills, competition, and evaluation from artists and fans," within which the boundaries between performer and audience are more fluid than in other performance settings.[174]

Within the scene documented by Morgan, the key place that nurtured an underground hip-hop ethos was the Good Life Café, located in the Crenshaw district of South Central Los Angeles. Opened as a health food restaurant by community activist B. Hall and a partner, in 1989 the café started an after-hours open mic on Thursday nights where anyone who wanted to get on the microphone and test their MC skills could do so. Quickly it became established as a hub of an emerging underground scene in the city and a proving ground where those who exhibited considerable skill were applauded and those whose skills were found lacking were encouraged to "please pass the mic."[175] Ultimate value was placed on the ability of participants to freestyle, a demonstration of verbal dexterity and lyrical flow that was contingent on improvisatory, in-the-moment creativity. An added constraint was the prohibition of the use of obscene language, which was justified by Hall as a mechanism to foster "the atmosphere of a serious arts workshop."[176] When the Good Life drew attention from *The Source* in 1993, it stood in marked contrast to the gangsta style that had defined L.A. hip-hop and had recently ascended to commercial dominance with the success of Dr. Dre's 1992 album, *The Chronic*. As detailed there, "Performers sign up on a first come first served, and a no cursing rule is enforced by cutting the sound on an act if they curse," while the style displayed by Good Life MCs was "more concerned with lyrical skills and the ability to style artistically than how many body bags the coroner has to collect after the show."[177]

One of the leading groups to emerge from the Good Life scene was Freestyle Fellowship, whose name alone conveyed the value attached to spontaneous lyrical invention. Fellowship members Myka 9, P.E.A.C.E., Self Jupiter, Aceyalone, and DJ Kiilu had all been active in the L.A. hip-hop scene, but the Good Life provided the forum where their individual skills could coalesce. According to Kiilu, speaking to photographer and journalist Brian Cross, "I couldn't believe there was really some good rap in LA that I could respect, until I heard Mike and that's what brought me down there." Expanding on the shared values of the group's members, he continued: "I think the common vector that brings us all together is that everybody's B-boy, everybody remembers the old school . . . I always like to show that I'm down with hiphop in some way."[178] Myka 9 adds another layer of connotation when explaining the drive behind his creative efforts:

> I think that what really brought it all together was our drive to really be singled out from all other MCs. Style was of the essence . . . Niggers have got their mouths busted and their nose busted behind rap, they have got slammed and pistols pulled on them behind some fuckin' hiphop and that's part of the reason why I have started to distinct myself with style. I am working to make that distinction, and that the reason why we're a fellowship of freestylers because freestyles are the ultimate forms of expression.[179]

Myka 9 voices here a powerful impulse to produce "a new style nobody can deal with," to use Fab Five Freddy's resonant phrase,[180] but with an added dimension: that style also becomes a strategy for survival and a vehicle of protest against the everyday violence confronted by African Americans. In this regard, he exemplifies Morgan's description of the underground as a space where difficult truths can be spoken in order to uphold the humanity of the participants.

The Good Life Café did not exist in isolation. New York gave rise to the Lyricist Lounge, where the emphasis was less on freestyling but similarly oriented toward lyrical invention above all. It was also specifically designed to be a place where artists who did not already have record deals or significant exposure could get onstage during a time when the number of active hip-hop clubs in New York had declined. Started in 1991 in an apartment on the Lower East Side of Manhattan, the Lounge moved several times over the course of the 1990s as its audience increased and it required larger quarters. Its legend grew as several artists later to gain renown appeared there early in their rise, most famously Notorious B.I.G., and at a certain point a diverse array of established performers such as Q-Tip, Puff Daddy, and Ol' Dirty Bastard began making appearances to reassert their credibility as lyrically-minded artists.[181] Washington, DC, housed a less star-studded organization, the Freestyle Union, which sponsored an open mic workshop and a more performance-oriented open mic on Saturday and Sunday nights at a venue called the Kaffa House, a restaurant and club in the U Street district. The DC organization was headed by a female artist, Toni Blackman, who also belonged to a collective of female rappers and musicians called CipHer that gave weekly performances.[182] In these instances and others, effort was directed toward creating alternative spaces that were locally oriented and designed to maximize participation, countering the gatekeeping practices that governed the broader world of commercial hip-hop performance.

* * *

About the emergence of the rock "underground" in the 1970s, which accompanied the rise of punk, philosopher Bernard Gendron has observed: "The reigning assumption in rock writing of the late 1960s . . . was that the underground was a temporary way station for innovative musical movements toward mainstream success. This view shifted in the early 1970s . . . The idea of a permanent underground began slowly to seep in."[183] A parallel transition occurred in hip-hop during the 1990s, evinced in the push to create spaces such as the Good Life and its companions. Yet in hip-hop, as in rock, the dividing line between underground and mainstream was never as absolute as the partisans of the former would have wished. The Lyricist Lounge in particular served as a way station for many up-and-coming rap stars even as it also provided a venue for others to take the mic who may otherwise not have had a chance. Even the Freestyle Fellowship found its way to a record deal.

These tensions between different ideas and functions of the underground led critic Will Ashon to observe that the underground's standing as a sphere where hip-hop "authenticity" was preserved ran up against two fundamental problems: there were many different formulations of authenticity in circulation; and more pointedly, "everyone wants authenticity" whether they identified with the underground or not, "so authenticity becomes a marketing tool."[184] Ashon worried that "underground hip-hop" had become just another stylistic category, marked by its departure from the prevalent rap-meets-R&B sound that had come to dominate the genre commercially. Looking at the trajectory of specific artists, or the fluid relationship that existed between independent and major record labels, this was a legitimate concern and one that was hardly limited to hip-hop but that characterized all avenues of "independent" culture as it existed at the time. Concentrating on performance venues like the Good Life Café or Washington, DC's Kaffa House gives us another vantage point, however, where something more like the permanent underground alluded to by Gendron could take root. Even if the venues in question are themselves transient, for as long as they last, they provide a sort of refuge from the market imperatives of late capitalism, where the sheer fact of performance is what matters.

Like jazz and rock before it, "real" hip-hop does not only dwell in one kind of space or inhere in one kind of performance. Jay-Z, among the most corporate-minded of rappers, celebrates the cipher—a street version of the freestyle open mics fostered by the Lyricist Lounge and the Good Life Café—as the founding space of hip-hop creativity.[185] He also valorizes the kinds of large-scale concert tours that have been a part of his career since 1997 as an expression of the artist's work ethic, a means to legitimate and authenticate the cash flow. In a section of *Decoded* subtitled "I work goddamn hard," Jay-Z offers the following insights about touring:

> Tours are the most lucrative aspect of a recording artist's career . . . [They] can also be stressful beyond belief. Every night you're in a different city, every crowd brings a different vibe, every show is subtly different . . . It becomes less about your innate charisma and talent . . . and more about being able to meet the mental and physical challenge of it. A tour requires stamina, willpower, and the ability to self-motivate, to hype yourself into game mode night after night.[186]

In light of the acquisitive materialism that came to dominate so much of commercial hip-hop during the 1990s, the arena tour could rightly be seen as the truest expression of the era's values in the live performance realm. That it remained to a significant degree off limits, or at least hard to break into, for so many artists during the period when rap's commercial success escalated dramatically was a sign of how the live music industry operated according to its own more exclusionary rules relative to the recording sector, handed down from long-standing patterns of segregation and reconstituted during the time of arena rock's ascendancy. From Run-DMC to Public Enemy to Ice-T to Jay-Z, the most successful touring rap artists have used the restrictiveness of the arena and festival concert economy to their advantage, highlighting the singularity of their presence and finding creative ways to work around the presiding system. In this, they exemplify the pointed dictum offered by media scholar S. Craig Watkins: "how capitalism has become black youth's"—and black America's more generally—"greatest friend and greatest foe."[187]

10
Conclusion
A Homecoming

Beyoncé was scheduled to headline the Coachella Valley Music and Arts Festival in 2017, but an unplanned pregnancy prevented her from appearing. Paul Tollett, the festival's principal producer and co-founder, quickly enlisted a more than suitable replacement in Lady Gaga, who became only the second woman to headline one of the festival's days—the other being Björk. When Beyoncé performed in 2018, she became the third, as well as the first African American woman to assume the headlining slot. Her elaborately staged show played upon this fact from multiple angles. She juxtaposed a wide cross-section of music from throughout her two-decade career with snippets and excerpts of songs from other artists, creating a sort of continuum of black musical creativity. On stage with her was a large cast of musicians and dancers, appearing on a set shaped like a pyramid to evoke an Afrocentric view of history and culture, but also styled as a set of bleachers akin to those used in a college sports stadium. As Beyoncé explained in the film that she produced of her Coachella performance, after spending a year giving birth and getting used to her new life as the mother of infant twins along with her six-year-old daughter, Blue Ivy, her return to the stage was a sort of homecoming.[1] But not just any homecoming: Beyoncé designed the show to have the air of a homecoming at a Historically Black College or University (HBCU), importing a set of cultural practices typically reserved for African American eyes and ears into the predominantly white cultural space of Coachella.

About a third of the way through Beyoncé's set, after her performance of the track "Flawless" from her self-titled 2013 album, the voice of top hip-hop producer DJ Khaled announces to the audience, "Check this out. After Beyoncé perform, after she done the decks, Coachella gotta rename Coachella to Beychella. New name alert: Beychella!" The name Beychella was Beyoncé's way of laying claim to the festival through her performance as if to say, Coachella is not allowing me to be its guest, rather I am allowing it to be my host. This bravado comes through again, tempered with a touch of humility, at a later point in the show when she stands at the top of the pyramid-shaped stage centerpiece and says, "Coachella, thank you for allowing me to be the first black woman to headline Coachella." These moments heighten the sense of occasion, producing the feeling that Beyoncé's sheer presence at the festival was an instance of history in the making. That the "Beychella" tag got picked up by media outlets around the US and the globe indicated Beyoncé's ability to control the narrative surrounding her performance and at least temporarily, insinuate her own personal brand onto the identity of the festival. Conversely, though, the gesture works because Coachella was by that point the most recognizable brand in the world of twenty-first-century festival production. When Beyoncé addresses "Coachella" and offers thanks for allowing her to be the first black female headliner, she appears to be speaking to the audience, but she also reinforces how much the festival has assumed an identity that encompasses and supersedes its participants, audience, and performers alike.

In this concluding chapter, I use Beyoncé's 2018 performance at Coachella as a medium to reflect on some of the ways in which live music has evolved in the twenty-first century. That her appearance caused such a stir shows the persistent power of musical stardom and celebrity, much as it was during the time of Jenny Lind. The terms of Beyoncé's breakthrough also represent the continued limits that have been faced by African American artists and other artists of color, and especially by women of color. Her now-husband Jay-Z celebrated his ability to perform at Madison Square Garden at a time when the venue had been largely closed to African American hip-hop artists, but he did so implicitly. Beyoncé much more loudly highlights and commemorates her achievement as the first black woman to headline Coachella to draw attention to the fact that such events have followed the pattern long entrenched in the live music industry, wherein black artists are too often assigned a marginal or secondary place.

Beyoncé's performance further commanded attention because festivals have become so central to US musical life and the music economy in the twenty-first century. This conclusion continues the consideration of the festival revival explored in the last chapter with the discussion of 1990s music festivals such as Lollapalooza and Smokin' Grooves. Coachella is one of a proliferating number of such events that grew in the past two decades, nearly all of which abandoned the touring festival model of the 1990s for the single location, multi-day, multi-act festival concept that had prevailed from the 1950s through the 1980s. Bonnaroo, Austin City Limits, Outside Lands,

Electric Daisy Carnival, Stagecoach—these are just some of the festivals that have reshaped the US concert industry, building a festival season that lasts throughout the warm weather months of the year and parallels the long-standing prevalence of rock, pop, and dance music festivals in Europe. Collectively these events typify the continuing power of the live music experience in an era when much of our daily lives has become filtered through our interaction with screens and online content of various sorts. And yet, as I alluded to in this book's introduction, there is no absolute line to be drawn between liveness and other modes of mediation. Contemporary festivals are very much multimedia events in their own right and Beyoncé's Coachella performance is emblematic of that tendency.

Behind the rise of music festivals designed on the model of Coachella and the magnified visibility they confer upon superstar artists like Beyoncé is a larger transformation in the organization of the live music industry. That transformation began in the late 1990s when a company called SFX began buying out several of the major regional popular music concert promoters who had dominated the industry since the late 1960s, the figures who built the network that allowed arena and stadium rock to grow and flourish, as was discussed in Chapter 8. The move toward consolidation in the live music industry continued and intensified in the 2000s, when SFX was bought out by the radio and communications mega-corporation Clear Channel, which soon thereafter spun off its live music division into a separate company called Live Nation Entertainment. Further developments solidified the expansionist tendencies of the era: the creation of Live Nation's principal competitor in the realm of concert promotion, AEG Live; and the merger between Live Nation and Ticketmaster, the largest concert ticket seller in the US and global market, which was finalized in 2010. These changes happened against the backdrop of a recorded music economy that was in rapid decline due to the widespread exchange of music on the Internet, which allowed live music to assume a level of predominance in the music industry writ large that it had not enjoyed for half a century.

The festival revival has been both a stimulus to the concert industry's revamped economy of scale and an outgrowth of it. Many of the largest and most successful festivals in the US are owned by either Live Nation Entertainment or AEG Live. Coachella is owned by the latter but did not begin that way. The story of Coachella's evolution from an independent festival produced by a regionally based promoter to a signpost of the new live music economy can be taken as an allegory for the ways that live music has evolved in the age of consolidation. And that story begins with Goldenvoice, a Southern California concert promotion company with roots in the punk and alternative music scene of Los Angeles and its environs.

* * *

Asked about his new year's resolution for 1984, Gary Tovar replied, "To have safer shows."[2] At the time, Tovar had been promoting shows under the Goldenvoice banner for just over two years, starting with a December 1981 show at La Casa de la Raza in Santa Barbara that was headlined by Orange County punk band T.S.O.L.[3] The Southern California punk scene had been known for some years already for its out-of-control shows, having given rise to slam dancing, the physically intense style of crowd interaction in which participants deliberately "slam" their bodies into one another. Enhancing the scene's aggression were the tactics of the police departments in Los Angeles, Orange County, and surrounding areas, which targeted punk shows for their perceived threat to public order, forcibly stopping shows and often driving key venues out of business.[4] By the early 1980s the scene was highly combustible. Tovar embraced the risk involved in promoting punk shows in the region. From the start, his goal was to promote punk shows on a larger scale than had been feasible or sustainable up to that time in Southern California. Several of his early shows ended in confrontations between fans and the police, but Tovar operated on the assumption that a bigger venue would actually afford more safety than the smaller spaces where punk shows were typically housed. He explained to the *Los Angeles Times* in 1984: "I refuse to use small places anymore where a lot of kids are standing around outside because they can't get in. I'd rather use an oversize venue so there won't be any more incidents like the Exploited show," a concert he promoted in Huntington Beach in 1983 that ended in a near riot.[5]

Tovar's efforts drew the attention of *Billboard* in February 1983, which wrote, "Over the past 18 months, such groups as Black Flag, the Exploited, Angelic Upstarts, Dead Kennedys, T.S.O.L., Anti-Pasti, Circle Jerks, U.K. Subs and Fear have performed concerts in California in front of crowds ranging in size from 500 to 3,000." Interviewed for the piece, Tovar described the challenge of finding suitable venues given the violent reputation punk shows had acquired: "A lot of dance places are in a slump, so they are willing to take a chance. I've had to have concerts everywhere from Mexican restaurants to Ukrainian halls."[6] The shows that really solidified his reputation, though, were held at the Olympic Auditorium, a large-capacity venue in downtown

Los Angeles. The Olympic had enough space that Tovar could sell four thousand tickets and avoid a crush at the door or outside the hall. It also allowed him to import artists from overseas such as pioneering British punk and post-punk artists the Damned and Siouxsie and the Banshees, whose appeal would have been too big for a small club. Tovar's shows at the Olympic helped him pursue an adventurous booking policy in which the best of the local scene was showcased along with performers that had a larger international profile. Figure 10.1 depicts an ad for a typical Goldenvoice bill at the venue. Meanwhile, its location in downtown L.A. allowed Tovar to draw people from disparate points of the region, as he recalled: "[The Olympic] was centrally located—east, west, north, south, all gathered in the middle."[7] Although he stopped using the Olympic in 1985, Tovar continued to book shows of comparable size at venues such as the Hollywood Palladium and the Santa Monica Civic Auditorium. Over time, the scale of these shows

Figure 10.1 Advertisement for a Goldenvoice show at the Olympic Auditorium headlined by Southern California hardcore band Suicidal Tendencies, also featuring British punk band One Way System, and two more California groups, the Vandals and Pariah. Goldenvoice's shows at the Olympic demonstrated a market for live punk much larger than other promoters had found or were willing to risk presenting. From the *L.A. Weekly* (October 18, 1984).

contributed to a growing recognition that punk and its offshoots were not limited in their appeal to a small clutch of diehard fans.

Goldenvoice focused its efforts on punk and other strains of alternative or independent rock and pop, but the company was not entirely single-minded. As the 1980s proceeded, Tovar also promoted the occasional hip-hop show in the Los Angeles area. This too was stepping into controversial territory, for rap music like punk had earned a reputation for violent and disorderly shows, as we saw in Chapter 9. A year after the infamous 1986 Run-D.M.C. concert at the Long Beach Arena that ended in disarray, Tovar co-promoted a concert featuring New York hip-hop group U.T.F.O. at the Hollywood Palladium that was plagued by reports of violence. The following year, Goldenvoice promoted a creative, multi-genre bill that featured hip-hop groups Public Enemy and Stetsasonic alongside the rock bands Living Colour and Fishbone at the Santa Monica Civic Auditorium. That show, too, was marred by altercations, reportedly instigated by gang members in attendance, but also drew notice for the relative diversity of the audience: "all sorts appeared to be on hand—from white collegiate types to heavy metal fans to colors-wearing homeboys."[8] Tovar, characteristically, asserted that the violence at rap concerts was blown out of proportion by media, and attributed the exaggeration to racism: "People don't want to deal with blacks, and every stereotype you can think of comes into people's minds." He even drew a parallel to his work promoting punk shows: "There's still that scare factor."[9]

Pushing boundaries as he did, Tovar helped to lay the groundwork for the coalition of alternative music artists and fans that came together in the Lollapalooza festivals of the next decade. Indeed, Goldenvoice worked closely throughout the 1980s with key bands who would figure significantly in the popularization of Lollapalooza, most notably Jane's Addiction and the Red Hot Chili Peppers, which headlined the first two years of the touring festival. Throughout the 1990s, Goldenvoice served as the Southern California promoter of Lollapalooza. Yet Tovar himself ran into trouble just as that next wave of activity was getting underway. In March 1991, he was arrested for his involvement in a large marijuana dealing enterprise, through which Tovar would arrange for the purchase of quantities of the drug in Arizona and distribute it in California and other areas.[10] As he later explained, the money he earned from marijuana trafficking allowed Tovar to keep Goldenvoice running, since the concert business itself tended to run at a loss.[11] Imprisoned upon his arrest, Tovar would ultimately serve seven years in prison. Meanwhile, he turned over control of Goldenvoice to two associates who had been working for him since the mid-1980s, Paul Tollett and Rick Van Santen, pictured in Figure 10.2. Eight years later, that duo would go on to create the Coachella Valley Music and Arts festival.

* * *

A key moment in the origin story of Coachella happened just two years after Tollett and Van Santen took over, in November 1993. Pearl Jam was coming to Southern California and wanted a venue that would allow them to avoid having the tickets handled by Ticketmaster. The band's conflict with the ticketing mega-corporation—which led to widely-publicized congressional hearings in 1995—had been fueled by a recent episode in its hometown of Seattle where Pearl Jam wanted to perform a free show. Required to distribute tickets by the city of Seattle for security reasons, the band turned to Ticketmaster, but then became upset the with company when it insisted on charging a $1.50 service charge for an otherwise free event.[12] Ultimately, Pearl Jam handled the tickets for the free concert without Ticketmaster, and then grew determined to avoid reliance on the company for its future performances. Seeking an alternate venue for the band's Southern

Figure 10.2 Coachella co-founders Rick Van Santen (left) and Paul Tollett photographed at the Empire Polo Grounds, 2003. Photograph by Myung Chun. Courtesy of *Los Angeles Times*/Getty Images.

California appearance, Goldenvoice settled on the Empire Polo Club in Indio, California. An exclusive polo club started in 1987, the setting was in some ways a risky choice for Goldenvoice, largely untested as a concert venue and more than a two-hour drive from the urban and suburban population centers of Los Angeles and Orange County. Yet the concert sold out, with a capacity of twenty-five thousand—the majority coming from outside Indio and its immediate surroundings—and with no major incidents, Empire owner Alexander Haagen III and the city of Indio were willing to consider other, similar events in the future.[13]

With the Empire Polo Club grounds proven to be a successful outdoor venue, the idea for a Goldenvoice-produced festival gestated slowly over the rest of the decade. As with Lollapalooza founders Perry Farrell and Marc Geiger, Tollett and Van Santen drew significant inspiration from the festival scene in Europe and especially the U.K., where the Glastonbury festival provided a compelling model. In 1997, Tollett even prepared a pamphlet extolling the potential virtues of the Empire Polo Grounds as a festival site and distributed it to artists and managers at Glastonbury.[14] Also influential was the burgeoning rave and electronic dance music scene in Southern California during the 1990s, out of which another of the era's major festivals emerged, the Electric Daisy Carnival. Although Tollett and Van Santen cut their teeth in the punk and alternative scene, Tollett had followed the rise of electronic dance music closely and collaborated with many of its key promoters, including EDC founder Pasquale Rotella. Consequently, when Coachella got off the ground, according to dance music historian Michaelangelo Matos, it "was more attuned to electronic dance music than any other rock festival."[15]

Further stimulus for Goldenvoice to establish a festival came from the changing financial landscape of concert promotion in the late 1990s. Goldenvoice was unquestionably one of the dominant Southern California promoters during this era, arguably second only to Avalon Attractions, with whom they routinely co-promoted shows. Independent regional promoters such as Goldenvoice faced increased competition, however, from larger companies that were being built through buyouts and consolidation on a national scale. The biggest moves were being made by SFX, a corporation owned by Robert F.X. Sillerman that began as a radio company and then expanded into live music promotion. In 1996, Sillerman purchased Delsener-Slater Enterprises, the dominant New York City promoter, on the assumption that radio and live music promotion had obvious synergies between them. The following March, SFX purchased Sunshine Productions, based in Indianapolis but with a reach into several neighboring states. As 1997 proceeded, Sillerman sold the broadcasting wing of his company and spun off the concert promotion wing into a separate corporation called SFX Entertainment.[16] That new entity then went on a further buying spree. By December of that year, SFX owned Bill Graham Presents, the company founded by the legendary Bay Area promoter; Concert/Southern Promotions, founded by Atlanta promoter Alex Cooley; the Contemporary Group, based in St. Louis; and Pace Entertainment, which covered Texas, New Orleans, and other parts of the Southeast.[17] This suite of deals intensified and formalized the impulse toward nationalization of the concert promotion industry displayed by the likes of Concerts West in the 1970s. As *Pollstar* observed in its business summary of 1997, "What had once been a business of small locally-based entrepreneurs is rapidly becoming a business dominated by large publicly traded corporations."[18]

One effect of industry consolidation for independent companies like Goldenvoice was that it drove up the guaranteed fees that top artists expected for their concert appearances. SFX influenced the national concert market by inflating the fees that it paid to artists, seeking to maximize its market share even if it meant cutting into the profits. Goldenvoice could not afford to keep up with its more highly capitalized competitors, something that Tollett explained in a 2003 interview: "We were getting our ass kicked financially. We were losing a lot of bands. And we couldn't compete with the money."[19] In the face of these increasing financial pressures, Tollett and Van Santen saw the mounting of a music festival as a way to carve out a new niche for Goldenvoice. For SFX and other larger competitors such as House of Blues, which had also recently expanded its imprint, festivals made little sense because they owned many of the venues where they promoted shows. In Tollett's words, a big festival "would take acts out of the amphitheaters they own."[20] Festivals therefore represented a fairly wide-open opportunity that Goldenvoice determined to pursue.

* * *

On July 12, 1999, the first public indication of the coming Coachella Valley Music and Arts Festival appeared in the *Desert Sun*, the daily newspaper of Palm Springs and its surrounding area, which includes Indio. "Polo Club Requesting Permit for Fall Music Fest," read the headline, while the accompanying article offered only scant details about the planned event except that it would be produced by Goldenvoice.[21] Five days later, more details emerged, including the news that the Indio City Council had approved the planned festival and pledged $90,000 to support traffic control and public safety.[22] The dates were set for October 9 and 10, and Beck was teased as a featured artist in what was otherwise described as an alternative music festival.

By the end of July, news of the festival hit the *Los Angeles Times*, which referred to the event as a possible "Woodstock West," evoking the recent Woodstock '99 festival commemorating the thirtieth anniversary of the original Woodstock.[23] Woodstock '99, held July 23–25 at the decommissioned Griffiss Air Force Base in Rome, New York, was the biggest US music festival in recent memory, and its gross of more than $28 million made it by far the highest grossing single live music event in North American history until that point.[24] Yet the festival was generally considered to be an exercise in bad planning. Water shortages and physically uncomfortable surroundings contributed to a restless atmosphere that led to violent outbursts by the crowd and widespread reports of sexual harassment and assault directed at female audience members. Woodstock '99 ensured that the Coachella festival would be subjected to heightened public scrutiny, and Goldenvoice responded with a festival design that included "extra toilets, creating more shade, bringing in benches and tables for eating areas, stepping up cleaning crews and trash collection, and keeping the crowd at well below capacity."[25] While Woodstock had a paid attendance of more than 200,000, Goldenvoice limited the number of tickets they sold for the first Coachella festival to 35,000 per day, even though the Empire Polo Grounds had the room to accommodate twice that many.

When the *Los Angeles Times* headlined its review of the Coachella debut, "Triumph of the Anti-Woodstock," it may have been hype, but it also suggested that Goldenvoice had succeeded in producing a model of American rock festival that diverged from the norm.[26] Festival goers found five performance areas: one main stage, a second smaller outdoor theater, one larger covered tent area, and two smaller tents. The main stage and outdoor theater were largely the province of the performers that fell under the "rock" category such as Beck, Perry Farrell, Morrissey, Spiritualized, Medeski, Martin, and Wood, and At the Drive in on day one; and Rage Against the Machine, Tool, Ben Harper, Pavement, and Cibo Matto on day two. Even on these main stages, the more rock-oriented artists were juxtaposed with shorter DJ sets, and several major electronic music artists such as Chemical Brothers, DJ Shadow, and Moby appeared in full-length sets. Meanwhile, the tents were almost entirely the province of electronic music artists, featuring a wide range of high-profile and up-and-coming artists including Detroit techno pioneers Carl Craig and Richie Hawtin, Bay Area scratch virtuosi DJ Q-Bert and Mixmaster Mike, and Washington, DC-based Thievery Corporation.[27] The distribution of the audience across the various stages adapted the multi-stage model of folk and jazz festivals to the rock festival to a degree hitherto untested, and the relative intimacy of the smaller tent areas offered an atmosphere quite removed from more conventionally staged mass music festivals. Meanwhile, the intermixing of guitar-based rock and electronic beats achieved something closer to parity than earlier efforts such as the final 1997 installment of Lollapalooza, which had pursued something similar. Perry Farrell himself observed, "Musically, this is taking a leap ... [Lollapalooza] was rock bands, guitars, but this also has the deejay culture ... electronic and organic together, and it's wonderful."[28]

Coachella did not draw widespread notice in its first year, but the reviews that appeared were full of praise. Writing for *Rolling Stone*, Mark Healy invoked the tagline offered by the *Los Angeles Times*: "Coachella made space, comfort and collective cool a priority; booked acts based on artistry rather than radio play; and not only succeeded in starting a viable new American tradition but also earned the title 'the anti-Woodstock.'"[29] For Healy and *L.A. Times* pop critic Robert Hilburn alike, a true test of the singularity of the atmosphere at Coachella came with Rage Against the Machine's Sunday night set. RATM had also appeared at Woodstock '99, where the band's fiery approach—a hard-driving rap-metal hybrid with outspoken left-progressive lyrics—appeared to dovetail with that event's most unruly tendencies. Apprehension surrounded the band's Coachella performance, and a representative of the festival even came out prior to the band's set to encourage the audience to remain peaceful. Hilburn described a particular moment of heightened intensity during the new RATM song, "Guerilla Radio," where vocalist Zach de la Rocha screamed his closing lines in a way that sounded like a call to arms: "It was an electrifying moment, but it also brought a tension to the festival grounds ... As thousands of bodies swirled and jerked on the lawn with startling force, you wondered whether somehow it wasn't going to get out of hand, a la Woodstock 99."[30] This forceful reaction never got out of hand, though, and the crowd's energy remained contained through the remainder of the band's set. Healy observed that "the crowd was too cooked ... to kick up more than the usual dust for the charged, channeled fury of Rage"—referencing the fact that temperatures had been over one-hundred degrees throughout both days of the festival.[31] Less cynically, he also offered the hope that Coachella would start a "new festival tradition."

Professional recognition came from *Pollstar*, which chose Coachella as the Music Festival of the Year for 1999, while also selecting Goldenvoice as its Independent Promoter of the Year and Paul Tollett as recipient of the Bill Graham Award for Promoter of the Year. In its write-up of the award for the festival, *Pollstar* cited Coachella as "evidence that ingenuity still plays a vital role in live music," and continued: "Coachella was modeled after European festivals that meld a variety of music styles and create a unique, communal experience in the process. DJs and electronica ruled the daytime from three huge dance tents, while the nights rocked with passion and innovation rather than commercialism."[32] By these measures, Coachella demonstrated that an independent promoter could succeed in the midst of industry consolidation.

The festival also offered a cautionary tale. The limit of 35,000 attendees per day proved to be overly optimistic. Day one of the festival barely drew half that number. While day two attracted a larger audience, the turnout was not sufficient to allow Goldenvoice to break even, let alone turn a profit. In the end, Tollett recalled later, the company lost "between eight hundred and fifty thousand and a million." He attributed the loss to various factors: the overwhelming heat, the unfortunate coincidence of Woodstock '99 with the time when tickets for Coachella went on sale, and the fact that they only announced the festival two months before it was scheduled, not nearly enough lead time for an event of that size.[33] The losses were a huge setback for Goldenvoice and jeopardized any chance that there would be a second Coachella festival. However, Tollett and his Goldenvoice associates—Van Santen, Moss Jacobs, and Lauren Matsui—used the years of goodwill they had built to dig themselves out of the financial hole left by Coachella. Working closely with artists and their agents, they got several key performers to accept deferred payment or even a reduced fee to help the company remain solvent. As Tom Morello of Rage Against the Machine remembered, "At the end of the weekend, they asked us to give half the money back. And we did."[34]

There would be a second Coachella, but the losses incurred in 1999 led the next installment of the festival to be pushed back to April 2001. In the extended gap between the first Coachella and the second, another corporate partner entered the picture. AEG, or the Anschutz Entertainment Group, grew out of Denver businessman Philip Anschutz's partial or majority ownership of several sports teams including two major Los Angeles organizations, the Lakers and the Kings; and arena complexes that included the Los

Angeles Forum and the Staples Center. In the late 1990s, the company began to take a larger interest in live music promotion as a way to control more of the entertainment that could be featured in the arenas under its ownership. AEG expanded its concert promotion footprint in December 2000 with the acquisition of Concerts West, a company that had been spun off from the original organization headed by Jerry Weintraub after it was purchased by SFX.[35] Three months later, in March 2001, AEG acquired Goldenvoice, merging it with Concerts West while retaining Tollett and Van Santen as co-presidents.[36]

With Concerts West and Goldenvoice in tow, AEG was newly competitive with the two largest promoters of the era, SFX and House of Blues, pushing the trend of industry consolidation further forward. Goldenvoice, in turn, relinquished its standing as one of the strongest independent promoters still standing, but Van Santen and Tollett both insisted that the deal did not require them to forsake control of their daily operations. Interviewed at the time, Van Santen emphasized that AEG was "letting us do exactly what we want to do and what we've been doing," but gave "more juice" to Goldenvoice's projects.[37] Tollett made the same point years later while adding that the experience of assuming control of Goldenvoice upon Gary Tovar's arrest had been a hardship: "When Rick [Van Santen] and I took over, it was hard. We never ran businesses, and I didn't enjoy that end of it. I wanted to promote concerts."[38]

At first Coachella was not included in the deal. Tollett and Van Santen retained separate ownership of the festival until Van Santen's sudden death at the age of forty-one due to complications from the flu in late 2003. Shortly thereafter, AEG bought into Coachella but left Tollett with a controlling interest.[39] Even prior to that point, the new infusion of resources provided by AEG enabled Tollett to allow the festival to grow slowly without fear that the bottom would fall out. Not until 2004 would the festival turn a profit when advance sale tickets sold out for the first time on the strength of a lineup headed by Radiohead and veteran indie rock artists the Cure and the Pixies.[40] By comparison, the Bonnaroo festival sold 60,000 tickets for its June 2002 debut before it even had a chance to issue advertisements in traditional media or make tickets available through Ticketmaster.[41] Begun through the collaboration of independent promoters Ashley Capps and Jonathan Mayers, the new festival's success capitalized on the value of the Internet as a direct marketing tool and the strength of the jam band fan community on which Bonnaroo drew. Financially speaking, Bonnaroo dominated the US festival scene for the next five years, with its grosses from 2003 forward routinely placing in the *Pollstar* list of top forty all-time highest-grossing concerts in North America. Coachella would not achieve the same distinction until 2006, when it reported gross earnings of over $10 million for the first time.[42]

More broadly, 2006 was something of a tipping point in the growth of festivals as more than a marginal aspect of the overall US live music business. Two other major festivals had by then arisen with comparable visibility to Coachella and Bonnaroo: Austin City Limits and the re-booted Lollapalooza. All four festivals used the model of the "destination" festival that was pioneered by Newport Jazz and Folk, which Coachella had popularized for the new century and Bonnaroo had consolidated, drawing attendees from across the US and even internationally. None of them used purpose-built venues, with Coachella's Empire Polo Grounds finding its analogue in the public parks that housed Lollapalooza (Chicago's Grant Park) and Austin City Limits (Austin's Zilker Park), or in the case of Bonnaroo, a large area of farmland in Manchester, Tennessee. In 2006, all four festivals appeared among the top 20 highest grossing concert events of the year as reported by *Pollstar*, with a combined gross of well over $40 million.[43] As they did so, they marked a rising trend wherein festivals appeared to be supplanting the outdoor amphitheaters that had dominated the US summer concert season for two decades. When factoring in the already established but still expanding European festival scene, bands could now organize a whole summer of touring around festivals in a manner that would not have been feasible even five years earlier.[44] Washington, DC promoter Seth Hurwitz said of this changing concert landscape: "The festival circuit is the new amphitheater circuit ... The big, big acts have somewhere to play besides amphitheaters that is not as challenging as a stadium."[45]

This new wave of festival activity in the twenty-first century derived from the earlier wave that thrived from the 1950s through the 1970s, but also reflected the changing circumstances of the live music industry. US festivals from Newport Jazz to Monterey Pop to the New Orleans Jazz and Heritage Festival in its early years were defined by a running tension between commercial imperatives and a drive to embody some sense of commitment to a larger social good. In the case of the Newport Jazz and Folk festivals, this latter impulse was embodied in the nonprofit character of both festivals at their time of creation as they sought to promote the art and culture attached to the music they featured. Rock festivals defined the social good more through the amorphous values of the counterculture and an abiding sense that festival time was, at least ideally, removed from the rhythms and patterns of ordinary daily life. Coachella, Bonnaroo, and the other festivals that have dominated the past two decades retain some sense of this countercultural orientation, that a festival can and should be a break from the ordinary. They are also, however, more squarely commercial enterprises than their predecessors were allowed to be.

I do not mean to romanticize festivals of the more distant past, which had their own contradictions and fault lines, as I discussed in Chapter 7. Nonetheless, it is important to acknowledge the very different context that gave rise to the mass festivals of the twenty-first century. Rock and pop music festivals were revitalized as a solution to the problem of how to remain competitive in a live music industry within which consolidation was making it harder to operate independently. Once the festival model became established as a viable commercial enterprise through the success of Coachella and its successors, it was quickly absorbed into the industry as a regular feature of the annual concert season, and the major promoters for whom festivals at first did not make good economic sense bought into the phenomenon and made it their own.

As of April 2020, Live Nation Entertainment—the corporation created first from the ashes of SFX after its sale to Clear Channel in 2000, and then through the merger between Live Nation and Ticketmaster that was finalized in 2010—had ownership of more than one-hundred different festivals in the US and globally. These included Austin City Limits, Bonnaroo, and Lollapalooza, as well as the various Electric Daisy Carnival events.[46] Principal competitor AEG Live owned more than twenty festivals, including Coachella, the Goldenvoice-produced Stagecoach country music festival that also occurs at the Empire Polo Grounds, and the New Orleans Jazz and Heritage Festival, which it began to co-produce in 2004.[47] Another Goldenvoice/AEG Live event, 2016's Desert Trip—often called "Oldchella" because of its lineup featuring rock music veterans Bob Dylan, Paul McCartney, the Rolling Stones, Roger Waters, the Who, and Neil Young—is now the highest grossing single live music event ever staged, earning over $160 million.[48] And as festivals have become part of the new normal of live music promotion, Coachella's reach and influence have only grown stronger. In 2017, the year before Beyoncé's performance at the festival, Coachella reported gross earnings of more than $114 million over its two weekends, more than ten times what it had earned in 2006. The next highest-grossing festival of the year—San Francisco's Outside Lands—earned barely a quarter of that amount, at nearly $28 million.[49] Retaining some of the "alternative" aura that defined it at its inception, Coachella has grown to encompass an older generation of arena rock performers as well as chart-topping pop acts. To headline Coachella is like a coronation, placing an artist at a certain pinnacle of notoriety.

* * *

Beyoncé did not necessarily need a boost to her notoriety when she was booked to headline Coachella. She had already performed at not one, but two Super Bowl halftime shows, and was a *zeitgeist* performer on a scale that at least matched, if not exceeded that of her husband, Jay-Z.

Crucially, Beyoncé had also become a major touring artist by the time of her 2018 Coachella performance. Her rise in this regard began at the end of the previous decade. Throughout the 2000s, the barriers that had inhibited the success of African American artists in the live music sphere remained very much in place, with only a small handful of black performers able to break through from year to year. In 2008, two hip-hop tours—by Kanye West and Jay-Z partnering with R&B singer Mary J. Blige—ranked in the top thirty North American tours of the year according to *Pollstar*, an unusually strong showing.[50] The next year, 2009, Beyoncé broke through with her *I Am . . .* tour, in support of her 2008 album, *I Am . . . Sasha Fierce*, which grossed $26.4 million and placed number thirty-four on *Pollstar*'s year-end list for North American tours. Even more impressive was her ranking on the chart for Worldwide Concert Tours, where Beyoncé's tour grossed $86 million globally, placing her at number 12 and in the company of artists such as U2, AC/DC, Bruce Springsteen, and Madonna.[51] From that point forward, her concert tours routinely appeared in the upper echelon of top grossing tours throughout the 2010s, and her 2016 Formation tour in support of her album *Lemonade* ranked as the top-grossing North American concert tour of the year—making her the first black artist to top the list since Tina Turner in 2000.[52] At decade's end, she was the sixth highest-earning touring artist in the entire industry, with overall revenue of more than $857 million since 2010. The only other African American artist to join her in the top twenty was Jay-Z at number seventeen, with whom she had jointly toured twice, in 2014 and 2018.[53] For Beyoncé and Jay-Z, their success—individually and jointly—in the realm of concert touring has contributed to their visibility as icons of exceptional black achievement in the face of continued racial inequality.

That inequality extended to the realm of festival production, where the position of black artists remained much as it had been throughout the 1990s. From its inception, Coachella had made room for a small proportion of African American artists, typically distributed between its various genre strongholds: alternative and indie (Rage Against the Machine, Ben Harper, Zap Mama, TV on the Radio), techno and electronic dance music (Juan Atkins, Carl Craig, Derrick May, Tricky), and hip-hop (Jurassic 5, the Roots, Gangstarr, KRS-One, Black Star). Tellingly, the first hip-hop headliner at the festival, in 2003, was the Beastie Boys. In 2006, Kanye West was added to the main stage lineup so late that he did not appear on that year's poster. Prince became the first full-fledged black headliner at the festival in 2008. Two years later, in 2010, Jay-Z became Coachella's first black hip-hop headliner.[54] From that point forward, hip-hop artists have been regular headliners most years and have accounted for some of the most widely remembered performances at Coachella, prominent among them being the hologram "resurrection" of Tupac Shakur that was staged as part of the 2012 appearance of Dr. Dre and Snoop Dogg. Unsurprisingly, all of these headlining hip-hop slots in the 2010s have been filled by African American men. The cultural logic underpinning this trend remained largely unchanged from that which led Ice-T and Ice Cube to be the principal representatives of hip-hop at the first Lollapalooza festivals. Black masculinity retains significant commodity value in the pop music marketplace, and festivals like Coachella remain relatively "safe spaces" where African American hip-hop performers can appear before large crowds of young, predominantly white fans in a live music industry that is still scared of putting black artists in front of black audiences.

Female artists have featured less prominently at Coachella for most of its history, and black female artists especially. Gina Arnold points out that as recently as 2015—a year in which the three main headline acts for the festival were AC/DC, Jack White, and Drake—there were twenty-six female artists out of a total of one-hundred sixty, about 16 percent of the overall number.[55] Two years later, in 2017, that number had barely changed, according to data compiled by Rob Mitchum and Diego Garcia-Olano for *Pitchfork*. Of 150 artists at that year's festival, twenty-one were identified as female and another sixteen as mixed gender (including at least one woman or non-binary person), comprising just under 25 percent of the total performers booked. That proportion was consistent with the larger industry trend, which showed an average of 14 percent female artists and an additional 12 percent of mixed gender performers for twenty-three major festivals surveyed by Mitchum and Garcia-Olano.⁵⁶ A year later, in 2018, the overall picture showed incremental improvement, with the proportion of female artists at twenty major festivals rising to 19 percent, along with 11 percent mixed gender performers. Coachella demonstrated a larger increase, jumping to 34 percent of combined female and mixed gender performers, or fifty-seven out of the festival's total of 165. Of those artists, fifteen were black women or included black women.⁵⁷ Beyoncé's headline appearance placed her at the top of a very narrow field which, even at that, was improved from what it had been just a year earlier.⁵⁸

Eight years prior to her Coachella "homecoming," Beyoncé had a sort of debut at Coachella. In 2010, she joined Jay-Z on stage for the next to last song of his set, "Young Forever." Her presence was unannounced and was doubly surprising because the recorded version—the closing track on Jay-Z's 2009 album, *The Blueprint 3*, remaking a 1984 synth-pop hit by the group Alphaville—featured the vocals of white male British singer Mr. Hudson. Introducing Beyoncé, Jay-Z declares, "I'm not even going to say her name, I'm just going to let her speak for herself." Over a soft synthesizer bed, Beyoncé owns the first verse and chorus, Jay-Z only interrupting her in the lead-up to the chorus to impel the audience to sing along with her.⁵⁹ Jay-Z takes over for verse two, but Beyoncé sings each chorus, standing in for the song's sentimental celebration of eternal youth. At the conclusion, with Beyoncé taking her turn at an extended final chorus, fireworks shoot off from behind the stage into the desert sky. For *Rolling Stone* critic Jenny Eliscu, Beyoncé's appearance "felt like the biggest and best Coachella surprise imaginable."⁶⁰ More revealing was the response of *Hollywood Reporter* reviewer Darryl Morden, who observed, "while [Beyoncé's] music is as non-Coachella as it comes, it was hard to deny it was one cool festival moment."⁶¹ This line marks the evolution of Beyoncé and Coachella over the course of nearly a decade and the barriers that had to be overcome for her to be invited to headline the festival in her own right. In 2018, no longer just an unannounced surprise, Beyoncé had the license to make Coachella over—at least temporarily—into a space where a black female artist would not be made to feel outside.

* * *

"Ladies and gentlemen, welcome to Beyoncé Homecoming 2018." A male announcer's voice gets the crowd's attention, giving way to a black female drummer dressed in an elaborately designed majorette's outfit.⁶² The drummer starts to hit her drum with single taps, then double, and then accelerates rapidly, all the while staring fiercely into the camera that carries her sound and image to the two large video screens that are on either side of the main festival stage. On a catwalk-style platform that extends several yards away from the main stage into the audience, the majorette ends her drum roll and blows into a whistle that calls the rest of her line into action. Three men holding black fabric flags sweep to the side, each flag emblazoned with a single letter, "B-Δ-K," representing the letters of an imagined Greek organization comprised of Beyoncé and the members of her troupe. Behind the flag bearers stand a line of female dancers dressed in tight bodysuits imprinted with the visage of an Egyptian sphinx. They twirl to the left and right, leaving a path in the middle, at the end of which stands Beyoncé. At first, she has her back to the dancers, allowing the camera to focus in close-up on the elaborate jeweled cape that adorns her, imprinted with her image and the same three letters, B-Δ-K. After a pause, she turns and walks forward, wearing a Nefertiti-styled headdress and a jeweled bodysuit that matches the opulence of her cape. As she begins her march toward the stage, a brass band plays a swaggering riff from the song, "Do Watcha Wanna," by the esteemed Rebirth Brass Band of New Orleans. Once arrived at the stage, Beyoncé walks into the wings while her dancers do a routine in front of the giant pyramid-shaped stage set where the brass band and other troupe members are already perched. After another minute passes during which the dancers dance and the brass band swings, Beyoncé rises at the top of the pyramid like an apparition, re-costumed in a sorority sweatshirt, booty shorts, and tassled knee-high boots. She dances hard, then stops and gazes silently at the audience for a full minute as they chant her name, before asking, "Coachella, y'all ready?" If this is a homecoming, there is no doubt who the queen is.

During the first documentary interlude in the film that Beyoncé produced from her Coachella performance, *Homecoming*, the singer says of her experience: "I grew up in Houston, Texas, visiting Prairie View. We rehearsed at TSU for many years in the Third Ward, and I always dreamed of going to an HBCU. My college was Destiny's Child. My college was traveling around the world, and life was my teacher." Unapologetic about her life and career having moved her in a direction that did not include attending college, Beyoncé nonetheless represents the HBCU as an aspirational goal. In this, she joins a lineage that extends back to the feats of the Fisk Jubilee Singers, another group of African American performers who expanded the field of black cultural representation. As I discussed in Chapter 2, Fisk University was part of a wave of black colleges and universities founded in the aftermath of the Civil War, designed to provide educational opportunities for recently freed African Americans who were otherwise shut out from the vast majority of existing institutions of higher learning. Music was central to the mission of many of these schools from the time of their inception, as the example of the Jubilee Singers would attest. Beyoncé's decision to make HBCUs the focus of her Coachella performance paid tribute to this legacy and to the continued relevance of these schools as places that encourage black social, political, and artistic advancement.

For much of their history, HBCUs have embodied what scholars of African American life have called the ideology of racial uplift. There is more than a trace of the uplift ideology inherited from earlier generations of middle-class, upwardly mobile African Americans in Beyoncé's choice to use an HBCU homecoming event as the framework for her Coachella show. Characterized by historian Kevin Gaines, from the late nineteenth century into the first decades of the twentieth, "For many black elites, uplift came to mean an emphasis on self-help, racial solidarity, temperance, thrift, chastity, social purity, patriarchal authority, and the accumulation of wealth."[63] Beyoncé's feminism may make her an unlikely representative of patriarchal authority but many of these other values underlie the narratives that she has spun around her career, including her appearance at Coachella. As Ann Powers has observed, there is a touch of something conservative in Beyoncé's vision of black female self-empowerment,[64] not least in its embrace of wealth as a sign of achievement, audible even in what is considered her most politically radical song, "Formation," which concludes with the advice to the "ladies" addressed in the lyrics, "Always stay gracious, your best revenge is your paper."

At the same time, the HBCU represents a distinctly non-assimilationist image of racial uplift. These institutions have given rise to a unique black youth culture that has only intermittently become subject to wider representation. To bring the stepping routines and marching band styles common to HBCUs to the Coachella stage, Beyoncé relied upon a talent pool of dancers and musicians who had considerable experience working in that setting. Most of the musicians that accompanied Beyoncé were recruited by Don Roberts, a former high school band director who gained notoriety as the musical director for the 2002 film, *Drumline*, and created a touring professional black marching band largely comprised of HBCU alums, several of whose members performed at Coachella.[65] Another key contributor was choreographer Jamal Josef, a graduate of Voorhees College in South Carolina who took a lead role in teaching Beyoncé and her dancers the art of stepping.

A demonstrative and physically demanding dance style largely identified with African American fraternities and sororities, stepping is also a highly codified cultural form with strict guidelines for doing it right. Josef impressed upon Beyoncé that in bringing these moves before the largely white audience at Coachella, she would have to do earn the respect of the African American Greek community, explaining that if she messed up "they will rip you to shreds and come for blood."[66] For Josef and other members of Beyoncé's performance troupe such as trombonist Wayne Westley, a graduate of Florida A&M University, having their work featured at the festival marked a significant moment of validation for the culture associated with HBCUs. Said Westley, interviewed by National Public Radio, "I think it opened the eyes to a lot of individuals who may have not known what HBCUs are or what they're about and the culture they have . . . If we didn't have them, when they first started, we wouldn't be here because, you know, back in the day, those were the only colleges black people could attend because of segregation."[67]

Three songs into her Coachella performance, Beyoncé renders a shortened version of the first verse of "Lift Every Voice and Sing," a song that stands for the values embedded in HBCUs. Commonly referred to as the "black national anthem," the song was composed by brothers James Weldon Johnson and J. Rosamond Johnson in 1900, when both men worked at black educational institutions in and around Jacksonville, Florida. In her probing history of the song, interdisciplinary scholar Imani Perry connects "Lift Every Voice" to two distinguishing patterns of African American cultural life: associationalism and formalism. Associationalism refers to the impulse demonstrated by African Americans to create a wide range of social organizations that provided a sense of structure, connection, and community in the face of the violence and restrictiveness of life under Jim Crow segregation. Such associations—whether women's social clubs, Greek student organizations, or fraternal lodges—were largely the province of "race men" and women such as the Johnson brothers, who conducted much of their lives in the service of black people.[68] Through its popularity among members of these associations, "Lift Every Voice and Sing" gained status and became invested with representative importance as an emblem of African American experience. Black formalism, in turn, refers to "ritual practices with embedded norms, codes of conduct, and routine, dignified ways of doing and being."[69] According to Perry, this quality characterizes much of the cultural work of black organizations, and crucially, it "describes practices that were primarily internal to the black community, rather than those based upon a white gaze or an aspiration for white acceptance."[70] The rigor of black formalism sets it apart from folk culture but it is not, by Perry's account, a move toward "highbrow" respectability. Rather, it stands as a meeting ground for vernacular and classical tendencies, not unlike that found in the concert spirituals sung by the Fisk Jubilee Singers.

Echoes of black formalism are evident in the abbreviated version of "Lift Every Voice and Sing" that Beyoncé performed at Coachella. While the song is about to begin, the dancers and musicians shift position, several of them moving down from the bleachers onto the stage to form a human triangle that outlines the pyramidal shape of the set, at the center of which Beyoncé stands alone. In unison, the performers step hard and issue a shouted "Ah" that announces a sudden transition, made more dramatic by flames that issue from the side of the stage. The violin section of Beyoncé's accompanying orchestra, comprised entirely of black women, comes to the foreground more than at any other point in the show. They produce a quiet drone that provides the foundation for the song, punctuated intermittently by vigorous cascades of steps and further shouts of "Ah" by the whole aggregation. Beyonce's singing is precise and understated through much of the song, but she highlights certain words with dramatic use of melisma, most prominently at the end of the line, "Let our rejoicing rise," when she extends the note of the last word upward for several seconds while the violins swell accordingly alongside her, the effect followed by yet another instance of collective stepping and shouting. With that, she skips ahead to the last line of the song's opening verse, envisioning a moment in the future when "victory is won." The brief performance merges respectability and spectacle, the body and the spirit, a poignant evocation of the cultural past and a forceful gesture toward a hopeful future, the latter further signaled by the bouncing synthesized sound that announces the start of the next song, "Formation."

Not all parts of Beyoncé's Coachella performance adhered steadfastly to the aesthetics of black formalism and the HBCU setting. During a segment positioned roughly halfway through the nearly two-hour show, she spotlighted another facet of her style that has been integral to her mounting success as a live music artist: her incorporation of the sonic and visual signifiers of rock. Beyoncé moved in this direction in 2006 when she put out a call for musicians to audition for an all-female band to accompany her on the tour for her second solo album, *B'Day*. The resulting band was dubbed Suga Mama.[71] Headed by guitarist Bibi McGill, who served as musical director, the musicians of Suga Mama moved fluently between the styles of

R&B, funk, soul, pop, and rock, enabling Beyoncé to effectively represent the stylistic range of her recorded work on stage. Some version of Suga Mama remained in place until 2014, performing alongside Beyoncé on all her major tours throughout that period and conferring upon her live work a rock-inflected edginess that was not always so evident on her recordings. Although the musicians of Suga Mama sometimes accompanied Beyoncé in the studio, they were first and foremost a touring band. As such, they indicate that for Beyoncé, as for her hip-hop counterparts during the 1980s and early 1990s, rock instrumentation and aesthetics were a key element of her strategy to break through the barriers that kept black artists on the margins of the live music industry.

Suga Mama was no longer with Beyoncé by the time of her Coachella performance, but she assembled a new group of female musicians playing the standard rock and funk band instruments (electric guitar, bass, drums, keyboards) for her appearance. During most of the show they stand largely out of view on the wings of the stage, overshadowed by the drummers, horns, and string section that formed the core of Beyoncé's Coachella "orchestra." That changes when the ensemble moves into the song "Don't Hurt Yourself." One of the more lacerating bursts of anger featured on *Lemonade*, directed at Jay-Z for his infidelity, "Don't Hurt Yourself" is also the most "rock"-oriented song on the album, marked by a guest appearance by indie rock luminary Jack White on guitar. At Coachella, the song's beginning brings the violins to the foreground once again, but this time, out in front, stand the two guitarists and a bass player who belong to the "rock band" portion of the collective. The three lead the charge as the whole orchestra bursts into the song's pounding riff, and bang their heads demonstratively while Beyoncé spits out the song's opening line, "Who the fuck do you think I is?" When the whole orchestra interjects the main riff from the Led Zeppelin epic "Kashmir" after the chorus, the song's already high quotient of heaviness rises to a new peak. Making the gesture all the more powerful is the inclusion of the sampled voice of Malcolm X toward the song's end, immediately on the heels of the Led Zeppelin quotation, suggesting that for Beyoncé, rock is not a "white" form she invokes opportunistically but is integral to her own brand of blackness.

Reflecting on the overall impact and reception of Beyoncé's Coachella performance, I think back to the music critic Hermann Saroni's praise of Jenny Lind, following her New York debut: "Not the great artist alone do we worship, but the *true woman* ... Her mission is not alone to delight and enchant, but to bless and elevate."⁷² Beyoncé's womanhood is unquestionably celebrated throughout the show, and in the resulting documentary film of her performance. In *Homecoming*, we see multiple scenes of Beyoncé working hard to get in shape for the festival. The preparation required months of rehearsal that was more challenging for the fact that she had just given birth to twins, which left her dealing with enhanced motherly duties and a body that was transformed and unaccustomed to the demands of a two-hour, dance-intensive show. As she narrates the experience in *Homecoming*, the rigors of bodily discipline were inseparable from the psychological process of rediscovering the sense of self that allowed her to feel comfortable returning to the stage after so many months away. In one portion of the film she explains in voiceover that she was limiting her food intake to get her body into the shape she felt was necessary for the show: "no bread, no carbs, no sugar, no dairy, no meat, no fish, no alcohol. And, I'm hungry . . . It's not like before when I could rehearse, you know, 15 hours straight. I have children, I have a husband. I have to take care of my body." We see time pass, and the way her body adapts to the constant routine of choreography and supervision, to the point where, as the festival approaches, she proclaims with pride that she feels like a "new woman, in a new chapter of my life." The change is registered by the fact that after so many months of self-deprivation, she can fit into one of her old, form-fitting stage costumes.

Later in the film, her accomplishment appears in a different light when, in a playful scene, she stands beside her oldest daughter Blue Ivy, feeding her lines from "Lift Every Voice and Sing," which the girl then sings back to the camera with pride. Here Beyoncé's achievement is no longer just her own. She celebrates the strength of family ties and the continuity of cultural traditions—as well as the ability to mix those traditions with sounds and styles that are markedly contemporary and not narrowly defined according to a strict notion of black identity. In this vein, the struggle she undertook to prepare her Coachella performance can be understood as a response to the problem identified by scholar Maureen Mahon in her study of black rock artists: "the refusal, disinclination, and inability to deal with the breadth and complexity of contemporary African American people and culture."⁷³

Reviewing the performance, pop critic Spencer Kornhaber mused on how Beyoncé manipulated the mass choreography of the festival setting. Whereas pop stars like Madonna present themselves as sovereign figures who expect something like "fealty" from their audiences, claimed Kornhaber, Beyoncé manages to express something less hierarchical and more inclusive: "she channels the dynamism of mass movement to make statements that are, relentlessly, democratizing."[74] In this too, we hear echoes of the reception of Jenny Lind, whose crowds were taken to be a sign of some democratic impulse let loose by her combination of virtue, refinement, and charisma. Yet there is a key difference between the two that goes beyond the simple opposition of white and black. Lind, the nineteenth-century diva, never dramatized any clear sense of solidarity with a larger collective in the substance of what she did on the concert stage. Beyoncé, now a twenty-first-century diva, made that solidarity the centerpiece of her Coachella performance. It was there in the combined orchestra and dance troupe of more than one-hundred members, whom she stood among and not just in front of for much of the show, as seen in Figure 10.3. It was there in the line of female dancers that followed her as she implored, "Okay ladies, now let's get in formation." And, it underpinned the most celebrated of the guest appearances that governed the last segment of the show, her reunion with her former Destiny's Child partners, Michelle Williams and Kelly Rowland. Immediately preceded by the words of contemporary Nigerian author Chimamanda Ngozi Adichie, "Feminist: a person who believes in the social, political, and economic equality of the sexes," the Destiny's Child portion of the show served at once as a sort of mass wish fulfillment for Beyoncé's dedicated fan base, a pivotal moment in the larger career summary that her Coachella set offered, and a testament to the power of raising women's voices in harmony. When the three singers stood center stage imploring, "Say My Name," the transformation of Coachella to Beychella was all but complete.

Longtime Goldenvoice producer Raymond Roker said in a recent interview, "Beyoncé could have played Madison Square Garden, the Staples Center or any massive celebrated venue. That performance would not have been as important as Coachella . . . That opened the door so wide. I mean, she is now the biggest performance Coachella's ever had. A black woman. That script could not have been conceived fifteen years ago."[75] Beyoncé's Coachella set changed the narrative of the festival, providing a necessary intervention in an annual event that, for all of its talk of inclusiveness, has remained overarchingly white.[76] Whether her accomplishment changes the trajectory of Coachella, or of music festivals more broadly, remains to be seen. What Beychella clearly demonstrates is that live music remains a critical space where struggles occur over who can claim space in the public sphere and how different constituencies should be represented. Beychella mattered because as a black woman Beyoncé laid claim to a space that had

Figure 10.3 Beyoncé stands in the middle of the pyramid stage set that she used for her 2018 Coachella performances, surrounded by the large troupe of dancers and musicians that accompanied her appearances. Photograph by Kevin Mazur. Courtesy of Getty Images.

previously been inaccessible to her and others like her. Its significance was heightened because she did so at a time when historical and political events had raised consciousness around the continued exclusion and oppression of women and people of color in the US. Finally, the impact of Beychella was so profound because Coachella gave the artist a platform where her actions achieved maximum visibility. Music festivals in the age of consolidation have moved far from the countercultural norms of an earlier era, but they continue to be invested with the promise of social change because we still hold faith in the agency of musical crowds.

* * *

Speaking to an audience of live music industry insiders at the 2004 Concert Industry Consortium—an event founded by the people behind *Pollstar*—Perry Farrell explained his thought process when he receives an invitation to play a festival. His mind moves first to the question of the festival setting because "like buying a house, it's location, location, location." Then he thinks of the lineup, and of course, how much he will be paid. From there, Farrell's attention turns to the less tangible elements of the event: "I start to think to myself about what's going to happen that night. I start to imagine the crowd and I start to look out at the crowd. What's cool about a crowd is that they instantly start to take over, wherever you are. You can have planned this place for a year; they start walking through the gates, it's their place."[77] This vision has motivated much of the history of live music that I have surveyed in this book: the sense that when you bring a crowd of people together in conjunction with music, whether at a mass festival or in the confines of an intimate club, anything can happen.

As I completed work on this book in April 2020, the possibilities attached to the live music experience withered away. The global pandemic associated with COVID-19 effectively put a halt to public life as we had known it for the past century. At a time when any social gathering—public or private, indoors or out—carried risk, live music events were no longer tenable. Coachella, originally scheduled for the weekends of April 10–12 and April 17–19, 2020, was postponed until October, and then canceled for the year. The festival skipped 2021 entirely and the next installment is planned for April 2022. As a whole, the concert industry has been steeped in uncertainty since the pandemic hit. Reporting on the situation in April 2020, the *Los Angeles Times* noted, "A disease that looked like a vague disruption just a month and a half ago could be an extinction-level event for the live business for at least a year to come."[78] Sixteen months later, in August 2021, live music has made a return of sorts, but venues throughout the US remain shuttered, some permanently and others still awaiting a time when it might be safe to return. Outdoor shows are the safer choice but will not be sustainable through cold weather months. Some venues are requiring proof of vaccination to attend, while others have announced mask mandates. As new variants of COVID-19 continue to emerge, it is hard not to wonder if live music will once again go into remission in the months to come.

The last live music event I attended before the pandemic had fully taken hold was on March 6, 2020. It was a very small show at an out-of-the-way venue in the back room of a bar, featuring 75 Dollar Bill, an experimental duo comprised of guitarist Che Chen and percussionist Rick Brown. Even then, in the early stages of the pandemic hitting the northeastern US, I was concerned about contagion, but decided that the risk was low enough that it was worth taking the chance. By the time my own band was scheduled to play our next gig just over two weeks later, on March 21, the decision was all but inevitable: the show could not go on. On March 10, Massachusetts governor Charlie Baker declared a State of Emergency due to the health crisis, and other restrictions would roll out in the ensuing weeks. Although the formal prohibition of gatherings of ten or more people was not made official until March 31, the scale and seriousness of the situation was readily apparent well before that time and one by one, local venues and promoters began to announce that all scheduled events were canceled until further notice.

In the face of the evaporation of live music opportunities, musicians took to livestreaming performances, sometimes from empty concert halls, more often from within their own homes or studios. The practice is not new, but it assumed a new salience in the transformed environment. To date, livestreaming has tended to be supplemental to the work that performing musicians do. It can help to maintain a connection to fans and offers a means of communication that combines performance with the more personally directed sort of outreach characteristic of social media. As music and media critic Cherie Hu points out, "From the fan's perspective, the 'stage' in a livestream is just the screen, and the audience is the chat room. There's a diminished sense of hierarchy between artist and the fan, leading to interactions that can be much more social, interactive, and intimate."[79] Hu further stresses that livestreaming was never designed to supplant the more standard live music experience, and efforts to generate revenue from it remain sorely underdeveloped. Advising artists who might be considering livestreams as a way to earn income that has been lost through regular live performance channels, Hu offers caution along multiple lines: because "everyday consumers aren't used to paying for musical livestreams," and furthermore, "even if you *did* want to put your livestream behind a paywall and have fans buy tickets for access just like in real life, there aren't many platforms around with that capability anyway."[80] That may change as the loss of live performance opportunities becomes more entrenched, but either way, solving the problem of monetization will not solve the larger quandaries posed by the situation at hand.

I contributed to the mounting discourse on the place of music in the pandemic on a couple of occasions. For a *New York Times* article on the proliferating practice of people singing from balconies and other semi-public settings, often in unison with others, I offered that communal singing is "like touching someone without touching them," and so can help to redress the situation in which our ability to be near other people, to feel the momentary and accidental touch of their bodies against ours, has become unavailable.[81] Speaking with Spencer Kornhaber of *The Atlantic*, I reflected on the larger implications of the pandemic, positing that live music is one of the essential things that makes us feel like we belong to some larger social collective: "If we lose [live music], we're losing a really key part of the social fabric."[82] Now a designated "expert" on live music as a result of the research I have done for this book, I continue to struggle for explanations as to what sort of impact the current health crisis will have. Mostly, I have been overwhelmed by a sense of loss regarding an aspect of life that for me and so many of the people I know has been a regular source of sustenance, stimulation, security, and belonging. My conviction that live music is an integral element of modern public life has been fortified, but I never imagined that I would see it, and so much of the public life that surrounded it, all but disappear.

Throughout this book I have brought a critical perspective to the topic of live music. I have documented how musical performance became industrialized and how live music is a cultural field in which power and hierarchy are always at work, even when artists appear at their most subversive. Closing this history at a moment of unprecedented crisis in the very conditions that allow live music to thrive, however, I am drawn to a vision that is more hopeful and can lead us toward restoration of the values and practices that lead us to want to participate in live music in the first place. Barbara Ehrenreich outlined some of these values in the closing pages of her study of what she calls "collective joy." Commenting on the importance of festivity, she suggests:

> While hierarchy is about exclusion, festivity generates inclusiveness. The music invites everyone to dance; shared food briefly undermines the privilege of class ... No source of human difference or identity is immune to the carnival challenge ... At the height of festivity, we step out of our assigned roles and statuses—of gender, ethnicity, tribe, and rank—and into a brief utopia defined by egalitarianism, creativity, and mutual love.[83]

In a less idealistic vein, but one that remains optimistic at its core, media theorist Nancy Baym says of the work that musicians do in forming relationships with their audiences that there is much more at issue than whether those musicians can earn a living, important as that is. Rather, what is at stake is "how they, their audiences, and ultimately all of us relating through commercial platforms in market systems can hold on to our basic humanity and help one another flourish."[84] Live music, in its many manifestations, has been a primary resource for allowing us to retain some basic sense of humanity in this manner and sometimes against great odds. Its return is essential to our recovery.

Notes

Preface and Acknowledgments

1. Tim Alberta, "Elvis Reenters the Building," *The Atlantic* 327, no. 5 (June 2021): 25.

Introduction

1. Louis Moreau Gottschalk, *Notes of a Pianist*, ed. Jeanne Behrend (Princeton, NJ: Princeton University Press, 2006), 217.
2. Gottschalk, *Notes of a Pianist*, 116.
3. Master itinerary for 1977 Led Zeppelin US tour, first leg. John Vogel Papers, Box 1, Folder 13, Rock and Roll Hall of Fame Library and Archives.
4. Mitzie Calder, cover letter and travel itinerary for 1977 Led Zeppelin US tour, first leg. John Vogel Papers, Box 1, Folder 13, Rock and Roll Hall of Fame Library and Archives.
5. On the different sorts of spaces that serve as venues for live music, and the distinction between "dedicated" spaces and "adapted" ones, see Robert Kronenburg, *Live Architecture: Venues, Stages and Arena for Popular Music* (London: Routledge, 2012).
6. Philip Auslander, *Liveness: Performance in a Mediatized Culture* (London: Routledge, 1999), 51.
7. Auslander, *Liveness*, 51.
8. George Foster, *New York by Gas-Light and other Urban Sketches*, ed. and with an introduction by Stuart Blumin (Berkeley and Los Angeles: University of California Press, 1990), 141–142.
9. Foster, *New York by Gas-Light*, 143; Eric Lott, *Love and Theft: Blackface Minstrelsy and the American Working Class* (New York: Oxford University Press, 1993), 85. More recently, Dale Cockrell has returned to this evocative passage in Foster's book to illustrate his discussion of Pete Williams' place in his study of music, sex, and New York underworld nightlife, *Everybody's Doin' It: Sex, Music, and Dance in New York, 1850–1917* (New York: W.W. Norton and Company, 2019), 35–36.
10. John S. Dwight, "Jenny Lind's First Concert," *New York Daily Tribune* (September 12, 1850): 1.
11. P. David Marshall, *Celebrity and Power: Fame in Contemporary Culture* (Minneapolis: University of Minnesota Press, 1997), 6.

12. Kyle Buchanan and Dee Lockett, "What It Was Like to Be in the Audience for Beyoncé's Historic Coachella Show," *Vulture* (April 17, 2019), https://www.vulture.com/2019/04/what-it-was-like-to-be-in-the-audience-for-beychella.html.
13. Buchanan and Lockett, "What It Was Like."
14. Elias Canetti, *Crowds and Power*, trans. Carol Stewart (New York: Noonday Press, 1984), 18; Steve Waksman, *This Ain't the Summer of Love: Conflict and Crossover in Heavy Metal and Punk* (Berkeley and Los Angeles: University of California Press, 2009), 48. See also Gina Arnold, *Half a Million Strong: Crowds and Power from Woodstock to Coachella* (Iowa City: University of Iowa Press, 2018), 126.
15. John Philip Sousa, "The Menace of Mechanical Music," *Appleton's Magazine* 8 (1906): 278–284.
16. Arthur Loesser, *Men, Women and Pianos: A Social History* (New York: Simon and Schuster, 1954); Richard Leppert, *The Sight of Sound: Music, Representation, and the History of the Body* (Berkeley and Los Angeles: University of California Press, 1993); Ruth Solie, "'Girling' at the Parlor Piano," *Music in Other Words: Victorian Conversations* (Berkeley and Los Angeles: University of California Press, 2004), 85–117.
17. Dwight, "The Virtuoso Age in Music," *The Harbinger* 1 (November 15, 1845): 362–364; Dwight, "The Virtuoso Age in Music, Part Two," *The Harbinger* 1 (November 22, 1845): 378–381.
18. On Liszt, see Dana Gooley, *The Virtuoso Liszt* (Cambridge: Cambridge University Press, 2004); and Leppert, "Cultural Contradiction, Idolatry, and the Piano Virtuoso: Franz Liszt," in *Piano Roles: Three-hundred Years of Life with the Piano*, ed. James Parakilas (New Haven, CT: Yale University Press, 1999), 200–223. About the impact of touring European piano virtuosos in the US, see R. Allen Lott, *From Paris to Peoria: How European Piano Virtuosos Brought Classical Music to the American Heartland* (New York: Oxford University Press, 2003). For the most thorough account of Gottschalk's career, see S. Frederick Starr, *Bamboula! The Life and Times of Louis Moreau Gottschalk* (New York: Oxford University Press, 1995).
19. Jürgen Habermas, *The Structural Transformation of the Public Sphere: An Inquiry into a Category of Bourgeois Society*, trans. Thomas Burger (Cambridge, MA: MIT Press, 1991), 37.
20. Habermas, *The Structural Transformation of the Public Sphere*, 39–40. For an insightful treatment of these changes in the context of British concert life, see Simon McVeigh, *Concert Life in London from Mozart to Haydn* (Cambridge: Cambridge University Press, 1993). On the situation of music in France, and the impact of the French Revolution on Parisian musical life, see James Johnson, *Listening in Paris: A Cultural History* (Berkeley and Los Angeles: University of California Press, 1995). For a valuable comparative history of concert life in three major European capitals, see William Weber, *Music and the Middle Class: The Social Structure of Concert Life in London, Paris and Vienna* (New York: Holmes & Meier, 1975).
21. Oscar Sonneck, in his pioneering research, dated the founding of the St. Cecilia Society to 1762, but the Society's most authoritative current-day historian, Nicholas Butler, has demonstrated that 1766 is the proper date. See Sonneck, *Early Concert-Life*

in America (1731–1800) (Leipzig: Breitkopf & Härtel, 1907), 16; Butler, *Votaries of Apollo: The St. Cecilia Society and the Patronage of Concert Music in Charleston, South Carolina, 1766–1820* (Columbia, SC: University of South Carolina Press, 2007), 43–44.
22. Butler, *Votaries of Apollo*, 81–82.
23. Benedict Anderson, *Imagined Communities: Reflections on the Origin and Spread of Nationalism* (London: Verso, 1991).
24. Lawrence Levine, *Highbrow/Lowbrow: The Emergence of Cultural Hierarchy in America* (Cambridge, MA: Harvard University Press, 1988), 177.
25. Bernard Gendron, *Between Montmartre and the Mudd Club: Popular Music and the Avant-Garde* (Chicago: University of Chicago Press, 2002), 6.
26. Advertisement for *The Dulcimer*, by I.B. Woodbury. *Boston Recorder* (January 20, 1853): 11.
27. "Live Music and Drama," *Worcester Daily Spy* (January 12, 1890): 5.
28. "Gustav Cook: He Makes His First Speech in Dallas Last Night," *Weekly Times-Herald* (July 5, 1890): 4; "The Y.M.C.A.," *Dallas Morning News* (March 27, 1892): 12; "Republican Rally Tonight," *Rockford Daily Register-Gazette* (October 26, 1898): 7.
29. Advertisement for the F.B. Haviland Publishing Co., *New York Clipper* (February 2, 1906): 1288.
30. Advertisement for the McKinley Music Co., *New York Clipper* (May 14, 1919): 22.
31. W. Stephen Bush, "Exhibition Wins," *The Moving Picture World* (February 26, 1916): 1278.
32. See Rick Altman, *Silent Film Sound* (New York: Columbia University Press, 2004).
33. Advertisement for C.G. Conn, Ltd., musical instrument company. *Photoplay* (October 1921): 105. Emphases in the original text.
34. James Kraft, *From Stage to Studio: Musicians and the Sound Revolution, 1890–1950* (Baltimore: Johns Hopkins University Press, 1996), 51–54.
35. Advertisement for the American Federation of Musicians, *Musical America* 49, no. 22 (November 25, 1929): 19.
36. Advertisement for the American Federation of Musicians, *Musical America* 50, no. 2 (January 25, 1930): 43.
37. Advertisement for the American Federation of Musicians, *Musical America* 51, no. 16 (October 25, 1931): 21.
38. Advertisement for the American Federation of Musicians, *Musical America* 51, no. 18 (November 25, 1931): 21.
39. Michael Roberts, *Tell Tchaikovsky the News: Rock 'n' Roll, the Labor Question, and the Musicians' Union, 1942–1968* (Durham, NC: Duke University Press, 2014).
40. See, for example, Ian Inglis, ed., *Performance and Popular Music: History, Place and Time* (Aldershot: Ashgate, 2006); and Corbin Reiff, *Lighters in the Sky: The All-Time Greatest Concerts, 1960–2016* (New York: Lesser Gods, 2017).
41. Some excellent examples of this latter approach include Catherine Tackley, *Benny Goodman's Famous 1938 Carnegie Hall Jazz Concert* (Oxford: Oxford University Press, 2012); John Fass Morton, *Backstory in Blue: Ellington at Newport '56* (New Brunswick: Rutgers University Press, 2008); and Elijah Wald, *Dylan Goes*

Electric: Newport, Seeger, Dylan, and the Night That Split the Sixties (New York: Dey St., 2015).
42. Representative of the breadth of works about Woodstock are Robert Spitz, *Barefoot in Babylon: The Creation of the Woodstock Music Festival, 1969* (New York: Viking Press, 1969); Joel Makower, *Woodstock: The Oral History* (New York: Doubleday, 1989); Joel Rosenman, John Roberts, and Robert Pilpel, *Young Men of Unlimited Capital: The Inside Story of the Legendary Woodstock Festival Told by the Two Who Paid for It* (New York: Harcourt Brace Jovanovich, 1974); Michael Lang with Holly-George Warren, *The Road to Woodstock* (New York: Ecco, 2009); and Andy Bennett, ed., *Remembering Woodstock* (Aldershot: Ashgate, 2004).
43. Richard Peterson and Roger Kern, "Changing Highbrow Taste: From Snob to Omnivore," *American Sociological Review* 61, no. 5 (October 1996): 900–907.
44. Peter Tschmuck, *Creativity and Innovation in the Music Industry*, 2nd ed. (Berlin: Springer, 2012), 181–182.
45. "A Record Year," *Pollstar* (December 31, 1999): 10.
46. "Concert Industry Ticket Sales," *Pollstar* (January 18, 2010): 6.
47. On the diversification of live music revenue streams, see Dean Budnick and Josh Baron, *Ticket Masters: The Rise of the Concert Industry and How the Public Got Scalped* (Toronto: ECW Press, 2011); and Simon Frith, "Live Music Matters," *Scottish Music Review* 1, no. 1 (2007): 5.
48. Among the new wave of work on music festivals is George McKay, ed., *The Pop Festival: History, Music, Media, Culture* (New York: Bloomsbury, 2015); Jonathan Wynn, *Music/City: American Festivals and Placemaking in Austin, Nashville, and Newport* (Chicago: University of Chicago Press, 2016); Chris Anderton, *Music Festivals in the UK: Beyond the Carnivalesque* (London: Routledge, 2019); and Arnold, *Half a Million Strong*.
49. Simon Frith, Matt Brennan, Martin Cloonan, and Emma Webster, *The History of Live Music in Britain*, vol. 1, *1950–1967: From Dance Hall to the 100 Club* (Farnham: Ashgate, 2013); Frith, Brennan, Cloonan, and Webster, *The History of Live Music in Britain*, vol. 2, *1968–1984: From Hyde Park to the Hacienda* (London: Routledge, 2019); Frith, Brennan, Cloonan, and Webster, *The History of Live Music in Britain*, vol. 3, *1985–2015: From Live Aid to Live Nation* (Abingdon: Routledge, 2021).
50. Frith et.al., *History of Live Music in Britain*: 1:62.

Chapter 1

1. John S. Dwight, "The Farewell Concert," *Dwight's Journal of Music* 1, no. 8 (May 29, 1852): 61.
2. Gustavus Stadler highlights this same feature in Dwight's reviews of Lind's earlier Castle Garden concerts, noting that the critic's descriptions of Lind's concerts "specifically thematize the mass audience response as a model of civic behavior." See Stadler, *Troubling Minds: The Cultural Politics of Genius in the United States, 1840–1890* (Minneapolis: University of Minnesota Press, 2006), 57.

3. John Dizikes, *Opera in America: A Cultural History* (New Haven, CT: Yale University Press, 1993); Katherine Preston, *Opera on the Road: Traveling Opera Troupes in the United States, 1825–1860* (Urbana: University of Illinois Press, 1993); R. Allen Lott, *From Paris to Peoria: How European Piano Virtuosos Brought Classical Music to the American Heartland* (Oxford: Oxford University Press, 2003).

4. Eric Lott, *Love and Theft: Blackface Minstrelsy and the American Working Class* (New York: Oxford University Press, 1993); W.T. Lhamon, *Raising Cain: Blackface Performance from Jim Crow to Hip Hop* (Cambridge, MA: Harvard University Press, 1998); Dale Cockrell, *Demons of Disorder: Early Blackface Minstrels and Their World* (Cambridge: Cambridge University Press, 1997).

5. Lott, *Love and Theft*, 64.

6. The most thorough account of the Astor Place Riot remains Peter Buckley, "To the Opera House: Culture and Society in New York City, 1820–1860" (PhD diss., State University of New York at Stony Brook, 1984).

7. P.T. Barnum, *Struggles and Triumphs*, edited and abridged by Carl Bode (New York: Penguin, 1981), 171.

8. Barnum, *Struggles and Triumphs*, 171.

9. On Lind's Berlin debut, see Henry Scott Holland and W.S. Rockstro, *Memoir of Madame Jenny Lind-Goldschmidt*, vol. 5, *Her Early Art-Life and Dramatic Career, 1820–1851* (London: John Murray, 1891), 211–216.

10. George Biddlecombe, "The Construction of a Cultural Icon: The Case of Jenny Lind," *Nineteenth-Century British Music Studies*, ed. Peter Horton and Bennett Zon (Aldershot: Ashgate, 2006), 3: 47–48.

11. Barnum, *Struggles and Triumphs*, 184.

12. Mark Samples, "The Humbug and the Nightingale: P.T. Barnum, Jenny Lind, and the Branding of a Star Singer for American Reception," *Musical Quarterly* 99, nos. 3/4 (Fall/Winter 2016): 288.

13. William Weber, *The Great Transformation in Musical Taste: Concert Programming from Haydn to Brahms* (Cambridge: Cambridge University Press, 2008), 122.

14. Lawrence Levine, *Highbrow/Lowbrow: The Emergence of Cultural Hierarchy in America* (Cambridge, MA: Harvard University Press, 1988), 120.

15. Barnum, *Struggles and Triumphs*, 175; Holland and Rockstro, *Memoir of Madame Jenny Lind-Goldschmidt*, 367.

16. Mary Kelley, *Private Woman, Public Stage: Literary Domesticity in Nineteenth-Century America* (New York: Oxford University Press, 1984); Jane Tompkins, *Sensational Designs: The Cultural Work of American Fiction, 1790–1860* (New York: Oxford University Press, 1985).

17. Glenn Hendler, *Public Sentiments: Structures of Feeling in Nineteenth-Century American Literature* (Chapel Hill: University of North Carolina Press, 2001), 32.

18. Bluford Adams, *E Pluribus Barnum: The Great Showman and the Making of U.S. Popular Culture* (Minneapolis: University of Minnesota Press, 1997), 41.

19. W. Porter Ware and Thaddeus Lockard, *P.T. Barnum Presents Jenny Lind: The American Tour of the Swedish Nightingale* (Baton Rouge: Louisiana State University Press, 1980), 9.

20. Advertisements for the music publishers Samuel Jollie, William Hall and Son, and William Vanderbeek, *Morning Courier and New York Enquirer* (August 29, 1850): 2. All subsequent discussion of these ads is based on the versions that appear in this edition.
21. On the social significance of Jenny Lind's whiteness, see Jennifer Stoever, *The Sonic Color Line: Race and the Cultural Politics of Listening* (New York: New York University Press, 2016), 78.
22. Charles Hamm, *Yesterdays: Popular Song in America* (New York: W.W. Norton & Company, 1979), 76.
23. Levine, *Highbrow/Lowbrow*, 108.
24. Gina Arnold, *Half a Million Strong: Crowds and Power from Woodstock to Coachella* (Iowa City: University of Iowa Press, 2018), 13–14. Emphasis in original.
25. Buckley, "To the Opera House," 61.
26. Sean Wilentz, *Chants Democratic: New York City and the Rise of the American Working Class, 1788–1850* (New York: Oxford University Press, 2004), 258; Levine, *Highbrow/Lowbrow*, 25–27.
27. Preston, *Opera on the Road*, 135.
28. Vera Brodsky Lawrence, *Strong on Music: The New York Music Scene in the Days of George Templeton Strong*, vol. 1, *Resonances, 1836–1850* (Oxford: Oxford University Press, 1988), 455. Also see "Astor Place Opera House," *The Albion* (November 27, 1847): 576.
29. On the varied uses to which opera houses were put, see Ann Satterthwaite, *Local Glories: Opera Houses on Main Street Where Art and Community Meet* (New York: Oxford University Press, 2016), 10.
30. For the text of the card supporting Macready and the list of supporters, see the *Evening Post* (May 9, 1849): 2. The card was published widely in New York newspapers.
31. Buckley, "To the Opera House," 64.
32. For details of the riot, see "Alarming Riot at the Astor Place Theater," *Evening Post* (May 11, 1849): 2; "Another Shameful Riot: Attack on the Opera House," *New York Daily Tribune* (May 11, 1849): 2; and "Dreadful Riot and Bloodshed at the Astor Place Theater," *Weekly Herald* (May 12, 1849): 1.
33. "Riot and Loss of Life," *New York Commercial Advertiser* (May 11, 1849): 2.
34. "The Macready Riots," *New York Atlas* (May 13, 1849): 2.
35. "After-Lesson of the Astor Place Riot," *Home Journal* (May 26, 1849): 2.
36. Richard Butsch, *The Citizen Audience: Crowds, Publics, and Individuals* (New York: Routledge, 2008), 30.
37. The details of Lind's arrival and her initial concerts are primarily based on my reading of three daily newspapers (*New York Daily Tribune, New York Herald, Morning Courier and New York Enquirer*) and two weekly or biweekly music magazines (*The Message Bird, Saroni's Musical Times*). Supplementing these sources is Charles Rosenberg, *Jenny Lind in America* (New York: Stringer & Townsend, 1851), a contemporary account of the first year of Lind's American tour by a British journalist who traveled with the singer; and two detailed historical accounts, that in Ware and Lockard, *P.T. Barnum Presents Jenny Lind*; and Vera Brodsky Lawrence, *Strong*

on Music: The New York Music Scene in the Days of George Templeton Strong, vol. 2, Reverberations, 1850–1856 (Chicago: University of Chicago Press, 1995).
38. See Mary Ryan, Civic Wars: Democracy and Public Life in the American City During the Nineteenth Century (Berkeley and Los Angeles: University of California Press, 1997), 58–59.
39. "Arrival of the Atlantic," Morning Courier and New York Enquirer (September 2, 1850): 1.
40. "Arrival of Jenny Lind," New York Daily Tribune (September 2, 1850): 1.
41. "Arrival of Jenny Lind," New York Herald (September 2, 1850): 4.
42. A tenuous connection, admittedly, but it is worth noting that Lind's date of arrival roughly coincided with the passage of the national Fugitive Slave Law that required citizens of Northern states to cooperate with the rule of slavery. Discourse on slavery and its implications for national governance was thus much in the air at the time, and while it was not often directly brought to bear upon Lind, detecting traces of it in accounts of her endeavors is not without grounds.
43. The same Herald article makes this point more explicitly a few paragraphs further on, where the writer offers the following description: "[Lind's] whole countenance is highly intellectual; but what strikes the spectator most is the lofty and dignified benevolence that shines from every feature . . . Jenny Lind appears before thousands while she sings; but her nature is retiring and modest. Other women are admired by the public; Jenny Lind is loved and respected as much as she is admired."
44. Music historian Richard Crawford observed of the singer's reception: "Lind's arrival, her persona, travels, deeds and foibles, and perhaps most of all, Americans' embrace of her visit were received not simply as an artistic enterprise or a commercial venture. They were *news*, reported throughout the country." Crawford, America's Musical Life: A History (New York: W.W. Norton & Company, 2001), 187.
45. Lawrence, Strong on Music, vol. 2, Reverberations, 165.
46. Advertisement for Jenny Lind's debut concert at Castle Garden, New York Herald (September 5, 1850): 3.
47. Neil Harris, Humbug: The Art of P.T. Barnum (Boston, MA: Little, Brown and Company, 1973), 28.
48. "Jenny Lind—Her First Concert—Price of Tickets, & c.," New York Daily Tribune (September 4, 1850): 1.
49. "The Jenny Lind Ticket-Auction," New York Daily Tribune (September 9, 1850): 1.
50. "The Jenny Lind Ticket-Auction—Second Day," New York Daily Tribune (September 10, 1850): 1. Barnum reveals in his autobiography that the total receipts wound up being much less than was reported in the newspapers, because many of the tickets purchased at auction were never claimed. By his account, the first concert earned $17,864.05 in ticket sales. See Barnum, Struggles and Triumphs, 195.
51. Daniel Cavicchi, Listening and Longing: Music Lovers in the Age of Barnum (Middletown, CT: Wesleyan University Press, 2011), 35.
52. Ossian Dodge, "Ossian's Serenade," sheet music published by Oliver Ditson (Boston, MA, 1850). A copy of this song resides in the sheet music holdings of the American Antiquarian Society, Worcester, MA.

53. This announcement appeared in all three of the daily newspapers that I have surveyed, the *New York Daily Tribune*, the *New York Herald*, and the *Morning Courier and New York Enquirer*.
54. "Jenny Lind," *The Message Bird*, no. 29 (October 1, 1850): 471.
55. "Jenny Lind's First Concert in New York—Triumphant Success and Tremendous Excitement in Castle Garden," *New York Herald* (September 12, 1850): 1.
56. Richard Grant White, "Jenny Lind's First Concert," *Morning Courier and New York Enquirer* (September 12, 1850): 2.
57. Herrman Saroni, "Jenny Lind," *Saroni's Musical Times* 1, no. 51 (September 14, 1850): 603.
58. Since the receipts for the first concert were less than anticipated, Lind actually earned less than the reported $10,000 for the concert. Barnum thus arranged with Lind that the amount would be taken from her share of the profits of the first two of her New York concerts, still amounting to $10,000 overall. See Barnum, *Struggles and Triumphs*, 196.
59. The full text of Barnum's speech to the audience, including the details of Lind's charitable contributions, was reproduced in the *New York Herald* (September 12, 1850): 1.
60. Saroni, "Jenny Lind," 603.
61. Dizikes, *Opera in America*, 3–4.
62. Stoever, *The Sonic Color Line*, 36.
63. White, "Jenny Lind," *Morning Courier and New York Enquirer* (September 18, 1850): 2.
64. White, "Jenny Lind," 2.
65. White, "Jenny Lind," 2.
66. "Jenny Lind's Singing," *Evening Post* (September 17, 1850): 2.
67. "Jenny Lind's Second Concert at Castle Garden," *New York Herald* (September 14, 1850): 2.
68. "Jenny Lind, the Northern Light," *New York Herald* (September 17, 1850): 4.
69. Dwight, "Jenny Lind's Second Concert at Castle Garden," *New York Daily Tribune* (September 14, 1850): 1.
70. Dwight, "Jenny Lind's Third Concert," *New York Daily Tribune* (September 18, 1850): 1.
71. Dwight, "Jenny Lind's Third Concert," 1.
72. Gustavus Stadler further explains the logic underpinning Dwight's aesthetic assumptions: "Lind's singing replaces the sensual intensity ascribed to female Italian singers with a more 'integral and whole' presence ... in which the corporeal and the intellectual are intertwined. Erotics can't be strictly associated with body; aesthetics can't be strictly associated with intellect. The audience response is so powerful, so *sublime*, because it makes such a distinction unimportant." See Stadler, *Troubling Minds*, 65.
73. Dwight, "Jenny Lind's First Concert," *New York Daily Tribune* (September 12, 1850): 1.
74. Dwight, "Jenny Lind's Fourth Concert," *New York Daily Tribune* (September 20, 1850): 1.
75. Saroni, "Jenny Lind's Concerts," *Saroni's Musical Times* 2, no. 9 (November 23, 1850): 87.

76. Dwight, "Jenny Lind's Fifth Concert," *New York Daily Tribune* (September 23, 1850): 1.
77. Advertisement for Jenny Lind's Castle Garden concerts, *New York Herald* (September 14, 1850): 3. The same announcement appeared in all major New York daily newspapers that day.
78. "The Second Concert," *The Evening Post* (September 14, 1850): 2.
79. "Jenny Lind's Fifth Concert," *New York Herald* (September 22, 1850): 2; Dwight, "Jenny Lind's Fifth Concert," 1.
80. "Jenny Lind's Sixth Concert," *New York Herald* (September 25, 1850): 2.
81. Advertisement for Jenny Lind's two concerts at Fitchburg Station Hall, *Boston Courier* (October 11, 1850): 3.
82. "The Concert Last Night," *Boston Evening Transcript* (October 12, 1850): 2.
83. "Farewell Concert of Jenny Lind," *Boston Courier* (October 14, 1850): 2.
84. "The Jenny Lind Concert," *Daily Atlas* (October 14, 1850): 2.
85. "The Concert of Saturday Evening," *Boston Daily Bee* (October 14, 1850): 2; "Jenny Lind's Last Concert," *Boston Herald* (October 14, 1850): 2.
86. One of 'Em, "Barnum's Meanness," *Boston Herald* (October 17, 1850): 2.
87. Letter to the editor, *Gloucester Telegraph* (October 16, 1850): 2.
88. Cited in Cavicchi, *Listening and Longing*, 167.
89. "Cheap Clocks," *Portsmouth Journal* (July 4, 1851): n.p.
90. "Jenny Lind in Cincinnati," *Pittsburgh Daily Post* (April 19, 1851): 2.
91. "Jenny Lind," *Pittsburgh Daily Post* (April 28, 1851): 2; "The True Version of the Jenny Lind Affair," *Pittsburgh Daily Post* (April 29, 1851): 3.
92. Adams, *E Pluribus Barnum*, 65.
93. Barnum, *Struggles and Triumphs*, 191–192.
94. Ware and Lockard, *P.T. Barnum Presents Jenny Lind*, 94–98.
95. "Jenny Lind Excitement—the Concert & c.," *Springfield Republican* (July 1, 1851): 2.
96. "Jenny Lind's Tuesday Evening Concert," *Springfield Republican* (July 2, 1851): 2.
97. *The Seventh Census of the United States, 1850* (Washington, DC: Robert Armstrong, Printer), 123, 130.
98. "Jenny Lind at Northampton," *Springfield Republican* (July 4, 1851): 2; "Jenny Lind at Northampton," *Hampshire Gazette* (July 8, 1851): 2.
99. "Jenny Lind's Concert," *Hampshire Gazette* (July 8, 1851): 3.
100. "The Jenny Lind Concert at Hartford—Riot & c.," *Boston Evening Herald* (July 7, 1851): 2.
101. "The Riot at Jenny Lind's Concert in Hartford, on Saturday Evening," *Boston Herald* (July 8, 1851): 4.
102. "Jenny Lind's Concert," *Connecticut Courant* (July 12, 1851): 2.
103. "Jenny Lind's Concert," *Connecticut Courant*, 2.
104. "Wall St. Criticism," *New York Daily Tribune* (September 17, 1850): 3.
105. Karen Halttunen, *Confidence Men and Painted Women: A Study of Middle-Class Culture in America, 1830–1870* (New Haven, CT: Yale University Press, 1982), 93. Also see Steve Waksman, "A Woman's Place: Staging Femininity in Live Music from Jenny Lind to the Jazz Age," *The Routledge Research Companion to Popular Music and Gender*, ed. Stan Hawkins (London and New York: Routledge, 2017), 220.

Chapter 2

1. Gustavus Pike, *The Jubilee Singers and Their Campaign for Twenty Thousand Dollars* (Boston, MA: Lee and Shepard, 1873), 109.
2. Pike, *The Jubilee Singers*, 107.
3. The key recent works are Andrew Ward, *Dark Midnight When I Rise: The Story of the Fisk Jubilee Singers* (New York: Amistad, 2001); Toni Anderson, *"Tell Them We Are Singing for Jesus": The Original Fisk Jubilee Singers and Christian Reconstruction, 1871–1878* (Macon, GA: Mercer University Press, 2010); Sandra Graham, "The Fisk Jubilee Singers and the Concert Spiritual: The Beginnings of an American Tradition" (PhD diss., New York University, 2001); and Graham, *Spirituals and the Birth of a Black Entertainment Industry* (Urbana: University of Illinois Press, 2018). Lynn Abbott and Doug Seroff also discuss the Jubilee Singers extensively in *Out of Sight: The Rise of African American Popular Music, 1889–1895* (Jackson: University of Mississippi Press, 2003), but concentrate entirely on the post-1878 career of the ensemble when it was only nominally associated with Fisk University.
4. For an influential statement on these issues, see Dena Epstein, "Black Spirituals: Their Emergence into Public Knowledge," *Black Music Research Journal* 10, no. 1 (Spring 1990): 58–64. Graham analyzes the relationship of the "concert spiritual," that performed by the Jubilee Singers, to vernacular African American religious song at length in *Spirituals and the Birth of a Black Entertainment Industry*, 48–81.
5. See Eileen Southern's discussion of African American participation in antebellum concert life in *The Music of Black Americans: A History*, 2nd ed. (New York: W.W. Norton & Company, 1983), 103–116.
6. Robert Toll compiled an extensive list of African American minstrel troupes in an appendix to his history of blackface minstrelsy, *Blacking Up: The Minstrel Show in Nineteenth-century America* (New York: Oxford University Press, 1974), 275–280. Only seven of these troupes appeared before 1865, compared to the several dozen that appeared after that date.
7. Graham, "The Fisk Jubilee Singers," 61–63; Ward, *Dark Midnight When I Rise*, 83.
8. Anderson provides a good account of the AMA's concerns, stressing the organization's commitment to what she terms principles of "Christian reconstruction." See *"Tell Them We Are Singing for Jesus,"* 31.
9. For an insightful dissection of the power dynamics that inhered in the cultural and financial arrangements surrounding the Jubilee Singers, see Graham, "On the Road to Freedom: The Contracts of the Fisk Jubilee Singers," *American Music* 24 no. 1 (Spring 2006): 1–29.
10. Ward, *Dark Midnight When I Rise*, 123–124.
11. Graham, "The Fisk Jubilee Singers," 125–126.
12. Ella Sheppard Moore, "Historical Sketch of the Jubilee Singers," in *Music in the U.S.A.: A Documentary Companion*, ed. Judith Tick (New York: Oxford University Press, 2008), 260–261.
13. "Remarkable Praise Meetings," *Cincinnati Daily Gazette* (October 9, 1871): 4.

14. Epstein, *Sinful Tunes and Spirituals: Black Folk Music to the Civil War* (Urbana, IL: University of Illinois Press, 2003), 244–245.
15. "Remarkable Praise Meetings," 4.
16. "Remarkable Praise Meetings," 4. I have not uncovered the original notice in the *Cincinnati Commercial*, but the same passage is reproduced verbatim in Pike, *The Jubilee Singers*, 77.
17. Reproduced in Graham, "The Fisk Jubilee Singers," 133.
18. Hermann Saroni, "To the Readers of Saroni's Musical Times," *Saroni's Musical Times* 3, no. 18 (July 26, 1851): 193.
19. Willie Lee Rose, *Rehearsal for Reconstruction: The Port Royal Experiment* (Indianapolis: Bobbs-Merrill, 1964). Epstein devotes a chapter to the Port Royal Experiment in *Sinful Tunes and Spirituals*, 252–273, in which she makes mention of Spaulding's account.
20. H.G. Spaulding, "Under the Palmetto," *Continental Monthly* 4, no. 2 (August 1863): 197–200. On the significance of the shout, or the ring shout as it has often been called, see Sterling Stuckey, *Slave Culture: Nationalist Theory and the Foundations of Black America* (New York: Oxford University Press, 1987), 3–97; and Samuel Floyd, *The Power of Black Music: Interpreting Its History from Africa to the United States* (New York: Oxford University Press, 1995).
21. Spaulding, "Under the Palmetto," 200.
22. William Francis Allen, Charles Pickard Ware, and Lucy McKim Garrison, eds., *Slave Songs of the United States: The Classic 1867 Anthology* (New York: Dover, 1995), i.
23. Allen, Ware, and Garrison, *Slave Songs*, iii.
24. Allen, Ware, and Garrison, *Slave Songs*, vii.
25. Allen, Ware, and Garrison, *Slave Songs*, iii.
26. Theodore Cuyler, "Our Native Music—The Jubilee Singers," *New York Tribune* (January 19, 1872): 5.
27. Jon Cruz, *Culture on the Margins: The Black Spiritual and the Rise of American Cultural Interpretation* (Princeton, NJ: Princeton University Press, 1999), 3.
28. Cuyler, "Our Native Music," 5.
29. Graham, "The Fisk Jubilee Singers," 229.
30. Floyd, *The Power of Black Music*, 61.
31. "The Fisk University Club," *Brainard's Musical World* 9, no. 99 (March 1872): 38.
32. "The Jubilee Singers," *Loomis' Musical and Masonic Journal* 5, no. 8 (March 1872): 144.
33. James McKim, "Negro Songs," *Dwight's Journal of Music* 21, no. 19 (August 9, 1862): 148–149; Lucy McKim, "Songs of the Port Royal 'Contrabands,'" *Dwight's Journal of Music* 22, no. 6 (November 8, 1862): 254–255.
34. "Negro Folk Songs," *Dwight's Journal of Music* 32, no. 26 (April 5, 1873): 411–412.
35. "Negro Folk Songs," 413.
36. Cuyler, "The Hampton Negro Singers," *New York Evangelist* (April 10, 1873): 1.
37. Jennifer Stoever discusses the way that the reception of the Jubilee Singers among white critics was shaped by what she calls the "sonic color line." See Stoever, *The Sonic Color Line: Race and the Cultural Politics of Listening* (New York: New York University Press, 2016), 153.

38. Leon Litwack, *Been in the Storm So Long: The Aftermath of Slavery* (New York: Vintage, 1979), 212.
39. Litwack, *Been in the Storm So Long*, 177.
40. Graham, "The Fisk Jubilee Singers," 119; Anderson, 43.
41. Quoted in Anderson, *"Tell Them We Are Singing for Jesus,"* 44.
42. Sheppard Moore, "Historical Sketch of the Jubilee Singers," 262.
43. Patrick Gilmore, *History of the National Peace Jubilee and Great Musical Festival: Held in the City of Boston* (Whitefish, MT: Kessinger Publishing, 2008), 13.
44. Gilmore depicts Dwight in less-than-flattering terms in his history of the Jubilee, as a naysayer whose elitist leanings made him unable to grasp the beneficial aspects of his project; see Gilmore, *History of the National Peace Jubilee and Great Musical Festival*, 53–58. Dwight, for his part, reserved comment until the Jubilee began, at which point he admitted that the event resulted in something better than he had expected, but still chafed at the "bigger is better" mentality that he believed to underlay Gilmore's outlook. Dwight, "The Peace Jubilee," *Dwight's Journal of Music* 29, no. 7 (June 19, 1869): 55. Joseph Horowitz uses the ideological conflict between Gilmore and Dwight as the opening to his book, *Classical Music in America: A History* (New York: W.W. Norton and Company, 2007), 15–25.
45. All program information comes from the official program of the Jubilee, published in the *Official Monthly Bulletin of the Great National Celebration of Peace and Musical Festival*, no. 4 (May/June 1869): 2–9; and Gilmore, *History of the National Peace Jubilee and Great Musical Festival*, 432–444.
46. Gilmore, *History of the National Peace Jubilee and Great Musical Festival*, 40–43.
47. Gilmore, *History of the National Peace Jubilee and Great Musical Festival*, 658.
48. Southern, *The Music of Black Americans*, 227.
49. "Let Them in," *Zion's Herald* 49, no. 17 (April 25, 1872): 200. I have found no other evidence to support the tantalizing suggestion made here, that the Jubilee Singers approached Gilmore, rather than the other way around, but I do think it's a credible suggestion if not clearly factual.
50. Ward, *Dark Midnight When I Rise*, 190–193; Anderson, *"Tell Them We Are Singing for Jesus,"* 218–221.
51. The *New York Herald*, for example, commented that, "Madame Parepa-Rosa then sang Gounod's 'Ave Maria.' Her voice was not sufficient to fill the immense building, though the tones were pure and expressive as usual." Quoted in Gilmore, *History of the National Peace Jubilee and Great Musical Festival*, 510.
52. For a useful short history of the transformation of "John Brown's Body" into "Battle Hymn of the Republic," see Sarah Vowell, "John Brown's Body," *The Rose and the Briar: Death, Love and Liberty in the American Ballad*, ed. Greil Marcus and Sean Wilentz (New York: W.W. Norton and Company, 2005), 81–89.
53. Sheppard Moore, "Historical Sketch of the Jubilee Singers," 264.
54. Program, World's Peace Jubilee and International Musical Festival, Sixth Day, June 22, 1872 (Boston, MA: Alfred Mudge and Son, 1872), 2.
55. On the career of the Hyers Sisters, see James Trotter, *Music and Some Highly Musical People* (New York: Johnson Reprint Corporation, 1968), 160–179; Southern, 250–251.
56. Sheppard Moore, "Historical Sketch of the Jubilee Singers," 264.

57. "The World's Peace Jubilee," *Boston Journal* (June 24, 1872): 4.
58. J.B.T. Marsh, *The Story of the Jubilee Singers with Their Songs* (Boston: Houghton, Mifflin and Company, 1880), 41. Sheppard repeats the anecdote about the German cellist in her own account of the event, written some thirty years after that of Marsh.
59. "Yesterday," *Boston Globe* (June 24, 1872): 8.
60. "From the Jubilee, by a Lady Correspondent," *Galveston News* (July 3, 1872): 1.
61. The best account of the day appeared as "The Jubilee. A Popular Programme—Visit of President Grant," *Chicago Tribune* (June 26, 1872): 6.
62. Details about this meeting can be found in Ward, *Dark Midnight When I Rise*, 175–177.
63. "Snubbing Sambo," *Cincinnati Enquirer* (February 25, 1872): 5. Reprinted from the *New York Telegram*.
64. Eric Foner, *A Short History of Reconstruction* (New York: Harper & Row, 1990), 37.
65. Sandra Graham pointedly asserts of the contractual arrangements between the Jubilee Singers and the AMA: "in sense being a Jubilee Singer meant being enslaved all over again." Graham, "On the Road to Freedom," 7.
66. "The Jubilee Singers," *Boston Daily Advertiser* (March 15, 1872): 4.
67. Foner, *A Short History of Reconstruction*, 226. The Bill was also to bar discrimination in public schools, but that provision was dropped in the version that was passed by Congress, as it was deemed too offensive to southern Democrats and moderate Republicans. The compromised version of the bill that was passed ultimately had little effect and fell victim to the dissolution of the effort to reform southern social relations that culminated in the election of 1876, when Republican Rutherford Hayes won the presidency on the condition that military occupation of the South be ended. Some years later, in 1883, the Supreme Court ruled the bill unconstitutional.
68. "Introductory Overture," *New York Clipper* (March 13, 1875): 398.
69. Details of this incident were reported in an untitled notice that appeared in the Middletown, Connecticut newspaper, the *Daily Constitution* (February 13, 1873): 3.
70. Pike, *The Singing Campaign for Ten Thousand Pounds* (Freeport, NY: Books for Libraries Press, 1971), 9.
71. Pike, *The Singing Campaign for Ten Thousand Pounds*, 10–11; Marsh, 45–46.
72. Sterling Stuckey offers insightful commentary on Garnet's career and ideas in *Slave Culture*, 138–192. A short but useful history of Shiloh Presbyterian Church can be found on the website *Mapping the African American Past*, developed by Columbia University, http://maap.columbia.edu/place/37.html.
73. "Colored Watch Meeting at Shiloh Church," *New York Times* (January 1, 1872): 1.
74. "The Fifteenth Amendment—Religious Anniversary of Its Adoption," *New York Times* (March 31, 1873): 5.
75. Southern, *The Music of Black Americans*, 107–109.
76. Quoted in Paul Gilroy, *The Black Atlantic: Modernity and Double Consciousness* (Cambridge, MA: Harvard University Press, 1993), 116.
77. Gilroy, *The Black Atlantic*, 88–92.
78. Pike includes a reproduction of the invitation, which bore the Earl of Shaftesbury's name, in *The Singing Campaign for Ten Thousand Pounds*, 31.
79. "The Jubilee Singers," *The Standard* (May 7, 1873): 2.

80. Michael Pickering, *Blackface Minstrelsy in Britain* (Aldershot: Ashgate, 2008), 15.
81. "The Jubilee Singers," *The Standard*, 2.
82. "The Jubilee Singers," *The Orchestra* 20, no. 502 (May 9, 1873): 86.
83. "The Jubilee Singers," *The Tonic Sol-Fa Reporter* (May 15, 1873): 152.
84. Cruz traces the emergence of this more culturally grounded type of analysis concerning the spiritual in *Culture on the Margins*, arguing that over time the spiritual was understood less as testimony concerning the emotional truth of black experience under slavery than as cultural artifact bearing specific traits associated with African American culture.
85. "The Jubilee Singers," *Tonic Sol-Fa Reporter*, 153.
86. Pike, *The Singing Campaign for Ten Thousand Pounds*, 38; Ward, *Dark Midnight When I Rise*, 211.
87. "The Jubilee Singers," *Indianapolis Sentinel* (July 29, 1873): 7. The *Sentinel* article notes that Porter's letter first appeared in the *Nashville Republican*. Porter later wrote another version of the Jubilee Singers' meeting with Queen Victoria in "The Jubilee Singers on the Ocean and in Europe," *Fisk University News* (October 1911), which has been more widely cited. I have found no other citations for this earlier letter by Porter, but the details are consistent with other accounts of the event, and the singer's perspective is distinctly revealing.
88. The meeting with Gladstone was the more widely reported of these two episodes in the Fisk Jubilee Singers' British career and generated a detailed letter from the English activist clergyman Newman Hall that was published in the *Boston Globe*. See "Jubilee Singers in England: Newman Hall's Account of Their Visit to Gladstone," *Boston Globe* (August 27, 1873): 3.
89. Pike, *The Singing Campaign for Ten Thousand Pounds*, 94–95.
90. Pike, *The Singing Campaign for Ten Thousand Pounds*, 172.
91. In his book on the first phase of the Jubilee Singers' American touring efforts, Pike offered a useful overview of the publicity techniques employed in conjunction with the troupe, which consisted of four methods: "by giving a notice . . . in each of the leading dailies, as well as the weekly religious papers of the city; by placing large posters in conspicuous places . . . ; by distributing, in stores, and at private residences, little slips, called *dodgers*, containing favorable testimonials; and last, though by no means least, by preparing notices to be read in all the churches in the region." Pike, *The Jubilee Singers*, 142.
92. The biographical information here is principally drawn from Anderson, 172–186. For the best account of Loudin's latter-day career with the Jubilee Singers, see Abbott and Seroff, *Out of Sight*, esp. 3–27, 73–89, 455–461.
93. "American Negroes in England," *New York Herald* (October 3, 1875): 15. This same piece would also be reprinted in England; see "A Coloured Man's Experience of the English People," *Huddersfield Daily Chronicle* (January 21, 1876): 4.
94. W.E.B. DuBois, *The Souls of Black Folk* (New York: Dover Publications, 1994), 2.
95. Gilroy, *The Black Atlantic*, 117.
96. Details about the Slave Circular, and the political debates that surrounded it, can be found in William Mulligan, "The Fugitive Slave Circulars, 1875–1876," *Journal*

of Imperial and Commonwealth History 37, no. 2 (June 2009): 183–205. According to Mulligan, the primary geographic region with which the Slave Circular was concerned was East Africa and the Persian Gulf, where the slave trade remained active.
97. "The Jubilee Singers," *Lancaster Gazette* (December 11, 1875): n.p.
98. "The Jubilee Singers at Durham," *Northern Echo* (December 17, 1875): 4.
99. A digitized version of this sheet music can be found at https://jscholarship.library.jhu.edu/handle/1774.2/8572, an online resource built from the collections of Johns Hopkins University. Sandra Graham offers details of the publication and a couple selected press notices regarding its performance in an appendix to "The Fisk Jubilee Singers and the Concert Spiritual," 488–489. Although the sheet music is undated, I believe it was published in early 1876, based on a short announcement listed in "The Musical World," *The Tonic Sol-Fa Reporter* (February 1, 1876): 39.
100. "The Jubilee Singers—The Slave Circular," *Blackburn Standard* (February 5, 1876): 5.
101. "The Jubilee Singers and Politics," *Blackburn Standard* (February 5, 1876): 5.
102. See Gillian Rodger, *Champagne Charlie and Pretty Jemima: Variety Theater in the Nineteenth Century* (Urbana: University of Illinois Press, 2010).
103. Graham provides the most thorough study of the expansion of jubilee singing beyond the Fisk troupe, and documents the work of many competing organizations, in *Spirituals and the Birth of a Black Entertainment Industry*. Robert Toll analyzes the incursion of jubilee singing and greater religious content into blackface minstrelsy as a result of the influence of the Fisk Singers, *Blacking Up*, 236–244. Abbott and Seroff track the continued proliferation of such ensembles in the last two decades of the nineteenth century, after the collapse of the original Fisk troupe, in *Out of Sight*.

Chapter 3

1. "Mirror Interviews: Tony Pastor," *New York Dramatic Mirror* (July 27, 1895). Tony Pastor clippings file, New York Public Library.
2. "Mirror Interviews: Tony Pastor."
3. Lynn Abbott and Doug Seroff, *Out of Sight: The Rise of African American Popular Music, 1889–1895* (Oxford, MS: University of Mississippi Press, 2003), 444.
4. This story comes from an undated article in the Ernest Hogan clippings file, New York Public Library.
5. Abbott and Seroff, *Out of Sight*, 445.
6. See Lawrence Levine, *Highbrow/Lowbrow: The Emergence of Cultural Hierarchy in America* (Cambridge, MA: Harvard University Press, 1988); Joseph Horowitz, *Classical Music in America: A History* (New York: W.W. Norton & Company, 2007); William Weber, *The Great Transformation in Musical Taste: Concert Programming from Haydn to Brahms* (Cambridge: Cambridge University Press, 2008).
7. Isidore Witmark and Isaac Goldberg, *The Story of the House of Witmark: From Ragtime to Swingtime* (New York: L. Furman, 1939), 68.

8. For firsthand accounts of song plugging, see Edward Marks, *They All Sang: From Tony Pastor to Rudy Vallee* (New York: Viking Press, 1934); and Charles Harris, *After the Ball: Forty Years of Melody* (New York: Frank-Maurice, Inc., 1926). For an excellent historical consideration of song plugging in the context of Tin Pan Alley's new production and sales methods, see David Suisman, *Selling Sounds: The Commercial Revolution in American Music* (Cambridge, MA: Harvard University Press, 2009).
9. "Dramatic," *New York Clipper* (October 9, 1875): 223.
10. On the broad contours of vaudeville history, see Douglas Gilbert, *American Vaudeville: Its Life and Times* (New York: Whittlesey House, 1940); Robert Snyder, *The Voice of the City: Vaudeville and Popular Culture in New York* (New York: Oxford University Press, 1989); Alison Kibler, *Rank Ladies: Gender and Cultural Hierarchy in American Vaudeville* (Chapel Hill, NC: University of North Carolina Press, 1999); Arthur Wertheim, *Vaudeville Wars: How the Keith-Albee and Orpheum Circuits Controlled the Big-time and Its Performers* (New York: Palgrave Macmillan, 2006); and Trav S.D., *No Applause—Just Throw Money: The Book That Made Vaudeville Famous* (New York: Faber and Faber, Inc., 2005).
11. Advertisement for Brooks, Dickson and Hickey theatrical circuit, *New York Clipper* (May 8, 1880): 55.
12. Advertisement for J.H. Haverly's Amusement Enterprises, *New York Clipper* (May 8, 1880): 56.
13. The classic statement on the "culture industry" remains the chapter "The Culture Industry: Enlightenment as Mass Deception," in Max Horkheimer and Thedor Adorno, *Dialectic of Enlightenment: Philosophical Fragments*, ed. Gunzelin Schmid Noerr and trans. Edmund Jephcott (Stanford, CA: Stanford University Press, 2002), 94–136. Although the phrase "culture industry" is laden with considerable ideological baggage, stemming from Horkheimer and Adorno's deeply pessimistic appraisal, I continue to find it the best way to characterize the processes under discussion, whereby cultural and entertainment forms become subject to processes of mass production.
14. Wertheim, *Vaudeville Wars*, 7.
15. Wertheim, *Vaudeville Wars*, 95–105, 117–133; Snyder, *The Voice of the City*, 35–37, 65–66.
16. Parker Zellers, *Tony Pastor: Dean of the Vaudeville Stage* (Ypsilanti, MI: Eastern Michigan University Press, 1971); Armond Fields, *Tony Pastor: Father of Vaudeville* (Jefferson, NC: McFarland & Co., 2007).
17. "The Late Tony Pastor," *Philadelphia Telegraph* (September 5, 1908). Robinson Locke Collection, Ser. 2, Vol. 284: Tony Pastor clippings, New York Public Library.
18. "Pastor Looks Far Back." Undated news item in Townsend Walsh scrapbook, New York Public Library.
19. Gillian Rodger, *Champagne Charlie and Pretty Jemima: Variety Theater in the Nineteenth Century* (Urbana, IL: University of Illinois Press, 2010), 156.
20. On the evolution of burlesque, see Robert Allen, *Horrible Prettiness: Burlesque and American Culture* (Chapel Hill, NC: University of North Carolina Press, 1991).

21. Pastor's year of birth is a point of great uncertainty in published accounts of his life. The various biographies of him that appeared in the *New York Clipper* and other publications contemporary with his lifetime most commonly gave the year as 1837, with 1835 also appearing occasionally. Yet Armond Fields, Pastor's most recent and thorough biographer, gives the birthdate of April 26, 1833, and so I am taking that date as the correct one. See Fields, *Tony Pastor*, 6.
22. See, for instance, the biography of Pastor that appeared on the occasion of his twenty-fifth anniversary as a theater owner and manager in the *New York Clipper* (March 29, 1890): 33. Fields questions the veracity of Pastor's association with Barnum and suggests that at the very least, if he did in fact appear at Barnum's Museum, he did not likely do so in the company of the more seasoned minstrel performers with which he claimed to have performed at the time. Fields, *Tony Pastor*, 8.
23. Undated article, *New York Clipper*. The article is clearly written during Pastor's time at 444 Broadway, and after he had already been there for at least a season, so it likely dates from 1862–1864. Tony Pastor clippings file, New York Public Library.
24. On the Bowery b'hoy and working class male culture in New York city, see Peter Buckley, "To the Opera House: Culture and Society in New York City, 1820–1860" (PhD diss., State University of New York at Stony Brook, 1984), especially 294–409; and Sean Wilentz, *Chants Democratic: New York City and the Rise of the American Working Class, 1788–1850*, twentieth anniversary ed. (New York: Oxford University Press, 2004), 300–301.
25. The best consideration of the sexual geography of New York City during the nineteenth century can be found in Timothy Gilfoyle, *City of Eros: New York City, Prostitution, and the Commercialization of Sex, 1790–1920* (New York: W.W. Norton and Company, 1992).
26. Brooks McNamara, *The New York Concert Saloon: The Devil's Own Nights* (Cambridge, UK: Cambridge University Press, 2002), 87.
27. Maretzek was an articulate observer of the musical life of New York City and published two memoirs that offer valuable firsthand accounts of mid-nineteenth-century developments. See especially *Crotchets and Quavers, or, Revelations of an Opera Manager in America* (New York: Da Capo, 1966), which includes Maretzek's impressions of the Jenny Lind phenomenon and his account of his experience with the Astor Place Opera House.
28. Advertisement for Tony Pastor's Opera House, *New York Herald* (September 6, 1865): 7.
29. Richard Butsch discusses the changes in American theatrical culture heralded by the rise of matinees and the effort to attract more women to the theater in *The Making of American Audiences: From Stage to Television* (Cambridge: Cambridge University Press, 2000), 66–80.
30. "Amusements," *New York Morning Telegraph* (April 25, 1875): 6.
31. "A Saturday Night Scene in the Bowery," *New York Times* (January 31, 1875): 2.
32. Zellers, *Tony Pastor*, 51.
33. See Pastor's ads in the *New York Times* (October 17, 1875): 11; and *New York Times* (October 26, 1875): 7.

34. Fields, *Tony Pastor*, 83.
35. Program for Tony Pastor's Opera House, April 3, 1871. Tony Pastor Collection, New York Public Library, Box 5.
36. Program for Tony Pastor's Opera House, October 4, 1875. Tony Pastor Collection, New York Public Library, Box 5.
37. Eric Lott, *Love and Theft: Blackface Minstrelsy and the American Working Class* (New York: Oxford University Press, 1993), 141.
38. Raymond Knapp, *The American Musical and the Formation of National Identity* (Princeton, NJ: Princeton University Press, 2005), 32.
39. "Tony Pastor's Theater," *New York Clipper* (March 1, 1879): 390.
40. "Tony Pastor's Theater," *New York Clipper* (March 15, 1879): 406.
41. Gilfoyle, *City of Eros*, 210.
42. "How to Get to Tony Pastor's." Undated handbill. Tony Pastor clippings file, New York Public Library.
43. Tony Pastor's 14th Street Theater. Poster. Tony Pastor Collection, New York Public Library, Box 6, folder 4. The poster is undated, but the designation of Pastor's theater as "new" on the marquee, as well as other details of the street scene, lead me to think it was produced during the first decade of Pastor's residency on 14th Street.
44. The *New York Clipper* review of Pastor's opening night at his 14th Street Theater, on October 24, 1881, recounted: "As his contribution towards the happiness of his auditors, the proprietor sang 'The Strawberry Blonde,' 'Lula, the Beautiful Hebrew Girl,' 'I'll Give You a Pointer on That,' and 'Yum, Yum, Yum,' and, as the auditors' special contribution towards the happiness of Tony, they handed up to him a large floral horseshoe as a prayer for good luck in the new house whose latchstring was then put outside for the first time by New York's favorite comic singer." "Tony Pastor's New Fourteenth Street Theater," *New York Clipper* (October 29, 1881): 522.
45. "Tony Pastor's Theater," *New York Clipper* (February 23, 1884): 834.
46. Again from the *Clipper*, concerning Pastor's 1885 engagement at the Academy of Music: "It is almost unnecessary to add that the Academy of Music held an audience noticeable not only as to numbers but also as to selectness, it embracing hundreds of ladies and children, as well as scores of males who rarely attend a variety entertainment unless it is Tony Pastor." "Tony Pastor's Two Theaters," *New York Clipper* (February 28, 1885): 792.
47. Snyder, *The Voice of the City*, 21.
48. Popular music historian Keir Keightley has offered convincing proof that, despite a long-standing assumption that the phrase "Tin Pan Alley" had become standard by the end of the nineteenth century, the first clear printed usage of the term in reference to music publishing and the popular music industry does not appear until 1903, in a newspaper article by the journalist Roy McCardell. See Keightley, "Taking Popular Music (and Tin Pan Alley and Jazz) Seriously," *Journal of Popular Music Studies* 22, no. 1 (March 2010): 92.
49. Charles Hamm, *Yesterdays: Popular Song in America* (New York: W.W. Norton & Company, 1979), 285.
50. Witmark and Goldberg, *The Story of the House of Witmark*, 73.

51. "City Summary," *New York Clipper* (June 15, 1878): 94. The article describes the demonstration of Edison's device as follows: "There is nothing hidden about it—you see a small cylinder, around which the operator places a sheet of tinfoil; then he talks into the mouthpiece, turning a small wheel, which revolves the cylinder all the time he thus talks. This done, he rises, fixes a longer funnel to the apparatus . . . and revolves the cylinder again, reproducing all the words and sounds as he had given them . . . [The resulting sounds] are loud enough to be heard in the remotest part of the hall; distinct enough in articulation to be fairly understood; but the precise tone of the voice is not clearly given."

52. The early history of sound recording is beyond the scope of this chapter. For background on the advent of the phonograph and the impact of sound recording in the late nineteenth century and early twentieth centuries, see Roland Gelatt, *The Fabulous Phonograph: From Edison to Stereo* (New York: Appleton-Century, 1954); Evan Eisenberg, *The Recording Angel: The Experience of Music from Aristotle to Zappa* (New York: Penguin, 1987); Andre Millard, *America on Record: A History of Recorded Sound* (New York: Cambridge University Press, 1995); William Kenney, *Recorded Music in American Life: The Phonograph and Popular Memory, 1890–1945* (New York: Oxford University Press, 1999); Jonathan Sterne, *The Audible Past: Cultural Origins of Sound Reproduction* (Durham, NC: Duke University Press, 2003); Mark Katz, *Capturing Sound: How Technology Has Changed Music* (Berkeley and Los Angeles: University of California Press, 2004); Greg Milner, *Perfecting Sound Forever: An Aural History of Recorded Music* (New York: Faber and Faber, 2009); and Patrick Feaster, "Phonography and the Recording in Popular Music," in *The Sage Handbook of Popular Music*, ed. Andy Bennett and Steve Waksman (London and Thousand Oaks, CA: Sage, 2015), 511–529.

53. On the nineteenth-century market for musical instruments, see Craig Roell, *The Piano in America, 1890–1940* (Chapel Hill, NC: University of North Carolina Press, 1989); Karen Linn, *That Half-Barbaric Twang: The Banjo in American Popular Culture* (Urbana, IL: University of Illinois Press, 1994); and Jeffrey Noonan, *The Guitar in America: Victorian Era to Jazz Age* (Jackson, MS: University Press of Mississippi, 2008).

54. Historian David Suisman says of Tin Pan Alley that its "essential impact . . . lay not in aesthetic innovation but in the relation between aesthetic forms and the industry's modern capitalist structure," which was shaped by two primary principles: "A firm's production had to rest on the systematic organization and application of knowledge . . . And the fundamental motivation of the business enterprise had to be financial profit." Suisman, *Selling Sounds*, 21.

55. Harris, *After the Ball*, 40.

56. Harris, *After the Ball*, 212–213.

57. Marks, *They All Sang*, 3, 16–17.

58. Marks, *They All Sang*, 128.

59. Suisman, *Selling Sounds*, 57.

60. *Tony Pastor's New Union Song Book* is bound with four other, similar collections of songs that were performed—and sometimes written—by Pastor during his

pre-Bowery career, into a single volume, *Tony Pastor's Complete Budget of Comic Songs* (New York: Dick and Fitzgerald, 1864).
61. "The Carte de Visite Album," in *Tony Pastor's Carte de Visite Album Songster* (New York: Dick and Fitzgerald, 1865), 5.
62. Andrea Volpe, "The Carte de Visite Craze," *New York Times* (August 6, 2013), http://opinionator.blogs.nytimes.com/2013/08/06/the-cartes-de-visite-craze.
63. "The Carte de Visite Album," 7.
64. Letter from Felix McGlennon to Tony Pastor, June 20, 1889. Tony Pastor Collection, New York Public Library, Box 1, Folder 5.
65. Letter from Matt Woodward to Tony Pastor, April 2, 1892. Tony Pastor Collection, New York Public Library, Box 1, Folder 5.
66. Letter from I.F. Farrar to Tony Pastor, August 1, 1876. Tony Pastor Collection, New York Public Library, Box 1, Folder 5.
67. Fields, *Tony Pastor*, 31.
68. *Tony Pastor's Music Box*. Tony Pastor Collection, New York Public Library, Box 3, Folder 15.
69. "A Saturday Night Scene on the Bowery."
70. "The Irish Queen Can Wait," *Fort Worth Morning Register* (October 27, 1897): 3. This article is reprinted from the *New York Sun*.
71. On the prevalence of women appearing as male impersonators in the variety theater, see Rodger, *Champagne Charlie and Pretty Jemima*, 127–146.
72. Kibler, *Rank Ladies*, 129. Lynn Abbott and Doug Seroff also credit Irwin for her early prominence as a "coon shouter" in *Ragged but Right: Black Traveling Shows, "Coon Songs," and the Dark Pathway to Blues and Jazz* (Jackson, MS: University of Mississippi Press, 2007), 16–17.
73. "Some People of the Stage," *Kansas City Star* (August 30, 1896): 5.
74. "The Stage," *Indianapolis Freeman* (October 3, 1896): 6.
75. For an insightful survey of the broader coon song phenomenon, see James Dormon, "Shaping the Popular Image of Post-Reconstruction American Blacks: The 'Coon Song' Phenomenon of the Gilded Age," *American Quarterly* 40, no. 4 (December 1988): 450–471.
76. Work on Bert Williams has grown significantly in recent years, and he has become the principal performing artist associated with this key transitional moment in the history of African American entertainment. See Thomas Riis, *Just Before Jazz: Black Musical Theater in New York, 1890–1915* (Washington, DC: Smithsonian Institution Press, 1989); Mel Watkins, *On the Real Side: A History of African American Comedy from Slavery to Chris Rock*, revised edition (Chicago: Chicago Review Press, 1999), 138–180; David Krasner, *Resistance, Parody, and Double Consciousness in African-American Theater, 1895–1910* (New York: St. Martin's Press, 1997); W.T. Lhamon, "Whittling on Dynamite: The Difference Bert Williams Makes," in *Listen Again: A Momentary History of Pop Music* (Durham, NC: Duke University Press, 2007), 7–25; Tim Brooks, *Lost Sounds: Blacks and the Birth of the Recording Industry, 1890–1919* (Urbana, IL: University of Illinois Press, 2004), 105–148; Louis Chode-Sokei, *The Last "Darky": Bert Williams, Black-on-Black Minstrelsy, and the African Diaspora* (Durham, NC: Duke University Press, 2006); Karen Sotiropoulos, *Staging*

Race: Black Performers in Turns of the Century America (Cambridge, MA: Harvard University Press, 2006); and Camille Forbes, *Introducing Bert Williams: Burnt Cork, Broadway, and the Story of America's First Great Black Star* (New York: Basic Civitas, 2008).

77. Abbott and Seroff, *Ragged but Right*, 6. Others who have expanded on Hogan's significance include Thomas Riis, whose study of African American musical theater treats Hogan's work in some detail; and Karen Sotiropoulos, who gives Hogan a relative amount of prominence in her analysis of African American performing artists at the turn of the twentieth century.
78. In fact there were several black minstrel troupes that carried the name "Georgia Minstrels" created in the years 1865–1866. The original such organization, according to Robert Toll, was Brooker and Clayton's Georgia Minstrels, and that troupe's success led to many imitators, just as the success of the Fisk Jubilee Singers did the same. See Toll, *Blacking Up: The Minstrel Show in Nineteenth-Century America* (New York: Oxford University Press, 1974), 199, 276.
79. Witmark and Goldberg, *The Story of the House of Witmark*, 133.
80. Witmark and Goldberg, *The Story of the House of Witmark*, 135.
81. James Weldon Johnson, *Black Manhattan* (New York: Arno Press, 1968), 114.
82. Hoffman's career with Witmark and Sons is briefly surveyed in Witmark and Goldberg, 169–170.
83. David Jasen and Gene Jones, *Spreadin' Rhythm Around: Black Popular Songwriters, 1880-1930* (New York: Routledge, 2005), 32.
84. Abbott and Seroff, *Ragged but Right*, 15.
85. All of these versions of Hogan's song except one—by Frank Finney—also appear in Abbott and Seroff, *Ragged but Right*, 15. However, I found these references independently in the contemporary sources where they appeared, mostly the *Indianapolis Freeman*.
86. Advertisement for Howley, Haviland & Co. Music Publishers, *New York Clipper* (September 3, 1898): 454.
87. Sotiropoulos, *Staging Race*, 75.
88. A 1901 editorial in the *Indianapolis Freeman* is representative of this opinion. Writing about ragtime music, the piece asserts: "It is said that 'rag time' music is going out of fashion. We are glad of it. More lies have been sprung over the footlights in rag time than otherwise. Take the vile lie, 'All Coon Look Alike to Me,' and that other, 'Every Race Has a Flag but the Coon.'... The music of rag time is tolerable, but most of the sentiment of it is false, degrading and intolerable." "Rag Time Music," *Indianapolis Freeman* (March 16, 1901): 4.
89. Elijah Wald, *How the Beatles Destroyed Rock 'n' Roll: An Alternative History of American Popular Music* (New York: Oxford University Press, 2009), 30.
90. Advertisement for Ernest Hogan, *New York Clipper* (July 3, 1897): 297.
91. An excellent, detailed account of the Black Patti's early career can be found in John Graziano, "The Early Life and Career of the 'Black Patti': The Odyssey of an African American Singer in the Late Nineteenth Century," *Journal of the American Musicological Society* 53, no. 3 (Fall 2000): 543–596. For the most complete treatment of Sissieretta Jones' life, see Maureen Lee, *Sissieretta Jones: "The Greatest Singer of Her*

Race," 1868–1933 (Columbia: University of South Carolina Press, 2012). Also see Eileen Southern, *The Music of Black Americans: A History*, 2nd ed. (New York: W.W. Norton & Company, 1983), 242–245; and Abbott and Seroff, *Out of Sight*, 27–40.

92. Graziano also questions whether the name, the Black Patti, which was meant to reflect the praise that Jones had drawn from critics, was invented more in the spirit of promotion. According to his research no published account calling Jones the "Black Patti" can be found prior to the point at which she and her managers began using it to advertise her talent. See Graziano, "The Early Life and Career of the 'Black Patti,'" 565–567.
93. Graziano, "The Early Life and Career of the 'Black Patti,'" 587.
94. Southern, *The Music of Black Americans*, 245.
95. "The Stage," *Indianapolis Freeman* (September 11, 1897): 5.
96. On the prevalence of the ideology of racial uplift among African American political leaders and intellectuals at the turn of the twentieth century, see Kevin Gaines, *Uplifting the Race: Black Leadership, Politics, and Culture in the Twentieth Century* (Chapel Hill, NC: University of North Carolina Press, 1996).
97. "Amusements," *Kalamazoo Gazette* (November 7, 1897): 1.
98. "Ohio," *New York Clipper* (December 11, 1897): 675.
99. "The Stage," *Indianapolis Freeman* (December 3, 1898): 5. All further quotations in this paragraph are from the same source.
100. Lester Walton, "Music and the Stage," *New York Age* (March 30, 1911): 6.
101. Tom Fletcher, *100 Years of the Negro in Show Business* (New York: Da Capo, 1984), 141.
102. Johnson, 120–122. On Hogan's involvement with the Smart Set, see Abbott and Seroff, *Ragged but Right*, 81–84.
103. Riis, *Just Before Jazz*, remains the best source for the musical theater productions that occupied Hogan in his later years.
104. Walton, "Music and the Stage," *New York Age* (June 18, 1908): 6.
105. Walton, "Music and the Stage," *New York Age* (June 25, 1908): 6.
106. For details of Handy's career, see W.C. Handy, *Father of the Blues: An Autobiography* (New York: Da Capo, 1969); and David Robertson, *W.C. Handy: The Life and Times of the Man Who Made the Blues* (New York: Alfred A. Knopf, 2009).
107. "Art of Making Merry," *Anaconda Standard* (December 27, 1903): 7.

Chapter 4

1. Lawrence Gushee, *Pioneers of Jazz: The Story of the Creole Band* (New York: Oxford University Press, 2005).
2. Gushee surveys the various accounts that have been given in *Pioneers of Jazz*, 169–175.
3. See Tim Brooks, *Lost Sounds: Blacks and the Birth of the Recording Industry, 1890–1919* (Urbana: University of Illinois Press, 2005), for a consideration of black recording activity in the years preceding the race record boom initiated by Smith and Bradford.

4. Contract between Reisenweber's Inc. and E.B. Edwards, D. Jos. LaRocca, Lawrence Shields, Anthony Sbarbaro, and Henry Ragas [the members of the Original Dixieland Jazz Band], May 25, 1918. Nick LaRocca Collection, Series 7—Business and Personal Documents, Box 1, Folder 2, Hogan Jazz Archive. A note on the front page of this contract explains that the band's original contract with Reisenweber's, from January 1917, was in the possession of Max Hart, the agent who booked the ODJB into the restaurant. I do not know whether it too included such a clause about the band's obligation to provide "jazz" music.

5. Kimberly Teal has pursued a parallel argument regarding the crucial role that venues play in giving meaning to jazz in *Jazz Places: How Performance Spaces Shape Jazz History* (Berkeley and Los Angeles: University of California Press, 2021). However, Teal's focus is on contemporary, twenty-first-century jazz venues and institutions, and so her study offers a valuable complement to the historical perspective offered in this chapter.

6. Lewis Erenberg, *Steppin' Out: New York Nightlife and the Transformation of American Culture, 1890–1930* (Chicago: University of Chicago Press, 1981); Shane Vogel, *The Scene of the Harlem Cabaret: Race, Sexuality, Performance* (Chicago: University of Chicago Press, 2009).

7. Franco Fabbri, "A Theory of Musical Genres: Two Applications," *Popular Music Perspectives*, ed. David Horn and Philip Tagg (Gotenburg, Sweden: International Association for the Study of Popular Music, 1981): 57.

8. This last example—heavy metal and arena rock—is a central topic in Steve Waksman, *This Ain't the Summer of Love: Conflict and Crossover in Heavy Metal and Punk* (Berkeley and Los Angeles: University of California Press, 2009).

9. Kathy Ogren provides a valuable overview of 1920s jazz venues in her book, *The Jazz Revolution: Twenties America and the Meaning of Jazz* (New York: Oxford University Press, 1989), 56–86.

10. Interview with Peter Bocage, January 29, 1959, reel 1, transcript p. 6. Hogan Jazz Archive Oral History Collection.

11. Donald Marquis, in his groundbreaking study of Buddy Bolden, *In Search of Buddy Bolden: First Man of Jazz*, revised edition (Baton Rouge: Louisiana State University Press, 2005), makes a convincing case that despite the assertions of Bocage and others who rejected the notion that Bolden was musically literate, there is good reason to believe that Bolden could read music, even if he did not typically rely on sheet music during the performances for which he became best known. See Marquis, *In Search of Buddy Bolden*, 104–106.

12. Efforts to document the history of jazz in New Orleans have given rise to a rich and varied literature that is, in many ways, the foundation for jazz historical scholarship writ large. Along with the valuable studies by Gushee and Marquis already cited, see Frederic Ramsey and Charles Edward Smith, eds., *Jazzmen: The Story of Hot Jazz Told in the Lives of the Men Who Created It*, rev. with a new introduction by Nat Hentoff (New York: Limelight Editions, 1985); Alan Lomax, *Mister Jelly Roll: The Fortunes of Jelly Roll Morton, New Orleans Creole and "Inventor of Jazz"* (Berkeley and Los Angeles: University of California Press, 1950); Thomas Brothers,

Louis Armstrong's New Orleans (W.W. Norton & Company, 2006); Charles Hersch, *Subversive Sounds: Race and the Birth of Jazz in New Orleans* (Chicago: University of Chicago Press, 2007); and Bruce Boyd Raeburn, *New Orleans Style and the Writing of American Jazz History* (Ann Arbor: University of Michigan Press, 2009).

13. Alan Lomax provides the classic account of the geographic and racial divide between "Uptown" and "Downtown" in New Orleans jazz in *Mister Jelly Roll*, 83–86.
14. Marquis, *In Search of Buddy Bolden*, 67–68.
15. Marquis, *In Search of Buddy Bolden*, 109.
16. John McCusker, *Creole Trombone: Kid Ory and the Early Years of Jazz* (Jackson: University Press of Mississippi, 2012), 59.
17. Louis Armstrong, *Satchmo: My Life in New Orleans*, rev. with an introduction by Dan Morgenstern (New York: Da Capo, 1986), 22–23.
18. Armstrong, *Satchmo*, 23.
19. Quoted in Brothers, *Louis Armstrong's New Orleans*, 89.
20. The word "jazz" was not in circulation during the time of Bolden's career, at least not in print. Bolden's music would most likely have been considered a sort of ragtime, although as Thomas Brothers explains, the variant of ragtime associated with musicians like Bolden was distinctly situated in New Orleans and not entirely of a piece with the more famous sort connected to the likes of pianist-composer Scott Joplin. In New Orleans ragtime was less likely to be fully composed, placed less emphasis on the piano and comparatively greater emphasis on string and horn instruments, and was defined primarily by a musician's ability to "rag" a tune, which meant to play variations on and around the more fixed, pre-arranged components. See Brothers, *Louis Armstrong's New Orleans*, 157–159.
21. New Orleans City Ordinance No. 3131. Donald Marquis Collection, Hogan Jazz Archive.
22. Letter from James Reynolds to Martin Behrman, June 3, 1911. Donald Marquis Collection, Hogan Jazz Archive.
23. Letter from L.W. Rawlings to James Reynolds, July 6, 1911. Donald Marquis Collection, Hogan Jazz Archive.
24. Statement to police by Joseph Ferrantelli, July 5, 1911. Donald Marquis Collection, Hogan Jazz Archive.
25. Poster advertising "A Grand Benefit Ball," December 19, 1910. Hogan Jazz Archive.
26. Poster advertising "A Grand Fancy Dress and Masquerade Ball," April 14, 1910. Hogan Jazz Archive.
27. Poster advertising "A Grand Lawn Party," August 9, 1909. Hogan Jazz Archive.
28. For background about Economy Hall, see McCusker, *Creole Trombone*, 101–102; Richard Allen, "Economy Hall," unpublished memo dated January 23, 1969, Hogan Jazz Archives.
29. Armstrong, *Satchmo*, 138.
30. Indeed Robichaux's centrality is such that the whole collection of posters housed at the Hogan Jazz Archive advertising these early twentieth-century dances comes from a corresponding collection of Robichaux's old sheet music, from his days as a bandleader. Robichaux used the concert posters to wrap and store pieces of sheet music.
31. Jempi Di Donder, "Professor Robichaux," *Footnote* (June/July 1989): 8.

32. Poster advertising "The First Grand Ball of the Season to be Given by the Young Men's Olympian Benefit Association Juniors," January 8, 1900. Hogan Jazz Archive.
33. Details about Lincoln and Johnson Parks can be found in Marquis, *In Search of Buddy Bolden*, 59–62.
34. Interview with Louis Jones, January 19, 1959, reel 1, transcript p. 17. Hogan Jazz Archive Oral History Collection.
35. Frederick Ramsey and Charles Edward Smith open their pivotal 1939 collection, *Jazzmen*, with an account of Bolden's gesture; while among more recent historians, Thomas Brothers paints the conflict between Bolden and Robichaux as a sort of class warfare in which Bolden symbolized the victory of working-class black masculinity through the force of his horn. See Ramsey and Smith, *Jazzmen*, 6; Brothers, *Louis Armstrong's New Orleans*, 152–153.
36. Interview with Bill Matthews, March 10, 1959, reel 3, transcript pp. 20–21. Hogan Jazz Archive Oral History Collection.
37. Poster advertising "A Grand Excursion Pic-Nic," September 24–25, 1907. Hogan Jazz Archive.
38. Advertisement for a Special Scenic Trip DeLuxe to San Diego and Tijuana, Mexico, *California Eagle* (July 29, 1922). Kid Ory files, Hogan Jazz Archive.
39. See McCusker, *Creole Trombone*, 144–150, for details about the making of Ory's first recordings.
40. Robin D.G. Kelley, *Race Rebels: Culture, Politics, and the Black Working Class* (New York: The Free Press, 1996), 57.
41. Posters advertising an "Excursion to Thibodeaux," March 14, year unknown; and "First Excursion to Covington, Abita Springs, and Slidell, La.," May 5, 1908. Hogan Jazz Archive.
42. William Kenney, *Jazz on the River* (Chicago: University of Chicago Press, 2005), 13.
43. Pops Foster with Tom Stoddard, *The Autobiography of Pops Foster, New Orleans Jazzman* (Berkeley and Los Angeles: University of California Press, 1971), 113.
44. Kenney, *Jazz on the River*, 34–35.
45. In his autobiography, Armstrong compared his time with Marable to that spent in Kid Ory's band, which he left to play on the riverboats: "Fate's [band] had a wide range and they played all the latest music because they could read at sight. Kid Ory's band could catch on to a tune quickly, and once they had it no one could outplay them. But I wanted to do more than fake the music all the time because there is more to music than just playing one style." Armstrong, *Satchmo*, 182.
46. Details about the membership of the Creole Band come from Gushee, *Pioneers of Jazz*, 23–59.
47. Gushee, *Pioneers of Jazz*, 94.
48. "Pantages Show Is Winner," *Portland Oregonian* (November 24, 1914).
49. Gushee, *Pioneers of Jazz*, 197.
50. Raeburn, "Early New Orleans Jazz in Theaters," *Louisiana History* 43, no. 1 (Winter 2002): 42.
51. Lowery's distinguished but largely unheralded career has been well documented in Clifford Watkins, *Showman: The Life and Music of Perry George Lowery* (Jackson: University Press of Mississippi, 2003).

52. "Artists' Forum," *Variety* (September 19, 1919): 7. For details concerning Sweatman's career, see Brooks, *Lost Sounds*, 337–354; Mark Berresford, *That's Got 'Em: The Life and Music of Wilbur Sweatman* (Jackson: University Press of Mississippi, 2010).
53. Dave Peyton, "The Musical Bunch: The Origin of Jazz," *Chicago Defender* (December 12, 1925): 7.
54. Garvin Bushell with Mark Tucker, *Jazz from the Beginning* (New York: Da Capo Press, 1998), 22.
55. Rex Stewart, *Boy Meets Horn*, ed. Claire Gordon (Ann Arbor, MI: University of Michigan Press, 1991), 47–48.
56. Foster, *The Autobiography of Pops Foster*, 120.
57. See Brothers, *Louis Armstrong: Master of Modernism* (New York: W.W. Norton & Company, 2014), 22, for a description of Oliver's proclivity toward showmanship and "freak" playing; and 86, on the secondary priority attached to harmony by Oliver's band in 1923 when it made a series of historic recordings with Louis Armstrong on second cornet.
58. Perry Bradford, *Born with the Blues: Perry Bradford's Own Story* (New York: Oak Publications, 1965), 99–100.
59. Tony Langston, "'Mamie Smith Co.' Fills the Avenue; 'Mexico' Enters Second Week at Grand," *Chicago Defender* (March 5, 1921): 4.
60. "Mamie Smith a Hit," *Chicago Defender* (March 5, 1921): 5.
61. Advertisement for Mamie Smith and OKeh Records, *Talking Machine World* (April 15, 1921): n.p.
62. Bradford, *Born with the Blues*, 128–129.
63. Erenberg treats Tucker as a paradigmatic cabaret artist; see *Steppin' Out*, 176–205.
64. Sophie Tucker, *Some of These Days: The Autobiography of Sophie Tucker* (Garden City, NY: Doubleday, Doran and Company, 1945), 63.
65. Susan Ecker and Lloyd Ecker, liner notes to Sophie Tucker, *Origins of the Red Hot Mama, 1910–1922*, Archeophone Records ARCH 5010, 2009, compact disc.
66. Sime Silverman, "Sophie Tucker and Her Five Kings of Syncopation," *Variety* (September 27, 1918): 17.
67. Wynn, "Show Reviews: Colonial," *Variety* (March 9, 1917): 15.
68. Jack Lait, "Show Reviews: Palace," *Variety* (March 5, 1920): 28.
69. Tucker, *Some of These Days*, 131.
70. W.V., "New Acts and Reappearances: Ted Lewis," *New York Clipper* (August 27, 1919): 10.
71. Abel Green, "New Shows This Week: Palace," *Variety* (May 21, 1924): 31.
72. Thomas DeLong, *Pops: Paul Whiteman, King of Jazz* (Piscataway, NJ: New Century Publishers, 1983), 13.
73. San Francisco's status as an incubator for jazz is often overlooked or downplayed, but the music took hold there at a very early date, and some have claimed that the city's Barbary Coast district has as much claim to being the place where jazz first arose as the African American district of New Orleans. See Tom Stoddard, *Jazz on the Barbary Coast* (Berkeley, CA: Heyday Books, 1998).
74. DeLong, *Pops*, 27–28.

75. Sime Silverman, "New Acts This Week: Paul Whiteman Orchestra," *Variety* (October 7, 1921): 21. According to DeLong, Whiteman accepted a fee of $900 for this initial week's run at the Palace, which was significantly less than he was receiving for his standing engagement at the Palais Royal, where he was earning $2500 weekly at the time. When Whiteman was re-booked at the Palace soon after his debut, his fee jumped to $2750 per week. See DeLong, *Pops*, 49.
76. Silverman, "Paul Whiteman Orchestra," 21.
77. "Presentations—New Acts: Ethel Waters," *Variety* (September 21, 1927): 26. Waters discusses her transition from playing for predominantly black audiences to predominantly white ones in her autobiography, *His Eye Is on the Sparrow*, written with Charles Samuels (Garden City, NY: Doubleday & Company, 1951), 173–177.
78. "Vaudefilms Soak St. Vaude," *Variety* (October 26, 1927): 29; "Vaude House Reviews: Palace," *Variety* (May 29, 1929): 40.
79. "Ellington's Silver Jubilee in *Down Beat*," *The Duke Ellington Reader*, ed. Mark Tucker (New York: Oxford University Press, 1995), 265.
80. "Leatrice Joy Sings Pleasingly at the Palace," *New York Times* (April 22, 1929): 30. Terry Teachout identifies this review as the first instance where the *Times* had commented on Ellington's music. See Teachout, *Duke: A Life of Duke Ellington* (New York: Gotham Books, 2013), 92.
81. Bige, "New Acts: Duke Ellington Band," *Variety* (April 24, 1929): 38.
82. Bige, "New Acts: Duke Ellington Band," 38.
83. Elijah Wald, *How the Beatles Destroyed Rock 'n' Roll: An Alternative History of American Popular Music* (New York: Oxford University Press, 2009), 56; Stoddard, *Jazz on the Barbary Coast*, 193.
84. William Kenney, *Chicago Jazz: A Cultural History, 1904–1930* (Chicago: University of Chicago Press, 1993), 66–67.
85. Gordon Seagrove, "Blues Is Jazz and Jazz Is Blues," *Chicago Tribune* (July 11, 1915): E8. Also see Wald, *How the Beatles*, 57, for discussion of this same article.
86. Seagrove, "Blues Is Jazz and Jazz Is Blues," E8.
87. "Cabarets," *Variety* (October 27, 1916): 12.
88. "Cabarets," *Variety* (November 3, 1916): 20.
89. Kenney, *Chicago Jazz*, 67. Details about Jack Laine and his connection to the younger white New Orleans jazz musicians who would draw attention upon moving to Chicago can be found in Charles Edward Smith, "White New Orleans," in Ramsey and Smith, *Jazzmen*, 39–58; and H.O. Brunn, *The Story of the Original Dixieland Jazz Band* (London: The Jazz Book Club, 1963), 17–25.
90. Brunn, *The Story of the Original Dixieland Jazz Band*, 30.
91. Casino Gardens publicity postcard, Nick LaRocca Collection, Series 6—Publicity, Folder 1 (1916), Hogan Jazz Archive.
92. The "Four Hundred Club" Room at Reisenweber's publicity postcard, Nick LaRocca Collection, Series 10—Scrapbooks, Box 22, Scrapbook 1 (1917-1936), Hogan Jazz Archive. This is one of several postcards portraying the different rooms at Reisenweber's that was saved by LaRocca. On this particular card, he wrote the annotation, "ODJB Room."
93. Erenberg, *Steppin' Out*, 123–124.

94. Vogel, *The Scene of the Harlem Cabaret*, 69.
95. "Cabarets," *Variety* (February 2, 1917): 8.
96. Vogel, *The Scene of the Harlem Cabaret*, 69.
97. Erenberg, *Steppin' Out*, 133.
98. On the political and social history of Prohibition, including the many ways in which the law was undermined, circumvented and subverted during the thirteen years that it was in place, see Daniel Okrent, *Last Call: The Rise and Fall of Prohibition* (New York: Scribner, 2011).
99. Burton Peretti, *Nightclub City: Politics and Amusement in Manhattan* (Philadelphia: University of Pennsylvania Press, 2007), 4.
100. Paul Chevigny, *Gigs: Jazz and the Cabaret Laws in New York City* (New York: Routledge, 1991), 55.
101. Chevigny, *Gigs*, 56; also see Peretti, *Nightclub City*, 66.
102. Timothy Gilfoyle, *City of Eros: New York City, Prostitution, and the Commercialization of Sex, 1790–1920* (New York: W.W. Norton & Company, 1992), 203.
103. David Levering Lewis, *When Harlem Was in Vogue* (New York: Penguin, 1997), 28; Jim Haskins, *The Cotton Club* (New York: Hippocrene Books, 1994), 25.
104. Gilfoyle, *City of Eros*, 209; Kevin Mumford, *Interzones: Black/White Sex Districts in Chicago and New York in the Early Twentieth Century* (New York: Columbia University Press, 1997), 28–30.
105. On the racial policies of these clubs, see Lewis, *When Harlem Was in Vogue*, 209–211; Haskins, *The Cotton Club*, 36–38. The Cotton Club was reputed to have been the most exclusionary of the major Harlem nightspots where admission of African Americans was concerned, but according to Jim Haskins, even at Small's Paradise where black patrons were admitted, "its prices successfully shielded the white downtowners from the 'colored rabble'" (38).
106. Sime Silverman, "Night Life of the World: Black Belt (Harlem, N.Y. City)," *Variety* (February 17, 1926): 8.
107. Wallace Thurman, "Negro Life in New York's Harlem: A Lively Picture of a Popular and Interesting Section [First Installment]," *The Light and Heebie Jeebies* (November 5, 1927): 46.
108. Thurman, "Negro Life in New York's Harlem, Installment Two," *The Light and Heebie Jeebies* (November 12, 1927): 10.
109. Thurman, "Negro Life, Installment Two," 10.
110. Jimmy Durante and Jack Kofoed, *Nightclubs* (New York: Alfred A. Knopf, 1931), 113.
111. Chad Heap, *Slumming: Sexual and Racial Encounters in American Nightlife, 1885–1940* (Chicago: University of Chicago Press, 2009), 196.
112. For more on the complicated and sometimes tense relationships between white and African Americans in 1920s Harlem, see Lewis, *When Harlem Was in Vogue*, 156–197; and Ann Douglas, *Terrible Honesty: Mongrel Manhattan in the 1920s* (New York: Farrar, Strauss and Giroux, 1995).
113. See John Gennari, *Blowin' Hot and Cool: Jazz and Its Critics* (Chicago: University of Chicago Press, 2006); and Raeburn, *New Orleans Style*.
114. Gushee, *Pioneers of Jazz*, 57–58, 71–77.
115. Stoddard, *Jazz on the Barbary Coast*, 42.

116. Stoddard, *Jazz on the Barbary Coast*, 13.
117. Stewart, *Boy Meets Horn*, 70.
118. Advertisement for the Savoy Ballroom, *New York Age* (March 20, 1926): 8.
119. Savoy Ballroom Reservation Guide (n.d.), Programs and Playbills Collection, Schomburg Center for Research in Black Culture.
120. "Plantation Frolics on List of Entertainment at New Savoy Ballroom," *The Light and Heebie Jeebies* (November 19, 1927): 4.
121. "Inaugural Ball at Savoy Triumphant Occasion," *The Light and Heebie Jeebies* (December 3, 1927): 28.
122. Brothers, *Louis Armstrong: Master of Modernism*, 290.
123. Peyton, "The Musical Bunch," *Chicago Defender* (April 28, 1928): 6.
124. Peyton, "The Musical Bunch," *Chicago Defender* (May 5, 1928): 6.
125. Nat Shapiro and Nat Hentoff, *Hear Me Talkin' to Ya: The Story of Jazz as Told by the Men Who Made It* (New York: Dover, 1955), 117–118.
126. Brothers, *Louis Armstrong: Master of Modernism*, 296–297.
127. Fabian Holt, *Genre in Popular Music* (Chicago: University of Chicago Press, 2007), 81.

Chapter 5

1. "'Modern' and 'Mod'ren' Music," *Musical America* (November 25, 1933): 16.
2. Marc Blitzstein, "Popular Music—An Invasion: 1923–1933," *Modern Music* 10, no. 2 (January/February 1933): 98.
3. Blitzstein, "Popular Music," 98. Mr. Damrosch here refers to Walter Damrosch; Mr. Koussevitzky to Serge Koussevitzky. Both were leading orchestral conductors of the era, whose endorsement of Gershwin gave his work a stamp of legitimacy. Similarly with the I.S.C.M., or International Society for Contemporary Music, a respected body that had selected Gershwin's work for inclusion at its annual music festival.
4. Blitzstein, "Popular Music," 102.
5. Lawrence Levine, *Highbrow/Lowbrow: The Emergence of Cultural Hierarchy in America* (Cambridge, MA: Harvard University Press, 1988), 177.
6. Levine, *Highbrow/Lowbrow*, 164.
7. Dates for these concert halls and many others can be found in the appendix to Michael Forsyth, *Buildings for Music: The Architect, the Musician, and the Listener from the Seventeenth Century to the Present Day* (Cambridge, MA: MIT Press, 1985), 329–333.
8. Paul DiMaggio, "Cultural Entrepreneurship in Nineteenth-Century Boston: The Creation of an Organizational Base for High Culture in America," *Media, Culture and Society* 4, no. 1 (January 1982): 35. For a social history of the rise of this new economic elite in New York City, see Sven Beckert, *The Monied Metropolis: New York City and the Consolidation of the American Bourgeoisie, 1850–1896* (Cambridge: Cambridge University Press, 2001).

9. Details about Leopold Damrosch come from Richard Schickel, *The World of Carnegie Hall* (New York: Julian Messner, Inc., 1960), 19–22; and Joseph Horowitz, *Classical Music in America—A History* (New York: W.W. Norton, 2007), 136, 150–153.
10. Beckert, *The Monied Metropolis*, 212.
11. Andrew Carnegie, "The Gospel of Wealth," in *The Gospel of Wealth and Other Timely Essays* (New York: The Century Co., 1900), 17–18.
12. Carnegie, "The Gospel of Wealth," 37–38.
13. Tim Page and Carnegie Hall, *Carnegie Hall Treasures* (New York: Harper Design, 2011), 16, 40.
14. Page and Carnegie Hall, *Carnegie Hall Treasures*, 46; Schickel, *The World of Carnegie Hall*, 30–31.
15. Forsyth, *Buildings for Music*, 225.
16. "It Stood the Test Well," *New York Times* (May 6, 1891): 5.
17. Emily Thompson, *The Soundscape of Modernity: Architectural Acoustics and the Culture of Listening in America, 1900–1933* (Cambridge, MA: MIT Press, 2002), 4.
18. Thompson, *The Soundscape of Modernity*, 41.
19. Scott DeVeaux, "The Emergence of the Jazz Concert, 1935–1945," *American Music* 7, no. 1 (Spring 1989): 8.
20. I have discussed this feature of the jazz concert, the presentation of the music as part of a historical or evolutionary narrative, in "Live Recollections: Uses of the Past in U.S. Concert Life," *IASPM@Journal* 1, no. 1 (2010): 5–8.
21. Gilbert Seldes, *The 7 Lively Arts* (Mineola, NY: Dover Publications, 2001), 99. This book is a reprint of the original edition, first issued in 1924.
22. John Howland effectively summarizes the place of Whiteman within debates concerning the jazz tradition in *Ellington Uptown: Duke Ellington, James P. Johnson, and the Birth of Concert Jazz* (Ann Arbor: University of Michigan Press, 2009), 144–145.
23. Elijah Wald, *How the Beatles Destroyed Rock 'n' Roll: An Alternative History of American Popular Music* (New York: Oxford University Press, 2009), 74.
24. For details on Grofé joining Whiteman's band, see Thomas DeLong, *Pops: Paul Whiteman, King of Jazz* (Piscataway, NJ: New Century Publishers, 1983), 36; and Don Rayno, *Paul Whiteman: Pioneer in American Music*, Vol. 1, *1890–1930* (Lanham, MD: Scarecrow Press, 2003), 35–36.
25. "The Band Craze," *Variety* (December 29, 1922): 14.
26. Among the more outspoken critics of Whiteman along these lines was the British music critic Ernest Newman, who expressed strong distaste for jazz in general and Whiteman in particular. Addressing Whiteman's practice of "jazzing the classics," Newman proclaimed: "Argument would be wasted on him and people of his way of thinking. All we musicians can do is to say to him and them 'Jazz hymns, ancient and modern and future, as much as you like—most of these are hardly above your own intellectual level—but keep your dirty paws off your betters.'" "British Music Critic Excoriates Jazz," *New York Times* (September 12, 1926): 1. Whiteman's stance on this issue is outlined in one of a series of articles he wrote for the *Boston Globe* in the weeks leading up to the Aeolian Hall concert. See Paul Whiteman, "Making Beautiful Dance Tunes out of Half-Forgotten Classics," *Boston Globe* (December 30,

1923): 46. Addressing "Song of India" in particular, he writes: "If you can take a brilliant, strongly melodic, strongly rhythmic number somewhere out of the world of 'great music,' and shape and fashion and set it as true gold ought to be set, you are doing no harm but an actual artistic service."
27. See "Tallest Building North of 23[d] Street Being Erected in Times Square District," *New York Times* (February 11, 1912): 21; "Building Changes Near Times Square," *New York Times* (March 17, 1912): 17.
28. "New York's Newest Music Hall," *New York Times* (October 27, 1912): 12. Reports on the capacity of the hall varied, and one review noted that it was said to hold 1,800, but also observed that it seemed much smaller to the eye. The figure of around 1,300 is in accord with later accounts of the hall's size.
29. "Gottfried Galston in Aeolian Hall," *New York Times* (November 3, 1912): 17; "New York Symphony in New Aeolian Hall," *New York Times* (November 9, 1912): 11.
30. Paul Whiteman and Mary McBride, *Jazz* (New York: J.H. Sears & Company, 1926): 94.
31. "Jazz to Vie for Recognition as National Music in U.S. Concert," *New York Tribune* (December 11, 1923): 12.
32. "First American Jazz Concert Will be Paul Whiteman's," *Variety* (December 13, 1923): 1, 7.
33. Whiteman and McBride, *Jazz*, 89.
34. Details concerning the program for the "Experiment in Modern Music" are drawn from the following sources: Whiteman and McBride, *Jazz*, 98–111; Rayno, *Paul Whiteman*, 71–86, 390–391; Thornton Hagert, liner notes to *An Experiment in Modern Music: Paul Whiteman at Aeolian Hall*, RCA Special Products DMM2-0518, 1981, LP; Samuel Charters and Leonard Kunstadt, *Jazz: A History of the New York Scene* (New York: Da Capo, 1981), 138–143. I have also benefited from the efforts of conductor Maurice Peress to reconstruct the concert at Aeolian Hall, released as *The Birth of Rhapsody in Blue: Paul Whiteman's Historic Aeolian Hall Concert of 1924* (Music Masters, 1986).
35. Whiteman and McBride, *Jazz*, 104.
36. Olin Downes, "A Concert of Jazz," *New York Times* (February 13, 1924): 16. Hagert suggests that Whiteman would learn from his Aeolian Hall concert that, "his audience enjoyed the 'discordant' old jazz, at least in small doses," and that when he would repeat the "Experiment" in later appearances, "the pretext that it was a thing to be despised became increasingly transparent." *An Experiment in Modern Music*.
37. Information about the size of Whiteman's recording and performance orchestras of the time come from Rayno, who has painstakingly reconstructed the details of all of Whiteman's recording sessions and also provides reliable material about his concert ensemble; Rayno, *Paul Whiteman*.
38. Whiteman and McBride, *Jazz*, 105.
39. Hagert, *An Experiment in Modern Music*.
40. Downes, "A Concert of Jazz;" Abel Green, "Whiteman's 'Jazz' Recital," *New York Clipper* (February 15, 1924): 15.
41. Howland, *Ellington Uptown*, 83.
42. Hagert, *An Experiment in Modern Music*.

43. Rayno, *Paul Whiteman*, 77–78; Hagert, *An Experiment in Modern Music*.
44. One of the more pointed evaluations of Gershwin's work, and the concert as a whole, came from Lawrence Gilman, critic for the *New York Tribune*. Gilman complained that Gershwin's *Rhapsody* had deficiencies that characterized the concert as a whole, calling the music offered by Whiteman "half alive. Its gorgeous vitality of rhythm and of instrumental color is impaired by melodic and harmonic anaemia of the most pernicious kind . . . Recall the most ambitious piece on yesterday's program, the 'Rhapsody in Blue' of Mr. Gershwin, and weep over the lifelessness of its melody and harmony, so derivative, so stale, so inexpressive. And then recall, for contrast, the rich inventiveness of the rhythms, the saliency and vividness of the orchestral color." Gilman, "Paul Whiteman and the Palais Royalists Extend Their Kingdom; Jazz at Aeolian Hall," *New York Tribune* (February 13, 1924): 9.
45. Virgil Thomson, "George Gershwin," *Modern Music* 13, no. 1 (November/December 1935): 13.
46. Wald, *How the Beatles Destroyed Rock 'n' Roll*, 78.
47. Wald, *How the Beatles Destroyed Rock 'n' Roll*, 235.
48. Levine, *Highbrow/Lowbrow*, 221–223.
49. F.D. Perkins, "Paul Whiteman in 2d 'Experiment' at Aeolian Hall," *New York Tribune* (March 8, 1924): 6; "Carnegie Hall Captured by Jazz a la Whiteman," *New York Herald-Tribune* (April 22, 1924): 11.
50. On Whiteman's eighth and final "Experiment in Modern Music," see DeLong, *Pops*, 232–233.
51. "New Acts This Week," *Variety* (May 13, 1925): 10.
52. "Whiteman with Publix for All Season," *Variety* (July 28, 1926): 4; "Whiteman Tours Publix," *Los Angeles Times* (August 9, 1926): A7.
53. See for example, "Whiteman Band Plays for Dance," *Los Angeles Times* (October 10, 1926): C23; Peggy Nye, "Sub-Deb-Rosa," *Los Angeles Times* (October 17, 1926); "Paul Whiteman Will Play for Dancers," *Boston Globe* (November 10, 1926): 8.
54. On the history of the League of Composers, and the conflicted relationship it had with the International Composers Guild, see Claire Reis, *Composer, Conductors and Critics* (Detroit, MI: Detroit Reprints in Music, 1974); Carol Oja, *Making Music Modern: New York in the 1920s* (New York: Oxford University Press, 2000), 177–200; R. Allen Lott, "'New Music for New Ears': The International Composers' Guild," *Journal of the American Musicological Society* 36, no. 2 (Summer 1983): 266–286; David Metzer, "The League of Composers: The Initial Years," *American Music* 15, no. 1 (Spring 1997): 45–69.
55. "Coming Events in Guild and League of Composers," *New York Tribune* (January 27, 1924): D6.
56. Reis, *Composer, Conductors and Critics*, 48; "Discussion and Demonstration of Jazz Next Week," *New York Tribune* (February 3, 1924): E6.
57. Green, "Whiteman's 'Jazz' Recital," 17.
58. For a full list of League of Composers programs from the organization's first season, 1923–1924, until 1929–1930, see Metzer, "The League of Composers," 59–66.
59. Olin Downes, "Facts and Figures of Programs as Played from October to May," *New York Times* (April 27, 1924): X6.

60. Oja, *Making Music Modern*, 189.
61. Aaron Copland, "America's Young Men of Promise," *Modern Music* 3, no. 3 (March/April 1926): 13–20.
62. William Weber suggests that after 1848, in both Europe and the US, the tendency to valorize older "classic" works and to give them greater priority on concert programs of "serious" music began to grow noticeably, although it would take several decades for the practice to become fully entrenched. See Weber, *The Great Transformation of Musical Taste: Concert Programming from Haydn to Brahms* (Cambridge: Cambridge University Press, 2008). According to Joseph Horowitz in his history of American classical music, the full move toward "sacralization," which entailed the rejection of contemporary culture and "enshrining dead European masters," did not occur until after World War I. See Horowitz, *Classical Music in America*, 252.
63. See Andreas Huyssen, *After the Great Divide: Modernism, Mass Culture, Postmodernism* (Bloomington: Indiana University Press, 1986); Diana Crane, *The Transformation of the Avant-Garde: The New York Art World, 1940–1985* (Chicago: University of Chicago Press, 1987); and Bernard Gendron, *Between Montmartre and the Mudd Club: Popular Music and the Avant-Garde* (Chicago: University of Chicago Press, 2002).
64. Virgil Thomson, *Virgil Thomson: An Autobiography* (New York: E.P. Dutton, 1985), 55; Aaron Copland and Vivian Perlis, *Copland: 1900 Through 1942* (New York: St. Martin's/Marek, 1984), 71.
65. Howard Pollack, Copland's biographer, discusses the evidence that Copland was drawing upon jazz even before he left for Paris; see Pollack, *Aaron Copland: The Life and Work of an Uncommon Man* (New York: Henry Holt and Company, 1999), 43–44. On Copland's absorption of jazz influence second-hand, through the work of European composers, see Copland and Perlis, *Copland: 1900 Through 1942*, 95.
66. Will Straw, "Systems of Articulation, Logics of Change: Communities and Scenes in Popular Music," *Cultural Studies* 5, no. 3 (October 1991): 374. I have drawn upon Straw's insight in a very different context to explain some of the ways in which the genres of heavy metal and punk were defined in relation to one another, specifically with regard to the New Wave of British Heavy Metal of the late 1970s and early 1980s. See Steve Waksman, *This Ain't the Summer of Love: Conflict and Crossover in Heavy Metal and Punk* (Berkeley and Los Angeles: University of California Press, 2009): 176.
67. Reis, *Composer, Conductors and Critics*, 33.
68. Thomas led a long career as a performer and, starting in 1859, a conductor in the US until his death in 1905, having made his mark most strongly while leading his own Theodore Thomas Orchestra, the New York Philharmonic, and then as the founding conductor of the Chicago Symphony Orchestra. Lawrence Levine assigns Thomas considerable priority as a figure that personified and transmitted "highbrow" cultural values in the musical realm in *Highbrow/Lowbrow*, 112–119; and Joseph Horowitz credits him with fortifying the American taste in Germanic concert repertory and also with developing a new standard of showmanship as an orchestra leader in *Classical Music in America*, 34–36. For the most detailed account of Thomas's career and achievements, see Ezra Schabas, *Theodore Thomas: America's Conductor and Builder of Orchestras, 1835–1905* (Urbana: University of Illinois Press, 1989).

69. Details of Toscanini's career are drawn from Joseph Horowitz, *Understanding Toscanini: A Social History of American Concert Life* (Berkeley and Los Angeles: University of California Press, 1987).
70. "Philharmonic Gets Toscanini for Five Years," *New York Herald Tribune* (May 24, 1927): 24; "Toscanini to Lead Here Five Years," *New York Times* (May 24, 1927): 23.
71. A. [Walter Kramer], "Six Conductors Heard with Four Local Orchestras: Toscanini Says Au Revoir," *Musical America* 52, no. 19 (December 10, 1932): 10.
72. Horowitz, *Understanding Toscanini*, 130–133.
73. "Scant Recognition Given American Music," *Musical America* 52, no. 9 (May 10, 1932): 5.
74. Theodor Adorno, "On the Fetish Character in Music and the Regression of Listening," in *Essays on Music*, selected with introduction, commentary and notes by Richard Leppert (Berkeley and Los Angeles: University of California Press, 2002), 293–296.
75. Horowitz, *Understanding Toscanini*, 119.
76. David Suisman, *Selling Sounds: The Commercial Revolution in American Music* (Cambridge, MA: Harvard University Press, 2009), 125–149; William Kenney, *Recorded Music in American Life: The Phonograph and Popular Memory, 1890–1945* (New York: Oxford University Press, 1999), 44–64.
77. James Doering, *The Great Orchestrator: Arthur Judson and American Arts Management* (Urbana: University of Illinois Press, 2013), 60.
78. See Catherine Parsons Smith, *Making Music in Los Angeles: Transforming the Popular* (Berkeley and Los Angeles: University of California Press, 2007), 132–153.
79. Doering, *The Great Orchestrator*, 135; "Manager Resigns in Stokowski Rift," *New York Times* (October 24, 1934): 24.
80. Doering, *The Great Orchestrator*, 173–193; Howard Shanet, *Philharmonic: A History of New York's Orchestra* (Garden City, NY: Doubleday and Company, 1975), 304–305.
81. Shanet *Philharmonic*, 324–325.
82. For a decade starting in 1927, Judson served as an agent for the League of Composers, while that organization was trying to raise its public profile and secure better engagements for its concerts. That he did so would suggest that his musical tastes did not strictly form the basis for his business decisions, although as Claire Reis recounts their relationship in her memoir, his aesthetic conservatism would come out whenever her plans threatened his sense of musical propriety. In her tactful phrase, "In those days his genius as a manager was opposed to new music." See Reis, *Composer, Conductors and Critics*, 92–93.
83. "Unites Concert Bureaus," *New York Times* (November 6, 1922): 16.
84. "New Radio Chain Will Broadcast All Over Nation," *New York Herald Tribune* (July 2, 1927): 11; "Plan Radio Chain East of Rockies," *New York Times* (July 2, 1927): 20; Doering, *The Great Orchestrator*, 88–89.
85. "Radio System and 7 Concert Bureaus Merge," *New York Herald Tribune* (December 11, 1930): 24; "7 Concert Groups Join Radio Merger," *New York Times* (December 11, 1930): 34.
86. "Prosperous Season Vouched for by New York Impresarios," *Musical America* (January 25, 1931): 15.

87. "Movies May Oust Music at Carnegie," *New York Times* (April 20, 1933): 20.
88. Bill Graham and Robert Greenfield, *Bill Graham Presents: My Life Inside Rock and Out* (New York: Da Capo, 2004), 116.
89. Hurok's biographer, Harlow Robinson, notes that there has always been uncertainty about Hurok's age. His given birth year is 1888, which would have made him eighteen at the time of his arrival in the US, but he may have been slightly older. See Robinson, *The Last Impresario: The Life, Times, and Legacy of Sol Hurok* (New York: Viking, 1994), 8–9.
90. Sol Hurok with Ruth Goode, *Impresario* (New York: Random House, 1946), 25.
91. Hurok and Goode, *Impresario*, 31.
92. Hurok claims that the phrase "the Hurok audience" appeared in the *New York Morning Telegraph*, but I have not been able to find any such reference. See Hurok and Goode, *Impresario*, 32. There is also considerable ambiguity as to the time frame of Hurok's concert series at the Hippodrome. Hurok is fuzzy with the dates in his memoir but suggests that it was around the middle of the 1910s. Harlow Robinson seems to take him at his word and places the start of Hurok's series in 1915. However, I have found no documentation in any New York papers to suggest that Hurok was presenting concerts at the Hippodrome before the fall of 1919. It could well be that his name would not have appeared prior to that time because he was an unknown figure, but Hurok did gain some newspaper recognition in the 1910s for his efforts with the Labor Lyceum. See Robinson, *The Last Impresario*, 41–44, for discussion of Hurok's association with the Hippodrome.
93. "Soviet Grants Hurok Rights on Performers," *New York Times* (August 3, 1930): 2.
94. Hurok and Goode, *Impresario*, 79.
95. Hurok and Goode, *Impresario*, 154; Robinson, *The Last Impresario*, 134–135. Also see H.T., "Art, Radio and Big Business," *New York Times* (March 15, 1931): 118.
96. Advertisement for N.B.C. Artists Service, *Musical America* 52, no. 2 (January 25, 1932): back cover.
97. Raymond Arsenault, *The Sound of Freedom: Marian Anderson, the Lincoln Memorial, and the Concert That Awakened America* (New York: Bloomsbury, 2009), 15.
98. Arsenault, *The Sound of Freedom*, 44.
99. Hurok and Goode, *Impresario*, 238.
100. Advertisement for Marian Anderson, Town Hall concert, *New York Herald Tribune* (December 15, 1935): E9.
101. Howard Taubman, "Marian Anderson in Concert Here," *New York Times* (December 31, 1935): 13.
102. See Arsenault, *The Sound of Freedom*, 129–130; "Mrs. F.D. Parries Queries on D.A.R.," *Boston Globe* (February 28, 1939): 13; "Has Mrs. Roosevelt Quit D.A.R. Over Marian Anderson Slight?" *New York Herald Tribune* (February 28, 1939): 1, 11; and "Mrs. Roosevelt Indicates She Has Resigned from D.A.R. Over Refusal of Hall to Negro," *New York Times* (February 28, 1939): 1, 5.
103. "School Board Picketed in Ban on Singer," *Washington Post* (February 20, 1939): 3. The board eventually modified its judgment but in a compromised way, stipulating that Anderson's appearance would be treated as an exception and should not be

taken as a sign that the "dual system" was being revoked. At the urging of civil rights organizations, Anderson refused to appear under such restrictive circumstances.

104. Hurok and Goode, *Impresario*, 258–259; Robinson, *The Last Impresario*, 236–237. Chapman was also given credit for the idea in some contemporary articles; see for example, Ernest Lindley, "Voice from the Temple," *Washington Post* (April 12, 1939): 9.
105. "School Ban Stands on Miss Anderson," *New York Times* (March 21, 1939): 31.
106. Edward Folliard, "Ickes Introduces Contralto at Lincoln Memorial; Many Officials Attend Concert," *Washington Post* (April 10, 1939): 1, 12; "Throng Honors Marian Anderson in Concert at Lincoln Memorial," *New York Times* (April 10, 1939): 15; "75,000 Hear Marian Anderson Sing for the First Time in Capital," *New York Herald Tribune* (April 10, 1939): 17; Jay Walz, "Anderson Sings at Lincoln Memorial," *Musical America* 59, no. 8 (April 25, 1939): 15.
107. Quoted in Arsenault, *The Sound of Freedom*, 154.
108. Hurok and Goode, *Impresario*, 260–261.
109. Irving Kolodin, liner notes to Benny Goodman, *Live at Carnegie Hall*, Columbia G2K 40244, 1987, CD; Ross Firestone, *Swing, Swing, Swing: The Life and Times of Benny Goodman* (New York: W.W. Norton & Company, 1993), 207; Catherine Tackley, *Benny Goodman's Famous 1938 Carnegie Hall Jazz Concert* (New York: Oxford University Press, 2012), 12–13.
110. Robinson, *The Last Impresario*, 221.
111. Kolodin, *Live at Carnegie Hall*.
112. Advertisement for S. Hurok, Inc., *New York Herald Tribune* (November 23, 1924): F19.
113. Abel Green, "Lopez Concert," *Variety* (November 26, 1924): 50.
114. Howland, *Ellington Uptown*, 87. On *Evolution of the Blues*, also see Green, "Lopez Concert," 51; and W.C. Handy, *Father of the Blues: An Autobiography*, ed. Arna Bontemps (New York: Da Capo, 1969), 218. Handy's work was in fact a regular presence in efforts to incorporate jazz and blues into more formal concert settings throughout the 1920s and 1930s, and he staged two of his own Carnegie Hall concerts in 1928 and again in 1938.
115. Gendron, *Between Montmartre and the Mudd Club*, 121–141; David Stowe, *Swing Changes: Big-Band Jazz in New Deal America* (Cambridge, MA: Harvard University Press, 1994); John Gennari, *Blowin' Hot and Cool: Jazz and Its Critics* (Chicago: University of Chicago Press, 2006).
116. Wilder Hobson, "Fifty-Second Street," in *Jazzmen: The Story of Hot Jazz Told in the Live of the Men Who Created It*, ed. Frederick Ramsey, Jr., and Charles Edward Smith (New York: Limelight Editions, 1985), 251.
117. Patrick Burke, *Come in and Hear the Truth: Jazz and Race on 52nd Street* (Chicago: University of Chicago Press, 2008), 40.
118. Green, "Swing It!" *Variety* (January 1, 1936): 188.
119. Hobson, "Fifty-Second Street," 249.
120. Benny Goodman and Irving Kolodin, *The Kingdom of Swing* (New York: Frederick Ungar Publishing, 1961), 198.
121. Goodman and Kolodin, *The Kingdom of Swing*, 208.

122. Carl Cons, "Society and Musicians Sit Spellbound by Brilliance of Goodman Band," *Down Beat* 3, no. 1 (December/January 1935-1936): 1. Also see Helen Oakley, "Chicago," *Metronome* 52, no. 1 (January 1936): 47; DeVeaux, "The Emergence of the Jazz Concert," 10-11.

123. "In Person Policy of NY Paramount Shows Public Trend," *Metronome* 52, no. 3 (March 1936): 16.

124. Cecelia Ager, "Going Places," *Variety* (March 10, 1937): 11; Firestone, *Swing, Swing, Swing*, 198-199; Goodman and Kolodin, *The Kingdom of Swing*, 218-219.

125. Annemarie Ewing, "Carnegie Hall Gets First Taste of Swing," *Down Beat* 5, no. 2 (February 1938): 7.

126. H.E.P., "'Goodman Came, Saw, and Laid a Golden Egg!'" *Down Beat* 5, no. 2 (February 1938): 1.

127. Firestone, *Swing, Swing, Swing,* 245-252; Goodman and Kolodin, *The Kingdom of Swing*, 242.

128. Kolodin, *Live at Carnegie Hall*.

129. Details from Firestone, *Swing, Swing, Swing*, 134-140, 164-166, 180-182.

130. On Europe's Carnegie Hall concerts, see Reid Badger, *A Life in Ragtime: A Biography of James Reese Europe* (New York: Oxford University Press, 1995), 63-74; and David Gilbert, *The Product of Our Souls: Ragtime, Race, and the Birth of the Manhattan Musical Marketplace* (Chapel Hill: University of North Carolina Press, 2015), 1-3, 178-182; and "Black Music Concerts in Carnegie Hall," *Black Perspective in Music* 6, no. 1 (Spring 1978): 71-88. On Handy's concert, see Howland, *Ellington Uptown*, 88-90 (and ff. for his extended consideration of Johnson's *Yamekraw*); W.C. Handy's Concert," *Variety* (May 2, 1928): 63.

131. Hammond's career and influence upon the jazz world have been discussed widely. For basic background, see John Hammond with Irving Townsend, *John Hammond on Record* (New York: Summit Books, 1977); and Dunstan Prial, *The Producer: John Hammond and the Soul of American Music* (New York: Farrar, Strauss, and Giroux, 2006). On Hammond's role as critic, see Gennari, *Blowin' Hot and Cool*, 19-59. On his connection to the broader cultural politics of the swing era, see Stowe, *Swing Changes*, 54-64. For an insightful and balanced contemporary portrait of Hammond and his place in the jazz world of the late 1930s, see Otis Ferguson, "John Hammond," in *In the Spirit of Jazz: The Otis Ferguson Reader*, ed. Dorothy Chamberlain and Robert Wilson (New York: Da Capo, 1997), 97-103.

132. The program notes for the first "From Spirituals to Swing" concert, along with select reviews, were reprinted as "An Early Black-Music Concert: From Spirituals to Swing," *Black Perspective in Music* 2, no. 2 (Fall 1974): 191-208. Recordings of the concert have been issued in multiple versions, with an initial release by the Vanguard label in 1959, reissued on CD in 1987. The most extensive recorded representation of the concert is the box set, *From Spirituals to Swing: The Legendary 1938 and 1939 Carnegie Hall Concerts Produced by John Hammond* (Santa Monica, CA: Vanguard, 1999), which includes music from both concerts, original liner notes from the 1959 release, and a full reproduction of the program for the 1938 concert.

133. "A Landmark in Ellington Criticism: R.D. Darrell's 'Black Beauty'," *The Duke Ellington Reader*, ed. Mark Tucker (New York: Oxford University Press, 1995), 57-65.

134. Copland, "Scores and Records," *Modern Music* 15, no. 2 (January/February 1938): 110.
135. John Hammond, "The Tragedy of Duke Ellington," *The Duke Ellington Reader*, 120.
136. Howland, *Ellington Uptown*, 182.
137. Tad Hershorn, *Norman Granz: The Man Who Used Jazz for Justice* (Berkeley and Los Angeles: University of California Press, 2011), 5.
138. DeVeaux, "The Emergence of the Jazz Concert," 15.
139. Ralph Ellison, "The Golden Age, Time Past," *Shadow and Act* (New York: Vintage, 1995), 199–213; Scott DeVeaux, *The Birth of Bebop: A Social and Musical History* (Berkeley and Los Angeles: University of California Press, 1997), 202–235.
140. Burke, *Come in and Hear the Truth*, 147–154.
141. William Kenney, "Jazz and the Concert Halls: The Eddie Condon Concerts, 1942–48," *American Music* 1, no. 2 (Summer 1983): 60–72; concert program, Eddie Condon jazz concert at Town Hall, December 1, 1945, Tad Hershorn/Norman Granz collection, Institute for Jazz Studies.
142. Hershorn, *Norman Granz*, 31–32.
143. John McDonough, Interview with Norman Granz, September 12, 1978, p. 6. Tad Hershorn/Norman Granz collection, Institute for Jazz Studies.
144. Hershorn, *Norman Granz*, 55; "Jazz Concert at Music Town," *California Eagle* (February 10, 1944): 12, Tad Hershorn/Norman Granz collection, Institute for Jazz Studies.
145. Parsons Smith, *Making Music in Los Angeles*, 97–104.
146. Hershorn, *Norman Granz*, 60–61.
147. Newspaper ad for the first "Jazz at the Philharmonic" concert, source and date unknown, Tad Hershorn/Norman Granz collection, Institute for Jazz Studies.
148. Much of the music from the first JATP concert, including the versions of "Lester Leaps In" and "Body and Soul," has been preserved on record; details of the recording of Granz's concerts will be discussed shortly. See *Jazz at the Philharmonic: The First Concert* (Verve/Polygram, 1994).
149. Mary Shaughnessy, *Les Paul: An American Original* (New York: William Morrow and Company, 1993), 118.
150. "LA Session Heps Kids; Granz to Do Second One," *Down Beat* (August 1, 1944): 12.
151. Hershorn, *Norman Granz*, 64.
152. McDonough, Interview with Norman Granz, March 6, 1989, 56. Tad Hershorn/Norman Granz Collection, Institute for Jazz Studies.
153. Letter from Norman Granz to Moe Asch, August 1945 (date unspecified except that it is a Friday). Tad Hershorn/Norman Granz collection, Institute for Jazz Studies.
154. Undated press release (circa 1945) announcing agreement between Norman Granz and Moe Asch/Disc Records. Tad Hershorn/Norman Granz collection, Institute for Jazz Studies.
155. Hershorn, *Norman Granz*, 83.
156. "Granz Setting up Co. to Market Jazz Disks," *Variety* (June 4, 1947): 40.
157. "Granz' First Disc Releases Out Soon," *Chicago Defender* (September 13, 1947): 18. Granz's Clef Records were distributed by Mercury, which itself had only been formed

in 1945 but was on its way to becoming one of the major labels of the pop record industry.

158. Russell would soon achieve wider notoriety as the founder of Dial Records, which grew from the Tempo shop and would release many of the best-regarded sides by Charlie Parker, for whom Russell would serve as record producer. Later Russell would write the first book-length biography of Parker, *Bird Lives: The High Life and Hard Times of Charlie (Yardbird) Parker* (New York: Charterhouse, 1973). For an overview of Russell's career and his relationship with Parker, see Gennari, *Blowin' Hot and Cool*, 299–338.

159. Ross Russell, "Be-bop Invades the West! Dizzy Gillespie Quintet Opens Monday at Berg's," *Jazz Tempo* 1, no. 1 (December 1945): 1. Tad Hershorn/Norman Granz Collection, Institute for Jazz Studies.

160. Russell, "Confetti," *Jazz Tempo* 1, no. 1 (December 1945): 2. Tad Hershorn/Norman Granz Collection, Institute for Jazz Studies.

161. Concert program for Jazz at the Philharmonic, fourth national tour (Spring 1947). Tad Hershorn/Norman Granz Collection, Institute for Jazz Studies.

162. "Eatery Wouldn't Serve 'Em, Negro Jazzers File Suit," *Variety* (October 15, 1947): 41; "Norman Granz and Jazz Stars Make It Hot for Michigan Restaurant," *Chicago Defender* (October 18, 1947): 1, 7; Hershorn, *Norman Granz*, 1–3.

163. Will Davidson, "Stream of Jazz Flows Jerkily in Svelte Setting," *Chicago Tribune* (May 15, 1946): 24.

164. "'Jazz at Philharmonic' Gets Hot 9G in Detroit," *Billboard* (June 1, 1946): 21.

165. Mike Levin, "Carnegie Bash Hits $4,400 Pot," *Down Beat* (July 1, 1946): 8.

166. Advertisement for Jazz at the Philharmonic, *Variety* (June 5, 1946): 36–37.

167. Concert program for Jazz at the Philharmonic, third national tour (Fall 1946). Tad Hershorn/Norman Granz Collection, Institute for Jazz Studies.

168. McDonough, Interview with Norman Granz, September 12, 1978, 78. Tad Hershorn/Norman Granz Collection, Institute for Jazz Studies.

169. Concert program for Jazz at the Philharmonic, seventeenth national tour (Fall 1956). Tad Hershorn/Norman Granz Collection, Institute for Jazz Studies.

170. Concert program for Jazz at the Philharmonic, tenth national tour (Fall 1950); concert program for Jazz at the Philharmonic, seventeenth national tour (Fall 1956). Tad Hershorn/Norman Granz Collection, Institute for Jazz Studies.

Chapter 6

1. Information about Sweatnam comes from Dailey Paskman and Sigmund Spaeth, *Gentlemen, Be Seated! A Parade of the Old-Time Minstrels* (Garden City, NY: Doubleday, Doran & Company, Inc., 1928), 92–93, 160–161.

2. Review of Billy Sweatnam with Bryant's Minstrels, *New York Clipper* (July 6, 1878): 118.

3. "Minstrel Jokes," *Grip* (December 16, 1882): 6. According to a notice that accompanies the article, it originally appeared in the *New York Journal*.

4. See Eric Lott, *Love and Theft: Blackface Minstrelsy and the American Working Class* (New York: Oxford University Press, 1993); and for an extension of the argument into the mid-twentieth century, Lott, "White Like Me: Racial Cross-Dressing and the Construction of American Whiteness," in *Cultures of United States Imperialism*, ed. Amy Kaplan and Donald Pease (Durham, NC: Duke University Press, 1994), 474–495.
5. Bill Griggs, "Alan Freed's Moondog Coronation Ball," *Rockin' 50s* (April 1992): 6; Tom Junod, "Oh, What a Night," *Life* 15, no. 13 (December 1, 1992): 36.
6. "Moondog Ball Is Halted as 6,000 Crash Arena Gate," *Cleveland Plain Dealer* (March 22, 1952): 1; Jane Scott, "30 Years Ago, 'Moon Dog' Howled," *Cleveland Plain Dealer* (March 14, 1982): D1, D12. Also see John Jackson, *Big Beat Heat: Alan Freed and the Early Years of Rock & Roll* (New York: Schirmer Books, 1991), 1–5.
7. Scott, "30 Years Ago," D1.
8. Quoted in Scott, "30 Years Ago," D1. Jackson suggests that the middle-class values of the *Call and Post* placed the newspaper at odds with the tenor of Freed's event; as he explains, for the reporters of the *Call and Post*, "Alan Freed's sin was not so much his championing of 'gutbucket' rhythm and blues as it was the encouraging of thousands of young blacks to make a public display of themselves to white society that historically attached a negative image to all blacks." Jackson, *Big Beat Heat*, 4.
9. Advertisement for WJW radio station. Publication and date unknown. John A. Jackson Papers, Box 3, Folder 11, Rock and Roll Hall of Fame Library and Archives.
10. On the significance of radio disc jockeys in the early rock and roll era, see Arnold Passman, *The Deejays: How the Tribal Chieftains of Radio Got to Where They're At* (New York: Macmillan, 1971); Wes Smith, *The Pied Pipers of Rock 'n' Roll: Radio Deejays of the 50s and 60s* (Marietta, GA: Longstreet Press, 1989); William Barlow, *Voice Over: The Making of Black Radio* (Philadelphia, PA: Temple University Press, 1999); and Marc Fisher, *Something in the Air: Radio, Rock, and the Revolution That Shaped a Generation* (New York: Random House, 2007).
11. Theodore Gracyk, *Rhythm and Noise: An Aesthetics of Rock* (Durham, NC: Duke University Press, 1996), 1. Other key works that have taken recording technology and techniques as their focus include Albin Zak, *The Poetics of Rock: Cutting Tracks, Making Records* (Berkeley and Los Angeles: University of California Press, 2001); Simon Frith and Simon Zagorski-Thomas, eds., *The Art of Record Production: An Introductory Reader for a New Academic Field* (Surrey, UK and Burlington, VT: Ashgate, 2012); and Zagorski-Thomas, *The Musicology of Record Production* (Cambridge: Cambridge University Press, 2014).
12. Gracyk, *Rhythm and Noise*, 13–16.
13. For details concerning Presley's relationship with Parker, see Peter Guralnick, *Last Train to Memphis: The Rise of Elvis Presley* (Boston, MA: Little, Brown and Company, 1994); and Scotty Moore with James Dickerson, *Scotty and Elvis: Aboard the Mystery Train* (Jackson: University of Mississippi Press, 2013).
14. Joe Hyams, "The Highest-Paid Movie Star Ever: Elvis Presley Now Makes Over a Million a Year," *New York Herald Tribune* (May 16, 1957): 16

15. Writing about Barnes, who doubled as a bandleader and columnist for the *Chicago Defender*, Lauterbach observes: "He plugged his band into the territory-band network and fused these previously separate entities into a more cohesive whole. He performed along the *Defender*'s underground circulation route, and learned how darktown functioned. In print, he ego-stroked the local fat cats and granted favors to those in the business who might help him." Lauterbach, *The Chitlin' Circuit and the Road to Rock 'n' Roll* (New York: W.W. Norton & Company, 2011), 41.
16. Lauterbach, *The Chitlin' Circuit*, 159.
17. On the rise of the honky-tonk during the Depression, and its connection to country music culture of the time, see Bill Malone, *Country Music U.S.A.*, rev. ed. (Austin: University of Texas Press, 1985), 153–155.
18. Richard Peterson, *Creating Country Music: Fabricating Authenticity* (Chicago: University of Chicago Press, 1997), 159–172.
19. Carl Perkins with David McGee, *Go, Cat, Go! The Life and Times of Carl Perkins, the King of Rockabilly* (New York: Hyperion, 1996), 65.
20. Perkins and McGee, *Go, Cat, Go!*, 68.
21. Guralnick, *Last Train to Memphis*, 129–130.
22. Moore and Dickerson, *Scotty and Elvis*, 75.
23. Greil Marcus, *Mystery Train: Images of America in Rock 'n' Roll Music*, 4th ed. (New York: Plume, 1997), 18.
24. On racial ventriloquy and radio broadcasting, see Barlow, *Voice Over*, 1–2, 157–175. For more detail on the white deejays who formed the core of Nashville's WLAC, see Smith, *The Pied Pipers of Rock 'n' Roll*, 53–116. On Hunter Hancock, see Fisher, *Something in the Air*, 29–36.
25. On the Southern response to, and reception of, rock 'n' roll, see Michael Bertrand, *Race, Rock, and Elvis* (Urbana: University of Illinois Press, 2005).
26. Chuck Berry, *The Autobiography* (New York: Fireside, 1987), 136; also see Bruce Pegg, *Brown Eyed Handsome Man: The Life and Hard Times of Chuck Berry* (New York: Routledge, 2002), 69. On Berry's status as "black hillbilly," see Steve Waksman, *Instruments of Desire: The Electric Guitar and the Shaping of Musical Experience* (Cambridge, MA: Harvard University Press, 1999), 159–161.
27. Berry, *The Autobiography*, 136.
28. Perkins and McGee, *Go, Cat, Go!*, 210–212.
29. Cliff Richardson, "Mixed Dancing Baffles Cops in Houston, Texas," *Pittsburgh Courier* (August 18, 1956): 2.
30. Details come from Richardson's account in the *Pittsburgh Courier*; and Bertrand, *Race, Rock, and Elvis*, 182. The Citizens Councils referred to by Richardson were organizations dedicated to the maintenance of racial segregation, whose members commonly accused rock 'n' roll of being part of a conspiracy to make young white people subject to the influence of African Americans and their culture.
31. Charles White, *The Life and Times of Little Richard* (New York: Pocket Books, 1985), 69.
32. My use of the term "streams" here is meant to evoke the work of Philip Ennis, whose study of the emergence of what he calls "rocknroll" remains one of the most detailed

and insightful accounts available. See Ennis, *The Seventh Stream: The Emergence of Rocknroll in American Popular Music* (Hanover, NH: Wesleyan University Press, 1992). As valuable as Ennis' work is, it is also typical in its treatment of live music as a relatively marginal phenomenon and much greater emphasis on radio and recordings as the primary media through which rock 'n' roll emerged.

33. Bob Rolontz, "Rhythm and Blues Notes," *Billboard* (June 6, 1953): 42. The name of this first R&B package show is hard to pin down. In this first account it is simply called "The Rhythm and Blues Show," but when *Billboard* referred to the show subsequently, it was called alternately, "The Big Rhythm and Blues Show," or "The Giant Rhythm and Blues Show." It may be that the show's title evolved over time, or that *Billboard*'s reporting was inconsistent; but all of these different names were clearly used by the publication to refer to the same show that toured in the summer of 1953 and then embarked on a second year of touring in 1954.

34. "New 'Top Ten R&B Show' to Do 60 One-Nighters," *Billboard* (November 27, 1954): 14.

35. Rolontz, "R&B Packages' Big-Time Hit Peaks All Around Solid Year," *Billboard* (January 29, 1955): 58.

36. Rolontz, "R&B Packages," 58.

37. John Broven, *Record Makers and Breakers: Voices of the Independent Rock 'n' Roll Pioneers* (Urbana: University of Illinois Press, 2009), 452.

38. "Major Agencies Booking Rhythm & Blues Talent," *Billboard* (February 4, 1956): 64.

39. Rick Coleman, *Blue Monday: Fats Domino and the Lost Dawn of Rock 'n' Roll* (New York: Da Capo, 2006), 147.

40. Ennis, *The Seventh Stream*, 9–10.

41. Hal Willard, "Musical Empire of Felds Has Capital in Back Room," *Washington Post* (September 30, 1956): D17. This article offers a brief but valuable overview of the Felds' entry into the music business.

42. Broven, *Record Makers and Breakers*, 278.

43. "Dealer Doings," *Billboard* (January 21, 1950): 26.

44. Gayle Wald, *Shout, Sister, Shout! The Untold Story of Rock-and-Roll Trailblazer Sister Rosetta Tharpe* (Boston, MA: Beacon Press, 2007), 110–111; "Religion Comes to DC; Spiritual 'Bash' a Smash," *Billboard* (July 22, 1950): 3, 38.

45. Wald, *Shout, Sister, Shout!*, 115–116, 121.

46. "Gov't Holds up Bids for Use of Amphitheater," *Billboard* (March 7, 1953): 1, 53; "Festival, Inc., Wins Fight for Wash'ton Arena," *Billboard* (April 11, 1953): 45; "Two-Way Plan Aids Box Office Takes and Disks," *Billboard* (April 3, 1954): 1, 12.

47. "Two-Way Plan," 12; "Winston-Salem Arena Premiere Draws 6,500," *Billboard* (October 1, 1955): 80.

48. "Two-Way Plan," 12.

49. Advertisement for a "Rock 'n' Roll Jamboree" sponsored by the Super Music stores, *Washington Post* (March 13, 1956): 18.

50. Tom Parkinson, "Feld Promotions Pack Halls, Fill Southeast Show Needs," *Billboard* (April 21, 1956): 62.

51. Robert Bird, "Anti-Semitism in White Councils," *New York Herald Tribune* (March 13, 1956): 1, 12; "Segregationist Wants Ban on Rock 'n' Roll," *New York Times* (March 30, 1956): 27; Rob Roy, "Bias Against 'Rock 'n' Roll' Latest Bombshell in Dixie," *Chicago Defender* (April 2, 1956): 19; Bertrand, *Race, Rock, and Elvis*, 163–164.
52. Brian Ward, *Just My Soul Responding: Rhythm and Blues, Black Consciousness, and Race Relations* (Berkeley and Los Angeles: University of California Press), 95–105.
53. "A Lesson for Nat Cole," *Chicago Defender* (April 12, 1956): 11.
54. "Promoters Holding to Southern Bookings, Despite Cole Incident," *Billboard* (April 21, 1956): 29.
55. Ward, *Just My Soul Responding*, 104.
56. Ren Grevatt, "On the Beat," *Billboard* (September 9, 1957): 64.
57. "Feld Show Bows to Jim Crowism," *Pittsburgh Courier* (October 5, 1957): 22.
58. Passman, *The Deejays*, 159–161, 205–217; Fisher, *Something in the Air*, 3–28.
59. Some of Freed's airchecks are now readily available through YouTube and other on-line resources, allowing for valuable exposure to his on-air announcing style as well as the selection of songs he played. For a strong example of Freed's DJ style during his tenure at Cleveland station WJW, listen to the excerpt from Freed's broadcast of April 6, 1954, available at https://www.youtube.com/watch?v=GqKRYJS6ORc. Accessed August 10, 2015. For more discussion of Freed's manner of presentation see Jackson, *Big Beat Heat*, 42–43.
60. Arnold Shaw, *Honkers and Shouters: The Golden Years of Rhythm & Blues* (New York: Collier Books, 1978), 513.
61. "Cleveland Arena Ball Draws Smaller Crowd," *Billboard* (May 31, 1952): 43.
62. Jackson, *Big Beat Heat*, 46; Junod, "Oh, What a Night," 34–35.
63. Advertisement for Freed's Moondog Moonlight Ball, *Call and Post* (June 21, 1952). John A. Jackson Papers, Box 3, Folder 11, Rock and Roll Hall of Fame Library and Archives.
64. Smith, *The Pied Pipers of Rock 'n' Roll*, 73.
65. Rolontz, "Alan Freed Attracts Mob in Newark," *Billboard* (May 15, 1954): 37.
66. Rolontz, "Alan Freed Attracts Mob in Newark," 37.
67. "Dear Mr. Moondog," *Our World* (August 1954): 33–35. John A. Jackson Papers, Box 3, Folder 11, Rock and Roll Hall of Fame Library and Archives.
68. Jackson, *Big Beat Heat*, 65; "Freed of WJW, to Start in N.Y. in Fall," *Billboard* (July 10, 1954): 15; Josephine Jablons, "'Moondog,' Blues, Jazz Disk Ace, Gets N.Y. Show," *New York Herald Tribune* (August 29, 1954): D5.
69. Letter of agreement between Robert Leder/WINS radio and Alan Freed, August 10, 1954. Alan Freed Collection, Box 1, Folder 25, Rock and Roll Hall of Fame Library and Archives.
70. "WINS Places Freed Show in 5 Markets," *Billboard* (August 28, 1954): 12.
71. George Brown, "'Moondog' in Radio Doghouse," *Pittsburgh Courier* (October 2, 1954): 4.
72. "Sightless Musician Sounds off in Court," *New York Times* (November 24, 1954): 25; "Freed Enjoined from Use of 'Moondog' Label," *Billboard* (December 4, 1954): 22.

John A. Jackson Papers, Box 3, Folder 12, Rock and Roll Hall of Fame Library and Archives.
73. Jackson, *Big Beat Heat*, 82.
74. "Freed Enjoined from Use of 'Moondog' Label," 22.
75. "Alan Freed to Promote 'Rock & Roll Ball' in N.Y.," *Variety* (December 22, 1954): 45. John A. Jackson Papers, Box 3, Folder 12, Rock and Roll Hall of Fame Library and Archives. On the photocopy of this article in Jackson's papers appears the written annotation: "Most likely, this is the first dance ever promoted as a 'rock and roll' dance."
76. Mail-order form for Alan Freed's "Rock 'n' Roll" Jubilee Ball, January 14th and 15th, 1955. John A. Jackson Collection, Box 3, Folder 12, Rock and Roll Hall of Fame Library and Archives.
77. Frederic Dannen, *Hit Men: Power Brokers and Fast Money Inside the Music Business* (New York: Vintage Books, 1991), 31–57.
78. Letter from Seig Music Corporation to the Gotham Broadcasting Corporation, January 1955. Alan Freed Collection, Box 1, Folder 26, Rock and Roll Hall of Fame Library and Archives. This letter did not mean that WINS and its parent Gotham Broadcasting Company had a clear trademark on the phrase "rock 'n' roll." Indeed, Levy, Freed and Platt had applied for such a trademark themselves after Freed changed the name of his show to "Rock 'n' Roll Party," although ultimately to no avail. See Jackson, *Big Beat Heat*, 85.
79. "Freed Ball Takes 24G at St. Nick," *Billboard* (January 22, 1955): 13.
80. "'Rock 'n Roll' Ball," *Cash Box* (January 29, 1955), n.p. Alan Freed Collection, Box 1, Folder 26, Rock and Roll Hall of Fame Library and Archives.
81. For a valuable historical overview of the change over time in the values attached to "crowds" and "masses" in American culture, see Richard Butsch, *The Citizen Audience: Crowds, Publics, and Individuals* (New York: Routledge, 2008).
82. "'Rock 'n Roll' Ball."
83. Dannen, *Hit Men*, 42.
84. Jackson, *Big Beat Heat*, 86.
85. Herm Schoenfeld, "R&B Big Beat in Pop Music," *Variety* (January 19, 1955): 49.
86. Schoenfeld, "R&B Big Beat in Pop Music," 54.
87. Schoenfeld, "R&B Big Beat in Pop Music," 54.
88. Quoted in Simon Frith, Matt Brennan, Martin Cloonan, and Emma Webster, *The History of Live Music in Britain*, Vol. 1, *1950–1967* (Farnham: Ashgate, 2013), 173.
89. Advertisement for *Rock, Rock, Rock! New York Times* (December 4, 1956): 48; Gary Kramer, "Rhythm & Blues Notes," *Billboard* (December 15, 1956): 62.
90. Smith, *The Pied Pipers of Rock 'n' Roll*, 158–159.
91. "WWRL Stages 'Dr. Jive' Teen Dance at Rockland Pal.," *Billboard* (April 16, 1955): 18; "Freed Breaks Record; Jive Big in Harlem," *Billboard* (April 23, 1955): 28.
92. Ted Fox, *Showtime at the Apollo: 50 Years of Great Entertainment from Harlem's World Famous Theater* (New York: Holt, Rinehart and Winston, 1983), 167–168; *The Apollo Theater Story* (New York: Apollo Operations Inc., 1966), n.p. Programs and Playbills Collection, Schomburg Center for Research in Black Culture.
93. Fox, *Showtime at the Apollo*, 175–176.

94. "Smalls Is Apollo Box-Office King," *Chicago Defender* (November 13, 1956): 15.
95. "R&B Is Broadway's Current Lullaby," *Billboard* (February 16, 1957): 23. In fact, the concentration of activity was not limited to New York. The *Chicago Defender* noted that during the same time frame, the Olympia stadium in Detroit hosted a substantial package show featuring Fats Domino, Chuck Berry, LaVern Baker and many others (this would have been the Detroit installment of Irvin Feld's "Greatest Show of 1957" tour); and Chicago was preparing for a big package show emceed by the city's popular disc jockey Al Benson, to be held at the Regal Theater. See "Rock 'n' Rollers Run Amuck Over Nation for Week," *Chicago Defender* (February 23, 1957): 8.
96. "Times Sq. Rock 'n' Rolls to Wild Teenage Beat," *Boston Globe* (February 23, 1957): 3; Harold Hutchings, "Rock 'n' Roll Addicts Take Over Times Sq.," *Chicago Tribune* (February 23, 1957): 1; Charles Quinn, "Rock-Roll Fans Mob Paramount, Set off Bedlam," *New York Herald Tribune* (February 23, 1957): A1; and Edith Evans Asbury, "Rock 'n' Roll Teen-Agers Tie up the Times Square Area," *New York Times* (February 23, 1957): 1, 12.
97. As listed on the program for the week's engagement, the full roster of artists was: Robin Robinson, the Duponts, Ruth Brown, the Cleftones, Bobby Charles, Frankie Lymon and the Teenagers, Nappy Brown, Maureen Cannon, Buddy Knox with Jimmy Bowen and the Rhythm Orchids, the Cadillacs, the Platters, and Alan Freed and his Orchestra with Sam (The Man) Taylor and Al Sears. Concert program for *Alan Freed Holiday Jubilee* (February 1957). Alan Freed Collection, Box 2, Folder 13, Rock and Roll Hall of Fame Library and Archives.
98. Asbury, "Rock 'n' Roll Teenagers," 1.
99. Quinn, "Rock-Roll Fans Mob Paramount," A1.
100. Jackson, *Big Beat Heat*, 159.
101. The best account of the rising stage effect appears in H.T.T., "Frenzy 'n' Furor Featured at Paramount," *New York Times* (February 23, 1957): 13.
102. Quinn, "Rock-Roll Fans Mob Paramount," A1.
103. Asbury, "Times Sq. 'Rocks' for Second Day," *New York Times* (February 24, 1957): 76.
104. Asbury, "Rock 'n' Roll Teen-Agers," 12.
105. Theodore Irwin, "Rock 'n Roll 'n Alan Freed," *Pageant* (July 1957): 56. Alan Freed Collection, Box 1, Folder 54, Rock and Roll Hall of Fame Library and Archives.
106. Irwin, "Rock 'n Roll 'n Alan Freed," 59.
107. Grevatt, "On the Beat," *Billboard* (January 20, 1958): 40.
108. Rolontz, "Two Big Shows Totaling 500G Cost to Rock and Roll Across Country," *Billboard* (February 24, 1958): 6.
109. On Shaw's role in booking the tour, see "Freed to Start 6 Week Tour of U.S. March 28th," *Cash Box* (January 4, 1958), n.p. Alan Freed Collection, Box 1, Folder 26, Rock and Roll Hall of Fame Library and Archives.
110. In August, Ren Grevatt wrote that many promoters were backing away from the term, "rock 'n' roll," to avoid its connotations of controversy. Freed was among those said to be avoiding its use: "Freed's on-the-air remarks now refer only to 'the big beat.'" Grevatt, "On the Beat," *Billboard* (August 11, 1958): 52.

111. *Alan Freed Presents the Big Beat*, concert program (April 1958). Alan Freed Collection, Box 2, Folder 14, Rock and Roll Hall of Fame Library and Archives.
112. "Rock 'n' Roll Show Wows 'Em—They Were Dancing in Aisles!" *Dayton Journal Herald* (April 5, 1958), n.p. Alan Freed Collection, Box 1, Folder 26, Rock and Roll Hall of Fame Library and Archives.
113. Pegg, *Brown Eyed Handsome Man*, 90–91.
114. Grevatt, "Touring R&R Shows Meet Gate Trouble," *Billboard* (April 28, 1958): 8.
115. "Boy Stabbed, Nearly Killed in Rock 'n' Roll Aftermath," *Boston Globe* (April 15, 1957): 13; Jackson, *Big Beat Heat*, 192.
116. Jackson, *Big Beat Heat*, 193–194.
117. "Ban on Rock 'n' Roll Aimed at Promoters," *Boston Globe* (May 6, 1958): 7.
118. "Rock and Roll Hoodlums Slug, Rob 15 in Melee," *Boston Globe* (May 5, 1958): 4; "15 Assaulted After Boston Jam Session," *Chicago Tribune* (May 5, 1958): C8.
119. "Boston Police O.K.'d Rock 'n' Roll License," *Boston Globe* (May 9, 1958): 1, 37; Jerome Sullivan, "Atty. Paul Smith to Represent Rock 'n' Roller," *Boston Globe* (May 15, 1958): 1, 8.
120. "New Haven Bans Rock-and-Rollers," *New York Herald-Tribune* (May 6, 1958): 17; "Rock 'n' Roll Show Ban Faces Court Test Today," *Boston Globe* (May 7, 1958): 1, 35; "Jury to Air Rock 'n' Roll Riot," *Boston Globe* (May 8, 1958): 1, 11; Paul Benzaquin, "Teens Orderly at Rock Show in Providence," *Boston Globe* (May 8, 1958): 1, 11; "Jersey Guard Bars Rock 'n' Roll Show in Newark Armory," *New York Times* (May 8, 1958): 31.
121. "City Rejects Bid for Show at Griffith Stadium," *Washington Post* (May 9, 1958): A3.
122. "Rock 'n' Roll Show Ban," 35.
123. Grevatt, "On the Beat," *Billboard* (May 19, 1958): 10.
124. Wallace Vaine, "Defender of Rock 'n' Roll Asks: What's Been Done About Hoodlums?" *Boston Globe* (May 8, 1958): 10.

Chapter 7

1. Minutes of the first meeting of the Board of Directors of the Jazz Festival of Newport, R.I., Inc., May 10, 1954. Newport Jazz Festival, Business Records and Related Papers, Box 2, Folder 3, Institute for Jazz Studies.
2. Articles of Association, the Jazz Festival of Newport, R.I., Inc., April 28, 1954. Newport Jazz Festival, Business Records and Related Papers, Box 2, Folder 1, Institute for Jazz Studies.
3. Michael Lydon, "The High Cost of Music and Love," *Rolling Stone*, no. 1 (November 9, 1967): 1.
4. Leo Marx, *The Machine in the Garden: Technology and the Pastoral Ideal in America* (London: Oxford University Press, 1964)
5. Scott Saul, *Freedom Is, Freedom Ain't: Jazz and the Making of the Sixties* (Cambridge, MA: Harvard University Press, 2003), 105.

6. Elijah Wald, *Dylan Goes Electric! Newport, Seeger, Dylan, and the Night That Split the Sixties* (New York: Dey St., 2015), 203–204.
7. By no means is largeness of scale a precondition for festivals. This chapter concentrates upon festivals that were distinguished for their size, what might be called "mass festivals," but there is a whole history of smaller scale festivals yet to be written in conjunction with genres and musical spheres such as free jazz and experimental music.
8. John S. Dwight, "Musical Festivals," *Dwight's Journal of Music* 3, no. 7 (May 21, 1853): 53–54.
9. Clyde Shive, Jr., "The 'First' Band Festival in America," *American Music* 15, no. 4 (Winter 1997): 446–458.
10. Robert Vitz, "'Im Wunderschonen Monat Mai': Organizing the Great Cincinnati May Festival of 1878," *American Music* 4, no. 3 (Autumn 1986): 324. Also see, Ezra Schabas, *Theodore Thomas: America's Conductor and Builder of Orchestras, 1835–1905* (Urbana: University of Illinois Press, 1989), 48–68.
11. See, for example, Barry Millington, "All in It Together: The *Gesamtkunstwerk* Revisited," *The Wagner Journal* 11, no. 1 (March 2017): 46–61.
12. Frederic Spotts, *Bayreuth: A History of the Wagner Festival* (New Haven, CT: Yale University Press, 1994), 7.
13. On Wagner's reception and influence in the US, including enthusiasm for his festival at Bayreuth, see Joseph Horowitz, *Wagner Nights: An American History* (Berkeley and Los Angeles: University of California Press, 1994).
14. Michael Steinberg, *Austria as Theater and Ideology: The Meaning of the Salzburg Festival* (Ithaca, NY: Cornell University Press, 2000), 21–22.
15. Anton Haefeli and Reinhard Oehlschlägel, "International Society for Contemporary Music," *Grove Music Online* (2001), accessed July 20, 2018. The ISCM festivals received regular coverage in the publications of the League of Composers, the notable American organization devoted to the promotion of modern art music whose history is briefly discussed in Chapter 5. For the first of several such reports, see Edwin Evans, "After the Festivals," *League of Composers' Review* 1, no. 3 (November 1924): 22–23.
16. Alfred Meyer, "Yaddo—A May Festival," *Modern Music* 9, no. 4 (May/June 1932): 172–176; Rudy Shackelford, "The Yaddo Festivals of American Music, 1932–1952," *Perspectives of New Music* 17, no. 1 (Autumn-Winter 1978): 92–125.
17. Irving Kolodin, "Yaddo Festival Brings Hearing of Native Works," *Musical America* 52, no. 9 (May 10, 1932): 3.
18. Ronald Cohen, *A History of Folk Music Festivals in the United States* (Lanham, MD: Scarecrow Press, 2008), 1. Also see Heike Bungert, "The Singing Festivals of German Americans, 1849–1914," *American Music* 34, no. 2 (Summer 2016): 141–179.
19. Gavin Campbell, *Music and the Making of a New South* (Chapel Hill: University of North Carolina Press, 2004), 100–142. It should be noted that classical music festivals were no less oriented toward white supremacy in their governing assumptions and practices. Lawrence Levine has made a strong argument concerning the intersection of "highbrow" cultural values and eugenicist assumptions about the inherent superiority and intelligence of white northern European peoples in *Highbrow/Lowbrow: The Emergence of Cultural Hierarchy in America* (Cambridge, MA: Harvard University Press, 1988), 221–224.

20. Cohen, *A History of Folk Music Festivals*, 6–9.
21. David Whisnant, *All That Is Native and Fine: The Politics of Culture in an American Region*, 25th anniversary ed. (Chapel Hill: University of North Carolina Press, 2009), 185.
22. Annabel Morris Buchanan, "Interstate Folk Festival Held in Virginia," *Musical America* 51, no. 14 (September 1931): 26.
23. George Pullen Jackson, "White Top Festival Keeps Folk Music Alive," *Musical America* 53, no. 14 (September 1933): 7.
24. Michael Ann Williams, *Staging Tradition: John Lair and Sarah Gertrude Knott* (Urbana: University of Illinois Press, 2006), 20.
25. Cohen, *A History of Folk Music Festivals*, 19.
26. The uneven power relationships that so often shaped the practice of folklore collecting and scholarship have received increasing comment in recent decades. In addition to Whisnant's groundbreaking work, see Benjamin Filene, *Romancing the Folk: Public Memory and American Roots Music* (Chapel Hill: University of North Carolina Press, 2000); and Karl Hagstrom Miller, *Segregating Sound: Inventing Folk and Pop Music in the Age of Jim Crow* (Durham, NC: Duke University Press, 2010).
27. "Plans Moving for Huge Summer Jazz Festival," *Down Beat* (June 16, 1954): 1.
28. "The Future ...," *Newport Jazz Festival #1 Program* (1954): 4. Ralph Gleason Files, Jeff Gold Collection, Box RG3, Rock and Roll Hall of Fame Library and Archives.
29. Journalist Andrew Pincus references the idea of Tanglewood as an "American Salzburg" in his portrait of the festival, *Scenes from Tanglewood* (Boston, MA: Northeastern University Press, 1989), 5–6.
30. On the structure of the Tanglewood season and the development of the Berkshire Music Center, see Peggy Daniel, *Tanglewood: A Group Memoir* (New York: Amadeus Press, 2008), 21–45; and Aaron Copland and Vivian Perlis, *Copland: 1900 Through 1942* (New York: St Martin's/Marek, 1984), 305–320.
31. For background on the Lenox school, which would run from 1957 to 1960, see Jeremy Yudkin, *The Lenox School of Jazz: A Vital Chapter in the History of American Music and Race Relations* (South Egremont, MA: Farshaw Publishing, 2006). John Gennari addresses the parallels between the Lenox School and the Newport Jazz Festival in *Blowin' Hot and Cool: Jazz and Its Critics* (Chicago: University of Chicago Press, 2006), 207–249.
32. George Wein with Nate Chinen, *Myself Among Others: A Life in Music* (New York: Da Capo, 2003), 136.
33. Wein and Chinen, *Myself Among Others*, 5.
34. Wein and Chinen, *Myself Among Others*, 52.
35. Wein and Chinen, *Myself Among Others*, 85.
36. Nat Hentoff, "Self-Promotion: It Pays," *Down Beat* (May 30, 1957): 15.
37. Hentoff, "Self-Promotion," 15.
38. George Wein, "Newport Sets Pace for Jazz Festivals Here and Abroad," *Fifth Annual Newport Jazz Festival Official Program* (1958): 16. Ralph Gleason Files, Jeff Gold Collection, Box RG3, Rock and Roll Hall of Fame Library and Archives.
39. Cleveland Amory, "High Society Blues," *Holiday* (July 1956): 92.

40. George McKay, *Circular Breathing: The Cultural Politics of Jazz in Britain* (Durham, NC: Duke University Press, 2005), 81. Also see McKay, "'The Pose . . . Is a Stance: Popular Music and the Cultural Politics of Festival in 1950s Britain," in *The Pop Festival: History, Music, Media, Culture*, ed. George McKay (New York: Bloomsbury, 2015), 13–31.
41. McKay, *Circular Breathing*, 73.
42. Details of the line-up on the opening night of the 1954 festival come from two sources: the official program produced for the festival, and the detailed script that was used to narrate the festival from the stage by emcee Stan Kenton, which will be discussed in more detail below. The script was the more accurate source for tracking the sequence of artists over the festival's two nights, suggesting that some program changes had to be made at the last minute. For the program, see *Newport Jazz Festival #1 Program* (1954): 10. Ralph Gleason Files, Jeff Gold Collection, Box RG3, Rock and Roll Hall of Fame Library and Archives. The script for the concert of Saturday night, July 17, is held in the Newport Jazz Festival, Business Records and Related Papers, 1954–1995, Box 1, Folder 4, Institute for Jazz Studies, Rutgers University, Newark.
43. The script on file at the Institute for Jazz Studies has no attribution of authorship, but John Gennari attributes it to Hentoff, based on a personal interview with Wein. See Gennari, *Blowin' Hot and Cool*, 228.
44. Newport Jazz Festival script, Saturday night, July 17, 1954. Newport Jazz Festival, Business Records and Related Papers, 1954–1995, Box 1, Folder 4, Institute for Jazz Studies, Rutgers University, Newark.
45. Gardner Dunton, "7,000 Crowd Newport for First Jazz Festival," *Providence Journal* (July 18, 1954): 1, 14. *New York Times* music critic Howard Taubman also noted the same restlessness in his post-festival commentary. See Taubman, "Newport Festival: Jazz Goes Respectable in Resort Town," *New York Times* (July 25, 1954): X7.
46. Dunton, "7,000 Crowd Newport," 1.
47. Cyrus Durgin, "Jazz Gives New Beat to Staid Newport Casino," *Boston Globe* (July 19, 1954): 1.
48. Taubman, "Newport Rocked by Jazz Festival," *New York Times* (July 19, 1954): 21.
49. Wein and the rest of the Newport board were hardly alone in this wish to maintain a boundary between the music they presented at the festival and rock 'n' roll. Matt Brennan has shown that jazz critics throughout the 1950s took a largely disparaging attitude toward rock 'n' roll. As Brennan observes: "if one looks at three common arguments used to dismiss jazz in the early twentieth century—namely jazz as mass culture appealing to the lowest common denominator of public taste, jazz as an agent of moral corruption, and jazz as an aesthetically primitive form of music—all of these arguments were employed by jazz critics and musicians only a few decades later to dismiss R&B and rock 'n' roll." Brennan, *When Genres Collide: Down Beat, Rolling Stone, and the Struggle Between Jazz and Rock* (New York: Bloomsbury, 2017), 87.
50. For a critique of this tendency in jazz history, see Christi Jay Wells, "*You* Can't Dance to It: Jazz Music and Choreographies of Listening," *Daedalus* 148, no. 2 (Spring 2019): 36–51.
51. Carter Harman, "Mood Indigo and Beyond," *Time* 68, no. 8 (August 20, 1956): 55.

52. The original *Ellington at Newport* album (Columbia CL934, 1957) contained just five songs from Ellington's set, including the three sections of an original suite composed by Ellington just for the occasion, the *Festival Suite*, and the Johnny Hodges feature, "Jeep's Blues," in addition to "Diminuendo and Crescendo in Blue." An expanded reissue offers the full concert played by Ellington and his Orchestra that night; see *Ellington at Newport 1956 (Complete)* (Columbia C2K 64932, 1999). A detailed account of Avakian's work with Columbia and his efforts to record Ellington's set can be found in John Fass Morton, *Backstory in Blue: Ellington at Newport'56* (New Brunswick, NJ: Rutgers University Press, 2008).
53. Bob Parent, "Newport Jazz in Pictures," *Down Beat* (August 22, 1956). George Wein Scrapbook, 1954–August 1958, Institute for Jazz Studies, Rutgers University, Newark.
54. Morton, *Backstory in Blue*, 179.
55. Duke Ellington, *Music Is My Mistress* (New York: Da Capo, 1973), 227.
56. Wein and Chinen, *Myself Among Others*, 154.
57. Wein and Chinen, *Myself Among Others*, 156.
58. James Kaull, "Jazz Festival Record Crowd Honors Louis Armstrong," *Newport Daily News* (July 5, 1957): 1, 4; Kaull, "Jazz Festival Again Breaks Mark at Gate with 11,500," *Newport Daily News* (July 6, 1957): 1, 9.
59. "Newport Fiesta Winds up with Big Surplus," *Billboard* (July 15, 1957): 25.
60. Bill Simon, "Jazz '57 Blooms in the Open Air," *Billboard* (August 19, 1957): 40.
61. Richard Gehman, "Newport Music Is Superb, but -," *Boston Advertiser* (July 7, 1957). George Wein Scrapbook, January 1957–August 1958, Institute for Jazz Studies, Rutgers University, Newark.
62. Whitney Balliett, "Musical Events: Jazz," *New Yorker* (July 20, 1957): 81.
63. Whitney Balliett, "Musical Events: Jazz," *New Yorker* (July 19, 1958): 88.
64. George Wein, "Words of Scorn for Critics," *Boston Herald* (July 28, 1957), 30. George Wein Scrapbook, January 1957–August 1958, Institute for Jazz Studies, Rutgers University, Newark.
65. George Wein, "'Non-Profit' Newport Festival Has Need to End in Black," *Boston Herald* (July 14, 1957): 37. George Wein Scrapbook, January 1957–August 1958, Institute for Jazz Studies, Rutgers University, Newark.
66. George Wein, "Small Concert Provides Music in Places Once By-passed," *Boston Herald* (October 6, 1957). George Wein Scrapbook, January 1957–August 1958, Institute for Jazz Studies, Rutgers University, Newark.
67. On the efforts by the US State Department to use jazz as a diplomatic resource, and the complex social dynamics that resulted between jazz musicians, US officials, and local populations, see Penny Von Eschen, *Satchmo Blows up the World: Jazz Ambassadors Play the Cold War* (Cambridge, MA: Harvard University Press, 2004). The Newport Jazz Festival collection at the Institute for Jazz Studies has significant documentation concerning the Brussels engagement.
68. Details about Sheraton's larger programming can be found in an article from Wein's scrapbook, "Sheraton Revives Spa; Promotes It with Music Festival," *Hotel World-Review* (July 19, 1958).
69. Wein and Chinen, *Myself Among Others*, 201–203.

70. "Newport Jazz Festival to Produce Three Festivals for Sheraton," undated press release. Newport Jazz Festival, Business Records and Related Papers, Box 1, Folder 25, Institute for Jazz Studies.
71. "Newport Expands to Join Sheraton's Jazz Promotion," *Billboard* (February 9, 1959): 3.
72. Minutes of the Meeting of the Board of Directors of the Newport Jazz Festival Held on March 20, 1959. Newport Jazz Festival, Business Records and Related Papers, Box 2, Folder 4, Institute for Jazz Studies.
73. On the broad contours of the folk revival, see Robert Cantwell, *When We Were Good: The Folk Revival* (Cambridge, MA: Harvard University Press, 1996).
74. Wein and Chinen, *Myself Among Others*, 96, 314.
75. Rick Massimo, *I Got a Song: A History of the Newport Folk Festival* (Middletown, CT: Wesleyan University Press, 2017), 18.
76. Wald, *Dylan Goes Electric!* 12–13.
77. Cohen, *A History of Folk Music Festivals*, 36–37.
78. Cohen, *A History of Folk Music Festivals*, 42–44. For more background on the Berkeley festival, see Michael Kramer, *The Berkeley Folk Music Festival Project*, an online resource documenting the festival's history, http://www.michaeljkramer.net/the-berkeley-folk-music-festival-project.
79. Artist information comes from the *First Annual Newport Folk Festival* program book (1959), held at the Smithsonian Folklife Archives.
80. Ren Grevatt and Paul Ackerman, "Folk Music Becomes Big Business in Pop Field," *Billboard* (July 13, 1959): 4, 8; "Lagging B.O. Dims Newport Folk Fiesta," *Billboard* (July 13, 1959): 4, 8.
81. Artist biography for Joan Baez, *Second Annual Newport Folk Festival* program book (1960), Smithsonian Folklife Archives.
82. Cohen, *A History of Folk Music Festivals*, 50; Eric Von Schmidt and Jim Rooney, *Baby, Let Me Follow You Down: The Illustrated Story of the Cambridge Folk Years*, 2nd ed. (Amherst: University of Massachusetts Press, 1994), 81–82.
83. Massimo, *I Got a Song*, 23.
84. Wein and Chinen, *Myself Among Others*, 316.
85. Irwin Silber and David Gahr, "Top Performers Highlight 1st Newport Folk Fest," *Sing Out* 9, no. 2 (Fall 1959): 21–22.
86. Robert Shelton, "Folk Joins Jazz at Newport," *New York Times* (July 19, 1959): X7.
87. Burt Goldblatt, *Newport Jazz Festival: The Illustrated History* (New York: The Dial Press, 1977), 67–71.
88. Richard Hurt, "Jazz Festivals Fighting It out? Like No, Man," *Boston Globe* (July 1, 1960): 27.
89. Jesse Walker, "Theatricals," *New York Amsterdam News* (July 2, 1960): 17.
90. *Bard College Jazz Festival* program, November 14–15, 1958. Ralph Gleason Files, Jeff Gold Collection, Box RG3, Rock and Roll Hall of Fame Library and Archives.
91. Ira Gitler, "Newport Revisited," *Newport Jazz Festival 7th Annual Official Program* (1960): 9–10. Ralph Gleason Files, Jeff Gold Collection, Box RG3, Rock and Roll Hall of Fame Library and Archives.
92. Gitler, "Newport Revisited," 10.

93. Bob Rolontz, "College Fans Jam Newport for 7th Annual Bash," *Billboard* (July 4, 1960): 14.
94. "Reasons Why Newport Curtailed Jazz Festival," *Boston Globe* (July 4, 1960): 45.
95. "Beer Cans, Bottles Fly as Mob Goes Berserk," *Boston Globe* (July 4, 1960): 36.
96. "The Disgraceful Battle of Newport," *New York Herald Tribune* (July 5, 1960): 12.
97. Olga Pierce Lytle, "Queens Private Line," *New York Amsterdam News* (July 16, 1960): 22.
98. Langston Hughes, "Gloomy Day at Newport," *Chicago Defender* (July 23, 1960): 10.
99. Shirley Baty, "The Fault Was Newport's," *New York Herald Tribune* (July 11, 1960): 14.
100. John Wilson, "The Good-by Newport Blues," *New York Times* (July 10, 1960): X9.
101. Nat Hentoff, "Bringing Dignity to Jazz," *The Jazz Life* (New York: Da Capo, 1985), 101–102. An earlier version of Hentoff's piece had run in the magazine, *Commweal*, a month after the festival and the riot.
102. Robert Kenney, "Wein Defends Festival, Blames Outsiders," *Boston Globe* (July 3, 1960): 7.
103. Bill Coss, "Jazz Fans Did Not Riot," *New York Herald Tribune* (July 8, 1960): 10.
104. Father Norman O'Connor, "Spirit of Newport Riot Came out of a Beer Can," *Boston Globe* (July 5, 1960): 1, 4.
105. Saul, *Freedom Is, Freedom Ain't*, 118.
106. Sid Bernstein with Arthur Aaron, *"It's Sid Bernstein Calling...": The Amazing Story of the Promoter Who Made Entertainment History* (Middle Village, NY: Jonathan David Publishers, 2002), 69–73.
107. Wein and Chinen, *Myself Among Others*, 232.
108. James Kaull, "Back to Newport," *Providence Bulletin* (July 6, 1962): 8.
109. Wein and Chinen, *Myself Among Others*, 318. Elijah Wald suggests that the idea to pay all festival artists the same fee came from Toshi, not Pete. See Wald, *Dylan Goes Electric*, 123.
110. Certificate of Incorporation, Newport Folk Foundation, Inc., March 8, 1963. Ralph Rinzler Collection, Smithsonian Folklife Archives, Box 5, Rinzler-Events-Newport, Bylaws and Contracts folder.
111. "Proposal for the Newport Folk Festival to be held in Newport July 1963 on the 26th, 27th and 28th," Alan Lomax Collection, Library of Congress Folklife Archive, Newport Folk Foundation—Memos, Correspondence—1963. All further material in this paragraph and the next is quoted and summarized from the same document. For a complementary discussion of the same proposal, see Massimo, *I Got a Song*, 31–32.
112. Irwin Silber, "Traditional Folk Artists Capture the Campus," *Sing Out* 14, no. 2 (April-May 1964): 12–13; John Cohen, "Folk Festivals: Rural, Urban and Commercial," *Newport Folk Festival 1964* program book, 22–23, Ralph Rinzler Collection, Smithsonian Folklife Archives, Box 7, Rinzler-Events-Newport, Program books 2.
113. John Cohen and Ralph Rinzler, "The University of Chicago Folk Festival," *Sing Out* 13, no. 2 (April-May 1963): 10.
114. Josh Dunson, "Slave Songs at the 'Sing for Freedom,'" *Broadside*, no. 46 (May 30, 1964): 9–10.

115. Cohen, "Folk Festivals," 23.
116. Program details come from the *Newport Folk Festival 1963* program book, Ralph Rinzler Collection, Smithsonian Folklife Archives, Box 7, Rinzler-Events-Newport, Program books 1.
117. "Newport Fest Spark to Hoots at All Levels," *Billboard* (August 17, 1963): 18.
118. Bob Dylan, "-for Dave Glover," *Newport Folk Festival 1963* program book.
119. Details about the funding given by the Foundation comes from two documents: "Summary of Proposed Expenditures out of Proceeds of 1963 Folk Festival," the minutes of a meeting of the special committee on disbursements dated October 1, 1963; and the minutes of the Newport Folk Foundation board, dated November 18th, 1963. Alan Lomax Collection, Library of Congress Folklife Archive, Newport Folk Foundation—Memos, Correspondence—1963.
120. Alan Lomax and Mike Seeger, memo to Newport Board concerning a scout and coordinator for traditional performers. Undated. Ralph Rinzler Collection, Smithsonian Folklife Archives, Box 5, Rinzler-Events-Newport, Correspondence 1.
121. Ralph Rinzler, "The Newport Folk Foundation: Keeping the Roots of Music Alive," *Newport Folk Festival 1964* program book, 6. Ralph Rinzler Collection, Smithsonian Folklife Archives, Box 7, Rinzler-Events-Newport, Program books 2.
122. Cantwell, *When We Were Good*, 298–299.
123. Robert Shelton, "'64 Folk Festival Ends in Newport," *New York Times* (July 27, 1964): 21.
124. "Newport (Notes)," *Broadside*, n. 49 (August 20, 1964): 11.
125. Paul Nelson, "Newport: The Folk Spectacle Comes of Age," *Sing Out* 14, no. 5 (November 1964): 6.
126. Paul Nelson, "A Voice of Dissent," *Newport Folk Festival 1965* program book, 19, 60. Ralph Rinzler Collection, Smithsonian Folklife Archives, Box 7, Rinzler-Events-Newport, Program books 3.
127. Massimo, *I Got a Song*, 69–91.
128. Steve Waksman, *Instruments of Desire: The Electric Guitar and the Shaping of Musical Experience* (Cambridge, MA: Harvard University Press, 1999), 2.
129. Wald, *Dylan Goes Electric!* 280.
130. Joe Boyd, *White Bicycles: Making Music in the 1960s* (London: Serpent's Tail, 2006), 103–105.
131. Rachel Lyons, transcribed interview with Bill Hanley and Rhoda Rosenberg, October 13, 2014, 13–14. New Orleans Jazz & Heritage Foundation Archive, Past Presidents and Founders Oral History Collection.
132. Jeff MacKay, "History Files: The Genesis of Clair Bros to Today," *ProSoundWeb* (November 20, 2013), https://www.prosoundweb.com/history-files-the-genesis-of-clair-bros-to-today.; Robert Greenfield, *Bear: The Life and Times of Augustus Owsley Stanley III* (New York: Thomas Dunne Books, 2016).
133. John Kane's recent book on Hanley, *The Last Seat in the House: The Story of Hanley Sound* (Jackson, MS: University of Mississippi Press, 2020), should go some way toward making Hanley's career and achievements more widely known.
134. For further details, see Kane, *The Last Seat in the House*, 44–47.

135. "10,000 Jazz Festival Fans to Hear Duke Ellington Open International Event," *Newport News* (July 3, 1958): 1, 4.
136. Lyons, interview with Hanley and Rosenberg, 5. Hanley tells another version of this story in an interview with Irv Joel conducted eleven years earlier, where he also names Rosenthal and claims that he was the one who actually did the mixing at the festival. See Irv Joel, interview with Bill Hanley, Audio Engineering Society Oral History Project, 2003.
137. Joel, interview with Hanley. On the JBL D130, see the relevant page of the Lansing Heritage website, designed to preserve the history of James B. Lansing's audio technology work (Lansing was the namesake of JBL), http://www.audioheritage.org/html/profiles/jbl/d130.htm. On the McIntosh MC75 and the broader history of the McIntosh Laboratory, Inc., audio products, see the website curated by Roger Russell, http://www.roger-russell.com/amplif1.htm.
138. Lyons, interview with Hanley and Rosenberg, 6.
139. Andy Coules, "Modern Pioneers: The History of PA," *ProSoundWeb* (December 22, 2017), https://www.prosoundweb.com/modern-pioneers-the-history-of-pa/2/.
140. Lyons, interview with Hanley and Rosenberg, 7.
141. Wein and Chinen, *Myself Among Others*, 232.
142. Advertisement for Hanley Sound Co., *Billboard* (March 19, 1966): 126.
143. Writes Beatles historian Steve Turner, "The [1966] Shea Stadium concert became an anticlimax. Almost exactly a year before the Beatles had played the same venue to a sellout audience of 55,600 . . . This time there were eleven thousand empty seats despite tickets having been on sale for over two months." Turner, *Beatles '66: The Revolutionary Year* (New York: Ecco, 2016), 299.
144. Bernstein and Aaron, *"It's Sid Bernstein Calling"*, 200.
145. Barry McKinnon, "Sockhops to Woodstock: An Interview with Bill Hanley," *Recording Engineer/Producer* 20, no. 1 (January 1989): 62.
146. McKinnon, "Sockhops to Woodstock," 62.
147. John Glatt, *Live at the Fillmore East: Getting Backstage and Personal with Rock's Greatest Legends* (Guilford, CT: Lyons Press, 2015), 129.
148. For details about the Magic Mountain Music Festival, see Harvey Kubernik and Kenneth Kubernik, *A Perfect Haze: The Illustrated History of the Monterey International Pop Festival* (Solana Beach, CA: Santa Monica Press, 2011), 54–60.
149. The classic account of the partnership between Lang, Kornfeld, Roberts, and Rosenman is that authored by the two money men in Joel Rosenman, John Roberts, and Robert Pilpel, *Young Men with Unlimited Capital: The Inside Story of the Legendary Woodstock Festival Told by the Two Who Paid for It* (New York: Harcourt Brace Jovanovich, 1974). Michael Lang has written his own version of events, many years after the fact; see Lang with Holly George-Warren, *The Road to Woodstock: From the Man Behind the Legendary Festival* (New York: Ecco, 2009). For general details about the production of the Woodstock festival, see Robert Spitz, *Barefoot in Babylon: The Creation of the Woodstock Music Festival, 1969* (New York: Viking Press, 1979); and Joel Makower, *Woodstock: The Oral History* (New York: Doubleday, 1989).

150. Makower, *Woodstock*, 147.
151. McKinnon, "Sockhops to Woodstock," 63.
152. Details come from Joel, interview with Hanley and Rosenberg; McKinnon, "Sockhops to Woodstock," 63. On the Crown DC300, see Gerald Stanley, "The Crown DC300 Amplifier Leads the Solid-State Revolution," *ProSoundWeb* (August 15, 2013), https://www.prosoundweb.com/history-files-the-crown-dc300-amplifier-leads-the-solid-state-revolution/.
153. Marc Myers, *Why Jazz Happened* (Berkeley and Los Angeles: University of California Press, 2013), 205.
154. Myers, *Why Jazz Happened*, 204.
155. Greil Marcus, "The Woodstock Festival," *Rolling Stone*, no. 42 (September 20, 1969): 17.
156. Myers, *Why Jazz Happened*, 205.
157. Joel, interview with Hanley and Rosenberg.
158. McKinnon, "Sockhops to Woodstock," 64.
159. Makower, *Woodstock*, 209.
160. Jerry Hopkins, Jim Marshall, and Baron Wolman, *Festival! The Book of American Music Celebrations* (New York: Collier, 1970), 154.
161. Rosenman, Roberts, and Pilpel, *Young Men with Unlimited Capital*, 137.
162. Lydon, "The High Cost of Music and Love," 1, 7.
163. Jerry Hopkins, "Festival Shucks," *Rolling Stone*, no. 36 (June 28, 1969): 11.
164. Miller Francis, Jr., "Atlanta International Pop Festival," *Great Speckled Bird* 2, no. 16 (June 30, 1969): 10–11.
165. Alex Cooley interview, part one, *Pollstar Pro*, https://vimeopro.com/user23430836/promoters-hall-of-fame-interviews/video/82023770. This content has since been taken down from the web, unfortunately, or at least made inaccessible to those without a paid subscription to *Pollstar*.
166. "Production and Crowd Communication." Undated memo. Alex Cooley Collection, Series 1, Box 1, Folder 20—Music festival materials, 1969, Georgia State University. All subsequent quotes in the next two paragraphs are from this document.
167. Marley Brant, *Join Together: Forty Years of the Rock Music Festival* (New York: Backbeat Books, 2008), 85.
168. "Why Dallas?" Undated memo. Alex Cooley Collection, Series 1, Box 1, Folder 20—Music festival materials, 1969, Georgia State University.
169. John Zeh, "Texas Pop: Heat, but Not So Hot," *Rolling Stone*, no. 45 (November 1, 1969): 14.
170. Alex Cooley interview, part one.
171. "A Proposal for the Symposium of Awareness." Undated memo. Alex Cooley Collection, Series 1, Box 1, Folder 22—Second Annual Atlanta International Pop Festival, Jul. 3-5, 1970, Georgia State University.
172. Michael Hill, "Pop," *Great Speckled Bird* 4, no. 29 (July 20, 1970): 12–13.
173. "Atlanta: the Biggest—and Maybe Last?" *Rolling Stone*, no. 64 (August 6, 1970): 14.
174. Wein, "Foreword from the Producer," *Jazz '69* [Newport Jazz Festival 1969 program book]. Ralph Gleason Files, Jeff Gold Collection, Box RG3, Rock and Roll Hall of Fame Library and Archives.

175. Brennan, *When Genres Collide*, 163.
176. "Rock Too Much for Newport," *Rolling Stone*, no. 39 (August 9, 1969): 10. *Rolling Stone*'s portrayal of Wein was markedly unsympathetic and undoubtedly exaggerated. Nonetheless, the pattern of his response to the performance, as reported by the magazine, fits well with that established during the early history of the festival. As for Sly Stone, this was but one of many instances where his band was perceived to be uniquely subject to fostering disorder, a point to be explored further in the next chapter.
177. Wein and Chinen, *Myself Among Others*, 286.
178. Minutes of Newport Folk Foundation board meeting, September 28, 1969. Ralph Rinzler Collection, Smithsonian Folklife Archives, Box 7, Rinzler-Events-Newport, Meeting Minutes 3.
179. Timothy Crouse, "600 Lames Wreck Newport Festival," *Rolling Stone*, no. 88 (August 5, 1971): 10.
180. Rachel Lyons and Kevin McCaffrey, transcribed interview with George Wein, April 30, 2008, 7–8. New Orleans Jazz & Heritage Foundation Archive, Past Presidents and Founders Oral History Collection.
181. Jonathan Wynn, *Music/City: American Festivals and Placemaking in Austin, Nashville, and Newport* (Chicago: University of Chicago Press, 2015), 226–232.
182. Bruce Boyd Raeburn, *New Orleans Style and the Writing of American Jazz History* (Ann Arbor: University of Michigan Press, 2009), 243.
183. Edmond Souchon, "Editorial," *The Second Line* 1, no. 2 (May 1950): 2.
184. Details from *Jazzfest '68: Official Program of the New Orleans International Jazz Festival Inc.*: 3. New Orleans Jazz Festival, 1968—Vertical Files—Planning documents. Hogan Jazz Archive, Tulane University.
185. Wein and Chinen, *Myself Among Others*, 353–354; Lyons and McCaffrey, interview with Wein, 2; Lyons and McCaffrey, transcribed interview with Earl Duffy, December 12, 2014, 6. New Orleans Jazz & Heritage Foundation Archive, Past Presidents and Founders Oral History Collection.
186. Wein and Chinen, *Myself Among Others*, 357.
187. Wein and Chinen, *Myself Among Others*, 359.
188. The particulars of the first Heritage Fair plan come from a New Orleans Jazz and Heritage Festival ticket order brochure for the 1970 festival, and the official program book for the event. New Orleans Jazz Festival 1970—Vertical Files. Hogan Jazz Archive, Tulane University.
189. Lyons and McCaffrey, interview with Wein, 8.
190. Allison Miner and Clare Beth Pierson, "Allison's Jazz Fest Memories," in Michael Smith and Allison Miner, *Jazz Fest Memories* (Gretna, LA: Pelican Publishing, 1997), 18.
191. Miner and Pierson, "Allison's Jazz Fest Memories," 19.
192. Lyons and McCaffrey, transcribed interview with George Wein, May 3, 2008, 8–9. New Orleans Jazz & Heritage Foundation Archive, Past Presidents and Founders Oral History Collection.

193. Kevin McCaffrey, ed., *The Incomplete, Year-by-Year, Selectively Quirky, Prime Facts Edition of the History of the New Orleans Jazz & Heritage Festival* (New Orleans: ePrime Publications, 2005), 297.
194. A VHS copy of this video is held at the New Orleans Jazz and Heritage Foundation Archive.
195. Miner and Pierson, "Allison's Jazz Fest Memories," 20–21.

Chapter 8

1. Information about Led Zeppelin's 1977 tour is drawn mainly from two sources: the master itinerary for the tour produced for Showco employees, retained in the papers of John Vogel, a lighting technician with the company, Box 1, Folder 13, Rock and Roll Hall of Fame Library and Archives; and the official Led Zeppelin website, which includes a detailed timeline of the band's touring history with supporting information, http://www.ledzeppelin.com/timeline/1977. Details concerning attendance figures can be found in Ritchie Yorke, *Led Zeppelin: The Definitive Biography* (Novato, CA: Underwood-Miller, 1993), 209–210. Other material about the tour appears in Stephen Davis, *Hammer of the Gods: The Led Zeppelin Saga* (New York: Ballantine Books 1985), 278–286; and Richard Cole, *Stairway to Heaven: Led Zeppelin Uncensored* (New York: HarperCollins, 1992), 333–359.
2. Information about the Rolling Stones 1978 tour comes primarily from the master itinerary for the tour, again held in the John Vogel Collection, Box 1, Folder 19, Rock and Roll Hall of Fame Library and Archives. Supporting details come from the website, Time Is on Our Side, maintained by Ian McPherson, http://www.timeisonourside.com/chron1978.html.
3. Steve Chapple and Reebee Garofalo, *Rock 'n' Roll Is Here to Pay: The History and Politics of the Music Industry* (Chicago: Nelson-Hall, 1977), 137–154.
4. Robert Duncan, *The Noise: Notes from a Rock 'n' Roll Era* (New York: Ticknor & Fields, 1984), 37.
5. See Bill Graham and Robert Greenfield, *Bill Graham Presents: My Life Inside Rock and Out* (New York: Da Capo, 2004), 354.
6. Steve Waksman, *This Ain't the Summer of Love: Conflict and Crossover in Heavy Metal and Punk* (Berkeley and Los Angeles: University of California Press, 2009); and Waksman, "Grand Funk Live! Staging Rock in the Age of the Arena," in *Listen Again: A Momentary History of Pop*, ed. Eric Weisbard (Durham, NC: Duke University Press, 2007), 157–171.
7. While the subject of arena rock is not quite as much of a scholarly blank slate as it was when I wrote about it a decade ago, there remains little work that truly excavates the mode of production that gave rise to the routine mounting of large-scale popular music concerts, and even less that treats the subject with any significant degree of historical perspective. The most notable recent publication on the topic, Robert

Edgar, Kristy Fairclough-Isaacs, Benjamin Halligan, and Nicola Spelman, eds., *The Arena Concert: Music, Media and Mass Entertainment* (New York: Bloomsbury Academic, 2015), considers the phenomenon primarily from the perspective of the twenty-first century, with a small section of essays devoted to "pre-history." Otherwise, the most substantial work on arena rock to date has been done in two as-yet unpublished doctoral dissertations: Michael Ethen, "A Spatial History of Arena Rock, 1964–1979" (PhD diss., Schulich School of Music, McGill University, 2011); and Gina Arnold, "Rock Crowds and Power: Race, Space, and Representation" (PhD diss., Stanford University, 2011).

8. Paul Gardner, "3,000 Fans Greet British Beatles," *New York Times* (February 8, 1964): 25.
9. Tom Wolfe, "Beatles Conquer New York," *Boston Globe* (February 8, 1964): 7.
10. Sid Bernstein with Arthur Aaron, *"It's Sid Bernstein Calling...": The Amazing Story of the Promoter Who Made Entertainment History* (Middle Village, NY: Jonathan David Publishers, 2002), 119–120. Beatles biographer Philip Norman confirms key parts of Bernstein's story, although suggests that the deal for the Beatles to play Carnegie Hall was finalized by one of Bernstein's associates at GAC, Norman Weiss. Bernstein claims that Weiss did not have anything to do with engaging the band to perform but that he did sign the Beatles to GAC, a move that led Bernstein to leave the company because he felt that he should have been more directly involved. See Philip Norman, *Shout! The Beatles in Their Generation*, rev. ed. (New York: Fireside, 2003), 226, 237–238.
11. Bernstein and Aaron, *"It's Sid Bernstein Calling"*, 138.
12. Robert Alden, "Wild-Eyed Mobs Pursue Beatles," *New York Times* (February 13, 1964): 26.
13. The best account of the events in Vancouver can be found in Larry Kane, *Ticket to Ride: Inside the Beatles' 1964 Tour That Changed the World* (Milwaukee, WI: Backbeat Books, 2003), 48–49. Also see Ethen, "A Spatial History of Arena Rock," 74–79.
14. Bernstein and Aaron, *"It's Sid Bernstein Calling"*, 167–168.
15. Howard Shubert, *Architecture on Ice: A History of the Hockey Arena* (Montreal and Kingston: McGill–Queen's University Press, 2016), 141.
16. Shubert, *Architecture on Ice*, 161.
17. A copy of one of these letters appears in Dave Schwensen, *The Beatles at Shea Stadium: The Story Behind Their Greatest Concert* (Chicago: North Shore Publishing, 2014), 51.
18. Bernstein claims in his memoir that he hired noted stage designer and concert producer Chip Monck (whose name he misspells as "Chip Munk") to build the stage for the Beatles concert at Shea Stadium. At the time Monck had worked on the Newport jazz and folk festivals and also had a long-standing association with the Village Gate nightclub in New York; his later acclaim would blossom after his work with Woodstock in 1969. However, I have found no other sources to verify that Monck was involved. See Bernstein and Aaron, *"It's Sid Bernstein Calling"*, 169–170.
19. Schwensen offers a concise but detailed account of the sequence of opening acts for the concert, 91–93.

20. The 9:14 P.M. time was reported in Claude Hall, "Beatlemonium at Stadium—Youngsters Get Carried Away," *Billboard* (August 28, 1965): 16. Also see Murray Schumach, "Shrieks of 55,000 Accompany Beatles," *New York Times* (August 16, 1965): 49.
21. "50,000 Hail Beatles in N.Y. Appearance," *Los Angeles Times* (August 16, 1965): 16.
22. Schumach, "Shrieks of 55,000 Accompany Beatles," 29.
23. The classic defense of the female pop audience as it took shape through Beatles fandom is Barbara Ehrenreich, Elizabeth Hess, and Gloria Jacobs, "Beatlemania: Girls Just Want to Have Fun," in *The Adoring Audience: Fan Culture and Popular Media*, ed. Lisa Lewis (London: Routledge, 1992), 84–106. Also see Norma Coates, "Teenyboppers, Groupies, and Other Grotesques: Girls and Women in Rock Culture in the 1960s and Early 1970s," *Journal of Popular Music Studies* 15, no. 1 (June 2003): 65–94.
24. Schwensen, *The Beatles at Shea Stadium*, 121.
25. Quoted in Schwensen, *The Beatles at Shea Stadium*, 133.
26. P.T. Barnum, *Struggles and Triumphs*, edited and abridged by Carl Bode (New York: Penguin, 1981), 171.
27. Graham and Greenfield, *Bill Graham Presents*.
28. Pat O'Day with Jim Ojala, *It Was All Just Rock 'n' Roll II: A Return to the Center of the Radio & Concert Universe* (Seattle: Ballard Publishing, 2003); Barry Fey, *Backstage Past* (Scottsdale, AZ: Lone Wolfe Press, 2011); Larry Magid with Robert Huber, *My Soul's Been Psychedelicized: Electric Factory, Four Decades in Posters and Photographs* (Philadelphia: Temple University Press, 2011); Pat DiCesare, *Hard Days Hard Nights: From the Beatles to the Doors to the Stones . . . Insider Stories from a Legendary Concert Promoter* (Terra Alta, WV: Headline Books, 2015); Jerry Weintraub with Rich Cohen, *When I Stop Talking, You'll Know I'm Dead: Useful Stories from a Persuasive Man* (New York: Twelve, 2010).
29. I have addressed this body of literature in "Writing the Life of the Concert Promoter," *Massachusetts Review* 57, no. 4 (Winter 2016): 784–793, from which portions of this section have been adapted. For a complementary perspective, see Matt Brennan and Emma Webster, "Why Concert Promoters Matter," *Scottish Music Review* 2, no. 1 (2011).
30. O'Day and Ojala, *It Was All Just Rock 'n' Roll II*, 237.
31. O'Day and Ojala, *It Was All Just Rock 'n' Roll II*, 240.
32. DiCesare, *Hard Days Hard Nights*, 24.
33. DiCesare, *Hard Days Hard Nights*, 25.
34. Weintraub and Cohen, *When I Stop Talking*, 52.
35. Aerosmith with Stephen Davis, *Walk This Way: The Autobiography of Aerosmith* (New York: Spike, 1999), 55; also see Waksman, *This Ain't the Summer of Love*, 32.
36. Weintraub and Cohen, *When I Stop Talking*, 80.
37. Details come from Peter Guralnick, *Careless Love: The Unmaking of Elvis Presley* (Boston, MA: Little, Brown and Company, 1999), 387–388.
38. On Graham's experience with the different incarnations of the Fillmore, see Graham and Greenfield, *Bill Graham Presents*; John Glatt, *Rage and Roll: Bill Graham and the Selling of Rock* (New York: Birch Lane Press, 1993); and Glatt, *Live at the Fillmore*

East and West: Getting Backstage and Personal with Rock's Greatest Legends (Guilford, CT: Lyons Press, 2015).
39. "Sol Hurok, Impresario, Dead at 85," Rolling Stone, no. 159 (April 25, 1974): 18.
40. Graham and Greenfield, Bill Graham Presents, 147. Other accounts of the clash between Graham and Helms appear in Charles Perry, The Haight-Ashbury: A History (New York: Vintage Books, 1984), 60; and Ralph Gleason, The Jefferson Airplane and the San Francisco Sound (New York: Ballantine Books, 1969), 289–290.
41. Perry, The Haight-Ashbury, 61–62.
42. Gleason, The Jefferson Airplane, 301.
43. David A Wiles, Letter to Ralph Gleason, dated October 23, 1968. Jeff Gold Collection, Box RG2, Rock and Roll Hall of Fame Library and Archives. For a discussion of this letter and its implications, see Waksman, "San Francisco's Fillmore Auditorium: From 'Dance-concerts' to 'Concerts,'" Live Music Exchange (November 1, 2012), http://livemusicexchange.org/blog/san-franciscos-fillmore-auditorium-from-dance-concerts-to-concerts-steve-waksman.
44. Sarah Hill, in her recent study of the 1960s San Francisco scene, cites Gleason himself observing some very similar trends in the ballrooms of the time. As Gleason wrote in his June 30, 1968, column in the San Francisco Chronicle: "People come to see the scene. People come to see the bands, the singers and the audience. They stand in front of the bandstand and they sit on the floor. They do not dance." Quoted in Hill, San Francisco and the Long 60s (New York and London: Bloomsbury Academic, 2016), 239, n39.
45. "Fillmore Bill Calls It Quits," Rolling Stone, no. 82 (May 27, 1971): 6.
46. Fred Goodman, The Mansion on the Hill: Dylan, Young, Geffen, Springsteen, and the Head-on Collision of Rock and Commerce (New York: Times Books 1997), 191.
47. Advertisement for Premier Talent Associates, Inc., Billboard (July 3, 1965): 21.
48. "Premier Nets $7.5 Mil. by Spanning Gap," Billboard (April 20, 1968): 1.
49. Advertisement for Premier Talent Associates, Inc., Billboard (December 27, 1969): T-27.
50. Advertisement for Premier Talent Associates, Inc., Billboard (November 6, 1971): 76.
51. "Something Must Happen," Billboard (November 14, 1970): R-63.
52. Loraine Alterman, "Foghat: Their Business Is Rock & Roll," Rolling Stone, no. 168 (August 29, 1974): 18.
53. Alterman, "Foghat," 27.
54. The following account mainly draws upon an extensive interview with Don Law conducted through a cooperative arrangement between the Rock and Roll Hall of Fame and the North American Concert Promoters Association, and hosted by Pollstar Pro, https://vimeopro.com/ user23430836/promoters-hall-of-fame-interviews/video/106021359. (This, and the other video interviews cited below as part of the Pollstar Pro collection, have all subsequently been removed from the web and are no longer accessible.) Goodman also addresses Barsalona's relationship with Don Law and the Tea Party in Mansion on the Hill, 28–30.
55. Don Law interview, Pollstar Pro.

56. Alex Cooley interview, part two, *Pollstar Pro*, https://vimeopro.com/user23430836/promoters-hall-of-fame-interviews/video/82023770.
57. Larry Magid interview, part one, *Pollstar Pro*, https://vimeopro.com/user23430836/promoters-hall-of-fame-interviews/video/106021365.
58. Peter Rudge interview, part one, *Pollstar Pro*, https://vimeopro.com/user23430836/promoters-hall-of-fame-interviews/video/152627323.
59. Weintraub and Cohen, *When I Stop Talking*, 83.
60. From Weintraub's memoir, one would get little sense that his takeover of Concerts West was anything more than a logical and cooperative business partnership. However, Seattle radio DJ and promoter Pat O'Day presents a very different version of the history of the company in his own memoir. According to O'Day, Concerts West began as his company, created as the result of a 1968 business deal where he divided up his existing dance promotion company and kept the division of the business that promoted the kinds of concerts that might be held in sports arenas (O'Day with Ojala, *It Was All Just Rock 'n' Roll II*, 134–35). He accuses his business partner Tom Hulett of having engaged in a series of shady dealings that led O'Day and other principals in the company to sell their shares, leaving Hulett to work with Weintraub (O'Day with Ojala, *It Was All Just Rock 'n' Roll II*, 355). None of these details appear in Weintraub's memoir, and he never mentions Pat O'Day by name.
61. Weintraub and Cohen, *When I Stop Talking*, 134.
62. Nat Freedland, "Rock Concert Promoters Eye Unity in Discussing Problems," *Billboard* (May 18, 1974): 1, 31.
63. Glatt, *Rage and Roll*, 159.
64. "Rock Promoters Meet, Try Rules for 'Our Thing,'" *Rolling Stone*, no. 162 (June 6, 1974): 20.
65. Fey, *Backstage Past*, 112.
66. Weintraub and Cohen, *When I Stop Talking*, 135.
67. Fey, *Backstage Past*, 235.
68. Sales pamphlet for Clark Transfer, Inc., Jules Fisher Collection, Box 1, Folder 19, Rock and Roll Hall of Fame Library and Archives.
69. Information on the company's history comes from "Clark Chronicles," a feature on the Clark Transfer website. https://clarktransfer.com/about/clark-chronicles.
70. Sam Cutler, *You Can't Always Get What You Want: My Life with the Rolling Stones, the Grateful Dead and Other Wonderful Reprobates* (Toronto: ECW Press, 2010), 72.
71. Philip Auslander, *Performing Glam Rock: Gender and Theatricality in Popular Music* (Ann Arbor: University of Michigan Press, 2006), 9–38; Waksman, *This Ain't the Summer of Love*, 70–103.
72. Robert Greenfield, *S.T.P.: A Journey Through America with the Rolling Stones* (New York: Da Capo, 2002), 10.
73. Peter Rudge interview, part one, *Pollstar Pro*.
74. "Rolling Stones Tour Underway," The Rolling Stones 1972 Tour press packet, Alex Cooley Collection, Box 3, Folder 22, Georgia State University.

75. "'72 Stones Tour Highlights New Concepts in Production and Security," The Rolling Stones 1972 Tour press packet, Alex Cooley Collection, Box 3, Folder 22, Georgia State University.
76. Official Tour Program, Rolling Stones Tour of the Americas '75, Alex Cooley Collection, Box 3, Folder 23, Georgia State University.
77. Information on Fisher's theatrical credits can be found at the *Broadway World* website, https://www.broadwayworld.com/people/Jules-Fisher.
78. The Concert Stage Design blog contains an excellent reconstruction of the production details for the 1975 Rolling Stones tour, "The Rolling Stones Tour of the Americas 1975—The Lotus Stage," which includes discussion of the inflatable phallus. http://concertstagedesign.blogspot.com/2011/04/the-rolling-stones-tour-of-americas.html.
79. Chet Flippo, "The Rolling Stones, Their 1975 Tour, World's Greatest Performing Band Bewilders the South, Baptized in Baton Rouge, Castrated in San Antone," *Rolling Stone*, no. 191 (July 17, 1975): 63.
80. "Rolling Stones Tour of the Americas '75: Staging, Lighting and Sound," The Rolling Stones 1975 Tour of the Americas press packet, Alex Cooley Collection, Box 3, Folder 27, Georgia State University.
81. The music selections memo and fabric samples are both included in the Jules Fisher Collection, Box 1, Folder 15, Rock and Roll Hall of Fame Library and Archives.
82. Memo from Jules Fisher to Mick Jagger, dated March 10, 1975, Jules Fisher Collection, Box 1, Folder 7, Rock and Roll Hall of Fame Library and Archives.
83. Memo from Stephen Bickford to Jules Fisher, dated March 20, 1975, Jules Fisher Collection, Box 1, Folder 7, Rock and Roll Hall of Fame Library and Archives.
84. Letter from Michael Crowley to Tim Mahoney, dated April 3, 1975, Jules Fisher Collection, Box 1, Folder 2, Rock and Roll Hall of Fame Library and Archives.
85. Memo from Jules Fisher to Robin Wagner [undated], Jules Fisher Collection, Box 1, Folder 7, Rock and Roll Hall of Fame Library and Archives.
86. George Clinton with Ben Greenman, *Brothas Be, Yo Like George, Ain't That Funkin' Kinda Hard on You?* (New York: Atria Books, 2014), 146.
87. Rickey Vincent, *Funk: The Music, the People, and the Rhythm of the One* (New York: St. Martin's Griffin, 1996), 258.
88. Clinton and Greenman, *Brothas Be*, 140.
89. P-Funk Mothership design drawings, Jules Fisher Collection, Box 1, Folder 15, Rock and Roll Hall of Fame Library and Archives.
90. Clinton and Greenman, *Brothas Be*, 156.
91. Clinton and Greenman, *Brothas Be*, 157.
92. Clinton and Greenman, *Brothas Be*, 169.
93. Jean Williams, "Washington Tiger Flower Co. Keeping Concert Tickets Down," *Billboard* (July 19, 1980): 32.
94. John Rockwell, "Joyous Musical 'Jivation' with the P-Funkadelics," *New York Times* (September 4, 1977): D1, D4.

95. Mikal Gilmore, "Commodores Break the Color Barrier," *Rolling Stone*, no. 250 (October 20, 1977): 16.
96. "Facility Ops Reform Demanded at Forum," *Billboard* (June 11, 1977): 16.
97. "Strategy Involved in Achieving Crossovers," *Billboard* (September 30, 1978): 43.
98. Frank Madison, "Bleak Future for Black Concert Promoters," *Billboard* (April 21, 1979): 35.
99. Nelson George, *The Death of Rhythm & Blues* (New York: E.P. Dutton, 1989), 163.
100. Vincent, *Funk*, 92.
101. Dalton Anthony, "A.K.A. Sly Stone: The Rise and Fall of Sylvester Stewart," in *Rip It Up: The Black Experience in Rock 'n' Roll*, ed. Kandia Crazy Horse (New York: Palgrave Macmillan, 2004), 51.
102. Joel Selvin, *On the Record: Sly and the Family Stone* (New York: Simon & Schuster, 1997), ch 7.
103. Marshall Rosenthal, "Chicago: The First Interracial Riot," *Rolling Stone*, no. 65 (September 3, 1970): 14.
104. DiCesare, *Hard Days Hard Nights*, 105.
105. DiCesare, *Hard Days Hard Nights*, 106.
106. Selvin, *On the Record*, ch 9.
107. Timothy Crouse, "The Struggle for Sly's Soul at the Garden," *Rolling Stone*, no. 93 (October 14, 1971): 1.
108. Crouse, "The Struggle for Sly's Soul," 8.
109. Crouse, "The Struggle for Sly's Soul," 8.
110. Greil Marcus, *Mystery Train: Images of America in Rock 'n' Roll Music*, 3rd ed. (New York: Dutton, 1990), 77.
111. Maurice White with Herb Powell, *My Life with Earth, Wind & Fire* (New York: HarperCollins, 2016), 180.
112. Bob Glassenberg, "Studio Track," *Billboard* (July 31, 1971): 4.
113. Wally Heider with Terry Stark, "The Story of Wally Heider Recording," *Mix* (February 1978). Available at: http://wallyheider.com/wordpress/2006/01/wallyinterview.
114. The Doors, *Absolutely Live*, Elektra Records EKS-9002, 1970, liner notes.
115. Photo booklet included with Yes, *Yessongs*, Atlantic Records K60045, 1973.
116. Rainbow, *On Stage*, Polydor 2657 016, 1977, liner notes.
117. Foghat, *Live*, Bearsville BRK 6971, 1977), liner notes.
118. The "liveness" of Kiss' first live album has long been a matter of dispute and speculation, although the band members and producer Eddie Kramer have admitted that substantial post-production was done to enhance the sound of the album and cover up wrong notes and performance glitches. See Nick Deriso, "How Kiss Came Alive!—By Using Some Studio Magic," *Ultimate Classic Rock* (September 15, 2015), http://ultimateclassicrock.com/kiss-alive.

Chapter 9

1. Eli Ellison, "The Highest Grossing Concert Tours of All Time," *Work + Money* (December 13, 2018), https://www.workandmoney.com/s/highest-grossing-concert-tours-ed51a7b3f92c4afb.
2. Jay-Z with Dream Hampton, *Decoded* (New York: Spiegel and Grau, 2010), 297.
3. Jay-Z and Hampton, *Decoded*, 297.
4. Details about the concert come from Christian Hoard, "Jay-Z Rocks the Garden," *Rolling Stone* (November 26, 2003), https://www.rollingstone.com/music/music-news/jay-z-rocks-the-garden-238251.
5. Footage of this performance can be found in *Fade to Black*, directed by Patrick Paulson and Michael John Warren (Los Angeles: Paramount, 2004).
6. Underground, local hip-hop scenes retain an emphasis on liveness that has been documented in a range of excellent local case studies. See, for example, Anthony Kwame Harrison, *Hip Hop Underground: The Integrity and Ethics of Racial Integration* (Philadelphia: Temple University Press, 2009); Marcyliena Morgan, *The Real Hip Hop: Battling for Knowledge, Power, and Respect in the LA Underground* (Durham, NC: Duke University Press, 2009); and Ali Colleen Neff, *Let the World Listen Right: The Mississippi Delta Hip-Hop Story* (Jackson: University Press of Mississippi, 2009).
7. Murray Forman, *The 'Hood Comes First: Race, Space, and Place in Rap and Hip-Hop* (Middletown, CT: Wesleyan University Press, 2002), 137.
8. On Bucano, see "The Industry Cosign Spotlight: Rocky Busano," *It Needs to Be CED* (November 3, 2016), http://itneedstobeced.com/industry-cosign-spotlight-rocky-bucano. On Pete "DJ" Jones and his association with Grandmaster Flash, see Jeff Chang, *Can't Stop Won't Stop: A History of the Hip-hop Generation* (New York: St. Martin's Press, 2005), 112–113; and Grandmaster Flash with David Ritz, *The Adventures of Grandmaster Flash: My Life, My Beats* (New York: Harlem Moon, 2008), 87–90.
9. Flyer for Stardust Room, June 30, 1978. Hip Hop and Party Event Flyers Collection, Cornell Hip Hop Collection. https://digital.library.cornell.edu/catalog/ss:1333842.
10. Details from Bambaataa's bio on the official website of the organization he founded, the Universal Zulu Nation. http://www.zulunation.com/afrika-bambaataa.
11. Flyer for T-Connection, April 4, 1981, https://digital.library.cornell.edu/catalog/ss:455277; flyer for Roller World Skating Rink, July 3, 1981, https://digital.library.cornell.edu/catalog/ss:455494. Hip Hop and Party Event Flyers Collection, Cornell Hip Hop Collection.
12. Dan Charnas, *The Big Payback: The History of the Business of Hip-Hop* (New York: New American Library, 2010), 59–60.
13. Amanda Lalonde, "Buddy Esquire and the Early Hip Hop Flyer," *Popular Music* 33, no. 1 (2014): 29.
14. Mark Katz, *Groove Music: The Art and Culture of the Hip-Hop DJ* (New York: Oxford University Press, 2012), 32–35.
15. "Paris Record Lending Club," *Billboard* (March 21, 1960): 11.

16. Gene Moskowitz, "What'll You Have—Nudes, Jazz, Food? Paris' Myriad of Cafés Has 'Em All," *Variety* (January 4, 1961): 239.
17. Abel Green, "Gotham Eyes Straight Dansapation Vs. Class Hotels' Show Policies," *Variety* (September 19, 1962): 59.
18. Abel Green, "Jumping Jet Set's Disk Den," *Variety* (April 1, 1964): 1.
19. Philip Dougherty, "Now the Latest Craze is 1-2-3, All Fall Down," *New York Times* (February 11, 1965): 43.
20. Nick Biro, "Seeburg's 'Instant Dance' Plan," *Billboard* (December 19, 1964): 1, 50, 54; "Seeburg Rolls on Discotheque Plan," *Billboard* (December 26, 1964): 3, 41.
21. Erik Quisling, and Austin Williams, *Straight Whisky: A Living History of Sex, Drugs, and Rock 'n' Roll on the Sunset Strip* (Chicago: Bonus Books, 2003); Jose, "Night Club Reviews: Phone Booth, NY," *Variety* (November 3, 1965): 52.
22. Ray Brack, "'Spinners' Irk Chicago Operators: Phonos Silent as Deejays Play Disks," *Billboard* (May 29, 1965): 43, 48.
23. Sarah Thornton, *Club Cultures: Music, Media and Subcultural Capital* (Hanover, NH: Wesleyan University Press, 1996), 41.
24. Joe Cohen, "Discotheque: Foe of Talent," *Variety* (February 5, 1964): 49.
25. Herm Schoenfeld, "Discotheque Rumble in AFM," *Variety* (June 17, 1964): 45.
26. "LA Discotheques Ruffle Feathers of AFM Local," *Billboard* (June 6, 1964): 1.
27. "Winter of AFM Discontent Over N.Y. Discotheques," *Variety* (March 10, 1965): 57, 60; "AFM Officials Mapping Fight Against Discotheques," *Billboard* (April 24, 1965): 1, 3.
28. Thornton, *Club Cultures*, 28–29.
29. Tim Lawrence, *Love Saves the Day: A History of American Dance Music Culture, 1970–1979* (Durham, NC: Duke University Press, 2003), 35.
30. Lawrence, *Love Saves the Day*, 107.
31. The following details are drawn principally from Chang, *Can't Stop Won't Stop*, 67–85; and Joseph Ewoodzie, *Break Beats in the Bronx: Rediscovering Hip-Hop's Early Years* (Chapel Hill: University of North Carolina Press, 2017), 17–20, 40–43.
32. Chang, *Can't Stop Won't Stop*, 79. Some disco DJs also showed a marked preference for percussive breaks, most notably Walter Gibbons. See Lawrence, *Love Saves the Day*, 215–217; Katz, *Groove Music*, 33.
33. Flash and Ritz, *The Adventures of Grandmaster Flash*, 43.
34. Flash and Ritz, *The Adventures of Grandmaster Flash*, 74–75.
35. Flash and Ritz, *The Adventures of Grandmaster Flash*, 76–79.
36. Ewoodzie, *Break Beats in the Bronx*, 75.
37. Mark Katz offers the following evocative description of the conditions according to which we can determine if a particular object or device, such as the turntable, should be considered a musical instrument: "It involves real-time sound manipulation; It has a body of techniques developed specifically for it; It has its own distinctive sound; The object itself is either specifically designed or modified for making music; The sound it generates is considered to be music by a community of listeners" (62).
38. Flyer for Castil Hill Park, August 22, 1981, https://digital.library.cornell.edu/catalog/ss:1333880. Hip Hop and Party Event Flyers Collection, Cornell Hip Hop Collection.

39. Tim Lawrence, *Life and Death on the New York Dance Floor, 1980–1983* (Durham, NC: Duke University Press, 2016), 177.
40. Steven Hager, "Afrika Bambaataa's Hip Hop," in *And It Don't Stop: The Best American Hip-Hop Journalism of the Last 25 Years*, ed. Raquel Cepeda (New York: Faber and Faber, 2004), 23–24.
41. Robert Palmer, "Pop: The Sugar Hill Gang," *New York Times* (March 13, 1981): C23.
42. Sally Banes, "To the Beat Y'all: Breaking Is Hard to Do," *Writing Dancing in the Age of Postmodernism* (Hanover, NH: Wesleyan University Press, 1994), 121–125; Chang, *Can't Stop Won't Stop*, 157; Lawrence, *Life and Death*, 173–174.
43. Ken Terry, "Rock Infiltrates Discos While Black Music Fills Rock Clubs; Sphere of Crossover Growing," *Variety* (March 25, 1981): 145, 153.
44. Robert Palmer, "'The Message' Is That Rap Is Now King in Rock Clubs," *New York Times* (September 3, 1982): C4.
45. Michael Diamond and Adam Horovitz, *Beastie Boys Book* (New York: Spiegel and Grau, 2018), 82–83.
46. Diamond and Horovitz, *Beastie Boys Book*, 85.
47. "Top Box Office," *Billboard* (April 5, 1980): 72.
48. Nelson George, "Rappin' with Kurtis Blow," *New York Amsterdam News* (July 19, 1980): 27.
49. Russell Simmons with Nelson George, *Life and Def: Sex, Drugs, Money, + God* (New York: Crown Publishers, 2001), 48–51.
50. Ronin Ro, *Raising Hell: The Reign, Ruin, and Redemption of Run-D.M.C. and Jam Master Jay* (New York: Amistad, 2005), 16.
51. "Who's Who at Norby Walters Associates," *New on the Charts* 8, no. 2 (February 1983): 14.
52. Roman Kozak, "Agency Expands into TV Production, Booking Rockers," *Billboard* (January 31, 1981): 36.
53. Said Jerry Ade, then Vice President for National Affairs at Norby Walters Associates, in a 1983 interview, "I think we are the only company in America that has taken black promoters seriously and helped develop a whole slew of black promoters, who are stable competent, reliable, dependable, honest and sincere. These are people who do business every week of the year . . . and we've helped develop them by continually feeding them entertainment so they could continue to make money." Roman Kozak, "Norby Walters' Ade Sees Black Tour Boom," *Billboard* (November 19, 1983): 47.
54. Radcliffe Joe and Nelson George, "Rapping DJs Set a Trend," *Billboard* (November 3, 1979): 64.
55. "Concert Reviews: Summer Festival (Felt Forum, N.Y.)," *Variety* (June 4, 1980): 68.
56. Advertisement for Chic with the Fatback Band and Kurtis Blow, *Nashville Tennessean* (July 13, 1980): 5; "Top Box Office," *Billboard* (September 6, 1980): 51.
57. Richard Nusser, "Big Sell Out—and How to Get It—Occupies Experts," *Billboard* (October 4, 1980): 46.
58. Robert Palmer, "Pop: Marley and Wailers on the Commodores' Bill," *New York Times* (September 23, 1980): C11.
59. Kozak, "Talent in Action: Commodores, Bob Marley, Kurtis Blow," *Billboard* (October 4, 1980): 47.

60. Philip Harrigan, "Commodores, Fatback Smoked; Kurtis Blows It," *Pittsburgh Courier* (September 27, 1980): A3.
61. Harrigan, "Rapping: The New Musical Art Form?" *Pittsburgh Courier* (February 21, 1981): A4.
62. "Top Box Office," *Billboard* (February 21, 1981): 31.
63. "Best of the Best," *The Source*, no. 100 (January 1998): 200.
64. "Boxscore," *Billboard* (August 11, 1984): 49.
65. Charnas, *The Big Payback*, 110–111.
66. Charnas, *The Big Payback*, 113.
67. Russ DeVault, "The Heartfixers' New Wave," *Atlanta Constitution* (August 31, 1984): 26.
68. DeVault, "Pool Q's to Hit Road with Lou Reed," *Atlanta Constitution* (September 14, 1984): 8P.
69. Harry Weinger, "Hip-Hop Heading for Huge Halls," *Billboard* (September 29, 1984): 40.
70. Lou Papineau, "Fresh Fest's Rappers, Breakdancers Draw 4500," *Boston Globe* (December 4, 1984): 78; Timothy Cox, "Rap/Break Crew Not to Be Misunderstood," *Pittsburgh Courier* (December 15, 1984): 2.
71. Cox, "Rap/Break Crew Not to Be Misunderstood," 2.
72. Terry Atkinson, "Rappers and Breakers in a Festival," *Los Angeles Times* (December 10, 1984): G1.
73. Papineau, "Fresh Fest's Rappers, Breakdancers Draw 4500," 78.
74. Atkinson, "Rappers and Breakers in a Festival," G1.
75. Cox, "Rap/Break Crew Not to Be Misunderstood," 2.
76. Ro, *Raising Hell*, 97.
77. "Def Jam Label Will Specialize in 'Real Street Music,'" *Billboard* (November 17, 1984): 56.
78. "The Fresh Fest: Rap's Columbus Scouts Out the New World," *Billboard* (April 20, 1985): R6. Simmons' claims here are supported by the numbers reported by *Variety*, which noted that the two shows at the Spectrum in Philadelphia earned a combined $268,114, out of a possible $384,428 if both shows had sold out. "Concert Grosses," *Variety* (November 14, 1984): 94.
79. Simmons and George, *Life and Def*, 68.
80. Nelson George, "The Rhythm and the Blues," *Billboard* (September 7, 1985): 46.
81. Ro, *Raising Hell*, 120.
82. "Boxscore," *Billboard* (July 19, 1986): 22; "Boxscore," *Billboard* (August 2, 1986): 24.
83. Tricia Rose, *Black Noise: Rap Music and Black Culture in Contemporary America* (Hanover, NH: Wesleyan University Press, 1994), 131.
84. Forman, *The 'Hood Comes First*, 139.
85. David Hinckley, "Let's Stop Giving Them a Bad Rap," *New York Daily News* (December 27, 1985): 5.
86. Hinckley, "Let's Stop Giving Them a Bad Rap," 6.
87. "7 Youths Injured in Concert Fights," *New York Times* (December 28, 1985): 28.

88. "Brawl Erupts at Rap Film in New York," *Washington Post* (December 1985): A10; "'Krush Groove' Concert Results in Stabbings; Garden Mulls Action," *Variety* (January 1, 1986): 132.
89. Charles Rogers, "Krushing Rap's Bad Rep Groove," *New York Amsterdam News* (January 4, 1986): 22.
90. "Boxscore," *Billboard* (January 18, 1986): 35.
91. Chang, *Can't Stop Won't Stop*, 245.
92. Details on the tour itinerary come from the website Setlist.fm. See https://www.setlist.fm/stats/concert-map/rundmc-63d68607.html?year=1986.
93. Christopher Weingarten, "The 50 Greatest Concerts of the Last 50 Years: Run-DMC 'Raising Hell' Tour," *Rolling Stone* (June 12, 2017), https://www.rollingstone.com/music/music-lists/the-50-greatest-concerts-of-the-last-50-years-127062/run-dmc-raising-hell-tour-194194.
94. Charnas, *The Big Payback*, 185; Ro, *Raising Hell*, 143–144, 150.
95. "18 Are Arrested After Rap Concert," *New York Times* (July 21, 1986): B3; "Violence Following N.Y. Rap Concert Prompts City Action," *Variety* (July 23, 1986): 70.
96. Ira Jeffries, "Police Action at Garden Frighten Concert Goers," *New York Amsterdam News* (August 9, 1986): 42; Nelson George, "Bad Rap for N.Y.C. Rap Concert?" *Billboard* (August 9, 1986): 26.
97. Brian Cross, *It's Not About a Salary: Rap, Race + Resistance in Los Angeles* (London: Verso, 1993), 156–157.
98. Ro, *Raising Hell*, 156.
99. Eric Hubler, "Rap Repercussions? Concert Violence Haunts Run-DMC Tour," *Washington Post* (August 19, 1986): C4.
100. Chris Morris, "Venue Reads Riot Act Following Melee," *Billboard* (August 30, 1986): 7.
101. Richard Harrington, "Run-DMC and the Rap Flap," *Washington Post* (August 29, 1986): C1.
102. "Violence Silences Rap Group," *Chicago Tribune* (August 19, 1986): 10.
103. Daryl Kelley, "L.B. Hunts Way to Stem Future Arena Violence," *Los Angeles Times* (August 21, 1986): A9.
104. George Ramos, "30 Injured at Long Beach Concert; L.A. Show Off," *Los Angeles Times* (August 18, 1986): 1.
105. Kelley, "L.B. Hunts," A9.
106. Steven Ivory, "Ticket Prices, Insurance up; Fewer Acts Take to Road," *Billboard* (September 27, 1986): B-8.
107. Richard Cromelin, "Beastie Boys Baptism," *Los Angeles Times* (February 9, 1987): G1.
108. Robert Lloyd, "The Beasties' Rap Bonanza," *Washington Post* (February 22, 1987): F11.
109. Jon Shecter, "Showdown," *The Source*, no. 22 (July 1991): 4.
110. Shecter, "Showdown," 4.
111. Rob Tannenbaum, "In Rap's Hometown, an Icy Reception," *New York Times* (April 18, 1991): H27. Also see David Hinckley, "Rap Fights Its Image—at Home," *New York Daily News Extra* (April 30, 1991): 1, 32.

112. Danyel Smith, "Banned in the U.S.A.," *The Source*, no. 17 (January 1991): 24.
113. Smith, "Banned in the U.S.A.," 27.
114. Jackie Paul, "Philly Report," *The Source* 3, no. 5 (September 1990): 50; AJ Shine, "The Philadelphia Story," *The Source*, no. 20 (May 1991): 40.
115. Lee Copeland, "Fear of a Rap Concert," *The Source*, no. 92 (May 1997): 100.
116. Copeland, "Fear of a Rap Concert," 104.
117. Copeland, "Fear of a Rap Concert," 102.
118. John Leland, "Do the Right Thing," *Spin* (September 1, 1989): 72.
119. The itinerary for the tour appears in a press release dated July 3, 1990, which is included in the Adler Hip Hop Archive, Cornell Hip Hop Collection.
120. Alan Light, "Public Enemy's Tour de Force," *Rolling Stone* (August 23, 1990): 29.
121. Light, "Public Enemy's Tour de Force," 29.
122. Chris Wilder, "Chuck D Interview," *The Source*, no. 21 (June 1991): 30.
123. Light, "Public Enemy's Tour de Force," 32.
124. Chuck D with Yusuf Jah, *Fight the Power: Rap, Race, and Reality* (New York: Delta, 1997), 127–128.
125. Kristine McKenna, "Clashing of the Clash in New York," *Los Angeles Times* (June 5, 1981): H12; Stephen Holden, "Rock-Rap: The Clash," *New York Times* (September 5, 1982): 56. Also see Katz, *Groove Music*, 98–99.
126. Craig Rosen, "Eclectic Tours Aim to Ignite Support for Up-and-Comers," *Billboard* (July 20, 1991): 82.
127. "Beats, Turntables and Guitar Solos," *The Source*, no. 24 (September 1991): 18.
128. Chuck D and Jah, *Fight the Power*, 129.
129. Jon Pareles, "Mix-and-Match Show with Snarling and Anger," *New York Times* (July 26, 1991): C3.
130. Scott Poulson-Bryant, "Striking Black," *Spin* (October 1, 1991): 46.
131. Gene Santoro, "The Turn on, Tune in, Burn out Tour," *Billboard* (August 24, 1991): 30.
132. Victoria Starr, "Anthrax, Public Enemy, Primus, Young Black Teenagers," *Billboard* (October 12, 1991): 35.
133. Jonathan Gold, "Anthrax, Public Enemy Fuse Rap, Metal," *Los Angeles Times* (October 21, 1991): F1.
134. Gold, "Anthrax, Public Enemy Fuse Rap, Metal," F8.
135. Chuck D and Jah, *Fight the Power*, 130.
136. Gold, "Anthrax, Public Enemy Fuse Rap, Metal," F8.
137. Peter Watrous, "The Garden Says It Can Handle Big Rap Show Friday," *New York Times* (January 1, 1992); William Bunch, "Garden Tightly 'Rapped' for Concert," *Newsday* (January 3, 1992). Adler Hip Hop Archive, Cornell Hip Hop Collection.
138. David Hinckley, "Rap Exhibits Its Good Side at Garden Show," *New York Daily News* (January 4, 1992): 3, 23; Mitch Gelman, "MSG's Rap Concert Runs Without Worry," *New York Newsday* (January 4, 1992); Don Broderick and Dan Aquilante, "All's Rap-turous at Garden Concert," *New York Post* (January 4, 1992); Jon Pareles, "The World of Hip-Hop Returns to the Garden," *New York Times* (January 6, 1992): C11, C13. Adler Hip Hop Archive, Cornell Hip Hop Collection.

139. Frank Owen, "The Rap Is Real and the Mood Is Mellow," *New York Newsday* (January 6, 1992). Adler Hip Hop Archive, Cornell Hip Hop Collection.
140. Kevin Powell, "Enemy Territory," *Vibe* 2, no. 7 (September 1994): 64.
141. Steve Hochman, "Cultivating a Common Denominator," *Los Angeles Times* (October 4, 1990): 405. Also see Chris Morris, "Diverse 'Tribes' to Unify in 2 Harmonious Calif. Shows," *Billboard* (October 6, 1990): 32.
142. Mike Boehm, "Diversity Captures a Following," *Los Angeles Times* (October 9, 1990): OCF1.
143. Gina Arnold, *Half a Million Strong: Crowds and Power from Woodstock to Coachella* (Iowa City: University of Iowa Press, 2018), 80.
144. "Concert Business Faces a Bleak Summer," *Pollstar* (May 27, 1991): 3.
145. Chris Morris, "A Gathering of the Tribes II," *Billboard* (August 3, 1991): 27; Kevin Zimmerman, "Rap Reaps Rock's Rewards," *Variety* (August 19, 1991): 53.
146. "A Lollapalooza of an Idea," *Pollstar* (November 29, 2001). https://www.pollstar.com/article/a-lollapalooza-of-an-idea-9416.
147. Gary Graff, "Banded Together: Package Deals Return to the U.S. Music Scene," *Detroit Free Press* (June 21, 1991): 7D.
148. Dean Budnick and Josh Baron, *Ticket Masters: The Rise of the Concert Industry and How the Public Got Scalped* (Toronto: ECW Press, 2011): 172.
149. Budnick and Baron, *Ticket Masters*, 174.
150. Upski, "We Use Words Like 'Mackadocious' (and Other Progress from the Front Lines of the White Struggle)," *The Source*, no. 44 (May 1993): 64.
151. Barry Shank, "From Rice to Ice: The Face of Race in Rock and Pop," in *The Cambridge Companion to Pop and Rock*, ed. Simon Frith, Will Straw, and John Street (Cambridge: Cambridge University Press, 2001), 269.
152. Greg Kot, "Ice-T Rocks the System," *Chicago Tribune* (July 28, 1991): O4.
153. Michele Vernon-Chesley, "More Than a Concert: Lollapalooza Offers Diverse Music, Politics," *Detroit Free-Press* (August 5, 1991): 1B.
154. Richard Harrington, "Lollapalooza: Heat with a Beat," *Washington Post* (August 17, 1991): C2.
155. David Fricke, "Lollapalooza," *Rolling Stone*, no. 613 (September 19, 1991): 86.
156. Footage of this can be seen in a video of the song uploaded to YouTube from an unspecified date on the 1991 Lollapalooza tour: "DON'T CALL ME NIGGER WHITEY (live 91) – Jane's Addiction & Body Count," Moody Hyadd, November 25, 2012, YouTube video, https://www.youtube.com/watch?v=H9p5LZSBl94.
157. Stoever's observations come from an unpublished paper delivered at the Experience Music Project Pop Conference in 2006, quoted in Arnold, *Half a Million Strong*, 100.
158. Eric Weisbard, "This Monkey's Gone to Heaven," *Spin* (July 1998): 64.
159. Eric Ducker, "How the Smokin' Grooves Tour Brought Rap to the Masses," *Pitchfork* (June 15, 2018), https://pitchfork.com/features/article/how-the-smokin-grooves-tour-brought-rap-to-the-masses.
160. Charles Aaron, "The Fugees," *Spin* (January 1, 1997): 54.
161. Brian McCollum, "Smokin' Grooves Proves Hip-Hop Can Go Live—and Live," *Detroit Free Press* (August 13, 1996): 3D.

162. Marc Allan, "Hip-Hop Show Reflects Some of the Problems with Live Performances," *Indianapolis Star* (August 18, 1996): C8.
163. "Smokin's Rap, Reggae Acts Fire up Sparse Crowd," *Cincinnati Enquirer* (August 21, 1996): E9.
164. Jon Pareles, "Peace Eases out Sex and Violence," *New York Times* (August 10, 1996): B8.
165. Dream Hampton, "The Trouble with Hip-Hop," *Detroit Free Press* (August 24, 1996): 4C.
166. J.R. Reynolds, "Black Promoters Say They're Excluded from Top R&B Gigs," *Billboard* (June 21, 1997): 18.
167. "Concert Promotion in Black and White," *Pollstar* (November 30, 1998): 4.
168. Gross receipts and rankings can be found in "1997 Top 100 Tours," *Pollstar* (January 5, 1998): 6–7; and "1998 Top 100 Tours," *Pollstar* (December 31, 1998): 8, 10.
169. Ducker, "How the Smokin' Grooves Tour Brought Rap to the Masses."
170. Nelson George, "Nationwide: America Raps Back," *Village Voice* (January 19, 1988). Reprinted at https://www.villagevoice.com/2019/04/03/hiphop-nation-america-raps-back.
171. See, for example, "The Hip-Hop Nation: Regional Rap Reports," *The Source* 2, no. 4 (June 1989): 32–37.
172. Mickey Hess, "The Rap Career," in *That's the Joint! The Hip-Hop Studies Reader*, 2nd ed., ed. Murray Forman and Mark Anthony Neal (New York: Routledge, 2012), 643.
173. Morgan, *The Real Hip Hop*, 16.
174. Morgan, *The Real Hip Hop*, 17.
175. Morgan, *The Real Hip Hop*, 36–38.
176. Brendan Mullen, "Down for the Good Life," *LA Weekly* (June 21, 2000), https://www.laweekly.com/down-for-the-good-life.
177. Akwanza Gleaves, "The Good Life Café," *The Source*, no. 41 (February 1993): 17.
178. Cross, *It's Not About a Salary*, 286.
179. Cross, *It's Not About a Salary*, 291.
180. Quoted in Rose, *Black Noise*, 38.
181. Reef, "The Lyricist Lounge," *The Source*, n. 41 (February 1993): 17; P.E. Cobb, "Lyricist Lounge Cold Lampin'," *Rap Pages* 7, no. 9 (September 1998): 55–57; Tracy Hopkins, "Hip-Hop Crusaders," *The Source*, no. 114 (March 1999): 97.
182. Mark Armstrong, "Free Styles at the Crossroads: Washington, D.C.," *The Source* (July 1997): 46.
183. Bernard Gendron, *Between Montmartre and the Mudd Club: Popular Music and the Avant-Garde* (Chicago: University of Chicago Press, 2002), 260.
184. Will Ashon, "Whose Underground Is It Anyway?" *The Source* (November 1999): 184.
185. Jay-Z and Hampton, *Decoded*, 4–5.
186. Jay-Z and Hampton, *Decoded*, 142.
187. S. Craig Watkins, *Hip Hop Matters: Politics, Pop Culture, and the Struggle for the Soul of a Movement* (Boston, MA: Beacon Press, 2005), 77.

Chapter 10

1. *Homecoming*, directed by Beyoncé Knowles-Carter (Los Gatos, CA: Netflix, 2019).
2. Craig Lee, Pleasant Gehman, and Miss Carri, "L.A. Dee Da's New Year's Resolutions," *L.A. Weekly* (December 30-January 5, 1984): 43.
3. Vickie Chang, "Gary Tovar Has His Goldenvoice," *OC Weekly* (December 15, 2011), http://www.ocweekly.com/2011-12-15/music/goldenvoice-gary-tovar-coachella-paul-tollet-gv30.
4. On the character of the Southern California punk scene at the time, see Brendan Mullen and Marc Spitz, *We Got the Neutron Bomb: The Untold Story of L.A. Punk* (New York: Three Rivers Press, 2001); Peter Belsito and Bob Davis, *Hardcore California: A History of Punk and New Wave* (San Francisco: Last Gasp, 1983); and Steven Blush, *American Hardcore: A Tribal History* (Los Angeles: Feral House, 2001).
5. Randy Lewis, "Tovar Helps Punk Acts Have a Voice," *Los Angeles Times* (March 30, 1984): G19.
6. Cary Darling, "Punk Rock Is Alive and Slamming," *Billboard* (February 19, 1983): 52.
7. Chang, "Gary Tovar Has His Goldenvoice."
8. Steve Hochman, "Rap-Meets-Rock Concert Marred by Violence," *Los Angeles Times* (December 19, 1988): G1.
9. Cary Darling, "L.A. —the Second Deffest City of Hip-Hop," *Los Angeles Times* (February 7, 1988): K70.
10. Mike Boehm, "Banding Together," *Los Angeles Times* (June 25, 1992): F3.
11. Chang, "Gary Tovar Has His Goldenvoice."
12. Kim Neely, *Five Against One: The Pearl Jam Story* (New York: Penguin, 1998): 176.
13. Jeff Dillon, "Jam-Packed: Pearl Jam (and 25,000 Pals) Rolled into Indio— and Rocked Empire Polo Grounds," *Palm Springs Desert Sun* (November 6, 1993): A1; Steve Hochman, "Pop Eye: Desert Dessert," *Los Angeles Times* (November 14, 1993): F66.
14. Geoff Boucher, "If You Build It, Will They Come?" *Los Angeles Times*, Weekend section (October 7, 1999): 8; John Seabrook, "The Immaculate Lineup," *New Yorker* (April 17, 2017): 34.
15. Michaelangelo Matos, *The Underground Is Massive: How Electronic Dance Music Conquered America* (New York: Dey St., 2015), 322.
16. Dean Budnick and Josh Baron, *Ticket Masters: The Rise of the Concert Industry and How the Public Got Scalped* (Toronto: ECW Press, 2011): 162–163; "Birth of a Concert Industry Giant," *Pollstar* (September 1, 1997): 1–2.
17. "SFX Deals Change the Concert Landscape," *Pollstar* (December 22, 1997): 1; Budnick and Baron, *Ticket Masters*, 169.
18. "1997 Concert Business Analysis," *Pollstar* (January 5, 1998): 9.
19. Susanne Ault, "Coachella Preserves Its Diverse Lineup of A-List Talent," *Billboard* (March 15, 2003): 18.
20. Boucher, "If You Build It," 12.
21. Mark Armstrong, "Polo Club Requesting Permit for Fall Music Fest," *Palm Springs Desert Sun* (July 12, 1999): B3.

22. Armstrong, "Alternative Music Gig Slated for Indio in Fall," *Palm Springs Desert Sun* (July 17, 1999): A1, A8.
23. "Woodstock West?" *Los Angeles Times*, Weekend section (July 29, 1999): 62.
24. "Top 20 Concert Grosses of All Time in North America," *Pollstar* (December 31, 1999): 8.
25. Boucher, "Post-Festival Stage Fright," *Los Angeles Times* (August 7, 1999): F18.
26. Robert Hilburn, "Triumph of the Anti-Woodstock," *Los Angeles Times* (October 12, 1999): F1.
27. Information about the lineups for the two days of the festival, including at which stages and tents artists appeared, comes from "Coachella Festival: the Lineup," *Palm Springs Desert Sun* (October 9, 1999): D3; and "Today's Lineup," *Palm Springs Desert Sun* (October 10, 1999): B5.
28. Geoff Boucher, "Heat Dampens but Doesn't Do in the First Coachella Music & Arts Festival," *Los Angeles Times* (October 11, 1999): F7.
29. Mark Healy, "Performance: Coachella Music and Arts Festival," *Rolling Stone* (November 25, 1999): 38.
30. Hilburn, "Triumph of the Anti-Woodstock," F5.
31. Healy, "Coachella Music and Arts Festival," 38.
32. "1999 Award Winners," *Pollstar* (February 28, 2000): 42.
33. John Seabrook, "The Immaculate Lineup," *New Yorker* (April 17, 2017): 34.
34. Randy Lewis and Randall Roberts, "How the First Coachella Upended the Festival Business," *Los Angeles Times* (April 11, 2019), https://www.latimes.com/entertainment/music/la-et-ms-coachella-history-festival-growth-concerts-20190411-story.html.
35. Jeff Leeds, "Anschutz Group Set to Buy Promotion Firm," *Los Angeles Times* (December 8, 2000): C6; Ray Waddell, "Concerts West Deal Boosts AEG," *Billboard* (December 16, 2000): 1.
36. Jeff Leeds, "Anschutz to Buy Concert Firm Goldenvoice," *Los Angeles Times* (March 7, 2001): C2; "New Goldenvoice in Los Angeles," *Pollstar* (March 12, 2001): 4.
37. Geoff Boucher, "Trying to Be Real Cool," *Los Angeles Times* (April 26, 2001): D7.
38. Mitchell Peters, "Paul Tollett," *Billboard* (April 28, 2007): 20.
39. Richard Cromelin, "Rick Van Santen, 41; L.A. Promoter Helped to Advance Punk Rock Bands," *Los Angeles Times* (January 3, 2004): B14; Seabrook, "The Immaculate Lineup," 34.
40. Bruce Fessier, "Coachella Sells Out for Day One," *Palm Springs Desert Sun* (April 20, 2004): A1.
41. Ray Waddell, "Jam-Band Fans Are Ready for Bonnaroo," *Billboard* (May 11, 2002): 18.
42. "Top 40 Concert Grosses of All Time in North America," *Pollstar* (January 15, 2007): 12. Bonnaroo's 2006 gross earnings of $14,731,723 placed it at number eight on the year's list of all-time grosses, while the festival's installments for 2003, 2004, and 2005 also appear. Coachella, with gross revenue of $10,331,326 for 2006, appeared at number thirty-six on the list.
43. "2006 Top 200 Concert Grosses," *Pollstar* (January 15, 2007): 32; Ray Waddell, "Festival Fever," *Billboard* (January 13, 2007): 14.

44. Evan Serpick, "Summer Fests Heat up," *Rolling Stone* (June 15, 2006): 18.
45. Ray Waddell, "Tour de Force," *Billboard* (May 17, 2008): 42.
46. Information is from Live Nation's website for its Festival Passport program. https://www.livenation.com/passport/fp/details.
47. Information is from the AEG Worldwide festival page. https://www.aegworldwide.com/divisions/music/festivals.
48. "2016 Year End Top 20 Worldwide Festival Grosses," *Pollstar* (January 6, 2017), https://www.pollstar.com/Chart/2017/01/2016YearEndTop20WorldwideFestivalGrosses_347.pdf.
49. "2017 Year End Top 20 Worldwide Festival Grosses," *Pollstar* (January 15, 2018). https://www.pollstar.com/Chart/2018/01/60-top20worldwidefestivalMoveAd_633.pdf.
50. "2008 Year End Top 100 North American Tours," *Pollstar* (January 19, 2009): 6.
51. "2009 Top 100 North American Tours," *Pollstar* (January 18, 2010): 10; "2009 Top Worldwide Concert Tours," *Pollstar* (January 18, 2010): 4.
52. "2016 Year End Top 200 North American Tours," *Pollstar* (January 6, 2017). https://www.pollstar.com/Chart/2017/01/2016YearEndTop200NorthAmericanTours_344.pdf.
53. "Top Touring Artists of the Decade," *Pollstar*, n.d. https://www.pollstar.com/top-touring-artists.
54. Coachella lineup information comes from the festival's official website, https://www.coachella.com/past-festivals.
55. Gina Arnold, *Half a Million Strong: Crowds and Power from Woodstock to Coachella* (Iowa City: University of Iowa Press, 2018), 120.
56. Rob Mitchum and Diego Garcia-Olano, "Are Music Festival Lineups Getting Worse?" *Pitchfork* (April 18, 2017), https://pitchfork.com/features/festival-report/10059-are-music-festival-lineups-getting-worse.
57. Mitchum and Garcia-Olano, "Tracking the Gender Balance of This Year's Music Festival Lineups," *Pitchfork* (May 1, 2018), https://pitchfork.com/features/festival-report/tracking-the-gender-balance-of-this-years-music-festival-lineups.
58. In 2019, the figures for gender representation at Coachella and other major festivals remained effectively unchanged, so there has not been a steady line of upward progress toward gender parity. See Allegra Frank, "Music's Biggest Stars Are Women. Music Festivals Would Make You Think Otherwise," *Vox* (April 23, 2019), https://www.vox.com/culture/2019/4/23/18285787/music-festival-lineups-women-gender-equity.
59. "Beyonce ft Jay-Z - Young Forever Live Coachella 2010," TheDBoy100, April 19, 2010, YouTube video, https://www.youtube.com/watch?v=EwH-tUH3Rf8.
60. Jenny Eliscu, "Coachella Opens Fest Season with Jay-Z, Pavement, Muse," *Rolling Stone* (May 13, 2010): 15.
61. Darryl Morden, "Coachella, Days 1-2," *Hollywood Reporter* (April 19, 2010): 10.
62. Performance details throughout this section are drawn from combined viewing of *Homecoming*, the Beyoncé-directed documentary of her Coachella performance, and videos posted on YouTube that present the full shows for both weekends of Beyoncé's

2018 Coachella appearance in a less expurgated fashion. See "Beyoncé – Coachella FULL SHOW," https://www.youtube.com/watch?v=S2d-lrcVf7I&ab_channel=Luca sNoleto; and "Beyoncé – The Beychella Show 2 2018 – Full Show – Second Show – Week 2," https://www.youtube.com/watch?v=lC9JUCHzC3s&ab_channel=BEYON CÉParis.

63. Kevin Gaines, *Uplifting the Race: Black Leadership, Politics, and Culture in the Twentieth Century* (Chapel Hill: University of North Carolina Press, 1996), 2.
64. Discussing Beyoncé's self-titled 2013 album, Powers writes: "*Beyoncé*, with its spicy by contained fantasies of monogamous love and female self-possession, stands out as a kind of protest, conservative in some ways and determinedly centered on female self-respect." Ann Powers, *Good Booty: Love and Sex, Black and White, Body and Soul in American Music* (New York: Dey St., 2017), 325.
65. Maya Jones, "Why Beyoncé Went with HBCUs at Coachella," *The Undefeated* (April 22, 2018), https://theundefeated.com/features/beyonce-coachella-hbcu-performers-life-changing-moment.
66. Britni Danielle, "Meet One of the Men Responsible for Teaching Beyoncé How to Step for Beychella," *Essence* (April 17, 2018), https://www.essence.com/culture/beychella-teaching-beyonce-step-dance.
67. Sidney Madden, "*Homecoming*, from the Bleachers: Members of Beyoncé's Marching Band Look Back," *NPR Music* (April 22, 2019), https://www.npr.org/2019/04/22/715985010/homecoming-from-the-bleachers-members-of-beyonc-s-marching-band-look-back.
68. Imani Perry, *May We Forever Stand: A History of the Black National Anthem* (Chapel Hill: University of North Carolina Press, 2018), 6.
69. Perry, *May We Forever Stand*, 7.
70. Perry, *May We Forever Stand*, 8.
71. For details about the formation of Suga Mama, see Malcolm Aimé-Musoni, "What's It Like to Be in Beyoncé's All-Female Band?" *Elle* (April 13, 2017), https://www.elle.com/culture/music/a44485/oral-history-beyonce-all-female-band-suga-mama.
72. Herrman Saroni, "Jenny Lind," *Saroni's Musical Times* 1, no. 51 (September 14, 1850): 603.
73. Maureen Mahon, *Right to Rock: The Black Rock Coalition and the Cultural Politics of Race* (Durham, NC: Duke University Press, 2004), 8.
74. Spencer Kornhaber, "Beyoncé Masters the Fierceness of Crowds," *The Atlantic* (April 16, 2018), https://www.theatlantic.com/entertainment/archive/2018/04/beyonce-coachella-crowds/558125.
75. Roker's comments come from the documentary film, *Coachella: 20 Years in the Desert*, directed by Chris Perkel (Los Angeles: Goldenvoice, 2020).
76. See Tomi Obaro, "How Beyoncé Called Out Coachella's Whiteness," *BuzzFeed News* (April 16, 2018), https://www.buzzfeednews.com/article/tomiobaro/how-beyonce-called-out-coachellas-whiteness; and Terri Burns, "What It's Like to Experience Coachella as a Black Person," *Teen Vogue* (April 25, 2017), https://www.teenvogue.com/story/what-its-like-to-experience-coachella-as-a-black-person.

77. Perry Farrell, "CIC Keynote Address: Lollapalooza of a Business," *Pollstar* (March 22, 2004): 31.
78. August Brown, "Artists, Live Industry Brace for a Year Without Concerts; 'Is There a Better Place for Spreading Disease?,'" *Los Angeles Times* (April 17, 2020), https://www.latimes.com/entertainment-arts/music/story/2020-04-17/coronavirus-concerts-live-music-return-2021.
79. Cherie Hu, "How Livestreaming Is Bridging the Gap Between Bands and Fans During the Coronavirus Outbreak," *Pitchfork* (March 17, 2020). https://pitchfork.com/thepitch/music-livestreaming-coronavirus.
80. Hu, "Virtual Music Events Directory," https://docs.google.com/document/d/11wWL_7I4BG76t0V2kw1a4yIeWxUSfGwMQFYdUWAgSnA/preview?fbclid=IwAR0BlVj3iDiIlTmtSOerTfk5mkIc_oul5Ns5n6cgs5_tj0NC8T9xOiDrT60.
81. Christoper Mele and Neil Vigdor, "Singalongs from Windowsills Lift Spirits During Coronavirus Crisis," *New York Times* (March 23, 2020), https://www.nytimes.com/2020/03/23/us/coronavirus-window-singalong.html.
82. Spencer Kornhaber, "Pop Music's Version of Life Doesn't Exist Anymore," *The Atlantic* (March 19, 2020), https://www.theatlantic.com/culture/archive/2020/03/what-good-is-pop-music-during-the-coronavirus-pandemic/607894.
83. Barbara Ehrenreich, *Dancing in the Streets: A History of Collective Joy* (New York: Metropolitan Books, 2006), 253.
84. Nancy Baym, *Playing to the Crowd: Musicians, Audiences, and the Intimate Work of Connection* (New York: New York University Press, 2018), 26.

Index

For the benefit of digital users, indexed terms that span two pages (e.g., 52–53) may, on occasion, appear on only one of those pages.

Tables and figures are indicated by *t* and *f* following the page number.

Abbott, Lynn, 152
Absolutely Live (Doors), 471–73
Academy of Music (New York), 132, 134, 140
acoustic design, for concert halls, 231–32
Adams, Bluford, 37, 72
Adichie, Chimamanda Ngozi, 563–64
Adidas endorsement deal for Run-D.M.C., 508–9
adolescent audiences. *See* young audiences
Adorno, Theodor, 251–52
advertising
    for Beatles' 1965 Shea Stadium concert, 425–26
    for Hogan in Black Patti Troubadours, 161*f*, 161–62
    by Hurok for Marian Anderson, 262
    Jazz at the Philharmonic concert series, 280, 286–87, 288*f*
    for jazz dances and events, 179–82, 181*f*, 183, 184*f*
    for Jenny Lind's US tour, 35–37, 38–41, 47, 50–51, 52–53
    for Rolling Stones' 1972 US tour, 450–51
    for Tony Pastor's Opera House, 132–33
    for Whiteman's "Experiment in Modern Music", 236–37
AEG (Anschutz Entertainment Group)/AEG Live, 542–43, 551–53, 554–55
Aeolian Company, 235–36
Aeolian Hall (New York), 226, 233–44, 240*f*, 245–46
AFM (American Federation of Musicians), 18–23, 20*f*, 22*f*, 487–88
African Americans, 27. *See also* racial discrimination/inequality; racial integration of musical entertainment; segregation; *specific African American artists*; *specific black music genres*
    anxieties surrounding hip-hop's move into mainstream, 506–7
    in arena rock, 457–69
    associationalism, 560–61
    black and tans, 199, 209–13
    black formalism, 560–61
    black public sphere, 160, 166
    black vaudeville, 153, 167–69, 191, 194
    booking agencies specialized in working with, 497
    chitlin' circuit, 300–1
    in classical music, 261–64, 274
    and Cliff Walk Manor music festival, 375
    in concert promotion, 460–61, 533–34
    concerts invoking music history of, 276–77
    connections to rock 'n' roll, 292–94
    coon songs, circulation of, 150–60, 157*t*, 158*t*
    coon songs, performance of, 160–67
    difficulties hip-hop faced in becoming established, 480–81
    diminishment of contributions to jazz, 233–34
    discourse of black musical authenticity, 85–93
    double-consciousness of, 114–15
    Freed's promotion of music by and for, 323–24, 325–26
    "From Spirituals to Swing" concerts, 275–76
    Harlem night clubs, 208–13

African Americans (cont.)
  Ice-T's use of N word, 528–29
  ideology of racial uplift, 559–60
  inclusion in Goodman's Carnegie Hall concert, 273–74
  inequality in live music sphere of 2000s, 555–57
  in Jazz at the Philharmonic concerts, 277–78, 284–86
  lack of involvement in Newport Jazz Festival riots, 379
  live recordings of, 469–70
  and merging of rock and rap on stage, 519
  migration of, 103, 185
  Moondog Coronation Ball, 294–98, 330–31
  New Orleans jazz dance halls, 178–79
  popular representations of in blackface minstrelsy, 80–81
  and rise of variety entertainment and vaudeville, 120–21
  at rock 'n' roll concerts, 297
  segregated jazz performances, 185–86
  segregation in post-emancipation era, 102–6
  spirituals as adding to acceptance of, 261–62
  and twenty-first century live music, 540–41
After Midnight club (Philadelphia), 514
agents. *See* booking agencies
Ager, Cecelia, 269–70
"Alan Freed's 'Rock 'n' Roll' Jubilee Ball" (New York), 326–27, 328–31
Albee, Edward Franklin (E.F.), 125–26, 126f, 148
Alen, Dick, 310–11
Alexander, Hinton, 108f
Alive! (Kiss), 475–77, 477f
"All Coons Look Alike to Me" (Hogan)
  circulation of, 150–60, 157t, 158t
  performances by Hogan, 160–67
Allan, Marc, 532–33
Allen, William Francis, 87
Altamont Speedway Free Festival, 381–82, 401, 409–10, 449, 450–51
Alterman, Loraine, 439–41

alternative music, 545–46. *See also* Coachella Valley Music and Arts Festival; Lollapalooza festivals
Amaturo, Matthew, 17–18
American Federation of Musicians (AFM), 18–23, 20f, 22f, 487–88
American Folk Song Festival, 352
American Missionary Association (AMA), 81
amphitheaters, 525–26, 553
Anastasio, Angelo, 508–9
Anderson, Benedict, 12–13
Anderson, Elaine, 364–65
Anderson, Marian, 261–64, 264f, 274
Anderson, Phebe, 82
Anderson Galleries (New York), 244–45, 246
Ann Arbor Blues and Jazz Festival, 411–12
Anschutz Entertainment Group (AEG)/AEG Live. *See* AEG (Anschutz Entertainment Group)/AEG Live
Anthology of American Folk Music (Smith), 369
Anthony, Dalton, 464
Anthrax, 520–21
Anti-Concert Saloon Bill (New York), 131–32
Apollo Theater (New York), 333
arena rap, 482
  criticism of, 499–500
  decline in support for concerts, 512–15
  Fresh Fest tour, 500–5, 503f
  golden age of, 500–5
  rap/rock cross-genre touring, 515–22
  restrictiveness of, 538–39
  Sugar Hill "Rappers Convention" tour, 499–500
  tours of Kurtis Blow, 495–99, 496f
  violence at concerts, 505–12
arena rock, 24–25, 343–44
  Alex Cooley and emergence of, 409
  Barnum's nineteenth-century version, 77
  Beatles' 1965 performance at Shea Stadium, 422–29, 426f
  booking agents, 438–48, 440f
  live recordings, 469–77, 477f
  overview, 418–22

Parliament-Funkadelic Earth Tour, 457–63, 459f
production codes, 448–57, 453f
promoters, 429–37
racial discontent in, 457–69
Sister Rosetta Tharpe and, 313–14
Sly Stone's unpredictability in performance, 463–69
sound engineering for, 396–97
Armstrong, Louis, 272
   in Marable's riverboat ensemble, 186–87
   memories of Funky Butt Hall, 177–78
   residency at Chicago Savoy, 219–21
Arnold, Gina, 42, 523–24, 556–57
art music. *See* highbrow forms of art and music
Asbury, Edith Evans, 335–36, 337
Asch, Moe, 283–84, 369
Ashburn, Benny, 497–98
Ashon, Will, 538
Associated Musical Bureaus, 255
Astbury, Ian, 522–25
Astor Place Opera House, 6–7, 33, 43–44, 131
Astor Place Riot, 33, 42–46
Atkinson, Terry, 502
Atlanta Pop Festival, 403–5, 404f, 408–9
auctions of tickets for Jenny Lind's concerts, 50–53
audience noise, on live recordings, 475–76
audio engineering
   Beatles' 1965 concert at Shea Stadium, 428
   Beatles' 1966 concert at Shea Stadium, 396–97
   at music festivals, 347, 392–401, 400f
Auslander, Philip, 5–6, 14
Austin City Limits Festival, 541–42, 553, 554–55
Austria, music festivals in, 350–51
authenticity, black musical, 85–93
Avalon Ballroom (San Francisco), 435–36
avant-garde, 248

Baez, Joan, 372, 387
Bailey, Albert, 156–57, 157t
Ballet Russe de Monte Carlo, 259–60
Balliett, Whitney, 366–67

ballrooms, jazz in, 216–21, 218f. *See also* rock ballrooms
Bambaataa, Afrika, 491–93
   expanding reach from community of origin, 491–95
   Hip-Hop Family Reunion shows, 483–85
Banes, Sally, 494
Barbary Coast district (San Francisco), 214–15
Bard College Jazz Festival, 375–76
Barnum, H.B., 306–7
Barnum, P.T., 24–25, 125–26
   concert model set by, 77
   and disturbances at Jenny Lind's concerts, 65–67, 69, 70–71
   legacy of, 429–30
   role in Jenny Lind's US tour, 33–37, 47, 50–53, 60
   termination of contract with Jenny Lind, 72–73
Baron, Josh, 525–26
Barsalona, Frank, 438–46, 440f
Bart, Ben, 300–1
"Battle Hymn of the Republic"/"Mine Eyes Have Seen the Glory" (Howe), 98–100
Baty, Shirley, 379–80
Baym, Nancy, 569
Bayreuth Festival (Germany), 350
Beastie Boys, 494–95, 505, 508, 511–12, 518–19, 556
beat matching, 489–90
Beatles, the
   1964 Civic Arena concert, 430–31
   1965 Seattle Center Coliseum, 430
   1965 Shea Stadium concert, 424–29, 426f
   1966 Shea Stadium concert, 396–97
   arrival in US, 422–23
   attempt to make highbrow art, 243–44
   Carnegie Hall concert, 423–25
   withdrawal from live performance, 449
Beaulieu Jazz Festival (U.K.), 359
bebop, 284, 285
Beecher, Henry Ward, 78, 84–85, 87–88
Belkin, Jules, 420
Belletti, Giovanni, 57, 58–59

Bellini, Vincenzo, 58
Benedict, Jules, 57, 58–60
Bennett, James Gordon, 132–33
Benny Goodman Quartet, 273
Benson, Al, 321–23
Beren, Peter, 401–2
Berg, Billy, 278–79
Berkeley Folk Festival, 370–71
Bernstein, Sid
   1961 Newport jazz festival, 381–82
   as promoter-memoirist, 429–30
   role in Beatles' tour of US, 396–97, 423–26, 426f, 429
Berry, Chuck, 305–6, 340–41
Bevan, Llewellyn D., 116
Beychella, 8–9, 540–42, 557–66, 565f
Beyoncé
   2018 Coachella Festival appearance, 8–9, 540–42, 557–66, 565f
   rise as major touring artist, 555
   surprise 2010 performance at Coachella, 557
Bickford, Stephen, 456
Biddlecombe, George, 34–35
"Big Beat" package tour, 338–43
Biggest Rock 'n' Roll Show of 1956, 314–18, 316f
"Biggest Show of Stars for 1957", 318
"Biggest Show of Stars for 1958", 338–39, 340–41
Bikel, Theodore, 383–84, 387
Bill Haley & His Comets, 314–15, 316f
Black, Bill, 302–3, 303f
Black, Brown, and Beige (Ellington), 276–77
Black, Durel, 413–14
black Americans. *See* African Americans; racial discrimination/inequality; racial integration of musical entertainment; segregation; *specific black artists*; *specific black music genres*
black and tans, 199, 209–13
black Lollapalooza. *See* Smokin' Grooves festival
Black Patti (Matilda Sissieretta Jones), 162
Black Patti Troubadours, 161–64
black public sphere, 160, 166

black vaudeville, 153, 167–69, 191, 194
blackface minstrelsy
   connections to rock 'n' roll, 292–94
   and coon songs, 150, 153–54, 156–57
   and discourse of black musical authenticity, 85–87, 88
   drawing attention to Lind's proximity to, 40–41
   Fisk Jubilee Singers and, 79–80, 84–85, 109–10, 118
   and popular representations of African Americans, 80–81
   and rise of provisional form of mass culture, 32
   Sophie Tucker and, 194
   variety entertainment and vaudeville as supplanting, 121
Blackman, Toni, 537–38
Blake, Ran, 375–76
Blige, Mary J., 555
Blitzstein, Marc, 225–26
Blood, Sweat, and Tears, 409–10
Blow, Kurtis (Curtis Walker), 491, 496f
   cross-genre touring, 518–19
   Fresh Fest Three tour, 505
   Fresh Fest tour, 501–5
   Krush Groove concert, 506–8
   performing career of, 495–99
"Blues Is Jazz and Jazz Is Blues" (Seagrove), 202
"Blues" number (Jazz at the Philharmonic), 281–82
Bocage, Peter, 175–76
"Body and Soul" (Jazz at the Philharmonic), 280–82
Body Count, 527–28
Bolden, Buddy
   origins of jazz linked to, 175–76
   performances in Funky Butt Hall, 176–78
   rivalry with John Robichaux, 182–83
Bongiovanni, Gary, 514–15
Bonnaroo festival, 541–42, 552–53, 554–55
booking agencies
   in arena rock era, 438–48, 440f
   and rock 'n' roll concerts, 308–11, 319–20

Boseman, Jesse, 533–34
Bow Wow Wow, 491–93
Bowery (New York), 131–32
Boyd, Joe, 392–93
Boyle, Jack, 420, 432–33, 445–46
Bradford, Perry, 192–94
Brathwaite, Fred (Fab Five Freddy), 484, 493–94, 537
breakdancing, 494, 500–2
Brennan, Matt, 26, 410
British artists. *See also specific artists*
    Premier Talent's focus on, 439
    theater riots aimed at, 42–43
Broadside magazine, 385–86
Broadway, 134–35
Bronx DJs, 488–91
Brooks, Dickson, and Hickey, 124–25
Brown, George, 325–26
Brown, James, 469–70
Brown, Paul, 341–42
Brown, Roy, 300–1
Brown, Vernon, 272f
Bryant, Willie, 325–26
Bucano, Rocky (Kool DJ Rock), 482–83
Buchanan, Annabel Morris, 352–53
Buchanan, Kyle, 9
Buckley, Peter, 44–45
Budnick, Dean, 525–26
Buffalo Booking Agency, 310–11
Bush, W. Stephen, 16–17
Bushell, Garvin, 190
Butler, Nicholas, 11–12
Butsch, Richard, 45–46
Butterfield Blues Band, 433–35
Byrd, Henry Roeland (Professor Longhair), 417

cabaret, 172–73
    black and tans, 209–13
    dance halls versus, 213–14
    jazz performances, 201–7
    New York laws regarding, 207–9
Calder, Mitzie, 3
Campbell, Clive (DJ Kool Herc), 483–85, 489–90
Canetti, Elias, 9
Cantwell, Robert, 388–89
Capps, Ashley, 552–53

Carnegie, Andrew, 229, 230
Carnegie Hall (New York), 228–29
    Beatles' concert at, 423–25
    Benny Goodman's concert at, 233, 264–75, 272f
    construction and design of, 230–31
    Duke Ellington's first concert at, 276–77
    "From Spirituals to Swing" concerts, 275–76
    Jazz at the Philharmonic concert at, 286
Carney, Harry, 272
Carpenter, John, 433–34
"Carte de Visite Album, The" (written for Tony Pastor), 145–46
Carter, Asa, 317
Carter Barron Amphitheater (Washington, DC), 314
Casey, Phil, 513–14
Casino Gardens (Chicago), 203–6
"Casta Diva" aria (Bellini), 58
Castle Garden (New York), 50
    crowds drawn by Jenny Lind at, 65–67
    Jenny Lind's debut concert at, 7–8, 12–13, 53–60, 54f, 56f, 227–28
    Jenny Lind's farewell concert at, 30–31
Cavicchi, Daniel, 52
CBS radio network, 255–56
celebrity, qualities of, 7–8
Cellar Door (Washington, DC), 432–33
centralization in live music industry. *See* consolidation in live music industry
Chang, Jeff, 489
Chapple, Steve, 421
Charleston Minstrels, 85–86
Charnas, Dan, 484, 508–9
Chedwick, Porky, 430–31
Chevigny, Paul, 207–8
Chicago, jazz origins in, 202–3. *See also specific artists; specific venues*
chitlin' circuit, 300–1
Christy Minstrels, 109–10
Chuck D, 516–22, 518f, 534–35
Cincinnati May Festival, 349–50
CipHer, 537–38
Civic Arena (Pittsburgh), 430–31
Civil Rights Bill of 1875, 104–5
civil rights movement, 385–86
Civil War, 85–87, 145

652 INDEX

Clair Brothers, 393–94, 401
Clark Transfer, 448, 449–50
class. *See* social class
classical music
   in 1920s America, 244–52
   Ellington as refashioning conventions of, 276–77
   and emergence of modern concert hall, 232
   growth of audiences during 1920s and 1930s, 252–53
   Hurok's role in audience growth, 253, 258–64
   Judson's role in audience growth, 253–58
   from mid-1920s to mid-1940s, 226–27
   music festivals, 349–52, 354–56
   outdoor concerts, 351–52
   rise of modern institution of, 122
   in swing era, 266
   visibility of black artists in, 274
   Whiteman's efforts to "jazz", 235, 241–43
classicization of music, 36
Clear Channel, 542, 554–55
Clef Records, 283–84
Cleveland Arena, 294–98, 295*f*
Cliff Walk Manor music festival, 374–75
Cline, Maggie, 149–50
Clinton, George, 457–61, 470, 530, 531*f*
Cloonan, Martin, 26
Coachella Valley Music and Arts Festival, 8–9, 481
   African American artists appearing at, 556
   Beyoncé's 2018 performance at, 540–42, 557–66, 565*f*
   Beyoncé's surprise 2010 performance at, 557
   evolution of, 542–43
   first version, 548–52
   gradual growth of, 552–53
   reach and influence of, 554–55
   women as featured less prominently at, 556–57
Cockrell, Dale, 32
Cohen, John, 372–73, 384–85, 386
Cohen, Lyor, 508–9
Cohen, Rich, 431
Cohen, Ronald, 352
Cole, Bob, 166–67
Cole, Nat "King", 281–82, 317
Coleman, Rick, 312
collective joy, 568–69
collectivity, experience of, 4, 9, 27
college folk festivals, 370–71
Collins, Arthur, 155–56
Collins, Tommy, 450
Columbia Concerts Corporation, 255–58, 257*f*
comic operas, 137–38
comic songs, 120, 122, 144–45, 239. *See also* vaudeville
commercial concert culture, 1. *See also* industrialization of liveness
   consolidation in, 420–21, 542–43, 547–48, 551–52
   emergence of vaudeville, 123–27, 126*f*
   Fisk Jubilee Singers and, 112–13
   and formation of modern public sphere, 11
   and growth of classical music audiences, 253, 266
   and highbrow musical values, 226–27
   Jazz at the Philharmonic concert series, 277–91
   Jenny Lind and, 7–8, 38–41, 39*f*, 76–77
   music festivals, 346–49, 382, 401–9, 404*f*, 416–17
   Newport Jazz Festival, 367
   pursuit of crowds in, 12–13
   rock 'n' roll concerts, 296–98
   and twenty-first century music festivals, 553–54
commercial dance halls, 214–16
commercial song production
   circulation of coon songs, 150–60, 157*t*, 158*t*
   Tin Pan Alley era, 122–23, 140–43
commodification of Jenny Lind, 76–77
Commodores, the, 462, 497–99
common forms of art and music. *See* lowbrow forms of art and music
communal singing, 568

composers
  and American classical music scene in 1920s, 247, 248–50
  Ellington's concert foregrounding role as, 276–77
composite live albums, 471, 472–75
Concert Management Arthur Judson, 253–54, 255–56, 261–62
concert music
  classical music scene of 1920s, 244–52
  concert halls and cultural hierarchy, 227–32
  and division between low and high culture, 224–27, 290–91
  Ellington's first Carnegie Hall concert, 276–77
  "From Spirituals to Swing" concerts, 275–76
  Goodman at Carnegie Hall, 264–75
  growth of audiences during 1920s and 1930s, 252–53
  Hurok's role in audience growth, 253, 258–64
  jazz as, overview of, 226–27, 346
  Jazz at the Philharmonic concert series, 277–90
  Judson's role in audience growth, 253–58
  Whiteman's "Experiment in Modern Music", 233–44, 240f
concert promotion
  African Americans in, 460–61, 462–63
  by Alan Freed, 297–98, 323–24, 326–33
  in arena rock era, 418–20, 429–37
  by Bill Graham, 429–30, 432–38
  booking agencies and, 308–11
  consolidation in industry, 542–43, 547–48, 551–52
  cooperation with booking agencies, 441–48
  by disc jockeys, 297, 319–23, 322f
  by Feld brothers, 311–18
  by George Wein, 356–57
  by Goldenvoice, 542–46, 544f
  by Jerry Weintraub, 445–48
  by Sid Bernstein, 423–26, 426f, 429
  twenty-first century music festivals, 542–43, 547–48, 554–55

concert saloons, 131–33
concert tours. *See also specific artists; specific tours*
  in arena rock era, 418–19
  implications beyond generation of revenue, 118–19
  live recordings from, 471, 472–75
  overview, 1–3
  production codes, 448–57, 453f
  rock careers built around, 439–41
concerts. *See* commercial concert culture; live music; *specific artists; specific concerts; specific music genres*
Concerts West, 418, 420, 432, 445–46, 551–52
Condon, Eddie, 278
conductors, 249–52
Confrey, Zez, 241–42
Conn wind instruments advertisement, 17–18
Conover, Willis, 414–15
Cons, Carl, 268–69
consolidation in live music industry, 420–21, 542–43, 547–48, 551–52
Cooley, Alex, 405–7, 408–9, 420, 443
coon songs
  circulation of, 150–60, 157t, 158t
  performances by Hogan, 160–67
Cooper, Anthony Ashley, Lord Shaftesbury, 108–9
"Cop Killer" (Ice-T), 527–28
Copeland, Lee, 514–15
Copland, Aaron, 248, 276, 351–52
Coss, Bill, 380
Costello, Fin, 476–77, 477f
Cotton, Elizabeth "Libba", 388–89
Cotton Club (New York), 199, 209–11
countercultural orientation of music festivals, 553–54
country music, 301–3, 307–8
COVID-19 pandemic, ix–x, 566–68
Cox, Timothy, 502–3
creative juxtaposition, 28–29
Creole Band, 171–72, 187–89
Criss, Peter, 475–76
Cromelin, Richard, 511–12
crooning vocals, 221
Crouse, Timothy, 467–68

crowds. *See also* arena rock
  "Alan Freed's 'Rock 'n' Roll' Jubilee
    Ball", 328–29
  Barnum's efforts to control at Lind's
    concerts, 53–55
  at "Big Beat" concert in Boston, 341–43
  discharge, 9
  disturbances at Jenny Lind's
    concerts, 69–76
  drawn by Jenny Lind, 31–34, 46, 47–
    50, 65–66
  and Ellington's 1956 Newport Jazz
    Festival appearance, 363–65
  focus on events drawing
    large, 27–28
  at Freed's engagement at
    Paramount, 334–37
  impulse to gather large, 12–13
  at Moondog Coronation Ball, 294–98
  National Peace Jubilee, 94–95
  at Newport Folk Festival, 373, 389–
    91, 391*f*
  at Newport Jazz Festival, 361–62,
    366, 376–81
  at pop music festivals, 405, 408–9
  and public sphere, 42–46
  and racial segregation, 305
  of vaudeville, 127
  at Woodstock, 401–3
  World's Peace Jubilee, 95–96
Crowley, Michael, 456
Cruz, Jon, 87–88
cultural capitalists, 228–29
cultural hierarchy, concert halls and,
  227–32. *See also* highbrow forms of
  art and music; lowbrow forms of art
  and music
Cuyler, Theodore, 87–89, 92
Cypress Hill, 529, 530

Dall, Caroline Healy, 71
Damrosch, Leopold, 229
Damrosch, Walter, 229, 230
dance/dancing
  breakdancing, 494, 500–2
  jazz dance halls, 176–80, 213–16
  move away from in rock ballrooms, 436
  at Newport Jazz Festival, 362, 363–65

racial integration at rock 'n' roll
  concerts, 306–7
rock 'n' roll concerts and, 337, 342–43
shimmy dance, 196–97
stepping dance style, 559–60
swing era, 267, 269–70
Whiteman orchestra's dance-ability, 244
Dane, Barbara, 391*f*
Darrell, R.D., 276
Daughters of the American Revolution
  (DAR), 263
Davey D, DJ, 495, 498
Davis, Miles, 410
Davis, Quint, 415–16
de la Rocha, Zach, 550–51
Death of Rhythm & Blues, The
  (George), 462–63
Def Jam Records, 503–4
Delsener, Ron, 420
Desert Trip festival, 554–55
Destiny's Child, 563–64
DeVeaux, Scott, 233, 278
Diamond, Michael (Mike D), 494–95
DiCesare, Pat, 429–31, 465–66
Dickens's Place (New York), 6–7, 13
Dickerson, Isaac, 82, 83*f*
Diddley, Bo, 371
DiMaggio, Paul, 228–29
"Diminuendo and Crescendo in Blue"
  (Ellington), 362–65
Disc company, 283–84
disc jockeys (DJs)
  concert promotion by, 297, 319–23, 322*f*
  early public appearances by, 485
  hip-hop, 485–91
  and racial integration of musical
    entertainment, 303–5
"Disco Extravaganza" event, 482–83
disco music, 482–85
discotheques, 485–88
"Dr. Jive Ball" (Harlem), 332–33
Dodge, Ossian, 52–53
Dollis, Bo, 415–16
"Don't Call Me Nigger, Whitey" (Sly and
  the Family Stone), 528–29
"Don't Hurt Yourself" (Beyoncé), 562
Don't Knock the Rock film, 332, 334
Doors, the, 471–73

double live albums, 472–73
double-consciousness, African American, 114–15
Downes, Olin, 238, 239, 246–47
DRB Productions, 482–83
Dre, Dr., 556
Driftwood, Jimmy, 388–89
DuBois, W.E.B., 106–7, 114–15, 118–19
Dulcimer, The (Woodbury) , 14
Duncan, Robert, 421
Dunn, Johnny, 189–91
Dunton, Gardner, 361
Durante, Jimmy, 212
Durgin, Cyrus, 361–62
Dwight, John S., 95
 on musical festivals, 349–50
 reviews of Jenny Lind's performances, 7, 30–31, 63–65
 sacralization and, 36
 sympathy for study of music of black Americans, 91–92
 on virtuoso pianists, 10–11
Dwight's Journal of Music, 30–31, 91–92, 95
Dylan, Bob, 1
 at 1963 Newport Folk Festival, 386–87
 at 1965 Newport Folk Festival, 348, 391–94

Eaglin, Snooks, 415–16, 417
Earth, Wind & Fire (EWF), 470
"Echo Song"/"The Herdsman's Song" (Jenny Lind), 58–59
economies of performance. *See also* Pastor, Tony; variety entertainment; vaudeville
 circulation of coon songs, 149–60, 157*t*, 158*t*
 effort to draw widest possible audiences, 127
 focus on novelty, 143–49
 overview, 120–23
 performances by Hogan, 160–67
 song plugging, 142–43
 and Tin Pan Alley, 142–49
Economy Hall (New Orleans), 180
Ehrenreich, Barbara, 568–69
Eldritch, Andrew, 519

Electric Daisy Carnival (EDC), 541–42, 547, 554–55
Electric Factory promotion company, 443–44
electric guitar, 391–92
electronic dance music, 547, 549–50
elevated forms of art and music. *See* highbrow forms of art and music
Eliscu, Jenny, 557
Ellington, Duke, 272, 273–74
 1956 appearance at Newport Jazz Festival, 362–65
 Ellington at Newport album, 362–63, 364–65
 first Carnegie Hall concert, 276–77
 vaudeville performances of, 199–201
emancipation from slavery, 93, 96–97, 102–6
Empire Polo Club (Indio, California), 546*f*, 546–47, 548–52
England
 festival culture in, 359, 525, 547
 Fisk Jubilee Singers in, 107, 108*f*, 108–17
 Slave Circular, 115–17
Ennis, Philip, 312
Epstein, Brian, 423, 424–26
Errico, Greg, 464–65
ethnic comedy in vaudeville, 157–59, 158*t*
ethnosympathy, 87–88
Europe, James Reese, 273–74
Europe '72 (Grateful Dead), 473–74
European music
 Fisk Jubilee Singers and, 88–93
 Hurok's focus on, 258–60
 influence on American musical landscape, 31
Evans, Greene, 82, 83*f*
Evolution of the Blues (Handy & Nussbaum), 265–66
EWF (Earth, Wind & Fire), 470
Ewing, Annemarie, 270–71
Ewoodzie, Joseph, 490–91
excursions, jazz, 183–87
"Experiment in Modern Music" (Whiteman), 240*f*
 comparisons to Goodman's Carnegie Hall concert, 270–73

656 INDEX

"Experiment in Modern Music" (Whiteman) (*cont.*)
  and emergence of jazz concert, 226, 233–44
  versus League of Composers program, 245–46

Fab Five Freddy (Fred Brathwaite), 484, 493–94, 537
Fabbri, Franco, 173–74
Family Dog, 432–35
Farrar, I.F., 147–48
Farrell, Perry, 528–29, 549–50, 566
Fat Boys, 501, 502–3, 504–5
Fat Water, 465
F.B. Haviland Publishing Co., 15–16, 16*f*
"Fear of a Rap Concert" (Copeland), 514–15
Feld, Irvin
  concert promotion by, 311–18, 316*f*
  direct competition with Freed, 338–39, 340–41
Feld, Israel, 311–18, 316*f*
Feld, Shirley, 313–14
Ferrantelli, Joseph, 178–79
Festival of American Folklife, 411–12
festivals, music. *See* music festivals; *specific music festivals*
festivity, 568–69
fetish, tendency to treat music as, 251–52
Fey, Barry, 420, 429–30, 432–33, 445–46, 447–48
Fields, Fannie, 157–58, 157*t*
Fifteenth Amendment, 106
Fight the Power (Chuck D), 517–18
Fillmore East (New York), 397–98, 432–33
Fillmore West (San Francisco), 432–37, 434*f*
film
  cross-promotion by Feld brothers, 314–15
  and early discourses surrounding live music, 16–17, 18–19
  and exposure to rock 'n' roll, 298–99
  Freed's career in, 331–32
Fishbone, 545
Fisher, Jules, 452–57, 458
Fisk Jubilee Singers, 83*f*, 90*f*, 558–59
  and discourse of black musical authenticity, 85–93
  effects of segregation on, 102–6
  gaining recognition, 80–85
  inspiration for name, 93–94
  legacy of, 117–19
  moral elevation of, 78–79, 117–18
  overseas ventures of, 106–17, 108*f*
  overview, 78–80
  at World's Peace Jubilee, 96–102, 97*f*
Fisk University, 81
Fitchburg Station Hall (Fitchburg, Massachusetts), 67–71, 68*f*
Fitzgerald, Ella, 360
Five Kings of Syncopation, 194–96
Flavor Flav, 516–22, 518*f*
Fletcher, Tom, 165–66
Flippo, Chet, 452–54
Floyd, Samuel, 89
flutter tongue technique, 190–91
FM Productions, 418
Foghat, 439, 441, 475
folk festivals. *See also* Newport Folk Festival
  emergence and evolution of, 352–54
  folk revival, 369–70, 384–86
  motives for creation of, 354–55
  overview, 346–49
  and political activism, 385–86
  precedent and competition in field, 370–71
  renewal of scene in 1970s, 411–12
Foner, Eric, 103
Fontana, D.J., 302–3
foreign artists in history of American music performance, 31. *See also specific artists*
Forman, Murray, 481, 505–6
Forrest, Edwin, 33–34, 44
Forster, Rumsey, 34–35
Forsyth, Michael, 230–31
Foster, George, 6–7
Foster, Pops, 185–86, 190–91
Four Hundred Club Room, Reisenweber's, 204–7, 205*f*
14th Street (New York)
  Tin Pan Alley, 140–41
  Tony Pastor's theater on, 138–40, 139*f*, 143

Francis, Miller, Jr., 403–5
Franklin, Aretha, 469–70
free festivals, 402, 405–6, 408–9, 411
Freebody Park (Newport), 363–64
Freed, Alan, 362
　"Big Beat" tour, 338–43
　comparison to Irvin Feld, 312, 315–17
　as concert promoter, 297–98, 323–24
　as disc jockey, 321, 322f, 323–28
　film career, 331–32
　Moondog Coronation Ball, 294–98, 295f
　Paramount Theater engagement, 334–37, 335f
　profile in *Pageant* magazine, 337–38
　use of all available media by, 298–99, 322f
　use of "rock 'n' roll" term, 326–28
Freedom Singers, 386, 387
Freestyle Fellowship, 536–37, 538
Freestyle Union (Washington, DC), 537–38
French Lick music festival, 367–68
Fresh, Doug E., 506–8
Fresh Fest Three tour, 505
Fresh Fest tour, 481, 500–5, 503f
Fresh Fest Two tour, 504–5
Frith, Simon, 26
"From Brass Bands to Bebop" concert, 356–57
"From Spirituals to Swing" concerts, 233, 275–76
front of house setup, for sound engineering, 395–96
Fugees, 530–33
Funky Butt Hall (New Orleans), 176–78

GAC (General Artists Corporation), 423, 438–39
Gahr, David, 373
Gaines, Kevin, 559
Gale Agency, 309, 310–11
Gang of Four, 519
gang violence at hip-hip concerts, 509–12
gangsta rap, 526–29. *See also* hip-hop
Garcia family troupe, 31–32
Garcia-Olano, Diego, 556–57
Garnet, Henry Highland, 105–6

Garofalo, Reebee, 421
Garrison, Lucy McKim, 87, 91–92
Gaskin, George, 155–56
Gathering of the Tribes festival, 522–26
Gehman, Richard, 366–67
Geiger, Marc, 525
Gendron, Bernard, 14, 248, 538
General Artists Corporation (GAC), 423, 438–39
genteel performance, 76–77
George, Nelson, 462–63, 504–5, 535
Georgia Graduates, 153
Georgia Old-Time Fiddlers Convention, 352
Germanic musical works, 64–65, 349–51
Germany, Bayreuth Festival in, 350
Gershwin, George, 225–26, 241–44
Get Your Ya-Yas Out (Rolling Stones), 471–73
Gibson, Bob, 372
Gibson & Stromberg publicity agency, 450–51
Gilbert, W.S., 137–38
Gillespie, Dizzy, 284, 285
Gillette, Captain, 102
Gilmore, Mikal, 462
Gilmore, Patrick, 80, 127
　National Peace Jubilee, 94–96
　World's Peace Jubilee, 95–97, 99–100, 101–2
Gilroy, Paul, 106–7, 114–15
Gitler, Ira, 376
Glastonbury festival (U.K.), 547
Glatt, John, 397–98
Gleason, Ralph, 436–37
Go, Johnny, Go! film, 332
"Go Down, Moses" spiritual (Fisk Jubilee Singers), 83–84
Gold, Jonathan, 520–21
Goldberg, Isaac, 122–23, 141, 153–54
Goldblatt, Burt, 374
Goldenvoice, 554–55
　evolution of idea for festival produced by, 546–48
　first Coachella festival, 548–52
　merger with AEG, 551–52
　roots in punk and alternative music scene, 542–46, 544f

Goldschmidt, Otto, 30, 72–73
Goldstein, Stanley, 398–99
Gonsalves, Paul, 362–65, 364*f*
Good Life Café (Los Angeles), 536–37
Goode, Ruth, 258–59
Goodman, Benny
  Benny Goodman Quartet, 273
  Carnegie Hall concert, 233, 264–75, 272*f*
  and emergent listening culture, 268–69, 271
  jam sessions, 278
  Paramount Theater stand, 269–71
Goodman, Fred, 438
Gordon, Georgia, 97–98, 108*f*
Gore, Tipper, 510–11
Gorman, Ross, 239–41, 242
gospel music, 275, 313–14
"Gospel of Wealth, The" (Carnegie), 230
Gottschalk, Louis Moreau, 1–2
Gough, John, 78
Gracyk, Theodore, 299
Graham, Bill, 410, 418
  as decrying move into arenas and stadiums, 421
  Hurok as role model for, 258–59
  as promoter, 429–30, 438
  as retooling rock concert presentation, 437
  tension with majority of promoters, 447
  venue ownership, 397–98, 432–37, 434*f*
Graham, Sandra, 82–83
Grand Funk Railroad, 24–25, 421
Grand Ole Opry, 302
"Grand Sacred Concert" (World's Peace Jubilee), 100–1
Grandmaster Flash (Joseph Saddler), 489–90, 493–94, 499–500, 504–5, 518–19
  Merry-Go-Round technique, 489–90
Grant, Ulysses S., 101–2
Granz, Norman
  comparison to Sol Hurok, 290–91
  early forays into concert promotion, 278–80
  first Jazz at the Philharmonic concert, 280–82
  Jazz at the Philharmonic recordings, 282–84

Jazz at the Philharmonic tours, 284–90
  overview, 277–78
Grasso, Frances, 488–89
Grateful Dead, 473–74
Gratitude (EWF), 470
great migration, 185
great performances, in analyses of live music, 23
Green, Abel, 197, 239, 245, 265–66, 267–68, 486
Greenfield, Robert, 450
"Greeting to America" (Taylor & Benedict), 59–60
Grevatt, Ren, 338–39, 342–43
Griff, Professor, 516–17, 520–21
Griffith Stadium concerts (Washington, DC), 313–14
Grofé, Ferde, 234–35, 242
Grossman, Albert, 369–70, 372, 382–83
Gushee, Lawrence, 171

Habermas, Jurgen, 11
Hager, Steven, 493–94
Hagert, Thornton, 241–42
Hale, Cecil, 462
Haley, Bill, 298–99, 314–17, 316*f*, 318
Hall, William, 38–40, 41
Halttunen, Karen, 76–77
Hamel, Reice, 471–72
Hamm, Charles, 40–41, 140–41, 147–48
Hammond, John, 273, 275–76
Hampton, Lionel, 273–74
Hampton Singers, 91–92
Handy, W.C., 168–69, 189–90, 265–66, 273–74
Hanley, Bill, 347
  Beatles' Shea Stadium concerts, 396–97
  Fillmore East, 397–98
  Newport festivals, 392–96
  Woodstock, 398–401, 400*f*
Hanlon, Jef, 331–32
"Hard Knock Life" tour (Jay-Z), 478
hard shell country, 301–2
Hardin, Louis Thomas ("Moondog"), 326
Harlem, New York
  night clubs, 208–13
  Savoy ballroom, 216–17, 218*f*

as territory of Tommy "Dr. Jive" Smalls, 332–33
Harrigan, Philip, 499–500
Harris, Charles K., 142–43, 152–53
Harris, Neil, 50–51
Hastings, Peter, 294–96
Haverly, J.H., 124–25
Hawkins, Coleman, 280–81
Hayes, Roland, 261–62
HBCUs (Historically Black College or Universities), 540, 557–61
headliners, anticipation of in package shows, 308
Healy, Mark, 550–51
Heavy D and the Boyz, 517
heavy metal, 24–25. *See also* arena rock
Heider, Wally, 471–72
Helms, Chet, 433–35
Henderson, Douglas "Jocko", 332–33, 334
Hendler, Glenn, 37
Hendrix, Jimi, 437, 463, 469–70
Hentoff, Nat, 360–61, 379–80
Herc, DJ Kool (Clive Campbell), 483–85, 489–90
"Herdsman's Song, The"/"Echo Song" (Jenny Lind), 58–59
Heritage Fair (New Orleans Jazz & Heritage Festival), 415, 416–17
Hershorn, Tad, 277–78
Hess, Mickey, 535–36
hierarchy, cultural, 227–32. *See also* highbrow forms of art and music; lowbrow forms of art and music
highbrow forms of art and music
  American classical music scene in 1920s, 244–47
  criticism of Jenny Lind related to, 64–65
  early discourses surrounding live music, 19–23
  Ellington's first Carnegie Hall concert, 276–77
  "From Spirituals to Swing" concerts, 275–76
  Goodman's Carnegie Hall concert, 264–75
  Hurok's role in audience growth, 253, 258–64
  jazz as typifying mingling of lowbrow and, 224–27, 290–91

jazz concerts, 233, 277–91
jazz festivals, 346
Judson's role in audience growth, 253–58
Lind's place on boundary of, 35–37
music festivals, 349–52, 353, 354–55
Newport Jazz Festival, 355–56, 358–59, 360–61, 362, 382
Pastor's alignment with, 131–34, 169
process of cultural stratification in America, 227–32
and rise of vaudeville, 122
rock ballrooms, 436
tension between lowbrow and, 13–14
variety entertainment and, 169–70
Whiteman's "Experiment in Modern Music", 233–44
Hilburn, Robert, 550–51
Hill, Edward Burlingame, 244–45
Hill, Michael, 408–9
hip-hop
  arena rap, 482
  at Coachella, 556
  decline in support for concerts, 512–15
  discotheques, 485–88
  early mixing techniques, 488–91
  expanding reach from communities of origin, 491–95
  festivals, 522–35
  Fresh Fest tour, 500–5, 503*f*
  golden age of arena rap, 500–5
  Goldenvoice promotion of, 545
  Jay-Z's Madison Square Garden concert, 478–81
  Kurtis Blow tours, 495–99, 496*f*
  music festivals, 531*f*
  package tours, 522–23, 524–25
  rap/rock cross-genre touring, 515–22
  regional spread of, 535
  success of records over live performance, 480–81
  Sugar Hill "Rappers Convention" tour, 499–500
  turntables, use in, 490–91
  underground, 535–39
  use of term, 483–84
  violence at concerts, 505–12
Hip-Hop Family Reunion shows, 483–85

Hippodrome (New York), 258–59
Historically Black College or Universities (HBCUs), 540, 557–61
history
    in Duke Ellington's first Carnegie Hall concert, 276–77
    in "From Spirituals to Swing" concerts, 275–76
    in Goodman's Carnegie Hall concert, 271–73
    and programming of first Newport Jazz Festival, 360–61
    in Whiteman's "Experiment in Modern Music", 238
Hjortsberg, Max, 72–73
H.M.S. Pinafore (Gilbert & Sullivan), 137–38
Hobson, Wilder, 267–68
Hodges, Johnny, 272*f*, 272
Hogan, Ernest, 151*f*
    circulation of "All Coons Look Alike to Me", 150–60, 157*t*, 158*t*
    and demand for novelty, 169–70
    feelings about "All Coons Look Alike to Me", 164–66
    later career, 165–66
    overview, 120–22
    performances by, 160–67
    realm of vaudeville occupied by, 167–69
    testimonial benefit in honor of, 166–67
Holiday, Billie, 278–79
Hollywood, DJ, 495–96
Hollywood Palladium (California), 511–12
Holman, Michael, 491–93
Holmes, Benjamin, 82, 83*f*
Holt, Fabian, 222
Homecoming film, 558–59, 562–63
honky tonks, 176–77, 301–3, 303*f*
Hooke, Jack, 342–43
Hopkins, Jerry, 402–3
Horowitz, Joseph, 251, 252
"hot" jazz, 234
Hotel Congress (Chicago), 268–69
House, Son, 388–89
House of Blues, 548, 552
Howe, Julia Ward, 98–99
Howland, John, 239–41, 265–66
Howley, Haviland & Co., 159

Hu, Cherie, 567–68
Hughes, Langston, 375, 379
Hulett, Tom, 432
Hurok, Sol, 260*f*
    as Bill Graham's personal hero, 433
    and classical/popular divide, 274–75
    comparison to Norman Granz, 290–91
    jazz concert promotion by, 264–66
    promotion of American music, 261–62
    role in growth of classical music audiences, 253, 258–64
Hurwitz, Seth, 553
Hyatt, George "Slim", 486–87
Hyers Sisters, 99–100
Hynes, John, 341–42

Ice Cube, 526–27, 529
ice shows, 450
Ice-T, 522–25, 526–29, 531–32
ideology of racial uplift, 559–60
imagined community, 12–13
improvisation, in Jazz at the Philharmonic concerts, 280–82
independent labels, 298, 319–20
industrialization of liveness
    Beatles' 1965 performance at Shea Stadium, 422–29, 426*f*
    booking agents, 438–48, 440*f*
    live recordings, 469–77, 477*f*
    overview, 418–22
    Parliament-Funkadelic Earth Tour, 457–63, 459*f*
    production codes, 448–57, 453*f*
    promoters, 429–37
    Sly Stone's unpredictability in performance, 463–69
inequality, live music and, 27. *See also* racial discrimination/inequality; women
insurance for rap concerts, 511, 513–14
International Composers' Guild, 244–45, 247
International Pop Festivals, Inc., 405–8
International Society for Contemporary Music (ISCM), 350–51
Irwin, May, 150
Irwin, Theodore, 337–38
Italian opera, 43–44, 61–64

INDEX 661

Jackson, George Pullen, 353
Jackson, Jennie, 82, 83f, 108f
Jackson, John, 326, 336–37, 341–42
Jackson, Julia, 97–98, 108f
Jacobs, Moss, 551
Jacquet, Illinois, 281–82
Jagger, Mick. *See* Rolling Stones
jam sessions, 278–79
Jane's Addiction, 528–29, 545–46
Jasen, David, 155–56
JATP. *See* Jazz at the Philharmonic concert series
Jay-Z, 541, 556
  at Coachella in 2010, 557
  insights about touring, 538–39
  success in sphere of live performance, 478–81, 555
jazz
  ballrooms, 216–21, 218f
  Bolden, influence of, 175–76
  cabaret performances, 201–7
  dance halls, 176–80, 213–16
  early appearances of term, 202
  early discourses surrounding live music, 17–18
  jam sessions, 278–79
  listening culture in, 267–69, 271, 278–79
  as listening music, 267–69, 271, 278–79
  media influence, 174–75
  night clubs, 207–13
  origins of, 175–79, 202–3
  performance conditions, effect on, 221–22
  places and venues, overview of, 172–75
  posters promoting dances and events, 179–82, 181f, 183, 184f
  in public parks, 182
  racially segregated performances, 185–86
  railroad excursions, 183–85
  recordings of, 171–72, 174–75, 183–85, 192–94, 193f
  as remade through shift into concert hall, 232
  speakeasies, 207–8, 211–12
  steamboat performances, 185–87
  "sweet" vs. "hot", 234
  swing era, 266–67, 268–75
  symphonic, 234–44, 276–77
  as typifying mingling of highbrow and lowbrow music, 224–27, 290–91
  vaudeville performances, 187–201, 193f
Jazz (Whiteman & McBride), 237
Jazz & Heritage Festival, New Orleans, 412–17
Jazz at the Philharmonic (JATP) concert series
  first concert, 280–82
  as model for integrated package shows, 307–8
  overview, 277–78
  recordings from, 282–84, 475
  tours, 284–90
jazz clubs, 172–73, 267–68, 278
jazz concerts
  and American classical music scene in 1920s, 248
  "From Spirituals to Swing", 275–76
  Goodman at Carnegie Hall, 264–75
  Hurok's promotion of, 264–66
  Jazz at the Philharmonic, 277–91
  League of Composers' lecture-recital, 244–47
  overview, 226–27
  as remaking jazz, 232
  Whiteman's "Experiment in Modern Music", 226, 233–44, 240f
jazz festivals. *See also* Newport Jazz Festival
  aura of idealism surrounding, 346–49
  fusion with rock, 409–11
  in Newport in 1961, 381–82
  renewal of scene in 1970s, 411–17
  in United Kingdom, 359
Jazz Hounds, 189–90
Jethro Tull, 410
J.H. Haverly's Amusement Enterprises, 124–25
Jim Mahoney and Associates, 454
Jimi Hendrix Experience, 463
Johnson, Angelo, 285
Johnson, Bill, 214
Johnson, Frank, 106–7
Johnson, J. Rosamond, 166–67, 560–61
Johnson, James Weldon, 154–55, 560–61

Jollie, Samuel, 38, 41
Jones, Gene, 155–56
Jones, Jo, 375
Jones, Louis, 182
Jones, Matilda Sissieretta (Black Patti), 162
Jones, Pete "DJ", 482–83
Josef, Jamal, 559–60
Jubilee, in collective memory of African Americans, 93
jubilee singing troupes, 117–18. *See also* Fisk Jubilee Singers
Judson, Arthur
  and management of Marian Anderson, 261–62
  role in audience growth of classical music, 253–58
jukeboxes, 486–87

Kapralik, David, 466
Keisker, Marion, 293
Keith, Benjamin Franklin (B.F.), 125–26, 126f, 148, 444–45
Kelley, Robin, 184–85
Kenton, Stan, 360–61
Kibler, Alison, 150
Kid 'n Play, 517
Kiilu, DJ, 536–37
Kimbro, Edmund, 417
Kingston Trio, 372–73
Kirk, Roland, 409–10
Kirkendall, Carol, 513–14
Kiss, 475–77, 477f
Knapp, Raymond, 137
Knickerbocker movie house (New York), 16–17
Knott, Sarah Gertrude, 353–54
Kolodin, Irving, 264–65, 271, 351–52
Kool DJ Rock (Rocky Bucano), 482–83
Kornfeld, Artie, 398
Kornhaber, Spencer, 563–64
Koussevitzky, Serge, 249–50
Kozak, Roman, 498
Kraft, James, 18–19
Kramer, A. Walter, 250–51
Krefetz, Lou, 309
Krupa, Gene, 273
Krush Groove Christmas Party, 506–8

Lait, Jack, 195
Lalonde, Amanda, 484–85
Lambert, Olaf, 414–15
Lang, Michael, 398
Lang, Paul Henry, 254
large-scale events, focus on, 27–28. *See also* crowds; music festivals; *specific artists; specific events; specific music genres*
Latinos, Sleepy Lagoon Defense Fund for, 280
Lauterbach, Preston, 300–1
Law, Don, 420, 432–33, 442–43, 445–46
Lawrence, Tim, 488–89
Le Club (New York City), 486
League of Composers, 225, 244–47
Led Zeppelin, 2–3, 418–19
Leder, Bob, 324–25
Leland, John, 516–17
LeProtti, Sid, 214–15
"Lester Leaps In" (Young), 280–82
Levine, Lawrence, 13–14, 36, 41, 227–29, 243, 247–48
Levy, Morris, 327–28, 329
Lewis, Cara, 530, 533–34
Lewis, Jerry Lee, 340–41
Lewis, Mabel, 97–98
Lewis, Ted, 17–18, 196–97
Lhamon, W.T., 32
L'Hommedieu, Sam, 432–33
"Lift Every Voice and Sing" (Johnson & Johnson), 560–61
lighting, on Rolling Stones' 1975 US tour, 452–54, 455–56. *See also* staging of arena rock
Lincoln Memorial, Marian Anderson's performance at, 263–64, 264f
Lind, Jenny, 24–25, 127, 174
  arrival in US, 47–50, 48f, 422–23
  Barnum's role in US tour, 34–37
  branding, 35–37
  comparison to Beyoncé, 562–64
  criticism of, 60–65
  crowds and public sphere, 42–46
  debate over cultural underpinnings of approach, 60–64
  disturbances at concerts of, 65–76
  early career, 34–35

INDEX 663

farewell concert in US, 30–31
mass appeal of, 31–34
model set by, 76–77
moral elevation and, 31, 36–37, 49–50, 60, 76–77
re-unification of divided cultural fields by, 227–28
tensions arising over appearances of, 33–34
ticket auctions for concerts, 50–53
US concert debut of, 7–8, 12–13, 53–60, 54f, 56f, 227–28
use of image and reputation for commercial purposes, 38–41, 39f
listening music. *See also* concert music
conversion of rock into, 435–36
jazz as, 267–69, 271, 278–79
Liszt, Franz, 10–11
Litwack, Leon, 93
Live Dead (Grateful Dead), 473
live music. *See also* industrialization of liveness; music festivals; *specific artists*; *specific events*; *specific music genres*
American Federation of Musicians campaign promoting, 18–23, 20f, 22f
aura attributed to, 6–9
broader questions covered in book, 23–27
consolidation in industry, 420–21, 542–43, 547–48, 551–52
early discourses surrounding, 14–23, 16f, 20f, 22f
effect of COVID-19 pandemic on, ix–x, 566–68
enabling conditions of, 3–4
in era before mechanical reproduction, 5–6, 9–14
and formation of modern public sphere, 11–13
need for restoration of, 568–69
organizing principles in book, 27–29
overview, 1–3
qualities defining, 4–5
on radio, 320
revenues from, 25–26
scholarship on, rise in, 26

Live Nation Entertainment, 542–43, 554–55
live recordings
of arena concerts, 421–22, 469–77, 477f
of Jazz at the Philharmonic concerts, 282–84
live sound engineering, 347, 392–401, 400f
Liveness (Auslander), 5–6
"Livery Stable Blues" (ODJB), 238
livestreaming, 567–68
Living Colour, 545
LL Cool J, 505, 506–8
Lockard, Thaddeus, 38, 72–73
Lockett, Dee, 8–9
Lollapalooza festivals, 554–55
first wave of tours, 523–30
Goldenvoice and, 545–46
hip-hop in, 481, 523–24, 526–29
intermixing of rock and electronic beats at, 549–50
new wave of activity in the twenty-first century, 553
Lomax, Alan, 353–54, 388
Long Beach Arena (California), 505–6, 509–12
Lopez, Vincent, 244–45, 265–66
Lorillard, Elaine, 345, 358f, 358–59, 374–75
Lorillard, Louis, 345, 358f, 358–59, 367–68, 372–73
Lott, Eric, 6–7, 32, 136–37, 293
"love and theft" dual trope, 293
Loudin, Frederic, 107, 108f, 113–17
Louisiana Hayride, 302–3, 303f
Love and Theft (Lott), 6–7
lowbrow forms of art and music. *See also* popular culture; *specific music genres*; vaudeville
jazz as typifying mingling of highbrow and, 224–27, 290–91
jazz concerts, 233
Jenny Lind's place on boundary of, 35–37
process of cultural stratification in America, 227–32
and rise of variety entertainment and vaudeville, 122
tension between highbrow and, 13–14
variety entertainment and, 131–33

Lunsford, Bascom Lamar, 352
Lydon, Michael, 402–3
Lyricist Lounge (New York), 537–38

Mack, Greg, 509–10
Macready, William, 33–34, 42–43, 44–45
Madison Square Garden (New York)
   Jay-Z's retirement concert, 478–81
   Krush Groove concert, 506–8
   Kurtis Blow performance at, 498
   Public Enemy performance at, 521–22
   Run-D.M.C. Raising Hell tour concert at, 508–9
   Sly and the Family Stone concerts at, 465–66, 467–68
Magid, Larry, 420, 429–30, 432–33, 443–44
Mahler, Gustav, 249–50
Mahon, Maureen, 563
Mahoney, Tim, 456
Malibran, Maria, 31–32, 61
Marable, Fate, 186–87
Marcus, Greil, 303–4, 400–1, 468
Mardi Gras Indians, 415–16
Maretzek, Max, 132–33
Marks, Edward, 143
Marquis, Donald, 178
Marsh, J.B.T., 100
Marshall, P. David, 7–8
Marx, John, 519
Marx, Leo, 347
mass culture. *See also* popular culture
   and American classical music scene, 252–53
   concert music and, 226–27
   Jenny Lind and, 31–34, 46, 55–57
   negative view of in 1950s, 329
   vaudeville and, 125, 127
mass music festivals. *See* music festivals
Massimo, Rick, 370, 391–92
Massine, Leonide, 259–60, 260*f*
matinees, at variety theaters, 133
Matos, Michaelangelo, 547
Matson, George, 510–11
Matsui, Lauren, 551
Matthews, Bill, 182–83
May Festival (Cincinnati), 349–50
"Maybellene" (Berry), 305–6

Mayers, Jonathan, 552–53
McBride, Mary, 237
McClain, Billy, 156–58, 157*t*
McCollum, Brian, 532–33
McDaniels, Daryl, 504–5
McGee, David, 301–2
McGill, Bibi, 561–62
McGlennon, Felix, 146
McKay, George, 359
McKim, James, 91–92
McKinley Music Co., 15–16
McLaren, Malcolm, 491–93
McMichen, Clayton, 388–89
McNamara, Brooks, 131–32
Meachum, Joe, 462–63
mechanical reproduction of music. *See also* recordings
   and early discourses surrounding live music, 15–16, 18–23, 20*f*, 22*f*
   live music in era before, 5–6, 9–14
media. *See also* film; radio; television
   coverage of Krush Groove concert, 506–8
   and exposure to rock 'n' roll, 298–99
mediatization, 5–6, 9
"Menace of Mechanical Music, The" (Sousa), 9–10
Metropolitan Opera House (New York), 265–66
Metropolitan Theater (New York), 134–38
Michigan Womyn's Music Festival, 411–12
middlebrow, 237–38, 252
Mike D (Michael Diamond), 494–95
Milhaud, Darius, 248
"Mine Eyes Have Seen the Glory"/"Battle Hymn of the Republic" (Howe), 98–100
Miner, Allison, 415–17
Mingus, Charles, 374–75
Mr. Rock and Roll film, 332
Mitchum, Rob, 556–57
mobile music, jazz as, 183–87
"'Modern' and 'Mod'ren' Music" (*Musical America*), 224–25
modern music
   and American classical music scene in 1920s, 244–49
   debate over definitions of, 224–26

Modern Music journal, 225–26, 247
Monck, Chip, 347, 396, 398, 450–51
monopoly in live music industry, 420–21. *See also* consolidation in live music industry
Monterey Pop Festival, 346–47, 402–3
"Moondog" (Hardin, Louis Thomas), 326
Moondog Coronation Ball (Cleveland), 294–98, 295f, 330–31
Moondog Coronation Ball (Newark), 324
Moondog Maytime Ball (Cleveland), 323
Moondog Moonlight Ball (Cleveland), 323–24
"Moondog Rock 'n' Roll Party" radio show, 326
Moore, Josephine, 97–98
Moore, Scotty, 301–3, 303f
moral elevation. *See also* highbrow forms of art and music
  of Fisk Jubilee Singers, 78–79, 117–18
  Jenny Lind and, 31, 36–37, 49–50, 60, 76–77
  of variety theater, 133, 134–35, 140
Morden, Darryl, 557
Morello, Tom, 551
Morgan, Henry, 97–98
Morgan, Marcyliena, 535–36
Morrison, Jim, 472–73
Morrow, Kevin, 530
Morton, John Fass, 364–65
Mothers of Invention, the, 409–10
Mothership stage prop, P-Funk Earth Tour, 457–60, 459f
Mountain Dance and Folk Festival, 352
movie theaters
  Benny Goodman performances in, 269–71
  concerts by Freed at, 331–33, 334–37, 335f
  conversion of vaudeville houses into, 199
  and early discourses surrounding live music, 16–17, 18–19
  Whiteman orchestra performances at, 244
Mudd Club (New York City), 493–94

music festivals. *See also specific music festivals*
  and contests over cultural values, 347–49
  evolution of, 349–55
  fusion of styles at, 409–17
  Goldenvoice's idea for, evolution of, 546–48
  halt in momentum of, 420
  hip-hop, 521–35, 531f
  in nineteenth century, 349–50
  overview, 345–49
  profit motive behind, 346–48, 401–9, 404f
  and promise of social change, 564–66
  racial inequality in, 523–24, 556
  renewal of scene in 1970s, 411–17
  role in twenty-first century live music industry, 541–43, 553–55
  social significance of, 42
  sound engineering at, 392–401, 400f
  women as featured less prominently at, 556–57
music publishing, Tin Pan Alley era, 122–23, 140–49
musical performance. *See* economies of performance; live music; *specific performances*; *specific performers*
musical societies, 11–12
"My Adidas" (Run-D.M.C.), 508–9
Myka 9, 536–37

Nager, Larry, 533
Nat Cole Trio, 281
Nathanson, Wynn, 264–65
National Folk Festival, 353–54
National Peace Jubilee, 94–97, 98, 127, 349–50
NBC radio network, 250, 255–56, 260–61
"Negro Folk Songs" (*New York Weekly Review*), 91–92
"Negro Life in New York's Harlem" (Thurman), 210–12
Nelson, Paul, 390–91
neo-classicists, 248–49
"Never Ending Tour" (Bob Dylan), 1
New Lost City Ramblers, 371

New Orleans jazz
  Funky Butt Hall, 176–78
  general discussion, 175–79
  origins of jazz linked to, 203
  posters promoting jazz dances and events, 179–82, 181f, 183, 184f
New Orleans Jazz & Heritage Festival, 412–17
New Orleans Jazz Club (NOJC), 412–14
New York by Gaslight (Foster), 6–7
New York City. *See also specific areas of New York; specific events; specific related persons; specific venues*
  Anti-Concert Saloon Bill, 131–32
  Broadway, 134–35
  cabaret laws, 207–9
  decline in support for hip-hop concerts, 512–13
  discotheques in, 485–88
  expansion of hip-hop in, 491–95
  Tin Pan Alley, 140–41
  underground hip-hop in, 537–38
New York Philharmonic, 250–52, 254
Newcleus, 501–5
Newport Casino, 358–59, 361, 363–64
Newport Folk Festival
  of 1960, 374
  Dylan's 1965 performance at, 348, 391–94
  emergence of, 369–73
  organized as nonprofit undertaking, 346–47
  reformation of after 1960 riot, 381–91, 391f
  scouts for, 388
  severing of bond between host city and, 410–11
  social good motive for, 553–54
  sound engineering at, 392–94
Newport Jazz Festival
  1956 appearance by Duke Ellington, 362–65
  broad popularity of, 366–69
  extension of Newport model to other settings, 367–69
  first version, 359–62
  inclusion of rock artists in 1969, 409–11
  inspiration for, 355–56, 358–59
  interplay between order and spontaneity at, 360–65
  Newport Folk Festival and, 369–73
  parallels with developments overseas, 359–60
  reformation of after riots, 381–82
  riot at 1960 version of, 348, 374–81, 378f
  riot of 1971, 411
  social good motive for, 345–46, 367, 553–54
  sound engineering at, 394
nightclubs
  in Prohibition years, 207–13, 267–68
  racial segregation at, 278–79
NOJC (New Orleans Jazz Club), 412–14
nonprofit music festivals, 345–47, 367, 382–84
Norma opera (Bellini), 58
North Alabama Citizens Council, 317, 318, 319–20
"Northern" character of Jenny Lind's talent, 61–64
Norton, John, 510–11
novelty, Tony Pastor's focus on, 143–49, 169–70
Nubian Productions, 483
Nussbaum, Joseph, 265–66

Oakley, Helen, 268–69
O'Connor, Norman, 380
O'Day, Pat, 429–30
ODJB. *See* Original Dixieland Jazz Band
Oja, Carol, 247
OKeh Records, 192–94, 193f
Oliver, Joe, 190–91
Olivier, Barry, 370–71
Olympic Auditorium (Los Angeles), 543–45, 544f
Omni arena (Atlanta), 501–2
On Stage (Rainbow), 474–75
Onyx Club (New York), 267–68
opening bands, in package shows, 308
opera
  comic, 137–38
  debate over Jenny Lind and, 61–64
  Italian, and class divisions in nineteenth century, 43–44

INDEX   667

in nineteenth century American
  culture, 40–41
opera houses, 131
orchestras
  American classical music scene in
    1920s, 246–47
  Paul Whiteman's, 238–39, 240f
  Philadelphia, 253–54
Original Dixieland Jazz Band (ODJB)
  Casino Gardens engagement, 203–4
  conflicted place in writing of jazz
    history, 233–34
  "Livery Stable Blues", 238
  origins of, 203
  recordings of, 171–72
  residency at Reisenweber's, 172, 204–
    7, 205f
Orioles, the, 333
Ory, Edward "Kid", 176–77, 180, 183–84
Ossman, Vess, 155–56
outdoor amphitheaters, 525–26, 553
outdoor classical music concerts, 351–52
outdoor concerts, growing trend
  toward, 254
outdoor music festivals, 347
Outside Lands Music and Arts Festival,
  541–42, 554–55
Owen, Frank, 521–22

Pace & Handy Music Company, 168
package shows. *See also* music festivals;
  specific shows
  Beatles' 1965 Shea Stadium
    concert, 426–27
  "Big Beat" tour, 338–43
  in early rock 'n' roll era, 307–11
  Freed's engagement at Paramount, 334–
    37, 335f
  Freed's promotional activities, 323–
    24, 326–33
  hip-hop, 495, 497–98, 499–500,
    506, 522
  move away from, 435–36
  promoted by Feld brothers, 314–18
  promoted by Tommy Smalls, 332–33
Palace Theatre (New York)
  Duke Ellington at, 199–201
  Paul Whiteman at, 197–99

Sophie Tucker at, 195–96
  Ted Lewis at, 196–97
Paley, William, 255–56
Palmer, Robert, 493–94, 498
Palomar Ballroom (Los Angeles), 268–69
Papadopoulos, George, 442
Papineau, Lou, 502–3
Paramount Theater (New York)
  Benny Goodman at, 269–71
  Freed's engagement at, 334–37, 335f
Pareles, Jon, 519–20
Parent, Bob, 363–64, 364f
Park Theater (Indianapolis), 163–64
Parker, Charlie, 284, 285
Parker, Colonel Tom, 432
Parliament-Funkadelic (P-Funk)
  Earth Tour, 457–63, 459f
  live album, 469–70
  Smokin' Grooves tour, 530, 531f
"Pas Ma Las" (Hogan), 120–21, 151–52
Pastor, Tony, 130f
  as commissioner of songs, 145–48
  dissatisfaction with "vaudeville"
    term, 128
  early career, 129–31
  focus on novelty, 143–49
  14th Street Theater, 138–40, 139f, 143
  later career, 149
  as laying claim to "vaudeville" term, 135
  Metropolitan Theater on
    Broadway, 134–38
  overview, 121–22, 128–29, 169–70
  role in promoting popular
    songs, 143–49
  sources of inspiration for songs, 120
  Tony Pastor's Opera House, 129–34
Paul, Les, 281–82
Peace Jubilees, 80, 94–102, 97f,
  127, 349–50
Pearl Jam, 546–47
Penniman, Richard Wayne (Little
  Richard), 306–7
performance, musical. *See* economies
  of performance; live music; *specific
  performances; specific performers*
Perkins, Carl, 301–2, 306–7
Perry, Charles, 435
Perry, Imani, 560–61

Peter, Paul, and Mary, 387
Peterson, Richard, 301–2
Peyton, Dave, 189, 219
P-Funk, 457–63, 469–70, 530, 531f. See Parliament-Funkadelic
Philadelphia Orchestra, 253–54
philanthropy, 228–29, 230
Philharmonic Auditorium (Los Angeles), 279–82
Phillips, Sam, 293
Phoebus lighting company, 456
phonograph, 141
piano, in nineteenth-century musical life, 10–11
Pickering, Michael, 109
Pike, Gustavus, 78–79, 103–4, 105, 112–13
Platters, the, 314–17, 316f
plugging songs, 142–43
police presence at music events
  hip-hop concerts, 509, 510–11
  After Midnight club, 514
  Newport Jazz Festival riots, 377–79, 378f
  punk music scene, 543
  rock 'n' roll concerts, 306–7, 323, 334–35, 337, 341–43
political activism, intersection of folk revival with, 385–86
politicization of crowds, 42–46
Poole, J.F., 137–38
pop music festivals, 402–9. See also music festivals; specific festivals
popular culture. See also lowbrow forms of art and music; specific popular music genres; vaudeville
  circulation of coon songs, 150–60, 157t, 158t
  and debate over definitions of modern music, 224–25
  emerging discourses of in nineteenth century, 40–41
  Fisk Jubilee Singers and minstrelsy in, 118
  folk revival, 369–70
  Jazz at the Philharmonic concert series, 277–91
  and move of jazz into concert hall, 226–27
  rise of variety entertainment and vaudeville, 122
  swing era, 266
  tension between highbrow and lowbrow culture, 13–14
  Tin Pan Alley, 122–23, 142–49
  variety entertainment and, 132–33
  Whiteman's "Experiment in Modern Music", 233–44
"Popular Music—An Invasion" (Blitzstein), 225–26
Port Royal, South Carolina, 85–86, 87
Porter, Maggie, 82, 83f, 108f, 111–12
Posnick, Nat, 424
postbellum public sphere
  discourse of black musical authenticity, 85–93
  Fisk Jubilee Singers and, 80
  segregation in, 102–6
Poulson-Bryant, Scott, 520
Powell, Teddy, 462–63
power relations, live music and, 27. See also racial discrimination/inequality; segregation
Powers, Ann, 559
Premier Talent agency, 438–46, 440f, 470
Presley, Elvis
  concerts by, 299–300
  at honky tonks, 302–3, 303f
  impact of television appearances, 298–99
  as recording artist, 299–300
  return to touring after army service, 432
  Weintraub's promotion efforts for, 445–46
Preston, Katherine, 43–44
Primus, 520–21
Prince, 556
private music making, 9–11
production codes
  arena rock, 448–57, 453f
  Parliament-Funkadelic Earth Tour, 457–63, 459f
professional success, live performance as linchpin of, 17–18
Professor Longhair (Henry Roeland Byrd), 417
Proffitt, Frank, 388–89

profit motive behind music festivals, 346–48, 401–9, 404f. *See also* commercial concert culture
Prohibition, 207–8, 209, 267–68
promoters. *See* concert promotion
prostitution, 131–32
Public Enemy, 516–22, 518f, 534–35, 545
public music making, 9–14. *See also* live music
public parks, jazz performances in, 182–83
public phenomenon, live music as, 4
public sphere
    black, 160, 166
    crowds and, 42–46
    postbellum, Fisk Jubilee Singers and, 80
    and racial segregation, 305
    role of music in, 11
publicity
    around Jenny Lind's US tour, 35–37, 38–41, 47, 50–51, 52–53
    for Beatles' 1965 Shea Stadium concert, 425–26
    drawn to acts of racial discrimination, 102–4
    for Hogan in Black Patti Troubadours, 161f, 161–62
    by Hurok for Marian Anderson, 262
    for Jazz at the Philharmonic concerts, 280, 286–87, 288f
    for jazz dances and events, 179–82, 181f, 183, 184f
    for Rolling Stones' 1972 US tour, 450–51
    for Tony Pastor's Opera House, 132–33
    for Whiteman's "Experiment in Modern Music", 236–37
Publix theater chain, 244
punk music scene, 494–95, 518–19, 543–45, 544f
"Punkin' to the Funk Rock" flyer, 491–93, 492f
Purcells dance hall (San Francisco), 214–15

Queen and Crescent Social Club (New Orleans), 180, 181f
Queen Latifah, 522–25
Queen Victoria of England, 111–12

R&B. *See* rhythm and blues; rock 'n' roll concerts
racial confusion in music, 303–4, 305–6
racial discrimination/inequality. *See also* segregation
    black promoters, 460–61, 533–34
    circulation of coon songs, 150–60, 157t, 158t
    in classical music, 274
    in early discourses surrounding live music, 21
    in England, 115–17
    experienced by Fisk Jubilee Singers, 102–6
    Granz's commitment to fight, 277–79, 284–86
    in international framework, 113–15
    in live music sphere of 2000s, 555–57
    Marian Anderson's Lincoln Memorial performance, 263–64
    related to violence at rap concerts, 545
racial integration of musical entertainment
    arena rock, 457–69
    black and tans, 199, 209–13
    Freed's engagement at Paramount, 334–35
    Moondog Coronation Ball in Newark, 324
    package shows, 307–8, 317–18
    in post-World War II, 303–5
    rock 'n' roll concerts, 297, 306–7, 319–20, 329, 330–31
    role of disc jockeys, 321–23
racial uplift, ideology of, 559–60
radio
    and advancement of classical music, 255–56
    and concert promotion, 294–97
    disc jockeys, influence of, 319–23, 322f
    and exposure to rock 'n' roll, 298–99
    live broadcasts, 320
    and racial integration of musical entertainment, 303–5
Radio City Music Hall (New York City), 520
Raeburn, Bruce Boyd, 412–13

Rage Against the Machine
    (RATM), 550–51
ragtime, 120–21, 155–56, 187–88. *See also*
    coon songs; jazz
railroad jazz excursions, 183–85
Rainbow, 474–75
Raising Hell tour, Run-D.M.C., 505–6, 508–12
rap/rock cross-genre touring, 515–22. *See also* arena rap; hip-hop
Rawlings, L.W., 178
record hops, 485
recordings
    of "All Coons Look Alike to Me", 155–56
    American Federation of Musicians campaign against, 18–23, 20f, 22f
    cross-promotion by Feld brothers, 314–15
    declining revenues from, 25–26
    discotheques, 485–88
    and early discourses surrounding live music, 15–16, 18–23, 20f, 22f
    early DJ mixing techniques, 488–89
    emergence as feature of radio programming, 320–23
    and growth of classical music audiences, 252–53
    of jazz, 171–72, 174–75, 183–85, 192–94, 193f
    Jazz at the Philharmonic, 282–84
    at Newport Jazz Festival, 362–63
    and racial integration of musical entertainment, 303–5
    rock 'n' roll, 298–300
Red Hot Chili Peppers, 545–46
refined forms of art and music. *See* highbrow forms of art and music
regional promoter networks, 445–46
Reid, Vernon, 528
Reis, Claire, 244–45, 249–50
Reisenweber's (New York), 172, 204–7, 205f
remote recording trucks, 471–72
repeatability, role in arena concerts, 421–22
respectability, Tony Pastor's emphasis on, 132, 133, 140, 169
reverberation time, 231–32

Reynolds, James, 178
Rhapsody in Blue (Gershwin), 241–44
Rhymes, Busta, 530, 531–32
rhythm and blues (R&B). *See also* rock 'n' roll concerts
    "Alan Freed's 'Rock 'n' Roll' Jubilee Ball" billed as, 328–30
    chitlin' circuit, 300–1
    package shows, 307–8, 309–11
    role of disc jockeys in promoting, 321–23
    shows at Apollo Theater, 333
"Rhythm and Blues Show, The" package, 309
Rhythm and Noise (Gracyk), 299
Richard, Little (Richard Wayne Penniman), 306–7
Richards, Keith, 468–69. *See also* Rolling Stones
Richardson, Cliff, 306–7
Rinzler, Ralph, 370–71, 384–85, 388–89
riots
    at 1960 Newport Jazz Festival, 348, 374–81, 378f
    at 1971 Newport Jazz Festival, 411
    Astor Place, 33, 42–46
    at Sly and the Family Stone concert, 465
    theater, in nineteenth century, 42–43
risk
    in business of American entertainment, 34
    involved in concert promotion, 429–30
riverboat jazz performances, 185–87
Ro, Ronin, 510
Roach, Max, 374–75
Roberts, Don, 559–60
Roberts, John, 398, 402
Roberts, Ken, 466–67
Roberts, Michael, 21–23
Robeson, Paul, 274
Robichaux, John, 180–83
Robinson, America, 107, 108f
Robinson, Harlow, 263–64, 265–66
Rock, Rock, Rock! film, 332
"Rock and Roll Dem" (Sweatnam), 292–94
Rock Around the Clock film, 314–15, 316f
rock ballrooms
    live recordings at, 471, 473

as providing primary elements for shows, 449
in San Francisco, 432–37
sound engineering for, 397–98
rock festivals. *See also* music festivals; *specific festivals*
fusion with other types of musical festivals, 409–11
overview, 346–49
profit motive behind, 402–9
reimagining of in 1990s, 521–24
social good motive for, 553–54
social significance of, 42
rock music. *See also* arena rock; *specific artists*
in Beyoncé's Coachella performance, 561–62, 563
conversion into listening music, 435–36
rap/rock cross-genre touring, 515–22
underground, 538
rock 'n' roll concerts. *See also* arena rock; *specific artists*; *specific concerts*
"Big Beat" tour, 338–43
chitlin' circuit, 300–1
disc jockeys, 319–23, 322*f*
Freed's engagement at Paramount, 334–37, 335*f*
Freed's promotional activities, 297–98, 323–24, 326–33
honky tonks, 301–3, 303*f*
and making of rock 'n' roll, 299–300
Moondog Coronation Ball, 294–98, 295*f*
Newport Jazz Festival and, 362
overview, 292–94
package shows, 307–11
racial segregation and, 303–7
and recordings, 298–300
role of Feld in promoting, 311–18
Super Attractions, 314–18
"Rock 'n' Roll Jamboree" (Washington, DC), 314–15
"Rock 'n' Roll" Jubilee Ball (New York), 328–31
"Rock 'n' Roll Party" radio show, 326
Rockwell, John, 461
Rodger, Gillian, 128–29
Rodzinski, Artur, 254

Rogers, Charles, 507–8
Roker, Raymond, 564–66
Roker, Renny, 462
Rolling Stones, 401, 468–69
1969 arena tour, 449
1972 US tour, 450–51
1975 US tour, 451–57, 453*f*
1978 US tour, 418–20
Get Your Ya-Yas Out album, 471–73
Rolontz, Bob, 309–10, 324, 338–39
Rose, Tricia, 505–6
Rosenman, Joel, 398
Rosenthal, Marshall, 465
Rosenthal, Myles, 394
Rothapfel, S.L., 16–17
Rothchild, Paul, 392–93
Rowland, Kelly, 563–64
Rudge, Peter, 444, 450–51
Run-D.M.C., 504–5
Fresh Fest tour, 500–5, 503*f*
Long Beach Arena concert, 505–6, 509–12
performance at Beastie Boys concert, 511–12
Raising Hell tour, 505–6, 508–12
Russell, Ross, 284–85
Russian artists, Hurok's focus on, 259–60
Rutling, Thomas, 82, 83*f*, 108*f*

S1W security organization, 516–17
Sabine, Wallace, 231–32
sacralization, 36–37, 228, 247–48
Saddler, Joseph (Grandmaster Flash), 489–90, 493–94, 499–500, 504–5, 518–19
St. Cecilia Society, 11–12
St. Nicholas Arena (New York), 326–27
saloons, concert, 131–33
Salzburg, Austria, music festivals in, 350–51
Samples, Mark, 35–36
Santoro, Gene, 520
Sargent, H.J., 123–24
Saroni, Herrman, 58–59, 60, 64–65, 85, 86–87, 562–63
Saul, Scott, 348, 380–81
Savoy ballroom
in Chicago, 217–21
in New York, 216–17, 218*f*

672 INDEX

Scher, John, 420
Schiffman, Frank, 333
Schoenfeld, Herm, 329–30
Schumach, Murray, 427
Schwensen, Dave, 428
scratching technique, 493–94
Scruggs, Earl, 372–73
Seagrove, Gordon, 202
Seeger, Mike, 388
Seeger, Pete, 382–84, 387, 392–93
Seeger, Toshi, 382–83
segregation
    effect on Fisk Jubilee Singers, 102–6
    Granz's commitment to desegregating jazz, 278–79
    Jazz at the Philharmonic as challenging, 277–78, 284–86
    at jazz performances, 185–86
    New Orleans Jazz & Heritage Festival and, 414–15
    package shows and, 317–18
    rock 'n' roll concerts and, 303–7
    in vaudeville theaters, 163–64
Seig Music Corporation, 327–28
Seldes, Gilbert, 233–34, 244–45
sentimentality
    in mid-nineteenth-century America, 36–37
    in variety theater, 136–37
serious music. *See* highbrow forms of art and music
Seroff, Doug, 152
Seventh Stream, The (Ennis), 312
Seward, Theodore, 116
Seyton, Charles, 72–73
SFX, 542, 547–48, 552, 554–55
Shakur, Tupac, 556
Sharp, Jeff, 510–11
Shaw, Arnold, 321
Shaw Artists Corporation, 309, 310–11, 339–40
Shea Stadium (New York)
    Beatles' 1965 concert at, 424–29, 426*f*
    Beatles' 1966 concert at, 396–97
Shecter, Jon, 512–13
sheet music, 15–16, 38–41, 39*f*, 141–42
Shelton, Robert, 373
Shepheard's (New York City), 486

Sheppard, Ella, 82–83, 83*f*, 93–94, 98–100, 108*f*
Sheraton Hotel corporation, 367–68
Shiloh Presbyterian Church (New York), 105–6
shimmy dance, 196–97
Showco, 418
Shubert, Howard, 425
Siano, Nicky, 488–89
Silber, Irwin, 373
silent film era, 16–17
Sillerman, Robert F.X., 547–48
Silverman, Sime, 198–99, 209–10, 212–13
Simmons, Joseph, 496–97
Simmons, Russell, 495–97, 501, 503–4
Simon, Bill, 366
Sisters of Mercy, 519–20
slam dancing, 543
Slave Circular (England), 115–17
slave culture, and discourse of black musical authenticity, 85–89
Slave Songs of the United States (Allen, Ware, and Garrison), 87
slavery, emancipation from, 93, 96–97, 102–6
Sleepy Lagoon Defense Fund, 280
slumming, 212
Sly and the Family Stone, 410, 463–69
Smalls, Tommy "Dr. Jive", 321–23, 332–33, 334
Small's Paradise (Harlem), 209–11, 210*f*
small-scale events, 27–28
Smith, Danyel, 513–14
Smith, Harry, 369
Smith, Mamie, 189–90, 191–94, 193*f*
Smokin' Grooves festival, 530–35, 531*f*
Snoop Dogg, 556
Snyder, Robert, 140
"So This Is Venice" (Paul Whiteman and His Orchestra), 239–41
social class
    and Astor Place Riot, 42–46
    and disturbances at Jenny Lind's concerts, 69–76
    and mass appeal of Jenny Lind, 32–34, 55–57
    mixing of at first Newport Jazz Festival, 361
    taste as marker of, 13–14

social Darwinism, 230
social relations of Harlem cabaret, 212–13
songs. *See also specific songs*
  comic, 120, 122, 144–45, 239
  commercial production of, 122–23, 140–43
  contest related to Jenny Lind's arrival in US, 47
  theatrical promotion of, 142–43
  topical, 120, 144–45, 385–86
sonic color line, 61–62
Sotiropoulos, Karen, 159–60
Souchon, Edmond, 412–13
Soul Sonic Force, 491–93
sound engineering
  Beatles' 1965 Shea Stadium concert, 428
  Beatles' 1966 Shea Stadium concert, 396–97
  at music festivals, 347, 392–401, 400f
sound films, 18–19. *See also* film
sound recordings. *See* recordings
soundscape of modernity, 231, 268
Sousa, John Philip, 9–10
Southern, Eileen, 96–97
Soviet artists, Hurok's focus on, 259–60
Spaulding, Henry George, 85–87
speakeasies, 207–8, 211–12
Spearhead, 530
spectacle over narrative, in variety theater, 136–37
Spence, Adam, 82–83
spirituals
  and discourse of black musical authenticity, 87–93
  Fisk Jubilee Singers and, 79–80, 82–84, 100–1, 110–11
  as key to acceptance for Marian Anderson, 261–62
Spotts, Frederic, 350
Stadium Concerts (New York), 254
stadium rock. *See* arena rock
Stagecoach Festival, 541–42, 554–55
staging of arena rock
  Parliament-Funkadelic Earth Tour, 457–58, 459f
  production codes, 448–57
  Rolling Stones' 1972 US tour, 450–51

Rolling Stones' 1975 US tour, 452–54, 453f, 456
"Standard of the Free, The" (Bevan & Seward), 115–16
Stanley, Augustus Owsley, 393–94
Stanley, Paul, 475–76
Stardust Room (New York City), 482–83
Starr, Victoria, 520–21
stars, qualities of, 7–8
steamboat jazz performances, 185–87
Steinberg, Michael, 350–51
Stein's Dixie Jass Band, 203
stepping dance style, 559–60
Stern, Debbie, 428–29
Stetsasonic, 545
Stewart, Rex, 190, 215, 216
Stock, Frederick, 249–50
Stoever, Jennifer, 61–62, 528–29
Stokowski, Leopold, 249–50, 253–54
Stone, Sly, 410, 463–69, 528–29
Storyville nightclub (Boston), 357–58
Stott, J. McEwen, 116–17
Stowe, Harriet Beecher, 14
"Straight up Nigga" (Ice-T), 528
Strauss, Johann, 99
Straw, Will, 248–49
Strong, Charlie, 465–66
Strong, George Templeton, 50
subscription concerts, 11–12
Suga Mama, 561–62
Sugar Cane Club (Harlem), 210–12
Sugar Hill "Rappers Convention" tour, 499–500
Sugarhill Gang, 491, 493–94, 499–500
Suisman, David, 143–44, 147–48
Sullivan, Arthur, 137–38
Sullivan, Ed, 423
Sullivan, John, 361
summertime concert programming, 254
Sunday Sacred Concert, at World's Peace Jubilee, 100–1
Super Attractions, 314–18
Super Music stores, 313, 314–15
Swatch Watch New York City Fresh Festival. *See* Fresh Fest tour
Sweatman, Wilbur, 189
Sweatnam, Willis P. "Billy", 292–94
"sweet" jazz, 234

swing era
  dance music in, 269–70
  emergent listening culture in, 268–69
  "From Spirituals to Swing" concerts, 275–76
  Goodman's Carnegie Hall concert, 270–75
  Goodman's Paramount Theater stand, 269–71
  overview, 266–67
symphonic jazz, 197–99, 234–44, 276–77
Symphony Hall (Boston), 231–32

talent agencies. *See* booking agencies
Talent Forums, 462
Tammany building (New York), 138
Tanglewood, 355–56
Tannenbaum, Rob, 513
taste, contests over, 13–14
Tate, Minnie, 82, 83*f*
Taubman, Howard, 254, 262, 361–62
Taylor, Bayard, 59–60
Taylor, Jerry, 377–79
Tea Party rock ballroom (Boston), 442–43
teenagers. *See* young audiences
television
  effect on radio industry, 320
  and exposure to rock 'n' roll, 298–99
temperance movement, 37
Ten Years After, 410
Tenderloin district (New York City), 208–9
Terminator X, 517, 518*f*
Texas Pop Festival, 407–8
"Thank You (Falettinme Be Mice Elf Again)" (Sly and the Family Stone), 464
Tharpe, Sister Rosetta, 313–14
theater. *See also* vaudeville
  organized groups with influence over, 124–26
  riots at, 42–43
  stigma attached to in mid-nineteenth-century America, 36–37
Theater Owners Booking Association (T.O.B.A.), 168
theatricality, rock and pop, 449–50
There's a Riot Goin' on (Sly and the Family Stone), 464, 468

This Ain't the Summer of Love (Waksman), 24–25
Thomas, B.W., 108*f*
Thomas, Jean, 352
Thomas, Theodore, 249–50
Thompson, Emily, 231
Thomson, Virgil, 242–43, 248
Thornton, Sarah, 487, 488
Thurman, Wallace, 210–13
Ticketmaster, 542, 546–47, 554–55
Tiger Flower promotion company, 460–61
Times Square (New York), 334–35
Tin Pan Alley
  circulation of coon songs, 150–60, 157*t*, 158*t*
  original location of, 140–41
  overview, 122–23
  relationship between variety/vaudeville and, 142–49, 169–70
  theatrical promotion of songs, 142–43
T.O.B.A. (Theater Owners Booking Association), 168
togetherness, live music and sense of, 27
Tollett, Paul, 545–46, 546*f*, 547, 548, 551–53
Tom Brown's Ragtime Band, 202
Tom Fields Associates, 456
Tony Pastor's 14th Street Theater (New York), 138–40, 139*f*, 143
Tony Pastor's Opera House (New York), 129–34, 135
Top Record Stars of 1956 tour, 306–7
"Top Ten R&B Show", 309
topical songs, 120, 144–45, 385–86
Tormey, Tim, 430–31
Toscanini, Arturo, 250–52
Tour of a Black Planet (Public Enemy), 516–17, 518*f*
touring piano virtuosos, 10–11
tours, concert. *See also specific artists*; *specific tours*
  in arena rock era, 418–19
  implications beyond generation of revenue, 118–19
  live recordings from, 471, 472–75
  overview, 1–3
  production codes, 448–57, 453*f*
  rock careers built around, 439–41

Tovar, Gary, 543–46
"T.P.'s Canal Boat Pinafore" (Poole), 137–38
traditional music
    and emergence of folk festivals, 352–54
    at Newport Folk Festival, 388–90
train jazz excursions, 183–85
transportation, for arena rock shows, 448–50, 456–57
Travel Service of America, 3
traveling ice shows, 450
Treacherous Three, 494–95
Tremont Temple (Boston), 67
Tribe Called Quest, A, 529, 530, 531–32
Tripler Hall (New York), 65–66
Tschmuck, Peter, 25–26
Tucker, Sophie, 194–96, 197
"Tune in, Turn on, Burn out" tour, 519–20
Turner, Tina, 555
Tuthill, William, 230–31
"Twenty Years of Jazz" segment, Goodman's Carnegie Hall concert, 271–73

Uncle Tom's Cabin (Stowe), 14
"Under the Palmetto" (Spaulding), 85–86
underground hip-hop, 535–39
union professionals, in arena rock era, 450
Union Sons Hall (New Orleans), 176–77
Union Square district (New York), 138, 140–41
United Booking Office (U.B.O.), 125–26
United Kingdom
    festival culture in, 359, 525, 547
    Fisk Jubilee Singers in, 107, 108f, 108–17
    Slave Circular, 115–17
Universal Attractions, 310–11
University of Chicago Folk Festival, 384–85
uplift ideology, 559–60
Urban Room concert, Goodman's (Chicago), 268–69
U.T.F.O., 545

Vaine, Wallace, 342–43
Van Santen, Rick, 545–46, 546f, 547, 548, 551–53

Vance, Clarice, 156–57, 157t
Vanderbeek, William, 40–41
variety entertainment. *See also* Pastor, Tony; vaudeville
    Apollo Theater, 333
    defined, 129
    Metropolitan Theater, 134–38
    moral elevation and, 133, 134–35, 140
    overview, 120–23
    package shows as inherited from, 308
    relationship between Tin Pan Alley and, 142–49
    respectable entertainment at, 132
    rise of, 117
    song plugging in, 142–43
    tensions between vaudeville and, 128–29
    Tony Pastor's Opera House, 129–34, 135
vaudeville. *See also* Pastor, Tony
    black, 153, 167–69, 191, 194
    circulation of "All Coons Look Alike to Me", 156–60
    crowds of, 127
    emergence of, 123–27, 126f
    Hogan's performances of coon songs, 160–67
    jazz performances in, 187–201, 193f
    Metropolitan Theater, 134–38
    overview, 121–23
    package shows as inherited from, 308
    relationship between Tin Pan Alley and, 142–49, 169–70
    residue of in Whiteman's "Experiment", 239–41
    song plugging in, 142–43
    tensions between variety and, 128–29
Vaudeville Theater (Louisville, Kentucky), 123–24
venues. *See also* arena rock; *specific venue types*; *specific venues*
    Feld brothers' deals with, 314
    jazz venues, 173–74
    for rock 'n' roll concerts, 343–44
Victor company, 252–53
Victoria, Queen of England, 111–12
Vincent, Rickey, 457–58, 463
violence at concerts, 505–12, 545. *See also* riots

virtuoso pianists, in nineteenth
  century, 10–11
Vitz, Robert, 349–50
Vogel, Shane, 206–7
Volpe, Andrea, 145–46
Volstead Act, 207–8

Wagner, Richard, 350
Wagner, Robin, 452, 456
Waksman, Steve, 23–25
Wald, Elijah, 160, 234, 243–44, 348,
  370, 391–92
Wald, Gayle, 313–14
"Walk This Way" (Run-D.M.C.), 508, 512
Walker, Cedric "Ricky", 501–2
Walker, Curtis. *See* Blow, Kurtis
Walker, Eliza, 82, 83*f*, 97–98
Walker, George, 166–67
Walters, Norby, 497–98
Walton, Lester, 164–65, 166–67
Ware, Charles Pickard, 87
Ware, W. Porter, 38, 72–73
Warrior Soul, 519
Waters, Ethel, 199
Watkins, Edmund, 97–98
Watson, Don, 450
Weavers, the, 369
Weber, William, 36, 64–65
Webster, Emma, 26
Wein, George
  approach to jazz, 356–59
  extension of Newport model to other
    settings, 367–69
  New Orleans Jazz & Heritage Festival,
    412, 414–17
  Newport Folk Festival, 369–70, 372–73
  Newport Jazz Festival, 345, 346, 356,
    358*f*, 358–59, 364–65, 367, 409–11
  reformation of festival production after
    riot, 382–84
  on riot at 1960 Newport Jazz
    Festival, 380
  use of Bill Hanley as sound engineer,
    394, 395–96
Wein, Joyce, 414–15
Weintraub, Jerry, 418, 420, 476–77
  career trajectory of, 431–32
  as promoter-memoirist, 429–30

  refusal to cooperate with Barsalona's
    network, 445–48
Weisbard, Eric, 530
West, Kanye, 555, 556
"West End Blues" (Armstrong), 220–21
Westley, Wayne, 559–60
Whettling, George, 220–21
Whisnant, David, 352–53
White, George, 78, 105
  appeals by at concerts, 103–4
  growing ambitions of, 81
  influence upon Fisk Jubilee
    Singers, 82–83
  inspiration for name of Jubilee
    Singers, 93–94
  manner of arranging songs in
    concerts, 89
  and World's Peace Jubilee, 97–99
White, Jack, 562
White, Maurice, 470
White, Richard Grant, 57–58, 62
White Top Folk Festival, 352–53
Whiteman, Paul, 17–18
  approach to jazz, 234–35
  comparisons to Goodman's Carnegie
    Hall concert, 270–73
  competing aims for jazz, 237–38
  conflicted place in writing of jazz
    history, 233–34
  "Experiment in Modern Music", 226,
    233–44, 240*f*, 245–46
  as middlebrow, 237–38, 252
  shift from cabaret to vaudeville, 197–99
whiteness, and claims of "highbrow"
  cultural value, 243
Who, the, 450
Whodini, 501, 504–5
Wiles, David A., 436–37
William Hall & Son, 38–40, 41
Williams, Bert, 121, 151–52, 166–67
Williams, Cootie, 272*f*, 272
Williams, Gus, 135–36
Williams, Michelle, 563–64
Williams, Paul, 294, 295*f*, 309
Williams, Valena Minor, 296–97
Wilson, John, 379–80
Wilson, Teddy, 273–74
Wimsatt, William "Upski", 526

WINS radio station, 324–25, 327–28
Witmark, Isidore, 141, 153–54
Witmark and Sons, 141, 153–54, 156–57
WJW radio station, 294–97
WNJR radio station, 324
Wolfe, Tom, 422–23
women. *See also specific female artists*
   coon shouters, 150
   as featured less prominently at music festivals, 556–57
   importance of Beyoncé's 2018 Coachella show for, 562–66
   and inequality in live music, 27
   in Jenny Lind's audiences, 32, 55
   private music making by in nineteenth century, 10
   use of sentimentality to gain access to public life, 36–37
   vaudeville as drawing to theater, 123–24, 133, 140
Woodbury, I.B., 14
Woodstock '99 festival, 549, 550–51
Woodstock Music and Art Fair
   crowds at, 401–3
   sound engineering for, 398–401, 400*f*
"Woodstock West". *See* Coachella Valley Music and Arts Festival
Woodward, Matt, 146
workshops, at Newport Folk Festival, 371–72, 384, 386, 390, 391*f*
World's Fair, Newport-associated performers at, 367–68
World's Peace Jubilee, 80, 95–102, 97*f*, 127, 349–50

Wynn, Jonathan, 412

Yaddo Music Festival, 351–52
Yarrow, Peter, 392–93
Yes, 474
Yessongs (Yes), 474
Young, Lester, 280–81
young audiences
   "Alan Freed's 'Rock 'n' Roll' Jubilee Ball", 328–30
   arena rock, 476–77, 477*f*
   Benny Goodman's Paramount Theater stand, 269–71
   at "Big Beat" concert in Boston, 341–43
   Freed's defense of, 337–38
   at Freed's engagement at Paramount, 334–37
   of hip-hop, 480–81
   Moondog Coronation Ball in Newark, 324
   music festivals and, 381
   and negative associations attached to rap, 506–7
   Newport Jazz Festival riots and, 376–81
   rock 'n' roll concerts and, 319–20
Young Black Teenagers, 519
"Young Forever" (Jay-Z), 557

Zappa, Frank, 409–10
Zeh, John, 408
Zellers, Parker, 134–35
Ziggy Marley and the Melody Makers, 530
Zimbalist, Efrem, 258–59
Zion's Herald journal, 96–97